T0338480

ADVANCED
ARTIFICIAL
INTELLIGENCE

Second Edition

Series on Intelligence Science

Series Editor: Zhongzhi Shi *(Chinese Academy of Sciences, China)*

Series on Intelligence Science Vol.4

ADVANCED ARTIFICIAL INTELLIGENCE

Second Edition

Probabilistic Modeling

Statistical Learning

Logical Reasoning

Brain Cognition

Zhongzhi SHI

Chinese Academy of Sciences, China

 World Scientific

NEW JERSEY · LONDON · SINGAPORE · BEIJING · SHANGHAI · HONG KONG · TAIPEI · CHENNAI · TOKYO

Published by

World Scientific Publishing Co. Pte. Ltd.

5 Toh Tuck Link, Singapore 596224

USA office: 27 Warren Street, Suite 401-402, Hackensack, NJ 07601

UK office: 57 Shelton Street, Covent Garden, London WC2H 9HE

Library of Congress Cataloging-in-Publication Data
Names: Shi, Zhongzhi, author.
Title: Advanced artificial intelligence / Zhongzhi Shi, Chinese Academy of Sciences, China.
Description: Second edition. | New Jersey : World Scientific, [2019] |
    Series: Series on intelligence science ; vol 4 | Includes bibliographical references.
Identifiers: LCCN 2019014024 | ISBN 9789811200878 (hc)
Subjects: LCSH: Artificial intelligence.
Classification: LCC Q335 .S4668 2019 | DDC 006.3--dc23
LC record available at https://lccn.loc.gov/2019014024

British Library Cataloguing-in-Publication Data
A catalogue record for this book is available from the British Library.

For any available supplementary material, please visit
https://www.worldscientific.com/worldscibooks/10.1142/11295#t=suppl

Desk Editor: Herbert Moses

Typeset by Stallion Press
Email: enquiries@stallionpress.com

Printed in Singapore

Preface

Artificial Intelligence's long-term goal is to build a human level of artificial intelligence (AI). AI was born 60 years ago, and this bumpy road has made encouraging progress; in particular, machine learning, data mining, computer vision, expert systems, natural language processing, planning, robotics, and related applications have brought good economic and social benefits. Widespread use of the Internet is also expanding the application of knowledge representation and reasoning, to build the semantic Web and improve the effectiveness of the rate of Internet information. The inevitable trend of information technology is intelligent. The intelligence revolution with the goal of replacing work performed by human brain work with machine intelligence will open up the history of humans post-civilization. If the steam engine created the industrial society, then the intelligent machine must also be able to magically create an intelligent society to realize social production automation and intelligence, which will thus promote great development of a knowledge-intensive economy.

Artificial intelligence is a branch of computer science — a discipline to study machine intelligence — that uses artificial methods and techniques for developing intelligent machines or intelligent systems to emulate, extend, and expand human intelligence and realize intelligent behavior. Artificial intelligence in general can be divided into symbolic intelligence and computational intelligence. Symbolic intelligence is the traditional symbolic artificial intelligence and is the basis of the physical symbol system to study the knowledge representation, acquisition, and reasoning process. The use of knowledge to solve problems is a basic concept — the most important feature of the current symbol of intelligence — so people often call the current stage of artificial intelligence knowledge as engineering. Knowledge engineering research emphasizes on knowledge information processing methods and technologies and promotes the development of artificial intelligence.

Computational intelligence includes neural computation, fuzzy system, genetic algorithms, evolutionary planning, and so on. To achieve intelligence revolution, we must better understand the human brain. Completely revealing the mysteries of the human brain is one of the biggest challenges natural sciences is facing. In the early 21st century, the U.S. National Science Foundation (NSF) and the U.S. Department of Commerce (DOC) jointly funded an ambitious program — Convergent Technology for Improving Human Performance — which viewed nanotechnology, biotechnology, information technology, and cognitive science as the four cutting-edge technologies of the 21st century. Cognitive science is a top priority area for development, advocating the development of integration of these four technologies and describing the prospects for such a science. Cognitive science is the guide of convergent technology because once we are able to know how, why, where, and when to understand the four levels of thinking, we can use nanotechnology along with biotechnology and biomedicine to achieve this aim and finally use information technology to manipulate and control it and make it work. This will have a tremendous impact on human society.

On the surface, symbolic intelligence and neural computing are completely different research methods, with the former based on knowledge and the latter on the data; the former uses reasoning, and the latter uses mapping. In 1996, the invited presentation on "Computers, Emotions and Common Sense" given by Minsky at the fourth Pacific Region International Conference on Artificial Intelligence was of the view that neural computation and symbolic computation can be combined and neural network is the foundation of the symbolic system. Hybrid system is committed to people, and it is this combination that is consistent with our proposed hierarchical model of the human mind.

New to this Edition

This edition captures the progresses in AI that have been made since the last edition in 2011. There has been a great deal of theoretical progress, particularly in areas such as probabilistic graphical inferences, machine learning, and computer vision. There have been algorithmic landmarks, such as deep learning and unsupervised learning. There have been important applications of AI technology, such as in practical speech recognition, machine translation, autonomous vehicles, and intelligent robotics. The major changes are as follows:

- Since 2006, deep learning has made great progress and plays an important role in machine learning. Deep learning establishes and simulates the human brain's hierarchical structure to extract the external input data's features from lower to higher, which can explain the external data. In 2016, AlphaGo unquestionably

defeated Li Shishi with a score of 3 to 1, thus opening up a wave of artificial intelligence.
- The following chapters from the first edition will be removed:
  Chapter 04 — Qualitative Reasoning
  Chapter 09 — Explanation-based Learning
  Chapter 11 — Rough Set
  Chapter 15 — Artificial Life.
- New material will be added with the following new chapters:
  Chapter 05 — Probabilistic Graphical Models
  Chapter 09 — Deep Learning
  Chapter 11 — Unsupervised Learning
  Chapter 15 — Internet Intelligence.
- We estimate that about 30% of the material is quite new. The remaining 70% has been revised.

This book is separated into 15 chapters. Chapter 1, the introduction, starts from the cognitive questions of artificial intelligence, describing the guiding ideology behind writing this book and provides an overview of the hot topics of current artificial intelligence research. Chapter 2 discusses the logic for artificial intelligence with a more systematic discussion of non-monotonic logic and agent-related logic systems. Chapter 3 provides information on constraint reasoning and introduces a number of practical constraints reasoning techniques. Chapter 4 describes the graphic model Bayesian networks for the connection probabilities among variables. Chapter 5 illustrates probabilistic graphical models. Over the years, the author and his colleagues have been engaged in case-based reasoning research, and the main results of this research constitute Chapter 6. Machine learning is the core of not only current artificial intelligence research but also knowledge discovery, data mining, and learnability and thus forms an important basis in the book and is discussed in Chapter 7, reflecting the latest progress in the field. Chapter 8 discusses support vector machines. Chapter 9 is related to deep learning, reflecting the latest progress of the field. Chapter 10 presents reinforcement learning; Chapter 11 describes unsupervised learning for big data; and Chapter 12 focuses on association rules. Evolutionary computation focusing on genetic algorithm is discussed in Chapter 13. In recent years, significant progress has been made in the distribution of intelligence, which, combined with the results of our study, is presented in Chapter 14 that discusses the main theories and key technologies for multi-agent systems. The final chapter addresses Internet intelligence and focuses on Semantic Web and crowd intelligence.

The author has set up an Advanced Artificial Intelligence course for Ph.D. and master's students at the University of Chinese Academy of Sciences since 1994. Based on those lecture notes, Science Press published the first, second, and third editions of this book in 1998, 2006, and 2011, respectively. The book has been identified as a key textbook for regular higher education and is widely used in China. In 2011, World Scientific had published the English edition.

This book can be regarded as a textbook for senior students or graduate students in the information field and related tertiary specialities. It is also suitable as a reference book for relevant scientific and technical personnel.

About the Author

 **Zhongzhi Shi** is a Professor at the Institute of Computing Technology, Chinese Academy of Sciences and a Fellow of CCF and CAAI. He is a senior member of the IEEE, AAAI, and ACM. His research interests mainly include intelligence science, artificial intelligence, multi-agent systems, and machine learning. He has been responsible for 973, 863 key projects of the NSFC. He has been awarded with various honors, such as the National Science and Technology Progress Award (2012), Beijing Municipal Science and Technology Award (2006), the Achievement Award of Wu Wenjun Artificial Intelligence Science and Technology by CAAI (2013), and the Achievement Award of Multi-Agent Systems by China Multi-Agent Systems Technical Group of AIPR, CCF (2016). He has published 16 books, including *Mind Computation, Intelligence Science, Advanced Artificial Intelligence*, and *Principles of Machine Learning* and published more than 500 academic papers. He served as chair of the machine learning and data mining group IFIP TC12, as Secretary-General of the China Computer Federation, and as Vice-Chair of the China Association of Artificial Intelligence.

Acknowledgments

I would like to take this opportunity to thank my family, particularly my wife Zhihua Yu and my children, Jing Shi and Jun Shi, for their support in the course of writing this book. I would also like to thank my organization, Institute of Computing Technology, Chinese Academy of Sciences, for providing a conductive environment to conduct research on artificial intelligence.

In the Intelligence Science Laboratory, there are 12 post-doctoral and 64 Ph.D. candidates and more than 130 master's students, and I thank all of them for their valuable work and contributions to this book; in particular, Rui Huang, Liang Chang, Wenjia Niu, Dapeng Zhang, Limin Chen, Zhiwei Shi, Zhixin Li, Qiuge Liu, Huifang Ma, Fen Lin, Zheng Zheng, Hui Peng, Zuqiang Meng, Jiwen Luo, Xi Liu, and Zhihua Cui have assisted in the first edition (English version) of this book.

The book collects and presents research efforts supported by the National Basic Research Priorities Programme (No. 2013CB329502, No. 2007CB311004, No. 2003CB317004), National Science Foundation of China (No. 61035003, Nos. 60775035, 60933004, 60970088), 863 National High-Tech Program (No. 2007AA01Z132), National Science and Technology Support Plan (No. 2006BAC08B06), Beijing Natural Science Foundation, the Knowledge Innovation Program of Chinese Academy of Sciences, and other funding agencies. I am very grateful for their financial support.

My special thanks to Science Press for publishing the first, second, and third editions of the Chinese version in the years 1998, 2006, and 2011, respectively. I am most grateful to the editorial staff and artists from World Scientific who provided all their support and help during the course of publishing this book.

Contents

Chapter 1

Introduction

Artificial intelligence emphasizes the creation of intelligent machines that work and react like humans. It is usually defined as the science and engineering of emulating, extending, and augmenting human intelligence through artificial means and techniques to make intelligent machines.

1.1 Brief History of AI

Artificial intelligence (AI) is usually defined as the science and engineering of imitating, extending, and augmenting human intelligence through artificial means and techniques to make intelligent machines. In 2005, John McCarthy pointed out that the long-term goal of AI is human-level AI (McCarthy, 2005).

In the history of human development, it is a never-ending pursuit to free people from both manual and mental labor with machines. The industrial revolutions enabled machines to perform heavy manual labor instead of people and thus lead to a considerable economic and social progress. To make machines help relieve mental labor, a long cherished aspiration is to create and make use of intelligent machines like human beings.

In ancient China, many mechanical devices and tools were invented to help accomplish mental tasks. The abacus was the most widely used classical calculator. The Water-powered Armillary Sphere and Celestial Globe Tower were used for astronomical observation and stellar analysis. The Houfeng Seismograph was an ancient seismometer used to detect and record tremors and earthquakes. The traditional Chinese theory of Yin and Yang reveals the philosophy of opposition, interrelation, and transformation, having an important impact on modern logic.

Aristotle (384–322 BC) proposed the first formal deductive reasoning system, syllogistic logic, in the Organon. Francis Bacon (1561–1626) established the inductive method in the Novum Organum (or "New Organon"). Gottfried Leibniz (1646–1716) constructed the first mechanical calculator capable of multiplication and division. He also enunciated the concepts of "characteristica universalis" and "calculus ratiocinator" to treat the operations of formal logic in a symbolic or algebraic way, which can be viewed as the sprout of the "thinking machine".

Since the 19th century, advancement in sciences and technologies such as Mathematical Logic, Automata Theory, Cybernetics, Information Theory, Computer Science, and Psychology laid the ideological, theoretical, and material foundation for the development of AI research. In the book *An Investigation of the Laws of Thought*, George Boole (1815–1864) developed the Boolean algebra, a form of symbolic logic to represent some basic rules for reasoning in thinking activities. Kurt Gödel (1906–1978) proved the incompleteness theorems. Alan Turing (1912–1954) introduced the Turing Machine — a model of the ideal intelligent computer — and initiated the automata theory. In 1943, Warren McCulloch (1899–1969) and Walter Pitts (1923–1969) developed the MP neuron, a pioneer work of Artificial Neural Networks research. In 1946, John Mauchly (1907–1980) and John Eckert (1919–1995) invented the Electronic Numerical Integrator And Computer (ENIAC), the first electronic computer. In 1948, Norbert Wiener (1894–1964) published a popular book of *Cybernetics*, and Claude Shannon (1916–2001) proposed the Information Theory.

In the real world, quite a number of problems are complex ones, most of the time without any algorithm to adopt; or even if there are calculation methods, they are still NP problems. Researchers might introduce heuristic knowledge to solve such problems, to simplify complex problems, and to find solutions in the vast search space. Usually, the introduction of domain-specific empirical knowledge will produce satisfactory solutions, though they might not be the mathematically optimal solutions. This kind of problem solving with its own remarkable characteristics led to the birth of AI. In 1956, the term "Artificial Intelligence" was coined, and the Dartmouth Summer Research Project on artificial intelligence, proposed by John McCarthy, Marvin Minsky, etc., was carried on at Dartmouth College with several American scientists of psychology, mathematics, computer science, and information theory. This well-known Dartmouth conference marked the beginning of the real sense of AI as a research field. Through dozens of years of research and development, great progress has been made in the discipline of AI. Many artificial intelligence expert systems have been developed and applied successfully. In domains such as Natural Language Processing, Machine Translation, Pattern Recognition, Robotics, and Image Processing, a lot of achievements have been made, and the applications span various areas of development.

In the 1950s, AI research mainly focused on game playing. In 1956, Arthur Samuel wrote the first heuristic game-playing program with learning ability. In the same year, Alan Newell, Herbert Simon, etc., invented a heuristic program called the Logic Theorist, which proved correct 38 of the first 52 theorems from the "Principia Mathematica". Their work heralded the beginning of research on cognitive psychology with computers. Noam Chomsky proposed the Syntactics, the pioneer work of Formal Language research. In 1958, John McCarthy invented the Lisp language, an important tool for AI research which can process not only numerical values but also symbols.

In the early 1960s, AI research mainly focused on search algorithms and general problem solving (GPS). Allen Newell *et al.*, published the General Problem Solver, a more powerful and universal heuristic program than other programs at that time. In 1961, Marvin Minsky published the seminal paper *Steps Toward Artificial Intelligence* which established a fairly unified terminology for AI research and established the subject as a well-defined scientific enterprise. In 1965, Edward Feigenbaum *et al.*, began work on the DENDRAL chemical analysis expert system, a milestone for AI applications, and initiated the shift from computer algorithms to knowledge representation as the focus of AI research. In 1965, Alan Robinson proposed the Resolution Principle. In 1968, Ross Quillian introduced the Semantic Network for knowledge representation. In 1969, International Joint Conferences on Artificial Intelligence (IJCAI) was founded, and since then, the IJCAI has been held biannually in odd-numbered years. *Artificial Intelligence*, an international journal edited by IJCAI, commenced publication in 1970.

In the early 1970s, AI research mainly focused on Natural Language Understanding and Knowledge Representation. In 1972, Terry Winograd published details of the SHRDLU program for understanding natural language. Alain Colmerauer developed Prolog language for AI programming at the University of Marseilles in France. In 1973, Roger Schank proposed the Conceptual Dependency Theory for Natural Language Understanding. In 1974, Marvin Minsky published the frame system theory, an important theory of Knowledge Representation. In 1977, Edward Feigenbaum published the well-known paper *The Art of Artificial Intelligence: Themes and Case Studies in Knowledge Engineering* in the 5th IJCAI. He stated that Knowledge Engineering is the art of bringing the principles and tools of AI research to bear on difficult applications problems requiring expert knowledge for their solution. The technical issues of acquiring this knowledge, representing it, and using it appropriately to construct and explain lines of reasoning are important problems in the design of knowledge-based systems.

In the 1980s, AI research developed prosperously. Expert systems were more and more widely used, development tools for expert systems appeared, and industrial AI thrived. Especially in 1982, Japan's Ministry of International Trade and Industry initiated the Fifth Generation Computer Systems project, which dramatically promoted the development of AI. Many countries also made similar plans for research in AI and intelligent computers. China also started the research of intelligent computer systems as an 863 National High-Tech Program.

During the past more than 60 years, great progress has been made in the field of AI research. Theories of Heuristic Searching Strategies, Non-monotonic Reasoning, Machine Learning, etc., have been proposed. Applications of AI, especially Expert Systems, Intelligent Decision-Making, Intelligent Robots, Natural Language Understandings, etc., also promoted the research of AI. Presently, Knowledge Engineering based on knowledge and information processing is a remarkable characteristic of AI.

However, just as with the development of any other discipline, there are also obstacles in the history of AI research. Even from the beginning, AI researchers had been criticized for their being too optimistic. In the early years of AI research, Herbert Simon and Allen Newell, two of the AI pioneers, optimistically predicted the following:

- Within 10 years, a digital computer will be the world's chess champion, unless the rules bar it from competition.
- Within 10 years, a digital computer will discover and prove an important new mathematical theorem.
- Within 10 years, a digital computer will write music that will be accepted by critics as possessing considerable aesthetic value.
- Within 10 years, most theories in psychology will take the form of computer programs or qualitative statements about the characteristics of computer programs.

These expectations haven't been completely realized even till date. A 3-year-old little child can easily figure out a tree in a picture, while a most powerful super computers have only reached a middle level as children in tree recognition. It is also very difficult to automatically understand even stories written for little children.

Some essential theories of AI still need improvements. No breakthrough progresses have been made for some key technologies such as Machine Learning, Non-monotonic Reasoning, Commonsense Knowledge Representation, and Uncertain Reasoning. It is also very difficult for global judgment, fuzzy information processing, multi-granular visual information processing, etc.

Conclusively, AI research is still in the first stage of Intelligence Science, an indispensable cross discipline which is dedicated to joint research on basic theories and technologies of intelligence by Brain Science, Cognitive Science, Artificial Intelligence, and others. Brain Science explores the essence of brain and investigates the principles and models of natural intelligence at the molecular, cellular, and behavioral levels. Cognitive Science studies human mental activities, such as perception, learning, memory, thinking, and consciousness. AI research aims at imitating, extending, and augmenting human intelligence through artificial means and techniques, and finally achieving machine intelligence. These three disciplines work together to explore new concepts, new theories, and new methodologies for Intelligence Science, opening up prospects for a successful and brilliant future in the 21st century (Shi, 2006a).

1.2 Cognitive Issues of AI

Cognition is generally referred to as the process of knowing or understanding relative to affection, motivation, or volition. Definitions of cognition can be briefly summarized into five main categories according to the American psychologist Houston:

(1) Cognition is the process of information processing.
(2) Cognition involves symbol processing in psychology.
(3) Cognition deals with problem solving.
(4) Cognition studies mind and intelligence.
(5) Cognition consists of a series of activities, such as perception, memory, thinking, judgment, reasoning, problem solving, learning, imagination, concept forming, language using, etc.

Cognitive psychologist David H. Dodd, etc., held that cognition involves the three aspects of adaptation, structure, and process, i.e., cognition is the process of information processing in certain mental structures for certain objectives.

Cognitive Science is the science of human perceptions and mental information processing, spanning from perceptual input to complex problem solving, including intellectual activities from individuals to the whole society, and investigating characteristics of both human intelligence and machine intelligence (Shi, 1990a). As an important theoretical foundation for AI, Cognitive Science is an interdisciplinary field developed from Modern Psychology, Information Science, Neuroscience, Mathematics, Scientific Linguistics, Anthropology, Natural Philosophy, etc.

The maturing and development of Cognitive Science marked a new stage of research on human-centered cognitive and intelligent activities. Research on

Cognitive Science will enable self-understanding and self-control and lift human knowledge and intelligence to an unprecedented level. Moreover, it will lay theoretical foundations for the intelligence revolution, knowledge revolution, and information revolution, as well as provide new concepts, new ideas, and new methodologies for the development of intelligent computer systems.

Promoted by works of Allen Newell and Herbert Simon, research related to cognitive science originated in the late 1950s (Newell and Simon, 1972, 1976; Simon, 1986). Cognitive scientists proposed better models for mind and thinking than the simplified model about humans developed by behaviorism scientists. Cognitive Science research aims at illustrating and explaining how information is processed during cognitive activities. It involves a variety of problems including perception, language, learning, memory, thinking, problem solving, creativity, attention, as well as the impact of environment and social culture on cognition.

In 1991, the representative journal *Artificial Intelligence* published a special issue on the foundation of AI in its 47th volume, in which trends about AI research are discussed. In this special issue, David Kirsh discussed five foundational questions for AI research (Kirsh, 1991):

(1) *Pre-eminence of knowledge and conceptualization*: Intelligence that transcends insect-level intelligence requires declarative knowledge and some form of reasoning-like computation — call this cognition. Core AI is the study of the conceptualizations of the world presupposed and used by intelligent systems during cognition.

(2) *Disembodiment*: Cognition and the knowledge, it presupposes, can be studied largely in abstraction from the details of perception and motor control.

(3) *Kinematics of cognition are language-like*: It is possible to describe the trajectory of knowledge states or informational states created during cognition using a vocabulary very much like English or some regimented logic–mathematical version of English.

(4) *Learning can be added later*: The kinematics of cognition and the domain knowledge needed for cognition can be studied separately from the study of concept learning, psychological development, and evolutionary change.

(5) *Uniform architecture*: There is a single architecture underlying virtually all cognition.

All these questions are cognitive problems critical to AI research that should be discussed from the perspective of fundamental theories of Cognitive Science. These questions have become the watershed for different academic schools of AI research, as different academic schools usually have different answers to them.

1.3 Hierarchical Model of Thought

Thought is the reflection of the objective realities, i.e., the conscious, indirect, and general reflection, in a conscious human brain on the essential attributes and internal laws about the objective realities. Currently, we are in a stage emphasizing self-knowledge and self-recognition with the development of the Cognitive Science. In 1984, Professor Xuesen Qian advocated the Noetic Science research (Qian, 1986).

Human thought mainly involves perceptual thought, imagery thought, abstract thought, and inspirational thought. Perceptual thought is the primary level of thought. When people begin to understand the world, perceptual materials are simply organized to form self-consistent information; thus, only phenomena are understood. The form of thought based on this process is perceptual thought. Perceptual thought about the surface phenomena of all kinds of things can be obtained in practice via direct contact with the objective environment through sensorial mechanisms such as by using eyes, ears, nose, tongue, and bodies, and thus, its sources and contents are objective and substantial.

Imagery thought mainly relies on generalization through methods of typification and the introduction of imagery materials in thinking. It is common to all higher organisms. Imagery thought corresponds to the connection theories of neural mechanisms. AI topics related to imagery thought include Pattern Recognition, Image Processing, Visual Information Processing, etc.

Abstract thought is a form of thought based on abstract concepts, through thinking with symbol information processing. Only with the emergence of language is abstract thought possible: language and thought boost each other and promote each other. Thus, the physical symbol system can be viewed as the basis of abstract thought.

Little research has been done on inspirational thought. Some researchers hold that inspirational thought is the extension of imagery thought to subconsciousness, during which a person does not realize that part of his brain is processing information, while some others argue that inspirational thought is sudden enlightenment. Despite all these disagreements, inspirational thought is very important to creative thinking and needs further research.

In the process of human thinking, attention plays an important role. Attention sets a certain orientation and concentration for noetic activities to ensure that one can promptly respond to the changes of the objective realities and be better accustomed to the environment. Attention limits the number of parallel thought processes. Thus, for most conscious activities, the brain works serially, with the exception of parallel looking and listening.

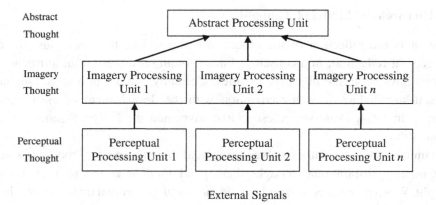

Fig. 1.1. Hierarchical model of thought

Based on the above analysis, we propose a hierarchical model of human thought, as shown in Figure 1.1 (Shi, 1990a, 1992a, 1994). In the figure, perceptual thought is the simplest form of thought, which is constructed from the surface phenomena through sensories such as eyes, ears, nose, tongue, and bodies. Imagery thought is based on the connection theories of neural networks for highly parallel processing. Abstract thought is based on the theory of physical symbol system in which abstract concepts are represented with languages. With the effect of attention, different forms of thought are processed serially most of the time.

The model of thought studies the interrelationships among these three forms of thought, as well as the microprocesses of transformation from one form to the other. Presently, much progress has been made. For example, attractors of neural networks can be used to represent problems such as associative memory and image recognition. Yet, there is still a long way to go for a thorough understanding and application of the whole model. For example, further research is needed on the microprocess from imagery thought to logical thought.

1.4 Symbolic Intelligence

What is intelligence? Intelligence involves purposeful actions, reasonable thinking, as well as comprehensive capabilities to effectively adapt to the environment. Generally speaking, intelligence is one's capabilities to understand the objective world and apply knowledge to solve problems. Intelligence of an individual consists of comprehensive capabilities such as capability to perceive and understand objective things, the objective world, and oneself; capability to gain experience and acquire knowledge through learning; capability to comprehend knowledge and apply knowledge and experience for problem analysis and problem solving; capabilities of association, reasoning, judgment, and decision-making; capability of linguistic abstraction and generalization; capabilities of discovery, invention, creativity, and innovation; capability to timely, promptly, and reasonably cope with the complex environments; capability for predictions of and insights into the development and changes of things. People live in a society, and thus, their intelligence is interrelated with the social environments. With the continuous development of human society, concepts of intelligence also evolve gradually.

Artificial Intelligence, compared with natural intelligence of humans, aims at imitating, extending, and augmenting human intelligence through artificial means and techniques to achieve certain machine intelligence. The science of AI focuses on computational models of intelligent behaviors; develops computer systems for noetic activities such as perception, reasoning, learning, association, decision-making, etc.; and solves complex problems that only human experts can solve.

In the history of AI research, different levels of thought are studied from different views of symbolicism, connectionism, and behaviorism.

Symbolicism is also known as traditional AI. It is based on the physical symbol system hypothesis proposed by Alan Newell and Herbert Simon, which states that a physical symbol system has necessary and sufficient means for general intelligent action. A physical symbol system consists of a set of entities, called symbols, which are physical patterns that can occur as components of another type of entity called an expression (or symbol structure). The system also contains a collection of processes that operate on expressions to produce other expressions: processes of creation, modification, reproduction, and destruction.

Connectionism, also known as neural computing, focuses on the essentials and capabilities for non-programmatical, adaptative, and brain-like information processing. The research field has been rapidly developing in recent years, with a great number of neural network mechanisms, models, and algorithms emerging continuously. Neural network systems are open neural network environments providing typical and practically valuable neural network models. The open system enables the convenient addition of new network models to the existing system, so that new network algorithms can be debugged and modified with the user-friendly interfaces and variety of tools provided by the system. Moreover, it is also convenient to improve existing network models; thus, the system provides an excellent environment to develop new algorithms.

Neural computing investigates the brain functionalities based on the nervous system of human brains and studies the dynamic actions and collaborative information processing capabilities of large numbers of simple neurons. The research focuses on the simulation and imitation of human cognition, including processes of perception and consciousness, imagery thought, distributed memory, self-learning, and self-organization. Neural computing is particularly competent in parallel search, associative memory, self-organization of spatiotemporal data and statistical descriptions, and automatic knowledge acquisition through interrelated activities. It is generally considered that neural networks better fit low-level pattern processing.

Basic characteristics of neural networks include the following: (a) Distributed information storage, (b) parallel information processing, and (c) capabilities of self-organization and self-learning (Shi, 1993). Owing to these characteristics, neural networks provide a new means for information processing with computers. With more and more applications and in-depth research of artificial neural networks, researchers have found many problems of existing models and algorithms, and even met with some difficulties of the nonlinear theories or approximation theory. Despite these problems and difficulties, we believe that with in-depth and extensive applications, neural networks will continue to develop and promote current techniques. The theory of neural field we proposed is such a new kind of attempt.

Currently, integration of symbol processing systems and neural network models is an important research direction. Fuzzy neural networks integrate fuzzy logic and neural networks, taking each other's advantages in theory, methodology, and application, to develop systems with certain learning and dynamic knowledge acquisition capabilities.

Behaviorism, also known as behavior-based AI, in many respects reflects the behavior physiological views in AI. Rodney Brooks brought forward theories of intelligence without representation (Brooks, 1991a) and intelligence without reasoning (Brooks, 1991b) and stated that intelligence is determined by the dynamics of interaction with the world.

These three research genres investigate different aspects of human natural intelligence corresponding to different layers in the model of human thought. Roughly categorizing, it can be presumed that Symbolism focuses on abstract thought, Connectionism focuses on imagery thought, and Behaviorism focuses on perceptual thought. The comparisons of Symbolism, Connectionism, and Behaviorism are shown in Table 1.1

Some researchers classify AI research into two categories: symbolic intelligence and computational intelligence. Symbolic intelligence, also known as traditional AI, solves problems through reasoning based on knowledge. Computational intelligence solves problems based on connections trained from example data. Artificial Neural Networks, Genetic Algorithms, Fuzzy Systems, Evolutionary Programming, Artificial Life, etc., are included in computational intelligence.

Table 1.1. Comparisons of symbolism, connectionism, and behaviorism

	Symbolicism	Connectionism	Behaviorism
Perceptual level	Discrete	Continuous	Continuous
Representation level	Symbolic	Continuous	Behavioral
Problem-solving level	Top-down	Bottom-up	Bottom-up
Processing level	Serial	Parallel	Parallel
Operational level	Reasoning	Connection	Interaction
System level	Local	Distributed	Distributed
Basic level	Logic	Simulant	Intuitional judgment

Presently, traditional AI mainly focuses on knowledge-based problem solving. From a practical point of view, AI is the science of knowledge engineering: taking knowledge as the object and investigating knowledge representation, acquisition, and application. This book mainly introduces and discusses traditional AI. For computational intelligence, please refer to the book *Neural Networks* by Zhongzhi Shi (2009).

1.5 Research Approaches of Artificial Intelligence

During the development of AI since the 1950s, many academic schools have been formed, each holding its specific research methodologies, academic views, and research focuses. This section introduces some research methodologies of AI, focusing mainly on the cognitive school, logical school, and behavioral school.

1.5.1 *Cognitive School*

Cognitive school, with representative researchers such as Herbert Simon, Marvin Minsky, and Allen Newell, focuses on functional simulation with computers based on human noetic activities. In the 1950s, Newell and Simon advocated the "heuristic program" together and worked out the "Logic Theorist" computer program to simulate the thinking process of mathematical theorem proving. Then in the early 1960s, they developed the "General Problem Solver (GPS)", which simulates the common principles of human problem solving with three steps: first, set the initial problem-solving plan; then, apply axioms, theorems, and rules to solve the problems according to the plan; and then continually proceed with the means-end analysis and modify the problem solving until the goal is achieved. Thus, the GPS possesses a certain universality.

In 1976, Newell and Simon proposed the physical symbol system premise and stated that a physical symbol system has the necessary and sufficient means for general intelligent action. Thus, an information processing system can be viewed as a concrete physical system, such as human neural system, computer construction system, etc. Each physical pattern is a symbol, as long as it can be distinguished from the other patterns. For example, different English characters are different symbols. Operation on symbols relies on comparison among different symbols, i.e., distinguishing which symbols are the same and which ones are different. Thus, the fundamental task and functionality of a physical symbol system is to identify the same characters and distinguish different ones.

In the 1980s, Newell *et al.*, focused on the SOAR system, a symbolic cognitive architecture for general problem solving, based on the Chunking mechanism for learning and rule-based memory for representation of operators, search control, etc.

Minsky took the view of psychics, holding that in daily activities, people apply plenty of knowledge acquired and collected from previous experiences. Such knowledge is stored in the brain in a structure similar to a frame. Thus, he proposed the frame knowledge representation structure in the 1970s. In the 1980s, Minsky believed that there is no unified theory for human intelligence. In the famous book *Society of Mind* he published in 1985, Minsky pointed out that the society of mind is a vast society of individually simple agents with certain thinking capabilities.

1.5.2 *Logical School*

Logical school, with representative researchers such as John McCarthy and Nils Nilsson, holds the logical perspective for AI research, i.e., describes the objective world through formalization. This academic school believes the following:

- Intelligent machines will have knowledge of their environment.
- The most versatile intelligent machines will represent much of their knowledge about their environment declaratively.
- For the most versatile machines, the language in which declarative knowledge is represented must be at least as expressive as first-order predicate calculus.

Logical school focuses on conceptual knowledge representation, model theoretic semantics, deductive reasoning, etc., in AI research. McCarthy claimed that everything can be represented with the unified frame of logics, and commonsense reasoning will be difficult without some form of non-monotonic reasoning.

1.5.3 *Behavioral School*

Most AI research is based on very abstract and simple models for the real world. Rodney Brooks argued that it is necessary to go beyond this ivory tower of abstract models and take the complex real world as the background instead, so that AI theories and technologies can be tested in real-world problem solving and improved on these tests.

In 1991, Brooks brought forward theories of intelligence without representation and intelligence without reason and stated that intelligence is determined by the dynamics of interaction with the world. He simply called this work as "robots" or "behavior-based robots". There are a number of key aspects characterizing this style of work as follows (Brooks, 1991b):

- *Situatedness*: The robots are situated in the world, and the world directly influences the behavior of the system.
- *Embodiment*: The robots have bodies and experience the world directly.
- *Intelligence*: The source of intelligence is not limited to just the computational engine. It also comes from the situation in the world.
- *Emergence*: The intelligence of the system emerges from the system's interactions with the world and sometimes indirect interactions between its components.

Based on these ideas, Brooks programmed autonomous mobile robots, based on layered, asynchronous, and distributed networks of augmented finite-state machines, each one being a comparatively independent unit for functionalities of advance, balance, prowl, etc. The robot walked successfully, and thus initiated a new approach to Robotics.

Different academic schools of AI research have different answers to the five foundational cognitive questions introduced in Section 1.2. The logical school (represented by Nils Nilsson) holds positive answers to questions 1–4 and a neutral answer to question 5; the cognitive school (represented by Allen Newell) holds positive answers to questions 1, 3, and 5; while the behavioral school (represented by Rodney Brooks) holds negative answers to all questions 1–5.

1.6 Automated Reasoning

Reasoning is the cognitive process of logically inferring a new judgment (conclusion) from one or more already known judgments (precondition). It is the reflection of the objective relationships in mind. People usually solve problems based on prior knowledge and make conclusions through reasoning. Theories and technologies of automated reasoning are important bases for research fields of program derivation, proof of program correctness, expert systems, intelligent robots, etc.

Early works of automated reasoning focused on automated theorem proving. Pioneer work includes the Logic Theorist developed by Herbert Simon and Allen

Newell. In 1956, Alan Robinson proposed the Resolution Principle, making great progress in research on automated reasoning. The resolution principle is easily applicable and logically complete; thus, it becomes the computing model for the logic programming language Prolog. Though some methods outperforming the Resolution Principle in some aspects appeared later, e.g., natural deductive reasoning and term rewriting systems, yet they are limited due to the combination problem and the computational intractability essentially.

For a practical system, there always exist some non-deductive cases. Thus, various reasoning algorithms have been proposed, which even weaken the attempt of finding a universal fundamental principle for AI. From the practical perspective, each reasoning algorithm conforms to its specific, domain-related strategies based on different knowledge representation techniques. On the contrary, it is undoubtedly useful to find a universal reasoning theory. In fact, an important impetus for AI theoretical research is to find more general and universal reasoning algorithms.

An important achievement of automated reasoning research is non-monotonic reasoning, a pseudo-induction system. The so-called "non-monotonic reasoning" is the reasoning process in which adding new positive axioms to the system may invalidate some already proved theorems. Obviously, non-monotonic reasoning is more complex than monotonic reasoning. In non-monotonic reasoning, first hypotheses are made; then standard logical reasoning is carried out; if inconsistence appears, then backtracking is done to eliminate inconsistence, and a new hypothesis is established.

Raymond Reiter first set forth the closed world assumption (CWA) for non-monotonic reasoning in 1978 (Reiter, 1978) and proposed the Default Reasoning (Reiter, 1980). In 1979, Jon Doyle developed the truth maintenance system (TMS) (Doyle, 1979). In 1980, John McCarthy formalized the theory of Circumscription (McCarthy, 1980). Circumscription of a predict P means to exclude most models based on P and select only a minimum set of models in which P is assigned to true. Different circumscription criteria will produce different minimizations of predicates.

Quantitative simulation with computers is commonly applied for scientific computing. Yet, people often predict or explain system behaviors without detailed calculation data. Such problem solving cannot be achieved simply through deduction; thus, qualitative reasoning is proposed in AI for representation and reasoning without precise quantitative information. In qualitative reasoning, physical systems or procedures can be decomposed into subsystems or model fragments, each with structuralized specifications of the subsystem itself and its interrelationships with other subsystems. Through approaches such as causal ordering and compositional modeling, functionalities and behaviors of the real physical systems can be qualitatively represented. Typical qualitative reasoning techniques include the following: qualitative differential equation (QDE)-based modeling and reasoning by Johan de Kleer, process-centered modeling and reasoning by Kenneth Forbus, and constraint-centered qualitative simulation by Benjamin Kuipers. Combined approaches of quantitative and qualitative reasoning will have a great impact on scientific decision-making of expert systems.

Uncertainty is ubiquitous to real-world problems, which results from the deviation of people's subjective cognition from the objective realities. Various causes may reflect such deviation and bring about uncertainty, such as randomicity of things, incompleteness, unreliability, imprecision and inconsistency of human knowledge, and vagueness and ambiguousness of natural language. With respect to different causes of uncertainty, different theories and reasoning methodologies have been proposed. In AI and knowledge engineering, representative approaches of uncertainty theories and reasoning methodologies are introduced in the following.

Probability theory is widely used to process randomicity and uncertainty of human knowledge. Bayesian theory has been successfully applied in the PROSPEC-TOR expert system, yet it relies on the assigned prior probabilities. The MYCIN model-based certainty factors, adopting some assumptions and principles for conjunction of hypothesis, is a simple and effective method, though it lacks well-established theoretical foundations.

The Dempster–Shafer theory of evidence introduces the concept of belief function to extend classical probabilities and describes that belief function satisfies a set of axioms weaker than probability axioms. Thus, belief function can be viewed as a superset of the existing probability functions. With belief function, even without precise probabilities, constrains on probability distributions can be set based on prior domain knowledge. The theory has well-established theoretical foundations, yet its definition and computation are comparatively complex. In recent years, this theory of evidence has gained more and more research focuses, and many research achievements and application systems have been developed. For example, Lotfi Zadeh illustrated how the Dempster–Shafer theory can be viewed as an instance of inference from second-order relations and applied it in a relational database.

In 1965, Lotfi Zadeh proposed the Fuzzy Set, based on which a research series has been carried out, including fuzzy logic, fuzzy decision-making, probability theory, etc. For reasoning with natural language, Zadeh introduced fuzzy quantization to represent fuzzy propositions in natural language; defined concepts of linguistic variable, linguistic value, and probability distribution; and developed possibility theory and approximate reasoning. His work has attracted much research focus. Fuzzy mathematics has been widely applied to expert systems and intelligent controllers, as well as for the research of fuzzy computer. Chinese researchers have done much work in theoretical research and practical applications, drawing the attention of international academics. However, many theoretical problems still remain to be solved in this domain. There are also some different views and disputes, such as what is the basis for fuzzy logic? What about the problem of consistency and completeness of fuzzy logic? In the future, research focuses of uncertain reasoning may be centralized on the following three aspects: first, to solve existing problems of current uncertainty theories; second, to study the efficient and effective discrimination capabilities and judgment mechanisms of human beings for new theories and new methodologies to deal with uncertainties; and third, to explore methods and technologies to synthetically process varieties of uncertainties.

Theorem proving is a kind of specific intelligent behavior of humans that not only relies on logic deductions based on premises but also requires certain intuitive skills. Automated theorem proving adopts a suit of symbol systems to formalize the process of human theorem proving into symbol calculation that can automatically be implemented by computers, i.e., to mechanize the intelligence process of reasoning and deduction. The mechanical theorem proving in elementary geometry and differential geometry proposed by Professor Wenjun Wu of the Chinese Academy of Sciences is highly valued all over the world.

1.7 Machine Learning

Knowledge, knowledge representation, and knowledge-based reasoning algorithms are always considered the heart of AI, while machine learning can be viewed as the most critical problem. For hundreds of years, psychologists and philosophers held the belief that the basic mechanism of learning is trying to transfer successful behaviors from one practice to other similar practices. Learning is the process of acquiring knowledge, gaining experience, improving performance, discovering rules, and adapting to environments. Figure 1.2 illustrates a simple model of learning with the four basic elements of a learning system (Simon, 1983). The environment provides external information, similar to a supervisor. The learning unit processes information provided by the environment, corresponding to various learning algorithms. The knowledge base stores knowledge in certain knowledge representation formalisms. The performing unit accomplishes certain tasks based on the knowledge in the knowledge base and sends the execution results to the learning unit through feedbacks. The system can be gradually improved through learning. Research on machine learning not only enables machines to automatically acquire knowledge and obtain intelligence but also uncovers principles and secrets of human thinking

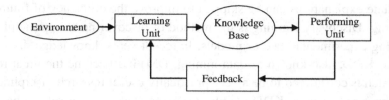

Fig. 1.2. Simple model of learning

and learning and even helps to improve the efficiency of human learning. Research on machine learning also has a great impact on memory storage patterns, information input methods, and computer architectures.

Research in machine learning roughly experienced four stages. The first and initial stage was learning without knowledge, focusing on neural models, and self-adaptative and self-organization systems based on decision theories. However, as neural models and decision theories were fairly restricted and only achieved limited success, the research passion gradually decreased. The second stage in the 1960s was the low tide, focusing mainly on symbolic concept acquisition. Then in the third stage, interest in machine learning rejuvenated and many distinctive algorithms appeared since Patrick Winston's important paper *Learning Structural Descriptions from Examples* in 1975. More importantly, it was then popularly recognized that a learning system would not learn high-level concepts without background knowledge. Thus, great amount of knowledge was introduced to learning systems as background knowledge, bringing about a new era and new prospects for machine learning research. Due to the mass applications of expert systems and problem-solving systems, knowledge acquisition has become the key bottleneck, the solution of which relies heavily on the advances of machine learning research. There comes the fourth stage and another climax of machine learning research.

The main paradigms of machine learning include inductive learning, analytical learning, discovery learning, genetic learning, connection learning, etc. (Shi, 1992b). Inductive learning has been most extensively studied in the past, focused mainly on general concept description and concept clustering, and proposed algorithms such as the AQ algorithms, version space algorithm, and ID3 algorithm. Analogical learning analyzes similarities of the target problem with previously known source problems and then applies the solutions from the source problems to the target problem. Analytical learning, e.g., explanation-based learning, chunking, etc., learns from training examples guided by domain knowledge. Explanation-based learning extracts general principles from a concrete problem-solving process which can be applied to other similar problems. As learned knowledge is stored in the knowledge base, intermediate explanations can be skipped to improve the efficiency of future problem solving. Discovery learning is the method of discovering new principles from the existing experimental data or models. In recent years, knowledge discovery in databases (KDD, also known as data mining, DM) has become the great research focus, which is considered to be a very practically useful research discipline by AI and database researchers. KDD mainly discovers classification rules, characteristic rules, association rules, differentiation rules, evolution rules, exceptional rules, etc., through the methods of statistical analysis, machine learning, neural networks, multidimensional database, etc. Genetic learning based on the classic genetic algorithm is designed to simulate biological evolution via reproduction and variation and Darwin's natural selection paradigm. It takes each variant of a concept as an individual of the species and evaluates different mutations and recombinations based on objective fitness functions, so as to select the fittest offsprings for survival. Connection learning recognizes different input patterns through training the neural networks with typical example instances.

Machine learning research is still in its primary stage and needs extensive research efforts. Progress in machine learning research will enable breakthroughs in AI and knowledge engineering research. In the future, research focuses of machine learning will include cognitive models for the learning process, computational learning theories, new learning algorithms, machine learning systems integrating multiple learning strategies, etc.

1.8 Distributed Artificial Intelligence

Studies of human intellectual behaviors show that most human activities involve social groups consisting of multiple individuals, and large-scale complex problem solving also involves cooperation of several professionals or organizations. "Cooperation" is a major aspect of human intelligence pervasive in the human society, and thus the motivation for research in distributed artificial intelligence (DAI).

With the development of computer network, computer communication and concurrent programming technologies since the 1980s, DAI is gradually becoming a new research focus in the field of AI. DAI is a subfield of AI investigating how logically and physically distributed agents cooperate with each other to perform intelligent behaviors. It enables collaborated and coordinated knowledge, skills, and planning; solves single-objective and multi-objective problems; and provides an effective means for the design and construction of large-scale complex intelligent systems or computers to support cooperation.

The term DAI was coined by American researchers, and the first International Workshop on distributed artificial intelligence was held at MIT in Boston, USA in

1980. From then on, all kinds of conferences on DAI or DAI-related topics have been held continually all over the world, which greatly promote the development and popularization of DAI technologies and gradually deepen and broaden the research and applications of the science of DAI. With the increase in scale, scope, and complexity of new computer-based information systems, decision support systems, and knowledge-based systems, as well as the requirement to encode more complex knowledge in these systems, applications and development of DAI technologies are becoming increasingly important to these systems.

Research on DAI can be generally categorized into two domains: distributed problem solving (DPS) and multi-agent system (MAS), both sharing the same research paradigm yet adopt different problem-solving means. The goal of DPS is to establish large-granularity cooperative clusters to accomplish the common problem-solving objectives. In a pure DPS system, problems are resolved into subtasks, specific task executors are designed to solve the corresponding subtasks, and all interaction strategies are incorporated as an integral part of the system. Such systems feature top-down design, since the whole system is established to solve the predefined objectives at the top end.

On the contrary, a pure MAS system generally comprises pre-existing autonomous and heterogeneous agents without a common objective. Research on MAS involves coordinations and cooperations in knowledge, plan, and behavior among groups of autonomous intelligent agents, so that they can jointly take actions or solve problems. Though the agent here is also a task executor, it is "open" to other peer agents and can deal with both single objective and multiple objectives.

Nowadays, applications of computers are becoming more and more extensive, and problems to be solved are becoming more and more complex, which makes centralized control of the problem-solving process and centralized processing of data, information, and knowledge more and more difficult. Such distributed and concurrent processing of data and knowledge signifies great potential along with many pending difficulties to the development of AI. The spatial distribution, temporal concurrency, and logical dependent relationships of multiple agents make the problem solving more complex in multi-agent systems than in single-agent systems.

Despite such difficulties, research on DAI is feasible, desirable, and important for the following reasons:

(1) *Technical foundations*: Advances in technologies such as hardware architecture of the processors and communication between the processors make it possible to interconnect a great number of asynchronous processors. Such a connection might be in the form of tightly coupled systems based on shared or distributed

memory, or loosely coupled systems based on local networks, or even very loosely connected systems based on geographically distributed communication networks.

(2) *Distributed problem solving*: Many AI applications are distributed in nature. They might be spatially distributed, such as the explanation and integration of spatially distributed sensors, or the control of robots cooperating for work in a factory. They might also be functionally distributed, such as the integration of several professional medical diagnosis systems to solve complex cases. They might even be scheduling distributed, for example, in a factory, the production line is composed of several working procedures, each scheduled by an expert system.

(3) *System integration*: DAI systems support modular design and implementation well. A complex system can be resolved into several comparatively simple and task-specific submodules, in order that the system can be easily constructed, debugged, and maintained. It is more flexible to handle errors of decomposed submodules than a single integral module. On the contrary, great economic and social benefit will be gained if the many existing centralized AI application systems can be used to construct distributed AI systems with minor modifications. For example, it will be extremely time-saving and practically effective if existing independent systems of liver diagnosis system, stomach diagnosis system, intestines diagnose system, etc., can be slightly modified to construct a complex expert system to diagnose digestive tract diseases. The plug-in approach we proposed for agent construction is an effective means to integrate existing AI systems.

(4) *New approach to intelligent behavior*: Implement intelligent behavior with intelligent agents. To become societies of mind, AI systems should have functions for interaction with the environment, as well as capabilities to cooperate and coordinate with each other.

(5) *Meanings in cognitive science*: DAI can be used for research and verification of the problems and theories in sociology, psychology, management, etc. Cooperative MAS based on belief, knowledge, hope, intention, promise, attention, object, cooperation, etc., provides an effective means to understand and simulate the cognitive problems.

Therefore, no matter technically or socially, the emergence and development of DAI systems is imperative. It is also natural to apply DAI technologies to solve large-scale martial problems. Presently, research in this domain has seen certain achievements in China.

MAS is a branch of DAI research. In a multi-agent system, an agent is an autonomous entity which continuously interacts with the environment and co-exists with other peer agents in the same environment. In other words, agent is an entity whose mental states consist of components such as belief, desire, and intention. In a multi-agent system, the agents can be either homogeneous or heterogeneous, and the relationships among them can be either cooperative or competitive. A common characteristic of DAI and MAS is distributed behaviors of entities or agents. Multi-agent systems feature bottom-up design because in practice, the distributed automatic individual agents are defined first, and then problem solving is accomplished with one or more agents. Both single objective and multiple objectives can be achieved. Research on MAS is dedicated to analysis and design of large-scale complex cooperative intelligent systems such as large-scale knowledge and information systems and intelligent robots, based on theories of problem solving through concurrent computing and mutual cooperation among logically or physically distributed multiple agents.

At present, MAS is a very active research direction that aims at simulation of human rational behaviors for applications in domains such as real-world and society simulation, robotics, intelligent machines, etc. An agent is characterized with features of autonomy, interaction with the environment, cooperation, communication, longevity, adaptability, real time, etc. In order to survive and work in the constantly changing environment of the real world, agents should not only react to emergencies promptly but also make middle- or short-term plans based on certain tactics, and then predict the future state through modeling and analysis of the world and other agents, as well as cooperate or negotiate with other agents using the communication language.

To achieve these features, agent architecture should be studied because architectures and functions of agents are closely related with each other: improper architecture may greatly limit the functions, while appropriate architecture may well support high-level intelligence of agents. We proposed a compound architecture for an agent, which systematically integrates multiple parallel and comparatively independent yet interactional forms of mind, including reaction, planning, modeling, communication, decision-making, etc. A multi-agent environment (MAGE) is implemented through the agent kernel-based plug-in approach we proposed for agent construction (Shi *et al.*, 2003). With MAGE and the plug-in approach, compound agents can be conveniently constructed and debugged.

1.9 Artificial Thought Model

Development of computers can be roughly divided into two stages. In the first stage, the Von Neumann architecture is applied for numerical computation, document processing, and database management and query. All these applications have specific algorithms, though somewhat difficult in programming. The second stage focuses on symbolic and logical processing, in which knowledge and information processing mainly base on reasoning. How to choose an effective algorithm is the key problem to this stage of research. All these applications are well-defined and explicitly represented problems of the ideal world. However, many real-world problems are ill-structured, such as pattern recognition, problem solving, and learning from incomplete information, etc. These problems are in the category of intuitive information processing.

For intuitive information processing, theories and technologies of flexible information processing should be studied. Flexibility in the real world has the following characteristics:

- integrate varieties of complex and intricately related information containing ambiguity or uncertainty information;
- actively acquire necessary information and knowledge, and learn general knowledge inductively from examples;
- automatically adapt to users and changing environment;
- self-organization based on the object for processing;
- error-tolerant information processing.

Actually, human neural networks capable of large-scale parallel and distributed information processing inherently support flexible information processing. Thus, we proposed the artificial thought model in Figure 1.3.

The artificial thought model in Figure 1.3 clearly illustrates that artificial thought is based on open autonomous systems, takes full advantage of varieties

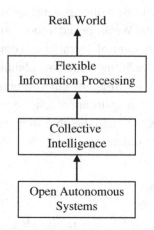

Fig. 1.3. Artificial thought model

of information processing patterns to achieve collective intelligence, then proceeds with flexible information processing, and finally solves real-world problems.

1.10 Knowledge-Based Systems

An important impetus for AI research is to construct knowledge-based systems to automatically solve difficult problems. Ever since the 1980s, knowledge engineering has become the most remarkable characteristic of AI applications. Knowledge-based systems (KBS) include expert system, knowledge-based system, intelligent decision support system, etc. In 1965, DENDRAL, which was designed to illustrate organic chemistry structures, developed to a series of expert system programs. Such systems mainly include two parts: one is the knowledge base, which represents and stores the set of task-related specific domain knowledge, including not only facts about the related domain but also heuristic knowledge at an expert level; the other is the inference engine, which includes a series of inference methodologies to retrieve the reasoning path, and thus form premises, satisfy objectives, solve problems, etc. As different mechanisms and concepts can be adopted, the inference engines have multiple patterns.

In knowledge-based systems, knowledge will be stored in the computer in defined structures for knowledge management, problem solving, and knowledge sharing. Projects and software of "knowledge-based management system (KBMS)" have been initiated and developed all over the world, such as in America, Japan (the NTT Company), as well as China. A remarkable characteristic of KBMS is the integration of inference and query, which improves the maintenance of the knowledge base and provides useful development environment for specific domain knowledge-based systems.

Decision Support System (DSS) evolved from the management information system (MIS), with its concept initiated in the early 1970s. It developed fast as an important tool to improve the competitiveness and productivity of companies as well as to decide on the successfulness of a company. DSS has been adopted by various levels of decision-makers abroad and has attracted much attention in China. Decision support techniques are critical to support scientific decision-making. Early DSS was based on MIS and included some standard models, such as the operational research model and the econometric model. In 1980, Ralph Sprague proposed a DSS structure based on a database, model base, and dialog generation and management software, which had a great impact on later research and applications. In recent years, AI technologies have been gradually applied to DSS, and thus came into being the intelligent decision support system (IDSS). In 1986, the author proposed the intelligent decision system composed of a database, model base, and knowledge base (Shi, 1988b), which improved the level of scientific management by providing an effective means to solve semi-structured and ill-structured decision problems. Characteristics of IDSS include the application of AI techniques to DSS and the integration of database and information retrieval techniques with model-based qualitative analysis techniques. In the 1990s, we developed the Group DSS (GDSS) based on MAS technologies, which attracted enormous research interest.

Building intelligent systems can imitate, extend, and augment human intelligence to achieve certain "machine intelligence", which has great theoretical meaning and practical value. Intelligent systems can be roughly classified into four categories according to the knowledge contained and the paradigms processed: single-domain single-paradigm intelligent system, multi-domain single-paradigm intelligent system, single-domain multi-paradigm intelligent system, and multi-domain multi-paradigm intelligent system.

1. Single-domain single-paradigm intelligent system

Such systems contain knowledge about a single domain and process only problems of a single paradigm. Examples of such systems include the first and second generation of expert systems, as well as the intelligent control system.

Expert systems apply domain-specific knowledge and reasoning methods to solve complex and specific problems usually settled only by human experts, so as to construct intelligent computer programs with similar problem-solving capabilities as experts. They can make explanations about decision-making procedures and learn to acquire related problem-solving knowledge. The first generation of expert systems (such as DENDRAL, MACSYMA, etc.) had highly professional and specific problem-solving capabilities, yet they lacked completeness and portability in architecture and were weak in problem solving. The second generation of expert systems (such as MYCIN, CASNET, PROSPECTOR, HEARSAY, etc.) were subject-specific professional application systems. They were complete in architecture with better portability and were improved in aspects such as human–machine interface, explanation mechanisms, knowledge acquisition, uncertain reasoning, enhanced expert system knowledge representation, heuristics and generality of reasoning, etc.

2. Multi-domain single-paradigm intelligent system

Such systems contain knowledge about multiple domains, yet only process problems of a certain paradigm. Examples include most distributed problem-solving systems and multi-expert systems. Generally, expert system development tools and environments are used to construct such large-scale synthetic intelligent systems.

Since intelligent systems are widely applied to various domains such as engineering technology, social economics, national defense affairs, and ecological environment, and several requirements are put forward for intelligent systems. To solve the many real-world problems such as medical diagnosis, economic planning, military commanding, financial projects, crop planting, and environment protection, expert knowledge and experience of multiple domains might be involved. Many existing expert systems are single-subject, specific microexpert systems, which might not satisfy the users' practical demands. To construct multi-domain single-paradigm intelligent systems might be an approach to meet the users' requirements in certain degrees. Some characteristics of such systems are as follows:

(1) solve the user's real-world complex problems;
(2) adopt knowledge and experience of multiple domains, disciplines, and professionals for cooperative problem solving;
(3) based on distributed open software, hardware, and network environment;
(4) constructed with expert system development tools and environments;
(5) achieve knowledge sharing and knowledge reuse.

3. Single-domain multi-paradigm intelligent system

Such systems contain knowledge of only a single domain, yet process problems of multiple paradigms. Examples include the compound intelligent system. Generally, knowledge can be acquired through neural network training, and then transformed into production rules to be used in problem solving by inference engines.

Multiple mechanisms can be used to process a single problem in problem solving. Take an illness diagnosis system as an example, both symbolic reasoning and artificial neural networks can be used. Then, compare and integrate the results of different methods processing the same problem, through which correct results might be obtained and unilateralism can be avoided.

4. Multi-domain multi-paradigm intelligent system

Figure 1.4 illustrates the sketch map of such systems which contain knowledge of multiple domains and process problems of different paradigms. Collective intelligence in the figure means that when processing multiple paradigms, different processing mechanisms work separately, accomplish different duties, and cooperate with each other, so as to represent collective intelligent behaviors.

Synthetical DSS and KBS belong to this category of intelligent systems. In such systems, reasoning-based abstract thought is based on symbolic processing, while imagery thought such as pattern recognition and image processing applies neural network computing.

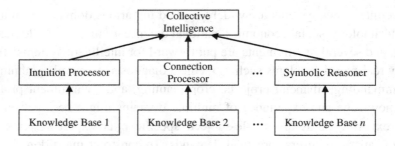

Fig. 1.4.   Multi-domain multi-paradigm intelligent system

Most intelligence problems are ill-structured and continuously changing, and are thus difficult to solve with a single specific algorithm. A plausible approach to solve such intelligence problems is to construct human–machine united open systems which interact with the environment. An open system is one which may always run into unexpected results during the system processing and can receive external new information at any time.

Based on a summary and analysis of the design methods and implementation technologies of existing KBS, intelligent agent technologies are studied to construct large-scale synthetical KBS with functionalities of multiple knowledge representation, synthetical knowledge base, self-organization and cooperation, automatic knowledge acquisition, continually improved intelligent behaviors, etc. Such systems are the primary means to construct multi-domain multi-paradigm intelligent systems.

Exercises

1.1 What is artificial intelligence (AI)? What is the research objective of AI?

1.2 Briefly introduce the main stages of development in the history of AI.

1.3 What are the five fundamental questions for AI research?

1.4 What is the physical symbol system? What is the physical symbol system's assumption?

1.5 What is symbolic intelligence? What is computational intelligence?

1.6 Describe the simple model of machine learning and its basic elements.

1.7 What is distributed artificial intelligence (DAI)? What are the main research domains of DAI?

1.8 Refer to relevant literature and discuss whether the following tasks can be solved by current computers:

(a) Defeat an international grandmaster in the world's chess competition;
(b) Defeat a 9 duan professional in a game of Go;
(c) Discover and prove a new mathematical theorem;
(d) Find bugs in the programs automatically.

1.9 How should we classify knowledge-based systems? How should we achieve collective intelligence behaviors?

Chapter 2

Logic Foundation

Logic is a primary tool in the study of computer science as well as in the study of artificial intelligence. McCarthy claimed human-level artificial intelligence (AI) is logical AI based on the formalizing of commonsense knowledge and reasoning in mathematical logic.

2.1 Introduction

Logic as a formal science was founded by Aristotle. Leibniz reaffirmed Aristotle's logical developing direction of mathematics form and founded the mathematical logic. From the thirties of the last century, various mathematical methods were extensively introduced and used in the mathematical logic with the result that mathematical logic has become one branch of mathematics and is as important as algebra and geometry. Mathematical logic has spread out many branches such as model theory, set theory, recursion theory, and proof theory.

Logic is a primary tool in the study of computer science as well as in the study of artificial intelligence. It is widely used in many domains, such as semasiology, logic programming language, theory of software specification and validation, theory of database, theory of knowledge base, intelligent system, and study of robots. The objective of computer science is essentially coincident with the goal of logic. On the one hand, the objective of computer science is to simulate with the computer the function and behavior of the human brain and bring the computer to be an extension of the brain. Here, the simulation of the function and behavior of the human brain is infact to simulate the thinking process of persons. On the other hand, logic is a subject focused on the discipline and law of human's thinking. Therefore, the methods and results obtained in logic are naturally selected and put to use during the research of computer science. Furthermore, the intelligent behavior of human beings is largely expressed by language and character; therefore, simulation of human natural language is the point of departure for the simulation of human thinking process. In 2005, McCarthy wrote "I think the best hope for human-level AI is logical AI, based on the formalizing of commonsense knowledge and reasoning in mathematical logic" (McCarthy, 2005).

Language is the starting point for the study of human's thinking in the logic, as well as for the simulation of human's thinking in computer science. Topics related to language are important issues that run through the domain of computer science. Many subjects of computer science, such as programming languages and their formal semantics, knowledge representation and reasoning, and the natural language processing, are all related to language. Generally speaking, representation and reasoning are two basic topics in computer science and artificial intelligence. Much of the intelligent behavior relies on a direct representation of knowledge, for which the formal logic provides an important approach.

Knowledge, especially the so-called common knowledge, is the foundation of intelligent behavior. Intelligent behavior, such as analyzing, conjecturing, forecasting, and deciding, are all based on the utilization of knowledge. Accordingly, in order to simulate with the computer the intelligent behavior, one should first make knowledge represented in the computer, and then enable the computer to utilize and reason about the knowledge. Representation and reasoning are two basic topics on knowledge in the study of artificial intelligence. They are entirely coincident with the two topics focused by the study of natural language, i.e., the accurate structure and reasoning of natural languages. Therefore, the methods and results obtained in logic are also useful for the study of knowledge in artificial intelligence. The ability of representation and the performance of reasoning are a pair of contradictions for any logic system applied to intelligent systems. A trade-off between such a pair is often necessary.

The logic applied in the majority of logic-based intelligent systems is first-order logic or its extensions. The representation ability of first-order logic is so strong that many experts believe that all the knowledge representation problems arising in the research of artificial intelligence can be carried out within the framework of first-order logic. First-order logic is suitable for representing knowledge with uncertainty. For example, the expression $\exists x P(x)$ states that there exists an object for which property P holds, while it is not pointed out which one is such an object. For another example, the expression $P \vee Q$ states that at least one of P and Q holds, but it is not determined whether P (or Q) really holds. Furthermore, first-order logic is equipped with a complete axiom system, which can be treated as a standard of reference in the designing of strategies and algorithms on reasoning. Although first-order logic is capable of representing majority of knowledge, it is not convenient and concise for many applications. Driven by various requirements, lots of logic systems have been proposed and studied; in the following, we enumerate some typical examples:

(1) In order to represent knowledge epistemically, such as belief, awareness, desire, intention, goal and commitment, various modal logics were proposed.
(2) In order to represent knowledge which is related to time, various temporal logics were proposed.
(3) In order to represent knowledge with uncertainty, the so-called fuzzy logic was proposed. As a system built upon the natural language directly, fuzzy logic adopts many elements from the natural language. According to Zadeh, the founder of fuzzy logic, fuzzy logic can be regarded as a computing system on words; in other words, fuzzy logic can be defined by the formula "fuzzy logic = computing with words".
(4) Knowledge of humans is closely interrelated to human activities. Accordingly, knowledge on behavior or action is important for intelligent systems. Compared with various static elements of logic, action is distinguished by the fact that the execution of actions will affect the properties of intelligent systems. Representation and reasoning about actions are classical topics in the study of artificial intelligence; many problems, such as the frame problem and the qualification problem, were put forward and well studied. Many logic systems, such as the dynamic logic and the dynamic description logic, were also proposed.
(5) Computer-aided decision-making has become one of the important applications of the computer. Persons always hold their predilections when they are making a decision. In order to represent the rule and simulate the behavior of people's decision-making process, it is inevitable to deal with predilection. As a result, based on management science, a family of so-called partial logics was proposed and studied.
(6) Time is one of the most important terms present in intelligent systems. Some adverbs, such as occasionally, frequently, and often, are used in the natural language to represent time. Knowledge about the time which is described by these adverbs cannot be represented with classical temporal logic. Therefore, an approach similar to the integral of mathematics was introduced into logic. With the resulted logic, time as described by various adverbs can be formally represented and operated.

2.2 Logic Programming

In this section, we give a brief introduction to the logic programming language Prolog. Prolog was first developed by a group around Alain Colmerauer at the University of Marseilles, France, in the early 1970s. Prolog was one of the first logic programming languages, and it is now a major Artificial Intelligence and Expert Systems programming language.

Prolog is declarative in style rather than procedural. Users just need to represent the facts and rules over which the execution is triggered by running queries; the execution is then carried out accordingly to find a resolution refutation of the negated query. In other words, users just need to tell the Prolog engine what to do but not how to do it. Furthermore, Prolog holds the following features:

(1) Prolog is a unification of data and program. Prolog provides a basic data structure called "terms". Both data and programs of prolog can be constructed over terms. This property is fit for the intelligent program since the outputs of certain programs can be executed as newly generated programs.
(2) Prolog supports the automatic backtracking and pattern-matching, which are two of the most useful and basic mechanisms used in intelligent systems.
(3) Prolog uses recursion. Recursion is extensively used in the Prolog program and data structure, so that a data structure with big size can be manipulated by a short program. In general, the length of a program represented with Prolog is only 10% of that which is written with the C++ language.

All these features make Prolog suitable for encoding intelligent programs and suitable for applications such as natural language processing, theorem proving, and expert systems.

2.2.1 *Definitions of Logic Programming*

First, we introduce the Horn clause which is the constituent of logic programs. A clause consists of two parts: the head and the body. As an IF-THEN rule, the condition portion of a clause is called the head and the conclusion portion of it is called the body.

Definition 2.1. A Horn clause is a clause that contains at most one literal (proposition/predicate) at the head.

Horn clauses in Prolog can be separated into three groups as follows:

(1) Clauses without conditions (facts): A;

(2) Clauses with conditions (rules): $A :\text{-} B_1, \ldots, B_n$;
(3) Goal clauses (queries): $? :\text{-} B_1, \ldots, B_n$.

Semantics of the above Horn clauses is informally described as follows:

(1) Clause A states that A is true for any assignments on variables.
(2) Clause $A :\text{-} B_1, \ldots, B_n$ states that for any assignments on variables: if $B_1, \ldots,$ and B_n are evaluated to be true, then A must also be true.
(3) The goal clause $? :\text{-} B_1, \ldots, B_n$ represents a query that will be executed. Execution of a Prolog program is initiated by the user's posting of a query; the Prolog engine tries to find a resolution refutation of the negated query.

For example, here are two Horn clauses:

(a) $W(X, Y) :\text{-} P(X), Q(Y)$.
(b) $?-R(X, Y), Q(Y)$.

The Horn clause indexed by (a) is a rule, with $P(X)$, $Q(Y)$ as the body and $W(X, Y)$ as the head. The Horn clause indexed by (b) is a query with $R(X, Y)$, $Q(Y)$ as the body. The intuition of the query indexed by (b) is that whether $R(X, Y)$ and $Q(Y)$ hold and what are the values of X and Y in the case that $R(X, Y) \wedge Q(Y)$ holds.

We will now formally define Logic Programs.

Definition 2.2. A logic program is a collection of Horn clauses. In the logic program, clauses with the same predicate symbol are called the definition of the predicate.

For example, the following two rules form a logic program:

$$\text{Father}(X, Y) :\text{-} \text{Child}(Y, X), \text{Male}(X).$$
$$\text{Son}(Y, X) :\text{-} \text{Child}(Y, X), \text{Male}(Y).$$

This program can also be extended with the following facts:

$$\text{Child(xiao-li, lao-li)}.$$
$$\text{Male(xiao-li)}.$$
$$\text{Male(lao-li)}.$$

Taking these rules and facts as inputs of the Prolog engine, we can compile and execute it. Then the following queries can be carried out:

(1) query: ?- Father(X, Y), we will get the result Father(lao-li, xiao-li);
(2) query: ?- Son(Y, X), we will get the result Son(xiao-li, lao-li).

2.2.2 *Data Structure and Recursion in Prolog*

An important and powerful tool in problem solving and programming, recursion is extensively used in data structures and programs of Prolog.

Term is a basic data structure in Prolog. Everything, including program and data, is expressed in the form of term. Terms of Prolog are defined recursively by the following BNF rule:

⟨term⟩ ::= ⟨constant⟩ | ⟨variable⟩ | ⟨structure⟩ | (⟨term⟩)

where structures are also called compound terms and are generated by the BNF rule

⟨structure⟩ ::= ⟨function⟩ (⟨term⟩ {, ⟨term⟩ })

⟨function⟩ ::= ⟨atom⟩

List is an important data structure supported by Prolog. A list can be represented as a binary function $cons(X, Y)$, with X as the head of the list and Y as the tail. The tail Y of a list $cons(X, Y)$ is also a list which can be generated by deleting the element X from $cons(X, Y)$. Elements of a list can be atoms, structures, terms, and lists. Table 2.1 shows some notations on lists that can be used in Prolog.

Finally, we present an example on which recursion is used in programs of Prolog. Consider a simple predicate that checks if an element is a member of a list. It has the two clauses as follows:

$member(X, [X|\_])$.

$member(X, [\_|Y])$:- $member(X, Y)$.

In this example, the predicate member is recursively defined, with the first Horn clause being the boundary condition and the second the recursive case.

2.2.3 *SLD Resolution*

SLD resolution is the basic inference rule used in logic programming. It is also the primary computation procedure used in PROLOG. Here, the name SLD is an

Table 2.1. Prolog list structure

[ ] or nil	empty table
[a]	cons(a, nil)
[a, b]	cons(a, cons(b, nil))
[a, b, c]	cons(a, cons(b, cons(c, nil)))
[X|Y]	cons(X,Y)
[a, b | c]	cons(a, cons(b,c))

abbreviation of "Linear resolution with Selection function for Definite clauses". First, we introduce definitions on the definite clause.

Definition 2.3. A Definite clause is a clause of the form

$$A :\text{-} B_1, B_2, \ldots, B_n$$

where the head is a positive literal; the body is composed of zero, one, or more literals.

Definition 2.4. A definite program is a collection of definite clauses.

Definition 2.5. A definite goal is a clause of the form

$$? :\text{-} B_1, B_2, \ldots, B_n$$

where the head is empty.

Let P and G be a program and a goal, respectively, then the solving process for the corresponding logic program is to seek an SLD resolution for $P \cup \{G\}$. Two rules should be decided for the resolution process: one is the computation rule on how to select the sub-goal; the other is the search strategy on how to go through the program. Theoretically, any search strategy used in artificial intelligence can be adopted. However, in practice, strategies should be selected according to their efficiency. The standard SLD resolution process is as follows:

(1) Sub-goals are selected with a "left then right" strategy.
(2) The program is gone through with a strategy based on the depth-first search and the backtracking method.
(3) Clauses of the program P are selected with the same priority of their appearance in the program.
(4) The occur-check is omitted from the unification algorithm.

There are some characteristics for such a resolution process.

1. There exists a simple and efficient method for the realization of depth-first search strategy

The depth-first search strategy can be realized with just a goal stack. A goal stack for the SLD tree consists of branches which are going through it. Correspondingly, the search process is composed of the pop and push operators on the stack. In the case that the sub-goal on the top of the stack is unified with the head of some clause of the program P, the corresponding resolvent will be put into stack. While in the case that no clause could be unified, a backtracking operator will be triggered with

Table 2.2.   Prolog goal stack

?-$p(X, b)$.	G is put into stack
?-$p(X, b)$. ?- $q(X, Y), p(Y, b)$.	A resolvent is put into stack
?-$p(X, b)$. ?- $q(X, Y), p(Y, b)$. ?- $p(b, b)$.	A resolvent is put into stack
?-$p(X, b)$. ?- $q(X, Y), p(Y, b)$. ?- $p(b, b)$. ?-$q(b, W), p(W, b)$	A resolvent is put into stack
?-$p(X, b)$. ?- $q(X, Y), p(Y, b)$. ?- $p(b, b)$. □	An element is popped, then the resolvent □ is put into stack
?-$p(X, b)$.	The pop operation is triggered for three times
□	The resolvent □ is put into stack
	□ is popped

the result that an element was popped from the stack; in this case, the resulted stack should be inspected for unification.

Example 2.1. Consider the following program:

$$p(X, Z) :- q(X, Y), p(Y, Z).$$

$$p(X, X).$$

$$q(a, b).$$

Let "?-$p(X, b)$" be the goal. Then the evolvement of the goal stack is as follows:

2. Completeness of SLD resolution process is destroyed by the depth-first search strategy

This problem can be partially solved according to change in the order of sub-goals and the order of clauses of the program. For example, consider the following program:

(1) $p(f(X)) :- p(X)$.
(2) $p(a)$.

Let "?-$p(Y)$" be the goal. Then it is obvious that the SLD resolution process will fall into an endless loop. However, if we exchange the order of clause (1) and clause (2), then we will get the result $Y = a, Y = f(a), \ldots$.

Consider another program as follows:

(1) $q(f(X)) :- q(X)$.
(2) $q(a)$.
(3) $r(a)$.

Let "$G: ?\text{-}q(Y), r(Y)$" be the goal. Then the SLD resolution process will fall into an endless loop. However, if we exchange the order of sub-goals contained in G and get the goal "$G: ?\text{-} r(Y), q(Y)$", then we will get the result $Y = a$ after the SLD resolution process.

In order to guarantee the completeness of the SLD resolution process, the width-first search strategy must be embodied in the search rules of Prolog. However, as a result, both the time and space efficiency of the process will be decreased, and the complexity of the process is increased. A trade-off is to maintain the depth-first search strategy that is used in Prolog and supplement it with some programs which embody other search strategies and are written with the Prolog language.

3. Soundness of SLD resolution is not guaranteed without occur-check

Occur-check is a time-consuming operation in the unification algorithm. In the case that occur-check is called, the time needed for every unification process is linear to the size of the table; consequently, the time needed for the append operation on predications is $O(n_2)$; here, n is the length of the table. Since a small pattern of the unification process in the Prolog program uses occur-check, the occur-check operator is omitted from unification algorithms of most Prolog systems.

In fact, without the occur check, we no longer have the soundness of SLD resolution. A sub-goal cannot be unified with a clause in the case some variables occur in the term. However, since the occur-check is omitted, the unification will still be executed and reach a wrong result. For example, let "$p(Y, f(Y))$" and "$?\text{-}p(X, X)$" be the program and the goal, respectively. Then the unification algorithm will generate a replacement $\theta = \{Y/X, f(Y)/Y\}$ for the pair $\{p(X, X), p(Y, f(Y))\}$. Such a mistake will be covered if the variable Y is not used in the SLD resolution anymore. However, once the variable Y is used again, the resolution process will fall into an endless loop.

2.2.4 *Non-Logic Components: CUT*

Program is the embodiment of algorithm. Algorithm in the logic programming is characterized with the following formula:

$$\text{algorithm} = \text{logic} + \text{control},$$

where the logic component determines the function of the algorithm; the control component determines the strategy which will be used to realize the function. Theoretically, a programmer just needs to specify the logic component, and then the corresponding control component can be automatically determined by the logic programming system. However, most Prolog systems in practice cannot reach such automation. As set forth, in order to guarantee a valid execution of the program, a programmer has to take the order of clauses into consideration. Another problem is the fact that an endless branch might be generated during the SLD resolution according to the depth-first search strategy adopted by Prolog. In such a situation, the goal stack used in the resolution algorithm will be overflowed and bring the resolution process into an error state. The "CUT" component is introduced to solve this problem.

From the point of declarative semantics, CUT is a non-logical control component. Represented as the character "!", CUT can be treated as an atomic component and inserted into clauses of the program or the order. Declarative semantics of a program is not affected by any "!" which appeared in the program or in the order.

From the point of operational semantics, some control information is carried by the CUT component. For example, let G be the following goal:

$$?- A_1, \ldots, A_{m-1}, A_m, A_{m+1}, \ldots, A_k$$

Let the following, which is denoted by C, be one of the clauses of the program:

$$A :- B_1, \ldots, B_i, !, B_{i+1}, \ldots, B_q$$

Consider the state that sub-goals $A_1, \ldots, A_{m-1}$ have been solved, and let G' be the current goal. Suppose Am can be unified with A. After the unification operation, the body of the clause C is added into the goal G'. Now, a cut "!" is contained in the current goal G'. We call Am a cut point and call the current goal G' as the father-goal of "!". Now, it is the turn to solve sub-goals $B_1, \ldots, B_i, !, B_{i+1}, \ldots, Bq$ one by one. As a typical sub-goal, "!" is valid and can be jumped over. Suppose a backtracking is triggered by the fact that some sub-goals behind "!" cannot be unified, then the goal stack will be tracked back to $Am - 1$, the sub-goal prior to the cut point Am. From the point of SLD tree, all the nodes which are rooted by the father-goal of "!" and are still accessed will be cut out.

For example, let P be the following program:

(1) $p(a)$.
(2) $p(b)$.
(3) $q(b)$.
(4) $r(X) :- p(X), q(X)$.
(5) $r(c)$.

Let G be the sub-goal "$?-r(X)$". Then the SLD tree generated during the process of SLD resolution is presented, as shown in Figure 2.1. However, if a cut is inserted into clause (4) of program P, i.e., clause (4) of program P is changed

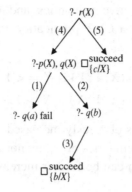

Fig. 2.1. A SLD tree without !

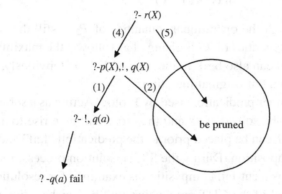

Fig. 2.2. A SLD tree with !

as follows:

$(4)'\ r(X) :\text{-}\ p(X),\ !,\ q(X)$

then the corresponding SLD tree as shown in Figure 2.2 is achieved. In the latter case, no solution will be generated since a critical part is cut out from this SLD tree.

According to the example, the soundness of the SLD resolution might be destroyed by the CUT mechanism. Furthermore, incorporation of the CUT mechanism will cause inconsistency between the declarative semantics and the operational semantics of logic programming. For example, let P be the following program which is designed to calculate the maximum value of two data.

$$max(X, Y, Y) :\text{-}\ X =< Y.$$

$$max(X, Y, X) :\text{-}\ X > Y.$$

We can check that declarative semantics and operational semantics of P are consistent. Now, we insert a CUT predication into P and get the following program P_1:

$$max(X, Y, Y) :\text{-} X =< Y, !.$$
$$max(X, Y, X) :\text{-} X > Y.$$

Efficiency of the program is obviously increased although both the declarative semantics and the operational semantics of P_1 are not changed with respect to those of P. Efficiency of the program can be further increased if we replace P_1 with the following program P_2:

$$max(X, Y, Y) :\text{-} X =< Y, !.$$
$$max(X, Y, X).$$

However, although the operational semantics of P_2 is still the same as that of P_1, the declarative semantics of P_2 is changed as follows: the maximum value of X and Y is always X, it can also be Y in the case of $X \leq Y$. Obviously, the semantics of P_2 is different from our original intention.

The "fail" is another predication used by Prolog. Acting as a sub-goal, the predication "fail" cannot be solved at all and therefore will give rise to a backtracking. The predication CUT can be placed prior to the predication "fail" and forms the so-called "cut-fail" composition. During the SLD resolution process, in the case that a clause which contains a cut-fail composition is examined for resolution, the resolution of the father-goal of the CUT predication will be finished directly. Therefore, the efficiency of search will be increased.

For example, consider the following program P:

(1) strong(X):- heart_disease(X), fail.
(2) strong(X):- tuberculosis(X), fail.
(3) strong(X):- nearsight(X), fail.
(4) strong(X).
(5) heart_ disease(Zhang).

Let "?- strong(Zhang)" be the goal. According to the first clause of program P, the goal "strong(Zhang)" can be first unified with a resolvent "heart_disease(Zhang), fail"; then a backtracking will be triggered by the "fail" after the unification of "heart_disease(Zhang)". In the following steps, sub-goals "tuberculosis(Zhang)" (or "nearsight(Zhang)") which are generated according to the second clause (resp., the third clause) cannot be unified. Finally, the goal "strong(Zhang)" will be unified according to the forth clause of P and produce a positive result. Backtracking is triggered three times in this example. We can reduce the backtracking accordingly to place a CUT prior to the "fail" occurring in the *P*. For example, the first three clauses of *P* can be changed as follows:

(1) strong(*X*):- heart_disease(*X*),!, fail.
(2) strong(*X*):- tuberculosis(*X*),!, fail.
(3) strong(*X*):- nearsight(*X*),!, fail.

Then, according to first clause of the program, a backtracking will be triggered by the "fail" after the unification of the goal "strong(Zhang)" and unification of the newly generated sub-goal "heart_disease(Zhang)". Since "strong(Zhang)" is the father-goal of the CUT contained in the first clause of *P*, it will be popped from the goal stack also. Therefore, the SLD resolution will be finished right away and return a negative result.

Since first-order logic is undecidable, there is no terminable algorithm to decide whether *G* is a logic inference of *P*, for *G* and *P* any program and any goal, respectively. Certainly, SLD resolution algorithm will return a corresponding result if G is a logic inference of *P*. However, in the case that *G* is not a logic inference of *P*, the SLD resolution process (or any other algorithm) will fall into an endless loop. In order to solve this problem, the rule "negation as failure" is introduced into logic programming. For any clause *G*, if it cannot be proved, then the rule will enable the result that ¬*G* is reasonable.

Based on the "negation as failure" rule, the predication "not" is defined in Prolog as follows:

$$\text{not}(A) \text{ :- call}(A), !, \text{fail.}$$

$$\text{not}(A).$$

Here "call" is a system predication and "call(*A*)" will trigger the system to solve the sub-goal "*A*". If the answer of the sub-goal "*A*" is positive, then a backtracking will be triggered by the "fail" occurring in the first clause, and the SLD resolution will be finished right away; in this case, result for the clause "not(*A*)" is negative. However, if the answer of the sub-goal "*A*" is negative, then a backtracking will be triggered right away so that the "fail" occurring in the first clause will not be visited; in this case, result for the clause "not(*A*)" is positive according to the second clause.

2.3 Non-Monotonic Logic

Driven by the development of the intelligence science, various non-classical logics were proposed and studied since the 1980s. Non-monotonic is one of these logics (McDermott and Doyle, 1980).

The human understanding of the world is a dialectical developing process which obeys the negation-of-negation law. During the cognitive process, man's understanding of the objective world is always uncertain and incomplete; it will be negative or complete and some new knowledge is acquired as well. As pointed by Karl Popper, the process of scientific discovery is a process of falsification. Under certain conditions and environment, every theory always has its historical limitations. Along with the increase of human understandings of the world and along with the development of scientific research, old theories will not meet the new needs and will be overthrown by the new discovery; based upon this understanding, old theories are negated and new theories are born. In this sense, the growth of human knowledge is in fact a non-monotonic development process.

Classical logics, such as the formal logic and the deductive logic, are all monotonic in their dealing with the human cognitive process. With these logics, new knowledge acquired according to rigorous logic inference must be consistent with the old knowledge. In other words, if there is a knowledge base A and it is known that A implies the knowledge B, i.e., $A \rightarrow B$, then the knowledge B can be inferenced by these logics. However, as stated above, human cognitive process is in fact non-monotonic and is not consistent with such a process at all.

Non-monotonic reasoning is characterized by the fact that the theorem set of an inference system is not monotonically increased along with the progress of inference. Formally, let F be the set of knowledge held by humans at some stage of the cognitive process, and let $F(t)$ be the corresponding function on time t. Then the set $F(t)$ is not monotonically increased along with the progress of time. In other words, $F(t_1) \subseteq F(t_2)$ will not always hold for any $t_1 < t_2$. At the same time, human understanding of the world is in fact enhanced. A basic reason for such a phenomenon is the incomplete knowledge base used in the reasoning process. Non-monotonic logic is a family of tools for the processing of incomplete knowledge.

Inference rules used in monotonic logics are monotonic. Let Γ be the set of inference rules of a monotonic logic, then the language $\text{Th}(\Gamma) = \{A | \Gamma \rightarrow A\}$ determined by these rules holds the following monotonicity:

(1) $\Gamma \in \text{Th}(\Gamma)$
(2) if $\Gamma_1 \subseteq \Gamma_2$, then $\text{Th}(\Gamma_1) \subseteq \text{Th}(\Gamma_2)$
(3) $\text{Th}(\text{Th}(\Gamma)) = \text{Th}(\Gamma)$ (idempotence)

    where (3) is also called as fixed point. A marked feature of monotonic inference rules is that the language determined by them is a bounded least fixed point, i.e., $\text{Th}(\Gamma_1) = \cap\{s | \Gamma_1 \rightarrow S \text{ and } \text{Th}(S) = \Gamma_2\}$.

In order to deal with the property of non-monotonic logic, the following inference rule is introduced:

(4) if $\Gamma \neg \vdash \neg P$, then $\Gamma | \sim MP$

Here, M is a modal operator. The rule states that if $\neg P$ cannot be deduced from Γ, then P is in default treated as true.

It is obvious that a fixed point $\text{Th}(\Gamma) = \Gamma$ cannot be guaranteed any more as well as the inference rule (4) being incorporated into monotonic inference systems. In order to solve this problem, we can first introduce an operator NM as follows: For any first-order theory Γ and any formula set $S \subseteq L$, set

(5) $NM\Gamma(S) = \text{Th}(\Gamma \cup AS\Gamma(S))$,

where $AS\Gamma(S)$ is a default set of S and is defined as follows:

(6) $AS\Gamma(S) = \{MP | P \in L \wedge P \in S\} - \text{Th}(\Gamma)$

Then, $\text{Th}(\Gamma)$ can be defined as the set of theorems that can be deduced from Γ non-monotonically, i.e.,

(7) $\text{Th}(\Gamma) =$ the least fixed point of $NM\Gamma$

Rule (7) is designed to blend the inference rule (4) into the first-order theory Γ so that reasoning can be carried out with a closed style. However, since the definition of $\text{Th}(\Gamma)$ is too strong, not only the calculation but also the existence of $\text{Th}(\Gamma)$ cannot be guaranteed. Therefore, the definition of $\text{Th}(\Gamma)$ is revised as follows:

(8) $\text{Th}(\Gamma) = \cap(\{L\} \cup \{S | NM\Gamma(S) = S\})$

Now, let L be the language determined by these rules, then L must be a fixed point according to $NM\Gamma(L) = L$.

Furthermore, according to these rules, Γ is inconsistent if $\text{Th}(\Gamma)$ does not exist. The definition of $\text{Th}(\Gamma)$ presented in (8) can also be rewritten as follows:

(9) $\text{Th}(\Gamma) = \{P | \Gamma | \sim P\}$

where $\Gamma | \sim P$ represents $P \in \text{Th}(\Gamma)$. We also use $\text{FP}(\Gamma)$ to denote the set $\{S | NM\Gamma(S) = S\}$ and call each element of this set as a fixed point of the theory Γ.

There are three major schools on non-monotonic reasoning: the circumscription theory proposed by McCarthy (1980), the default logic proposed by Reiter (1980), and the autoepistemic logic proposed by Moore (1985). In the circumscription theory, a formula S is true with respect to a limited range if and only if S cannot be proved to be true w.r.t. a bigger range. In the default logic, "a formula S is true in default" means that "S is true if there is no evidence to prove the false of S". In the autoepistemic logic, S is true if S is not believed and there are no facts which are inconsistent with S.

Various non-monotonic logic systems have been proposed by embracing the non-monotonic reasoning into formal logics. These non-monotonic logics can be roughly divided into two categories: non-monotonic logics based on minimization, and non-monotonic logics based on fixed point. Non-monotonic logics based on minimization can again be divided into two groups: one is based on the minimization of model, such as the logic with the closed world assumption and the circumscription proposed by McCarthy, and the other is based on the minimization of knowledge model, such as the ignorance proposed by Konolige. Non-monotonic logics based on a fixed point can be divided into default logics and autoepistemic logics. The non-monotonic logic NML proposed by McDermott and Doyle (1980) is a general default logic and was used for studying the general foundation of non-monotonic logics, and the default logic proposed by Reiter is a first-order formalization of default rules. Autoepistemic logic was first proposed by Moore (1985) to solve the so-called Hanks–McDermott problem on non-monotonic logics.

2.4 Closed World Assumption

With respect to any base set *KB* of beliefs, the closed world assumption (CWA) provides an approach to complete the theory $T(KB)$ which is defined by *KB*. Here, a theory $T(KB)$ is complete if either every ground atom in the language or its negation is in the theory. The basic idea of the CWA is that everything about the world is known (i.e., the world is closed); therefore, if a ground atom P cannot be proved according to the theory, then P will be considered to be negative. The CWA completes the theory by including the negation of a ground atom in the completed theory whenever that ground atom does not logically follow from *KB*.

One of the important applications of the CWA is to complete the database system. For example, let *KB* be the following database which contains information about contiguities of countries:

> Neighbor(China, Russia).
>
> Neighbor(China, Mongolia).
>
> $\forall x \forall y (\text{Neighbor}(x, y) \leftrightarrow \text{Neighbor}(y, x))$.

Then, it is obvious that T(*KB*) is incomplete since neither Neighbor(Russia, Mongolia) nor ¬ Neighbor(Russia, Mongolia) can be logically inferred from *KB*. According to the CWA, the database *KB* can be completed by adding the assertion ¬ Neighbor(Russia, Mongolia) into it. It is obvious that the CWA is non-monotonic because the set of augmented beliefs would shrink if we added a new positive ground literal to *KB*.

Let KB_{asm} be the set of all of the assertions added into *KB* during the completing process. According to the CWA, it is obvious that for any ground atom P

$$\neg P \in KB_{\text{asm}} \text{ if and only if } P \notin T(KB)$$

For example, with respect to the database *KB* presented in the previous example, we have $KB_{\text{asm}} = \{\neg \text{neighbor(Russia, Mongolia)}\}$.

Let CWA(*KB*) be the CWA-augmented theory, i.e., CWA(*KB*) = T(*KB* $\cup$ KB_{asm}). It is obvious that CWA(*KB*) is more powerful compared with T(*KB*), since many results that cannot be deduced from *KB* can now be derived from $KB \cup KB_{\text{asm}}$.

The augmented theory CWA(*KB*) might be inconsistent. For example, let $KB = \{P(A) \vee P(B)\}$, then it is $KB_{\text{asm}} = \{\neg P(A), \neg P(B)\}$ since neither P(A) nor P(B) can be derived from *KB*; therefore, the set $KB \cup KB_{\text{asm}}$ is inconsistent. Inconsistency of the CWA-augmented theory is an important problem that needs to be solved.

Theorem 2.1. *CWA(KB) is consistent if and only if, for every positive ground literal clause $P_1 \vee P_2 \vee \ldots \vee P_n$ that follows from KB, there is at least one ground literal P_i which is entailed by KB.*

In other words, CWA(*KB*) is inconsistent if and only if there are positive ground literals $P_1, P_2, \ldots, P_n$ such that $KB \models P_1 \vee P_2 \vee \ldots \vee P_n$ and $KB \not\models P_i$ for each $1 \leq i \leq n$.

Example 2.2. Let $KB = \{P(A) \vee P(B)\}$. It is obvious that CWA(*KB*) is inconsistent.

Example 2.3. Let $KB = \{\forall x (P(x) \vee Q(x)), P(A), Q(B)\}$. With respect to the atoms *A* and *B*, *KB* will be augmented with $\neg P(B)$ and $\neg Q(A)$ and will result in a consistent theory. However, if there is an atom *C*, then the resulted theory is inconsistent since it is both $(P(x) \vee Q(x)) \not\models P(C)$ and $(P(x) \vee Q(x)) \not\models Q(C)$.

Generally speaking, the theory augmented by the CWA might be inconsistent. However, if the knowledge base *KB* is composed of Horn clauses and is consistent, then the augmented theory CWA(*KB*) is also consistent. That is, we have the following theorem:

Theorem 2.2. *If the clause form of KB is Horn and consistent, then the CWA augmentation CWA(KB) is consistent.*

The condition that *KB* should be Horn is too strong for many applications. In fact, according to Theorem 2.1, such a condition is not absolutely necessary for the CWA augmentation of *KB* to be consistent. An attempt to weaken this condition leads to the idea of the CWA with respect to a predicate *P*. Under that convention, if *KB* is Horn in some predicate *P* and *P* is not provable from *KB*, then we can just add the negation of *P* into the set KB_{asm}. Here, we say that a set of clauses is Horn in a predict *P* if there is at most one positive occurrence of *P* in each clause.

For example, suppose KB is $\{P(A) \vee Q(A), P(A) \vee R(A)\}$. It is obvious that KB is Horn in the predicate P, even though both $P(A) \vee Q(A)$ and $P(A) \vee R(A)$ are not Horn clauses. Set $KB_{asm} = \{\neg P(A)\}$, then we have $KB \cup KB_{asm} \models Q(A)$ and $KB \cup KB_{asm} \models R(A)$, and thereby get a consistent augmented theory CWA' (KB) with respect to the predicate P.

But in fact, with respect to some predicate, consistency of the augmented theory cannot be guaranteed still. For example, let $KB = \{P(A) \vee Q, P(B) \vee \neg Q\}$ and let P be the particular predicate; then we have $KB_{asm} = \{\neg P(A), \neg P(B)\}$. Since $KB \models P(A) \vee P(B)$, the augmented theory CWA'(KB) with respect to the predicate P is inconsistent.

2.5 Default Logic

Default reasoning is a family of plausible reasoning. The intuition of various forms of default reasoning is to derive conclusions based upon patterns of inference of the following form:

> In the ordinary situation A holds,
> In the typical situation A holds,
> Then it is a default assumption that A holds.

A typical example of default reasoning is about the statement "birds fly". As we know, the statement "birds fly" is different from the statement "All birds will fly", since there are many exceptions such as the penguins, ostriches, and Maltese falcon. Given a particular bird, we will conclude that flies according to the following plausible proposition:

> In the ordinary situation birds can fly, or
> In the typical situation birds can fly, or
> If x is a bird, then it is a default assumption that x can flies.

However, if we know that this bird is an ostrich according to our subsequent discovery, we will revise our conclusion with a new result that this bird cannot fly. Therefore, it is obvious that what is reflected in this example is a process of plausible reasoning instead of deductive reasoning.

Based on the study of reasoning about incomplete specified worlds, a logic system named default logic was proposed by Reiter in 1980 (Reiter, 1980).

"By default" is an ordinary technology used in computer program designing. For example, let P be a program, let Q be a procedure specified in P, and let x be a variable that occurs in both P and Q. Then, the type of x which occurs in P will "by default" be the type of x which occurs in Q, unless the type of x is redeclared in Q. In other words, with the "by default" technology, operations of the system will be carried out according to predetermined rules, unless other requirements are explicitly specified by the programmer.

The idea of "by default" is introduced into logic by Reiter and forms the so-called default logic. In classical logics, new facts about a world are deduced from the known facts; all the facts that can be deduced are determined by facts contained in the knowledge base. In the default logic, knowledge base can be expanded with default knowledge so that more facts can be deduced in spite of the fact that the default knowledge may be unreliable.

Default rules used in default logic are of the following form:

$$\frac{\alpha(\overline{x}) : M\beta_1(\overline{x}), \ldots, M\beta_m(\overline{x})}{W(\overline{x})} \tag{2.1}$$

It can also be represented as follows:

$$\alpha(\overline{x}) : M\beta_1(\overline{x}), \ldots, M\beta_m(\overline{x}) \to W(\overline{x}) \tag{2.2}$$

Here, $\overline{x}$ is a parameter vector, $\alpha(\overline{x})$ is called the prerequisite of the default rule, $W(\overline{x})$ is the consequent, $\beta_i(\overline{x})$ is the default condition, and M is the default operator. The default rule is to be read as "If the prerequisite $\alpha(\overline{x})$ holds and it is consistent to assume $\beta_1(\overline{x}), \ldots, \beta_m(\overline{x})$, then infer that the consequent holds." For example, consider the following default rule:

$$\frac{\text{bird}(x) : M\,\text{flies}(x)}{\text{flies}(x)}$$

It states that if x is a bird and it is consistent to assume that x can fly, then it is inferred that x can fly.

A default rule is closed if and only if none of $\alpha, \beta_1, \ldots, \beta_m, W$ contains a free variable.

Definition 2.6. A default theory is a pair (D,W), where D is a set of default rules and W a set of closed formulas.

A default theory (D, W) is closed iff every default rule contained in D is closed. Default theory is non-monotonic. For example, suppose $T = \langle W, D \rangle$ is a default theory with $D = \{\frac{:MA}{B}\}$ and $W = \varnothing$, then formula B can be derived from T. However, if we add the knowledge $\neg A$ into W and get the default theory $T' = \langle D, W' \rangle$, where $W' = \{\neg A\}$, then formula B cannot be derived from T' any more, despite the fact that T' is an extension of T together with $W' \supseteq W$.

Example 2.4. Suppose $W = \{\text{bird(tweety)}, \forall x (\text{ostrich}(x) \rightarrow \neg \text{flies}(x))\}$, and

$$D = \left\{ \frac{\text{bird}(x) : M \text{ flies}(x)}{\text{flies}(x)} \right\}$$

Then the formula flies(tweety) can be deduced from the default theory. However, if we add the knowledge ostrich(tweety) into W, then flies(tweety) cannot be deduced any more.

Example 2.5. Suppose $W = \{\text{feathers(tweety)}\}$, and

$$D = \left\{ \frac{\text{bird}(x) : M \text{ flies}(x)}{\text{flies}(x)}, \frac{\text{feathers}(x) : M \text{ bird}(x)}{\text{bird}(x)} \right\}$$

Then the formula flies(tweety) can be deduced from the default theory. However, it cannot be deduced any more if we add the following knowledge into W:

$$\text{ostrich(tweety)},$$

$$\forall x (\text{ostrich}(x) \rightarrow \neg \text{flies}(x))$$

$$\forall x (\text{ostrich}(x) \rightarrow \text{feathers}(x)).$$

Definition 2.7. Let $\Delta = \langle D, W \rangle$ be a closed default theory. Γ is an operator defined w.r.t. Δ such that, for any set S of closed formulas, $\Gamma(S)$ is the smallest set satisfying the following three properties:

(1) $W \subseteq \Gamma(S)$;
(2) $\Gamma(S)$ is deductively closed, i.e., $\text{Th}(\Gamma(S)) = \Gamma(S)$;
(3) For any default rule $\alpha : M\beta_1, \ldots, M\beta_m \rightarrow w$ contained in D: if $\alpha \in \Gamma(S)$ and $\neg\beta 1, \ldots, \neg\beta m \notin S$, then it must be $w \in \Gamma(S)$.

Definition 2.8. A set E of closed formulas is an extension for $\Delta = \langle D, W \rangle$ iff E is a fixed point of the operator Γ w.r.t. Δ, i.e., iff $\Gamma(E) = E$.

Definition 2.9. A formula F can be deduced from a default theory $\Delta = \langle D, W \rangle$, in symbols $\Delta |\!\sim F$, iff F is contained in the extension of Δ.

Example 2.6. Suppose $D = \{\frac{:MA}{\neg A}\}$ and $W = \varnothing$. Then the default theory $\Delta = \langle D, W \rangle$ has no extension.

The result of this example can be demonstrated as follows. Suppose there is a fixed point E of the operator Γ w.r.t. Δ, then: (a) If $\neg A \notin E$, we will get $\neg A \in E$ according to the third property of Definition 2.7 and arrive at a contradiction.

(b) If $\neg A \in E$, then the default rule of D must has been applied in such a way that $\neg A$ was added into E; therefore, it must be $\neg A \notin E$ otherwise the rule cannot be applied. So, we arrive at a contradiction again. As a result, there is no fixed point of the operator Γ w.r.t. Δ, i.e., the default theory $\Delta = \langle D, W \rangle$ has no extension.

Example 2.7. Suppose $D = \left\{ \frac{:MA}{\neg B'}, \frac{:MB}{\neg C'}, \frac{:MC}{\neg F} \right\}$, $W = \varnothing$. Then the default theory $\Delta = \langle D, W \rangle$ has a unique extension $E = \text{Th}(\{\neg B, \neg F\})$.

For this example, it is easy to demonstrate that E is a fixed point of the operator Γ w.r.t. Δ. However, for any set $S \subseteq \{\neg B, \neg C, \neg F\}$ except $\{\neg B, \neg F\}$, we can demonstrate that $\text{Th}(S)$ is not a fixed point of Γ w.r.t. Δ.

Example 2.8. Suppose $D = \left\{ \frac{:MA}{A}, \frac{B:MC}{C}, \frac{F \vee A:ME}{E}, \frac{C \wedge E:M\neg A, M(F \vee A)}{G} \right\}$, $W = \{B, C \rightarrow F \vee A, A \wedge C \rightarrow \neg E\}$. Then there are three extensions for the default theory $\Delta = \langle D, W \rangle$:

$$E1 = \text{Th}(W \cup \{A, C\}),$$

$$E2 = \text{Th}(W \cup \{A, E\}),$$

$$E3 = \text{Th}(W \cup \{C, E, G\}).$$

According to the above example, we can see that not all default theories have their extensions; at the same time, the number of extensions for a default theory is not limited to be one. Effective default reasoning on a default theory is based on the existence of extensions. Therefore, it is important to study and discuss the conditions about the existence of extension.

Theorem 2.3. *Let E be a set of closed formulas, and let $\Delta = \langle D, W \rangle$ be a closed default theory. Define $E0 = W$ and for $i > 0$ it is*

$$E_{i+1} = \text{Th}(E_i) \cup \{w | (\alpha : M\beta_1, \ldots, M\beta_m \rightarrow w) \in D, \alpha \in E_i, \neg\beta_1, \ldots, \neg\beta_m \notin E\},$$

Then E is an extension for Δ iff $E = \cup_{i=0}^{\infty} E_i$.

With this theorem, the three extensions of Example 2.8 can be examined to be right.

There is a special default rule $\frac{:M\neg A}{\neg A}$. A natural question about this is whether the extension of a default theory determined by this default rule is the same as the corresponding CWA-augmented theory. Answer for this question is negative. For example, suppose $W = \{P \vee Q\}$ and $D = \{\frac{:M\neg P}{\neg P}, \frac{:M\neg Q}{\neg Q}\}$. Then it is obvious that CWA(Δ) is inconsistent, but the set $\{P \vee Q, \neg P\}$ and $\{P \vee Q, \neg Q\}$ as all consistent extensions for Δ.

Example 2.9. Suppose $D = \left\{ \frac{:MA}{\neg A} \right\}$, $W = \{A, \neg A\}$. Then the extension for $\Delta = \langle D, W \rangle$ is $E = \text{Th}(W)$.

This example is surprising since the extension for Δ is inconsistent. In fact, some conclusions on the inconsistency of extensions have been summed up:

(1) A closed default theory $\langle D, W \rangle$ has an inconsistent extension if and only if the formula set W is inconsistent.

Let E be an extension for $\langle D, W \rangle$. The result can be demonstrated as follows. On the one hand, if W is inconsistent, then the extension E is also inconsistent since $W \subseteq E$. On the other hand, if E is inconsistent, then any default rule of D can be applied since any formula can be deduced from E; therefore, according to Theorem 2.3, we will get the result that $E = T_h(W)$. So, W is also inconsistent.

(2) If a closed default theory has an inconsistent extension, then this is the unique extension for this default theory.

In the case that there are more than one extensions for a default theory, some conclusions on the relationship between these extensions have been summed up also:

(3) If E and F are extensions for a closed normal default theory and if $E \subseteq F$, then $E = F$.

(4) Suppose $\Delta_1 = \langle D_1, W_1 \rangle$ and $\Delta_2 = \langle D_2, W_2 \rangle$ are two different default theories, and that $W_1 \subseteq W_2$. Suppose further that extensions of Δ_2 are consistent. Then extensions of Δ_1 are also consistent.

Definition 2.10. A default rule is normal iff it has the following form:

$$\frac{A : MB}{B} \tag{2.3}$$

where A and B are any formulas. A default theory $\Delta = \langle D, W \rangle$ is normal iff every default rule of D is normal.

Normal default theories hold the following properties:

(1) Every closed normal default theory has an extension.

(2) Suppose E and F are distinct extensions for a closed normal default theory, then $E \cup F$ must be inconsistent.

(3) Suppose $\Delta = \langle D, W \rangle$ is a closed normal default theory, and that $D' \subseteq D$. Suppose further that E_1' and E_2' are distinct extensions of $\langle D', W \rangle$. Then Δ has distinct extensions E_1 and E_2 such that $E_1' \subseteq E_1$ and $E_2' \subseteq E_2$.

2.6 Circumscription Logic

Circumscription logic (CIRC) was proposed by McCarthy for non-monotonic reasoning. The basic idea of circumscription logic is that "the objects that can be shown to have a certain property P by reasoning from certain facts A are all the objects that satisfy P" (McCarthy, 1980). During the process of human informal reasoning, the objects that have been shown to have a certain property P are often treated as all the objects that satisfy P; such a treatment will be used in the further reasoning and will not be revised until other objects are discovered to have the property P. For example, it was initially guessed by the famous mathematician Erdos that the mathematical equation $xxyy = zz$ has only two trivial solutions: $x = 1$, $y = z$ and $y = 1$, $x = z$. But later it was proved by the Chinese mathematician Zhao He that this mathematical equation has infinite number of trivial solutions and therefore overthrew Erdos's guess.

Circumscription logic is based on minimization. In the following, starting with a propositional circumscription which is based on the minimal model, we first introduce basic definitions of circumscription. Then we will introduce some basic results on predicate circumscription.

Definition 2.11. Let p_1, p_2 be two satisfying truth assignments for a propositional language L_0. Then p_1 is called smaller than p_2, written as $p_1 \succeq p_2$, if and only if $p_2(x) = 1$ for any proposition x which holds $p_1(x) = 1$.

Definition 2.12. Let p be a satisfying truth assignment of a formula A. We say that p is a minimal satisfying assignment of A if and only if there is no other satisfying truth assignment p' of A such that $p' \succeq p$.

Definition 2.13. A formula B is called a minimal entailment of formula A, written as $A \models_M B$, if and only if B is true with respect to any minimal model of A.

Minimal model is non-monotonic. The following example reflects the property of minimal model:

$$p \models_M \neg q$$
$$p \vee q \models_M \neg p \ \vee \neg q \qquad (2.4)$$
$$p, q, p \vee q \models_M p \wedge q$$

Definition 2.14. Let $Z = \{z_1, z_2, \ldots, z_n\}$ be all the propositions occurring in formula A. Then, a satisfying truth assignment P is called a $\succeq^{Z-}$ minimal satisfying assignment of A if and only if there is no other satisfying truth assignment

P' of A such that $P \succeq^Z P'$, where, $P \succeq^Z P'$ if and only if $P'(z) = 1$ for any proposition z which holds $z \in Z$ and $P(z) = 1$.

Definition 2.15. Let $P = \{p_1, p_2, \ldots, p_n\}$ be all the propositions occurring in formula A. Then, formula φ is entailed by the propositional circumscription of P in A, written as $A \vDash_P \varphi$, if and only if φ is true with respect to any $\succeq^{Z-}$ minimal satisfying assignment of A.

The propositional circumscription $\mathrm{CIRC}(A, P)$ is defined as the following formula:

$$A(P) \wedge \forall P'(A(P') \wedge P' \to P)) \to (P \to P') \tag{2.5}$$

where $A(P')$ is the result of replacing all occurrences of P in A by P'. If we use $P' \succ P$ to replace $P' \to P$, then $\mathrm{CIRC}(A, P)$ can also be rewritten as

$$A(P) \wedge \neg \exists P'(A(P') \wedge P' \succ P) \tag{2.6}$$

Therefore, logical inferences in the propositional circumscription can be represented as schemas of the form $A \vDash_P \varphi$ or $\mathrm{CIRC}(A, P) \vDash \varphi$. The following theorem on the soundness and completeness has been proved

Theorem 2.4. $A \vdash_P \varphi$ *if and only if* $A \vDash_P \varphi$.

In the following, we advance the idea of propositional circumscription into predicate circumscription.

Definition 2.16. Let T be a formula of a first-order language L, and let ρ be a set of predicates contained in T. Let $M[T]$ and $M^*[T]$ be two models of T. Then, $M^*[T]$ is called smaller than $M[T]$, written as $M^*[T] \succeq M[T]$, if and only if

(1) M and M^* have the same domain;
(2) all the relations and functions occurring in T, except these contained in ρ, have the same interpretation in M and M^*;
(3) the extension of ρ in M^* is a subset of ρ in M.

A model M of T is called $\succeq$ P-minimal if and only if there is no other model M' of T such that $M \succeq_P M'$.

Definition 2.17. M_m is a minimal model of ρ if and only if $M = M_m$ for any model M such that $M \succeq_\rho M_m$.

For example, let the domain be $D = \{1, 2\}$,

$$T = \forall x \exists y (P(y) \wedge Q(x, y))$$
$$= [(P(1) \wedge Q(1, 1)) \vee (P(2) \wedge Q(1, 2))] \wedge [(P(1) \wedge Q(2, 1)) \vee (P(2)$$
$$\wedge Q(2, 2))]$$

Let M and M^* be the following models:

M:	$P(1)$	$P(2)$	$Q(1, 1)$	$Q(1, 2)$	$Q(2, 1)$	$Q(2, 2)$
	True	True	False	True	False	True
M^*:	$P(1)$	$P(2)$	$Q(1, 1)$	$Q(1, 2)$	$Q(2, 1)$	$Q(2, 2)$
	False	True	False	True	False	True

Then, model M and model M^* have the same true assignments on Q. At the same time, P is true in both (1) and (2) of model M; however, for model M^*, P is true in just (2). Therefore, we have $M^* \succeq_P M$. Furthermore, since $M^* \neq M$, we have $M^* \succ_P M$.

Let T be a set of beliefs, and let P be a predicate occurring in T. During the extension process, we should seek formula φ_P such that for any model M of $T \wedge \varphi_P$ there is no model M^* of T which satisfies

$$M^* \succ_P M$$

Formula $T \wedge \varphi_P$ which satisfies such a principle of minimization is called circumscription of P on T.

Let P^* be a predicate constant which has the same number of variables as that of P. Then, it can be demonstrated that any model of the following formula is a minimal model of P on T

$$(\forall x P^*(x) \rightarrow P(x)) \wedge \neg(\forall x P(x) \rightarrow P^*(x)) \wedge T(P^*)$$

Therefore, any model of the following formula is a minimal model of P on T

$$\neg((\forall x P^*(x)) \rightarrow P(x)) \wedge \neg(\forall x P(x) \rightarrow P^*(x)) \wedge T(P^*))$$

As a result, the following is a circumscription formula of P on T

$$\phi_P = \forall P^* \neg((\forall x P^*(x) \rightarrow P(x)) \wedge \neg(\forall x P(x) \rightarrow P^*(x)) \wedge T(P^*))$$

Definition 2.18. A formula ϕ is entailed by the predicate circumscription of P in A, written as $T \vDash_P \phi$ or $\text{CIRC}(T, P) \vDash \phi$, if and only if ϕ is true with respect to all the $\succeq^P$-minimal model of P.

The predicate circumscription $\text{CIRC}(T, P)$ of P in T is defined as

$$\text{CIRC}(T, P) = T \wedge \forall P^* \neg((\forall x)(P^*(x) \rightarrow P(x)) \wedge \neg(\forall x)(P(x)$$
$$\rightarrow P^*(x)) \wedge T(P^*)) \tag{2.7}$$

It can also be rewritten as

$$\text{CIRC}(T, P) = T \wedge \forall P^* ((T(P^*) \wedge (\forall x)(P^*(x) \rightarrow P(x)))$$
$$\rightarrow (\forall x)(P(x) \rightarrow P^*(x))) \tag{2.8}$$

Since it is a formula of high-order logic, we can rewrite it as

$$\phi_P = \forall P^* ((T(P^*) \wedge (\forall x)(P^*(x) \rightarrow P(x))) \rightarrow (\forall x)(P(x) \rightarrow P^*(x))) \tag{2.9}$$

It states that if there is a P^* such that $T(P^*)$ and $\forall x(P^*(x) \rightarrow P(X))$, then $\forall x(P(x) \rightarrow P^*(x))$ can be deduced as a conclusion.

If we use $P \wedge P'$ to replace P^* (here, P' is a predicate constant with the same number of variables as that of P), then $\text{CIRC}(T, P)$ can be written as

$$\phi_P = T(P \wedge P')\forall x(P(x) \wedge P'(x) \rightarrow P(x)) \rightarrow \forall x)(P(x) \rightarrow P(x) \wedge P'(x)) \tag{2.10}$$

Therefore, we get the formulas

$$T(P \wedge P') \rightarrow (\forall x)(P(x) \rightarrow P'(x)) \tag{2.11}$$

If we replace $(\forall x)(P^* x) \rightarrow P(x))$ by $P^* \succeq P$, then

$$P^* \succ P \text{ represents } (P^* \succeq P) \wedge \neg(P \succeq P^*), \text{ and}$$
$$P^* = P \text{ represents } (P^* \succeq P) \wedge (P \succeq P^*)$$

Therefore, we get

$$\phi_P = \forall P^*(T(P^*) \wedge (P^* \succeq P) \rightarrow (P \succeq P^*)) \tag{2.12}$$

That is, $\phi_P = \forall P^*(T(P^*) \rightarrow \neg(P^* \succ P))$

$$= \neg(\exists P^*)(T(P^*) \wedge (P^* \succ P)) \tag{2.13}$$

Theorem 2.5. *Let T be a formula of a first-order language, and let P be a predicate contained in T. Then, for any P' such that $T(P) \vdash T(P') \wedge (P' \succeq P)$, it must be*

$$\text{CIRC}(T, P) = T(P) \wedge (P = P') \tag{2.14}$$

According to this theorem, if $T(P') \wedge (P' \succeq P)$ can be deduced from $T(P)$, then $P = P'$ is the circumscription formula of P in T.

2.7 Non-Monotonic Logic NML

The non-monotonic logic NML proposed by McDermott and Doyle is a general default logic for the study of general foundation of non-monotonic logics (McDermott and Doyle, 1980). McDermott and Doyle modify a standard first-order logic by introducing a modal operator $\Diamond$, which is called the compatibility operator. For example, the following is a formula of NML:

$$\forall x (\mathrm{Bird}(x) \wedge \Diamond \mathrm{Fly}(x) \rightarrow \mathrm{Fly}(x))$$

It states that if x is a bird and if it is consistent by assertion that x can fly, then x can fly.

According to the example, it is obvious that default assumptions of the default theory can be represented in NML, and therefore, default theory can be treated as a special case of NML. However, in the non-monotonic logic, $\Diamond A$ is treated as a proposition in the formation of formulas; but in the default theory, $\Diamond A$ can only appear in default rules. Therefore, there are many fundamental differences between NML and the default theory.

In the following, starting with the compatibility operator $\Diamond$, we give an introduction to the non-monotonic reasoning mechanisms.

First, according to the intuitive sense of $\Diamond$, we might introduce the following rule from the point of syntax

$$\text{if } |\text{-}/\neg A, \text{ then } |\text{-} \Diamond A$$

It states that if the negation of A is not derivable, then A is compatible. We can see that rules like this are in fact unsuitable, since the negation of each formula which is not a theorem will be accepted as formula, and consequently, the non-monotonic logic is eliminated.

Therefore, McDermott and Doyle adopted a different form as follows:

$$\text{if } |\text{-}/\neg A, \text{ then} |\sim \Diamond A$$

Here, the notation $|\sim$ is introduced to represent non-monotonic inference, just like that used in the default theory.

We can also distinguish $|\sim$ from the inference relation $|\text{-}$ of first-order logic according to the following discussion. We know that in the monotonic first-order logic it is:

$$T \subseteq S \rightarrow \mathrm{Th}(T) \subseteq \mathrm{Th}(S)$$

Suppose

$$T \mathrel{|\text{-}} \text{fly(tweety)} \tag{2.15}$$

and

$$S = T \cup \{\neg\text{fly(tweety)}\} \tag{2.16}$$

Then, since $T \mathrel{|\text{-}} \text{fly(tweety)}$ and $T \subseteq S$, we will get

$$S \mathrel{|\text{-}} \text{fly(tweety)} \tag{2.17}$$

At the same time, since $\neg\text{fly(tweety)} \in S$, we have

$$S \mathrel{|\text{-}} \neg\text{fly(tweety)} \tag{2.18}$$

Therefore, it is obvious that $\text{Th}(T) \subseteq \text{Th}(S)$ does not hold. So, the notation $\mathrel{|\sim}$ is different from $\mathrel{|\text{-}}$.

Let FC be a first-order predicate calculus system with the compatibility operator $\Diamond$ embraced in, and let LFC be the set of all the formulas of FC. Then, for any set $\Gamma \subseteq \text{LFC}$, $\text{Th}(\Gamma)$ is defined as

$$\text{Th}(\Gamma) = \{A | \Gamma \mathrel{|\text{-}_{FC}} A\}$$

$\text{Th}(\Gamma)$ can also be defined according to another approach. For any set $S \subseteq \text{LFC}$, a non-monotonic operator $\text{NM}\Gamma$ is first defined as

$$\text{NM}_\Gamma(S) = \text{Th}(\Gamma \cup \text{ASM}_\Gamma(S))$$

where $\text{ASM}\Gamma(S)$ is the assumption set of S and is defined as

$$\text{ASM}_\Gamma(S) = \{\Diamond Q | Q \in L_{FC} \wedge \neg Q \notin S\}$$

then, $\text{Th}(\Gamma)$ can be defined as

$$\text{Th}(\Gamma) = \cap(\{L_{FC}\} \cup \{S | \text{NM}_\Gamma(S) = S\})$$

According to this definition, we can see that $\text{Th}(\Gamma)$ is the intersection of all fixed points of $\text{NM}\Gamma$, or the entire language if there are no fixed points.

Now, the non-monotonic inference $\mathrel{|\sim}$ can be defined as: $\Gamma \mathrel{|\sim} P$ if and only if $P \in \text{Th}(\Gamma)$.

It should be noted that $\Gamma \mathrel{|\sim} P$ requires that P is contained in each fixed point of $\text{NM}\Gamma$ in the case that there are fixed points. However, in the default theory, what is needed for P to be provable in Δ is just that P is contained in one of Δ's extension, i.e., P is contained in one of the fixed points.

Example 2.10. Suppose Γ is an axiom theory which contains $\Diamond P \rightarrow \neg Q$ and $\Diamond Q \rightarrow \neg P$, i.e.,

$$\Gamma = \text{FC} \cup \{\Diamond P \rightarrow \neg Q, \Diamond Q \rightarrow \neg P\}$$

Then there are two fixed points for this theory: $(P, \neg Q)$ and $(\neg P, Q)$.

However, for another theory $\Gamma = \text{FC} \cup \{\Diamond P \rightarrow \neg P\}$, we can demonstrate that it has no fixed points. The demonstration is as follows. Suppose $\text{NM}\Gamma(S) = S'$. If $\neg P \notin S$, then we will have $\Diamond P \in \text{ASM}\Gamma(S)$ and consequently $\neg P \in S'$. On the contrary, if $\neg P \in S$, then we will have $\Diamond P \notin \text{ASM}\Gamma(S)$, and consequently, $\neg P \notin S'$. Therefore, S will never be equal with S', i.e., there is no fixed point for $\text{NM}\Gamma$.

The above phenomenon can be further explained according to the following results:

$$\{\Diamond P \rightarrow \neg Q, \Diamond Q \rightarrow \neg P\} |\!\!\sim \ (\neg P \vee \neg Q)$$

$$\{\Diamond P \rightarrow \neg P\} |\!\!\sim \text{contradiction}$$

McDermott and Doyle pointed out the following two problems on the reasoning process of NML

(1) $\Diamond A$ cannot be deduced from $\Diamond (A \wedge B)$
(2) What can be deduced from $\{\Diamond P \rightarrow Q, \neg Q\}$ is surprising.

In order to overcome these problems, McDermott and Doyle introduced another modal operator $\Box$ called necessity. The relationship between $\Diamond$ and $\Box$ is as follows:

$$\Box P \equiv \neg \Diamond \neg P$$

$$\Diamond P \equiv \neg \Box \neg P$$

Here, the first definition states that P is necessary if and only if its negation is incompatible; the second definition states that P is compatible if and only if its negation is not necessary.

2.8 Autoepistemic Logic

2.8.1 *Moore System* $\mathscr{L}_\mathbf{B}$

Autoepistemic logic was proposed by Moore as an approach to represent and reason about the knowledge and beliefs of agents (Moore, 1985). It can be treated as a modal logic with a modal operator **B** which is informally interpreted as "believe" or "know". Once the beliefs of agents are represented as logical formulas, then a basic task of autoepistemic logic is to describe the conditions which should be satisfied by these formulas. Intuitively, an agent should believe these facts that can be deduced from its current beliefs.

An autoepistemic theory T is sound with respect to an initial set of premises A if and only if every autoepistemic interpretation of T in which all the formulas of A are true is an autoepistemic model of T. The beliefs of an ideally rational agent should satisfy the following conditions:

(1) If $P_1, \ldots, P_n \in T$, and $P_1, \ldots, P_n \vdash Q$, then $Q \in T$ (where $\vdash$ means ordinary tautological consequence).
(2) If $P \in T$, then $\mathbf{B}P \in T$.
(3) If $P \notin T$, then $\neg \mathbf{B}P \in T$.
   No further conditions could be drawn by an ideally rational agent in such a state; therefore, the state of belief characterized by such a theory is also described by Moore as stable autoepistemic theories. If a stable autoepistemic theory T is consistent, it will satisfy the following two conditions:
(4) If $\mathbf{B}P \in T$, then $P \in T$.
(5) If $\neg \mathbf{B}P \in T$, then $P \notin T$.

An autoepistemic logic named $\mathscr{L}_B$ was proposed and studied by Moore. This logic is built of a countable set of propositional letters, the logical connectives $\neg$ and $\wedge$, and a modal connective $\mathbf{B}$.

2.8.2 $O\mathscr{L}$ *Logic*

Based on the autoepistemic logic $\mathscr{L}_B$, Levesque introduced another modal connective $\mathbf{O}$ and built the logic $\mathbf{O}\mathscr{L}$. Therefore, there are two modal operators, $\mathbf{B}$ and $\mathbf{O}$, where $\mathbf{B}\phi$ is read as "ϕ is believed" and $\mathbf{O}\phi$ is read as "ϕ is all that is believed" (Levesque, 1990). Formulas of $\mathscr{L}_B$ and $\mathbf{O}\phi$ are formed as usual as that of ordinary logic. The objective formulas are those without any $\mathbf{B}$ and $\mathbf{O}$ operators; the subjective formulas are those where all non-logical symbols occur within the scope of $\mathbf{B}$ or $\mathbf{O}$. Formulas without $\mathbf{O}$ operators are called basic.

Similar to that of classical propositional logic, any formula of the autoepistemic logic $\mathbf{B}\phi$ can be transformed into a (disjunctive or conjunctive) normal form.

Theorem 2.6. (Theorem on Moore disjunctive normal form). *Any formula $\psi \in \mathscr{L}_B$ can be logically equivalently transformed into a formula for m $\psi_1 \vee \psi_2 \vee \ldots \vee \psi_k$, where each $\psi_i (1 \leq i \leq k)$ is an objective formula with* *the form*

$$\mathbf{B}\phi_{i,1} \wedge \dots \wedge \mathbf{B}\phi_{i,mi} \wedge \neg\mathbf{B}\phi_{i,1} \wedge \dots \wedge \neg\mathbf{B}\phi_{i,ni} \wedge \psi_{ii}.$$

Let L be a countable set of propositional letters. Let 2^L be the set of all the functions from the elements of L to $\{0, 1\}$, i.e., 2^L is the set of all the assignments of L. Let W be a subset of 2^L and w be an element of 2^L. Then, the truth relation $W, w \vDash \psi$ for any formula of the logic $\mathscr{L}_B$ or the logic $\mathbf{O}\mathscr{L}$ can be defined according to the following definitions.

Definition 2.19. For any formula ψ of the logic $\mathscr{L}_B$, the truth relation $W, w \vDash \psi$ is defined inductively as follows:

(1) for any propositional letter p, $W, w \vDash p$ iff $w(p) = 1$;
(2) $W, w \vDash \neg\psi$ iff $W, w| \neq \psi$;
(3) $W, w \vDash (\psi \wedge \varphi)$ iff $W, w \vDash \psi$ and $W, w \vDash \varphi$;
(4) $W, w \vDash \mathbf{B}\psi$ iff $W, w' \vDash \psi$ for every $w' \in W$.

Definition 2.20. For any formula ψ of the logic $\mathbf{O}\mathscr{L}$, $W, w \vDash \mathbf{O}\mathscr{L}$ iff $W, w \vDash \mathbf{B}\phi$ and for every w', if $W, w' \vDash \varphi$ then $w' \in W$.

Therefore, the rule for $\mathbf{O}$ is in fact a very simple modification of the rule for $\mathbf{B}$. This can also be seen by rewriting both rules as follows:

$$W, w \vDash \mathbf{B}\psi \text{ iff } w' \in W \Rightarrow W, w' \vDash \psi \text{ for every } w';$$

$$W, w \vDash \mathbf{O}\psi \text{ iff } w' \in W \Leftrightarrow W, w' \vDash \psi \text{ for every } w'.$$

The modal operator $\mathbf{O}$ is closely related to stable expansion. To a certain extent, the operator $\mathbf{O}$ can be used to describe stable expansions, as shown by the following theorem and corollary.

Theorem 2.7. (Stable expansion). *For any basic formula ψ and any maximal set of assignments W, $W \vDash \mathbf{O}\psi$ iff the set $\{\psi | \psi$ is a basic formula and $W \vDash \mathbf{B}\psi\}$ is a stable expansion of $\{\psi\}$.*

Corollary 2.1. *A formula ψ has exactly as many stable expansions as there are maximal sets of assignments where $\mathbf{O}\psi$ is true.*

2.8.3 *Theorems on Normal Forms*

Theorems on normal forms play important roles in the study of stable set and stable expansion. In the following, we reinspect these theorems from the point of semantics.

Definition 2.21. For any basic formula ψ, rank(ψ) is inductively defined as follows:

(1) if ψ is an objective formula, then rank(ψ) = 0;
(2) if $\psi = \psi_1 \wedge \psi_2$, then rank ($\psi$) = Max(rank($\psi_1$), rank($\psi_2$));
(3) if $\psi = \neg\varphi$, then rank(ψ) = rank(φ);
(4) if $\psi = B\varphi$, then rank(ψ) = rank(φ) + 1.

Lemma 2.1. *The modal operator* **B** *has the following properties:*

(1) $\vDash \mathbf{B}(\mathbf{B}(\psi)) \leftrightarrow \mathbf{B}(\psi)$;
(2) $\vDash \mathbf{B}(\neg\mathbf{B}(\psi)) \leftrightarrow \neg\mathbf{B}(\psi)$;
(3) $\vDash \mathbf{B}(\mathbf{B}(\psi) \wedge \varphi) \leftrightarrow \mathbf{B}(\psi) \wedge \mathbf{B}(\varphi)$;
(4) $\vDash \mathbf{B}(\neg\mathbf{B}(\psi) \wedge \varphi) \leftrightarrow \neg\mathbf{B}(\psi) \wedge \mathbf{B}(\varphi)$;
(5) $\vDash \mathbf{B}(\mathbf{B})(\psi) \vee \varphi) \leftrightarrow \mathbf{B}(\psi) \vee \mathbf{B}(\varphi)$;
(6) $\vDash \mathbf{B}(\neg\mathbf{B}(\psi) \vee \varphi) \leftrightarrow \neg\mathbf{B}(\psi) \vee \mathbf{B}(\varphi)$.

Lemma 2.2. $\vDash \mathbf{B}(\mathbf{B}(\psi_1) \vee \ldots \vee \mathbf{B}(\psi_s) \vee \neg\mathbf{B}(\varphi_1) \vee \ldots \neg\mathbf{B}(\varphi_t) \vee \varphi) \leftrightarrow (\mathbf{B}(\psi_1) \vee \ldots \vee \mathbf{B}(\psi_s) \vee \neg\mathbf{B}(\varphi_1) \vee \ldots \neg\mathbf{B}(\varphi_t) \vee B(\varphi))$.

Theorem 2.8. (Theorem on Conjunctive normal form). *For any formula* $\psi \in \mathcal{L}_B$, *it is* φ $\mathcal{L}$-*equivalent with some formula of the form* $\psi_1 \wedge \psi_2 \wedge \ldots \wedge \psi_k$, *where each* $\psi_i (1 \leq i \leq k)$ *is of the form* $B\varphi i, 1 \vee \ldots \vee B\varphi_{i,mi} \vee \neg B\varphi_{i,1} \vee \ldots \vee \neg B\varphi_{i,ni} \vee \varphi_{ii}$ *with* $\varphi_{i,j}, \varphi_{i,n} (1 \leq i \leq k, 1 \leq j \leq m_i, 1 \leq n \leq n_i)$ *and* ψ_{ii} *objective formulas.*

Proof. By induction on the value of rank(ψ). If rank(ψ) = 1, then the result is obvious according to Theorem 2.6.

Suppose rank(ψ) = N and suppose the result holds for any formula φ with rank(φ) < N. Then, according to Theorem 2.6, we have

$$\psi = \psi^1 \vee \psi^2 \vee \ldots \vee \psi^k,$$

where each ψ^i ($1 \leq i \leq k$) is of the form

$$\mathbf{B}\varphi_1^i \wedge \ldots \wedge \mathbf{B}\varphi_{mi}^i \wedge \neg\mathbf{B}\varphi_1^i \wedge \ldots \wedge \neg\mathbf{B}\varphi_{ni}^i \wedge \psi_{ii}.$$

According to the induction hypothesis, we have

$$\text{rank}(\varphi_j^i) \leq N - 1, \quad \text{rank}(\varphi_t^i) \leq N - 1, \quad \text{and} \quad \text{rank}(\psi^{ii}) = 0.$$

Therefore, both φ_j^i and φ_t^i can be equivalently transformed into formulas whose rank values are less or equivalent to 1. Without loss of generality, we let φ_j^i be a formula of the form

$$\chi_1 \wedge \ldots \wedge \chi_d,$$

where each $\chi_h (1 \leq h \leq d)$ is of the form

$$\mathbf{B}\chi_{h,1} \vee \ldots \vee \mathbf{B}\chi_{h,uh} \vee \neg\mathbf{B}\chi'_{h,1} \vee \ldots \vee \neg\mathbf{B}\chi'_{h,vh} \vee \chi_{hh}$$

and $\chi_{h,j}, \chi'_{h,n} (1 \leq h \leq d, 1 \leq j \leq u_h, 1 \leq n \leq v_h)$, and χ_{hh} are all objective formulas.

According to the semantic definition, the formula $\mathbf{B}\varphi^i_j$ is equivalent to

$$\mathbf{B}(\chi_1) \wedge \ldots \wedge \mathbf{B}(\chi_d) \tag{2.19}$$

Furthermore, according to Lemma 2.2, each $B(\chi_h)$ is equivalent to

$$\mathbf{B}\chi_{h,1} \vee \ldots \vee \mathbf{B}\chi_{h,uh} \vee \neg\mathbf{B}\chi'_{h,1} \vee \ldots \vee \neg\mathbf{B}\chi'_{h,vh} \vee \mathbf{B}\chi_{hh} \tag{2.20}$$

where $\chi_{h,j}, \chi'_{h,n} (1 \leq h \leq d, 1 \leq j \leq u_h, 1 \leq n \leq v_h)$, and χ_{hh} are all objective formulas.

Now, use expressions of the form (2.20) to replace each occurrence of $\mathbf{B}\chi h$, and use expressions of the form (2.19) to replace each occurrence of φ^i_j, we will get a formula ψ' which is $\psi \mathscr{L}$-equivalent with ψ and satisfies $\text{rank}(\psi') = \text{rank}(\psi) + 1$. Finally, the proof can be completed by transforming the formula ψ' into a conjunctive normal form. □

We can also reach the following result according to the duality property:

Corollary 2.2. (Theorem on disjunctive normal form). *For any formula* $\psi \in \mathscr{L}_B$, *it is* $\psi \mathscr{L}$-*equivalent with some formula of the form* $\psi_1 \vee \psi_2 \vee \ldots \vee \psi_k$, *where each* $\psi_i (1 \leq i \leq k)$ *is of the form* $\mathbf{B}\varphi_{i,1} \wedge \ldots \wedge \mathbf{B}\varphi_{i,mi} \wedge \neg\mathbf{B}\varphi_{i,1} \wedge \ldots \wedge \neg\mathbf{B}\varphi_{i,ni} \wedge \psi_{ii}$ *with* $\varphi_{i,j}, \varphi_{i,n}, (1 \leq i \leq k, 1 \leq j \leq m_i, 1 \leq n \leq n_i)$ *and* ψ_{ii} *objective formulas.*

2.8.4 ◇-Mark and a Kind of Course of Judging for Stable Expansion

First, we introduce the ◇-mark. Let L be a countable set of propositional letters, and let 2^L be the set of all the assignments of L.

Definition 2.22. (◇-mark). For any basic formula ψ, its ◇-mark $\Diamond\psi$ is inductively defined as follows:

(1) for any propositional letter $p, \Diamond p = \{w | w \in 2^L \text{ and } w(p) = 1\}$;
(2) if $\psi = \neg\varphi$, then $\Diamond\neg\varphi = \sim \Diamond\varphi = 2^L - \Diamond\varphi$, where $\sim$ is the complementary operator on sets;

(3) if $\psi = \psi_1 \wedge \psi_2$, then $\Diamond\psi_1 \wedge \psi_2 = \Diamond\psi_1 \cap \Diamond\psi_2$, where $\cap$ is the intersection operator on sets;

(4) if $\psi = \mathbf{B}\varphi$, $\Diamond\mathbf{B}\varphi = \Diamond\varphi$.

Lemma 2.3. *Let ψ and φ be objective formulas, then*

(1) $\vdash \psi \rightarrow \varphi$ *if and only if* $\Diamond\psi \subseteq \Diamond\varphi$;

(2) $\{\psi, \varphi\}$ *is satisfiable if and only if* $\Diamond\psi \cap \Diamond\varphi \neq \emptyset$.

Now, from the point of set theory, we can redefine the semantics of autoepistemic logic according to the following theorem.

Theorem 2.9. *Let ψ and φ be objective formulas, and let W, w be a model with $W \subseteq 2^L$ and $w \in 2^L$. Then*

(1) $W, w \vDash \psi$ *iff* $w \in \Diamond\psi$;

(2) $W, w \vDash \psi \wedge \varphi$ *iff* $W, w \vDash \psi$ *and* $W, w \vDash \varphi$;

(3) $W, w \vDash \neg\psi$ *iff* $W \notin \Diamond\psi$;

(4) $W, w \vDash \mathbf{B}\psi$ *iff* $W \subseteq \Diamond\psi$.

Next, we introduce the **O**-property.

Definition 2.23. Let ψ be a basic formula which is represented in the disjunctive normal form $\psi_1 \vee \psi_2 \vee \ldots \vee \psi_k$, where each ψ_i $(1 \leq i \leq k)$ is of the form $B\varphi_{i,1} \wedge \ldots \wedge B\varphi_{i,mi} \wedge \neg B\varphi_{i,1} \wedge \ldots \wedge \neg B\varphi_{i,ni} \wedge \varphi_{ii}$ with ψ_{ii} an objective formula. Let J be a subset of $\{1, \ldots, k\}$. We say that J has the **O**-property if and only if the following conditions hold:

(1) $\cup j \in J \Diamond\psi_{jj} \vDash \mathbf{B}\varphi_{r,1} \wedge \ldots \wedge \mathbf{B}\,\varphi_{r,mr} \wedge \neg\,\mathbf{B}\varphi_{r,1} \wedge \ldots \wedge \neg\,\mathbf{B}\,\varphi_{rnr}$ for each $r \in J$, and

(2) $\cup j \in J \Diamond\psi_{jj} \nvDash \mathbf{B}\varphi_{t,1} \wedge \ldots \wedge \mathbf{B}\varphi_{t,mt} \wedge \neg\,\mathbf{B}\,\varphi_{t,1} \wedge \ldots \wedge \neg\,\mathbf{B}\,\varphi_{t,nt}$ for each $t \notin J$.

The **O**-property of J can be decided according to the following two approaches:

Lemma 2.4. (The set theory approach). *J has the **O**-property if and only if the following conditions hold (here $\Diamond J$ is the abbreviation of $\cup j \in J \Diamond\psi_{jj}$):*

(1) $\Diamond J \subseteq \Diamond\varphi_{r,p1}$ *and* $\Diamond J \nsubseteq \Diamond\varphi_{r,p2}$ *for each* $r \in J$, $1 \leq p_1 \leq m_r$ *and* $1 \leq p_2 \leq n_r$, *and*

(2) *For each* $t \notin J$, *there must be a* q_1 *with* $1 \leq q_1 \leq m_t$ *or a* q_2 *with* $1 \leq q_2 \leq n_t$ *such that* $\Diamond J \nsubseteq \Diamond\varphi_{t,q1}$ *or* $\Diamond J \subseteq \Diamond\varphi_{t,q2}$.

Lemma 2.5. (The semantic approach). *J has the $\mathbf{O}$-property if and only if the following formula set is satisfiable:*

$$\{\psi^J \to \varphi_{r,p1} | r \in J \text{ and } 1 \le p_1 \le m_r\} \cup \{\neg\varphi_{r,p2} | r \in J \text{ and } 1 \le p_2 \le n_r\}$$

$$\cup \{\psi^J\} \cup \{\vee_{t \notin J, 1 \le q1 \le mt}\{\psi^J \wedge \neg\varphi_{t,q1}\} \vee \vee_{t \notin J}, 1 \le q2 \le nt\{\psi^J \to \varphi_{t,q2}\}\}.$$

Here, ψ^J is the abbreviation of $\vee_{j \in J}\psi_{jj}$.

According to theorems on normal forms and either Lemma 2.4 or Lemma 2.5, we can conclude that for any set $J \subseteq \{1, \ldots, k\}$, it is decidable to examine whether J has the $\mathbf{O}$-property.

Theorem 2.10. *Let ψ be a basic formula which is represented in the disjunctive normal form $\psi_1 \vee \psi_2 \vee \ldots \vee \psi_k$, where each $\psi_i (1 \le i \le k)$ is of the form $\mathbf{B}\varphi_{i,1} \wedge \ldots \wedge \mathbf{B}\varphi_{i,mi} \wedge \neg \mathbf{B}\varphi_{i,1} \wedge \ldots \wedge \neg \mathbf{B}\varphi_{i,ni} \wedge \varphi_{ii}$ with ψ_{ii} an objective formula. Then, for any set $J \subseteq \{1, \ldots, k\}$, there is a decision procedure to decide whether J has the $\mathbf{O}$-property.*

Furthermore, according to Lemma 2.5 and the fact that SAT problem is NP-completed, we can conclude that it is also an NP-completed problem to decide whether any set $J \subseteq \{1, \ldots, k\}$ has the $\mathbf{O}$-property.

With the help of $\diamond$-mark and $\mathbf{O}$-property, we can construct a procedure to decide the stable expansions of a basic formula.

Theorem 2.11. *Let ψ be a basic formula which is represented in the disjunctive normal form $\psi_1 \vee \psi_2 \vee \ldots \vee \psi_k$, where each $\psi_i (1 \le i \le k)$ is of the form $\mathbf{B}\varphi_{i,1} \wedge \ldots \wedge \mathbf{B}\varphi_{i,mi} \wedge \neg \mathbf{B}\varphi_{i,1} \wedge \ldots \wedge \neg \mathbf{B}\varphi_{i,ni} \wedge \psi_{ii}$ with ψ_{ii} an objective formula, and let W, w be a model. Then, $W, w \vDash \mathbf{O}\psi$ if and only if there exists a set $J \subseteq \{1, \ldots, k\}$ which has the $\mathbf{O}$-property and satisfies $W = \cup_{j \in J}\diamond\psi_{jj} = \diamond\cup_{j \in J}\psi_{jj}$.*

Proof. Recalling the definition, $W, w \vDash \mathbf{O}\psi$ if and only if

(1) $W, w \vDash \mathbf{B}\psi$, and
(2) $w' \in W$ for any w' which satisfies $W, w' \vDash \psi$.

Now, suppose $W, w \vDash \mathbf{O}\psi$. Then we can construct a set $J = \{j | W, w \vDash \mathbf{B}\varphi_{j,1} \wedge \ldots \wedge \mathbf{B}\varphi_{j,mj} \wedge \neg \mathbf{B}\varphi_{j,1} \wedge \ldots \wedge \neg \mathbf{B} \varphi_{j,mj}\}$. It is easy to demonstrate that J has the $\mathbf{O}$-property; furthermore, according to (1) we will get $W \subseteq \cup_{j \in J}\diamond\psi_{jj}$, and according to (2) we will get $\cup_{j \in J}\diamond\psi_{jj} \subseteq W$. Therefore, we have $W = \cup_{j \in J}\diamond\psi_{jj}$. The other direction can be similarly demonstrated. $\square$

Corollary 2.3. *The number of stable expansions of the basic formula ψ is equivalent to the number of sets which have the $\mathbf{O}$-property and are subsets of $\{1, \ldots, k\}$.*

Corollary 2.4. *The basic formula ψ has exactly one stable expansion if and only if there is only one subset of $\{1, \ldots, k\}$ that has the **O**-property.*

In what follows, we give some examples.

Example 2.11. Suppose ψ is $\mathbf{B}p$. Then ψ can be transformed as $\mathbf{B}p \wedge \neg\mathbf{B}(r \wedge \neg r) \wedge (q \vee \neg q)$. Therefore, there is no stable expansion for ψ, since $\Diamond(q \vee \neg q)$, i.e., 2^L, is the only maximal set for examine.

Example 2.12. Suppose ψ is p. Then ψ can be transformed as $\mathbf{B}(q \vee \neg q) \wedge \neg\mathbf{B}(r \wedge \neg r) \wedge p$. Therefore, there is just one stable expansion since $\Diamond p \subseteq \Diamond(q \vee \neg q) = 2^L$ and $\Diamond p \not\subseteq \Diamond(r \wedge \neg r) = \emptyset$.

Example 2.13. Suppose ψ is $(\neg\mathbf{B}p \to q) \wedge (\neg\mathbf{B}q \to p)$. Then ψ can be transformed as $(\mathbf{B}p \wedge \mathbf{B}q) \vee (\mathbf{B}p \wedge p) \vee (\mathbf{B}q \wedge q) \vee (p \wedge q)$. Therefore, there are four maximal sets, $\Diamond_p \wedge_q, \Diamond_p \vee_q, \Diamond_p$ and $\Diamond_q$, which might have the O-property. It can be easily examined that $\Diamond_p$ and $\Diamond_q$ are the only two sets that have the O-property. Therefore, there are just two stable expansions for ψ.

Finally, we can present a procedure to determine the stable expansions of basic formulas:

Inputs: a basic formula ψ.
Initial state: $N = 0$.

1. Transform ψ into a disjunctive normal form ψ' with rank$(\psi') = 1$;
   Let k be the number of disjunctive branches of ψ';
   Set $2^K = 2^k$, where 2^k is a set that is composed of all the subsets of the set $\{1, \ldots, k\}$.
2. Repeat the following operation until $2^K = \emptyset$: take out an element J from 2^K, if J has the **O**-property
   then set $N = N + 1$.
   Outputs: N (i.e., the number of stable expansions of ψ).

2.9 Truth Maintenance System

Truth Maintenance System (TMS) is a problem solver subsystem for recording and maintaining beliefs in a knowledge base (Doyle, 1979). The relationship between TMS and default inference is similar to the relationship between production system and first-order logic. A truth maintenance system is composed of two basic operations: (a) Make assumptions according to incomplete and finite information, and take these assumptions as a part of beliefs and (b) revise the current set of beliefs when discoveries contradict these assumptions.

There are two basic data structures in TMS: nodes, which represent beliefs, and justifications, which represent reasons for beliefs. Some fundamental actions are supported by the TMS. First, it can create a new node, to which some statements of a belief will be attached. Second, it can add (or retract) a new justification for a node to represent a step of an argument for the belief represented by the node. Finally, the TMS can mark a node as a contradiction to represent the inconsistency of any set of beliefs which enter into an argument for the node. In this case, the TMS invokes the truth maintenance procedure to make any necessary revisions in the set of beliefs. The TMS locates the set of nodes to update by finding those nodes whose well-founded arguments depend on changed nodes. When this happens, another process of the TMS, dependency-directed backtracking, is also carried out to analyze the well-founded argument of the contradiction node; then the contradiction can be eliminated according to "locate" and "delete" assumptions occurring in the argument.

The TMS provides two services: truth maintenance and dependency-directed backtracking. Both these services are carried out on the basis of the representation of reasons for beliefs.

1. Representation of Reasons for Beliefs

A node may have several justifications, each justification representing a different reason for believing the node. A node is believed if and only if at least one of its justifications is valid, i.e., at least one of its justifications can be deduced from the current knowledge base (where these beliefs are generated according to assumptions and are also included in this knowledge base).

In the TMS, each proposition or each rule can be represented as a node. Each node is of the following two types:

(1) the IN-node which has at least one valid justification, and
(2) the OUT-node which has no valid justifications.

Therefore, there are four states for the knowledge of each proposition p: an IN-node for p, an OUT-node for p, an IN-node for $\neg p$, and an OUT-node for $\neg p$.

Each node has its justifications. The TMS employs two forms for justifications, called support-list (SL) and conditional-proof (CP) justifications. The former is used to represent reasons for believing the node, while the latter is used to record the reasons for contradiction.

Each SL justification is of the following form:

$$(SL(\langle \text{ IN-list}\rangle)(\langle \text{ OUT-list }\rangle))$$ (2.21)

An SL justification is valid if and only if each node in its IN-list is IN-node, and each node in its OUT-list is OUT-node.

For example, consider the following SL justifications:

(1) It is now summer. (SL ( ) ( ))
(2) The weather is very humid. (SL (1) ( ))

In this example, IN-list and OUT-list of the SL justification of node (1) are all empty, it means, that the justification of node (1) is always valid and therefore node (1) will always be an IN-node. We call nodes of this type as premise. IN-list of the SL justification of node (2) is composed of node (1), it means that node (2) is believed if node (1) is an IN-node. According to this example, we can see that the inference of TMS is in fact similar to the inference of the predicate logic. The difference between them is that premises in the TMS can be retracted and correspondingly the knowledge base can be revised.

Based on the above example, we add an item to the OUT-list of node (2) and get the following SL justifications:

(1) It is now summer. (SL ( ) ( ))
(2) The weather is very humid. (SL (1) (3))
(3) The weather is very dry.

In this case, the condition for node (2) to be believed is that node (1) is an IN-node and node (3) is an OUT-node. All of these SL justifications state that "if it is now summer and there is no evidence to prove that the weather is very dry, then it can be derived that the weather is very humid". We call nodes whose SL justification has a non-empty OUT-list as assumptions.

Each CP justification is of the following form:

$$(\text{CP} \langle \text{consequent} \rangle \langle \text{IN-hypotheses} \rangle \langle \text{OUT-hypotheses} \rangle) \qquad (2.22)$$

A CP justification is valid if (1) the consequent node is an IN-node, (2) each node of the IN-hypotheses is an IN-node, and (3) each node of the OUT-hypotheses is an OUT-node.

The set of hypotheses must be divided into two disjoint subsets, since nodes may be derived both from some IN-nodes and some OUT-nodes.

2. Default Assumptions

Let $\{F_1, \ldots, F_n\}$ be the set of alternative default nodes, let G be a node which represents the reason for making an assumption to choose the default. To make *Fi* the default, justify it with the following SL justification:

$$(\text{SL } (G)(F_1, \ldots, F_{i-1}, F_{i+1}, \ldots, F_n)) \tag{2.23}$$

If no additional information about the value exists, none of the alternative nodes except F_i will have a valid justification, so F_i will be an IN-node and each F_j with $j \neq i$ will be an OUT-node. However, if a valid justification is added to some other alternative node and cause that alternative to become an IN-node, then the above SL justification will be invalid and make F_i an OUT-node. Consider the case that F_i has been selected as the default assumption and a contradiction is derived from F_i, then the dependency-directed backtracking mechanism will recognize F_i as an assumption because it depends on the other alternative nodes being OUT. The backtracker may then justify one of the other alternative nodes, say F_j, and make F_i an OUT-node, where the backtracker-produced justification for F_j will have the following form

$$(\text{SL}\langle\text{various nodes}\rangle\langle\text{remainder nodes}\rangle) \tag{2.24}$$

where $\langle$remainder nodes$\rangle$ represent the set of nodes except F_i and F_j.

The above approach will not work in the case that the complete set of alternatives cannot be known in advance but must be discovered piecemeal. To solve this problem, we can use a slightly different set of justifications with which the set of alternatives can be gradually extended.

Retain the above notation and let $\neg F_i$ be a node which represents the negation of F_i. Then, arrange F_i to be believed if $\neg F_i$ is an OUT-node, and set up justifications so that if F_j is distinct from F_i then F_j supports $\neg F_i$. That is, F_i is justified with

$$(\text{SL}(G)(\neg F_i)) \tag{2.25}$$

and $\neg F_i$ is justified with

$$(\text{SL}(F_j) \quad (j \neq i)) \tag{2.26}$$

where F_j is an alternative distinct from F_i.

According to these justifications, F_i will be assumed if no reasons exist for using any other alternative. However, if some contradiction is derived from F_i, then $\neg F_i$ will become an IN-node and correspondingly F_i will become an OUT-node. The dependency-directed backtracking mechanism will be used to recognize the cause of the contradiction and construct a new default assumption.

3. Dependency-Directed Backtracking

When the TMS makes a contradiction node as an IN-node, it will invoke the dependency-directed backtracking to find and remove at least one of the current assumptions in order to make the contradiction node as an OUT-node. Let C be the contradiction node. The dependency-directed backtracking is composed of the following three steps.

Step 1. Trace through the foundations of the contradiction node C to find the set $S = \{A_1, \ldots, A_n\}$ which is composed of maximal assumptions underlying C, where A_i is called a maximal assumption underlying C if and only if A_i is in C's foundations and there is no other assumption B in the foundations of C such that A_i is in the foundations of B.

Step 2. Create a new node NG to represent the inconsistency of S. NG is also called as nogood node for representing the following formula:

$$A_1 \wedge \ldots \wedge A_n \to \text{false}$$

which is equivalent with

$$\neg(A_1 \wedge \ldots \wedge A_n) \tag{1}$$

Node NG has the following CP justification:

$$(\text{CP C S}()) \tag{2}$$

Step 3. Select some maximal assumption A_i from S. Let $D_1, \ldots, D_k$ be the OUT-nodes in the OUT-list of A_i's supporting justification. Select D_j from this set and justify it with

$$(\text{SL}(\text{NG}A_1 \ldots A_{i-1}A_{i+1} \ldots A_n)(D_1 \ldots D_{j-1}D_{j+1} \ldots D_k)) \tag{3}$$

If the TMS finds other arguments so that the contradiction node C is still an IN-node after the addition of the new justification for Dj, then repeat this backtracking procedure.

As an example, consider a program to schedule a meeting. First, suppose the date for the meeting is Wednesday. The corresponding knowledge base is as follows:

(1) The date for the meeting is Wednesday (SL ( ) (2)).
(2) The date for the meeting is not Wednesday.

Here, node (1) is an IN-node since there are no arguments for the statement "the date for the meeting is not Wednesday".

Next, suppose it can be deduced from beliefs represented in other nodes, nodes (32), (40), and (61), such that the time for the meeting is 14:00. Then the corresponding knowledge base of the TMS is as follows:

(1) The date for the meeting is Wednesday (SL ( ) (2)).
(2) The date for the meeting is not Wednesday.
(3) The time for the meeting is 14:00 (SL (32, 40, 61) ( )).
   Now, suppose a previously scheduled meeting rules out the combination of the date of Wednesday and the time of 14:00, by supporting a new node with node (1) and node (3) and then declaring this new node to be a contradiction:
(4) Contradiction (SL (1, 3) ( )).
   Then the dependency-directed backtracking system will trace the foundations of node (4) to find two assumptions, (1) and (3), both maximal. Correspondingly, the following nogood node is constructed to record the result.
(5) nogood (CP 4 (1, 3) ( )).
   The TMS arbitrarily selects node (1) and justifies (1)'s only OUT antecedent (2), and correspondingly changes node (2) as follows:

(2) The date for the meeting is not Wednesday (SL (5) ( )).

Now, node (2) and node (5) are IN-nodes, and consequently, node (1) and node (4) are OUT-nodes. Therefore, the contradiction is eliminated.

de Kleer pointed out some limitations of TMS and correspondingly proposed an assumption-based TMS (ATMS) (de Kleer, 1986). A typical characteristic of ATMS is the capability of working with multiple contradictory assumptions at once.

The ATMS consists of two components: a problem solver and a TMS. The problem solver includes all domain knowledge and inference procedures. Every inference made is communicated to the TMS. The TMS's job is to determine what data are believed and disbelieved given the justifications records thus far.

An ATMS justification describes how a node is derived from other nodes and is of the following form:

$$A_1, A_2, \ldots, A_n \Rightarrow D$$

where D is the node being justified and is called the consequent; $A_1, A_2, \ldots, A_n$ is a list of nodes and is called the antecedents. The non-logical notation "$\Rightarrow$" is used here because the ATMS does not allow negated literals and treats implication unconventionally.

Limited to the space, detailed discussion of ATMS is omitted here. Readers may refer to relevant literatures.

2.10 Situation Calculus

Action is a basic concept in many branches of computer science. For example, in the branch of database theory, delete, insert, and update of data are frequently used operations (or actions). These operations play an important role in the database. Another example is the multi-agent system of distributed artificial intelligence, where various behaviors (or actions) of agents are the basis of the cooperation of agents. The knowledge and beliefs of agents is an important research topic for a multi-agent system, where the update and revision of knowledge and beliefs are also based on the study of action theory.

Situation calculus is the most commonly used formalism for the study and process of actions. With respect to the progress of a database, Fangzhen Lin and Reiter embed situation calculus into a many-sorted first-order logic framework **LR** and established a formal foundation for action (Lin and Reiter, 1994). In the **LR** framework, individuals are divided into three sorts: state, action, and object. Based on these three sorts, to characterize ab action, they described the pre-condition (under which the action could be performed) and the effect (the change of the world after the execution of the action) by sentences of **LR**. In **LR**, a system with actions was treated uniformly as a logic theory which was called basic action theory. The **LR** framework and the corresponding basic action theory provide a theoretical foundation for the study of actions.

Based on the **LR** framework, we present a many-sorted logic for the representation and reasoning about actions (Tian and Shi, 1997). In this logic, actions are treated as functions rather than individual sorts. Such a treatment is more coincident with the intuitive understanding of actions and also has a clear semantics in the model theory. In the logic, the so-called minimal action theory is introduced to characterize systems with actions; a model theory is correspondingly established to analyze the progression in the minimal action theory; finally, some results on the definability of progression in the minimal action theory are presented.

2.10.1 *Many-Sorted Logic for Situation Calculus*

LR is defined to be a many-sorted first-order logic (Lin and Reiter, 1994). In its signature $\mathscr{L}$, there are three sorts: sort s for state, sort o for object, and sort a for action. The constant S_0 of sort s is used to denote the initial state. There is a distinguished binary function **do** of type $\langle a, s; s \rangle$; $do(a, s)$ denotes the successor state to s resulting from performing the action a. The binary relation **Poss** of type $\langle a, s \rangle$ is also introduced; $Poss(a, s)$ means that it is possible to perform the action

a in the state s. Finally, a binary relation of type $\langle s, s \rangle$ is introduced to denote the sequential relation between states.

A relation symbol is called to be state independent if all its parameters are of sort o. A function symbol is called to be state independent if all of its parameters as well as its function value are of sort o. A relation symbol is called to be a fluent if there is a parameter of sort s while the other parameters are of sort o. The number of state-independent relations, state-independent functions, and fluents are all supposed to be limit in $\mathscr{L}$.

Term, atom formula, and formula of **LR** are defined in the usual way.

For any state term st, $\mathscr{L}_{st}$ is defined to be the subset of $\mathscr{L}$ that does not mention any other state terms except st, which does not quantify over state variables, and does not mention Poss and $<$. Formally, $\mathscr{L}_{st}$ is the smallest set satisfying the following conditions:

(1) if $\psi \in \mathscr{L}$ and it does not mention any state term, then $\psi \in \mathscr{L}_{st}$;
(2) for every fluent $F(x_1, \ldots, x_n, st) \in \mathscr{L}_s$, $F(x_1, \ldots, x_n, st) \in \mathscr{L}_{st}$;
(3) if $\psi, \varphi \in \mathscr{L}_{st}$, then $\neg\psi, \psi \wedge \varphi, \psi \vee \varphi, \varphi \rightarrow \psi, \psi \leftrightarrow \varphi, (\forall x)\psi, (\exists x)\psi, (\forall a)\psi$, and $(\exists a)\psi$ are all in $\mathscr{L}_{st}$, where x and a are variables of sort o and sort a, respectively.

$\mathscr{L}_{st}^2$ is defined to denote the second-order extension of $\mathscr{L}_{st}$ by n-ary predicate variables on the domain of sort o, $n \geq 0$. Formally, $\mathscr{L}_{st}^2$ is the smallest set satisfying the following conditions:

(1) $\mathscr{L}_{st} \subseteq \mathscr{L}_{st}^2$;
(2) if p is an n-ary predicate variable on domain of sort o, and $x_1, \ldots, x_n$ are terms of sort o, then $p(x_1, \ldots, x_n) \in \mathscr{L}_{st}^2$;
(3) if $\psi, \varphi \in \mathscr{L}_{st}^2$, then $\neg\psi, \psi \wedge \varphi, \psi \vee \varphi, \varphi \rightarrow \psi, \psi \leftrightarrow \varphi, (\forall p)\psi$, $(\exists p)\psi, (\forall x)\psi, (\exists x)\psi, (\forall a)\psi$, and $(\exists a)\psi$ are all in $\mathscr{L}_{st}^2$, where x and a are variables of sort o and sort a, respectively, and p is an n-ary predicate variable on domain of sort o.

2.10.2 Basic Action Theory in LR

A basic action theory D is of the following form:

$$\mathbf{D} = \sum \cup D_{ss} \cup D_{ap} \cup D_{una} \cup D_{s0} \tag{2.27}$$

where

(1) $\sum$ is a set of logic formulas stating that the domain of sort s is a branching temporal structure, with S_0 the root and ***do*** the successive function. Formally, it contains the following axioms:

$S_0 \neq \text{do}(a, s)$

$\text{do}(a_1, s_1) = \text{do}(a_2, s_2) \rightarrow (a_1 = a_2 \wedge s_1 = s_2)$

$\forall P[(P(S_0) \wedge \forall a, s(P(s) \rightarrow P(\text{do}(a, s)))) \rightarrow \forall s P(s)]$

$\neg(s < S_0)$;

$s < \text{do}(a, s') \leftrightarrow (\text{Poss}(a, s') \wedge s \leq s')$

(2) D_{ss} is a set of logic sentences expressing the effect after an action is performed. Generally, each sentence is of the form

$$\text{Poss}(a, s) \rightarrow (F(\overrightarrow{x}, \text{do}(a, s)) \rightarrow \psi_F(\overrightarrow{x}, a, s)) \tag{2.28}$$

where F is a fluent and ψ_F is a logic formula in $\mathscr{L}_s$

(3) D_{ap} is a set of logic sentences expressing the pre-condition under which an action could be performed. Each sentence has the following general form:

$$\text{Poss}(A(\overrightarrow{x}, s)) \rightarrow \psi_A(\overrightarrow{x}, s) \tag{2.29}$$

where A is an action and ψ_A is a logic formula in $\mathscr{L}_S$.

(4) D_{una} is a set of logic formulas expressing that two actions performed on two groups of objects will not have the same effect unless these two actions as well as these two groups of objects are the same, respectively. Generally, each pair of formulas is of the following forms:

$$A(\overrightarrow{x}) \neq A'(\overrightarrow{y})$$

$$A(\overrightarrow{x}) = A(\overrightarrow{y}) \rightarrow (\overrightarrow{x} = \overrightarrow{y})$$

(5) D_{S0} is a finite set of logic formulas in $\mathscr{L}_{S0}$ and is called the initial condition of the action theory.

2.11 Frame Problem

The frame problem, first described by McCarthy and Hayes, arises when we attempt to describe the effects of actions or events using logic. Using classical logic, if we describe the changes when a particular kind of action is performed or a particular kind of event occurs, we also have to describe what does not change. Otherwise, we cannot use the description to draw any useful conclusions.

When we use the apparatus of first-order logic to describe the effects of actions, the description of what does not change is considerably larger than the description of what does change. However, when we describe the effects of actions, we should be able to concentrate on what these changes are and be able to take what does not change for granted. Therefore, the frame problem is the problem of constructing a formal framework that enables us to do just this (Shanahan, 1997).

2.11.1 *Frame Axiom*

First, let's consider the Block World example and represent it with the situation calculus. Let Σ be the conjunction of the following formulas of the initial situation S_0.

$$\text{Holds(On}(C,\text{Table}), S_0)$$
$$\text{Holds(On}(B, C), S_0)$$
$$\text{Holds(On}(A, B), S_0)$$
$$\text{Holds(On}(D, \text{Table}), S_0)$$
$$\text{Holds(Clear}(A), S_0)$$
$$\text{Holds(Clear}(D), S_0)$$
$$\text{Holds(Clear(Table)}, S_0)$$

Suppose there is a single action Move and this action is described by the following effect axioms:

$$\text{Holds(On}(x,y), \text{Result(Move}(x, y), s)) \leftarrow \text{Holds(Clear}(x), s) \wedge$$
$$\text{Holds(Clear}(y), s) \wedge x \neq y \wedge x \neq \text{Table}$$

$$\text{Holds(Clear}(z), \text{Result(Move}(x, y), s)) \leftarrow \text{Holds(Clear}(x), s) \wedge$$
$$\text{Holds(Clear}(y), s) \wedge \text{Holds(On}(x, z), s) \wedge \quad x \neq y \wedge y \neq z$$

Let Δ be the conjunction of these formulas. Then, $\Delta \wedge \Sigma$ entails many of the conclusions we would expect. For example, we have

$$\Delta \wedge \Sigma| = \text{Holds(On}(A, D), \text{Result(Move}(A, D), S_0))$$

However, many conclusions we would like to be able to draw are absent. For example, although B is on C in S_0, and moving A to D doesn't change this fact, we do not have

$$\Delta \wedge \Sigma| = \text{Holds(On}(B, C), \text{Result(Move}(A, D), S0))$$

In other words, although we have captured what does change as the result of an action, we have failed to represent what doesn't change. In general, the effect of an action is limited to a certain range, majority of fluents are unaffected by the action. We need to capture the persistence of fluents that are unaffected by an action. To do this, we have to add some frame axioms.

For example, the following is a frame axiom for the fluent "On":

$$Holds(On(v, w), Result(Move(x, y),s)) \leftarrow Holds(On(v, w), s) \wedge x \neq v$$

It states that if v is on w in the situation s and v is not the block x which will be moved, then v is still on w when the action Move(x, y) is executed. Based on this axiom, the set Δ and Σ, the formula $Holds(On(B, C), Result(Move(A, D), S0))$ can now be deduced.

Similarly, we can add the following frame axiom for the fluent "Clear":

$$Holds(Clear(x), Result(Move(y, z), s)) \leftarrow Holds(Clear(x), s) \wedge x \neq z$$

Next, we introduce a fluent "Color" and an action "Paint" for the Block World:

(1) Color(x, c): block x has color c.
(2) Paint(x, c): painting block x color c.

Paint(x, c) has no pre-conditions since painting is always successful; the effect of Paint(x, c) is that x has color c. Therefore, the following formula should be added into Δ:

$$Holds(Color(x, c), Result(Paint(x, c), s))$$

Correspondingly, suppose each block has red color in the initial situation S_0 and therefore we add the following formula into Σ

$$Holds(Color(x, Red), S_0)$$

In the real world, we know that the color of a block will not be affected by moving it. However, based on the current representation of Σ and Δ, the following result cannot be reached at all:

$$\Delta \wedge \Sigma \models Holds(Color(A, Red), Result(Move(A, D), S_0))$$

In order to get this result, we need to add the following frame axioms into Δ:

$$Holds(Color(x, c), Result(Move(y, z), s)) \leftarrow Holds(Color(x, c), s)$$

$$Holds(Color(x, c_1), Result(Paint(y, c_2), s)) \leftarrow Holds(Color(x, c_1), s) \wedge x \neq y$$

These axioms state that the color of any block x will not be affected by moving it, and the color of x will not be affected by the painting of any other block.

Similarly, with respect to the action "Paint", we need to introduce the following frame axioms, which state that values of the fluent "On" and the fluent "Clear" will not be affected by the action "Paint":

$$\text{Holds(On}(x, y), \text{Result(Paint}(z, c), s\,)) \leftarrow \text{Holds(On}(x, y), s)$$
$$\text{Holds(Clear}(x), \text{Result(Paint}(y, c), s)) \leftarrow \text{Holds(Clear}(x), s)$$

In general, because most fluents are unaffected by most actions, every time we add a new fluent we are going to have to add roughly as many new frame axioms as there are actions in the domain, and every time we add a new action we are going to have to add roughly as many frame axioms as there are fluents in the domain. Therefore, if there are n fluents and m actions for a domain, then the total number of frame axioms will be of the order of $n \times m$ (Shanahan, 1997).

In the following, we consider a more succinct approach of expressing the information in the frame axioms. This approach is remaining in the realm of classical first-order logic and does not need to modify the situation calculus significantly. First, note that all frame axioms have the following similar form:

$$\text{Holds}(f, \text{Result}(a, s)) \leftarrow \text{Holds}(f, s) \wedge \Pi$$

where f is a fluent, a is an action, and Π is a conjunction. So, we can use the following frame axiom:

$$\text{Holds}(f, \text{Result}(a, s)) \leftarrow \text{Holds}(f, s) \wedge \neg\text{Affects}(a, f, s)$$

Furthermore, corresponding to each frame axiom, we need to introduce an axiom for the formula $\neg\text{Affects}(a, f, s)$. For example, the following axioms should be introduced for the Block World example:

$$\neg\,\text{Affects(Move}(x, y), \text{On}(v, w), s) \leftarrow x \neq v$$
$$\neg\,\text{Affects(Paint}(z, c), \text{On}(x, y), s)$$
$$\neg\,\text{Affects(Move}(y, z), \text{Clear}(x), s) \leftarrow x \neq z$$
$$\neg\,\text{Affects(Paint}(y, c), \text{Clear}(x), s)$$
$$\neg\,\text{Affects(Move}(y, z), \text{Color}(x, c), s)$$
$$\neg\,\text{Affects(Paint}(y, c2), \text{Color}(x, c1), s) \leftarrow x \neq v$$

With these frame axioms, we can draw exactly the same conclusions. If we employ an implication in place of the simple negation, the number of formulas can be further cut down and result in the following three formulas.

$$\text{Affects}(a, \text{On}(x, z), s) \rightarrow a = \text{Move}(x, y)$$
$$\text{Affects}(a, \text{Clear}(x), s) \rightarrow a = \text{Move}(x, y)$$
$$\text{Affects}(a, \text{Color}(x, c2), s) \rightarrow a = \text{Paint}(x, c1)$$

These formulas are known as explanation closure axioms. Explanation closure axioms are an effective substitute for frame axioms and are much more succinct. They form the basis of a whole class of monotonic solutions to the frame problem.

2.11.2 *Criteria for a Solution to the Frame Problem*

How can we represent the effects of actions in a formal, logical way without having to write out all the frame axioms? This is the frame problem. Various approaches have been proposed for the frame problem. This leads us to consider what the criteria are for an acceptable solution. Shanahan offered three criteria on a satisfactory solution (Shanahan, 1997):

(1) representational parsimony;
(2) expressive flexibility;
(3) elaboration tolerance.

The criterion of representational parsimony is the essence of the frame problem; it requires that representation of the effects of actions should be compact. It is difficult to quantify the compactness precisely. A reasonable guideline is that the size of the representation should be roughly proportional to the complexity of the domain, where a good indication of the complexity of the domain is the total number of actions plus the total number of fluents.

A compact solution of the frame problem should be to carry over to more complicated domains. That is to say, we have to see that the solution meets the second criterion, that of expressive flexibility. What is meant by a more complicated domain is not simply one with a larger number of fluents and actions, but rather one with features that demand a little extra thought before they can be represented. Some features are listed as follows:

(1) ramifications;
(2) concurrent actions;
(3) non-deterministic actions;
(4) continuous change.

An action will have ramifications beyond its immediate effects if we have to take into account domain constraints. A domain constraint (sometimes called a state constraint) is simply a constraint on what combinations of fluents may hold in the same situation. For example, suppose three are three blocks which are on top of each other. Let Stack(x, y, z) be a fluent which denotes that blocks x, y, and z are a stack. Then we could write effect axioms for Stack like those previously written for On, Clear, and Color. However, taking into account the domain constraints, we write the effect axiom for Stack as follows:

$$\text{Holds}(\text{Stack}(x, y, z), s) \leftarrow x \neq \text{Table} \wedge \text{Holds}(\text{On}(y, x), s) \wedge \text{Holds}(\text{On}(z, y), s)$$

In the Blocks World examples considered so far, no two actions are ever performed at the same time. But concurrent actions and events are ubiquitous in everyday life. For example, there are concurrent actions if a block is moved by more than one person.

Another feature of complicated domains that can trouble a potential solution is the presence of non-deterministic actions or actions whose effects are not completely known. For example, when we toss a coin, we known it will come down either heads or tails, but we cannot say which.

Finally, we have the issue of continuous change. Continuous changes are also ubiquitous in everyday life, such as speeding cars, filling vessels, and so on. In the Blocks World examples considered so far, all changes are discrete. This doesn't mean that the change being represented is discrete, but rather for the convenience of abstraction. However, such representations are not always appropriate, since the continuous variation of some quantity is the salient feature of the domain in question. Continuous change is particularly hard to represent in the situation calculus and this is one of the motivations for study in the event calculus in which continuous change can be represented without too much difficulty.

The final criterion in the list is elaboration tolerance. A representation is elaboration tolerant to the extent that the effort required to add new information to the representation is proportional to the complexity of that information. During the process that expands a situation calculus theory with adding a new action, if there are n fluents which will be directly affected, then it might require the addition of roughly n new sentences. But it should not necessitate the complete reconstruction of the old theory; facts about the effects should be gracefully absorbed into the old theory.

When the domain includes actions with ramifications, it is not enough to simply expand the explanation closure axioms. It calls for reconstruction and brings a great improvement to the original system. Such a reconstruction is expensive for any monotonic mechanisms. The goal of elaboration tolerance seems to be impossible to achieve if we remain in the realm of monotonic mechanisms. To solve this problem, many non-monotonic reasoning mechanisms were proposed by AI researchers, such as the circumscription proposed by McCarthy (1980) and the default logic proposed by Reiter (1980). In fact, frame problem is one of the driving forces for the study of non-monotonic reasoning. The core idea of non-monotonic solution to the frame problem is to formalize the commonsense law of inertia. One component of this law is as follows: normally, given any action and any fluent, the action doesn't affect the fluent.

More generally, we want to write down just the effect axioms, declare the default assumption that "nothing else changes", and then appeal to some non-monotonic formalism to work out the consequences. Since the early 1980s, there have been several candidates for such a formalism. Two of the most common are default logic and circumscription. Logic programming's negation-as-failure is another candidate, so long as its semantic is properly defined.

2.11.3 *Non-Monotonic Solving Approach of the Frame Problem*

Non-monotonic reasoning was first adopted by McCarthy to solve the frame problem. Circumscription was proposed by McCarthy and applied in a solution of the frame problem. Circumscription allows us to declare that the extensions of certain predicates are to be minimized. For example, consider a formula set Γ from which the formula $P(A)$ can be deduced, but from which we cannot show either $P(x)$ or $\neg P(x)$ for any x other than A. It follows from the circumscription of Γ minimizing P, written as CIRC[Γ; P], that $P(x)$ is false for any x unless Γ demands that it is true. So, $\neg P(B)$ will follow from CIRC[Γ; P].

The way to apply circumscription to the frame problem is to minimize the predicate Affects (McCarthy calls the predicate Ab rather than Affects). However, minimizing Affects in a naïve way will yield counterintuitive results.

According to the viewpoint of McCarthy, Hayes, and Sandewall, formalization of the commonsense law of inertia is the pivot for a non-monotonic solution to the frame problem. Here, the commonsense law of inertia states that inertia is normal and change is exceptional. One component of this commonsense law is the following default rule: normally, given any action (or event type) and any fluent, the action does not affect the fluent.

Consider the following universal frame axiom:

$$F_1 : [\text{Holds}(f, \text{Result}(a, s)) \leftrightarrow \text{Holds}(f, s)] \leftarrow \neg\text{Affects}(a, f, s) \qquad (2.30)$$

It says that the fluents that hold after an action takes place are the same as those that hold beforehand, except for those the action affects. This leaves us the tricky job of specifying exactly which fluents are not affected by exactly which actions, which is the essence of the frame problem.

If we simply replace the Affects predicate by the predicate Ab proposed by McCarthy, then we will get axioms of the following form:

$$F_2 : [\text{Holds}(f, \text{Result}(a, s)) \leftrightarrow \text{Holds}(f, s)] \leftarrow \neg\text{Ab}(a, f, s) \qquad (2.31)$$

Let Σ be the conjunction of effect axioms, domain constraints, and observation sentences. The obvious way to augment Σ with the commonsense law of inertia is to conjoint it with (F_2) and then circumscribe it, minimizing Ab and allowing Holds to vary. In other words, we consider $\text{CIRC}[\Sigma \wedge (F_2); \text{Ab}; \text{Holds}]$.

The approach of minimising Ab and allowing Holds to vary seems a sound approach to solve the frame problem. However, as McDermott and Hanks showed in 1968, this approach fails to generate the conclusions we require even with extremely straightforward examples. They distilled the essence of the difficulty into a simple example, the so-called Yale shooting problem.

In the Yale shooting problem, someone is killed by a gunshot. The formalization is composed of the following:

(1) three actions: Load, Wait, and Shoot;
(2) two fluents: Alive and Loaded;
(3) two effect axioms: the Load action puts a bullet in the gun, and the victim dies after a Shoot action as long as the gun is loaded at the time, i.e.:

$$Y_1: \text{Holds}(\text{Loaded}, \ \text{Result}(\text{Load}, s)) \qquad (2.32)$$

$$Y_2: \neg\text{Holds}(\text{Alive}, \ \text{Result}(\text{Shoot}, s)) \leftarrow \text{Holds}(\text{Loaded}, s) \qquad (2.33)$$

(4) two observation sentences about the initial situation $S0$: the victim is alive in the initial situation, and the gun is unloaded, i.e.:

$$Y_3: \text{Hold}(\text{Alive}, S_0) \qquad (2.34)$$

$$Y_4: \neg\text{Holds}(\text{Loaded}, S_0) \qquad (2.35)$$

Finally, a predicate UNA is introduced to guarantee the uniqueness of names of actions and fluents. Formally, $\text{UNA}(f_1, f_2, \ldots, f_k)$ is defined as:

$$f_i(x_1, x_2, \ldots, x_m) \neq f_j(y_1, y_2, \ldots, y_n) \quad \text{for all } i < j < k$$

and

$$f_i(x_1, x_2, \ldots, x_n) = f_i(y_1, y_2, \ldots, y_n) \rightarrow (x_1 = y_1 \wedge x_2 = y_2 \wedge \ldots \wedge x_n = y_n)$$
for all $i < k$.

With the predicate UNA, the following formulas are added for the Yale shooting problem

$$Y_5: \text{UNA(Load, Wait, Shoot)} \tag{2.36}$$

$$Y_6: \text{UNA(Alive, Loaded)} \tag{2.37}$$

$$Y_7: \text{UNA}(S_0, \text{Result}) \tag{2.38}$$

Now, consider the situation that is obtained after the sequence of actions: Load, Wait, Shoot, i.e., consider the situation Result(Shoot, Result(Wait, Result(Load, S_0))). What do fluents hold in this situation if the circumscription policy is applied to these formulas? Intuitively, the gun will be loaded after the Load action, it remaining Loaded after the Wait action, and the victim will die after the Shoot action; therefore, we expect the circumscription of (Y_1) to (Y_7) to have the following consequence:

$$\neg\text{Holds(Alive, Result(Shoot, Result(Wait, Result(Load, }S_0)))) \tag{2.39}$$

However, (2.37) does not follow from the circumscription.

Proposition 2.1. (The Hanks–McDermott problem). *If Σ is the conjunction of (Y_1) to (Y_7), then*

$$\text{CIRC}[\Sigma \wedge (F2); \text{Ab}; \text{Holds}] \mid \neq$$
$$\neg\text{Holds(Alive, Result(Shoot, Result(Wait, Result(Load, }S_0))))$$

This proposition can be proved as follows:
Consider any model M of $\Sigma \wedge (F_2)$ that meets the following criteria:

$M \models \text{Holds(Loaded, Result(Load, }S_0))$

$M \models \neg \text{Holds(Loaded, Result(Wait, Result(Load, }S_0))))$

$M \models \text{Holds(Alive, Result(Shoot, Result(Wait, Result(Load, }S_0))))$

It is easy to see that such models exist, and they will have the following properties:

$M \models \text{Ab(Load, Loaded, }S_0)$

$M \models \text{Ab(Wait, Loaded, Result(Load, }S_0))$

$M \models \neg\text{Ab(Shoot, Alive, Result(Wait, Result(Load, }S_0)))$

Then, with respect to the predicate Ab and Holds, it is obvious that we cannot remove either of the above properties and still have a model. Therefore, some of those models are minimal. Furthermore, since in any of these models, we have

$$M| = \text{Holds(Alive, Result(Shoot, Result(Wait, Result(Load, } S_0))))$$

We also have

$$\text{CIRC}[\Sigma \wedge (F_2); \text{Ab} ; \text{Holds}] | \neq \neg \text{Holds(Alive, Result(Shoot, Result(Wait, Result(Load, } S_0))))$$

The Hanks and McFermott problem arises from a failure to respect the directionality of time. This failure is most dramatically highlighted when default logic is used to address the frame problem.

Definition 2.23. A default theory is a pair $\langle \Delta, \Sigma \rangle$, where Δ is a set of default rules and Σ is a sentence of first-order predicate calculus.

Σ encapsulates certain knowledge of the domain, from which we can draw deductively valid inferences, while Δ represents the default knowledge, from which we draw defeasible conclusions.

The default theory $\langle \Delta, \Sigma \rangle$ considered here is:

$$\Delta = \left\{ \frac{: \neg Ab(a, f, s)}{\neg Ab(a, f, s)} \right\}$$

and Σ is the conjunction of (Y_1) to (Y_4) with (F_2).

Definition 2.24. A set of well-formed formulas is an extension of a default theory $\langle \Delta, \Sigma \rangle$ if it is a fixed point of the operator Γ. Here, the operator is defined as follows. If S is a set of well-formed formulas with no free variables, then $\Gamma(S)$ is the smallest set such that

(1) $\Sigma \subseteq \Gamma(S)$;
(2) if ϕ is a logical consequence of $\Gamma(S)$, then $\phi \in \Gamma(S)$;
(3) if Δ includes the default rule

$$\frac{\phi_1(\bar{x}) : \phi_2(\bar{x})}{\phi_3(\bar{x})}$$

and $\phi_1(\tau_1 \ldots \tau_n) \in \Gamma(S)$ and $\neg\phi_2(\tau_1 \ldots \tau_n) \notin \Gamma(S)$, then $\phi_3(\tau_1 \ldots \tau_n) \in \Gamma(S)$, where each τ_i is a non-variable term.

Each extension of a default theory will represent an acceptable set of beliefs. The way to construct extensions is natural: start with a set containing just Σ and its logical consequences, then repeatedly choose an applicable default, add its consequence, and form the corresponding deductive closure, until nothing more can be added.

More precisely, given a default theory $\langle \Delta, \Sigma \rangle$, the corresponding extensions can be constructed according to the following algorithm:

$S' := \{\}$
$S := \Sigma \cup$ logical consequences of Σ
While $S \neq S'$
  $S' := S$
  Choose any ϕ_1, ϕ_2, ϕ_3 and $\tau_1, \ldots, \tau_n$ such that

$$\frac{\phi_1(\bar{x}) : \phi_2(\bar{x})}{\phi_3(\bar{x})} \text{ in } \Delta \text{ and } \phi_1(\tau_1 \ldots \tau_n) \in S \text{ and } \neg\phi_2(\tau_1 \ldots \tau_n) \notin S$$

  $S := S \cup \phi_3(\tau_1 \ldots \tau_n)$
  $S := S \cup$ logical consequences of S
End While

This algorithm will not terminate in many cases, since the default rules will be applicable an infinite number of times. However, in such cases, each intermediate S is a subset of some extension, so we can still use the algorithm to obtain useful information by executing the loop a finite number of times.

Now, we can apply this algorithm to the default theory representing the Yale shooting problem. We start with the set $S = \Sigma \cup$, the logical consequences of Σ. Then we might choose to add

$$\neg \text{Ab(Wait, Loaded, Result(Load, } S_0))$$

The default rule permits this since it is consistent with S. Next, we add in the logical consequences of the new addition: the following is added according to (F_2):

$$\text{Holds(Loaded, Result(Wait, Result(Load, } S_0)))$$

and correspondingly the following is added according to (Y_2):

$$\neg\text{Holds(Alive, Result(Shoot, Result(Wait, Result(Load, } S_0)))).$$

We would need to iterate the algorithm forever to obtain an extension, but we have already shown that extensions exist that include the above intended consequence.

Now, we get anomalous extensions, simply by making a different choice when we apply the default rule. Again, we start with the set $S = \Sigma \cup$ the logical consequences of Σ. But in this time, applying the default rules, let's choose to add

$$\neg\text{Ab(Shoot, Alive, Result(Wait, Result(Load, } S_0)))$$

This sentence is consistent with S, so the default rule permits its addition. Now, we add in the logical consequences of this new addition with the result that the following is added:

$$\neg Holds(Loaded, Result(Wait, Result(Load, S_0)))$$

Since we already had

$$Holds(Loaded, Result(Load, S_0))$$

and taken together, these two sentences give us

$$Ab(Wait, Loaded, Result(Load, S_0))$$

This gives us the undesired consequence:

$$Holds(Alive, Result(Shoot, Result(Wait, Result(Load, S_0)))).$$

Therefore, with respect to the Yale shooting problem, the default logic will yield anomalous extension in just the same way that circumscription yields anomalous models. In other words, the Hanks–McDermott problem is not merely a problem for circumscription. The exercise of showing how it arises with default logic offers an insight into why the difficulty arises. The intended extension arises when the default rule is applied in a chronological order (i.e., earliest abnormalities are considered first); the anomalous extension arises when the default rules are applied in the reverse chronological order (i.e., later abnormalities are considered first). Therefore, the intended extension is the result of postponing change until as late as possible. Based on this result, a technique named chronological minimization was proposed.

The Hanks–McDermott problem can be solved by the chronological minimization approach. But the Yale shooting problem is just one example. There are still other examples, where chronological minimization supplies counterintuitive conclusions. The best example of these is the stolen car problem.

The stolen car problem is a family of explanation problems. In an explanation problem, we know that certain fluents hold in some situations other than the initial situation, and we want to know the cause for holding of these fluents. In the stolen car scenario, a person parks the car in the morning and goes to work. According to the commonsense law of inertia, it can be inferred by default that the car is still in the car park at lunch time. However, when this person returns to the car park in the evening, he finds that the car has gone. Now, the problem is to reason backward in time to the causes of the car's disappearance. In this case, the only reasonable explanation is that the car was stolen sometime between morning and evening. Therefore, the default assumption that the car was still in the car park at lunch time is open to question.

The stolen car problem can be represented by the following three sentences. Here, two successive Wait actions are used to represent the interval between morning and evening implicitly; the fluent Stolen represents that the car is not in the car park.

$$SC1: \quad \neg Holds(Stolen, S_0) \tag{2.40}$$

$$SC2: \quad S_2 = Result(Wait, Result(Wait, S_0)) \tag{2.41}$$

$$SC3: \quad Holds(Stolen, S_2) \tag{2.42}$$

Furthermore, let (Arb1) and (Arb2) be the following axioms:

$$Arb1: \ Result(a1, s1) = Result(a2, s2) \rightarrow a1 = a2 \wedge s1 = s2 \tag{2.43}$$

$$Arb2: \ S_0 \neq Result(a, s) \tag{2.44}$$

Then, with chronological minimization, it will be manifested that the car disappeared during the second Wait, i.e.,

$$Ab(Wait, Stolen, Result(Wait, S_0)) \wedge \neg Ab(Wait, Stolen, S_0)$$

But in fact, the car could equally well have disappeared during the first Wait, and we would like the formalization of the commonsense law of inertia to respect this possibility. In other words, what we would like is to be able to manifest the following result

$$Ab(Wait, Stolen, Result(Wait, S_0)) \vee Ab(Wait, Stolen, S_0)$$

and also that there exist two models $M1$ and $M2$ such that

$$M1 \models Ab(Wait, Stolen, Result(Wait, S_0))$$

and

$$M2 \models Ab(Wait, Stolen, S_0).$$

2.12 Dynamic Description Logic

2.12.1 *Description Logic*

Description logic is a kind of formalization of knowledge representation based on object, and it is also called concept representation language or terminological logic. Description logic is a decidable subclass of first-order logic. It has well-defined semantics and possesses strong expression capability. One description logic system consists of four parts: constructors which represent concept and role, TBox subsumption assertion, ABox instance assertion, and reasoning mechanism of TBox and ABox. The representation capability and reasoning capability of description logic system lie on the aforementioned four elements and different hypotheses (Baader *et al.*, 2003).

There are two essential elements, i.e., concept and role, in description logic. Concept is interpreted as a subclass of domain. Role represents interrelation between individuals, and it is a kind of binary relation of domain set.

In certain domains, a knowledge base $K = \langle T, A \rangle$ consists of two parts: TBox T and ABox A. TBox is a finite set of subsumption assertions, and it is also called terminological axiom set. The general format of subsumption assertion is $C \subseteq D$, where C and D are concepts. ABox is a finite set of instance assertions. Its format is $C(a)$, where a is individual name; or its format is $P(a, b)$, where P is a primitive role, a and b are two individual names.

In general, TBox is an axiom set which describes the domain structure, and it has two functions: one is to introduce concept name, the other is to declare subsumption relationship of concepts. The process of introducing concept name is expressed by $A \doteq C$ or $A \subseteq C$, where A is the concept which is introduced. The format of subsumption assertion of concepts is $C \subseteq D$. As to concept definition and subsumption relation definition, the following conclusion comes into existence:

$$C \doteq D \Leftrightarrow C \subseteq D \text{ and } C \subseteq D.$$

ABox is an instance assertion set, and its function is to declare the attribute of individual or relationship of individuals. There are two kinds of formats: one is to declare the relationship of the individual and concept, the other is to declare the relationship of two individuals. In ABox, as to arbitrary individual a and concept C, the assertion which decides whether individual a is a member of concept C is called concept instance assertion, i.e., concept assertion. $a \in C$ is denoted as $C(a)$; $a \notin C$ is denoted as $\neg C(a)$.

Given two individuals a, b, and a role R, if individual a and individual b satisfy role R, then aRb is role instance assertion, and it is denoted as $R(a, b)$.

In general, according to the constructor provided, the description logic may construct a complex concept and role based on a simple concept and role. Description logic includes the following constructors at least: intersection ($\cap$), union ($\cup$), negation ($\neg$), existential quantification ($\exists$), and value restriction ($\forall$). The description logic which possesses these constructors is called ALC. Based on ALC, different constructors may be added to it, so that different description logics may be formed. For example, if number restrictions "$\leq$" and "$\geq$" are added to the description logic

Table 2.3.   Syntax and semantics of ALC

Constructor	Syntax	Semantics	Example
Primitive concept	A	$A^I \forall \Delta^I$	Human
Primitive concept	P	$P^I \subseteq \Delta^I \times \Delta^I$	has-child
Top	$\top$	Δ^I	True
Bottom	$\bot$	Φ	False
Intersection	$C \cap D$	$C^I \cap D^I$	Human $\cap$ Male
Union	$C \cup D$	$C^I \cup D^I$	Doctor $\cup$ Lawyer
Negation	$\neg C$	$\Delta^I - C^I$	$\neg$Male
Existential quantification	$\exists R.C$	$\{x \vert \exists y, (x, y) \in R^I \wedge y \in C^I\}$	$\exists$ has-child.Male
Value restriction	$\forall R.C$	$\{x \vert \forall y, (x, y) \in R^I \Rightarrow y \in C^I\}$	$\forall$ has-child.Male

ALC, then a new kind of description logic ALCN is formed. Table 2.3 shows the syntax and semantics of description logic ALC.

An interpretation $I = (\Delta^I, \cdot^I)$ consists of a domain Δ^I and an interpretation function $\cdot I$, where the interpretation function $\cdot I$ maps each primitive concept to the subset of domain Δ^I and maps each primitive role to the subset of domain $\Delta^I \times \Delta^I$. With respect to an interpretation, the concept of ALC is interpreted as a domain subset, and the role is interpreted as a binary relation:

(1) an interpretation I is a model of subsumption assertion $C \subseteq D$, if and only if $C^I \subseteq D^I$;

(2) an interpretation I is a model of $C(a)$, if and only if $a \in C^I$; an interpretation I is a model of $P(a, b)$, if and only if $(a, b) \in P^I$;

(3) an interpretation I is a model of knowledge base K, if and only if I is a model of each subsumption assertion and instance assertion of knowledge base K;

(4) if knowledge base K has a mode l, then K is satisfiable;

(5) as to each model of knowledge base K, if assertion δ is satisfiable, then we say that knowledge base K logically implicates δ, and it is denoted as $K| = \delta$.

(6) as to concept C, if knowledge base K has a model I, and $C^I \neq \phi$, then concept C is satisfiable. The concept C of knowledge base K is satisfiable if and only if $K| \neq C \subseteq \bot$.

The basic reasoning problems of description logic include concept of satisfiability, concept of subsumption relation, instance checking, consistency checking, and so on, where the concept of satisfiability is the most basic reasoning problem, other reasoning problems may be reduced to the concept of satisfiability problem.

In description logic, reasoning problem may be reduced to the concept of satisfiability problem through the following properties. As to concepts C, D, there exist the following propositions:

(1) $C \subseteq D \Leftrightarrow C \sqcap \neg D$ is unsatisfiable;
(2) $C \doteq D$ (concept C and D are equivalent) $\Leftrightarrow$ both $(C \sqcap \neg D)$ and $(D \sqcap \neg C)$ are unsatisfiable;
(3) C and D are disjoint $\Leftrightarrow C \sqcap D$ is unsatisfiable.

2.12.2 *Syntax of Dynamic Description Logic*

Dynamic description logic (DDL) is formed by extending the traditional description logic (Shi *et al.*, 2005), while the traditional description logic has many species. Here, DDL is studied based on description logic ALC.

Definition 2.25. The primitive symbols in DDL are as follows:

- concept names: $C_1, C_2, \ldots$;
- role names: $R_1, R_2, \ldots$;
- individual constant: $a, b, c, \ldots$;
- individual variable: $x, y, z, \ldots$;
- concept operator: $\neg, \sqcap, \sqcup$ and quantifier $\exists, \forall$;
- formula operator: $\neg, \wedge, \rightarrow$ and quantifier $\forall$;
- action names: $A_1, A_2, \ldots$;
- action constructs: ;(sequence), $\cup$(choice), *(iteration), ?(test);
- action variable: $\alpha, \beta, \ldots$;
- formula variable: $\phi, \psi, \pi, \ldots$;
- state variable: $u, v, w, \ldots$.

Definition 2.26. Concepts in DDL are defined as follows:

(1) primitive concept P, top$\perp$ and bottom $\perp$ are concepts;
(2) if C and D are concepts, then $\neg C, C \sqcap D$, and $C \sqcup D$ are concepts;
(3) if C is concept and R is role, then $\exists R.C$ and $\forall R.C$ are concepts;
(4) if C is concept and α is action, then $[\alpha]C$ is action too.

Definition 2.27. Formulas in DDL are defined as follows, where C is concept, R is role, a, b are individual constants, and x, y are individual variables:

(1) $C(a)$ and $R(a, b)$ are called assertion formulas;
(2) $C(x)$ and $R(x, y)$ are called general formulas;
(3) both assertion formulas and general formulas are all formulas;
(4) if φ and ψ are formulas, then $\neg \varphi, \varphi \wedge \psi, \varphi \rightarrow \psi$, and $\forall x \varphi$ are all formulas;
(5) if φ is formula, then $[\alpha]\varphi$ is also formula.

Definition 2.28. A finite set of $\{a_1/x_1, \ldots, a_n/x_n\}$ is an instance substitution, where $a_1, \ldots, a_n$ are instance constants, which are called substitution items, $x_1, \ldots, x_n$ are variables which are called substitution bases, $x_i \neq x_j$ for each pair i, j in $\{1, \ldots, n\}$ such that $i \neq j$.

Definition 2.29. Let φ be a formula, let $x_1, \ldots, x_n$ be all the variables occurring in φ, and let $a_1, \ldots, a_n$ be instance constants. If $\varphi\prime$ is a substitution result of φ with $\{a_1/x_1, \ldots, a_n/x_n\}$, then φ' is called an instance formula of φ.

Definition 2.30. A condition in DDL is an expression of the form: $\forall C, C(p)$, $R(p, q), p = q$, or $p \neq q$, where N_C is a set of individual constants, N_X is a set of individual variables, N_I is the union N_C and N_X, $p, q \in N_I$, C is a concept of DDL, and R is a role of DDL.

Definition 2.31. *An action description is of the form* $A(x_1, \ldots, x_n) \equiv (P_A, E_A)$, where

(1) A is the action name;
(2) $x_1, \ldots, x_n$ are individual variables, which denote the objects on which the action operates;
(3) P_A is the set of *pre-conditions*, which must be satisfied before the action is executed, i.e., $P_A = \{con | con \in condition\}$;
(4) E_A is the set of post-conditions, which denotes the effects of the action; E_A is a set of pair *head/body*, where head $= \{con | con \in condition\}$, body is a condition.

Remarks are as follows:

(1) Action defines the transition relation of state, i.e., an action A transits a state u to a state v, if action A can produce state v under state u. The transition relation depends on whether states u, v satisfy the pre-conditions and post-conditions of action A. The transition relation is denoted as $uTAv$.
(2) Because some states that happened before action A may influence the post-condition of action A, there is some difference between pre-conditions and post-conditions. As to post-conditions of head/body, if each condition of head can be satisfied in state u, then each condition of body can also be satisfied in state v.

Definition 2.32. Let $A(x_1, \ldots, x_n) \equiv (P_A, E_A)$ be an action description and let $A(a_1, \ldots, a_n)$ be the substitution of $A(x_1, \ldots, x_n)$ by $\{a_1/x_1, \ldots, a_n/x_n\}$. Then $A(a_1, \ldots, a_n)$ is called an action instance of $A(x_1, \ldots, x_n).A(a_1, \ldots, a_n)$

is called atom action, $P_A(a_1, \ldots, a_n)$ is the pre-condition of $A(a_1, \ldots, a_n)$ and $E_A(a_1, \ldots, a_n)$ is the result set of $A(a_1, \ldots, a_n)$.

Definition 2.33. Actions in DDL are defined as follows:

(1) atomic action $A(a_1, \ldots, a_n)$ is action;
(2) if α and β are actions, then $\alpha; \beta$, $\alpha \cup \beta$, and α^* are all actions;
(3) if φ is an assertion formula, then φ? is action.

2.12.3 *Semantics of Dynamic Description Logic*

The semantics of DDL can be illustrated by a structure composed of the following components:

(1) non-empty set Δ, which is the set of all individuals discussed in a specified domain;
(2) the set of state W, which is the set of all states of the world in a specified domain;
(3) an interpretation I which explains each individual, concept, and role in DDL as follows:

    (a) Each individual constant is interpreted as an element of Δ;
    (b) Each concept is interpreted as a subset of Δ;
    (c) Each role is interpreted as a binary relation on Δ.

(4) each action is mapped into a binary relation on W.

    Next, we will explain the semantics of DDL in detail. First, for a state u in DDL, an explanation $I(u) = (\Delta, \bullet^{I(u)})$ in u is composed of two components, written as $I(u) = (\Delta, \bullet^{I(u)})$, where explanation function $\bullet^{I(u)}$ maps each concept into a subset of Δ and maps each role into a binary relation on $\Delta \times \Delta$.

- $\top^{I(u)} = \Delta$;
- $\bot^{I(u)} = \emptyset$;
- $C^{I(u)} \subseteq \Delta$;
- $R^{I(u)} \subseteq \Delta \times \Delta$;
- $(\neg C)^{I(u)} = \Delta - C^{I(u)}$;
- $(\neg R)^{I(u)} = \Delta \times \Delta - R^{I(u)}$;
- $(C \sqcap D)^{I(u)} = C^{I(u)} \bigcap D^{I(u)}$;
- $(C \sqcup D)^{I(u)} = C^{I(u)} \bigcup D^{I(u)}$;
- $(\exists R.C)^{I(u)} = \{x | \exists y.((x, y) \in R^{I(u)} \wedge y \in C^{I(u)})\}$;
- $(\forall R.C)^{I(u)} = \{x | \forall y.((x, y) \in R^{I(u)} \Rightarrow y \in C^{I(u)})\}$;
- $([\alpha]C)^{I(u)} = \{x | uT_\alpha v \wedge x \in (C)^{I(v)}\}$.

Since the interpretation of the object name does not depend on the particular world, we use the rigid designator and assume that each individual name is uniform and does not change with a change in state. Usually, we write $aI(u)$ as a for short.

Given action $A(x_1, \ldots, x_n) \equiv (P_A, E_A)$, N_X^A is a variable set which happened in action A, $I = (\Delta^I, \cdot^I)$ is an interpretation, and map $\gamma : N_X^A \to \Delta^I$ is a variable evaluation which happened in action A. As to individual constant $a \in N^C$ of ABox of DDL, $\cdot^I$ interprets a as an element of Δ^I, i.e., $a^I \in \Delta^I$. As to individual variable or individual constant $p \in N^I$, their interpretation is given in the following

$$p^{I,\gamma} = \begin{cases} \gamma(p), \text{if } p \in N_X \\ p^I, \text{if } p \in N_C \end{cases},$$

then the condition interpretations of DDL are as follows:

- if $C^I = \Delta^I$, then I and γ satisfy condition $\forall C$;
- if $a^{I,\gamma} \in C^I$, then I and γ satisfy condition $C(a)$;
- if $a^{I,\gamma} = b^{I,\gamma}$, then I and γ satisfy condition $a = b$;
- if $a^{I,\gamma} \neq b^{I,\gamma}$, then I and γ satisfy condition $a \# b$;
- if $\langle a^{I,\gamma}, b^{I,\gamma} \rangle \in R^I$, then I and γ satisfy condition $R(a, b)$.

In each state u, assertion formulas connect individual constants to concepts and roles. So, there are two kinds of assertion formulas: concept assertions with the form of $C(a)$ and role assertions with the form of $R(a_1, a_2)$. As to concept assertions, they declare the relation of individual constant and concept, i.e., the relation of element and set. Semantics of concept assertion can be interpreted as follows:

- $u \models C(a)$ iff $a \in C^{I(u)}$;
- $u \models \neg C(a)$ iff $a \notin C^{I(u)}$.

For example, under certain state, individual constant a denotes a block, and this means individual constant a belongs to the concept of block, and it is denoted as $\text{Block}(a)$; individual constant b is a button, and it is denoted as $\text{Button}(b)$.

Role assertions declare the relation of two individual objects or the attribute of an individual object. It is a binary relation, and its semantics can be explained as follows:

- $u \models R(a_1, a_2)$ iff $(a_1, a_2) \in R^{I(u)}$;
- $u \models \neg R(a_1, a_2)$ iff $(a_1, a_2) \notin R^{I(u)}$.

For example, under certain state, agent a_1 and agent a_2 are acquaintances, and this is denoted as *hasAquaintance*(a_1, a_2); object a presses on object b, and it is denoted as *On* (a, b). Role assertions may also declare some attributes of the individual object. For example, Button b_1 is in o pen state, and it is denoted as *hasState*(b_1, O_N); the length of object a is 10, and it is denoted as *hasLength(a, 10)*.

Analogously, for a particular state u, those formulas that are composed of assertion formulas can be interpreted as follows, where φ and ψ are assertion formulas:

- $u \models \neg\phi$ iff $u \models \phi$;
- $u \models \phi \wedge \psi$ iff $u \models \phi$ and $u \models \psi$;
- $u \models \phi \rightarrow \psi$ iff $u \models \phi \Rightarrow u \models \psi$.

Action execution results in change of world state, so action may also be defined as a state transition relationship. But the process of action change is the process of individual attribute change or individual relation change in fact, so under certain states, all individual attributes, relation description, and so on consist of the world state description. These individual attributes and relation descriptions may be defined based on the action description (Definition 2.33). State in DDL corresponds to all condition interpretations of action description under corresponding state in fact, so action may be interpreted based on the aforementioned condition interpretation and description logic interpretation. Before the action of DDL is defined, state transition (one state transits to an another state under action) is defined first.

Definition 2.34. Given two interpretations $I(u) = (\Delta, \bullet^{I(u)})$ and $I(v) = (\Delta, \bullet^{I(v)})$, under state u and v, an action $\alpha = (P\alpha, E\alpha)$ can produce state v when applied to state u (written $u \rightarrow_\alpha v$), if there exists an assignment map $\gamma.N_X^\alpha \rightarrow \Delta$, such that γ, $I(u)$, and $I(v)$ satisfy the following conditions:

(1) $I(u)$ and γ satisfy each condition of pre-conditions P_α;
(2) as to each pair head/body of post-conditions E_α, if $I(u)$ and γ satisfy head, then $I(v)$ and γ satisfy body.

In this case, we can say that action α can produce state v when applied to state u and assignment map γ, and it is denoted as $u \rightarrow_\alpha^\gamma v$.

The semantics of atomic and complex actions are defined as follows:

- $\alpha = \{\langle u, v\rangle | u, v \in W, u \rightarrow_\alpha^\gamma v\}$;
- $\alpha; \beta = \{\langle u, v\rangle | u, v, w \in W, u \rightarrow_\alpha^\gamma w \wedge w \rightarrow_\beta^\gamma v\}$;
- $\alpha \bigcup \beta = \{\langle u, v\rangle | u, v \in W, u \rightarrow_\alpha^\gamma v \vee u \rightarrow_\beta^\gamma v\}$;
- $\alpha^* = \{\langle u, v\rangle | u, v \in W, u \rightarrow_\alpha^\gamma v \vee u \rightarrow_{\alpha;\alpha}^\gamma v \vee u \rightarrow_{\alpha;\alpha;\alpha}^\gamma v \vee \ldots\}$;
- $\phi? = \{\langle u, u\rangle | u \in W, u \models \phi\}$.

Because the aforementioned action interpretation is based on the description logic, some new concepts about action may be given, and these new concepts supplement description logics.

Definition 2.35. Given action α (primitive action or complex action), if there exist two interpretations $I(u) = (\Delta, \bullet^{I(u)})$ and $I(v) = (\Delta, \bullet^{I(v)})$ that satisfy $u \to_\alpha v$, then action α is realizable.

Definition 2.36. Given action α (primitive action or complex action), if there exists an interpretation $I(u) = (\Delta, \bullet^{I(u)})$ corresponding to ABox A, and an interpretation $I(v) = (\Delta, \bullet^{I(v)})$ corresponding to ABox A and TBox T, and $u \to_\alpha v$ is satisfied, then action a is realizable corresponding to ABox A.

Definition 2.37. Given two actions α and β (primitive action or complex action), as to arbitrary interpretations $I(u) = (\Delta, \bullet^{I(u)})$ and $I(v) = (\Delta, \bullet^{I(v)})$), the following condition is satisfied: if the existence of $u \to_\alpha v$ can make $u \to_\beta v$ come true, then action β subsumes action α, denoted as $\alpha \subseteq \beta$.

Definition 2.38. Given two actions α and β (primitive action or complex action), an arbitrary interpretation $I(u) = (\Delta, \bullet^{I(u)})$ corresponding to ABox A of DDL, and an arbitrary interpretation $I(v) = (\Delta, \bullet^{I(v)})$ corresponding to ABox A and TBox T, the following condition is satisfied: if the existence of $u \to_\alpha v$ can make $u \to_\beta v$ come true, then action β subsumes action α corresponding to ABox A, denoted as $\alpha \subseteq A\beta$.

Remark. Similar to Definitions 2.37 and 2.39, action realization or subsumption corresponding to TBox T may also be defined. In order to understand the action subsumption, the following is a simple example.

Given four action descriptions: $\alpha_1 = (\{A(a), \neg A(b)\}, \{\Phi/\neg A(a), \Phi/A(b)\})$; $\alpha_2 = (\{A(c), \neg A(d)\}, \{\Phi/\neg A(c), \Phi/A(d)\})$; $\alpha_3 = (\{A(x), \neg A(y)\}, \{\Phi/\neg A(x), \Phi/A(y)\})$; and $\alpha_4 = (\{A(y), \neg A(x)\}, \{\Phi/\neg A(y), \Phi/A(x)\})$, where a, b, c, d are individual constants and x, y are individual variables, then we have $a1 \subseteq a3$, $a2 \subseteq a3$, $a1 \subseteq a4$, $a2 \subseteq a4$, $a3 \subseteq a4$, and $a4 \subseteq a3$, but there is no subsumption relation between α_1 and α_2.

Exercises

2.1 What is monotonic reasoning? What is non-monotonic reasoning?

2.2 How are default rules represented in the default theory? What are the representation forms that exist there?

2.3 A default theory is a pair $T = \langle W, D \rangle$, with D being a set of default rules and W a set of closed formulas. Represent the following sentences with such a default theory.

(1) Some mollusks have shells.
(2) Cephalopods are mollusks.
(3) Not all cephalopods have shells.

2.4 Both the closed world assumption and the circumscription are formalisms for non-monotonic reasoning. Exposit these two formalisms and compare the difference between them.

2.5 Represent the following situations with the truth maintenance system:

(1) It is now summer.
(2) The weather is very humid.
(3) The weather is very dry.

2.6 How to maintain the consistence of a knowledge base by the truth maintenance system? Illustrate it with an example.

2.7 Represent the following monkey-and-bananas problem with situation calculus. The world is composed of a monkey in a room, a bunch of bananas hanging from the ceiling, and a box that can be moved by the monkey. The bananas are out of the reach of the monkey; however, the box will enable the monkey to reach the bananas if the monkey climbs on it. The actions available to the monkey include *Go* from one place to another, *Push* an object from one place to another, *ClimbUp* onto or *ClimbDown* from an object, and *Grasp* or *Ungrasp* an object. Initially, the monkey is at A, the bananas at B, and the box at C. The question is: How will the monkey get the bananas?

2.8 What are the basic elements of the description logic?

2.9 How are actions represented in the dynamic description logic?

Chapter 3

Constraint Reasoning

Constraint reasoning has been proven to be an effective technique for representing and reasoning a variety of real-world decision problems. This includes problems in automatic reasoning and reactive and deliberative autonomous control.

3.1 Introduction

A constraint usually refers to relational expressions which include several variables and is used to represent conditions which these variables must satisfy. Constraint representation has been widely applied to various fields in artificial intelligence, including qualitative reasoning, model-based diagnosis, nature language understanding, scenery analysis, task scheduling, system dispose, scientific experiment planning, design and analysis of machinery and electronic apparatus, and so on. Design of a constraint satisfaction system is a difficult and complex task because a constraint satisfaction problem is generally an NP problem which must be solved by using various strategies and heuristic information. From the view of knowledge representation, many important problems need studying, such as representing abstract and default reasoning and so on. Non-monotonic reasoning has enough expressing ability, but it has low reasoning efficiency and even becomes non-calculated. Furthermore, it is inconvenient for non-monotonic reasoning to express heuristic information and meta information. Semantic network can also represent abstract and default information; however, it does not have enough problem-solving abilities. The constraint representation with abstract type can remedy deficiencies of both non-monotonic reasoning and semantic network in expression. The study on constraint representation and default reasoning in type hierarchy is very meaningful.

In constraint reasoning, to solve the contradictions between narrowing search space and controlling reasoning cost, we proposed an integrated search algorithm for constraint satisfaction and designed appropriate forms of strategy such as intelligent backtracking, constraint propagation, variable instantiation ordering, etc. By combining these strategies organically, the search space can be reduced effectively with reasonable calculation cost and the existing experimental result shows that this algorithm is superior to other similar algorithms. In addition, some special relations have been realized, such as equality and inequality reasoning, unit sharing strategy of identical relation, and the combination of inequality graph and interval reasoning. These realizations combine the evaluation of constraint expression and symbol relation together and strengthen the symbolic deduction ability of constraint reasoning. In constraint languages, we designed SCL — an object-oriented constraint language. SCL realizes an integrated constraint reasoning with default constraint representation and adopts a certain-type control of regular language (e.g., condition structure), while confining the uncertain part to the data. As a result, constraint propagation with intelligent backtracking can be used to reduce the uncertainty and narrow the search space. At the same time, such regular structure also improves code readability and makes language studying easy. We have also realized constraint representation embedded in C++ so that the constraint programming design fully utilizes the abundant computational resources of C++.

A constraint satisfaction problem (abbreviated as CSP) includes a set of variables and constraints between variables. In general, variables represent field parameters, and each variable has a fixed value domain. One variable's value domain may be limited, for example, one Boolean domain only contains two values. The value domain may be dispersed and limitless (e.g., integer domain) and may be continuous as well (e.g., real number domain). Constraints can be used to describe field object's property, interrelation, task requirement, goal, and so on. The goal of a constraint satisfaction problem is to find one or more assignments of all variables in order to satisfy all constraints.

Constraint representation is easy to understand, code, and realize. Constraint representation has the following advantages:

(1) Constraint representation allows to represent domain knowledge in a declarative way, and it has a strong expressing ability. The application only needs to define goal conditions and data interrelation in a problem. Therefore, constraint representation has the resembling characteristics of logic representation.

(2) Constraint representation allows the variable domain to contain arbitrary values, while the proposition only fetches true or false values. Thus, constraint

representation can keep some structural information of the problem, such as variable domain size, variable interrelation, etc., in order to offer heuristic information for problem solving.

(3) Constraint representation is easy to be implemented in parallel because information propagation in constraint networks can be regarded as running at the same time.

(4) Constraint representation is suitable for systems with a gradual increase in complexity. Constraint can be added to a constraint network in a gradual manner.

(5) Constraint representation is easy to connect with problem-solving models of the field. Mathematical planning, equation solving, and other techniques can be embedded into the constraint system naturally.

Many constraint reasoning methods have been proposed after many years of study. According to the data type of a node in the constraint network, constraint reasoning can be classified into the following categories:

(1) **Relation reasoning:** New constraint relation reasoned out in the reasoning process will be added into constraint network. Kuiper's ENV system, Simmon's Quantity Lattice system, and Brooks' CMS system all belong to relation reasoning.

(2) **Mark reasoning:** Mark each node with a set of possible values, which will be limited by constraint in constraint propagation.

(3) **Value reasoning:** The node is marked with a constant value. Constraints obtain values of unmarked nodes by using already marked node values. SKETCHPAD and THINGLAB both use value reasoning.

(4) **Expression reasoning:** It is an extension of value reasoning, and the node might be marked with other node expressions. The different expressions of the marked node should be equal and the result is equations need to be solved. CONSTRAINTS uses this kind of reasoning.

The value of a constraint variable may be a number or not, i.e., symbolic value. In general, the values of symbolic variable form a limited set. Therefore, after constraint propagation stops, an exhaustive search can be done to decide the consistency of a symbolic variable. While the number variable usually has limitless value domain, it is impossible to carry out the exhaustive search.

The above four kinds of constraint reasoning all have some shortcomings. For example, value reasoning can not be used in inequality constraint but can be used in equation constraint. Relation reasoning and mark reasoning are difficult to control, thus preventing their entry to limitless circulation. In relation reasoning, it is difficult to decide whether new constraints are useful for solving a given problem. Mark reasoning can be used as a constraint with arbitrary form and is thus much better than other reasonings.

Existing constraint representation can be classified into several categories according to complexity, which are listed below:

- unary predicate;
- order relation language, which only includes partial-order relation of the real variable;
- equations similar to "$x - y > c$" or "$x - y \geq c$";
- linear equation and inequality of a unit coefficient, that is, all coefficients are $-1, 0, 1$;
- linear equation and inequality of arbitrary coefficient;
- Boolean combination of constraints;
- algebra and triangular equation.

Compared with several important marks such as symbols, interval, and real numbers, unary predicate is the simplest constraint.

The partial-order relation appears in the systems that only care about relations of the quantity. Some systems only care about event order without considering its time interval, such as NOAH system. In NOAH system, operations in each level of planning are appointed toward the partial-order relation.

The inequality similar to $x - y \geq c$ is very useful for only knowing the differences between variables, and these inequality constraints are widely used in TMM and many task planning applications.

In the measure space of scalar multiplication, sometimes it is very useful to define the quotient of two numbers. This kind of expression and difference definition is isomorphism, and isomorphism mapping is the logarithm function. Allen and Kantz used the Boolean combination of quotient and order relation to implement temporal reasoning.

The linear equation with unit coefficient is very useful for commonsense reasoning because this kind of relation is good enough to describe the conservation rule in qualitative reasoning. The conservation law affirms that the change in a value is equal to the sum of its increase minus the sum of its decrease. If we are only interested in state change, then we can only take three variable values $+, -$, and 0 and the equation coefficient is always unit coefficient.

The linear inequality is a kind of widely used constraint. Boolean combination of constraints is widely used in physical reasoning, circuit design, and planning.

Nonlinear equations and inequality are frequently involved in physical reasoning. In geometry reasoning, algebra and triangular equations are also involved frequently.

At present, research on constraint reasoning is mainly concentrated on two aspects: constraint search and constraint languages. The main research of constraint search focuses on constraint satisfaction in a definite domain. For the definite domain, the constraint satisfaction problem is generally an NP problem. At present, there are several methods to solve CSP which are as follows:

- backtracking,
- constraint propagation,
- intelligent backtracking and truth maintenance,
- variable order instantiation,
- local revision.

Constraint language is another main research aspect for constraint reasoning. The following are several typical constraint languages:

1. CONSTRAINTS

CONSTRAINTS is a circuit-based constraint representation language. As a constraint representation language, CONSTRAINTS uses symbolic technology to solve mathematical equations. In CONSTRAINTS, functions of physical parts and device structure are represented by constraints, which are generally linear equations, inequalities, and condition expressions. Constraint variables are usually the real variables of the physical quantity and are sometimes assigned dispersed values as well, such as the state of the switch, working state of a triode, and so on. The system adopts expression reasoning and value reasoning and realizes dependence-directed backtracking.

One advantage of CONSTRAINTS is to represent constraints at type hierarchy and adopt a constraint to represent the function and structure of physical devices. One shortcoming of using constraints is the lack of methods which are similar to object-oriented language, and thus cannot define particular class concepts. Meanwhile, the constraint propagation method is monotonous. It lacks the interval propagation mechanism on the real domain and domain propagation mechanism in the definite domain.

2. Bertrand

Bertrand is an advanced constraint language developed by Leler, and its computational model is a system based on enhanced term rewriting. On the whole, Bertrand adds the assignment function and type mechanism based on a term rewriting system, which makes Bertrand capable of solving linear equations about real numbers and rational numbers. Bertrand also includes the function of abstracting data type. It has already been used for solving some problems in graphics and circuit.

Bertrand still cannot be regarded as a real constraint language, but a generating tool for the constraint satisfaction system. Basically, it offers nothing to solve dispersed constraints and it doesn't offer a propagation mechanism for interval propagation and order relation in the real number domain. Bertrand can only offer value propagation.

3. Constraint logic programming language — CHIP

The main research on constraint language concentrates on constraint logic programming language, which aims to combine constraint satisfaction technology and logic programming. Such languages introduce constraint propagation (mainly arc consistency technology) on the basis of Prolog in order to improve search efficiency and strengthen expressing ability. Constraint handling in Prolog (CHIP) is such a constraint logic programming language with great influence. The goal of CHIP is to solve a major kind of composition problem simply, conveniently, flexibly, and effectively. CHIP strengthens the ability of logic programming through offering several kinds of new computational domains: definite domain, Boolean item, and rational item. For all computational domains, CHIP offers an effective constraint-solving technology, including consistency technology of the definite domain, unified technology for the Boolean domain, and pure type for the rational domain as well as a general delay computing technology.

CHIP is mainly applied to two fields: operations research and hardware design. However, CHIP lacks the type mechanism which is extremely important for expressing the domain concept.

4. Constraint hierarchy and HCLP

"Soft constraint" solving problem is a very interesting and important practical problem. In this research, the most influential work is from Borning *et al.* (Freeman-Benson and Borning, 1992). Borning presented the concept of constraint hierarchy in order to solve the "overly constrained" problem of graph design. The idea is that a system can not only satisfy "Hard constraint" but also allow users to present as much "soft constraint" as possible. These soft constraints are divided into several priority grades, which are also called constraint hierarchy.

Constraint hierarchy is a definite set of marked constraints. Given a constraint level H, H_0 is a set of constraints that must be satisfied in H. H_1 is the strongest constraint of non-essential constraints and H_n is the weakest, in which n denotes the grade of non-essential constraints.

The evaluation of a constraint set is a function which maps a free variable into an element of D domain. A solution of constraint hierarchy is a set of evaluation of free variables. Evaluation in a solving set must at least satisfy essential constraints. In addition, the solving set should also satisfy the constraints of other evaluations. Among evaluations that satisfy essential constraints, there do not exist more evaluations that satisfy a non-essential constraint than evaluations in the solving set. There are a variety of methods to compare the degree of satisfaction of which evaluation satisfies the constraint. The method selected depends on the specific application.

At the beginning, the evaluation of constraint hierarchy uses some methods to make constraint hierarchy be satisfied to the greatest extent. But these methods do not have the declarative advantage of the constraint representation system. Therefore, Wilson (1987) and Freeman-Benson and Borning (1992) designed the hierarchical constraint logic programming language, HCLP, on the basis of constraint logic programming, which embeds constraint hierarchy into Prolog and makes a hierarchical constraint system to be built totally on declarative representation. The minimal model theory of non-monotonic theory is used to define the semantics of the HCLP model. HCLP first utilizes the backtracking method of common logic programming to obtain a necessary solution, which may include limited variable domains rather than variable values. Meanwhile, it also generates all constraints of current instantiations (constraint hierarchy), and then gradually limits the necessary solution by the generated constraint from a stronger constraint to a weaker one until inconsistent situations appear. As to the constraints in the same hierarchy, different orders of using constraints will lead to different solutions.

The solution of constraint hierarchy is simple and swift, but incomplete, because the generated solution may not correspond to the minimal model of the whole logic programming but a minimum model of reasoning path.

5. Object-oriented constraint language

COPS system, developed by the intelligent information processing laboratory of Institute of Computing Technology (ICT), Chinese Academy of Sciences, utilizes object-oriented technology and combines declarative constraint representation and constraint hierarchy together. COPS absorbs regular language (mainly object-oriented programming language) in form. The solution inside COPS is realized by using a constraint-reasoning mechanism, which combines declarative constraint representation and constraint hierarchy to realize structured encapsulation of knowledge. By taking full advantage of constraint representation and hierarchy, COPS tries to become a constraint satisfaction system with a strong expressing ability and high solving efficiency. The design of COPS considers requirement of software engineering and tries to determine uncertain problems: to realize iterative computation, COPS does not utilize only iteration statements but allows both the selection and iteration statements; through overload of class methods, a constraint may have multiple implementations, which can improve the execution efficiency of a program. COPS system is also an open system of gradual increment, in which users can realize the new data type and constraint relation through hierarchy definition. The constraint representation language COPS has a lot of characteristics of artificial intelligence programming languages, such as constraint propagation, target-oriented and data-driven problem solving, limited backtracking, inheritance of object hierarchy, and so on.

6. ILOG

ILOG Company established in 1987, whose general headquarters is in Paris, France and California, U.S.A., is the world's leading provider of software component suites in optimization, visualization, and business rule management fields and applies the optimization algorithms to business software. The products of ILOG are widely used in telecommunications, traffic, national defense, electricity, delivery, etc. ILOG Solver represents constraints by using modeling language.

3.2 Backtracking

Generate-and-test method is the simplest and most direct way to solve constraint satisfaction problems. Each possible combination of the variables is generated and then tested until a successful tested combination is found. This method is obviously less effective. Backtracking is a direct improvement of the generate-and-test method. In backtracking, the variables are instantiated in a fixed order. When a new variable violates a former instantiated variable, backtracking is performed to try other instantiated variables until all values of the domain are tried. When all values result in failure, it backtracks the most recently instantiated variable and assigns it again.

Suppose the solution of CSP is made up of vectors with uncertain lengths, i.e., $(x_1, x_2, \ldots)$, which satisfies all constraints. X_i is the value domain of variable x_i, then the feasible solution space of CSP is $X_1 \times X_2 \times \ldots \times X_n$, where n is the number of variables.

At the beginning of backtracking, partial solution is a null vector. Then choose a variable x_1 from the variable set and add it into a partial solution. Usually, x_1 takes the minimum element of X_1. The candidates of x_1 chosen under various constraints will form a subset S_1 of X_1. The constraints can be used to find out candidates from partial solution $(x_1, x_2, \ldots, x_{k-1})$ to $(x_1, x_2, \ldots, x_{k-1}, x_k)$. If $(x_1, x_2, \ldots, x_{k-1}, x_k)$ does not allow x_k to take any value, then $S_k = \phi$. On this condition, backtracking is done and a new permission value is assigned for x_{k-1}. If x_{k-1} does not have new permission value, further backtracking to x_{k-2} is done and so on. Suppose $T(x_1, x_2, \ldots, x_{k-1})$ denotes all fetching values of x_k. If partial solution $(x_1, x_2, \ldots, x_k)$ does not allow to have a new expansion node, then the bounding function $BT_k(x_1, x_2, \ldots, x_k)$ is false, otherwise true. The backtracking algorithm with only one solution is as follows:

Algorithm 3.1 (Backtracking Algorithm).

> Input: A CSP problem
> Output: Complete solution or return no solution
> procedure BACKTRACK
> > begin
> > $k = 1$;
> > > while $k > 0$ do
> > > > If x_k has unchecked value to make
> > > > > $x_k \in T(x_1, x_2, \ldots, x_{k-1})$ *and*
> > > > > $BT_k(x_1, x_2, \ldots, x_k) =$ true
> > > > then if $(x_1, x_2, \ldots, x_k)$ satisfy all constraints
> > > > > then return(0) ; /* return one solution */
> > > > > else $k = k + 1$;
> > > > end if;
> > > > else $k = k - 1$;
> > > endwhile
> > return(1) ; /*Return no solution */
> end BACKTRACK

Although backtracking is better than the generate-and-test method, it still has low efficiency for non-trivial problems. This is because search in different paths of the space keeps failing for the same reasons. Some researchers think that the thrashing is caused by the so-called "local inconsistency". The simplest cause of thrashing concerns the so-called "node inconsistency". If a variable v_i contains a value a that does not satisfy the unary constraint on v_i, then the instantiation of v_i to a always results in inconsistency. Another possible source of thrashing is the so-called "arc inconsistency", which is illustrated by the following example: Suppose the variables are instantiated in the order $v_1, v_2, \ldots, v_i, \ldots, v_j, \ldots, v_n$. Suppose also that the binary constraint between v_i and v_j is such that for $v_i = a$, there is no value for v_j that would satisfy such a constraint. The search will fail while instantiation is tried with v_j and the failure will be repeated for each possible combination that the variables $v_r (i < r < j)$ can take.

Thrashing because of node inconsistency can be eliminated by removing those values from the domains of each variable that does not satisfy unary constraint. The thrashing because of arc inconsistency can be eliminated by the arc consistency algorithm. In Section 3.3, the formal definition of arc consistency and the corresponding algorithm will be presented.

3.3 Constraint Propagation

If for every value x in the current domain v_i, there is some value y in the domain of v_j such that $v_i = x$ and $v_j = y$, which are permitted by the constraint between v_i and v_j, then arc(v_i, v_j) is arc consistent. The concept of arc consistency is directional, that is, if an arc(v_i, v_j) is consistent, then it does not automatically mean that arc(v_j, v_i) is consistent. For example, if the current domain of v_1 is $\{a\}$, the current domain of v_2 is $\{a, b\}$, and the constraint between v_1 and v_2 is unequal, then arc(v_1, v_2) is consistent but arc(v_2, v_1) is not consistent. Because there does not exist any value of v_1 to satisfy the unequal constraint for $v_2 = b$. Obviously, an arc(v_i, v_j) can be made consistent by deleting those values which do not satisfy constraints. Furthermore, deletions of such values do not affect any solution of original CSP. The following algorithm demonstrates such a deletion operation.

Algorithm 3.2 (Revised Constraint Propagation Algorithm (Mackworth, 1977)).

```
procedure REVISE(Vi, Vj)
DELETE←false;
for each x ∈ Di do
        if there is no such Vj ∈ Dj
        such that (x, Vj) is consistent,
        then
            delete x from Di;
                DELETE←true;
        endif
    endfor
    return DELETE;
    end REVISE
```

To make every arc of a constraint network consistent, it is not sufficient to execute REVISE for each arc just once. Once REVISE reduces the variable v_i, then each previously revised arc(v_i, v_j) has to be revised again because the domain of v_i might become smaller than before. The following algorithm obtains arc consistency for the whole constraint network:

Algorithm 3.3 (Constraint Propagation Algorithm AC-1 (Mackworth, 1977)).

```
procedure AC-1
Q←{(Vi,Vj) ∈ arcs(G), i ≠ j};
repeat
  CHANGE←false;
  for each (Vi,Vj) ∈ Q do
    CHANGE←REVISE(Vi,Vj) ∨ CHANGE;
  endfor;
until not(CHANGE) ;
end AC-1
```

The main shortcoming of AC-1 is that a successful revision will force all arcs to be revised in the next iteration, although only a small number of arcs are affected . AC-3 performs re-revision only for those arcs that are possibly affected by a previous revision, which improves AC-1 algorithm.

Algorithm 3.4 (Constraint Propagation Algorithm AC-3 (Mackworth, 1977)).

```
procedure AC-3
Q←{(Vi,Vj) ∈ arcs(G), i ≠ j};
while Q not empty
  select and delete any arc(Vk,Vm) from Q;
  if (REVISE(Vk,Vm)) then
    Q←{(Vi,Vk) such that (Vi,Vk) ∈ arcs(G), i ≠ k, i ≠ m}
  End if;
End while;
end AC-3
```

The famous algorithm of Waltz (1975) is a special case of this algorithm and is similar to another algorithm AC-2 proposed by Mackworth. Suppose that the domain size for each variable is d, and the total number of constraints networks is e. The complexity of the arc-consistency algorithm proposed by Mackworth is $O(ed^3)$. Mohr and Henderson proposed another arc-consistency algorithm (Mohr, 1986), whose complexity is $O(ed^2)$. Therefore, Mohr and Henderson's algorithm is optimal when considering the worst-case complexity.

Given an arc-consistent constraint network, is there an instantiation of the variable from the current domains that make the variable become a solution to CSP? If the domain size of each variable becomes 1 after obtaining arc consistency, then the network has exactly one solution. Otherwise, the answer is no in general. Nevertheless, arc-consistent algorithms reduce the search space of backtracking.

Since the arc-consistency algorithm does not have enough ability to replace backtracking, can another stronger consistent algorithm eliminate the search needed for backtracking? The notion of K consistency captures different degrees of consistency for different values of K. A constraint network is K consistent if the following is true: Choose values of any $K - 1$ variables that satisfy all the constraints among these variables, then choose any Kth variable. A value for this variable exists that satisfies all the constraints among these K variables. The exactly formal description is as follows.

Suppose that the variables $x_1, x_2, \ldots, x_{k-1}$ are instantiated by values $a_1, a_2, \ldots, a_{k-1}$ separately. If each value of $a_1, a_2, \ldots, a_{k-1}$ satisfies all the constraints among $x_1, x_2, \ldots, x_{k-1}$, x_k, then for a variable x_k, there is a value a_k to make the value of $a_1, a_2, \ldots, a_{k-1}, a_k$ satisfy all the constraints among $x_1, x_2, \ldots, x_{k-1}$, x_k.

A constraint network is strong K consistent if it is J consistent for all $J \leq K$. Node consistency is equivalent to strong 1 consistency. Arc consistency is equivalent to strong 2 consistency. Algorithms exist to make a constraint network strong K consistent for $K > 2$ (Cooper, 1989). If an n-node constraint network is strong n consistent, then a solution to CSP can be found without any search. However, the worst-case complexity of the algorithm for obtaining n consistency in a n-node constraint network is also exponential.

However, the algorithm shows multinomial complexity for a constraint network with a special structure. The simplest case is that the arc-consistent algorithm can be used to solve the tree-structured constraint network within linear time complexity.

3.4 Constraint Propagation in Tree Search

Two different methods for solving CSP have been discussed above: backtracking and constraint propagation. In the first method, different combinations of variable assignments are tested until a complete solution is found. This approach suffers from thrashing. In the second method, constraints between different variables are propagated to derive a simpler problem. Although any CSP can always be solved by achieving n consistency, the efficiency of this approach is usually lower than backtracking. Furthermore, the k-consistency ($k < n$) algorithm does not ensure the achievement of a global consistent solution. An integrated method is to embed constraint propagation inside a backtracking algorithm, as follows.

At first, a root node is created to solve the original CSP. When a node is visited, a constraint propagation algorithm is used to achieve a desired consistency. If at a node, the domain of each variable contains only one value and the corresponding CSP is arc consistent, then the node represents a solution. If in the process of constraint propagation at a node, the domain of any variable becomes null, then the node is pruned. Otherwise, select one variable (whose domain size >1), and then a new CSP node is created for each possible assignment of this variable. Each new CSP node is depicted as a successor node of the node representing the current CSP. All these nodes are visited by a depth-first backtracking algorithm.

The problem now is how and to what extent constraints propagate at each node. If no constraint propagation occurs, then the method reverts to backtracking. If m-consistency algorithm is used to achieve m consistency for m CSP nodes which are unassigned, it would completely eliminate backtracking and result is poor efficiency. Experience indicates that a limited-constraint propagation whose consistency is generally not stronger than arc consistency can achieve the best efficiency.

3.5 Intelligent Backtracking and Truth Maintenance

Another method to overcome the drawbacks of standard backtracking is intelligent backtracking, in which backtracking is done directly to the variable that caused the failure. To see how intelligent backtracking works, consider the following example.

Suppose that variables v_1, v_2, and v_3 have been assigned values a_1, b_3, and c_2, respectively. Suppose that none of the values of v_3 were found compatible with the values b_1 and b_2 of v_2. Now suppose that all possible values of v_4 conflict with the choice of $v_1 = a_1$. The conflict is caused by the inappropriate choice of v_1, so the intelligent backtracking method will perform backtracking to v_1 and also undo the assignments of v_2 and v_3.

Although this kind of method can find the correct backtracking node according to the failed source, it has not totally avoided the redundant path. Dependency-directed backtracking is a method to eliminate the drawback and is widely used in truth maintenance system (TMS) developed by Doyle.

A TMS-based problem solver consists of two components: an inference engine and a TMS. The inference engine is used to derive new facts from old ones, while

TMS records the justifications of the derivations. New joining of facts might make some existing assumptions not true. Therefore, the maintenance of justifications can abolish those assumptions not true any more. The method used for CSP is described as follows.

When a variable is assigned some value, a justification for this value is created. Then similarly, a default value is assigned to some other variable and is justified. At this time, the system checks whether the current assignments violate any constraint. If they do, then a new node is created which denotes that the pair of values for the two variables are contradictory. This node is also used to justify other value assignment. This process continues until a consistent assignment is found for all the variables. Such a system never performs redundant backtracking and never repeats any computation.

Although the amount of search performed by such a system is minimal, the cost of determining the source of constraint violation is high. Because reasoning steps are exponentially increasing, the time and space complexity for storing and search are exponential. Hence, the overall method can take more time than even simple backtracking for a variety of problems.

Assumption-based truth maintenance system (ATMS) is another relevant work developed by de Kleer. The ATMS evolves from the TMS. TMS can be regarded as constraint propagation, and ATMS is the expansion of TMS. TMS only maintains single context, while ATMS attempts to search for multiple contexts at the same time. Therefore, each fact derived is corresponding to assumptions that make the fact true. A conclusion may be true in multiple contexts. The assumptions differ from the justifications in the fact that they are believed unless there is evidence to the contradiction and can thus be proven false. The advantage of ATMS lies in the fact that some temporary assumptions are shared and are not needed to be created separately. The number of temporary assumptions is usually exponentially increasing, and therefore, the procedure of assumption creation has exponential complexity. The ATMS has the following shortcomings:

- It is designed for complete solutions; for one solution unnecessary search is always done.
- It costs a lot of time and space for maintaining all contexts.
- It is difficult to correct mistakes.

It is very difficult for this method to estimate storage requirement, and all derivations and assumptions should be recorded, which makes the method difficult to apply to large-scale systems. Thus, de Kleer and Williams proposed to use backtracking in order to control ATMS again, which is also similar to an intelligent backtracking method.

3.6 Variable Instantiation Ordering and Assignment Ordering

Another improvement for standard backtracking is variable instantiation ordering. Experiments show that this ordering can have a substantial impact on the efficiency of backtrack search. Several heuristics have been developed for selecting variable ordering. One method is selecting the variable with the fewest value of domains for instantiation. Thus, the order of variable instantiation is, in general, determined dynamically, which is different in different branches of the search tree. Purdom and Brown extensively studied the heuristic, as well as its variants (Purdom and Brown, 1983), and the results show that they have substantial improvements over the standard backtracking method.

Another heuristic is to first instantiate those variables that participate in the highest number of constraints. This approach tries to ensure that the unsuccessful branches of search tree are pruned early.

Recall that the tree-structured constraint network can be solved without back-tracking. Any given constraint network can be made a tree after deleting certain vertices. This set of vertices is called the *cycle cutset*. If a small cycle cutset can be found, then a good heuristic is to first instantiate all the variables in the cycle cutset and then solve the resulting tree-structured CSPs.

3.7 Local Revision Search

At present, most algorithms are constructive methods based on the tree search. But another method to solve combination problem draws people's attention for its surprising experimental results recently, that is, the so-called "local revision" (Gu, 1992). First, this method produces a global but not an inconsistent variable assignment, then modifies some variable value according to the contradiction appearing in order to reduce the assignments that violates constraints, and repeats the process again until a consistent assignment is achieved. This method follows a simple rule: Find a variable which causes the contradiction, then select a new assignment to it, such that assignments can reduce contradictions to the least. The basic idea of this method is as follows:

Given a set of variables, a set of binary constraints, and an assignment of each variable, if two variable values violate a constraint, then the two variables are contradictory.

The process is to select a contradictory variable and assign a new value to it in order to reduce contradictions to the least.

Local revision search is very effective, and the main reason is that, more information is provided by variable assignments; thus, the next transforming state will reduce the contradictions tremendously.

Local revision search has shortcomings as well. First, the strategy is incomplete. When the solution of a problem does not exist, the search may not stop. When the density of solution is low, the search efficiency is very low too. We compared revision search and tree search on a graph-coloring problem, and the results showed that when there were less edges in the graph, revision search was better; otherwise, tree search had higher efficiency. If the problem has no solution, however, revision search will not stop.

At present, a new research direction of constraint search is studying the difficulty distribution of CSP. Although CSP is generally an NP problem, a large amount of CSPs can be solved during the tolerated time. The real intractable problems account for a small number.

3.8 Graph-Based Backjumping

Graph-based backjumping is a kind of dependency-directed method in which dependency information comes from graph structure of constraint network. A constraint graph consists of a vertex that denotes a variable and an edge that denotes a constraint (binary constraint). The edge between two vertices denotes that there exists a binary constraint between these two variables denoted by vertices. In graph-based backjumping, whenever a failure comes out at some variable X, the algorithm always goes back to the recent assigned variable connected to X in graph. The graph-based backjumping is described as follows:

Algorithm 3.5 (Forward Propagation Algorithm).

Forward($x_1, \ldots, x_i, P$)
begin
    if $i = n$ then Exit and Return current assignment;
        $C_{i+1} \leftarrow$ compute Candidates($x_1, \ldots, x_i, x_{i+1}$);
        if C_{i+1} not null, then
        $x_{i+1} \leftarrow$ The first element in C_{i+1};

Delete x_{i+1} from C_{i+1}
Forward $(x_1, \ldots, x_i, x_{i+1}, P)$;
    else
Jumpback $(x_1, \ldots, x_i, P)$;
  endif
end

Where, P is a set of variables which will be backtracked.

Algorithm 3.6 (Jumpback Algorithm).

Jumpback $(x_1, \ldots, x_i, x_{i+1}, P)$
begin
if $i = 0$, then Exit without solution;
    PARENTS $\leftarrow$ Parents(x_{i+1});
    $P \leftarrow P \cup$ PARENTS;
    $P \leftarrow P_{-x_j}$; j is the biggest serial number of variables in P,
If $C_j \neq \phi$, then
        $x_j =$ first in C_j;
        Delete x_j from C_j;
    Forward $(x_1, \ldots, x_j, P)$;
  else
        Jumpback $(x_1, \ldots, x_{j-1}, x_j, P)$;
  endif;
  end

3.9 Influence-Based Backjumping

We improved graph-based backjumping to form a new influence-based backjumping. First of all, our goal is to utilize not only static connection relation but also dynamic relevant information. The key problem is how to limit the cost of computing resources that is caused by introducing dynamic information within reasonable scope. Through exquisite design of the algorithm and data structure, we succeeded in solving this problem.

Influence-based backjumping — Influence-based-Backjumping, Most-constrained-first, Domain-filtering (IBMD) integrates three strategies: most-constrained-first, domain filtering, and backjumping. Most-constrained first refers to selecting the variable with minimum "degree of freedom" to assign each time. The "degree of freedom" is mainly measured by the current domain of variable because it is the most important and easiest quantity to calculate. The calculation can also be measured with the help of the connection degree of the variable in the constraint network. The most-constrained-first strategy is a very effective improvement for fixed-variable instantiation ordering.

Domain filtering refers to deleting the value inconsistent with assigned variable values from a variable domain. This is a constraint propagation technology with small cost. When a new variable is assigned, all those unassigned variable values which are inconsistent with this assignment will be deleted. The assignment is tentative, so deleted values must be stored. When some assignment is revoked, all deleted values caused by this assignment must be recovered.

The backjumping that we designed is different from traditional dependency-directed backtracking, including graph-based backjumping. The traditional dependency-directed backtracking records explicitly assumption sets on which reasoning will rely. Once one-step backtrack is done, the assumption set of the revoked variable will be merged into the assumption set of the recently assigned variables, which causes a lot of time cost and space cost. In order to avoid such cost, our backjumping does not backjump according to the recorded assumption set. In fact, we do not need these records at all. Our backjumping method backjumps according to the actual influence from one assignment to a variable in the filtering process. One assignment has influence on the variable v_i, if and only if at least one value of the current domain has been deleted in the filtering process caused by that assignment. Obviously, the influence is calculated more accurately than the connection relation of network — because connection relation is a possible data relevance, while influence relation is actual data dependence. Therefore, perhaps some two variables are connected in constraint graph, but do not influence each other under the current context. The space cost of influence-based backjumping is less than that of graph-based backjumping. Furthermore, influence-based backjumping leads to less time cost as well.

In IBMD, each instantiated variable stores a set of influenced variables. Given IBMD's context (all assignments of instantiated variables), a variable v_i is influenced by v_j if and only if the instantiations of v_j reduce the current domain of v_i to some extent.

IBMD includes forward instantiation and backward backtracking. In forward instantiation, select the variable whose current domain is minimal to assign at first. After the variable v_i is assigned, domain filtering will be carried out. For all unassigned variables v_j, delete those values in its domain D_j which are contradicting with assignment of v_i. If D_j becomes null, this means that the assignment of v_i contradicts with the previous variable assignment, and therefore backtracking begins. Backtracking first recovers values which have been deleted because of variable v_i instantiation. If all values of v_i have been tried, then backtracking continues going to the previous variable v_h. If v_h has no influence on v_j or other variables, all of whose values have been tried, or v_h has been already tried for all values, then make v_h as the previous instantiation variable and repeat the backtracking. Suppose that the procedure stops at variable v_g and the latest variable that influences v_g is v_f, then delete the instantiation value of v_g from D_g and record v_g and its instantiation value into the influence set of v_f. Then assign v_g with the new value again, thus going back to forward instantiation backtracking. The algorithm written in C is as follows:

Algorithm 3.7 (Influence-based Backjumping Algorithm (Liao *et al.*, 1994)).

```
IBMD()
{
  int var, failvar;
  while (uninstantiated ! =nil ) {
   var =mostConstrained() ;
      /*Choose a variable to instantiate */
   a[var] =domain[var][0]; /* Assign a value. */
      while ((failvar =propagate(var) )! =SUCCESS) {
        /*While inconsistent */
         if ((var =backjump(failvar) ==nil) return(0) ;
         /*If back up to top, exit */
         a[var] =domain[var][0]; /*Else reinstantiate var */
      }
  }
  return(1) ;
}
```

Algorithm 3.8 (Backjumping Algorithm (Liao, 1994)).

```
backjump (failvar)
int failvar;
   {
      int assignedVar, sourceVar;
      failedVarSet =makeVariableSet() ;
      addVariableSet(failvar, failedVarSet) ;
       /*Initialize the set of failed variables */
      while ((assignedVar =lastAssigned[ASSIGNEDHEAD]) ! =TOP)
        { /*Until go back to top */
```

```
        retract(assignedVar) ; { /*Retract the influences of the variable */
        if (relevant) /*The instantiation influence failedVarSet */
            if (! exhausted(assignedVar) )break;
            else addVariableSet(assignedVar, failedVarSet) ;
        }
    }
    if (assignedVar ==TOP) return(nil) ;
    for(sourceVar =lastAssigned[assignedVar];
      sourceVar ! =TOP && ! isCulpit(sourceVar) ;
        sourceVar =lastAssigned[sourceVar]) ;
        /*Find last variable that is relevant to the failure */
        domainfilter(sourceVar, assignedVar, a[assignedVar]) ;
        /*Filter the current value and record the influence */
    return(assignedVar) ;
    }
```

In the program, function mostConstrained() selects the minimum variable of the current domain and moves this variable from the unassigned variable table uninstantiated to the already assigned variable table instantiated. Propagate() is used for domain filtering. If some variable domain is null after domain filtering, then return this variable, otherwise return 0. Function retract() carries on backjumping and returns the backjumped variable. If backjumping goes to the top, then it will return a nil value. Array a[] is used for storing assigned values of each variable. Two-dimensional array domain[][] is used to record the state of each assigned value of each variable that is belonging to the current domain or has been deleted by some instantiated variable. The values which belong to the current domain are chained together with the suffix, as well as those values that have been deleted by the same variable instantiation.

The algorithm implements an exhaustive search and thus has exponential time complexity. The space complexity is $O(n(n + d))$, where n is the number of the variable and d is the size of the variable domain (suppose all variables have equal domain size).

IBMD has been used to test a series of examples and compared with some other algorithms, which include backtracking (BT), conflict-based backtracking (CBJ), the algorithm only adopting most-constrained-first method (MCF), and the algorithm only adopting most-constrained-first and domain filtering methods (MD). The experimental results show that IBMD is superior to these algorithms to some extent. For example, N queen's problem is solved with IBMD on the workstation sparc-1. For $N = 100$, IBMD algorithm takes less than 2 seconds. On the same machine, BT algorithm takes more than 10 seconds for the 2 queen's problem. For $N \geq 30$, BT algorithm takes several hours at least. For $N = 50$, MCF algorithm takes more than 10 seconds and takes several hours for $N \geq 60$. For N queen's problem, MD algorithm and IBMD algorithm nearly have the same performance and IBMD is slightly superior to MD. There are several reasons here. First of all, in the N queen's problem, there is little one-step backtracking. Domain filtering strategy can reduce much "out-layer" inconsistency. However, "deep-layer" inconsistency involves many other variables. Second, the extra cost of IBMD is less than that of MD. Table 3.1 shows the execution time of different algorithms operating on N queen's problem.

We have also tested the graph-coloring case. When the connection degree of vertices is small (≤ 7), backtracking is hardly used and the IBMD performance is equivalent to MD performance. When increasing the connection degree, IBMD performance is obviously superior to MD.

Compare the IBMD algorithm with other similar algorithms as follows:

(1) **Compared with backjumping (BJ):** BJ can only backjump to the latest variable caused by inconsistent variables. But if the latest variable has already tried all

Table 3.1. Execution time of running N queen's problem (unit: sec)

n	BT	CBJ	IBMD	n	BT	CBJ	IBMD
8	0.0	0.0	0.0	26	324.0	323.6	0.0
9	0.0	0.0	0.0	27	389.4	389.5	0.0
10	0.0	0.0	0.0	28	2810.2	2799.0	0.0
11	0.0	0.0	0.0	29	1511.1	1517.2	0.0
12	0.1	0.0	0.0	30	*	*	0.1
13	0.0	0.1	0.0	40	*	*	0.3
14	0.5	0.5	0.0	50	*	*	1.8
15	0.4	0.5	0.0	60	*	*	0.7
16	3.3	3.7	0.0	70	*	*	1.4
17	1.9	2.2	0.0	80	*	*	1.0
18	16.9	17.9	0.0	90	*	*	1155.7
19	1.1	1.3	0.0	100	*	*	1.8
20	101.6	105.5	0.0	110	*	*	158.9
21	4.6	4.7	0.0	120	*	*	*
22	1068.1	1048.4	0.0	130	*	*	11.5
23	16.2	16.2	0.0	140	*	*	*
24	290.5	289.6	0.0	160	*	*	7.1
25	35.8	35.9	0.0	200	*	*	14.0

Note: "*" represents time ≥ 2 hours.

values, backtracking is the same as common backtracking. Therefore, BJ is very limited in improvement of performance. However, IBMD can backtrack continuously until it finds a variable, which is correlated with the inconsistency and not all values have been tried.

(2) **Compared with graph-based backjumping:** The topology connection of a constraint network is an approximation of actual data dependence. Under a particular context, two graph-relevant variables will probably not influence each other. What the IBMD utilized is the actual influence.

(3) **Compared with conflict-based backjumping:** Prosser *et al.* proposed some improvement of backjumping at the IJCAI conference in 1993, such as conflict-based backjumping (CBJ). The starting points of IBMD and CBJ are similar, but in realizing the results, they differ a lot. CBJ has one drawback. Each variable has a dependence variable set. When backjumping is done once, the merger of sets should be carried out, and therefore, CBJ results in a very large time cost. However, this problem does not exist in IBMD algorithm.

One aspect by which IBMD is superior to all other algorithms described above is that it combines the most-constrained-first and domain filtering strategies together.

3.10 Constraint Relation Processing

3.10.1 *Unit Sharing Strategy for Identical Relation*

In constraint reasoning, if two variables always take the same value, then the relation between these two variables is identical in relation, which is a kind of important constraint relation. For instance, two devices are connected in series in the circuit, which means that the electric current through one device is equal to that through the other device. A square can be defined as a rectangle whose length and width are equal. Although an identical relation can be processed by a common constraint relation, it is necessary to carry out special processing for its popularity and special semantic. As a result, it can avoid the low efficiency of a common CSP solver; more importantly, it can directly reduce the computing scale of CSP. Because the two equal variables should take the same value, they can be regarded as the same variables in computing. This is the basic idea of unit sharing strategy.

A simple method to realize unit sharing strategy is that of replacing equal variables with a new variable; however, this will lead to global variable replacement of the constraint network. Meanwhile, consider that some equal relations are defined after making some assignment assumptions, and therefore, the original variable information before being equated must be kept. So, we use a binary tree to represent variable information. For the equation $x = y$, if x and y have already been assigned, then determine whether they are equal and return the Boolean value. If x is assigned but y is not, then determine whether the values of x belong to the domain of y. If the condition is not true, then return "inconsistence" information (failure information). Otherwise, assign the value of x to y. If x and y are not assigned yet, then create a new variable node $com(x, y)$ which is called common node of x and y and its two branch nodes are x and y, respectively. The domain of $com(x, y)$ is the intersection set of domains of x and y. If the intersection set is null, then return "inconsistent" information (fail information). Constraint connections between x or y and other nodes are all merged into $com(x, y)$. All operations on x or y will later be implemented by operating on $com(x, y)$.

In general, when a variable involves a lot of equation constraints, such as the equation set $\{x = y, y = z, x = u\}$, our method will form a big binary tree.

The root node of the binary tree gathers all the information of all branch nodes. It becomes an agent for all leaf nodes of the binary tree. The node set of the current visited variable is all the root node sets of such a binary tree (including the isolation node).

For tree search, it is necessary to consider that the equation is made after assumption assignment. After assumption assignment is revoked, the equivalent relation of assertions is no longer tenable, which should be revoked as well. The method is to revoke its corresponding common node. The equation reasoner offers to enquire the equal relation of any two variables with the same type, even if they are not assigned. This strategy has the following advantages, which certainly may be interrelated:

(1) The complexity of constraint search is mainly dependent on the number of constraint variables. The unit sharing strategy merges two or more variables with identical relations into one variable. Therefore, the strategy can be used to reduce search space.

(2) Make the constraint reasoner finds inconsistencies relevant to identical relations before variables are assigned. For example, for constraints $\{x = y, y = z, x \neq z\}$, even x, y, and z are not assigned yet, so the system can check out inconsistency of constraints.

(3) Make constraint propagation run. The unit sharing strategy of identical relations reduces the number of unknown variables and reduces the number of unknown variables of one constraint relation as well. In general, only when the number of unknown variables in one constraint relation is less enough can constraint

propagation be carried on. Constraint propagation at an early time is equivalent to pruning branches close to the root node of the search tree ahead of time, and therefore can reduce the search space greatly.

For example, for the constraint $r(x, y, z)$ which includes three enumerated variables x, y, and z, after x is instantiated, if y and z are different variables, in general we can perform consistency refinement for the domain of y or z. If there exists one constraint $y = z$, it means that the unassigned variable is only one. Therefore, constraint propagation can be carried out.

(4) Make constraint language have the ability of pattern matching in symbol processing.

In order to explain the advantage of such a strategy, we consider taking qualitative add operation of qualitative physic implemented by COPE language as an example. One physical quantity that varies in real domain can be characterized by a qualitative variable for its positive and negative aspects. One qualitative variable can take three values: position, negation, and zero:

$$\text{enum qualitative \{pos, neg, zero\};}$$

Qualitative add operation can be defined as follows:

```
qualsum (x, y, z)
enum qualitative x, y, z;
{
    if (x = y) z = x;
    if (x = zero) z = y;
    if (y = zero) z = x;
}
```

If we have constraint program

```
main
{
enum qualitative u, v, w;
w = zero;
qualsum(u, w, v);
qualsum(u, v, w);
}
```

We do not need to take any tentative search to achieve the only solution, which is $\{u = \text{zero}, v = \text{zero}, w = \text{zero}\}$. By qualsum$(u, w, v)$ and $w = \text{zero}$, we have $u = v$, which makes qualsum(u, v, w) reason out $u = w =$ zero. Thus, $v = u =$ zero.

3.10.2 *Interval Propagation*

In addition to equality relation, the most common relation is the inequality relation. Especially for the analysis and design of electronic apparatus, the use of inequality is particularly important. The most basic reasoning of inequality representation is to test a variable value. That is, if the variable value is already known, then calculate and check whether the variable value satisfies the inequality. Simply put, this kind of calculation can only be used for generate-and-test strategy, which has the lowest efficiency. We have realized stronger inequality reasoning.

A commonly used inequality reasoning is interval reasoning, i.e., the interval propagation in constraint network. Given the interval limit of some variables, other variables' interval limit can be reasoned out by ordering the relation among variables. For example, suppose that constraint $x > y$ and the interval of variables x and y are $[l_x, g_x]$ and $[l_y, g_y]$, respectively, then after the constraints propagate, the interval of variables x and y are as follows

$$[\max(l_x, l_y), g_x],$$

$$[l_y, \min(g_x, g_y)].$$

If $g_x < l_y$, then it means contradiction.

This reasoning can be promoted to a more complicated equation or inequality as well. Consider the equation $x + y = z$, and the current interval of variables x, y, and z are $[l_x, g_x]$, $[l_y, g_y]$, and $[l_z, g_z]$, respectively; if $l_x + l_y > g_z$ or $g_x + g_y < l_z$, it means the contradiction. Otherwise, the z's new interval values of $[l_z', g_z']$ are the following:

$$l_z' = \max(l_x + l_y, l_z),$$

$$g_z' = \min(g_x + g_y, g_z).$$

x's new interval values of $[l_x', g_x']$ are the following:

$$l_x' = \max(l_z - g_y, l_x),$$

$$g_x' = \min(g_z - l_y, g_x).$$

y's new interval values of $[l_y', g_y']$ are the following:

$$l_y' = \max(l_z - g_x, l_y),$$

$$g_y' = \min(g_z - l_x, g_y).$$

3.10.3 *Inequality Graph*

In many AI applications such as qualitative reasoning, temporal reasoning, and activity planning, what is important is the relative relation among the variables. Therefore, the reasoning of ordering relation is very important. This is actually the reasoning on axioms of inequality, such as identical relation, partial-order relation, etc.

All inequalities which are similar to $x \leq y$ and $x \neq y$ are used to make up an inequality graph. The relation $x \geq y$ is represented as $y \leq x$, $x < y$ is represented as $x \leq y$, and $x \neq y$, and $x > y$ is represented as $y \leq x$ with $x \neq y$ (identical relation has been implemented by unit sharing strategy).

Definition 3.1. (Positive Cycle). A inequality graph is a marked graph $\langle V, E \rangle$, in which V is a set of nodes and E is a set of xry *relations, where* $x, y \in V$ and r denotes $\leq$ or $\neq$ relation. A positive path in the graph is a node series $v_1, v_2, \ldots, v_i$, such that for $i (i = 2, \ldots, l)$, $(v_{i-1} \leq v_i)$ is an edge in the graph. If $v_1 = v_l$, then the path is called positive cycle.

Obviously, the inequality graph has the following properties.

Property 3.1. In a positive cycle, if $\neq$ relation does not exist between any two nodes, then all nodes denote the same variables in this cycle.

Property 3.2. There exists a positive cycle in an inequality graph if there exists $\neq$ relation between any two nodes in the cycle, then the inequality graph contains inconsistency.

Property 3.1 can be used to carry out equivalent transformation on an inequality graph to make it exclude the positive cycle. The method is merging all nodes of the positive cycle into one single node according to unit sharing strategy for all positive cycles of the graph. The resultant graph obtained is called a reduced inequality graph.

Property 3.2 can be used to define the inconsistency of the inequality graph.

Definition 3.2. One inequality graph is inconsistent if and only if in this graph there exists an edge in which two variable nodes have "$\neq$" relation.

Theorem 3.1. *One inequality graph is inconsistent if and only if in its reduced graph there exists one edge with "$\neq$" relation from one variable node to itself.*

On the basis of these two facts, the inequality reasoner carries out graph traversal. If a positive cycle is found, then use unit sharing strategy to merge the cycle into one variable node. If one variable's domain is null or one variable has one $\neq$ relation pointed to itself, then report the inconsistency. It is easy to prove the completeness of operations described above for partial-order relation and identical relation. Given a set W including identical relations, inequality relations, and partial-order relations and the set G of axiom on identical relation and partial-order relation, then $W \cup G$ is inconsistent if and only if the inequality graph corresponding to W is inconsistent.

Compared with the deductive method, the graph operation method is much more effective because the graph traversal has linear complexity.

3.10.4 *Inequality Reasoning*

The inequality graph reflects the structural characteristic of inequality. When the variable node in the inequality graph is limited by interval, besides the operation of the inequality graph, constraints propagate in the inequality graph. All these operations are caused after the inequality graph receives an outside input. The outside inputs include adding a relation expression xry into the network, where x and y are variables or constants, but at least one variable; r is one of relations $=, \neq, <, \leq, >, \geq$.

For r is $=$, if the variables x and y are both not assigned, then merge them into one variable node according to unit sharing strategy, check whether a positive cycle is generated, and possibly simplify and check the consistency of the inequality graph. If the new node domain is smaller to some extent than the domain of x or y, then propagate the interval along the inequality graph. If x and y are both assigned variables or constants, then decide whether their values are equal; if there exists only one unassigned variable and the value of another variable drops on this unassigned variable domain, then assign the value to the unassigned variable and propagate constraints; otherwise, report the inconsistency.

For r is $\leq$, if the variables x and y are already assigned, then decide whether $\leq$ relation is tenable; otherwise, carry on consistency limit to the interval of x and y. If the limited interval of the x or y is smaller to some extent, then propagate the interval along the inequality graph. If these two variables are both not unassigned, then add an edge with relation $\neq$ into this inequality graph, check whether positive cycle generates, and possibly simplify and check the consistency of the inequality graph.

For r is $\neq$, if the variables x and y are both already assigned, then decide whether $\neq$ relation is tenable.

For $x < y$, $x > y$, and $x \geq y$, their equivalent transformations are $(x \leq y) \wedge (x \neq y)$, $(y \leq x) \wedge (x \neq y)$, and $y \leq x$, respectively.

Inequality reasoner offers inquiry of inequality relation between any two variables with the same type, even if they are not assigned. The method which combines symbol reasoning and interval propagation not only regards inequality as the internal predicate to reduce the reasoning cost but also eliminates redundancy and reduces the solution scale of the problem. Furthermore, as a general inequality reasoner, it can carry out symbol reasoning before the situation where the variable is not assigned or even added an interval limit. For example, the system can check the inequality set and find out if $\{x \leq y, y \leq z, x > z\}$ contains inconsistency. Inequality reasoning makes a system have a function of propagating partial relation. The function has been used widely in qualitative reasoning. By realizing operations of equality and inequality reasoning, the system increases the reasoning depth, avoids more generated tests, and thus reduces search space.

3.11 Constraint Reasoning System COPS

A main function of the constraint reasoning system is to offer common and effective constraint reasoning mechanism for a user. This reasoning mechanism should overcome the search problem caused by uncertainty. Constraint propagation is also a technology to reduce uncertainty. From the language representation view, we think that the uncertain part should be explicitly marked out and limited to the data part. In this way, the data relevance can be identified, and the data domain can be operated, which thus makes constraint propagation and intelligent backtracking reduce uncertainty and search space. Also, such a regular structure improves the readability of the code and makes language studying easy so that special search technology, such as constraint propagation and intelligent backtracking, can be used. The logic programming language Prolog uses the inductive proof method of Horn clause, a technology of tentative solving, as a unified computing mechanism. Although Prolog is simple, it is very difficult to use.

In the constraint reasoning system COPS, constraint programming language COPS combines object-oriented technology, logic programming, production system, and constraint representation together. COPS absorbs basic forms of object-oriented programming language, applies constraint propagation and heuristic mechanism into solving, combines declarative constraint representation and type hierarchy together, and realizes structural knowledge encapsulation (Shi *et al.*, 1996). COPS language has the following characteristics:

- combines type hierarchy and constraint representation together;
- realizes default constraint reasoning;
- realizes conditional constraint and other part of regular programming;
- realizes effective constraint reasoning.

1. Constraint and Rule

A constraint is a predicate expression:

$$P(t_1, \ldots, t_n),$$

where $t_1, \ldots, t_n$ are items, which typically include a variable; P is a predicate symbol, and the predicate can be an internal function such as sum, times, eq (equal), neq (not equal), ge (greater than or equal to), or gt (greater than), which can also be defined by users.

Conditional constraint has the following forms:

```
if {
condition₁: constraint₁;
   ...
conditionₙ: constraintₙ
}
```

where, $condition_1, \ldots, condition_n$ are Boolean expression. $Constraint_1, \ldots,$ $constraint_n$ is a constraint or a constraint table having { }.

The rule is used for defining a new function, method, predicate, or adding a constraint to an object. The form of the rule is

```
RULE [class: : ]Predicate (variable or constant) (Boolean expression)
{
constraint₁;
   ...
constraintₙ;
CASE
Boolean expression₁: constraint₁;
   ...
Boolean expressionₘ: constraintₘ;
}
For example:
RULE multiple(INTEGER: *x, INTEGER: y, INTEGER: z) (neq(y, 0))
{
  equal(x, divide(z, y));
}
```

which defines the constraint relation among three variables x, y, and $z : x = z \div y$.

2. Class Definition

In COPS system, entity of the problem field is defined as class, and entity's internal attributes and relations are encapsulated in class. Multiple entities with a certain relation can be encapsulated in a high-level class. The definition of class in COPS is similar to class definition in C++:

```
CLASS [class name] [: super class name]
{
        //Attribute definition
        Data type: Attribute name;

        . . .
        //Rule definition
        Rule name;

        . . .
        //Function definition
        Function name;

        . . .
        //Method definition
        Method name;

    . . .

}
```

The whole COPS program is made up of class definition and rule. COPS language keeps the style of relational declarative language while offering class and method of object-oriented language. In this way, COPS not only strengthens the regulatory and flexibility aspect of programming but also improves readability and usage. COPS language can make the user focus on the problem description and not care about the solution in detail. Because COPS language is very similar to object-oriented language (C++), its description is clear and it is easy to use and it can fully utilize the encapsulation and inheritance mechanism to expand and reuse. COPS system has already been used for the simulation of a circuit successfully.

3. Constraint Reasoning in COPS

In COPS system, constraint reasoning mainly depends on production composition and constraint propagation, which have the heuristic characteristics of ranked conditional term-rewriting system, utilizing state information of problem solution, default rule, assumption reasoning, propagation in different areas, etc. The key algorithm of COPS system is as follows:

Algorithm 3.9 Main-COPS which is a core algorithm in COPS.

1. procedure main _ COPS
2. {
3.   Invoke yacc program, generate internal structure;
4.   Initialize;
5.   Set up COPS constant trueNode;
6.   Allocate memory for global variable;
7.   Interpreter the program with internal structure;
8.   Construct constraint network for unsolved constraint and variable;
9.   While trigger the constraint of constraint network
10.   Interpreter triggered constraint
11. }

Yet another compiler compiler (Yacc) is a another compiler of compiler. It transforms context-free grammar into a table set of a simple automachine, which carries out an LR grammar analysis program. The output file y.tab.c must be compiled by C compiler and produces the program yyparse, which must be installed together with the lexical analyzer yylex, main program, and error handler yyerror.

The interpreter of the algorithm is as follows:

Interpreter:
{
    switch (constraint type)
    case Constant:
            return Constant:
    case global variable:
       interprete global variable:
    case local variable or argument:
            interprete local variable or argument:
    case object-attribute pair:
            interprete object-attribute pair:
    case function call:
            interprete function call:
    case method call:
            interprete method call:
    case CASE expression:
            interprete CASE expression:
    . . .

default:

report error

}

COPS system fully utilizes the encapsulation and inheritance mechanism to expand and reuse. Through overloading a member function, COPS realizes the constraint solution efficiently and flexibly. We can also design a new solution class and add many methods of constraint solution to improve the weakness that the original system only had a single strategy. At present, the main problem to solve is the message passing across different classes, value propagation for sharing variables, and composition exploding in consistency maintenance. In the future, we plan to apply constraint technology to a multi-agent system in order to solve cooperation and negation problems and apply constraint reasoning to solve multi-goals problem in an intelligent decision support system.

3.12　ILOG Solver

Constraint program is a computing system about constraints. Its input is a group of constraints and problems to solve and output is the solution scheme. The algorithms to solve the problem are all basic functions of constraint programming language. What the programmer has to face is how to describe problem as a model consisting of constraints, and the description language should be very close to natural language. If the problem is regarded as a kind of constraint, then the solution is to achieve one or several constraints, each of which is a sufficient condition of the given constraints, that is, the obtained constraints should satisfy the given constraints. Then, constraint programming can be called constraint-oriented programming method.

ILOG Company was established in 1987 and is the leading French provider of the software component suite in optimization, visualization, and business rule management areas. In the past, ILOG Company was carrying out development and innovation of the enterprise software package and service constantly and made customers optimize the flexibility of business treatment, and thus improved the operation efficiency of these companies. There are more than 1,000 global companies and 300 software suppliers using ILOG. With the development of China's economy, ILOG Company has seen the broad development prospect of the Chinese market and set up a representative office in Beijing in August 2002, which commands the market of Greater China region including Hong Kong, Macao, and Taiwan.

Constraint planning is a program in the computer system based on constraint rule. The idea of constraint planning is to describe constraints of problems to solve them and finally find a scheme which satisfies all constraints. The key of realizing planning and scheduling is resource scheduling based on constraint rule and constraint, and optimizing the plan to reach the goal that you need. ILOG Solver is used to solve complicated processes like multiple operations, multiple resources, etc., for dispersed manufacturing and solve ordering problem such as optimizing ordering (Flowshop scheduling) for the manufacturing of repeating type or procedure type. ILOG Solver is a constraint programming language which embeds the process-oriented language. It combines object-oriented programming and constraint logic programming together, includes logic variable, and solves problems through increment-type constraint satisfaction and backtracking. The main language components in the ILOG Solver are as follows:

```
variables : C ++ object                    //variable
    integer variable CtIntVar
    floating variable CtFloatVar
    boolean variable CtBoolVar
Memory Management                 // memory management
    new:
    delete:
Constraints                        // constraint
    CtTell(x == (y + z));
    Basic constraints: =,¡'Ü,¡'Ý, <>, +, -, *,/, subset, superset, union,
                 intersection, member, boolean or, boolean and, boolean not,
                 boolean xor,
    CtTell((x == 0)||(y  == 0));
    CtIfThen (x < 100, x = x + 1) ;
Search                         // search
    CTGOALn: how to execute CTGOAL1(CtInstantiate, CtIntVar* x)
    {
        CtInt a = x-> chooseValue() ;
        CtOr(Constraint(x == a),
        CtAnd(Constraint(x ! = a),
        CtInstantiate(x) ));
    }
Schedule                       // schedule
    CtSchedule class
        Global object: time original ··· timeMin
                       time horizon ··· timeMax
    Resources                     // resource
        CtResource
        CtDiscreteResource
```

> CtUnaryResource
> CtDiscreteEnergy
> CtStateResource
> Activities   // operation
> CtActivity class
> CtIntervalActivity

Activity is defined as the start time, end time, time span, operations requiring, providing, and consuming, and resource production.

Constraint planning has already drawn much attention from experts in each field because it is able to solve very difficult problems in reality. No matter whether we use the advanced genetic algorithm or use the simulation method of human–computer interaction, we need further studies on complex constraints of the manufacturing industry, multi-goals optimization, extensive search, and the uncertainty problem of workshop production. Event-based scheduling method is adopted here, in which at least one resource is idle. Two or more operations can use this resource, and operation selection rule (OSR) decides which operation is loaded. OSR is the key factor to determine the quality of planning. Independent operation selection rules are shown in detail as follows:

(1) **Early finish date:** Select early finished operation (maybe order finish date).
(2) **Highest priority first:** Select the operation with the highest priority (minimum value).
(3) **Lowest priority first:** Select the operation with the lowest priority (maximum value).
(4) **Highest order attribute field:** Select the operation with the highest (maximum) attribute field of order.
(5) **Lowest order attribute field:** Select the operation with the lowest (minimum) attribute field of order.
(6) **Dynamic highest attribute field of order:** Select the operation with dynamic highest (maximum) attribute field of order.
(7) **Dynamic lowest attribute field of order:** Select the operation with dynamic lowest (minimum) attribute field of order.
(8) **Planning record order:** Select the operation on a first-come first-served basis.
(9) **Key rate:** Select the operation with the minimum key rate:
    Key rate = planning working time left/(finish date–current date).

(10) **Real key rate:** Select the operation with the minimum real key rate:
Real key rate = real working time left/(finish date–current date).

(11) **Least remaining operation (static):** Select the operation with the least remaining operation time.

(12) **Longest waiting time:** Select the operation with the longest waiting time.

(13) **Shortest waiting time:** Select the operation with the shortest waiting time.

(14) **Maximum process time:** Select the operation with maximum process time.

(15) **Minimum process time:** Select the operation with minimum process time.

(16) **Minimum operation idle time:** Select the operation with minimum idle time:
idle time of the order = remaining finish time – remaining working time; idle time of operation = idle time of task/remaining operation number.

(17) **Minimum operation idle time:** Select the operation with minimum idle time in order.

(18) **Minimum time of work remaining:** Select the operation with minimum remaining work time in order.

Resource Selection Rule (RSR) selects an operation to be loaded in which resource of resource group exists.

(1) **Early ending time:** Select the resource first used to finish the operation.

(2) **Early start time:** Select the resource first used to start the operation.

(3) **Latest ending time:** Select the resource last used to finish the operation.

(4) **Same as the previous operation:** Select the resource used in the previous operation.

(5) **No-bottleneck early start time:** Select the resource no-bottleneck first used to start the operation.

Relevant selection rule refers to when an operation selection rule is selected, and then the corresponding resource selection rules are automatically selected.

(1) **Serial circulation order:** Select the operation with the same or the next maximum (minimum) serial value. When there is no operation with a maximum serial value, the order will be reverse and select the minimum operation.

(2) **Serial decreasing order:** Select the operation with the same or the next minimum serial value.

(3) **Serial increasing order:** Select the operation with the same or the next maximum serial value.

(4) **Minimum preparing series:** Select the operation with minimum preparing time and the recent serial value.

(5) **Minimum preparing time:** Select the operation with minimum preparing or changing time.

(6) **Serial circulation order of time zone:** Select the operation with the same or the next maximum (minimum) serial value. Only consider the operation of the order finished date in the particular time zone. When there is no operation with maximum serial value, the order will be opposite and select the minimum operation.

(7) **Serial decreasing order of time zone:** Select the operation with the same or the next minimum serial value. Only consider the operation of the order finished date in the particular time zone.

(8) **Serial increasing order of time zone:** Select the operation with the same or the next maximum serial value. Only consider the operation of the order finished date in the particular time zone.

(9) **Minimum preparing series of time zone:** Select the operation with minimum preparing time and recent serial value. Only consider the operation of the order finished date in the particular time zone.

(10) **Minimum preparing time of time zone:** Select the operation with minimum preparing time or changing time. Only consider the operation of the order finished date in the particular time zone.

In the following, we take house decoration as an example (see Figure 3.1), in which ILOG Scheduler is used to provide the planning scheme for description Suppose that the start task costs 1,000 Yuan each day, and total fund is 20,000 Yuan. When the project reaches the 15th day, funds can increase by 9,000 Yuan.

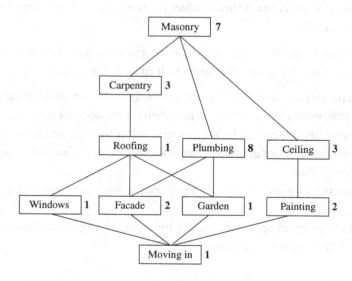

Fig. 3.1. House decoration operation solving principles of CSP

Adopt ILOG Scheduler to schedule, the constraint program is as follows:

```
CtSchedule* schedule = new CtSchedule(0, horizon);
// To create an operation with given duration.
CtIntervalActivity* act = new CtIntervalActivity(schedule, duration);

//To define constraint between act1 and act2.
act2->startsAfterEnd(act1,0);

//To create a total budget of limited funds (here 29000).
CtDiscreteResource* res =
new CtDiscreteResource(schedule, CtRequiredResource,capacity);
// To state that only 20000 is available in first 15 days
res->setCapacityMax(0,date,cap);
// To state that an operation act consumes c units of resources.
act->consumes(res, c);

CtBoolean IsUnScheduled(CtActivity* act){
// Return true if operation does not have a fixed start time.
if (act->getStartVariable()->isBound())
    return CtFalse;
else
    return CtTrue;
}
CtBoolean IsMoreUrgent(CtActivity* act1,
            CtActivity* act2){
// Returns true if act1 is more urgent than act2.
// Returns true if act2 is not limited (==0)
if (act2 == 0)
    return CtTrue;
else if (act1->getStartMax() < act2->getStartMax())
    return CtTrue;
else
    return CtFalse;
}
CtActivity* SelectActivity(CtSchedule* schedule){
// Returns the unscheduled activity with the smallest latest
// start time. Returns 0 if all activities are scheduled.
CtActivity* bestActivity = 0;
```

```
//Creates an iterator to iterate on all activities.
CtActivityIterator* iterator(schedule);
CtActivity* newActivity;
while(iterator.next(newactivity))
    if((IsUnScheduled(newActivity))
          && (IsMoreUrgent(newActivity, bestActivity)))
          bestactivity = newActivity;
return bestActivity;
}

void SolveProblem(CtSchedule* schedule){
// Solve the problem assuming constraints have been posted.
CtActivity* act = SelectActivity(schedule);
while (act !=0) {
    act->setStartTime(act->getStartMin());
    act = SelectActivity(schedule);
  }
}
```

ILOG Scheduler solves the above problem; the planning of the decoration process is illustrated in Figure 3.2.

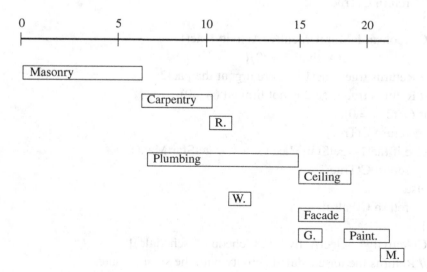

Fig. 3.2. Scheduling problem in house decoration

Exercises

3.1 What is constraint satisfaction problem? What categories can constraint reasoning be divided into?

3.2 What is arc consistency? Illustrate its asymmetry with examples.

3.3 Write constraint propagation AC-1 and AC-3 algorithms and compare the similarities and differences between them.

3.4 Try to write influence-based backjumping algorithm IBMD using programming language, and test it through N queen's question. Compare it with other constraint algorithms.

3.5 How can constraint reasoning system COPS solve a symbolic reasoning problem and also perform a numeric analysis?

3.6 Write a scheduling system of a workshop with ILOG Solver language.

Chapter 4

Bayesian Network

The basic Graphical Model can be broadly divided into two categories: the Bayesian network and the Markov random field. The main difference is that different types of graphs are used to express the relationship between variables: Bayesian network uses directed acyclic graph to express causality, and Markov random field uses undirected graph (undirected graph) to express the interaction between variables. This structural difference leads to a series of subtle differences in their modeling and inference. This chapter focuses on Bayesian network.

4.1 Introduction

Bayesian Network is a graphic model for describing the connection probabilities among variables. It provides a natural representation of casual relationship and is often used to explore potential relationships among data. In the network, nodes represent variables and directed links represent dependent relationships between variables. With firm mathematical foundation, Bayesian Theory offers a method for brief function calculation and describes the coincidence of brief and evidence, and it possesses the incremental learning property that brief varies along with the variation of evidence. In data mining, Bayesian networks can deal with incomplete or noisy data sets. It describes correlations among data with probabilistic measurement, thereby solving the problem of data inconsistency. It describes correlations among data with the graphical method, which has clear semantic meaning and understandable representation. It also makes predictions and analyses with casual relationships among data. Bayesian network is becoming one of the most remarkable data mining methods due to its unique properties, including unique knowledge representation of uncertain information, capability for handling probability, and incremental learning with prior knowledge.

4.1.1 *History of Bayesian Theory*

The foundational work of the Bayesian School is credited to Reverend Thomas Bayes' (1702–1761) *An Essay toward Solving a Problem in the Doctrine of Chances*. Maybe he felt the work was not perfect enough as this work was published not in his lifetime but posthumously by his friend. As the famous mathematician P. S. Laplace deduced Law of Succession based on Bayesian method, Bayesian method and theory began to be recognized. In the 19th century, because the problem of motivating and constructing prior probabilities was not adequately answered, Bayesian theory was not well accepted. Early in 20th century, B. de Finetti and H. Jeffreys made significant contribution to Bayesian theory. After World War II, Wald A. proposed the statistical decision theory. In this theory, Bayesian method played an important role. Besides, the development of information science also contributed to the reincarnation of Bayesian theory. In 1958, Bayes' paper was republished by *Biometrika*, the most historical statistical magazine in Britain. In the 1950s, H. Robbins suggested to combine empirical Bayesian approach and conventional statistical method. This novel approach captured the attention of the statistical research field and soon showed its merits and thus became an active research direction.

　　With the development of artificial intelligence, especially after the rise of machine learning and data mining, Bayesian theory gained increasingly more developments and applications. Its connotation has also varied greatly from its origin. In the 1980s, Bayesian networks were used for knowledge representation in expert systems. In the 1990s, Bayesian networks were applied to data mining and machine learning. Recently, more and more papers concerning Bayesian theory are being published, which cover most fields of artificial intelligence, including casual reasoning, uncertain knowledge representation, pattern recognition, clustering analysis, and so on. There is even an organization and a journal, *ISBA*, which focus especially on the progress on Bayesian theory.

4.1.2 *Basic Concepts of the Bayesian Method*

In Bayesian theory, all kinds of uncertainties are represented with probabilities. Learning and reasoning are implemented via probabilistic rules. The Bayesian learning results are distributions of random variables, which show the briefs to various possible results. The foundations of the Bayesian School are Bayesian theorem and Bayesian assumption. Bayesian theorem connects prior probabilities of events with their posterior probabilities. Assume that the joint probability density of random vectors $\mathbf{x}$ and $\boldsymbol{\theta}$ is $p(\mathbf{x}, \boldsymbol{\theta})$, and $p(\mathbf{x})$ and $p(\boldsymbol{\theta})$ give the marginal densities of $\mathbf{x}$ and $\boldsymbol{\theta}$, respectively. In common cases, $\mathbf{x}$ is an observation vector and $\boldsymbol{\theta}$ is an unknown parameter vector. The estimation of parameter $\boldsymbol{\theta}$ can be obtained with the observation vector via Bayesian theorem. The Bayesian theorem is denoted as follows:

$$p(\theta|x) = \frac{\pi(\theta)p(x|\theta)}{p(x)} = \frac{\pi(\theta)p(x|\theta)}{\int \pi(\theta)p(x|\theta)d\theta} \quad (\pi(\theta) \text{ is the prior of } \theta). \quad (4.1)$$

From this formula, we see that in the Bayesian method the estimation of a parameter needs prior information of the parameter and information from evidence. In contrast, traditional statistical method, e.g., maximum likelihood, only utilizes the information from evidence. The general process to estimate a parameter vector via Bayesian method is as follows:

(1) Regard unknown parameters as random vectors. This is the fundamental difference between Bayesian method and traditional statistical approach.
(2) Define the prior $\pi(\theta)$ based on previous knowledge of the parameter θ. This step is a controversial step and is debated by conventional statistical scientists.
(3) Calculate posterior density and make estimation of parameters according to the posterior distribution.

In the second step, if there is no previous knowledge to determine the prior $\pi(\theta)$ of a parameter, Bayes suggested to assume uniform distribution to be its distribution. This is called Bayesian assumption. Intuitively, Bayesian assumption is well accepted. Yet, it encounters a problem when no information about prior distribution is available, especially when the parameter is infinite. Empirical Bayes (EB) estimator combines a conventional statistical method and Bayesian method, so that it applies the conventional method to gain the marginal density $p(x)$, and then ascertains prior $\pi(\theta)$ with the following formula:

$$p(x) = \int_{-\infty}^{+\infty} \pi(\theta)p(x|\theta)d\theta.$$

4.1.3 *Applications of Bayesian Network in Data Mining*

1. Bayesian method in classification and regression analysis

Classification is to classify an object based on its feature vector and some constrains. In data mining, we mainly study how to learn classification rules from data or experiences. For classification, sometimes each feature vector corresponds to one class label (determinate classification); sometimes different classes can overlap, where samples from different classes are very similar and we can only tell the probabilities of a sample in all classes and choose a class for the sample according to the probabilities. Bayesian School provides two methods to handle this situation: one is selecting the class with maximum posterior probability; the other is selecting the class with maximum utility function or minimum lost function. Let the feature vector be $X = (x_1, x_2, \ldots, x_m)$, and class vector be $C = (c_1, c_2, \ldots, c_l)$. Classification then assigns a class c_i ($i \in (1, \ldots, l)$) to a feature vector X.

In the first method, the class c_i with maximum posterior probability will be selected, viz. $P(c_i|x) \geq P(c_j|x) \quad j \in (1, \ldots, l)$. In this case, the decision function is $r_i(x) = p(c_i|x)$. It has been proved that in this method the minimum classification error can be guaranteed.

The second method is often used in decision theory. It utilizes average benefit to evaluate decision risk, which has a close relationship with degrees of uncertainty. Let $L_{ij}(X)$ be the loss of misclassifying a feature vector X of class c_i to class c_j. The class with minimum loss of X is Minimize$_i$ $\{\sum_{j=1}^{l} L_{ij}(x) \cdot P(c_j|x)\}$. In this case, the decision function is $r_i(x) = \sum_{j=1}^{l} L_{ij}(x) \cdot P(c_j|x)$. If the diagonal elements of $L_{ij}(X)$ are all 0 and non-diagonal elements of $L_{ij}(X)$ are all 1, viz. correct classification makes no loss and misclassification has same loss, the first method and the second method are equal.

In data mining, the research on Bayesian classification mainly focuses on how to learn the distribution of feature vectors and the correlation among feature vectors from data so as to find the best $P(c_i|x)$ and $L_{ij}(X)$). By now successful models have been proposed, including Naïve Bayesian, Bayesian Network, and Bayesian Neural Network. The Bayesian classification method has been successfully applied to many fields, such as text classification, alphabet recognition, and economic prediction.

2. Bayesian method in casual reasoning and uncertain knowledge representation

The Bayesian network is a graph that describes the probabilistic relations of random variables. Currently, Bayesian network has been the primary method of uncertain knowledge representation in an expert system. Many algorithms have been proposed to learn Bayesian network from data. These techniques have gained reasonable success in data modeling, uncertainty reasoning, and so on.

Compared with other knowledge representation methods in data mining, such as rule representation, decision tree, and artificial neural networks, Bayesian network possesses the following merits in knowledge representation (Cooper *et al.* 1992):

(1) Bayesian network can conveniently handle incomplete data. For example, when we face a classification or regression problem with multiple correlative variables, the correlation among variables is not the key element for standard supervised learning algorithms. As a result, missing values will cause large predictive bias. Yet, Bayesian network can handle incomplete data with the probabilistic correlation of variables.

(2) Bayesian network can learn the casual relation of variables. Casual relation is a very important pattern in data mining, mainly because in data analysis, it is helpful for field knowledge understanding; it can also easily lead to precise prediction even under much interference. For example, some sale analyzers wonder whether increasing their advertisements will cause sales to increase. To get the answer, the analyzer must know whether the increase in advertisement is the cause of increase in sales with a Bayesian network. This question can be easily answered even without experimental data because the causal relation has been encoded in this network.

(3) The combination of Bayesian network and Bayesian statistics can take full advantage of field knowledge and information from data. Everyone with modeling experience knows that prior information or field knowledge is very important to modeling, especially when sample data are sparse or difficult to obtain. Some commercial expert systems, which are constructed purely based on field expert knowledge, are a perfect example. Bayesian network, which expresses a dependent relation with directed edge and uses probabilistic distribution to describe the strength of dependence, can integrate prior knowledge and sample information well.

(4) The combination of Bayesian network and other models can effectively avoid the problem of over-fitting.

3. Bayesian method in clustering and pattern discovery

Generally, clustering is a special case of model selection. Each clustering pattern can be viewed as a model. The task of clustering is to find a pattern, which best fits the nature of data, from many models based on analysis and some other strategies. Bayesian method integrates prior knowledge and characteristics of the current data to select the best model.

With Bayesian analysis, Vaithyanathan and Dom (1998) proposed a model-based hierarchical clustering method. By partitioning the feature set, they organized data in to a hierarchical structure. The features either have a unique distribution in different classes or have the same distribution in some classes. They also give the method to determine the model structure with marginal likelihood, including how to automatically determine the number of classes, depth of the model tree, and the feature subset of each class.

AutoClass is a typical system that implements clustering with the Bayesian method. This system automatically determines the number of classes and the complexity of model by searching all possible classifications in the model space. It allows for features in certain classes to have correlation and successive relations existing among classes (in the hierarchical structure of classes, some classes can share some model parameters). Detailed information about AutoClass can be found on the website http://ic-www.arc.nasa.gov/ic/projects/bayes-group/autoclass.

Here, we have only listed some typical applications of Bayesian method. The applications of Bayesian method in data mining are far more than just these. Bayesian neural network, which combines Bayesian method and neural network, and Bayes Point Machine, which combines Bayesian method and statistical learning, are all interesting examples of applications of Bayesian method. Interested readers can find more in the book by Amari (1985).

4.2 Foundation of Bayesian Probability

4.2.1 *Foundation of Probability Theory*

Probability is a branch of mathematics which focuses on the regularity of random phenomena. Random phenomena are phenomena for which different results appear under the same conditions. Random phenomena include individual random phenomena and substantive random phenomena. The regularity from the observation of substantive random phenomena is called statistical regularity.

Statistically, we conventionally call an observation, a registration, or an experiment about phenomenon a trial. A random trial is an observation on a random phenomenon. Under the same condition, random trials may lead to different results. But the sphere of all the possible results is estimable. The result of a random trial is both uncertain and predictable. Statistically, the result of a random trial is called a random event, in short an event.

A random event is the result that will appear or not appear in a random trial. In a random phenomenon, the frequency of a mark is the total number of times the mark appears in all trials.

Table 4.1. The result of sampling of product quality

Number of products examined	5	10	50	100	300	600	1,000	5,000	10,000
Number of qualified products	5	8	44	91	272	542	899	4,510	8,999
Frequency of qualification	1	0.8	0.88	0.91	0.907	0.892	0.899	0.902	0.8997

Example 4.1. To study the product quality of a factory, we make some random samplings. In each sampling, the number of samples is different. The result of sampling is recoded and presented in Table 4.1.

In the table, the number of products examined is the total number of products examined in one sample. The number of qualified products is the total number of qualified products in the examination. The frequency of qualification is the proportion of qualified products in all the products examined in one sample. From the table, we can easily see the relation between the number of a mark and the frequency of a mark. We can also find a statistical regularity. That is, as the number of products examined increases, the frequency of qualification inclines to 0.9 stably, or the frequency of qualification wavers around a fixed number $p = 0.9$. So, p is the statistical stable center of this series of trials. It represents the possibility of qualification of an examined product. The possibility is called probability.

Definition 4.1 (Statistical Probability). If in a number of repeated trials, the frequency of event A inclines to a constant p stably, it represents the possibility of appearance of event A, and we call this constant p the probability of event A, shortly $P(A)$:

$$p = P(A).$$

So, a probability is the stable center of a frequency. A probability of any event A is a non-negative real number that is not bigger than 1:

$$0 \leq P(A) \leq 1.$$

The statistical definition of probability has a close relationship with frequency and is easily understood. But it is a tough problem to find the probability of an arbitrary event with experiments. Sometimes it is even impossible. So we often calculate probability with the classical probabilistic method or geometrical probabilistic method.

Definition 4.2 (Classical Probability). Let a trial have only finite N possible results, or N basic events. If event A contains K possible results, we call K/N the probability of event A, shortly $P(A)$:

$$P(A) = K/N. \tag{4.2}$$

To calculate classical probability, we need to know the number of all the basic events. So, classical probability is restricted to cases of finite population. In the case of an infinite population or if the total number of basic events is unknown, the geometrical probability model is used to calculate the probability. Besides, geometrical probability also gives a general definition of probability.

Geometrical random trial: Assume Ω is a bounded domain of M-dimensional space, and $L(\Omega)$ is the volume of Ω. We consider the random trial that we throw a random point into Ω evenly and assume the following: (a) The random point may fall in any domain of Ω, but cannot fall outside of Ω. (b) The distribution of the random point in Ω is even, viz. the possibility that the random point falls into a domain is proportional to the volume of the domain and is independent of the position or the shape of the domain in Ω. Under the restrictions above, we call a trial a geometrical random trial where Ω is basic event space.

Event in a geometrical random trial: Assume that Ω is the basic event space of geometrical random trial, and A is a subset of Ω that can be measured with volume, where $L(A)$ is the M-dimensional volume of A. Then the event "random point falls in domain A" is represented with A. In Ω, a subset that can be measured with volume is called a measurable set. Each measurable set can be viewed as an event. The set of all measurable subsets is represented by F.

Definition 4.3 (Geometrical Probability). Assume that Ω is a basic event space of a geometrical random trial and F is the set of all measurable subsets of Ω. Then the probability of any event A in F is the ratio between the volume of A and that of Ω:

$$P(A) = V(A)/V(\Omega). \tag{4.3}$$

Definition 4.4 (Conditional Probability). The probability of an event A under the condition that event B has happened is denoted by $P(A|B)$. We call it the conditional probability of event A under condition B. $P(A)$ is called unconditional probability.

Example 4.2. There are two white balls and one black ball in a bag. Now we take out two balls in turn. The following questions arise: (a) What is the probability of the event that a white ball is picked the first time? (b) What is the probability of the event that a white ball is picked the second time when a white ball has been picked the first time?

Solution: Assume A is the event that a white ball is picked the first time, and B is the event that a white ball is picked the second time. Then $\{B|A\}$ is the event that a white ball is picked the second time when a white ball has been picked the first time. According to Definition 4.4, we have the following:

(1) No matter whether it is repeated sampling or non-repeated sampling, $P(A) = 2/3$.
(2) When sampling is non-repeated, $P(B|A) = 1/2$; when sampling is repeated, $P(B|A) = P(B) = 2/3$. The conditional probability equals non-conditional probability.

If the appearance of any of event A or B will not affect the probability of the other event, viz. $P(A) = P(A|B)$ or $P(B) = P(B|A)$. We call events A and B independent events.

Theorem 4.1 (Addition Theorem). *The probability of the sum of two mutually exclusive events equals the sum of the probabilities of the two events, that is,*

$$P(A + B) = P(A) + P(B).$$

The sum of probabilities of two mutually inverse events is 1. In other words, if $A + A^{-1} = \Omega$, A and A^{-1} are mutually inverse, then $P(A) + P(A^{-1}) = 1$, or $P(A) = 1 - P(A^{-1})$.

If A and B are two arbitrary events, then

$$P(A + B) = P(A) + P(B) - P(AB)$$

holds. This theorem can be generalized to the case that involves more than three events:

$$P(A + B + C) = P(A) + P(B) + P(C) - P(AB) - P(BC)$$

$$- P(CA) + P(ABC).$$

Theorem 4.2 (Multiplication Theorem). *Assume A and B are two mutually independent non-zero events, then the probability of the multiple event equals the multiplication of probabilities of events A and B, that is,*

$$P(A \cdot B) = P(A) \cdot P(B) \quad \text{or} \quad P(A \cdot B) = P(B) \cdot P(A).$$

Assume A and B are two arbitrary non-zero events, then the probability of the multiple event equals the multiplication of the probability of event A (or B) and the *conditional probability of event B (or A) under condition A (or B):*

$$P(A \cdot B) = P(A) \cdot P(B|A) \quad \text{or} \quad P(A \cdot B) = P(B) \cdot P(A|B).$$

This theorem can be generalized to the case that involves more than three events. When the probability of multiple events $P(A_1 A_2 \ldots A_{n-1}) > 0$, we have

$$P(A_1 A_2 \ldots A_n) = P(A_1) \cdot P(A_2|A_1) \cdot P(A_3|A_1 A_2) \ldots P(A_n|A_1 A_2 \ldots A_{n-1}).$$

If all the events are pairwise independent, we have

$$P(A_1 A_2 \ldots A_n) = P(A_1) \cdot P(A_2) \cdot P(A_3) \ldots P(A_n).$$

4.2.2 Bayesian Probability

(1) **Prior Probability:** A prior probability is the probability of an event that is gained from historical materials or subjective judgments. It is not verified and is estimated in the absence of evidence. So it is called prior probability. There are two kinds of prior probabilities. One is objective prior probability, which is calculated according to historical materials; the other is subjective prior probability, which is estimated purely based on the subjective experience when historical material is absent or incomplete.

(2) **Posterior Probability:** A posterior probability is the probability that is computed according to the prior probability and additional information from investigation via Bayesian formula.

(3) **Joint Probability:** The joint probability of two events is the probability of the intersection of the two events. It is also called multiplication formula.

(4) **Total Probability Formula:** Assume all the influence factors of event A are $B_1, B_2, \ldots$, and they satisfy $B_i \cdot B_j = \emptyset, (i \neq j)$ and $P(\cup B_i) = 1, P(B_i) > 0$, $i = 1, 2, \ldots$, then we have

$$P(A) = \sum P(B_i)P(A|B_i). \tag{4.4}$$

(5) **Bayesian Formula:** Bayesian formula, which is also called posterior probability formula or inverse probability formula, has wide applications.

Assume $P(B_i)$ is the prior probability, and $P(A_j|B_i)$ is the new information gained from investigation, where $i = 1, 2, \ldots, n$, and $j = 1, 2, \ldots, m$. Then the posterior probability calculated with Bayesian formula is

$$P(B_i|A_j) = \frac{P(B_i)P(A_j|B_i)}{\sum_{k=1}^{m} P(B_k)P(A_j|B_k)}. \tag{4.5}$$

Table 4.2. Daily outputs of three teams

	B_1	B_2	Total
Team A_1	2,000	1,000	3,000
Team A_2	1,500	500	2,000
Team A_3	500	500	1,000
Total	4,000	2,000	6,000

Example 4.3. One kind of product is made in a factory. Three work teams (A_1, A_2, and A_3) are in charge of two specifications (B_1 and B_2) of the product. Their daily outputs are listed in Table 4.2.

Now we randomly pick out one from the 6,000 products. Please answer the following questions.

1. Calculate the following probabilities with Classical Probability

(1) Calculate the probabilities that the picked product comes from the outputs of A_1, A_2, or A_3, respectively.

$$\text{Solution:} \quad P(A_1) = 3{,}000/6{,}000 = 1/2,$$
$$P(A_2) = 2{,}000/6{,}000 = 1/3,$$
$$P(A_3) = 1{,}000/6{,}000 = 1/6.$$

Calculate the probabilities that the picked product belongs to B_1 or B_2, respectively.

$$\text{Solution:} \quad P(B_1) = 4{,}000/6{,}000 = 2/3,$$
$$P(B_2) = 2{,}000/6{,}000 = 1/3.$$

(2) Calculate the probability that the pick product is B_1 and comes from A_1.

$$\text{Solution:} \quad P(A_1 \cdot B_1) = 2{,}000/6{,}000 = 1/3.$$

(3) If the fact that the product comes from A_1 is known, what is the probability that it belongs to B_1?

$$\text{Solution:} \quad P(B_1|A_1) = 2{,}000/3{,}000 = 2/3.$$

(4) If the product belongs to B_2, what is the probability that it comes from A_1, A_2, or A_3, respectively?

$$\text{Solution:}\quad P(A_1|B_2) = 1{,}000/2{,}000 = 1/2,$$
$$P(A_2|B_2) = 500/2{,}000 = 1/4,$$
$$P(A_3|B_2) = 500/2{,}000 = 1/4.$$

2. Calculate the following probabilities with Conditional Probability

(1) If a product comes from A_1, what is the probability that it belongs to B_1?

$$\text{Solution:}\quad P(B_1|A_1) = (1/3)/(1/2) = 2/3.$$

(2) If a product belongs to B_2, what is the probability that it comes from A_1, A_2, or A_3, respectively?

$$\text{Solution:}\quad P(A_1|B_2) = (1/6)/(1/3) = 1/2,$$
$$P(A_2|B_2) = (1/12)/(1/3) = 1/4,$$
$$P(A_3|B_2) = (1/12)/(1/3) = 1/4.$$

3. Calculate the following probabilities with Bayesian formula

(1) Known: $P(B_1) = 4000/6000 = 2/3,$
$$P(B_2) = 2000/6000 = 1/3,$$
$$P(A_1|B_1) = 1/2,$$
$$P(A_1|B_2) = 1/2.$$

Question: If a product comes from A_1, what is the probability that it belongs to B_2?

Solution: Calculate Joint Probabilities:

$$P(B_1)P(A_1|B_1) = (2/3)(1/2) = 1/3,$$
$$P(B_2)P(A_1|B_2) = (1/3)(1/2) = 1/6.$$

Calculate Total Probability:

$$P(A_1) = (1/3) + (1/6) = 1/2.$$

Calculate posterior probability according to Bayesian formula:

$$P(B_2|A_1) = (1/6) \div (1/2) = 1/3.$$

(2) Known: $P(A_1) = 3{,}000/6{,}000 = 1/2,$

$$P(A_2) = 2{,}000/6{,}000 = 1/3,$$

$$P(A_3) = 1{,}000/6{,}000 = 1/6,$$

$$P(B_2|A_1) = 1{,}000/3{,}000 = 1/3,$$

$$P(B_2|A_2) = 500/2{,}000 = 1/4,$$

$$P(B_2|A_3) = 500/1{,}000 = 1/2.$$

Question: If a product belongs to B_2, what is the probability that it comes from A_1, A_2, or A_3?

Solution: Calculate Joint Probabilities:

$$P(A_1)P(B_2|A_1) = (1/2)(1/3) = 1/6,$$

$$P(A_2)P(B_2|A_2) = (1/3)(1/4) = 1/12,$$

$$P(A_3)P(B_2|A_3) = (1/6)(1/2) = 1/12.$$

Calculate Total Probability P(B2):

$$P(B_2) = \sum P(A_i)P(B_2|A_i)$$

$$= (1/2)(1/3) + (1/3)(1/4) + (1/6)(1/2) = 1/3.$$

Calculate posterior probability according to Bayesian formula:

$$P(A_1|B_2) = (1/6) \div (1/3) = 1/2,$$

$$P(A_2|B_2) = (1/12) \div (1/3) = 1/4,$$

$$P(A_3|B_2) = (1/12) \div (1/3) = 1/4.$$

4.3 Bayesian Problem Solving

Bayesian learning theory utilizes prior information and sample data to estimate unknown data. Probabilities (joint probabilities and conditional probabilities) are the representation of prior information and sample data in Bayesian learning theory.

How to get the estimation of these probabilities (also called probabilistic density estimation) is a topic of much controversy in Bayesian learning theory. Bayesian density estimation focuses on how to estimate the distribution of unknown variables (vectors) and its parameters based on sample data and prior knowledge from human experts. It includes two steps. One is to determine prior distributions of unknown variables; the other is to get the parameters of these distributions. If we know nothing about previous information, the distribution is called non-informative prior distribution. If we know the distribution and seek its proper parameters, the distribution is called informative prior distribution. Because learning from data is the most elementary characteristic of data mining, non-informative prior distribution is the main subject of Bayesian learning theory research.

The first step of Bayesian problem solving is to select a Bayesian prior distribution. This is a key step. There are two common methods to select a prior distribution, namely, subjective method and objective method. The former makes use of human experience and expert knowledge to assign prior distribution. The latter is done by analyzing the characteristics of the data to get the statistical features of the data. It requires having a sufficient amount of data to get the true distribution of data. In practice, these two methods are often combined. Several common methods for prior distribution selection are listed in the following. Before we discuss these methods, we give some definitions first.

Let θ be the parameter of a model, $X = (x_1, x_2, \ldots, x_n)$ be the observed data, and $\pi(\theta)$ be the prior distribution of θ. $\pi(\theta)$ represents the brief of parameter θ when no evidence exists. $l(x_1, x_2, \ldots, x_n|\theta) \propto p(x_1, x_2, \ldots, x_n|\theta)$ is the likelihood function. It represents the brief of unknown data when parameter θ is known. $h(\theta|x_1, x_2, \ldots, x_n) \propto p(\theta|x_1, x_2, \ldots, x_n)$ is the brief of parameter θ after new evidence appears. Bayesian theorem describes the relation between them as follows:

$$h(\theta|x_1, x_2, \ldots, x_n)$$
$$= \frac{\pi(\theta)p(x_1, x_2, \ldots, x_n|\theta)}{\int \pi(\theta)p(x_1, x_2, \ldots, x_n|\theta)d\theta} \propto \pi(\theta)l(x_1, x_2, \ldots, x_n|\theta). \qquad (4.6)$$

Definition 4.5 (Kernel of Distribution Density). If $f(x)$, the distribution density of random variable z can be decomposed as $f(x), = cg(x)$, where c is a constant independent of x, we call $g(x)$ the kernel of $f(x)$, or short for $f(x) \propto g(x)$. If we know the kernel of distribution density, we can determine the corresponding constant according to the fact that the integral of distribution density in the whole space is 1. Therefore, the key to solving the distribution density of a random variable is to solve the kernel of its distribution density.

Definition 4.6 (Sufficient Statistic). To parameter θ, the statistic $t(x_1, x_2, \ldots, x_n)$ is sufficient if the posterior distribution of θ, $h(\theta|x_1, x_2, \ldots, x_n)$, is always a function of θ and $t(x_1, x_2, \ldots, x_n)$ in spite of its prior distribution.

This definition clearly states that the information of θ in data can be represented by its sufficient statistics. Sufficient statistics are connections between posterior distribution and data. Below, we give a theorem to judge whether a statistic is sufficient.

Theorem 4.3 (The Neyman–Fisher Factorization Theorem). *Let $f\theta(\mathbf{x})$ be the density or mass function for the random vector $\mathbf{x}$, parametrized by the vector θ. The statistic $t = T(\mathbf{x})$ is sufficient for θ if and only if there exist functions $a(\mathbf{x})$ (not depending on θ) and $b\theta(t)$ such that $f\theta(\mathbf{x}) = \mathbf{a}(\mathbf{x})\, \mathbf{b}\theta(\mathbf{t})$ for all possible values of $\mathbf{x}$.*

4.3.1 *Common Methods for Prior Distribution Selection*

1. Conjugate family of distributions

Raiffa and Schaifeer suggested using conjugate distributions as prior distributions, where the posterior distribution and the corresponding prior distribution are the same kind of distribution. The general description of conjugate distribution is as follows:

Definition 4.7. Let the conditional distribution of samples $x_1, x_2, \ldots, x_n$ under parameters θ be $p(x_1, x_2, \ldots, x_n|\theta)$. If the prior density function $\pi(\theta)$ and its resulting posterior density function $\pi(\theta|x)$ are in the same family, the prior density function $\pi(\theta)$ is said to be conjugate to the conditional distribution $p(x|\theta)$.

Definition 4.8. Let $P = \{p(x|\theta) : \theta \in \Theta\}$ be the density function family with parameters θ. $H = \pi(\theta)$ is the prior distribution family of θ. If for any given $p \in P$ and $\pi \in H$, the resulting posterior distribution $\pi(\theta|x)$ is always in family H, H is said to be the conjugate family to P.

When the density functions of data distribution and its prior are all exponential functions, the resulting function of their multiplication is the sample kind of exponential function. The only difference is a factor of proportionality. So we have the following theorem:

Theorem 4.4. *If for random variable Z, the kernel of its density function $f(x)$ is an exponential function, the density function belongs to the conjugate family.*

All the distributions with exponential kernel function compose the exponential family, which includes binary distribution, multinomial distribution, normal distribution, Gamma distribution, Poisson distribution, and Dirichlet distribution.

Conjugate distributions can provide a reasonable synthesis of historical trials and a reasonable precondition for future trials. The computation of non-conjugate distribution is rather difficult. In contrast, the computation of conjugate distribution is easy, where only multiplication with the prior is required. So, in fact, the conjugate family makes a firm foundation for the practical application of Bayesian learning.

2. Principle of maximum entropy

Entropy is used to quantify the uncertainty of an event in information theory. If a random variable x takes two different possible values, namely a and b, compare the following two case:

$$(1)\quad p(x = a) = 0.98,\quad p(x = b) = 0.02,$$
$$(2)\quad p(x = a) = 0.45,\quad p(x = b) = 0.55.$$

Obviously, the uncertainty of case 1 is much less than that of case 2. Intuitively, we can see that the uncertainty will reach maximum when the probabilities of the two values are equal.

Definition 4.9. Let x be a discrete random variable. It takes at most countable values $a_1, a_2, \ldots, a_k, \ldots$, and $p(x = a_i) = p_i$, $i = 1, 2, \ldots$. The entropy of x is $H(x) = -\sum_i p_i \ln p_i$. For a continuous random variable x, if the integral $H(x) = -\int p(x) \ln p(x)$ is meaningful, where $p(x)$ is the density of variable x, the integral is called the entropy of a continuous random variable.

According to the definition, when two random variables have the same distribution, they have equal entropy. So, entropy is only related to distribution.

Principle of maximum entropy: For non-information data, the best prior distribution is the distribution which makes the entropy maximum under parameters θ.

It can be proved that the entropy of a random variable, or vector, reaches maximum if and only if its distribution is uniform. Hence, the Bayesian assumption, which assumes non-information prior to be uniform, fits the principle of maximum entropy. It makes the entropy of a random variable, or vector, maximum. Below is the proof of the case of limited valued random variable.

Theorem 4.5. *Let random variable x take limited values $a_1, a_2, \ldots, a_n$. The corresponding probabilities are $p_1, p_2, \ldots, p_n$. The entropy $H(x)$ is maximum if and only if $p_1 = p_2 = \cdots = p_n = 1/n$.*

Proof. Consider $G(p_1, p_2, \ldots, p_n) = -\sum_{i=1}^{n} p_i \ln p_i + \lambda(\sum_{i=1}^{n} p_i - 1)$. To find its maximum, we let the partial derivative of G with respect to p_i be 0, and thus get the following equation:

$$0 = \frac{\partial G}{\partial p_i} = -\ln p_{i-1} + \lambda \quad (i = 1, 2, \ldots, n).$$

Solving the equations, we get $p_1 = p_2 = \cdots = p_n$. Because $\sum_{i=1}^{n} p_i = 1$, we have $p_1 = p_2 = \cdots = p_n = 1/n$. Here, the corresponding entropy is $-\sum_{i=1}^{n} \frac{1}{n} \ln \frac{1}{n} = \ln n$.

For a continuous random variable, the result is the same.

From above, when there is no information to determine prior distribution, the principle of maximum distribution is a reasonable choice for prior selection. There are many cases where no information is available to determine the prior, so Bayesian assumption is very important in these cases. □

3. Jeffrey's principle

Jeffrey had made a significant contribution to prior distribution selection. He proposed an invariance principle, which solved a conflict in Bayesian assumption very well and gave an approach to find prior density. Jeffrey's principle is composed of two parts: one is a reasonable requirement to prior distribution; the other is giving out a concrete approach to find a correct prior distribution fitting the requirement.

There is a conflict in Bayesian assumption: If we choose uniform as the distribution of parameter θ, once we take function $g(\theta)$ as parameter, it should also obey uniform distribution and vice versa. Yet, the above precondition cannot lead to the expected result. To solve the conflict, Jeffrey proposed an invariance request. That is, a reasonable principle for prior selection should have invariance.

If we choose $\pi(\theta)$ as the prior distribution of parameter θ, according to invariance principle, $\pi_g(g(\theta))$, the distribution of function $g(\theta)$ should satisfy the following:

$$\pi(\theta) = \pi_g(g(\theta))|g'(\theta)|. \tag{4.7}$$

The key point is how to find a prior distribution $\pi(\theta)$ to satisfy the above condition. Jeffrey skillfully utilized the invariance of the Fisher information matrix to find a required $\pi(\theta)$.

The distribution of parameter θ has the kernel of the square root of information matrix $I(\theta)$, viz. $\pi(\theta) \propto |I(\theta)|^{1/2}$, where $I(\theta) = E\left(\frac{\partial \ln p(x_1, x_2, \ldots, x_n; \theta)}{\partial \theta}\right) \left(\frac{\partial \ln p(x_1, x_2, \ldots, x_n; \theta)}{\partial \theta}\right)'$. The concrete deriving process is not presented here. Interested readers can find them in related references. It is noted that Jeffrey's principle is just a principle of finding a reasonable prior, while using the square root of the information matrix as the kernel of the prior is a concrete approach. They are different. In fact, we can seek other concrete approaches to embody the principle.

4.3.2 *Computational Learning*

Learning is the process by which a system can improve its behavior after running. Is the posterior distribution gained via Bayesian formula better than its corresponding prior? What is its learning mechanism? Here, we analyze normal distribution as an example to study the effect of prior information and sample data by changing parameters.

Let $x_1, x_2, \ldots, x_n$ be a sample from normal distribution $N(\theta, \sigma_1^2)$, where σ_1^2 is known and θ is unknown. To seek $\tilde{\theta}$, the estimation of θ, we take another normal distribution as the prior of θ. That is,

$$\pi(\theta) = N(\mu_0, \sigma_0^2).$$

The resulting posterior distribution of θ is also a normal distribution:

$$h(\theta|\bar{x}_1) = N(\alpha_1, d_1^2),$$

where

$$\bar{x}_1 = \sum_{i=1}^{n} \frac{x_i}{n}, \quad \alpha_1 = \left(\frac{1}{\sigma_0^2}\mu_0 + \frac{n}{\sigma_1^2}\bar{x}_1\right) \Big/ \left(\frac{1}{\sigma_0^2} + \frac{n}{\sigma_1^2}\right), \quad d_1^2 = \left(\frac{1}{\sigma_0^2} + \frac{n}{\sigma_1^2}\right)^{-1}.$$

Take α_1, the expectation of the posterior $h(\theta|\bar{x})$ as the estimation of θ, then we have

$$\tilde{\theta} = E(\theta|\bar{x}_1) \left(\frac{1}{\sigma_0^2}\mu_0 + \frac{n}{\sigma_1^2}\bar{x}_1\right) \cdot d_1^2. \tag{4.8}$$

Therefore, $\tilde{\theta}$, the estimation of θ, is the weighted average of μ_0, the expectation of prior, and $\bar{x}_1$, the sample mean. σ_0^2 is the variance of $N(\mu_0, \sigma_0^2)$, so its reciprocal, $1/\sigma_0^2$, is the precision of μ_0. Similarly, σ_1^2/n is the variance of sample mean $\bar{x}$, so its reciprocal is the precision of $\bar{x}_1$. Hence, we see that $\tilde{\theta}$ is the weighted average of μ_0 and $\bar{x}_1$, where the weights are their precisions, respectively. The smaller the variance, the bigger the weight. Besides, the bigger the sample size n, the smaller the variance σ_1^2/n, or the bigger the weight of sample mean. This means that when, n is quite large, the effect of the prior mean will be very small. This analysis illustrates that the posterior from the Bayesian formula integrates prior information and sample data.

The result is more reasonable than that based on merely prior information or sample data. The learning mechanism is effective. The analysis based on other conjugate prior distribution leads to a similar result.

According to the previous discussion, with the conjugate prior, we can use the posterior information as the prior of the next computation and seek the next posterior by integrating the information of more samples. If we repeat this process time after time, can we get posterior increasingly close to reality? We study this problem in the following.

Let new sample $x_1, x_2, \ldots, x_n$ be from normal distribution $N(\theta, \sigma_2^2)$, where σ_2^2 is known and θ is unknown. If we use the previous posterior $h(\theta|\bar{x}_1) = N(\alpha_1, d_1^2)$ as the prior of the next round of computation, then the new posterior is $h_1(\theta|\bar{x}_2) = N(\alpha_2, d_2^2)$, where

$$\bar{x}_2 = \sum_{i=1}^{n} \frac{x_i}{n}, \quad \alpha_2 = \left(\frac{1}{d_1^2}\alpha_1 + \frac{n}{\sigma_2^2}\bar{x}_2\right) \Big/ \left(\frac{1}{d_1^2} + \frac{n}{\sigma_2^2}\right), \quad d_2^2 = \left(\frac{1}{d_1^2} + \frac{n}{\sigma_2^2}\right)^{-1}$$

Now, $\alpha_2 = \left(\frac{1}{\sigma_0^2}\mu_0 + \frac{n}{\sigma_1^2}\bar{x}\right) \Big/ \left(\frac{1}{\sigma_0^2} + \frac{n}{\sigma_1^2}\right)$ uses the expectation of posterior $h_1(\theta|\bar{x}_2)$ as the estimation of θ. Because $\alpha_1 = \left(\frac{1}{\sigma_0^2}\mu_0 + \frac{n}{\sigma_1^2}\bar{x}_1\right) \cdot d_1^2$, we have

$$\alpha_2 = \left(\frac{1}{d_1^2}\alpha_1 + \frac{n}{\sigma_2^2}\bar{x}_2\right) \cdot d_2^2 = \left(\frac{1}{\sigma_0^2}\mu_0 + \frac{n}{\sigma_1^2}\bar{x}_1 + \frac{n}{\sigma_2^2}\bar{x}_2\right) \cdot d_2^2$$

$$= \left(\frac{1}{\sigma_0^2}\mu_0 + \frac{n}{\sigma_1^2}\bar{x}_1\right) \cdot d_2^2 + \frac{n}{\sigma_2^2}\bar{x}_2 \cdot d_2^2, \tag{4.9}$$

and $\frac{n}{\sigma_2^2} > 0$, so

$$d_2^2 = \left(\frac{1}{d_1^2} + \frac{n}{\sigma_2^2}\right)^{-1} = \left(\frac{1}{\sigma_0^2} + \frac{n}{\sigma_1^2} + \frac{n}{\sigma_2^2}\right)^{-1} < d_1^2 = \left(\frac{1}{\sigma_0^2} + \frac{n}{\sigma_1^2}\right)^{-1}.$$

In α_2, $\left(\frac{1}{\sigma_0^2}\mu_0 + \frac{n}{\sigma_1^2}\bar{x}_1\right) \cdot d_2^2 < \alpha_1$. It is clear that because of the addition of the new sample, the proportion of the original prior and the old sample declines. According to Equation (4.9), with the continuous increase of new sample (here we assume the sample size keeps invariant), we have

$$\alpha_m = \left(\frac{1}{\sigma_0^2}\mu_0 + \frac{n}{\sigma_1^2}\bar{x}_1 + \frac{n}{\sigma_2^2}\bar{x}_2 + \cdots + \frac{n}{\sigma_m^2}\bar{x}_m\right) \cdot d_m^2$$

$$= \left(\frac{1}{\sigma_0^2}\mu_0 + \sum_{k=1}^{m} \frac{n}{\sigma_k^2}\bar{x}_k\right) \cdot d_m^2 \quad (k = 1, 2, \ldots, m). \tag{4.10}$$

From Equation (4.10), if the variance of the new samples are the same, they equal a sample with the size $m \times n$. The above process weighted all the sample means with their precisions. The higher the precision, the bigger the weight. If the prior distribution is estimated precisely, we can use less sample data and only need a little computation. This is especially useful in the situation where the sample is hard to collect. It is also the point where the Bayesian approach outperforms other methods. Therefore, the determination of prior distribution in Bayesian learning is extremely important. If there is no prior information and we adopt non-information prior, with the increase of sample, the effect of the sample will become more and more salient. If the noise of the sample is small, the posterior will be increasingly close to its true value. The only issue is that significant computation is required.

4.3.3 *Steps in Bayesian Problem Solving*

The steps in Bayesian problem solving can be summarized as follows:

(1) Define the random variable. Set unknown parameters as random variable or vector, for short denoted as θ. The joint density $p(x_1, x_2, \ldots, x_n; \theta)$ of the sample $x_1, x_2, \ldots, x_n$ is regarded as the conditional density of $x_1, x_2, \ldots, x_n$ with respect to θ, denoted briefly as $p(x_1, x_2, \ldots, x_n | \theta)$ or $p(D|\theta)$.
(2) Determine the prior distribution density $p(\theta)$. Use conjugate distribution. If there is no information about prior distribution, then use Bayesian assumption of non-information prior distribution.
(3) Calculate posterior distribution density via Bayesian theorem.
(4) Make inference of the problem with the resulting posterior distribution density.

Take the case of a single variable and single parameter as an example. Consider the problem of thumbtack throwing. If we throw a thumbtack up in the air, the thumbtack will fall down and reset at one of two states: on its head or on its tail. Suppose we flip the thumbtack $N + 1$ times, from the first N observations, how can we get the probability of the case "head" in the $N + 1$th throw?

Step 1. Define a random variable Θ. The value θ corresponds to the possible value of the real probability of head. The density function $p(\theta)$ represents the uncertainty of Θ. The variable of the ith result is X_i $(i = 1, 2, \ldots, N + 1)$, and the set of observations is $D = \{X_1 = x_1, \ldots, X_n = x_n\}$. Our objective is to calculate $p(x_{N+1}|D)$.

Step 2. According to Bayesian theorem, we have, $p(\theta|D) = \frac{p(\theta)p(D|\theta)}{p(D)}$, where $p(D) = \int p(D|\theta)p(\theta)d\theta$, $p(D|\theta)$ is the binary likelihood function of sample. If θ, the value of Θ, is known, the observation value in D is independent; the probability of head (tail) is θ, the probability of tail is $(1 - \theta)$, then

$$p(\theta|D) = \frac{p(\theta)\theta^h(1 - \theta)^t}{p(D)}, \tag{4.11}$$

where h and t are the times of head and tail in the observation D, respectively. They are sufficient statistics of sample binary distribution.

Step 3. Seek the mean of Θ as the probability of case head in the $N + 1$th toss:

$$p(X_{N+1} = \text{heads}|D) = \int p(X_{N+1} = \text{heads}|\theta)p(\theta|D)d\theta$$

$$= \int \theta \cdot p(\theta|D)d\theta \equiv E_{p(\theta|D)}(\theta), \tag{4.12}$$

where $E_{p(\theta|D)}(\theta)$ is the expectation of θ under the distribution $p(\theta|D)$.

Step 4. Assign prior distribution and supper parameters for Θ.
The common method for prior assignment is to assume prior distribution first, and then to determine proper parameters. Here, we assume the prior distribution is Beta distribution:

$$p(\theta) = \text{Beta}(\theta|\alpha_h, \alpha_t) \equiv \frac{\Gamma(\alpha)}{\Gamma(\alpha_h)\Gamma(\alpha_t)}\theta^{\alpha_h-1}(1 - \theta)^{\alpha_t-1}, \tag{4.13}$$

where $\alpha_h > 0$ and $\alpha_t > 0$ are parameters of Beta distribution, $\alpha = \alpha_h + \alpha_t$, and $\Gamma(\cdot)$ is the Gamma function. To distinguish from parameter θ, σh and α_t are called "Supper Parameters". Because Beta distribution belongs to the conjugate family, the resulting posterior is also Beta distribution:

$$p(\theta|D) = \frac{\Gamma(\alpha + N)}{\Gamma(\alpha_h + h)\Gamma(\alpha_t + t)}\theta^{\alpha_h+h-1}(1 - \theta)^{\alpha_t+t-1}$$

$$= \text{Beta}(\theta|\alpha_h + h, \alpha_t + t). \tag{4.14}$$

To this distribution, its expectation of θ has a simple form as follows:

$$\int \theta \cdot \text{Beta}(\theta|\alpha_h, \alpha_t)d\theta = \frac{\alpha_h}{\alpha}. \tag{4.15}$$

Therefore, for a given Beta prior, we get the probability of head in the $N + 1$th toss as follows:

$$p(X_{N+1} = \text{heads}|D) = \frac{\alpha_h + h}{\alpha + N}. \tag{4.16}$$

There are many ways to determine the supper parameters of the prior Beta distribution $p(\theta)$, such as imagined future data and equivalent samples. Other methods can be found in the works of Winkler, Chaloner, and Duncan. In the method of imagined future data, two equations can be deduced from Equation (4.16), and two supper parameters α_h and α_t can be solved accordingly.

In the case of single variable multiple parameters (a single variable with multiple possible states), commonly X is regarded as a continuous variable with Gaussian distribution. Assume its physical density is $p(x|\theta)$, then we have

$$p(x|\theta) = (2\pi v)^{-1/2}e^{-(x-\mu)^2/2v^2},$$

where $\theta = \{\mu, v\}$.

Similar to the previous approach on binary distribution, we first assign the prior of parameters and then solve the posterior with the data $D = \{X_1 = x_1, X_2 = x_2, \ldots, X_N = x_N\}$ via Bayesian theorem:

$$P(\theta|D) = p(D|\theta)p(\theta)/p(D).$$

Next, we use the mean of Θ as the prediction as follows:

$$p(x_{N+!}|D) = \int p(x_{N+1}|\theta)p(\theta|D)d\theta. \tag{4.17}$$

For an exponential family, the computation is effective and close. In the case of multi samples, if the observed value of X is discrete, Dirichlet distribution can be used as the prior distribution, which can simplify the computation.

The computational learning mechanism of Bayesian theorem is to get the weighted average of the expectation of prior distribution and the mean of sample, where the higher the precision, the bigger the weight. Under the precondition that the prior is conjugate distribution, posterior information can be used as the prior in the next round of computation, so that it can be integrated with further obtained sample information. If this process is repeated time and again, the effect of the sample will be increasingly prominent. Because Bayesian method integrates prior information and posterior information, it can both avoid the subjective bias when using only prior information and avoid numerous blind searching and computation when sample information is limited. Besides, it can also avoid the affect of noise when utilizing only posterior information. Therefore, it is suitable for problems of data mining with statistical features and problems of knowledge discovery, especially the problems where the sample is hard to collect or the cost of collecting the sample is high. The key of effective learning with Bayesian method is determining the prior reasonably and precisely. Currently, there are only some principles for prior determination, and there is no operable whole theory to determine priors. In many cases, the reasonability and precision of prior distribution is hard to evaluate. Further research is required to solve these problems.

4.4 Naïve Bayesian Learning Model

In naïve Bayesian learning models, the training sample I is decomposed into feature vector X and decision class variable C. Here, it is assumed that all the weights in a feature vector are independent given the decision variable. In other words, each weight affects the decision variable independently. Although the assumption to some extent limits the sphere of the naïve Bayesian model, in practical applications, naïve Bayesian model can both exponentially reduce the complexity for model construction and express striking robustness and effectiveness even when the assumption is unsatisfied (Nigam *et al.*, 1998). It has been successfully applied in many data mining tasks, such as classification, clustering, model selection, and so on. Currently, many researchers are working to relax the limitation of independence among variables (Heckerman, 1997) so that the model can be applied more widely.

4.4.1 *Naïve Bayesian Learning Model*

Bayesian theorem tells us how to predict the class of the incoming sample given training samples. The rule of classification is maximum posterior probability, which is given in the following equation:

$$P(C_i|A) = P(C_i) * P(A|C_i)/P(A). \tag{4.18}$$

Here, A is a test sample to be classified and $P(Y|X)$ is the conditional probability of Y under the condition of X. The probabilities at the right side of the equation can be estimated from the training data. Suppose that the sample is represented as a vector of features. If all features are independent for the given classes, $P(A|C_i)$ can be decomposed as a product of factors: $P(a_1|C_i) \times P(a_2|C_i) \times \cdots \times P(a_m|C_i)$, where a_i is the ith feature of the test sample. Accordingly, the posterior computation equation can be rewritten as follows:

$$P(C_i|A) = \frac{P(C_i)}{P(A)} \prod_{j=1}^{m} P(a_j|C_i). \tag{4.19}$$

The entire process is called naïve Bayesian classification. In the common sense, only when the independent assumption holds, or when the correlation of features is very weak can the naïve Bayesian classifier achieve the optimal or sub-optimal result. Yet, the strong limited condition seems inconsistent with the fact that the naïve Bayesian classifier gains striking performance in many fields, including some fields where there is obvious dependence among features. In 16 out of the total 28 data sets of UCI, naïve Bayesian classifier outperforms the C4.5 algorithms and has similar performance with that of CN2 and PEBLS. Some research works report similar results (Clark and Niblett, 1989). At the same time, researchers have also successfully proposed some strategy to relax the limitation of independence among features (Nigam *et al.*, 1998).

The conditional probability in formula (4.19) can be gained using maximum likelihood estimation:

$$P(v_j|C_i) = \frac{\text{count}(v_j \wedge c_i)}{\text{count}(c_i)}. \tag{4.20}$$

To avoid zero probability, if the actual conditional probability is zero, it is assigned to be $0.5/N$, where N is the total number of examples.

Suppose that there are only two classes, namely class 0 and class 1, and $a_1, \ldots, a_k$ represent features of test set. Let $b_0 = P(C = 0)$, $b_1 = P(C = 1) = 1 - b_0$, $p_{j0} = P(A_j = a_j|C = 0)$, $p_{j1} = P(A_j = a_j|C = 0)$, then

$$p = P(C = 1|A_1 = a_1 \wedge \cdots \wedge A_k = a_k) = \left(\prod_{j=1}^{k} p_{j1}\right) b_1/z, \tag{4.21}$$

$$q = P(C = 0|A_1 = a_1 \wedge \cdots \wedge A_k = a_k) = \left(\prod_{j=1}^{k} p_{j0}\right) b_0/z, \tag{4.22}$$

where z is a constant. After taking logarithm on both sides of the above two equations, we subtract the second equation from the first one and get

$$\log p - \log q = \left(\sum_{j=1}^{k} \log p_{j1} - \log p_{j0}\right) + \log b_1 - \log b_0. \tag{4.23}$$

Here, let $w_j = \log p_{j1} - \log p_{j0}$, $b = \log b_1 - \log b_0$, then the above equation is written as:

$$\log (1 - p)/p = -\sum_{j=1}^{k} w_j - b. \tag{4.24}$$

After taking exponential on both sides of Equation (4.24) and rearranging, we have

$$p = \frac{1}{1 + e^{-\sum_{j=1}^{k} w_j - b}}. \tag{4.25}$$

To calculate this value, we assume that feature A_j has $v(j)$ possible values. Let

$$w_{jj'} = \log P(A_j = a_{jj'}|c = 1)$$

$$\log P(A_j = a_{jj'}|c = 0)(1 \leq j' \leq v(j)). \tag{4.26}$$

We have

$$P(C(x) = 1) = \frac{1}{1 + e^{-(\sum_{j=1}^{k} \sum_{j'}^{v(j)} I(A_j(x)=a_{jj'})w_{jj'}-b)}}, \tag{4.27}$$

where I is a characteristic function. If φ is true, then $I(\varphi) = 1$; else $I(\varphi) = 0$. In practical computation, Equation (4.27) can be calculated similar to Equation (4.20).

In fact, Equation (4.27) is a perception function with a sigmoid activation function. The input of this function is the possible value of all features. So, to some extent, naïve Bayesian classifier is equal to a perception model. Further research demonstrated that naïve Bayesian classifier can be generalized to logical regression with numerical features.

Consider Equation (4.20). If A_j takes discrete values, count($A_j = a_j \wedge C = c_i$) can be calculated directly from the training samples. If A_j is continuous, it should be discretized. In unsupervised discretization, a feature is discretized into M equally wide sections, where $M = 10$ commonly. We can also utilize a more complicated discretization method, such as supervised discretization method.

Let each A_j be a numerical feature (discrete or continuous). The logical regression model is given as follows:

$$\log \frac{P(C = 1|A_1 = a_1, \ldots, A_k = a_k)}{P(C = 0|A_1 = a_1, \ldots, A_k = a_k)} = \sum_{j=1}^{k} b_j a_j + b_0. \tag{4.28}$$

After transforming similar to that of Equation (4.24), we have

$$p = \frac{1}{1 + e^{-\sum_{j=1}^{k} b_j a_j - b_0}}. \tag{4.29}$$

Obviously, this is also a perception function with a sigmoid activation function. Its inputs are all feature values using function $f_j(\varphi)$ to replace $b_j a_j$. If the sphere of A_j is divided into M parts and the ith part is $[c_{j(i-1)}, c_{ji}]$, the function $f_j(\varphi)$ is given as follows:

$$b_j a_j = f_j(a_j) = \sum_{i=1}^{M} b_{ji} I(c_{j(i-1)} < a_j \leq c_{ji}), \tag{4.30}$$

where b_{ji} is a constant. According to Equations (4.29) and (4.30), we have

$$P(C(x) = 1) = \frac{1}{1 + e^{-(\sum_{j=1}^{k} \sum_{i}^{M} b_{ji} I(c_{j(i-1)} < a_j \leq c_{ji})) - b_0}}. \tag{4.31}$$

This is the final regression function. So, naïve Bayesian classifier is a non-parametric and nonlinear extension of logical regression. By setting $b_{ji} = (c_{j(i-1)} + c_{ij})/(2b_j)$, we can get a standard logical regression formula.

4.4.2 *Boosting of Naïve Bayesian Model*

In boosting, a series of classifiers will be built, and in each classifier in the series misclassified by previous classifier will be given more attention. Concretely, after learning classifier k, the weights of training examples that are misclassified by classifier k will increase, and classifier $k + 1$ will be learnt based on the newly weighted training examples. This process will be repeated T times. The final classifier is the synthesis of all the classifiers in series.

Initially, each training example is set with a weight. In the learning process, if some example is misclassified by one classifier, in the next learning round, the corresponding weight will be increased, so that the next classifier will pay more attention to it.

The boosting algorithm for binary classification problem is given by Freund and Schapire as the AdaBoost Algorithm (Freund and Schapire, 1995).

Algorithm 4.1 (AdaBoost Algorithm).

Input:
N training examples $< (x_1 , y_1 >, \cdots (x_N, y_N) >$
Distribution of the N training examples, D: w, where w is the weight vector of training example.
T: the number of rounds for training.
1. Initialize:
2. Initial weight vector of training examples: $w_i = 1/N\ i = 1, \ldots, N$
3. for $t = 1$ to T
4.   Given weights $w_i{}^t$, find a hypothesis $H^{(t)} : X \to [0, 1]$
5.   Estimation the general error of hypothesis $H^{(t)}$:
   $$e^{(t)} = \sum_{i=1}^{N} w_i{}^{(t)} \mid y_i - h_i{}^{(t)}(x_i)\mid$$
6.   Calculate $\beta^{(t)} = e^{(t)}/(1 - e^{(t)})$
7.   Renew the next round weights of examples with
   $$w_i{}^{(t+1)} = w_i{}^{(t)} (\beta^{(t)})^{1 - \mid y_i - h_i{}^{(t)}(x_i)\mid}$$
8.   Normalize $w_i{}^{(t+1)}$, so that they are summed up to 1
9. End for
10. Output

$$h(x) = \begin{cases} 1 & \text{if } \sum_{t=1}^{T} \left(\log \frac{i}{\beta^{(t)}}\right) h^{(t)}(x) \geq \frac{1}{2} \sum_{t=1}^{T} \left(\log \frac{i}{\beta^{(t)}}\right), \\ 0 & \text{otherwise.} \end{cases}$$

Here we assume that all the classifiers are effective. In other words for each classifier, the examples correctly classified are more than the ones misclassified, $e^t < 0.5$. Hence, $\beta^{(t)} < 1$. When $|y_i - h_i^{(t)}(x_i)|$ increases, $w_i^{(t+1)}$ will increase accordingly. The algorithm fulfills the idea of boosting.

Some notes on the algorithm:

(1) $h^{(t)}(x)$ is calculated via the output formula, and the result is either 0 or 1.
(2) The calculation of conditional probability $P(A_j = a_{jj'}|C = c)$ in formula (4.20). If we do not consider the weights, the computational basis for *count(condition)* is 1. For example, if there are k examples satisfying the condition, then *count(condition)* $= k$. If we consider the weights, the computational basis for each example is its weight. For example, if there are k examples satisfying the condition, then *count(condition)* $= \sum_i^k w_i$. In this case, the adjustment of weights embodies the idea of boosting.
(3) The output of the algorithm means that for an incoming input x, according to Step 6 in the algorithm, we can use the result of learning to generate the output by voting.

The final combined hypothesis can be defined as

$$H(x) = \frac{1}{1 + \prod_{t=1}^{T} (\beta^{(t)})^{2r(x)-1}},$$

where $r(x) = \frac{\sum_{t=1}^{T} (\log 1/\beta^t) H^{(t)}(x)}{\sum_{t=1}^{T} (\log 1/\beta^t)}$.

Below we will demonstrate that after boosting the representative capability of combined naïve Bayesian classifier equals to that of multiple layered perception model with one hidden layer. Let $\alpha = \prod_{t=1}^{T} \beta^t$ and $v^{(t)} = \log \beta^{(t)} / \log \alpha$, then

$$H(x) = \frac{1}{1 + \alpha^{2(\sum_{t=1}^{T} v^{(t)} H^{(t)}(x))-1}} = \frac{1}{1 + e^{\sum_{t=1}^{T} 2\log \beta^{(t)} H^{(t)}(x) - \sum_{t=1}^{T} \log \beta^{(t)}}}.$$

The output of the combined classifier is the output of a sigmoid function, which takes the outputs of single classifiers and their weights as its parameters. Since a naïve Bayesian classifier equals a perception machine, the combined classifier equals a perception network with a hidden layer.

The boosting naïve Bayesian method for multiple classification problems is as follows:

Algorithm 4.2 (Multiple Classification AdaBoost Algorithm).

Input:
N training examples $< (x_1, y_1) >, \cdots < (x_N, y_N) >$

Distribution of the N training examples, D: w, where w is the weight vector of training example.

T: the number of rounds for training.

1. Initialize:

   Initial weight vector of training examples $w_i = 1/N$, $i = (1, \ldots, N)$

2. *for* $t = 1$ *to* T

3.   Given weights $w_i{}'$, find a hypothesis $H^{(t)} : X \to Y$

4.   Estimation the general error of hypothesis $H^{(t)}$:

   $$e^{(t)} = \sum_{i=1}^{N} w_i^{(t)} I(y_i \neq h_i^{(t)}(x_i))$$

5.   Calculate $\beta^{(t)} = e^{(t)}/(1 - e^{(t)})$

6.   Renew the next round weights of examples with

   $$w_i^{(t+1)} = w_i^{(t)} (\beta^{(t)})^{1 - I(y_i = h_i^{(t)}(x_i))}$$

7.   Normalize $w_i^{(t+1)}$, so that they are summed up to 1

8. End for

9. Output:

$$h(x) = \arg\ \max_{y \in Y} \sum_{t=1}^{T} \left(\log \frac{i}{\beta^{(t)}} \right) I(h^{(t)}(x) = y)$$

where $I(\phi) = 1$ if $\phi = T$; $I(\phi) = 0$ otherwise.

4.4.3 *The Computational Complexity*

Suppose a sample in the sample space has f features, and each feature takes v values. The naïve Bayesian classifier deduced by Formula (4.27) will have $fv + 1$ parameters. These parameters are accumulatively learnt $2fv + 2$ times. In each learning process, each feature value of each training example will improve the final precision. So, the time complexity for n training examples is $O(nf)$, independent of v. Substantially, this time complexity is optimal. For boosting the naïve Bayesian classifier, the time complexity of each round is $O(nf)$. T round training corresponds to $O(Tnf)$. Notice that T is a constant. So the entire time complexity is still $O(nf)$.

For naïve Bayesian classifier, the primary computation is counting. Training examples can be processed either sequentially or in batches from disk or tape. So this method is perfectly suited for knowledge discovery on a large data set. The training set is not necessarily loaded to memory entirely, and part of it can be kept in disks or tapes. Yet, the boosting naïve Bayesian model also has the following problems:

(1) From the idea of boosting, when noise exists in the training set, the boosting method will take it as useful information and amplify its effect with a large weight. This will reduce the performance of boosting. If there are many noisy data, boosting will lead to worse result.

(2) Although theoretically boosting can achieve zero error rate for the training set, in its practical application of naïve Bayesian model, the 0 classification error seen in the training set is generally hardly guaranteed.

4.5 Construction of a Bayesian Network

4.5.1 *Structure of a Bayesian Network and Its Construction*

In short, Bayesian network is a directed acyclic graph with probabilistic notes. The graphic model can be utilized to represent the (physical or Bayesian) joint distribution of a large variable set. It can also be used to analyze correlations among numerous variables. With the capability of learning and statistical reasoning under the Bayesian theorem, it can fulfill many data mining tasks, such as prediction, classification, clustering, casual analysis, and so on.

Given a series of variables $X = \{x_1, x_2, \ldots, x_n\}$, a Bayesian network is composed of two components: one is network structure S, which represents the conditional independence among variables X; the other is local distribution set P, which is related to every variable. The two components define the joint probability of X. S is a directed acyclic graph. Nodes in S and variables in X are one to one correspondingly. Let x_i be a variable or node and Pa_i be the parent nodes of x_i in S. The absence of an arc between the nodes usually represents conditional independence. The joint probability of X is represented as

$$p(X) = \prod_{i=1}^{n} p(xi|Pa_i), \tag{4.32}$$

where $p(x_i|Pa_i)(i = 1, 2, \ldots, n)$ is the local probabilistic distribution in formula (4.32). The pair (S, P) represents the joint probabilistic distribution $p(X)$. If a Bayesian network is constructed merely based on prior information, the probabilistic distribution is Bayesian, or subjective. If the Bayesian network is constructed purely based on data, the distribution is physical, or objective.

To construct a Bayesian network, we should do the following tasks.

Step 1. Determine all the related variables and their explanations. To do so, we need to (a) determine the objective of the model, or make a reasonable explanation of given problem; (b) find as many as possible problem-related observations, and determine a subset that is worthy of constructing model; (c) translate these observations into mutually exclusive and exhaustive state variables. The result of these operations is not unique.

Step 2. Construct a directed acyclic graph which expresses a conditional independent assertion. According to the multiplication formula, we have

$$p(X) = \prod_{i=1}^{n} p(x_i|x_1, x_2, \ldots, x_{i-1})$$

$$= p(x_1)p(x_2|x_1)p(x_3|x_1, x_2) \ldots p(x_n|x_1, x_2, \ldots, x_{n-1}). \quad (4.33)$$

For any variable X, if there is a subset $\pi_i \subseteq \{x_1, x_2, \ldots, x_{i-1}\}$, then x_i and $\{x_1, x_2, \ldots, x_{i-1}\}\backslash\pi_i$ are conditional independent. That is, for any given X, the following equation holds:

$$p(x_i|x_1, x_2, \ldots, x_{i-1}) = p(x_i|\pi_i), \quad (i = 1, 2, \ldots, n). \quad (4.34)$$

According to Formulas (4.33) and (4.34), we have $p(x) = \prod_{i=1}^{n} p(x_i|\pi_i)$. The variable set $(\pi_1, \ldots, \pi_n)$ corresponds to the parent set $(Pa_1, \ldots, Pa_n)$. So the above equation can also be written as $p(X) = \prod_{i=1}^{n} p(x_i|Pa_i)$. To determine the structure of the Bayesian network, we need to (a) sort variables $x_1, x_2, \ldots, x_i$; and (b) determine the variable set $(\pi_1, \ldots, \pi_n)$ that satisfies formula (4.34).

Theoretically, finding a proper conditional independent sequence from n variables is a combination explosion problem, for it will require comparison among $n!$ different sequences. In practice, casual relation is often used to solve this problem. Generally, casual relation will correspond to a conditional independent assertion. So we can find a proper sequence by adding arrowed arcs from reason variables to result variables.

Step 3. Assign local probabilistic distribution $p(x_i|Pa_i)$. In the discrete case, we need to assign a distribution for each variable on each state of its parent nodes.

Obviously, the steps above may be intermingled but not purely performed in sequence.

4.5.2 *Probabilistic Distribution of Learning the Bayesian Network*

Consider the following problem: given the structure of a Bayesian network, how can we learn the probabilistic distribution, or how can we update its original prior, based on observed data? Here we use Bayesian approach, which integrates prior knowledge and data to improve existing knowledge. This technique can be applied to data mining. Assume that the physical joint distribution of variables $X = (x_1, x_2, \ldots, x_n)$ can be coded in some network structure S:

$$P(x|\theta_s, S^h) = \prod_{i=1}^{n} p(x_i|\mathbf{Pa}_i, \theta_i, S^h), \qquad (4.35)$$

where θ_i is the parameter vector of distribution $p(x_i|\mathbf{Pa}_i, \theta_i, S^h)$; θ_s is the vector of parameter groups $(\theta_1, \theta_2, \ldots, \theta_n)$; and S^h is the hypothesis that physical joint distribution can be decomposed in accordance with structure S. It is noted that the decomposition is not cross, or overlapped. For example, given $X = \{x_1, x_2\}$, any joint distribution of X can be decomposed to a no-arc network or a network with the only arc $x_1 \rightarrow x_2$. This is cross or overlapped. Besides, suppose we generate a random sample $D = \{x_1, \ldots, x_n\}$ based on the physical distribution of X. An element x_i of D represents an observed value of the sample and is called a case. We define a vector-valued variable Θ_S corresponding to parameter vector θ_s and assign a prior density function $p(\theta_s|S^h)$ to represent the uncertainty of Θ_S. Then the probability learning of the Bayesian network is described as: given a random sample D, calculated the posterior $p(\theta_s|D, S^h)$.

Below, we use unrestricted multinomial distribution to discuss the basic idea of probability learning. Assume that each variable $x_i \in X$ is discrete and has r_i possible values $x_i^1, x_i^2, \ldots, x_i^{r_i}$. Each local distribution function is a set of multinomial distributions, each of which corresponds to a composition of $\mathbf{Pa}_i$. That is to say, let

$$p(x_i^k|\mathbf{pa}_i^j, \theta_i, S^h) = \theta_{ijk} > 0$$

$$i = 1, 2, \ldots, n; \quad j = 1, 2, \ldots, q_i; \quad k = 1, 2, \ldots, r_i, \qquad (4.36)$$

where $\mathbf{pa}_i^1, \mathbf{pa}_i^2, \ldots, \mathbf{pa}_i^{q_i}$ represent the composition of $\mathbf{Pa}_i$; $q_i = \prod_{X_i \in Pa_i} r_i$; $\theta_i = ((\theta_{ijk})_{k=2}^{r_i})_{j=1}^{q_i}$ is parameter; θ_{ij1} is not included for $\theta_{ij1} = 1 - \sum_{k=2}^{r_i} \theta_{ijk}$ can be calculated from other parameters. For convenience, we define the parameter vector as follows:

$$\theta_{ij} = (\theta_{ij2}, \theta_{ij3}, \ldots, \theta_{ijr_i}), \quad (i = 1, 2, \ldots, n; \quad j = 1, 2, \ldots, q_i).$$

Given the local distribution functions above, we still require two assumptions to make the calculation of the posterior $p(\theta_s|D, S^h)$ close:

(1) There is no missing data in sample D, or D is complete;
(2) Parameter vectors are mutually independent, viz. $p(\theta_s|S^h) = \prod_{i=1}^{n} \prod_{j=1}^{q_i} p(\theta_{ij}|S^h)$. This is called parameter independence.

Under the above assumptions, for a given random sample D, parameters are independent:

$$p(\boldsymbol{\theta}_s|D, S^h) = \prod_{i=1}^{n} \prod_{j=1}^{q_i} p(\boldsymbol{\theta}_{ij}|D, S^h). \tag{4.37}$$

Then we can update each parameter vector θ_{ij} independently. Suppose each parameter θ_{ij} has the prior distribution of Dirichlet distribution $\mathrm{Dir}(\theta_{ij}|\alpha_{ij1}, \alpha_{ij2}, \ldots, \alpha_{ijr_i})$, we get the following posterior distribution:

$$p(\boldsymbol{\theta}_{ij}|D, S^h) = \mathrm{Dir}(\theta_{ij}|\alpha_{ij1} + N_{ij1}, \quad \alpha_{ij2} + N_{ij2}, \ldots, \alpha_{ijr_i} + N_{ijr_i}), \tag{4.38}$$

where N_{ijk} is the number of cases in D that satisfy $X_i = x_i^k$ and $\boldsymbol{Pa}_i = \boldsymbol{pa}_i^j$.

Now we can make an interesting prediction by seeking the mean of possible $\boldsymbol{\theta}_s$. For example, for the $N + 1$th case,

$$p(X_{N+1}|D, S^h) = \underset{p(\theta_s|D,S^h)}{E} \left(\prod_{i=1}^{r_i} \theta_{ijk} \right).$$

According to the parameter independence given D, we can calculate the expectation as follows:

$$p(x_{N+1}|D, S^h) = \int \prod_{i=1}^{n} \theta_{ijk}\, p(\boldsymbol{\theta}_s|D, S^h)\mathrm{d}\boldsymbol{\theta}$$

$$= \prod_{i=1}^{n} \int \theta_{ijk}\, p(\boldsymbol{\theta}_{ij}|D, S^h)\mathrm{d}\boldsymbol{\theta}_{ij},$$

and finally get

$$p(x_{N+1}|D, S^h) = \prod_{i=1}^{n} \frac{\alpha_{ijk} + N_{ijk}}{\alpha_{ij} + N_{ij}}, \tag{4.39}$$

where $\alpha_{ij} = \sum_{k=1}^{r_i} \alpha_{ijk}$ and $N_{ij} = \sum_{k=1}^{r_i} N_{ijk}$. Because unrestricted multinomial distribution belongs to the exponential family, the above computation is rather easy.

A Bayesian network with respect to variables X represents the joint distribution of X. So, no matter whether a Bayesian network is constructed from prior knowledge, or data, or integration of them, in principle, it can be used to deduce any interested probability. Yet, the precise or even approximately precise reasoning on a Bayesian network with discrete variables is NP hard. The current solution is to simplify computation based on some conditional independence, to construct a simple network topology for some specific reasoning problem, or to simplify the network structure at the cost of less precision loss. Even though it often requires considerable computation to construct a Bayesian network, for some problems, such as naïve Bayesian classification, using conditional independence can largely reduce computation without loss of much precision.

When sample data are incomplete, except for some special cases, we need to borrow an approximation method, such as Monte Carlo method, Gaussian approximation, EM algorithm to find maximum likelihood (ML) or maximum *a posteriori* (MAP), and so on. Although these algorithms are mature, the computational cost is large.

4.5.3 *Structure of Learning the Bayesian Network*

When the structure of a Bayesian network is undetermined, it is possible to learn both the network structure and the probabilities from data. Because in data mining, there are huge amount of data, and it is hard to tell the relation among variables, the structure learning problem is practically meaningful.

The network structure that represents the physical joint probability of X is improvable. According to Bayesian approach, we define a discrete variable to represent the uncertainty of network structure. The states of the variable correspond to all possible network structure hypotheses S^h. We set its prior as $p(S^h)$. For a given random sample D, which comes from the physical distribution of X, we calculate the posterior probability $p(S^h|D)$ and $p(\theta_S|D, S^h)$, where θ_S is a parameter vector. Then we use these posteriors to calculate the interested expectations.

The computation of $p(\theta_S|D, S^h)$ is similar to what we have illustrated in the previous section. The computation of $p(S^h|D)$ is theoretically easy. According to Bayesian theorem, we have

$$p(S^h|D) = p(S^h, D)/p(D) = p(S^h)p(D|S^h)/p(D), \qquad (4.40)$$

where $p(D)$ is a structure-independent normalizing constant and $p(D|S^h)$ is the marginal likelihood. To determine the posterior of the network structure, we need to only calculate marginal likelihood for each possible structure.

Under the precondition of unrestricted multinomial distribution, parameter independence, Dirichlet prior, and complete data, the parameter vector θ_{ij} can be updated independently. The marginal likelihood of data is exactly the multiplication of marginal likelihoods of each $i-j$ pair:

$$p(D|S^h) = \prod_{i=1}^{n} \prod_{j=1}^{q_i} \frac{\Gamma(\alpha_{ij})}{\Gamma(\alpha_{ij} + N_{ij})} \cdot \prod_{k=1}^{r_i} \frac{\Gamma(\alpha_{ijk} + N_{ijk})}{\Gamma(\alpha_{ijk})}. \qquad (4.41)$$

This formula was originally proposed by Cooper and Herskovits in 1992.

In common cases, the number of possible Bayesian networks with n variables is larger than exponential in n. It is intractable to exclude these hypotheses. Two approaches can be used to handle this problem, namely model selection and selective model averaging. The former approach is to select a "good" model from all the possible models (structure hypotheses) and use it as the correct model. The latter approach is to select a reasonable number of "good" models from all the possible models and pretend that these models are exhaustive. The questions are as follows: how to decide whether a model is "good" or not? How to search "good" models? Can a precise result can be obtained when these approaches are applied to Bayesian structure? There are some different definitions and corresponding computational methods about a "good" model. The last two questions are hardly capable of being answered theoretically. Some research work had demonstrated that using greedy algorithm to select a single good model often leads to precise prediction (Chickering and Heckerman, 1996). Applying the Monte Carlo method to perform selective model averaging is sometime effective as well. It may even result in better prediction. These results are somewhat largely responsible for the great deal of recent interest in learning with Bayesian network.

In 1995, Heckerman pointed out that under the precondition of parameter independence, parameter modularity, likelihood equivalence, and so on, the methods for learning Bayesian non-casual network can be applied to learning the casual network. In 1997, he suggested that under casual Markov condition, the casual relationship could be deduced from conditional independence and conditional correlation (Heckerman, 1997). This makes it possible for the corresponding effect to be predicted when interference is seen.

Below is a case study in which Heckerman *et al.* used Bayesian network to perform data mining and knowledge discovery. The data came from 10,318 Wisconsin high school seniors. Each student was described by the following variables and corresponding states

- Sex (SEX): male, female;
- Socioeconomic status (SES): low, lower middle, upper middle, high;
- Intelligence quotient (IQ): low, lower middle, upper middle, high;
- Parental encouragement (PE): low, high;
- College plans (CP): yes, no.

Our goal here is to discover the factors that affect the intention of high school seniors to attend college or to understand the possibly causal relationships among these variables. Data are described by the sufficient statistics in Table 4.3. In this

Table 4.3. Sufficient statistics

(Male)	4	349	13	64	9	207	33	72	12	126	38	54	10	67	49	43
	2	232	27	84	7	201	64	95	12	115	93	92	17	79	119	59
	8	166	47	91	6	120	74	110	17	92	148	100	6	42	198	73
	4	48	39	57	5	47	132	90	9	41	224	65	8	17	414	54
(Female)	5	454	9	44	5	312	14	47	8	216	20	35	13	96	28	24
	11	285	29	61	19	236	47	88	12	164	62	85	15	113	72	50
	7	163	36	72	13	193	75	90	12	174	91	100	20	81	142	77
	6	50	36	58	5	70	110	76	12	48	230	81	13	49	360	98

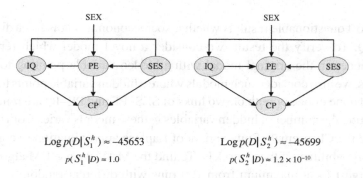

Fig. 4.1. Most likely network structures with no hidden variables

table, each entry represents a statistic of a state which cycles through all possible configurations. For example, the first entry indicates that the statistic for the configuration (SEX = male, SES = low, IQ = low, PE = low, CP = yes) is 4; the second entry states that the statistic for the configuration (SEX = male, SES = low, IQ = low, PE = low, CP = no) is 349. In the cycling of configuration of variables in the table, the last variable (CP) varies most quickly, and then PE, IQ, SES, and SEX vary more slowly. Thus, the upper four lines are the statistics for male students and the lower four lines are that for female students.

When analyzing data, we assume that there are no hidden variables. To generate priors for network parameters, we utilize an equivalent sample size of five and a prior network where $p(X|S_c^h)$ is uniform. Except that we exclude the structure where SEX and/or SES have parents and/or CP has children, we assume that all network structures are equally likely. Because the data set is complete, we use formulas (4.40) and (4.41) to calculate the posterior of the network structure. After searching all network structures exhaustively, we find the two most likely networks which are shown in Figure 4.1. Note that the posterior probabilities of the two most likely network structures are very close. If we adopt casual Markov assumption and assume that there are no hidden variables, the arcs in the two graphs can all be interpreted casually. Some of these results, such as the influence of socioeconomic status and IQ on the college plan, are not surprising. Some other results are very interesting: from both graphs, we can see that the influence of Sex on the College Plan is conveyed by the influence of Parental Encouragement. Besides, the only difference between the two graphs is the direction of the arc between PE and IQ. Two different casual relationships are seen, both of which seem reasonable. The network on the right in the below figure was in 1993 with a non-Bayesian method.

The most questionable result is whether socioeconomic status has a direct influence on IQ. To verify the result, we consider a novel model which replaces the direct influence in the original model with a hidden variable pointing to SES and IQ. Besides, we also consider such models where a hidden variable points to SES, IQ, and PE and none or one or both of two links of SES–PE and PE–IQ are removed. For each structure, the number of hidden variables in these models varies from two to six.

We use the Cheeseman–Stutz variant of Laplace approximation to compute the posterior probabilities of these models. To find the MAP, we use EM algorithm and take the largest local maximum from 100 runs with different random initials. The model with the highest MAP is shown in Figure 4.2. This model is 2×10^{10} times more likely than the best model containing no hidden variables about. Another most likely model contains a hidden variable and has an additional arc from the hidden variable to PE. This model is only 5×10^{-9} times less likely than the best model. Suppose that no reasonable models are ignored, strong evidence suggests that there is a hidden variable influencing the SES and IQ. An examination of the probabilities

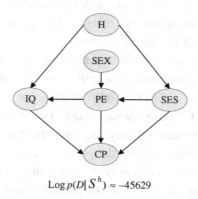

$$\text{Log}\, p(D|\, S^h) \approx -45629$$

Fig. 4.2.   The *a posteriori* most likely network structure with a hidden variable

in Figure 4.2 suggests that the hidden variable corresponds to some concept like "parent quality".

Using Bayesian method to learn the structure and probabilities of Bayesian network from prior information and sample information so as to construct a whole Bayesian network opens an avenue for applying Bayesian network to data mining and knowledge discovery. Compared with other data mining methods, such as rule-based method, decision tree, and artificial neural network, Bayesian network has the following characteristics:

(1) It can integrate prior and posterior information, so as to avoid subjective bias when using merely prior information, to avoid the large blind searching and computation when sample is lacking, and to avoid the influence from noise when using only posterior information. As long as the prior is determined properly, we can perform effective learning, especially when the sample is difficult or costly to gain.
(2) It can handle an incomplete data set.
(3) It can explore casual relations in data.
(4) There are mature and effective algorithms. Although probabilistic reasoning is NP hard for any arbitrary Bayesian network, in many practical problems, these operations can be either simplified by adding some constrains or solved by some approximation methods.

Yet, the computation of Bayesian network is huge. The Bayesian network seems less efficient than some other methods if a problem is also be resolved by other efficient approaches. Although there are some methods for prior determination, which is extremely important when a sample is hard to get, in practice, to find a reasonable prior involving many variables is still a difficult problem. Besides, a Bayesian network requires many assumptions as precondition. There are no ready rules to judge whether a practical problem satisfies the assumptions or not. These are problems that deserve further study. Still, it can be predicted that in data mining and knowledge discovery, especially in data mining with probabilistic statistical features, the Bayesian network will become a powerful tool.

4.6 Bayesian Latent Semantic Model

With the prevalence of Internet, Web information is increasing in an exponential manner. It has been a research focus of Web information processing as to how to organize the information reasonably so as to find the expected target in massive Web data, and how to effectively analyze the information so as to mine new and latently useful patterns in the massive Web data. The classification of Web information is an effective approach for improving search effectiveness and efficiency. For example, when searching with a Web search engine, if the class information of the query is available, the searching sphere will be limited and recall will be improved. Meanwhile, classification can provide good organization of information so as to help the user browse and filter information. Many big websites adopt this kind of information organization. For example, Yahoo maintains its Web catalog structure manually; Google uses some sorting mechanism to let the most user-related pages rank ahead, so as to make users' browse convenient. Deerwester *et al.* take the advantage of linear algebra and perform information filtering and latent semantic index (LSI) via singular value decomposition (SVD) (Deerwester *et al.* 1990). They project the high-dimensional representation of documents in vector space model (VSM) to a low-dimensional latent semantic space (LSS). This approach on the one hand reduces the scale of the problem and on the other hand, to some extent, avoids the over-sparse data. It gains preferable effects in many applications including language modeling, video retrieval, and protein database.

Clustering is one of main approaches in text mining. Its primary effects include the following: (a) By clustering search results, a website can provide users the required Web pages in terms of classes, so that users can quickly locate their expected targets, (b) generating the catalog automatically, (c) analyzing the commonness in Web pages by clustering them. The typical clustering algorithm is K-means clustering. Besides, some new clustering algorithms, such as self-organizing map (SOM), clustering with neural networks, and probability-based hierarchical Bayesian clustering (HBC), are also under intensive study and have many applications. Yet, most clustering algorithms are unsupervised algorithms, which search the solution space somewhat blindly. Thus, the clustering results often lack semantic characteristics. Meanwhile, in high-dimensional cases, selecting a proper distance metric becomes very difficult.

Web classification is one kind of supervised learning. By analyzing training data, classifiers can predict the class labels for unseen Web pages. Currently, there are many effective algorithms to classify Web pages, such as naïve Bayesian method and SVM. It is a pity that obtaining a large amount of classified training samples, which are necessary for training highly precise classifiers, is very costly. Besides, in practice, different classification architectures are often inconsistent. This makes daily maintaining of the Web catalog difficult. Kamal Nigam *et al.* proposed a method that can utilize documents with class labels and those without class labels to train a classifier. It only requires a small amount of labeled training samples, and one can learn a Bayesian classifier by integrating knowledge in the unlabeled samples (Nigam *et al.*, 1998).

Our basic idea for solving this problem is as follows. If some Web pages $D = \{d_1, d_2, \ldots, d_n\}$ consist of a description of some latent class variables $Z = \{z_1, z_2, \ldots, z_k\}$, first, by introducing Bayesian latent semantic model, we assign documents containing latent class variables to the corresponding class; then we utilize naïve Bayesian model to classify the documents containing no latent class variables with the knowledge in the previous step. According to the characteristics of these two steps, we define two likelihood functions and use the EM algorithm to find the local optimal solution with the maximum likelihood. This approach on the one hand avoids blind search in the solution space like unsupervised learning; on the other hand, it requires only some class variables but not a large amount of labeled training samples. It will release website managers from fussy training document labeling and improve the efficiency of Web page automatic classification. To distinguish from supervised learning and unsupervised learning, this approach is named semi-supervised learning.

The basic idea of latent semantic analysis (LSA) is to project the documents in a high-dimensional VSM to a low-dimensional latent semantic space. This projection is performed via singular value decomposition (SVD) on entry/document matrix $N_{m \times n}$. Concretely, according to linear algebra, any matrix Nm^*n can be decomposed as follows:

$$N = U \sum V^T, \tag{4.42}$$

where U, V are orthogonal matrixes ($UU^T = VV^T = I$); $\sum = \mathrm{diag}(a_1, a_2, \ldots, a_k, \ldots, a_v)$ ($a_1, a_2, \ldots, a_v$ are singular values) is a diagonal matrix. In latent semantic analysis, the approximation is gained by keeping k biggest singular values and setting others to 0:

$$\tilde{N} = U \widetilde{\sum} V^T \approx U \sum V^T = N. \tag{4.43}$$

Because the similarity between two documents can be represented with $NN^T \approx \tilde{N}\tilde{N}^T = U \widetilde{\sum}^2 U^T$, the coordinate of a document in the latent semantic space can be approximated by $U \widetilde{\sum}$. After projecting the representation of a document from high-dimensional space to low-dimensional semantic space, the sparsity of data, which exists in high-dimensional space, does not exist any more in the low-dimensional latent semantic space. This also indicates that even if there is no common factor between the two documents in the high-dimensional space, we may still find meaningful connections between them in the low-dimensional semantic space.

After the SVD and projecting documents from a high-dimensional space to a low-dimensional latent semantic space, the scale of the problem is effectively reduced. LSA has been successfully applied to many fields, including information filtering, text indexing, and video retrieval. Yet, SVD is sensitive to variation of data and seems stiff when prior information is lacking. These shortcomings limit its application.

According to our experiences, the description of any problem is developed centering on some theme. There are relative obvious boundaries between different themes. Because of differences in personal favors and interests, people's concerns on different themes vary. There is prior knowledge in different themes. Accordingly, we proposed the Bayesian latent semantic model for document generation.

Let document set be $D = \{d_1, d_2, \ldots, d_n\}$, and word set be $W = \{w_1, w_2, \ldots, w_m\}$. The generation model for document $d \in D$ can be expressed as follows:

(1) Choose document d at the probability of $P(d)$;
(2) Choose a latent theme z, which has the prior knowledge $p(z|\theta)$;
(3) Denote the probability that theme z contains document d by $p(z|d, \theta)$;
(4) Denote the probability of word $w \in W$ under the theme z by $p(w|z, \theta)$.

After this process, we get the observed pair (d, w). The latent theme z is omitted, and joint probability model is generated as follows:

$$p(d, w) = p(d)p(w|d), \tag{4.44}$$

$$p(w|d) = \sum_{z \in Z} p(w|z, \theta)p(z|d, \theta). \tag{4.45}$$

This model is a hybrid probabilistic model under the following independence assumptions:

(1) The generation of each observed pair (d, w) is relatively independent, and they are related via latent themes.
(2) The generation of word w is independent of any concrete document d. It only depends on latent theme variable z.

Formula (4.45) indicates that in some document d, the distribution of word w is the convex combination of latent themes. The weight of a theme in the combination is the probability at which document d belongs to the theme. Figure 4.3 illustrates the relationships between factors in the model.

According to Bayesian formula, we substitute Formula (4.45) into Formula (4.44) and get

$$p(d, w) = \sum_{z \in Z} p(z|\theta)p(w|z, \theta)p(d|z, \theta). \tag{4.46}$$

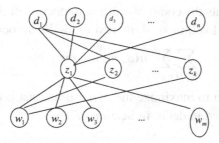

Fig. 4.3. Bayesian latent semantic model

Compared with LSA, Bayesian latent semantic model has a firm statistical foundation and avoids the data sensibility in LSA. It also utilizes prior information of latent theme variables to avoid being over stiff like the SVD. In the Bayesian latent semantic model, formula (4.42) can be rewritten as follows:

$$U = \{p(d_i|z_k)\}_{n\times k},$$

$$V = \{p(w_i|z_k)\}_{m\times k},$$

$$\tilde{\Sigma} = \mathrm{diag}(p(z_k), p(z_k), \ldots, p(z_k)).$$

So it has same representation form as that of SVD.

In LSA, the criterion for parameter selection is minimum least square loss. From the viewpoint of Bayesian learning, in our model, we have two applicable criteria: maximum *a posteriori* (MAP) and maximum likelihood (ML).

MAP estimation is applied to find the proper latent theme variable under the condition of document set D and word set W:

$$P(Z|D, W) = \prod_{z\in Z}\prod_{d\in D}\prod_{w\in W} p(z|d, w). \tag{4.47}$$

According to Bayesian formula, we have

$$p(z|d, w) = \frac{p(z)p(w|z)p(d|z)}{\sum_{z\in Z} p(z)p(w|z)p(d|z)}. \tag{4.48}$$

ML estimation is used to find a proper value of the following expression:

$$\prod_{d\in D}\prod_{w\in W} p(d, w)^{n(d,w)}, \tag{4.49}$$

where $n(d, w)$ represents the count of word w in document d. In practice, we often take a logarithm of the likelihood, shortened to log-likelihood:

$$\sum_{d \in D} \sum_{w \in W} n(d, w) \log p(d, w). \tag{4.50}$$

A general approach to maximize the two estimations is expectation maximum (EM), which is discussed in detail in Section 4.7.

4.7 Semi-Supervised Text Mining Algorithms

4.7.1 *Web Page Clustering*

Presently there are many algorithms for text classification, and they can achieve satisfactory precision and recall. Yet, the cost for obtaining labeled training documents is very high. Nigam *et al.* proposed an approach in which they used mix corpus including labeled and unlabeled documents to train a classifier and gained good classification results, but they still needed a certain number of labeled documents (Nigam *et al.* 1998). Web clustering merges related Web pages into one cluster with some similarity criterion. When dealing with high-dimensional and massive data, conventional clustering methods cannot achieve satisfactory effectiveness and efficiency. The reason is, on the one hand, unsupervised search in solution space is to some extent blind; on the other hand, common similarity metric, e.g., Euclidean distance, does not work well in high-dimensional space and it is hard to find proper similarity metric in this situation. Considering the characters of supervised learning and unsupervised learning, we proposed a semi-supervised learning algorithm. Under the framework of Bayesian latent semantic model, we can classify documents into different classes with some user-provided latent class variables. In this process, no labeled training documents are required.

The general model is described as follows: given a document set $D = \{d_1, d_2, \ldots, d_n\}$ and its word set $W = \{w_1, w_2, \ldots, w_m\}$, and a group of class variable $Z = \{z_1, z_2, \ldots, z_k\}$ with its prior information $\theta = \{\theta_1, \theta_2, \ldots, \theta_k\}$, try to seek a division $D_j (j \in (1, \ldots, k))$ of D, so that

$$\bigcup_{j=1}^{k} D_j = D, \quad D_i \cap D_j = \phi \ (i \neq j).$$

First, we divide D into two sets: $D = D_L \cup D_U$, where

$$D_L = \{d | \exists j, z_j \in d, j \in [1 \ldots k]\},$$

$$D_U = \{d | \forall j, z_j \notin d, j \in [1 \ldots k]\}.$$

In our algorithm, the classification process includes two stages

Stage 1. Utilize Bayesian latent semantic model with the parameters estimated based on EM algorithm to label the documents in D_L:

$$l(d) = z_j = \max_i \{p(d|z_i)\}. \tag{4.51}$$

Stage 2. Train a naïve Bayesian classifier with the labeled documents in D_L, and label documents in D_U with this classifier. Then, update the parameters of Bayesian latent semantic models with the EM algorithm.

4.7.2 Label Documents with Latent Classification Themes

Ideally, any document will not contain more than one latent class theme. In this case, we can easily label a document with its latent theme. In practice, however, the ideal status is hard to achieve. On the one hand, it is difficult to find such a latent theme; on the other hand, there may be multiple themes in one document. For example, a document labeled with "economics" may contain words of other themes, e.g., "politics" and/or "culture". We handle these cases by labeling them with the most related theme. Under ML criterion, after some rounds of EM iterations, we finally determine the theme of the test document according to Formula (4.51).

EM algorithm is one of the primary parameter estimation approaches for sparse data. It performs E step and M step alternately so as to find the most likely result. The general process of EM algorithm is described below.

(1) **E step:** calculate expectation based on the current parameters;
(2) **M step:** find the proper parameter with maximum likelihood based on the expectation in E step;
(3) Compute the likelihood with the renewed parameters. If the likelihood exceeds the predefined threshold or the number of iterations exceeds the predefined value, stop. Otherwise, go to Step (1).

In our algorithm, we adopt the following two steps to perform the iteration:

(1) In E step, we obtain the expectation via the following Bayesian formula:

$$P(z|d, w) = \frac{p(z)p(d|z)p(w|z)}{\sum_{z'} p(z')p(d|z')p(w|z')}. \tag{4.52}$$

In terms of probabilistic semantics, the formula explains the probability of word w in document d with latent theme variable z.

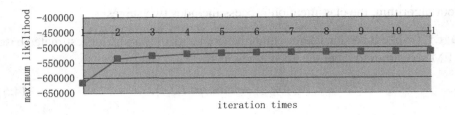

Fig. 4.4.   Relationship of iteration times and maximum likelihood

(2) In *M* step, we use the expectation from the above step to estimate the density of parameters:

$$p(w|z) = \frac{\sum_d n(d, w) p(z|d, w)}{\sum_{d, w'} n(d, w') p(z|d, w')}, \tag{4.53a}$$

$$p(d|z) = \frac{\sum_w n(d, w) p(z|d, w)}{\sum_{d', w} n(d', w) p(z|d', w)}, \tag{4.53b}$$

$$p(z) = \frac{\sum_{d, w} n(d, w) p(z|d, w)}{\sum_{d, w} n(d, w)}. \tag{4.53c}$$

Compared with SVD in LSA, EM algorithm has linear convergence time. It is simple and easy to implement, and it results in local optimal of likelihood function. Figure 4.4 shows the relation between iteration times and the corresponding maximum likelihood in our experiment.

4.7.3 *Learning Labeled and Unlabeled Data Based on Naïve Bayesian Model*

Conventional classification methods usually learn classifiers based on labeled training samples to classify unlabeled data. Yet, obtaining a large amount of labeled training samples is very costly and fussy. Kamal Nigam *et al.*'s research indicated that unlabeled data also contain useful information for learning classifiers. Accordingly, we use naïve Bayesian model as classifier and label the unlabeled training samples with a special non-label status; then, we estimate these labels with EM algorithm.

Here, we present the general description of text classification with a naïve Bayesian classifier: given the training document set $D = \{d_1, d_2, \ldots, d_n\}$ and its word set $W = \{w_1, w_2, \ldots, w_m\}$, each training document is represented as an $m + 1$ dimensional vector $d_i = \langle w_1, w_2, \ldots, w_m, c_i \rangle$, where $c_i \in C = \{c_1, c_2, \ldots, c_k\}$ is a class variable. The classification task is to predict the class of unseen document

$d = \langle w_1, w_2, \ldots, w_m \rangle$:

$$c = \max_{j \in 1, \ldots, k} \{ p(c_j | d, \theta),$$

where θ is the parameter of model.

To calculate the above expression, we expend the factor in the expression and get

$$p(d | c_j, \theta) = p(|d|) \prod_{k=1}^{|d|} p(w_k | c_j; \theta; w_q, q < k). \tag{4.54}$$

When computing Formula (4.54) with the naïve Bayesian model, we need to introduce the following independence assumptions:

(1) The generation of words in documents is independent of the content. That is to say, same words at different position of a document are independent.
(2) Words in a document are independent of the class of the documents.

Based on the above independence assumption and Bayesian formula, Equation (4.54) can be rewritten as

$$p(c_j | d, \theta) = \frac{p(c_j | \theta) p(d | c_j, \theta)}{p(d | \theta)}$$

$$= \frac{p(c_j | \theta) \prod_{r=1}^{m} p(w_r | c_j, \theta)}{\sum_{i=1}^{k} p(c_i | \theta) \prod_{r=1}^{m} p(w_r | c_i, \theta)}. \tag{4.55}$$

The learning task learns parameters of the model from prior information in training data. Here, we adopt multinomial distribution and Dirichlet conjugate distribution:

$$\theta_{c_j} = p(c_j | \theta) = \frac{\sum_{i=1}^{|D|} I(c(d_i) = c_j)}{|D|}, \tag{4.56a}$$

$$\theta_{w_t | c_j} = p(w_t | c_j, \theta) = \frac{\alpha_{jt} + \sum_{i=1}^{|D|} n(d_i, w_t) I(c(d_i) = c_j)}{\alpha_{j0} + \sum_{k=1}^{m} \sum_{i=1}^{|D|} n(d_i, w_k) I(c(d_i) = c_j)}, \tag{4.56b}$$

where $\alpha_{j0} = \sum_{i=1}^{k} \alpha_{ji}$ is the super-parameter of model; $c(\cdot)$ is the class labeling function $I(a = b)$ and is a characteristic function (if $a = b$, then $I(a = b) = 1$; otherwise $I(a = b) = 0$).

Although the applicable condition for naïve Bayesian model is somewhat harsh, numerous experiments demonstrate that even when independence assumption is unsatisfied, naïve Bayesian model can still work robustly. It has been one of the most popular methods for text classification.

Below, we will classify unlabeled documents according to MAP criterion based on the knowledge in these unlabeled documents.

Consider the entire sample set $D = D_L \cup D_U$, where D_L is the set of documents that has been labeled in the first stage. Assume that the generation of all samples in D is mutually independent; then, the following equation holds:

$$p(D|\theta) = \prod_{d_i \in D_U} \sum_{j=1}^{|C|} p(c_j|\theta)p(d_i|c_j, \theta) \cdot \prod_{d_i \in D_L} p(c(d_i)|\theta)p(d_i|c(d_i), \theta). \quad (4.57)$$

In the above equation, unlabeled documents are regarded as a mix model. Our learning task is to gain the maximum estimation of model parameter θ with the sample set D, and according to Bayesian theorem, we have

$$p(\theta|D) = \frac{p(\theta)p(D|\theta)}{P(D)}. \quad (4.58)$$

For a fixed sample set, $p(\theta)$ and $p(D)$ are both constants. Take logarithm on the both sides of Equation (4.58). We have

$$l(\theta|D) = \log p(\theta|D)$$

$$= \log \frac{p(\theta)}{p(D)} + \sum_{d_i \in D_U} \log \sum_{j=1}^{|C|} p(c_j|\theta)p(d_i|c_j, \theta) \quad (4.59)$$

$$+ \sum_{d_i \in D_L} \log p(c(d_i)|\theta)p(d_i|c(d_i), \theta).$$

To label the unlabeled documents, we need latent variables in LSA. Here we introduce k latent variables $Z = \{z_1, z_2, \ldots, z_k\}$, where each latent variable is an n-dimensional vector $z_i = \langle z_{i1}, z_{i2}, \ldots, z_{in} \rangle$, and if $c(d_j) = c_i$ then $z_{ij} = 1$, otherwise $z_{ij} = 0$. So, Equation (4.59) can be rewritten as follows:

$$l(\theta|D) = \log \frac{p(\theta)}{p(D)} + \sum_{i=1}^{|D|} \sum_{j=1}^{|C|} z_{ji} \log p(c_j|\theta)p(d_i|c_j, \theta_j). \quad (4.60)$$

In Equation (4.59), z_{ji} for labeled documents is known. The learning task maximizes model parameters and estimates z_{ji} of unlabeled documents.

Here, we still apply EM algorithm to gain knowledge about unlabeled documents. Yet, the process is somewhat different from the previous stage. In the kth iteration in E step, we will use the naïve Bayesian classifier to find the class label of unlabeled documents based on the current estimation of parameters:

$$p(d|c_j, \theta^k) = \frac{p(c_j|\theta^K) \prod_{r=1}^{m} p(w_r|c_j; \theta^k)}{\sum_{i=1}^{k} p(c_i|\theta^k) \prod_{r=1}^{m} p(w_r|c_i; \theta^k)}, \quad j \in 1, \ldots, k.$$

The class c_i corresponding to MAP is the expected label of the unlabeled documents

$$z_{id} = 1, \quad z_{jd} = 0 (j \neq i).$$

In step M, we maximize the estimation of the current parameters based on the expectation obtained from the just previous E step:

$$\theta_{c_j} = p(c_j|\theta) = \frac{\sum_{i=1}^{|D|} z_{ji}}{|D|}, \tag{4.61a}$$

$$\theta_{w_t|c_j} = p(w_t|c_j, \theta) = \frac{\alpha_j + \sum_{i=1}^{|D|} n(d_i, w_t) z_{ji}}{\alpha_0 + \sum_{k=1}^{m} \sum_{i=1}^{|D|} n(d_i, w_k) z_{ji}}. \tag{4.61b}$$

Organizing Web information into catalogs is an effective way to improve the effectiveness and efficiency of information retrieval. It can be achieved by learning classifiers with labeled documents and predicting the class label of a new Web page with the learnt classifiers. Yet, the acquisition of labeled training data is often costly and fussy. Web page clustering, which can cluster documents according to some similarity metric, can help to improve the retrieval. The problem is that the solution search of traditional clustering methods is somewhat blind and lacks semantic meaning. Thus, the effect of clustering is usually unsatisfactory. In this section, we proposed a semi-supervised learning algorithm. Under the framework of Bayesian latent semantic model, the new algorithm uses no labeled training data but only a few latent class/theme variables to assign documents to the corresponding class/theme. The algorithm includes two stages. In the first stage, it applies Bayesian latent semantic analysis to label documents which contain latent theme variable(s); in the second stage, it uses the naïve Bayesian model to label the documents without latent theme with the knowledge information in these documents. Experimental results demonstrate that the algorithm achieves high precision and recall. We will further investigate related issues, such as the influence of latent variable selection on the clustering result and how to implement word clustering under the framework of Bayesian latent semantic analysis.

Exercises

4.1 Explain conditional probability, prior probability, and posterior probability.
4.2 Describe Bayesian formula and explicate its significance thoroughly.

4.3 Describe some criteria for prior distribution selection.

4.4 What does "Naïve" mean in Naïve Bayesian classification? Briefly state the main ideas for improving Naïve Bayesian classification.

4.5 Describe the structure of Bayesian network and its construction and exemplify the usage of a Bayesian network.

4.6 What is semi-supervised text mining? Describe some applications of the Bayesian model in Web page clustering.

4.7 In recent years, with the development of Internet technology, Bayesian rules are widely applied. Exemplify two concrete applications of the Bayesian rules and explain the results.

Chapter 5

Probabilistic Graphic Models

Probabilistic graphical models are powerful tools for compactly representing complex probability distributions, efficiently computing (approximate) marginal and conditional distributions, and conveniently learning parameters and hyperparameters in probabilistic models. As a result, they have been widely used in applications that require some sort of automated probabilistic reasoning, such as computer vision and natural language processing, as a formal approach to deal with uncertainty.

5.1 Introduction

The probabilistic graphical models provide a description framework that allows us to abstract knowledge from different domains into a probabilistic model, summarizing the problems in various applications. In order to calculate the probability distribution of some variables in the probability model, knowledge representation and reasoning are separated (Koller and Friedman, 2009). The design of the model is mainly concerned with how to design a probabilistic model reflecting the nature of the problem according to the domain knowledge, while taking into account the feasibility of effective reasoning. The design of a reasoning algorithm only needs to care about how to reason effectively in a general or specific probability model. This degree of orthogonality greatly expands the application of probability model and speeds up its development.

Probabilistic graphical model is a kind of modeling and reasoning framework for describing the probabilistic model of this kind of representation. It provides the possibility to succinctly represent, effectively reason, and learn various types of probabilistic models. Historically, there have been examples of different disciplines using graphs to represent the correlation between variables in high-dimensional distributions. In the area of artificial intelligence, probabilistic methods began with early attempts to construct expert systems. By the end of the 1980s, due to a series of important advances in reasoning in Bayesian networks and general probabilistic graphical models, and the successful application of large-scale expert systems, the probabilistic method represented by the probabilistic graphical model was re-emphasized.

Nowadays, with the development of more than 20 years, the inference and learning of the probabilistic graph model have been widely used in machine learning, computer vision, natural language processing, speech recognition, expert system, user recommendation, social network mining, bioinformatics, and other research fields. It has become an indispensable part of artificial intelligence research. The research of probabilistic graphical model is in the ascendant, and the scope of application and research fever are continuing to grow.

Here, we introduce the important concepts of the probabilistic graphical model, containing inference, learning, and conditional independence. Most problems in artificial intelligence applications can be expressed formally as inferred problems in probabilistic models. In inference problems, the objective is to infer the value distribution of the variables in the set S of random variables of interest to us, and we use generative or discriminant models to model the problems and use general or discriminant models to model the problems. In the production model, we know the joint distribution of some interrelated variables including the set of interesting variables, and the observed values (or real values) of the observable variables. The objective is to compute the conditional probability of the target variables under the condition of the observable variables. In the variance model, we know the relationship between some interrelated variables including the set S of variables of interest and some other observable variables, that is, the conditional distribution under the condition of observable variables, and the observed values of observable variables. The objective is also to calculate the conditional probability of variables in the set S of variables of interest.

From a more general point of view, the learning problem can be seen as a special case of inferring the problem: the random variable we are interested in is the parameter or structure of the model. Therefore, the simple processing of the learning problem will be the same as the inferred problem. The difficulty, that is, the time and space complexity of the representation and calculation, is exponential with respect to the number of variables in the model, and we need an efficient learning algorithm that can handle the actual application data size.

Conditional independence is a core concept in the probabilistic graphical model, which runs through the representation, reasoning, and learning of the model.

The probabilistic graphical model combines probability theory with graph theory to provide a tool to visually represent the conditional independence between random variables. It is convenient for people to analyze the nature of the model, and at the same time make conclusions and algorithms related to graph theory that can be used to deal with the inference and learning problems of probabilistic models.

Consider the variable set A, B, C. If $P(A, B|C = c) = P(A|C = c) = P(B|C = c)$, $\forall c$ holds, we call the variable sets A and B as being independent of each other under condition C. At this time, it is easy to verify $P(A|B, C) = P(A|C)$, $P(B|A, C) = P(B|C)$. The conditional independence in the model is the basis for effective calculation of inferential and learning problems.

5.2 Graphic Theory

Graph theory is the study of graphs, which are mathematical structures used to model pairwise relations between objects. A graph in this context is made up of vertices, nodes, or points which are connected by edges, arcs, or lines. A graph may be undirected, meaning that there is no distinction between the two vertices associated with each edge, or its edges may be directed from one vertex to another.

In the most common sense of the term, a graph is an ordered pair $G = (V, E)$ comprising a set V of vertices or nodes or points together with a set E of edges or arcs or lines, which are two-element subsets of V. To avoid ambiguity, this type of graph may be described precisely as undirected and simple.

In computer science, graphs are used to represent networks of communication, data organization, computational devices, the flow of computation, etc. For instance, the link structure of a website can be represented by a directed graph, in which the vertices represent Web pages and directed edges represent links from one page to another. A similar approach can be taken to problems in social media, travel, biology, computer chip design, mapping the progression of neurodegenerative diseases, and many other fields. The development of algorithms to handle graphs is therefore of major interest in computer science. The transformation of graphs is often formalized and represented by graph rewrite systems. Complementary to graph transformation systems focusing on rule-based in-memory manipulation of graphs are graph databases geared toward transaction-safe and persistent storing and querying of graph-structured data.

There are different ways to store graphs in a computer system. The data structure used depends on both the graph structure and the algorithm used for manipulating the graph. Theoretically, one can distinguish between list and matrix structures, but in concrete applications the best structure is often a combination of both. List structures are often preferred for sparse graphs as they have smaller memory requirements. Matrix structures on the contrary provide faster access for some applications but can consume huge amounts of memory.

List structures include the incidence list, an array of pairs of vertices, and the adjacency list, which separately lists the neighbors of each vertex. Much like the incidence list, each vertex has a list of which vertices it is adjacent to.

Matrix structures include the incidence matrix, a matrix of 0's and 1's whose rows represent vertices and whose columns represent edges, and the adjacency matrix, in which both the rows and columns are indexed by vertices. In both cases, a 1 indicates two adjacent objects and a 0 indicates two non-adjacent objects. The Laplacian matrix is a modified form of the adjacency matrix that incorporates information about the degrees of the vertices and is useful in some calculations such as Kirchhoff's theorem on the number of spanning trees of a graph. The distance matrix, like the adjacency matrix, has both its rows and columns indexed by vertices, but rather than containing a 0 or a 1 in each cell it contains the length of a shortest path between two vertices.

5.3 Hidden Markov Model

Hidden Markov Model (HMM) is a statistical Markov model in which the system being modeled is assumed to be a Markov process with unobserved (i.e., hidden) states. It can be represented as the simplest dynamic Bayesian network. The mathematics behind the HMM were developed by Baum *et al.* (Baum and Petrie, 1966).

A basic HMM can be described as follows:

N = number of states

T = number of observations

$\theta_{i=1...N}$ = emission parameter for an observation associated with state i

$\phi_{i=1...N, j=1...N}$ = probability of transition from state i to state j

$\phi_{i=1...N}$ = N-dimensional vector, composed of $\phi_{i, j=1...N}$, the ith row of the

matrix $\phi_{i=1...N, j=1...N}$ (sum of it is 1)

$x_{i=1...T}$ = (Hidden) state at time t

$y_{i=1...T}$ = (Hidden) state at time t

$F(y|\theta)$ = probability distribution of an observation, parametrized on θ

$$x_{t=2...T} \sim \text{categorical } (\phi_{xt-1})$$

$$y_{t=1...T} \sim F(\theta_{xt}).$$

Note that in the above model, the prior distribution of the initial state x_1 is not specified. Typical learning models correspond to assuming a discrete uniform distribution over possible states.

In its discrete form, a hidden Markov process can be visualized as a generalization of the Urn problem with replacement (where each item from the urn is returned to the original urn before the next step). Consider this example: in a room that is not visible to an observer there is a genie. The room contains urns $X1, X2, X3, \ldots$ each of which contains a known mix of balls, each ball labeled $y1, y2, y3, \ldots$. The genie chooses an urn in that room and randomly draws a ball from that urn. It then puts the ball onto a conveyor belt, where the observer can observe the sequence of the balls but not the sequence of urns from which they were drawn. The genie has some procedure to choose urns; the choice of the urn for the nth ball depends only upon a random number and the choice of the urn for the $(n - 1)$th ball. The choice of urn does not directly depend on the urns chosen before this single previous urn; therefore, this is called a Markov process. It can be described by the upper part of Figure 5.1. The symbols in Figure 5.1 indicate the following:

X — states
y — possible observations
a — state transition probabilities
b — output probabilities

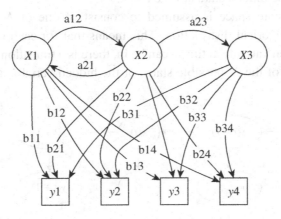

Fig. 5.1. Probabilistic parameters of a hidden Markov model

The Markov process itself cannot be observed, only the sequence of labeled balls; thus, this arrangement is called a "hidden Markov process". This is illustrated by the lower part of the diagram shown in Figure 5.1, where one can see that balls $y1$, $y2$, $y3$, and $y4$ can be drawn at each state. Even if the observer knows the composition of the urns and has just observed a sequence of three balls, e.g., $y1$, $y2$, and $y3$, on the conveyor belt, the observer still cannot be sure which urn (i.e., at which state) the genie has drawn the third ball from. However, the observer can work out other information, such as the likelihood that the third ball came from each of the urns.

Figure 5.2 shows the general architecture of an instantiated HMM. Each oval shape represents a random variable that can adopt any number of values. The random variable $x(t)$ is the hidden state at time t, ($x(t) \in \{x1, x2, x3\}$). The random variable $y(t)$ is the observation at time t (with $y(t) \in \{y1, y2, y3, y4\}$). The arrows in the diagram (often called a trellis diagram) denote conditional dependencies. From the diagram, it is clear that the conditional probability distribution of the hidden variable $x(t)$ at time t, given the values of the hidden variable x at all times, depends only on the value of the hidden variable $x(t-1)$; the values at time $t-2$ and before have no influence. This is called the Markov property. Similarly, the value of the observed variable $y(t)$ only depends on the value of the hidden variable $x(t)$ (both at time t).

In the standard type of hidden Markov model considered here, the state space of the hidden variables is discrete, while the observations themselves can either be discrete (typically generated from a categorical distribution) or continuous (typically from a Gaussian distribution). The parameters of a hidden Markov model are of two types, transition probabilities and emission probabilities (also known as output probabilities). The transition probabilities control the way the hidden state at time t is chosen given the hidden state at time $t-1$.

The hidden state space is assumed to consist of one of N possible values, modeled as a categorical distribution. This means that for each of the N possible states that a hidden variable at time t can be in, there is a transition probability from this state to each of the N possible states of the hidden variable at time $t+1$, for

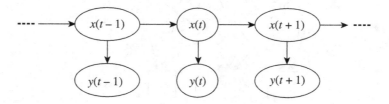

Fig. 5.2.   The general architecture of an instantiated HMM

a total of N^2 transition probabilities. Note that the set of transition probabilities for transitions from any given state must sum to 1. Thus, the $N \times N$ matrix of transition probabilities is a Markov matrix. Because any one transition probability can be determined once the others are known, there are a total of $N(N-1)$ transition parameters.

In addition, for each of the N possible states, there is a set of emission probabilities governing the distribution of the observed variable at a particular time given the state of the hidden variable at that time. The size of this set depends on the nature of the observed variable. For example, if the observed variable is discrete with M possible values, governed by a categorical distribution, there will be $M-1$ separate parameters, for a total of $N(M-1)$ emission parameters over all hidden states. On the contrary, if the observed variable is an M-dimensional vector distributed according to an arbitrary multivariate Gaussian distribution, there will be M parameters controlling the means and $\frac{M(M+1)}{2}$ parameters controlling the covariance matrix, for a total of $N\left(M + \frac{M(M+1)}{2}\right) = \frac{NM(M+3)}{2} = O(NM^2)$ emission parameters.

Figure 5.2 is a Markov Chain, in which probability of each event depends only on the state attained in the previous event. Based on this dependency, the joint probability distribution of all variables is as follows:

$$P(x_1, y_1, \ldots, x_n, y_n) = P(y_1)P(x_1|y_1) \prod_{i=1}^{n} P(y_1|y_{i-1})P(x_i|y_i). \tag{5.1}$$

In addition to structural information, the following three sets of parameters are required to determine a hidden Markov model:

(1) **State transition probability:** The probability that a model will be transferred between states, usually written as a matrix $A = [a_{ij}]_{N \times N}$, where

$$a_{ij} = P(y_{t+1} = s_j | y_t = s_i) \quad 1 \leq i \, j \leq N$$

indicates the probability that s_j is at the next time state if the state is s_i at any time t.

(2) **Output observation probability:** The model obtains the probability of each observation based on the current state, usually referred to as a matrix $B = [b_{ij}]_{N \times M}$, where

$$b_{ij} = P(x_t = o_j | y_t = s_i) \quad 1 \leq i \leq N \, 1 \leq j \leq M$$

indicates the probability that the observed value o_j is acquired in any state t, if the state is s_i.

(3) **Initial state probability:** The probability that the model will appear in each state at the initial moment, usually referred to as $\boldsymbol{\pi} = (\pi_1, \pi_2, \ldots, \pi_N)$, where

$$\pi_i = P(y_1 = s_i) \quad 1 \leq i \leq N$$

represents the probability that the initial state of the model is s_i.

By specifying the state space y, the observation space X, and the above three sets of parameters, it is possible to determine a hidden Markov model, usually referred to by parameters $\lambda = [\mathbf{A}, \mathbf{B}, \boldsymbol{\pi}]$.

In practical applications, people often pay attention to the three basic problems of the hidden Markov model:

(1) **Evaluation:** Given an HMM λ and an observation sequence $\mathbf{x}$, how to efficiently calculate the probability $P(\mathbf{x}|\lambda)$ of an observation sequence $\mathbf{x}$? — Forward algorithm, backward algorithm.
(2) **Decoding:** Given an HMM λ and an observation sequence $\mathbf{x}$, how to maximize $P(\mathbf{y}|\mathbf{x})$ and find the "most likely" state sequence $\mathbf{y}$? — Viterbi algorithm.
(3) **Learning (training):** Given several observation sequences $\mathbf{x}$ (the corresponding state sequence $\mathbf{y}$ may or may not be known), how to train the model parameter λ such that $P(\mathbf{x}|\lambda)$ is the largest Turn? — EM algorithm.

5.4 Conditional Random Field

The Conditional Random Field (CRF) is a typical discriminant model proposed by Lafferty *et al.* in 2001. It models the target sequence based on the observation sequence and focuses on solving the problem of serialized annotation. The conditional random field model has the advantages of both the discriminant model and the production model considering the transition probability between context markers to serialize. The form is characterized by global parameter optimization and decoding, which solves the label offset problem that is difficult to avoid by other discriminant models (such as the maximum entropy Markov model).

Suppose X is a random variable over data sequences to be labeled, and Y is a random variable over the corresponding label sequences. All components y_i of Y are assumed to range over a finite label alphabet $\mathcal{Y}$. For example, X might range over natural language sentences and Y might range over part-of-speech taggings of those sentences, with $\mathcal{Y}$ the set of possible part-of-speech tags. The random variables X and Y are jointly distributed, but in a discriminative framework we construct a conditional model $p(Y|X)$ from paired observation and label sequences and do not explicitly model the marginal $p(X)$.

Let $G = (V, E)$ be a graph such that $Y = (Y_v)_{v \in V}$, so that Y is indexed by the vertices of G. Then (X, Y) is a conditional random field in the case, when conditioned on X, the random variables Y_v obey the Markov property with respect to the graph: $p(Y_v|X, Y_w, w \neq v) = p(Y_v|X, Y_w, w \sim v)$, where $w \sim v$ means that w and v are neighbors in G.

CRF is mostly used in the field of natural language processing and image processing. In NLP, it is a probabilistic model for labeling and dividing sequence data. According to the definition of CRF, the relative sequence is the given observation sequence X and the output sequence Y is then passed. The conditional probability $p(Y|X)$ is defined to describe the model.

The output random variable of CRF is assumed to be an undirected graph model or a Markov random field, and the input random variable is not assumed to be a Markov random field. The graph model structure of CRF can theoretically be given arbitrarily, but we take it as common. It is a special conditional random field defined on a linear chain, called a linear chain conditional random field, which is shown in Figure 5.3.

A CRF is a random field globally conditioned on the observation X. G is a simple chain or line: $G = (V = \{1, 2, \ldots, m\}, E = \{(i, i+1)\})$. X may also have a natural graph structure. In general, it is not necessary to assume that X and Y have the same graphical structure, or even that X has any graphical structure at all. However, we will be most concerned with sequences $X = (X_1, X_2, \ldots, X_n)$ and $Y = (Y_1, Y_2, \ldots, Y_n)$.

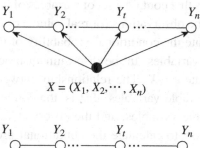

Fig. 5.3. Graph structure of a linear chain conditional random field

If the graph $G = (V, E)$ of Y is a tree, its cliques are the edges and vertices. The joint distribution over the label sequence Y given X has the form

$$p_\theta(y|x) = \frac{1}{Z} \exp \left(\sum_j \sum_{i=1}^{n-1} \lambda_j t_j(y_{i+1}, y_i, x, i) + \sum_k \sum_{i=1}^{n} \mu_k s_k(y_i, x, i) \right), \quad (5.2)$$

where $t_j(y_{i+1}, y_i, x, i)$ is a transfer eigenfunction defined at two adjacent mark positions i of the observed sequence used to characterize the relationship between the adjacent mark variables and the effect of the observed sequence on them. $s_k(y_i, x, i)$ is used to characterize the effect of an observation sequence on a marker variable, λ_j and μ_k are parameters, and Z is the canonical factor used to ensure that the probability of Equation (5.2) is correctly defined.

Conditional random field theories (CRFs) can be used in natural language processing tasks such as sequence tagging, data segmentation, and block analysis. It has been applied in Chinese natural language processing tasks such as Chinese word segmentation, Chinese name recognition, and ambiguity resolution, and it performs well.

5.5 Inference

The inference problem of the probabilistic graphical model is to use the joint probability distribution to answer the query problem in the case of known network structure and evidence. The goal is to infer the distribution of the values of the variables in the set X of random variables we are interested in, and we adopt a generative model or a discriminant model to model the problem and use a general or model-specific inference algorithm to calculate this distribution. In the generative model, we know some interconnected ones that contain a set of variables of interest. In the joint distribution of variables, and the observations (or real values) of the observable variables, the objective is to calculate the conditional probability of the target variable on the condition of observable variables. In the discriminant model, we know to include the set of variables of interest X. The relationship between some interconnected variables and other observable variables, that is, the conditional distribution under the condition of observable variables, and the observed values of observable variables. The objective is also to calculate the conditional probability of variables in the set X of variables of interest.

Some important algorithms used in probabilistic graphical model inference can be roughly divided into three categories:

(1) **Precise inference algorithm.** It can calculate the exact value of the edge distribution or conditional distribution of the query variable, but its computational

complexity increases exponentially with the tree width of the graph model, so the scope of application is limited.

(2) **Optimization-based inference algorithm.** The inference of the graph model is formalized into an optimization problem. By loosening the constraints of the optimization problem or adjusting the objective function of the optimization, the algorithm can obtain the approximate solution of the original problem at a lower time complexity. For most graph models that are difficult to reason accurately, it is not difficult to sample their variables.

(3) **Sampling-based inference algorithm.** Try to generate the sample of the obtained edge distribution or conditional distribution and use the empirical distribution of the sample to approximate the real distribution.

The inference in the general graph model is difficult. In terms of the complexity of reasoning in the worst case, we already know that we have a series of negative results: graph model exact reasoning is #P-complete; the approximate reasoning of the graph model relative error is NP-hard; the absolute error $\varepsilon \in (0, 1/2)$ graph model approximate reasoning has polynomial time complexity, but the evidence-based approximate reasoning is still NP-hard. However, the problems in practical applications often have good condition-independent structures, and thus the accurate inference and approximate inference algorithms of graph models bring many successful applications.

This section introduces the precise inference algorithm for the graph model. Section 5.6 introduces the approximate inference algorithm. The precise inference algorithm of the graph model is essentially a kind of dynamic programming algorithm which uses the factorization characteristic of joint distribution caused by conditional independence to compress the information transmitted between the variables of the graph model.

5.5.1 *Variable Elimination*

The variable elimination algorithm is the most intuitive and easily deduced precision inference algorithm, but it is the basis of other more advanced precision inference algorithms. Consider the joint distribution $P(A, B, C, D, E)$ defined by the Bayesian network; if we observe the variable $E = e$ and want to calculate the conditional probability $P(c|e)$ of the variable $C = c$, we can simply write

$$p(c|e) = \frac{1}{Z} \sum_{a,b,d} P(a, b, c, d, e), \tag{5.3}$$

where $Z = \sum_{a,b,d} P(a, b, c, d, e)$.

Utilizing the independence of the Bayesian network, the above summation can be reduced to

$$\sum_{a,b,d} P(a,b,c,d,e) = \sum_{a,b,d} P(a)P(b|a)P(c|b)P(d|b)P(e|c,d)$$

$$= \sum_{d}\left(P(e|c,d)\sum_{b}\left(P(c|b)P(d|b)\sum_{a}P(a)P(b|a)\right)\right).$$

(5.4)

In short, the variable elimination algorithm actually uses the multiplication–addition law and decomposes the product of multiple variables into the quadrature and summation of the partial variables. The disadvantages of the variable elimination algorithm are as follows: once the variable elimination can find the conditional distribution of the query variable, different queries will bring a lot of repeated calculations. In order to realize one calculation and multiple uses, the algorithm design needs to be performed more carefully. In order to ensure the correctness of the algorithm, it is necessary to ensure that all items related to the summation variable are within the summation symbol, which is the theoretical basis of the following two commonly used precision inference algorithms.

5.5.2 *Clique Tree*

In order to implement a more efficient algorithm for accurate reasoning, it is necessary to design a data structure that supports inference operations: clique tree. The clique tree is a tree structure with the following properties (Koller and Friedman, 2009):

(1) Each vertex of the cluster tree is a set of factors in the corresponding graph model.
(2) **Family retentivity:** Each factor in the original model belongs to at least one clique tree vertex.
(3) **Flow intersect:** If the variable X appears in the two vertices C_i and C_j of the clique tree, then X appears in each vertex between C_i and C_j. In the clique tree, the intersection of the variables of two adjacent vertices, $S_{ij} = C_i \cap C_j$, is called the cut set of two vertices.

Let Φ be a set of factors over X. A cluster tree over Φ that satisfies the running intersection property is called a clique tree (sometimes also called a junction tree or a join tree). In the case of a clique tree, the clusters are also called cliques.

From the same graph model, a variety of clique trees can be generated, and their inference costs are not the same, but finding the least cost of a clique tree is difficult. A better method is to find a good clique tree on the fully connected graph of the so-called "maximum elimination clique". Specify the order in which a variable is eliminated, and consider the clique generated when the variables are eliminated in turn. The largest clique generates a fully connected graph for the vertices, and the base of the cut set is used to weight the edges. The maximum weighted spanning tree of the fully connected graph is a better clique tree. This is because in the process of variable elimination, we only need to eliminate variables that do not appear in the cut set, so for a given set of vertices, the cut set contains more variables, and the computational cost is relatively small.

After the clique tree is generated, it is necessary to calculate the factor corresponding to the vertex of the clique tree. To do this, it is only necessary to traverse the set of the original model factor for each vertex. If the variable contained in the factor is a subset of the variables contained in the vertex of the cluster tree, then multiply it into the factor of the vertex. The set of factors corresponding to the clique tree is called the decomposable density because they are the result of the decomposition of the original probability distribution on the clique tree. With the clique tree and the decomposable density, you can execute the following exact reasoning algorithm.

1. Message passing

In the messaging algorithm, A passes a message to B if and only when node A receives a message from all neighbor nodes except neighbor node B. The message passing algorithm progresses as follows:

(1) Select a root node in the group tree and construct a single root tree from the root node.
(2) Recursively execute from the root node: If the child node of the node receives messages from all other neighbors, the child node passes the message to the node.
(3) Recursively execute from the root node: If the node receives a message from all neighbors except a certain child node, the node passes the message to the child node.

An abstract clique tree is shown in Figure 5.4 (Koller and Friedman, 2009). We can now specify a general variable elimination algorithm that can be implemented via message passing in a clique tree. Let message passing T be a clique tree with the cliques $C_1, \ldots, C_k$. We begin by multiplying the factors assigned to each clique, resulting in our initial potentials. We then use the clique tree data structure to pass

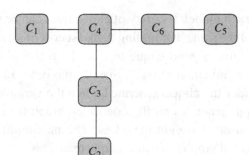

Fig. 5.4.   An abstract clique tree

messages between neighboring cliques, sending all messages toward the root clique. We describe the algorithm in abstract terms as follows:

Algorithm 5.1. Upward pass of variable elimination in clique tree.

Procedure CTree-SP-Upward (
Φ,   //Set of factors
T,   //Clique tree over Φ
α,   //Initial assignment of factors to cliques
Cr   //Some selected root clique
)
1. Initialize-Cliques
2. while C_r is not ready
3.   Let C_i be a ready clique
4. $\delta_{i \rightarrow pr(i)}(S_{i,pr(i)}) \leftarrow$ SP-Message$(i, p_r(i))$
5. $\beta r \leftarrow \psi\, r \cdot \Pi_{k \in NbCr}\delta_{k \rightarrow r}$
6. return βr

Procedure Initialize-Cliques (
)
1. for each clique C_i
2. $\psi_i(C_i) \leftarrow \Pi_{\phi j} : \alpha(\phi_j) = i\,\Phi j$
3.   end

Procedure SP-Message (
i,   //sending clique
j //receiving clique
)

1. $\psi(C_i) \leftarrow \psi_i \cdot \Pi_{k \in (Nbi-\{j\})} \delta_{k \rightarrow i}$
2. $\tau(S_{i,j}) \leftarrow \Sigma_{C_i - S_{i,j}} \psi(C_i)$
3. return $\tau(S_{i,j})$

2. Belief propagation

In the belief propagation algorithm, we attach a variable called belief to each node. At each step of the algorithm, each node simultaneously delivers a message to its neighbors. The content of the message is the current cut of the node. The belief is the edge distribution of variables. Each node updates its beliefs immediately after receiving messages from other nodes, multiplies its beliefs by the newly received message, and removes the last message received from the same node. If after the node receives the message of its neighbor node, its belief does not change any more, and the algorithm converges, it can be proved that for the belief propagation on the clique tree, after the message is transmitted twice between each pair of nodes, the algorithm will converge, and converge on the correct distribution (may need to be normalized).

The precise algorithm is shown in Algorithm 5.2.

Algorithm 5.2. Calibration using belief propagation in clique tree.

Procedure CTree-BU-Calibrate (

    Φ,   //Set of factors

    T //Clique tree over Φ

)

    1. Initialize-CTree
    2. **while** exists an uninformed clique in T
    3.   Select $(i - j) \in ET$
    4. BU-Message(i, j) $\frac{\sigma_{i \rightarrow j}}{\mu_{i,j}}$
    5. **return** $\{\beta_i\}$

Procedure Initialize-CTree (

)

    1. for each clique C_i
    2. $\beta_i \leftarrow \Pi_\phi : \alpha(\phi) = i \Phi$
    3. **for** each edge $(i - j) \in \varepsilon_T$
    4. $\mu_{i,j} \leftarrow 1$

Procedure BU-Message (

    i,   //sending clique

    j //receiving clique

)

1. $\sigma_{i \rightarrow j} \leftarrow \Sigma_{C_i - S_{i,j}} \beta i$
2.   //marginalize the clique over the sepset
3. $\beta_j \leftarrow \beta_j$
4. $\mu_{i,j} \leftarrow \sigma_{i \rightarrow j}$

Note that, as written, the message passing algorithm is underspecified: in line 3, we can select any pair of cliques C_i and C_j between which we will pass a message. Interestingly, we can make this choice arbitrarily, without damaging the correctness of the algorithm. For example, if C_i (for some reason) passes the same message to C_j a second time, the process of dividing out by the stored message reduces the message actually passed to 1, so that it has no influence. Furthermore, if C_i passes a message to C_j based on partial information, and then resends a more updated message later on, the effect is identical to simply sending the updated message once. Moreover, at convergence, regardless of the message passing steps used, we necessarily have a calibrated clique tree. This property follows from the fact that, in order for all message updates to have no effect, we need to have $\sigma_{i \rightarrow j} = \mu_{i,j} = \sigma_{j \rightarrow i}$ for all i, j, and so:

$$\sum_{C_i - S_{i,j}} \beta_i = \mu_{i,j} = \sum_{C_j - S_{i,j}} \beta_j.$$

Thus, at convergence, each pair of neighboring cliques i and j must agree on the variables in sepset, and the message $\mu_{i,j}$ is precisely the sepset marginal.

5.6 Approximate Inference

Precise inference methods usually require a large computational overhead, so approximate inference methods are more commonly used in real-world applications. The approximate inference methods are roughly divided into two categories: the first type is the sampling method, which uses the randomization method to complete the approximation; the second similarity uses the deterministic approximation to complete the approximation inference, and the typical representative is variational inference.

5.6.1 *Markov Chain Monte Carlo Methods*

Considering the stochastic process $\{X^{(1)}, \ldots, X^{(t)}\}$ on the random vector X state space, if the state transition matrix is properly selected and applied to X, the Markov chain can be constructed to make the distribution of $X^{(t)}$ converge to the posterior distribution. Therefore, this type of algorithm is called the MCMC (Markov Chain

Monte Carlo) algorithm (Neal, 1993). The MCMC algorithm determined by different state transition methods has different properties.

The Metropolis–Hastings (MH) algorithm is a Markov chain Monte Carlo method for obtaining a sequence of random samples from a probability distribution for which direct sampling is difficult. This sequence can be used to approximate the distribution (e.g., to generate a histogram) or to compute an integral. Metropolis–Hastings and other MCMC algorithms are generally used for sampling from multi-dimensional distributions, especially when the number of dimensions is high. Metropolis–Hastings algorithm thus is written as follows:

Algorithm 5.3 (Metropolis–Hastings (MH) Algorithm).

1. Initialize
2.   Pick an initial state x_0;
3.   Set $t = 0$;
4. Iterate
5.   Generate: randomly generate a candidate state x' according to $g(x'|x_t)$;
6.   Calculate: calculate the acceptance probability

$$A(x', x_t) = \min\left(1, \frac{P(x')\, g(x_t\,|\,x')}{P(x_t)\, g(x'\,|\,x_t)}\right)$$

7.   Accept or Reject:
8.   generate a uniform random number $u \in [0, 1]$);
9.   if $u \le A(x', x_t)$, accept the new state and set $x_{t+1} = x'$;
10.   if $u < A(x', x_t)$, reject the new state, and copy the old state forward
       $x_t + 1 = x_t$
11.   Increment: set $t = t + 1$.

Provided that the specified conditions are met, the empirical distribution of saved states $x_0, \ldots, x_T$ will approach $P(x)$. The number of iterations (T) required to effectively estimate $P(x)$ depends on the number of factors, including the relationship between $P(x)$ and the proposal distribution and the desired accuracy of estimation. For distribution on discrete state spaces, it has to be of the order of the autocorrelation time of the Markov process (Newman and Barkema, 1999).

It is important to notice that it is not clear, in a general problem, which distribution $g(x'|x)$ one should use or the number of iterations necessary for proper estimation; both are free parameters of the method which must be adjusted to the particular problem at hand.

Gibbs sampling can be seen as a special case of the Metropolis–Hastings algorithm. The Gibbs sampling algorithm assumes that for any variable X_i, we can sample from $p(x_i|x_{\bar{i}})$. Each step of the algorithm selects one variable in turn with other variables. The current value of the quantity is a condition, and its value is sampled from the conditional distribution of the variable.

The advantage of Gibbs sampling is that the algorithm is simple. The disadvantage is that only one variable can be updated at a time, which is less efficient. With improved blocked Gibbs pumping at each step, it is possible to simultaneously sample mutually independent variables. However, when sampling from $p(x_i|x_{\bar{i}})$ is difficult, Gibbs sampling is not applicable.

5.6.2 *Variational Inference*

Graph model variational inference is an approximate inference method based on the mathematical variational method. According to the conjugate duality of convex functions, the probabilistic inference problem of summing variables for joint probability distribution of graph model is transformed into the functional extreme

$$\ln p(\mathbf{x}|\Theta) = \sum_{i=1}^{N} \ln \left\{ \sum_{\mathbf{z}} p(x_i, \mathbf{z}|\Theta) \right\},$$

value problem of free distribution, and the upper/lower bounds of the objective function are calculated by the approximate solution of the functional extreme value.

The convex duality principle is the basis of the variational transformation of the graph model. For the convex function $f(x)$, by introducing the conjugate parameter λ and the conjugated dual function factory $f^*(\lambda)$, it is expressed as an optimization problem about conjugate parameter λ:

$$f(x) = \max_{\lambda}(\lambda^T x - f^*(\lambda)). \tag{5.5}$$

In 1994, Buntine proposed a plate notation for probabilistical graphical model (Buntine, 1994). A simple example is shown in Figure 5.5. N variables are dependent

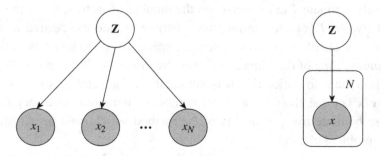

Fig. 5.5.   Illustration of plate notation

on other variables $\mathbf{z}$. In Figure 5.5, the probability density function of the joint distribution of all observed variables x is given as

$$p(x|\Theta) = \prod_{i=1}^{N} \sum_{\mathbf{z}} p(x_i, \mathbf{z}|\Theta). \tag{5.6}$$

The corresponding logarithmic likelihood function is

$$\ln p(\mathbf{x}|\Theta) = \sum_{i=1}^{N} \ln \left\{ \sum_{\mathbf{z}} p(x_i, \mathbf{z}|\Theta) \right\}, \tag{5.7}$$

where, $\mathbf{x} = \{x_1, x_2, \ldots, x_N\}$, Θ is distributable parameters of $\mathbf{x}$ and $\mathbf{z}$ obedience. Generally speaking, the corresponding inference task is to estimate the hidden variable $\mathbf{z}$ and the distributed parameter variable Θ mainly by the observed variable $\mathbf{x}$, that is, to solve the problem $p(\mathbf{z}|\mathbf{x}, \Theta)$ and Θ.

5.7 Probabilistic Graphical Model Learning

For complex, probabilistic models with no expert experience, if we have a certain amount of observation data, we usually want to obtain the parameters and even the structure of the model from the observation data. This is divided into several different cases: Bayesian network or Markov network; models with observables for all variables or models with only observable partial variables; and models with known structures or models with unknown structures. Different situations produce a series of problems of different difficulty.

In the criteria of parameter estimation, a commonly used estimation method is maximum likelihood estimation (MLE), which finds the parameter that maximizes the likelihood of observation data in the parameter space; the other is called the maximum *a posteriori* (MAP) estimation method and finds the parameter with the largest posterior probability in the parameter space. The following is a simple description. We only introduce the method of maximum likelihood estimation. The corresponding maximum *a posteriori* estimation can follow the same method for derivation. In the parameter estimation with missing data, we will also introduce the Bayesian inference method for the posterior distribution of the visual parameters as potential random variables.

5.7.1 *Estimating the Parameters of the Bayesian Network*

For parameter estimation of fully observable models, due to the large amount of information, the learning problem is the simplest of all types of learning problems.

However, even in this case, the learning algorithm costs of Bayesian networks and Markov networks are essentially different. We will see that the parameter estimation problem of a Bayesian network is decomposable and therefore easy to solve; but the Markov network lacks local normalization properties due to its factor, the model brought by the global normalization constant. The coupling between parameters increases the difficulty of learning.

For a Bayesian network G, remember that the variable set is X, the parameter is θ, and the observed sample is $D = \{X^{(1)}, \ldots, X^{(N)}\}$; then, the likelihood function is

$$L(\theta; D) = \prod_{i=1}^{N} \prod_{X_j \in X} p(x_j^{(i)} | u(x_j)^{(i)}; \theta_j). \tag{5.8}$$

Maximizing the likelihood function is equivalent to maximizing the logarithmic likelihood:

$$\max_{\theta} l\left(\theta; D = \sum_{X_j \in X} \max_{\theta_j} \sum_{i=1}^{N} \log p(x_j^{(i)} | u(x_j)^{(i)}; \theta_j)\right). \tag{5.9}$$

Thus, in fully observable Bayesian networks, the maximum likelihood parameter estimation problem can be decomposed into the parameter estimation problem for each conditional probability density.

5.7.2 *Estimating the Parameters of Markov Network*

For a Markov network H, it is convenient to study a kind of model called log-linear model. Remember that the set of factors is C, the parameter is θ, and the likelihood of log-linear model is defined as

$$p(y|\theta) = \frac{1}{Z(\theta)} \exp\left(\sum_{c} \theta_c^T \varphi_c(y)\right). \tag{5.10}$$

It can be proved that the log-likelihood function of the fully observable log-linear model is convex with respect to the parameter θ, so the gradient method can be used to solve the maximum likelihood estimation problem.

Another typical method called maximizing pseudo-likelihood attempts to avoid the difficulty of parameter estimation caused by normalization constants. This method defines log pseudo-likelihood as

$$l_{PL}(\theta) = \frac{1}{N} \sum_{i=1}^{N} \sum_{d=1}^{D} \log p(y_{id} | y_{i,\bar{d}}, \theta). \tag{5.11}$$

The goal of modifying the parameter estimation is to maximize the product of all conditional distributions (also known as combined likelihood). Under the new objective function, the parameter estimation problem can be decomposed into parameters of each conditional distribution similar to those in Bayesian networks. In the Gauss–Markov random field, the maximum pseudo-likelihood is equivalent to the maximum likelihood target, but this equivalence does not hold for the general model.

Algorithm 5.4 (Random Maximum Likelihood Algorithm for Fitting, MRF).
1. Random initialization weight
2. $k = 0, \eta = 1$
3. for each rounds do
4.   for each Small batch training samples of size B do
5.   for each $s = 1 : S$ do
6.   Sampling $y^{s,k} \sim p(y|\theta_k)$
7. $$\widehat{E}(\phi(y)) = \frac{1}{S}\sum_{s=1}^{S}\phi(y^{s,k})$$
8.   for each the ith sample in a small batch of training samples do
9. $g_{ik} = \phi(y_i) - \widehat{E}(\phi(y))$
10. $$g_k = \frac{1}{B}\sum_{i \in B}g_{ik}$$
11. $\theta_{k+1} = \theta_k - \eta g_k$
12. $k = k + 1$
13.   reduce step size η

5.8 Topic Model

The topic model is a kind of generated directed graph model, which is mainly used to process discrete data. It has a wide range of applications in information retrieval, text analysis, social network analysis, and natural language processing. The Latent Dirichlet Allocation (LDA) is an outstanding representative of the topic model. LDA looks at documents and topics from the perspective of a generative model. Assuming that each document contains multiple topics, θ_t is used to represent the proportion of each topic of the document d and $\theta_{t,k}$ represents the proportion of the document d contained in the topic t, and then the document d is generated by the following process:

(1) Randomly sampling a topic distribution θ_t according to the Dirichlet distribution with parameter α.

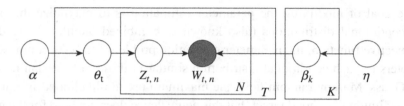

Fig. 5.6.   The plate notation of LDA

(2) Follow the steps below to generate the N words in the text:

(a) Assign a word according to θ_t to get the topic of the word n in the document d;
(b) Sampling randomly generated words according to the word frequency β_k corresponding to the assigned topic.

The plate notation can be used to represent the LDA model as shown in Figure 5.6. The Dirichlet distribution sampling of α generates T topic distributions corresponding to D articles, θ_t generates themes of the words and generates words according to the frequency distribution of the subject words. Then the probability distribution of the LDA model can be written as

$$p(W, z, \beta, \theta | \alpha, \eta) = \prod_{t=1}^{T} p(\theta_t | \alpha) \prod_{i=1}^{K} p(\beta_k | \eta) \left(\prod_{n=1}^{N} p(w_{t,n} | z_{t,n}, \beta_k) p(z_{t,n} | \theta_t) \right),$$

(5.12)

where, $p(\theta_t | \alpha)$ and $p(\beta_k | \eta)$ are usually set to K- and N-dimensional Dirichlet distributions with parameters α and η, for example,

$$p(\theta_t | \alpha) = \frac{\Gamma \left(\sum_k \alpha_k \right)}{\prod_k \Gamma(\alpha_k)} \prod_k \theta_{t,k}^{\alpha_k - 1},$$

(5.13)

where $\Gamma(\cdot)$ is Gamma function. Obviously, α and η are the parameters to be determined in model equation (5.12).

Here, we introduce the topic model from the perspective of text analysis. The hypothetical corpus is composed of K topics, and the content of each document is a mixture of different topics, represented by the T item distribution i. Each topic corresponding to a thesaurus of the subject represents the probability distribution of the kth thesaurus to produce different words. The process of generating documents is described by Algorithm 5.5.

Algorithm 5.5 The Text Generation Method of the Topic Model.
    Input: hyperparameter α, γ, K, V, N;
    Output: text corpus.
    1. for the first $k[1, \ldots, K]$ topics do
    2.   Probability distribution of sample vocabulary $\beta_k|\gamma \sim \mathrm{Dir}(\gamma 1_V)$
    3. for the $i \in [1, \ldots, D]$ document do
    4.   Sampling the subject distribution of the document $i\pi_i|\alpha \sim \mathrm{Dir}(\alpha 1_k)$
    5.   for the $l \in [1, \ldots, N_i]$ words do
    6.   Sampling the subject of the word $q_{il}|\pi_i \sim \mathrm{Cat}(\pi_i)$
    7.   Sampling words $y_{il}|q_{il} = k, \beta \sim \mathrm{Cat}(\beta_k)$

With the rise of large-scale applications such as the Internet and sensor networks, the scale of inference problems in graph models has also expanded rapidly. In this type of large-scale graph model application, how to perform approximate inference on graph models quickly and effectively is of concern to us. In view of the core problem, the current method mainly combines the following solutions: a well-designed message delivery scheduling method, using multi-core hardware to implement parallel and distributed reasoning, and selectively performing inference for query variables.

Exercises

5.1 What is Hidden Markov Model? Given an HMM λ and an observation sequence O, how to calculate the probability $P(O|\lambda)$ of an observation sequence O?

5.2 What is conditional random field? Please use the plate notation to indicate the conditional random field.

5.3 How to use conditional random field for Chinese word segmentation?

5.4 Provide a simple method for constructing a clique tree such that a given set of variables Y is guaranteed to be to together in some clique. Your algorithm should use a standard clique tree construction algorithm as a black box.

5.5 Assume that we have a clique tree T over X such that, for every pair of nodes $X, Y \in X$, there exists a clique that contains both X and Y. Prove that T must contain a single clique that contains all of X.

5.6 Let X be a node with parents $U = \{U_1, \ldots, U_k\}$, where $P(X|U)$ is a tree-CPD. Assume that we have a cluster consisting of X and U. In this question, you will show how to exploit the structure of the tree-CPD to perform message passing more efficiently.

(a) Consider a step where our cluster gets incoming messages about $U_1, \ldots, U_k$ and sends a message about X. Show how this step can be executed in time linear in the size of the tree-CPD of $P(X|U)$.

(b) Now, consider the step where our clique gets incoming messages about $U_1, \ldots, U_{k-1}$ and X and send a message about U_k. Show how this step can also be executed in time linear in the size of the tree-CPD.

5.7 Markov Chain Monte Carlo Methods is an approximate inference method. Explain how to apply Markov Chain Monte Carlo Methods to Go games.

5.8 Try to design an LDA algorithm without specifying the number of topics in advance and analyze the evolution of topics in Shakespeare's book *Romeo and Juliet*.

Chapter 6

Case-Based Reasoning

Case-based reasoning is the process of solving new problems based on the solutions of similar past problems. A case is a contextualized piece of knowledge representing an experience.

6.1 Overview

In order to solve a new problem, we often recall and search in the memory to find similar problems that have been successfully solved, and then reuse the knowledge required for these problem-solving methods to solve the new problems. For example, a doctor treats a patient by recalling another person who exhibited similar symptoms.

The new problem at hand is termed as target case, while the previous problems and their solutions in memory are base cases. Briefly speaking, case-based reasoning (CBR) solves new problems by adapting previously successful solutions to similar problems.

A case is a contextualized piece of knowledge representing an experience. It contains the past lesson that is the content of the case and the context in which the lesson can be used (Kolodner, 1993). Specifically speaking, a case should have the following characteristics:

(1) A case contains implicitly some concrete knowledge related to a certain context; this kind of knowledge is usually concerned with how to do something.
(2) Cases can be of all kinds, in different forms, and with different granularities. They can contain large or small time slices and effects of the application of the solution.
(3) Useful experiences are coded in cases. These experiences are helpful for the reasoners to reach the goal more easily, or predicate the possibility of failure.

Case-based reasoning is a relatively developed branch in Artificial Intelligence. It is a kind of reasoning based on previous practical experiences. From a traditional point of view, reasoning is a process of conclusion drawing by "cause–effect" chains, which has been used by many expert systems. CBR is quiet different in that knowledge is implicitly contained in cases, not in the form of rules explicitly. These cases record all sorts of relevant contexts in the past. CBR solves new problems by adapting previously successful solutions to similar problems, rather than by a reasoning chain. For a new problem, CBR retrieves the most relevant case from memory or in the case base, then adds revises it and produces a suitable solution to the present problem.

CBR is rational because there are two characteristics in reality: regulation and repetition. Actually speaking, there are certain regulations that exist in the world, and actions happening under similar conditions will produce similar results. As it goes, "reality takes shape in the memory alone", and the past experiences may carry some hints for the future.

The researches on CBR originate from the investigations on the mechanism of reasoning and learning from a cognitive perspective. From the children's simple activity to experts' cautious decisions, human affairs are usually accomplished with the help of people's recollection unconsciously or consciously. Mankind often acts according to experiences, and people are intelligent systems in some sense, so it is intuitive to apply such kind of reasoning based on experiences to researches and applications of Artificial Intelligence. Generally speaking, CBR has made the following contributions to Artificial Intelligence:

(1) **Knowledge acquisition:** This is a difficult process, often referred to as the knowledge acquisition bottleneck in knowledge-based systems. The biggest challenges to the implementation of knowledge-based systems are the elicitation of an explicit model of the domain and the implementation of knowledge often in the form of rules, which require teamwork between domain experts and knowledge engineers. Sometimes, creating an explicit model of the domain knowledge is extremely difficult. CBR does not require an explicit domain model, and the need for knowledge acquisition in CBR can be limited to establishing how to characterize cases.

(2) **Knowledge maintenance:** Knowledge update is necessary due to the incompleteness of the initial system knowledge. The newly generated knowledge may conflict with what systems already know, and thus a process of conflict elimination is necessary to maintain the consistency of the knowledge base. Knowledge maintenance in knowledge-based systems is difficult and expensive, while CBR

systems learn by acquiring new knowledge as cases, thus making maintenance easier.

(3) **Improvement in problem-solving efficiency:** Problem solving in CBR can reuse the previous solutions and need not start from scratch as in classic inferences. Particularly, the previous records can help advance the solutions doomed to failure.

(4) **Improvement in problem-solving quality:** The records of previous failure help in the current attempt to avoid failure in advance.

(5) **Improve user acceptance degree:** Users are ready to accept a conclusion only when they are shown how it is reached. CBR systems draw conclusions on the basis of historical facts. Facts speak louder than words; conclusions in CBR systems are more convincing.

The Key Laboratory of the Institute of Intelligent Information Processing, Institute of Computing Technology, Chinese Academy of Sciences, has carried out a series of researches on CBR. Zhongzhi Shi *et al.* proposed a memory network model and case-based search algorithm (Shi, 1992c) in 1991. Han Zhou developed EOFDS, a CBL-based design system for an internal combustion engine oil product (Zhou, 1993). In 1994, Xu developed a CBR-based weather forecast system, while two years later, Jun Wang developed FOREZ, a CBR-based predication and deployment system for Wang's Dam in Huanghe River. Shiren Ye designed and implemented a CBR-based system for fishing ground predication (Ye, 2001).

6.2 Basic Notations

Analogical problem solving is the process of finding a solution to a new problem by applying an analogy between the recalled similar old problems and the new problem, and by the analogy, new knowledge is generated through reasoning to help in problem solving. The solution to the new problem can also be generated on the analysis of, and after adjustment to, the previous problem solutions. So in addition to the ability to record the solutions to similar old problems, a computation model should also have learning skills, i.e., the skill of adjusting the solutions based on past useful experiences. When people can't obtain the solution to the problem after retrieval of old solutions and revision of those solutions to solve the existing problem, some other methods should be employed. So, analogy learning is a kind of learning based on knowledge (or experience). The general model of analogical problem solving is shown in Figure 6.1.

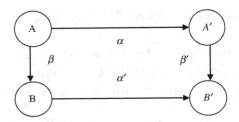

Fig. 6.1. The general model of analogical problem solving

Analogical problem solving can be formalized as follows: Suppose B is the solution to problem A, given a new problem A′ that is similar to A by some predefined criteria, how to get its solution B′? As shown in Figure 6.1, β represents the dependence between B and A and is called causality. α is the similarity of source domain A and the target domain A′. β', the dependence between B′ and A′, can be computed on the basis of β and α. The following are some definitions regarding analogy learning.

Definition 6.1 (Similarity). Suppose P_1 and P_2 are finite sets of predicates. If $q_1 \in P_1$, and $q_2 \in P_2$ are the same, then the ordered pair $\langle q_1, q_2 \rangle \in P_1 \times P_2$ is similar.

Definition 6.2 (Partial Match). Suppose s and t are finite sets of literals with shared constants. For $s \in S, t \in T$, as for Q, if $Q\theta \subseteq s \subseteq s \times t$, and there is a one-to-one mapping between $Q\theta$ and $v(Q)\theta$, then (Q, θ) is a general partial match of s and t.

Definition 6.3 (Intensity). Suppose (Q, θ) and (Q', θ') are two partial matches of $s \times t$. If there is a substitution ξ such that $Q'\xi \subseteq Q$, and for any $W \in v(Q')W\theta' = W\xi\theta$, then (Q, θ) is more intensive than (Q', θ'), written as $(Q, \theta) \geq (Q', \theta')$.

Definition 6.4 (Maximal Partial Match). (Q, θ) is a maximal partial match of $s \times t$ if for any partial match of $s \times t$, (Q', θ') such that $(Q, \theta) \geq (Q', \theta')$.

Definition 6.5 (Analogical Learning). Suppose $s_1, s_2 \in S, t_1 \in T, \beta \in S \times S, s_1 \times s_2 \in \beta$, and m is a maximal partial match of $s_1 \times t_1$. Analogical learning is the process of finding a t_2 such that $t_2 \in T$ on the basis of facts $t_1 \times t_2 \in \beta$ and that m is a maximal partial match of $s_2 \times t_2$.

6.3 Process Model

CBR is a kind of analogical reasoning. When a new problem is encountered, a set of similar cases is retrieved from memory according to some properties of the target case. But the result is coarse and might not be correct; so, we must verify their similarities, which makes us further explore more details of the target and potential base cases. Actually, some analogical mapping has already been carried out locally and tentatively at this stage. After this process, the potential base cases have already been arranged in a partial order according to the similarity with the target cases. We enter the stage of analogical mapping. We choose the most similar base case from the potential base case set and construct a one-to-one mapping between them. In the next step, we get a complete (or partial) solution to the new problem by utilizing this mapping and the solution of the base case. If the solution is a partial one, then add it to the initial descriptions of the target case and restart a new round of the whole analogy course. In the case that the suggested solution is not a valid solution to the target case, an explanation of the reason why it fails is given and the system will evoke the mending module to revise the suggested solution to get a confirmed one, which provides an opportunity to learn from failure. The system should record reasons to fail, in order to avoid the same mistakes in future. Finally, an evaluation on the validity of the analogical reasoning should be given. The whole analogy course is carried out in an accumulative manner. Figure 6.2 sketches the general structure of CBR.

CBR can be categorized into two types: problem-solving CBR and interpretive CBR. The former solves new problems by adapting solutions that were used to solve old problems; the latter utilizes previous cases as evidence for what it pleads.

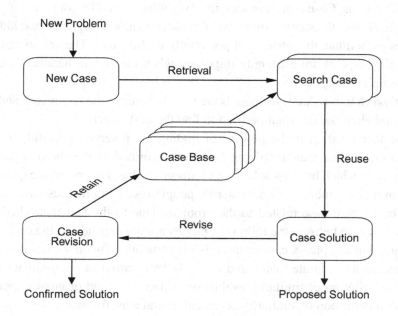

Fig. 6.2. Structure of CBR

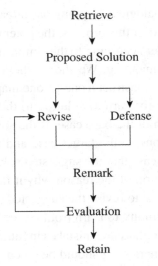

Fig. 6.3.   A CBR process

A CBR process is shown in Figure 6.3. The subjects that matter in CBR include the following:

(1) **Case Representation:** Efficiency is closely linked to case representation in CBR systems. Case representation involves what should be contained in a case, how to choose the storage structure of a case, and how to organize and index the cases to facilitate the retrieval of potentially useful cases. The organization and indexing aspects are especially important when the system handles thousands of complex cases.

(2) **Analysis Model:** Analysis models are used to analyze the target case and identify and elicit the information used to find the best match.

(3) **Case Retrieval:** It is the process of finding the potentially useful cases and choosing the best match utilizing the search information. It is the very similar to the way in which humans solves problems on the basis of previous experiences. When a new problem is encountered, people resort to previous cases and get the best match case related to the problem. Due to the fact that whether the retrieved case helps in the following phases mainly depends on the case quality obtained in this phase, case retrieval is very crucial. Generally speaking, it is by no means an accurate match and can only be a partial or approximate match. So, the criterion of similarity evaluation is necessary and of great importance. A good definition of similarity is critical to find a useful base case.

(4) **Analogical Mapping:** Construct the corresponding similarities between the target case and the base one.

(5) **Analogical Transformation:** Transform the information in the base case in the form that is easy to use in problem solving in the target case. The adaptation of the solution in the base case is involved in this process, which aims to construct the solution in the new situation. The consideration in this adaptation process includes the differences between the target case and the base one and the decision about which part of the base case can be reused in the target case. As to the simple classification question, we only need to apply the classification result of the base cases to the target base directly. There is no need to consider their differences in that the above process of case retrieval has already fulfilled the job. As for problem solving, the system needs to revise the solution of base case according to differences between the target case and base case.

The case reuse can be classified into two types in terms of the information reused: result reuse and method reuse. As regards the former, when the solution in the base case needs an adaptation, the system looks for prominent differences between the base case and the target one and then applies a set of adaptation rules to suggest a solution. The method reuse cares little about the solution stored in the retrieved case and reuses the algorithms, or rules, employed in the problem solving in the base cases to produce a new solution to the target case. In this process, information useful in the base case, such as the can operation of the operator, consideration of the sub goal, search route of success or failure, etc., are reconsidered and reinstanced in the target case, which is also referred to as Derivational adaptation.

(6) **Explanation:** Explain the failure in the transformation from solution in the base case to the generation of new solutions to the target case and provide the cause-and-effect analysis report. Make explanations in successful cases sometimes. Explanation-based indexing techniques, which determine the relevant features for each case, analyze each case to find which of their features are predictive. Cases are then indexed by those features. Indexing based on explanations is an important method as well.

(7) **Case revise:** Some revises are similar to analogical transformation. The input data for the revise process comprise a proposed solution and a failure report; sometimes an explanation might also be included. The revise process adapts the input solution to preclude the factors leading to failures.

Case revise happens when the proposed solution is regarded as not good, and so the first step in case revise is the evaluation of the proposed solution. Only in the cases in which the solution is evaluated to be not good is a revise process evoked.

The evaluation on a proposed solution can be fulfilled on the basis of feedbacks after the solution's application or by consulting domain experts. It takes some time to wait for a feedback, e.g., the effects of therapy on a patient. The method of simulation of a temporal environment is usually employed in solution evaluations because of the above consideration.

Mistake revise generally involves mistake finding and diagnosis of the reason. Looking for the reason is for explaining and analyzing the mistake, in order to find out the reason and modify the remedy to the case, revising the reason to ensure that the mistake does not recur. Certainly, revising can use the knowledge model of the field to go on mending and can be input and finished by users too.

(8) **Analogy Verification:** This proves the validation of the analogy mapping between the base cases and the target one.

(9) **Case Retention:** Once the solution to the new problem has been generated, it may be useful in solving future problems when the situation is similar to it. It is necessary to add it into the current case base. The retention of a newly generated solution is also a process of knowledge acquisition, or in other words, LEARNING. Case retention involves the choice of information that should be kept, the way to integrate the new case to the case base organically, and the work to revise and refine the base cases, such as generalization and abstraction.

Determining on what should be kept involves the following several considerations generally: description of the features involved, the result of the current problem solving, and the explanations on success or failure.

Additional indices should be assigned to the newly added cases to facilitate their retrieval. Indices should be constructed in such a way that the cases only be retrieved for related cases. For this reason, adjustments of the index contents, even the structure of case base, should be done, such as changes to the intensity of the indices or the weights of the feature concerned.

6.4 Case Representation

The brain's memory mechanism for knowledge is still an open problem. A wide range of knowledge representation methods, such as production rules, semantic network, frame, object-oriented representation, etc., have been employed in the present knowledge-based system, but it seems that they are unsuitable in learning systems, especially in the analogical learning systems. The reason is that the knowledge in memory should not only be structural and well-organized but also easy to retrieve, retain, and learn.

Many researches on memory have been launched extensively in the fields of physiology, psychology, etc. Psychological researchers focus on the general theory of memory and have proposed many conceptual models for memory. Some typical ones are episodic memory, semantic memory, associative memory, and Schank's dynamic memory theory.

Knowledge has some structure in nature. Experts adapt semantic memory in fulfilling some tasks to store information involved in problem solving. This kind of information memory method has the following advantages:

(1) facilitate information retrieval;
(2) organize the content easily into a tree-like level or network;
(3) confine the effects of knowledge change to a part and make it easy for information management;
(4) facilitate the sharing of knowledge.

In Schank's dynamic memory theory (Schank, 1982), knowledge is stored in structures of the following four types: memory organization packet (MOP), Scene, Script, and thematic organization packet (TOP). A MOP can contain some scenes, while each scene can contain many scripts. Meanwhile, Meta-MOPs may be contained in upper levels of MOP. Those structures form a network according to some predefined organizational principles and can be searched by indices.

6.4.1 *Semantic Memory Unit*

Semantic memory unit (SMU) refers to those concepts, modes, and themes that are involved in the course of knowledge's study, analysis, understanding, and memory, and the conceptual knowledge acquired in due course. In other words, SMUs are acquired by the system through "calculation" to elicit the factors that reflect the characteristics of knowledge and are well organized to link knowledge together.

The knowledge in our memory is a real memory and serves well for the future only when it is constructed on the basis of processing to some degree. SUM is not only the generation of a certain aspect of concrete problem and concrete knowledge, but the essential understanding of them. Using SMUs as centers, concrete knowledge and concrete problems can be linked in a well-organized manner in terms of the relationship between SMUs.

A critical question arises here: which factors of knowledge should be chosen as SMUs? Each kind of knowledge has its own inherent characteristics, and the choice tactics vary according to the characteristics of knowledge. As for some new knowledge, we generally regard concepts contained in the knowledge as primary memory targets. As knowledge accumulates, the system acquires the analytical capacity of the concrete problem, which can be used for analyzing themes of the concrete problem. Finally, some abstract conceptual understandings are summarized. For example, in astronomy, the fact that celestial bodies rotate around is a general understanding of the relation among the celestial bodies. The binary relation "rotate around" can be abstracted as an SMU. Through this vocabulary, we can associate it with not only concrete knowledge but also the concrete image. Another point in choice tactics is the consideration to abstract those important modes involved in knowledge as an SMU. These modes are not expressed as characters but as a special kind of expression method made up of some special symbols.

6.4.2 *Memory Network*

The knowledge we remember is not isolated, but is linked closely or loosely into a unified system in terms of a certain factor. We use the notation of memory network to summarize this aspect of knowledge (Shi, 1992c). A memory network is a network of SMUs constructed according to the relations among the component SUMs. Every node in a memory network represents an SMU, which can be described as having the following structure:

```
SMU =
    {
        SMU_NAME slot
        Constraint slots
        Taxonomy slots
        Causality slots
        Similarity slots
        Partonomy slots
        Case slots
        Theory slots
    }
```

(1) **SMU_NAME slot:** SUM slot for short, is the conceptual description of the SMU, usually a word or a phrase.

(2) **Constraint slots:** CON slots for short, these are the restraints on the SMU. Usually, they are just restraints on the description of the SMU and not in a structural manner. In addition, each constraint includes a CAS facet linked to a THY facet.

(3) **Taxonomy slots:** TAX slots for short, they define some parents and sons of this SMU in its involved taxonomy systems. So, they describe the classification among the nodes in the memory network.

(4) **Causality slots:** CAU slots for short, they define the cause and effect connections to other SMUs. The SUM may be the cause of other SMUs or the effect of other

SMUs. So, they describe the cause and effect connection among the nodes in the memory network.

(5) **Similarity slots:** SIM slots for short, these define the SUMs similar to the SUM and describe the similarity among the nodes in the memory network.

(6) **Partonomy slots:** PAR slots for short, these define the SUMs with whole-part relation to the SUM.

(7) **Case slots:** CAS slots for short, these define the set of cases relevant to the SUM.

(8) **Theory slots:** THY slots for short, these define the theory about the SUM.

The above eight kinds of slots can be divided into three classes. The first is the inter-SMU relations, including TAX slots, CAU slots, SIM slots, and PAR slots; the second type is the content and characteristics of the SUM's own, including SMU slot and THY slots; the last type is the information of cases related to the SMU, including CAS slots and CON slots. As for similar SMUs, we introduce special kind of nodes, i.e., the intention nodes MMU to express the fact that the SMUs linked to the SMU have similar intention with the SMU. Knowledge that is more special can be stored near the SMU by adding additional restraints to the SMU, and hence a lot of knowledge can be retrieved through the corresponding SMU. This makes the memory of knowledge layer in levels. PAR slots do not influence the retrieval of knowledge in our model; yet, they play an important role in the recall of knowledge. Through the whole-part connections, we can recall the knowledge of a certain theme or a certain field. The memory in THY slots is about the theories about SMU, e.g., the knowledge of "resource conflict". The knowledge can be represented by any ripe representation method, such as production rules, frames, and object-oriented formalisms. In some cases, this makes knowledge processing be done locally. In the memory network, the semantic relations among nodes guarantee the easy retrieval of knowledge relevant to a certain SMU.

It easy to see that the memory network is quite complicated; yet, it can really reflect the intricate inner relations among all kinds of knowledge. The complexity of the network makes the construction of the memory network and its learning process very complex as well. For people, the memory network is the result of long-term accumulation of studying and thinking. In this process, new nodes and knowledge are being created constantly; meanwhile, the knowledge about a certain node that has been not used for a long time is forgotten. It means that the construction process of the memory network is in fact a learning process of knowledge.

The memory network can account for the forgetfulness of knowledge in some sense. Some concrete contents of nearly unused knowledge are generally totally forgotten unconsciously; yet, some rough impressions about this kind of knowledge can be left in memory. It means that the memory network is long-term memory, while the memory of slots is of short term and will die away gradually or vanish. We can describe the above phenomenon with the notation of memory intensity. In general, the memory intensity is a function of time and recall. As time elapses, the memory intensity will be weakened, and after a recall, the memory intensity of the knowledge increases to some extent.

The memory network has some resemblance to the semantic network. It is a kind of model developed on the basis of the semantic network, and they both code information in networks: nodes to express information and arcs between nodes to express the semantic relations. Yet, there are many differences between them. The most primary difference is in the expression of information. The information expression power of the semantic network is confined to the network itself, namely, knowledge can only be represented by nodes and the connections among nodes. But the expression power of the memory network is far beyond the semantic network. It is capable of the following:

(1) store and use the theory and concrete cases represented in other representation methods;
(2) store special knowledge by adding restraints to the nodes;
(3) organize similar knowledge by intention nodes;
(4) have an agent as a memory unit that can finish certain tasks independently.

Serials of reasoning can be taken on the basis of memory network. The following are some examples:

(1) Knowledge can be inherited among nodes through the semantic relations. This point is similar to inheritance reasoning in semantic networks.
(2) Constraint satisfaction refers to the process of obtaining special knowledge within a node by imposing constraints on its content.
(3) As for the knowledge stored in THY slots, reasoning methods, i.e., forward and backward reasoning, information transmission, can be adapted according to the representation methods.
(4) CAS slots are about cases, so CBR methods can be adopted. Hence, case-based abstraction and generalization are operations that can be implemented in the memory network.

6.5 Case Indexing

The organization of cases includes two parts: the content of cases, which should be useful in problem solving, and the indices of cases, which reflect the differences among cases and are involved in the structure and the retrieval of cases.

Typically a case comprises the following three main components: the problem or scene that describes the problem to be solved and the states of world when the case occurred; the solution which states the solution to that problem; and/or the *result* that describes the new state of the world after the case occurred. The first two parts are the necessary parts in any CBR systems, while the result is optional.

(1) The *problem* or *scene* is the description of problems to be solved or the states of world to be understood. They generally include the following contents: The goal of the system when the case occurred, the tasks involved in the fulfillment of the goal, and all the characteristics of the world states or environments related to the possible solutions.

(2) The content of the *solution* is how the problem is solved under a particular situation. It may be just a simple solution to the problem or the process to reach this answer.

(3) The *result* records whether the solution has been implemented successfully and the situation after the solution's implementation. With the results, CBR can provide the cases that once worked successfully while providing proposed solutions; meanwhile, potential problems can be avoided with the records of previous failures. When a sufficient understanding of the problem is absent, CBR works better through the result parts.

Case indexing is an important aspect in retrieving and recalling the useful cases relevant to the new problem. Case indexing involves assigning indices to cases with the aim to facilitate their retrievals. Given a new case, the system can retrieve the relevant cases by their indices that characterize the cases in the case base, if any. The following are three principles for case indexing:

(1) The indices should be relevant to the concrete domain. The indices in the database are general enough to divide the database on average, and thus, the retrieval from the database can be faster. In CBR systems, however, indices should be predicative and concrete enough to simplify the access and retrieval of relevant cases.

(2) The indices should be predicative and abstract enough to allow for widening the future use of the case base.

(3) The indices should be concrete enough to be recognized in future. Extremely abstract indices will efface the differences among the cases.

6.6 Case Retrieval

Case retrieval is the process of finding the best match in the case base to the current problem. The knowledge in CBR systems is a history of solved problems in the past (i.e., cases), rather than a form of rules as that in other expert systems. A case in the case base contains the description of the problem and the situation when the case occurred. When a new case is added to the base, indices on its primary characteristics are also constructed. When a new problem is encountered, the system utilizes the knowledge of similarities and indices to retrieve the most similar cases to the current problem or situation. This retrieval process plays an important role in CBR in that the cases retrieved influence the quality of the current problems solving method. The process can be divided into three phases: feature identification, tentative matching, and final selection.

Feature Identification identifies the relevant features on the analysis of the problem. The features can be obtained by the following method: (a) Extract the features of the question directly from its description. For example, the system can extract some keywords from the problem description that is in natural languages. The extracted keywords can be viewed as features of the problem. (b) Elicit the features after a understanding of the problem, such as the feature elicitation in image analyzing and processing. (c) Obtain the feature from users by the human–machine interaction according to the context requirements or the knowledge model. The system utilizes users' answers heuristics to constrain and direct the search and make the retrieved case more accurate.

Tentative Matching finds a group of candidates from the case base to the current problem. It relies on the indices of the features fixed in Feature Identification. Retrieval of cases from the case base must be equipped with the ability to perform partial matches and construct a partial order on the similarities among cases, since in general there is no existing case that exactly matches the new case. The similarities can be computed in terms of syntax structures without the utilization of domain knowledge, or be estimated on the basis of a deep analysis and thorough understanding. Some well-known concrete methods are as follows: nearest neighbor, induction, knowledge-guided induction, and template retrieval; we can also give weights to the features reflecting their importance.

Final Selection chooses one or several cases with the most similarity to the target case from the tentative matches. It is closely related to the domain knowledge. First, explanations can be made by the knowledge engineers, or be computed based on the knowledge model. Then the system evaluates the explanations and arranges the candidates into a queue according to some criterion. The one that receives the highest rating becomes the best match, for example, the most relevant one or the one with the most rational explanations.

A normal course of case retrieval is sketched on the left-hand side of Figure 6.4. The input is the target case, i.e., the present case. It comprises the

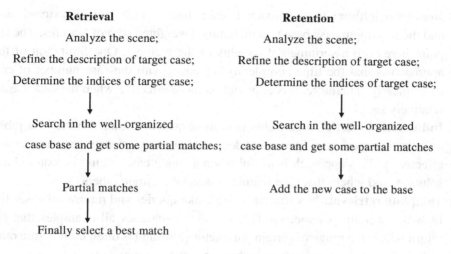

Fig. 6.4.   The process of retrieval and retention

current scene and reasoning goal. The scene is refined after an analysis. If there are cases similar to the target case in the case base, then the indices of the target case related to those similar cases can be calculated. The retrieval algorithms rely on the indices and the target case to search in the case base to find potentially useful cases. The algorithms need the ability to perform partial matches between the target case and cases in the base. Then the system retains a group of partial matches with potential use. Finally, the system ranks these partial matches and chooses the most useful case.

There are three key points in the case retrieval: the retrieval algorithms, matching function, and situation assessment. The following discussion focuses on the retrieval algorithms. Algorithms are closely linked to the data structures that they process. So we cannot isolate our discussion on the retrieval algorithms to the organization of case bases. Bases with different organization should be searched by different algorithms accordingly. Different organizational forms have both pros and cons, and the choice of these should be determined by the application in use.

A series of methods have been formed for case organization and retrieval in CBR: serial or parallel ones; flat or layered ones; ones with indices of small or great granularities to distinguish different examples. The most used methods are based on the inverted index, which can search in the case base serially or parallelly. The application system constructed by Kitano can already deal with more than 25,000 cases. Among the frequently used methods for case retrieval are nearest neighbor, induction, and template retrieval.

(1) **Nearest neighbor:** This approach assesses the similarity between stored cases and the new input case based on matching a weighted sum of features. The key point here is to determine the weights of the features. One limitation of this approach is that the time complexity increases with the case number of case base linearly. Therefore, this approach is more effective when the case base is relatively small.

(2) **Induction:** Induction algorithms determine which features do the best job of discriminating cases and generate a decision tree to organize the cases in memory effectively. This approach is useful when a single case feature is required as a solution, and where that case feature is dependent upon others.

(3) **Template retrieval:** It is similar to SQL-like queries and returns all cases that fit within certain parameters. This technique searches all examples that can return within the range of certain parameter value and is often used before other techniques, such as nearest neighbor, to limit the search space to a relevant section of the case base.

6.7 Similarity Relations in CBR

The process of retrieving the most similar cases to the current problem or situation is especially critical in that the successful retrieval of cases with high quality is a prerequisite for successful applications. Due to the fact that case retrieval is carried on the basis of similarity, the successful retrieval of similar cases is totally determined by the definition of "similarity". We cannot get useful cases using an inappropriate similarity measure assessment among the cases, let alone successful applications. Similarity is a core concept in case-based reasoning.

As indicated by case representation, a case comprises many attributes, and similar degrees among the cases are defined in terms of the similarity degrees among the component attributes. Among well-known similarities are semantic similarity, structural similarity, goal similarity, and individual similarity.

6.7.1 *Semantic Similarity*

If one case is analogical to another, then there must be some similarity among their semantics. One foundation in CBR is how to assess the similarity between cases in order to retrieve appropriate base cases. The analogies between the two cases can be classified into the following three types: positive analogy, negative analogy, and uncertain analogy. Positive analogy is the analogy determined by some similar aspects among cases, negative analogy is the one that is determined by the dissimilar aspects, and uncertain analogy is the analogy other than the above two types. One of the conditions for two analogical cases is that the essential property and causality of the model is not a part of negative analogy. The uncertain analogy makes the analogy have certain predicative aspects that are not necessarily true. To solve a problem analogically, there must be some similarity between the essential features of the base case and the target case, which is the foundation for the analogy.

Still some scholars define two types of similarity: surface similarity and structural similarity. Surface similarity is defined as similar aspects that are not the essential ones in the process of adapting past experiences to the new case. On the contrary, the ones that affect the adaptation process are structural similarities. A less strict definition for structural similarly is the semantic overlap of the relations. The two types of similarities play different roles in the analogy process. The surface one helps in the tentative analogy and individual identifications, while the structural one not only facilitates the analogical search but also plays a very great role in the construction of analogical mapping.

6.7.2 *Structural Similarity*

If there is a certain mapping between two structures, and this kind of corresponding relation can reserve structural consistency, then the structures are isomorphic. Structural consistency requires that the one-to-one mapping between two isomorphic structures guarantees the involved individuals and the component mappings are one-to-one relations too, and such mappings respect the previous corresponding relations among the individuals. Isomorphism has great effects on the validity of analogical reasoning.

The meaning of structural similarities is great for similarity-based retrievals. First, as we have found, analogy is still possible in the cases with dissimilar surface similarities when the cases' structures are similar. The atom and the solar system are totally different entities in different fields. At first sight, there are no essential connections between them. However, deep research can reveal their highly similar space structures. Second, the isomorphism or similarities among substructures can free us from the complex overall consideration and make us focus on the interesting parts locally. This is particularly important in cases where there are some local similarities between two cases that are dissimilar as a whole. For example, in the aspects of understanding of a story, stories are generally very different from each other; however, there may be surprising similarities in a certain plot, or a certain personality, etc. In planning, we should not merely consider the usability of the whole solution to the base case; moreover, we should also pay attention to the sub-solutions in case the whole solution is not appropriate. It is unwise to totally discard the proposed solution when it is proved to be insufficient.

The concept of isomorphism and structural similarity plays a very important role in our analogical retrieval model. The structural similarity facilitates the tentative retrieval of base cases, while isomorphism reminds us to give much higher priorities to those base cases with isomorphism or sub-isomorphism relations to the target case.

6.7.3 *Goal's Features*

The final purpose of problem solving is to fulfill the goal posed by the problem itself, and the goal directs people during the process of problem solving. In a set of cases similar to the current one, those with potential usefulness to the goal achievement should gain higher priority for consideration over the cases whose implicated goals are irrelevant to that of the target case.

Given a structure, when we add information about its goals to it, the resulting structure will gain more semantic similarity and structural consistency. In other words, the goal features will increase the dependability of our choice on the best match. Meanwhile, it can also constrain the search for the base case to a limited part. Keane's analogical retrieval model searches the base cases based on the analysis of the goals' features (Keane, 1988). Keane names the goal features as structural index in analogical retrieval.

However, can we ignore those base cases without any goal relevance? In fact, goal features is just an important additional restraint. If we emphasize goal features too much, we might lose potentially useful cases with a similar sub-structure by the filter of goal features, which is unwise.

6.7.4 *Individual Similarity*

Another emphasis in our model is the restraints posed by the classification information about individuals. Informally speaking, if two individuals have some similarities, then they belong to the same group. In concept clustering, we cluster the concept set in terms of the relevance or closeness among them. Relevance refers to the average of similar degrees between the features of the concepts. But here, we still cluster electric wires and rope into the same class because they both can be used to tie up things.

Sometimes, some individuals in a case play the primary role in problem solving. In those situations, these kind of cases should be used as the primary retrieval information to search the case base tentatively. After completing the tentative retrieval, we should pay more attention to the cases within the same class as the target case or having whole-part relations with the target case. The analogy among individuals helps us to identify them. The partial solutions to the case can help find the whole solution.

6.7.5 Similarity Assessment

(1) The similarity among numeric features:

$$\text{Sim}(V_i, V_j) = 1 - d(V_i, V_j) = 1 - d_{ij}$$

$$\text{or} \quad \text{Sim}(V_i, V_j) = \frac{1}{1 + d(V_i, V_j)} = \frac{1}{1 + d_{ij}}$$

$$d_{ij} = |V_i - V_j|$$

$$\text{or} \quad d_{ij} = \frac{|V_i - V_j|}{\max\{V_i, V_j\}}, \tag{6.1}$$

where V_i, V_j are two possible values for feature V.

(2) The similarity among categorical features.

The similar degree for categorical features is generally divided into two types: the simple method is to compare the corresponding values of the features. If the two are identical, the similar degree between the features is 0; otherwise, it is considered to be 1. Other methods may incorporate some differential ranking into the definitions of similarity according to the detailed relations among the feature values, rather than the simple 0-or-1 division. The former is actually similarity in quality, i.e., the division between to be or not to be, while the latter is similarity in quantity, a further discrimination among the features. Generally speaking, the former is common and suitable for all kinds of situations; the latter needs to be predefined and related to domain knowledge, and thus serves a special purpose. The above two kinds of similarity assessment methods have different application domains of their own.

(3) The similarity among ordered features.

Ordered features are the features lying between the numeric and the categorical ones, and thus, the similarity degrees for them lie between the quality and quantity assessments too. When the values for a feature are in order, we can assign different similarity degrees to different segments of the whole line of possible values. Compared with categorical features, the ordered features have more regular similarity assessment rules. Suppose the whole line of values can be divided into n segments, then the similarity between feature values in segments i and j can be defined as $1 - \frac{|i-j|}{n}$.

Features of different types can be transformed into each other. A feature can be delineated by a set of numbers sometimes or by ordered values too. For example, students' examination marks can be reflected by natural numbers from 0 to 100, or by different classes A, B, and C.

When we calculate the similar degrees among cases, we should consider a weighted sum of similar degrees of all features. The similar degrees among cases are often defined as distances. Typical distances are as follows:

(1) Manhattan distance:

$$d_{ij} = \sum_{k=1}^{N} |V_{ik} - V_{jk}|, \tag{6.2}$$

where V_{ik} and V_{jk} are the values of the kth feature of case i and j, respectively.
(2) Euclidean distance:

$$d_{ij} = \sqrt{\sum_{k=1}^{N} (V_{ik} - V_{jk})^2}. \tag{6.3}$$

(3) Minkowski distance:

$$d_{ij} = \left[\sum_{k=1}^{N} |V_{ik} - V_{jk}|^q \right]^{1/q}, \quad q > 0. \tag{6.4}$$

The above definitions are normal in that every feature influences the similarity among two cases equally. Actually, each feature contributes differently to similar degrees; therefore, we still need to add weights to features reflecting their importance. The above definitions can be rewritten as

$$d_{ij} = \sum_{k=1}^{N} w_k \, d(V_{ik}, V_{jk}), \tag{6.5}$$

where w_k is the weight of kth features of the cases, and normally $\sum_{k=1}^{N} w_k = 1$; and $d(V_{ik}, V_{jk})$ is the distance between the ith case and the jth one on the dimension of kth feature, which can be computed by the classical definition, or other definitions.

The similar degree between two cases can be defined in terms of the above definition of distances as

$$\text{SIM}_{ij} = 1 - d_{ik} \quad \text{if} \quad d_{ij} \in [0, 1]$$

$$\text{or}: \quad \text{SIM}_{ij} = \frac{1}{1 + d_{ij}} \quad \text{if} \quad d_{ij} \in [0, \infty). \tag{6.6}$$

In addition, the ReMind system developed by the Cognitive System Company employs the following definition to calculate similar degrees among cases:

$$\sum_{i=1}^{n} w_i \times \text{Sim}(f_i^I, f_i^R) / \sum_{i=1}^{n} w_i, \qquad (6.7)$$

where w_i is the weight of ith feature of the case, Sim is the similarity function, and f_{Ii} and f_R i are the values of ith feature of the target case and the potential base cases in the case base.

6.8 Case Reuse

Case reuse can be classified into two types in terms of the information reused: result reuse and method reuse. For the former, the adaptation is applied directly to the solution stored in cases. The system looks for prominent differences between the base case and the target one and then applies a set of adaptation rules to suggest a solution. Instead of the solutions stored, the method reuses the algorithms or rules employed in the problem solving in the base cases to produce a new solution to the target case, while the choice of adaptation methods is dependent on the concrete problems.

Case revise happens when the proposed solution is regarded as not good, so the first step is the evaluation on the proposed solution. Only in the cases in which the solution is evaluated to be not good can a revise process be evoked. The evaluation on a proposed solution can be fulfilled on the basis of feedbacks after the solution's application, or by consulting domain experts. It takes some time to wait for a feedback, e.g., the effects of therapy on a patient, while some kinds of real-time feedback are required in some situations.

Generally speaking, there is no existing case that exactly matches the new case, so in problem-solving CBR systems, it is necessary to transform or adapt the solutions of retrieved cases to the new problem. The revise process uses the description of the current problem and a suggested solution obtained in the reuse process to output a better solution.

The revision may be just simple a replacement of some components of the suggested solution, or it could be very complex and entail a revision of the whole structure of the suggested solution. Revision can take place in the process that the suggested solution forms, or be postponed until some exceptions arise during the execution of the suggested solution. Revision is generally fulfilled by adding new content to or deleting some content from the suggested solutions and replacement or retransformation of some parts of the suggested solution.

The revise methods can be classified into four types: substitution, transformation, special-purpose adaptation and repair, and derivational replay.

1. Substitution

Substitution is a class of structural adaptation techniques that obtain the suggested solution by appropriate component substitutions. It includes the following:

(1) Reinstantiation is used to instantiate features of an old solution with new features. For example, CHEF can reinstantiate chicken and snow peas in a Chinese recipe with beef and *broccoli*, thereby creating a new recipe.
(2) Parameter adjustment is a structural adaptation technique that compares specified parameters of the retrieved and current case to modify the solution in an appropriate direction. It is a heuristic method for parameters with numeric values and depends on the concrete models of input and output.
(3) Local search is the method using additional knowledge as heuristics to find replacement values. For example, in pastry design, in the absence of oranges, we can use this method to search for some fruit similar to oranges (such as apples) as a second choice with the help of knowledge about fruit.
(4) Query obtains the substitution content by the conditional queries to the case base or additional knowledge base.
(5) Specialized search performs a search of the case base and knowledge base at the same time, and uses the knowledge base as a heuristic to direct its search in the case bases.
(6) Case-based substitution uses other cases to propose a substitution.

2. Transformation

Transformation includes the following: (a) commonsense transformation, which replaces, deletes, or increases some components to the old solution by a basic and easily understood method of commonsense; the typical transformation method is "to delete the secondary components"; (b) model-guided repair, which uses a causal model to guide adaptation and is often used in diagnosis systems.

3. Special-purpose adaptation and repair

This kind of method is used mainly in the domain-dependent and structural adaptations. Various heuristics are used to index the potentially useful cases. Generally, the heuristics in this method serve by giving evaluations on approximate solutions and are controlled by rule-based production systems.

4. Derivational replay

The above three kinds of revise methods are based on adaptations of the solutions to the base cases. Derivational replay cares about how the solutions are derived and uses the method of deriving an old solution or solution piece to derive a solution in the new situation. Compared with the case-based substitution methods mentioned above, derivational replay is a kind of case-based revise method.

6.9 Case Retention

The process of case retention is similar to that of case retrieval. The word "remember" has two kinds of meanings: storage and retrieval. Incorporating the problem and solution to the case base as a new case involves the index mechanism to assign indices to the cases to facilitate its future retrieval and the insertion algorithms to store the new case in the appropriate place in the case base. Generally speaking, the search performed in case retention is the same as that in case retrieval. The insertion algorithms aim to find a place for the new case, while retrieval algorithms return the most similar cases. Arrangement on cases begins when potentially useful cases are returned, and the systems need to reorganize the case base after the insertion of new cases.

If the new problem has been solved successfully, the problem and solution should be stored as a new case for future use. Case retention is the process of learning and knowledge acquisition, which involves deciding what information to retain and in what form to retain it; how to index the case for future retrieval; how to integrate the new case into the case base; and how to organize and manage the case base.

Deciding what information to retain is based on the following considerations: Feature descriptions involved in the problem; the solution to the problem; and explanations on the success.

Additional indices should be assigned to the newly added cases to facilitate their retrieval. Indices should be constructed in such a way that the cases only be retrieved in the related cases. For this reason, adjustments to the index contents, even the structure of case base, should be done, such as changes on the intensity of the indices or the weights of the feature concerned.

As time goes by, the case base becomes larger and larger. This will cause great waste of the memory space and retrieval time. In light of this, the system should perform effective organization and management on the case base.

Retrieval, reuse, revise, and retention are the four main processes in a CBR cycle, and the reasoning process of CBR is also named as the Four-R process.

6.10 Instance-Based Learning

Instance-based learning (IBL) is a family of inductive learning methods closely linked to case-based learning (Aha *et al.*, 1991). The learning algorithms in IBL simply store the already classified instances, and when a new query instance is encountered, classify the instance into the same class as the most similar related instance retrieved from the instance base. Rather than complex index mechanisms, IBL uses the feature–value pairs as the primary representation method. This approach also does no revisions on instances, yet it has been proven to be very useful.

In the researches of learning from examples or supervised learning, a range of concept representation formalisms have been put forward, including rules, decision tree, connectionist networks, etc. All these methods predict the new instance based on the abstraction and generalization of the training instances. Instance-based learning can be viewed as an extension of the nearest neighbor method in that it uses the typical instances to denote the corresponding concepts directly, rather than generalizing a set of abstractions of the training instances. Its prediction about the new query is estimated under the similarity assumption, i.e., the classification results of similar instances are similar too. IBL retrieves a set of instances similar to the new instance and returns a result for the new query based on a systemic analysis of the retrieved results. The nearest neighbor learning is incremental and gains the best prediction accuracy for instances whose feature values are continuous, compared with other learning methods (Biberman, 1994).

The k-nearest neighbor algorithm (k-NN) is the general form of nearest neighbor method, where k is the number of most nearest neighbors. Two key points in the application of k-NN are the following: How to retrieve some instances similar to the instance from the instance base, and how to assess the retrieved results to from the prediction value for the present example. The former includes how to define the similarities among instances and the criteria for the choice of k. Weiss *et al.* provide better solutions in the cases where the feature values are symbols or discrete ones (Richter and Weiss, 1991). Aha gaven a method, named as cross validation, to determine the value of k (Aha, 1997).

6.10.1 *Learning Tasks of IBL*

In IBL, an instance is described as a set of feature–value pairs. Each instance contains several features, and missing feature values are tolerated. All instances are described by the same n features, which define an n-dimensional instance space. Exactly one of these features corresponds to the category feature, while the other $n - 1$ features are referred to as predictor features. IBL algorithms can learn a lot of overlapping concepts, yet in general the learning only involves exactly one category feature and the categories are disjoint and do not overlap, and the outputs are also basically simple.

Generally speaking, an output of IBL algorithms is a concept description, which is a function mapping from instances to categories: Given an instance in the instance space, the function gives a classification, i.e., a predication on this instance's category attribute. An instances-based concept description includes a set of stored instances, and possibly information about their performances in the past classification processes. This set of instance can change after each query instance is processed.

Classification function: It receives as input the similarity function's results and the classification performance records for the instances, and outputs a classification for i.

Concept description updater: It maintains records on classification performance and determines which instances should be incorporated in the concept description. IBL assumes that similar instances have similar classifications; thus, it classifies the new instances according to their most similar neighbors' classifications. Meanwhile, when prior knowledge is absent, IBL assumes that all features' contributions to classification are equal, i.e., feature weights reflecting their importance are identical in the similar function. This bias requires normalizations of each features' value domain.

Different from most other supervised learning algorithms, no explicit abstractions such as decision trees or decision inductions are needed in IBL algorithms. Most learning algorithms maintain a set of generalizations of instances to form their abstract representations and adopt simple matching to classify the represented instances. However, IBL algorithms do little in the representation phase in that they do not store explicit generalizations, yet there is more calculation on similarities among cases in the classification phase when a new instance is encountered.

The performance of IBL algorithms is generally assessed in terms of the following respects:

(1) Generalization capability refers to the ability to determine which concepts are describable and the learning power of the algorithms. IBL algorithms can PAC-learn any concept whose boundary is a union of a finite set of closed hypercurves of finite size.
(2) Classification accuracy.
(3) Learning rate.
(4) Incorporation costs are the overheads involved in updating the concept descriptions of a training instance, including classification costs.

(5) Storage requirement refers to the size of the concept descriptions which, for IBL algorithms, is defined as the number of saved instances used for classification decisions.

6.10.2 *Algorithm IB1*

The key idea of the IB1 algorithm is quite simple: Given an instance, it assumes that the instance is in the same category as its nearest neighbor. Yet, it must be acknowledged that IB1 will fail in the cases that the given attributes are logically inadequate for the description of the target concept.

Algorithm 6.1 (IB1 Algorithm).
  1. $CD \leftarrow \emptyset$ //CD=Concept description
  2. For each $x \in$ Training Set do
  3.   for each $y \in CD$ do
  4. $sim[y] \leftarrow$ similarity(x, y).
  5. $y_{max} \leftarrow$ some $y \in CD$ with maximal $sim[y]$
  6.   if class(x) =class (y_{max})
  7.   then classification $\leftarrow$ correct
  8.   else classification $\leftarrow$ incorrect
  9. $CD \leftarrow CD \cup \{x\}$

It is a fact that under general statistical assumptions, the nearest neighbor decision policy has a misclassification rate at most twice the optimal Bayes in the worst cases. This result is relatively weak in that it is obtained in the cases that the number of samples is unbounded.

6.10.3 *Reducing Storage Requirements*

In IB1 algorithm, only the instances that lie between the ε-neighborhood and the ε-core of C are used in the production of an accurate approximation of the target concept. The other instances have no contribution to the determination of the concept boundary. So, only keeping those useful instances will save a significant amount of memory space. However, without full knowledge of the concept boundary, this set is not known. But it can be approximated by the set of misclassified instances. This is the key idea of the algorithm IB2.

Algorithm 6.2 (IB2 Algorithm).
  1. $CD \leftarrow \emptyset$ //CD=Concept description
  2. For each $x \in$ Training Set do
  3.   For each $y \in CD$ do

4.   sim[y]←similarity (x, y)
5. y_{max} ←some $y \in$ CD with maximal sim[y].
6.   if class(x)=class (y)
7.   then classification ←correct
8.   else
9.   classification←incorrect
10.   CD←CD $\cup \{x\}$.

Different from IB1, the IB2 algorithm only saves misclassified instances, most of which lie between the ε-neighborhood and the ε-core of C (for some rationally small positive number ε) and is close to the boundary. In the cases where the instances vary greatly in their distance from the concept boundary, the reduction of storage requirements is significantly less in IB2.

The classification accuracy decreases more dramatically than that of IB1 does as the level of noise increases in that those noisy instances are almost always misclassified. Since IB2 saves only a small part of the non-noisy training instances, its saved noisy instances have more chance of being used to generate poor classifications.

IB3 is the improvement of IB2 that employs a "selective utilization filter" to determine which of the saved instances should be used to make classification decisions in such a way that IB3 is insensitive to noise.

Algorithm 6.3 (IB3).
1. CD← Ø //CD=Concept description
2. for each $x \in$ Training Set do
3. for each $y \in$ CD do
4.   sim[y]←similarity(x, y)
5.   if $\exists\{y \in$ CD|acceptable (y)} then
6. y_{max} ←some acceptable $y \in$ CD with maximal sim[y]
7.   else
8. i ←a randomly-selected value in [1,|CD|]
9. y_{max} ← some y $\in$ CD that is the i-th most similar instance to x
10.   if class(x)≠class(y_{max})
11.   then
12.   classification←correct
13.   else
14.   classification←incorrect
15.   CD←CD∪{x}
16. for each $y \in$ CD do
17.   if sim [y]≥sim[y_{max}]

18.   then
19.   update y's classification record
20.   if y's record is significantly poor
21.   then CD$\leftarrow$C-$\{y\}$.

The IB3 algorithm maintains a classification record, e.g., the number of correct and incorrect classification attempts, with each saved instance. A classification record is a summary of an instance's classification performance on the current training instances and hints the performance in the future. Meanwhile, IB3 employs a significance test to determine which instances are good classifiers and which ones are noisy. The noisy instances are discarded from the concept description. For each training instance i, all classification records are updated for instances that are at least as similar as i's most similar acceptable neighbor.

When no instance in storage is acceptable, we adopt a policy that assumes that at least one instance is acceptable. If none of the saved instances are acceptable, a random number y will be generated from $[1, n]$, where n is the number of saved instances. Then, the y most similar saved instances' classification records are updated. If there is at least one acceptable instance, say i, then the instances whose classification records need updating are those that are in the hypersphere, centered on i with radius equal to the normalized distance between i and its nearest neighbor.

IB3 employs the notion of confidence interval of the proportions test to determine whether an instance is acceptable, mediocre, or noisy. Confidence intervals are determined by both the instance's current classification accuracy and the observed relative frequency of the class it belongs to. The instance is acceptable in the cases where its accuracy interval's lower endpoint is greater than the class frequency interval's higher endpoint. Similarly, instances are noisy when their accuracy interval's higher endpoint is less than their class frequency interval's lower endpoint. If the two intervals overlap, then it is mediocre and a further decision process will be employed to decide whether the instance is to be accepted or discarded.

The learning performance IB3 is highly sensitive to the number of irrelevant features employed in instance descriptions. Meanwhile, with increasing dimensionality, its storage requirements increase exponentially, yet the learning rate decreases exponentially. IB3 cannot represent overlapping concepts and respects the assumption that every instance is a member of exactly one concept. Fortunately, this can be solved by learning a separate description for each concept.

IBL has the following advantages. The approach is simple and relatively robust, and its algorithms have a relatively relaxed concept bias. They learn piecewise-linear approximations of concepts incrementally with a faster learning rate than other algorithms when their bias is not satisfied by target concepts, especially when the boundary of the target concept is not parallel to the feature dimensions. Finally, the updating costs in IBL algorithms are relatively low. IBL updating costs include classification costs, which requires $O(|N| * |A|)$ feature examinations, where $|N|$ is the number of saved instances and $|A|$ is the number of features used in instance descriptions. C4.5 requires $O(|I| * |A|^2)$ feature examinations, where $|I|$ is the size of the training set. Meanwhile, parallel processing methods and index strategies can be employed to further reduce the computation complexity of IBL.

6.11 Forecast System for Central Fishing Ground

As indicated by psychological researches, humans are good at making decisions based on their past experiences. The restrictions posed by human memory capacity make it difficult for people to recall the appropriate cases correctly, especially when the number of cases is dauntingly big. Compared with people, computers have advantages in terms of "memory", i.e., computers can store a large number of cases and retrieve relevant ones fast. It is exactly the scope of case-based decision aiding to combine the merits of people and machine together to help in decision-making.

It has attracted extensive attention of countries from all over the world so as to employ the modern science and technology to develop marine resources, maintain and manage marine fishery resources well, and realize the sustainable development of sea fishery. The utilization of computer, remote sensing, automation, and geographical information system can not only offer macroscopic decision information for developing and managing in the sea fishery but also direct the microcosm concretely for the use of marine fishery resources.

Under the support of 863 Program, we launched researches on remote sensing information and resource assessment system for sea fishery, and the concerned system integration and case illustration for the better utilization of resources and development of fishery of the sea areas in our country. It serves to strengthen the new and high level of technology to support the functions of maintaining and utilizing the administrative skill of fishery resources of the marine-exclusive economic zone in the future. We use East China Sea (north latitude 25° to 34°, 130 of east longitude with west sea area) as the demonstration area for fishing ground prediction and lay a good foundation for the utilization and development of fishery resources in open seas and oceans. The fishing ground prediction utilizes technologies such as data mining, CBL, expert system, and analysis technology in remote sensing and sea fishery, and these come under the support of the geographical technology of information system, which together with the knowledge and experiences domain experts, implements Learning and Decision-support System for fishing ground analysis and prediction.

6.11.1 *Problem Analysis and Case Representation*

In addition to making assessment on fishery resources (medium- and long-term predictions), the important function of the system is to make a short-term prediction (the fishing ground center). The fishing ground refers to ocean areas with a high number of fishes or other economic marine animals in a certain season that are worth developing and utilizing. The central fishing ground is the fishing ground with higher average net product and gross total product. Accurate predictions can directly improve the product and efficiency of the fishery production and bring great economic benefits.

The migration of fish and the formation of the central fishing ground have been influenced by the following factors: temperature of sea water (including marine surface temperature, the temperature of marine ground floor), data about the platform, such as the salinity of sea water, salt gradient ion, the flow rate of Yangtze River, wind directions and velocities, and marine chlorophyll density. However, the migration of the fish is influenced by many factors and is too complicated to be described by using traditional mathematics methods and models. Furthermore, the knowledge of experts about fishing ground is inaccurate, and incomplete in some sense. Fortunately, we have already collected the data about fishery conditions in East China Sea for the past 20 years. These materials are very valuable in that a lot of useful information and knowledge can be elicited from them, which can then be used to predict the trend of the fishing ground. The system has adopted CBR as it is highly suitable in situations where there is little domain knowledge and many exceptions for the general rules, but only a large number of historical data that are available domains are described in terms of cases, and the problems are not totally understood.

As information about the state of the sea is usually collected weekly, for the sake of easy computation, we simplify the demand according to the actual conditions and take 1 week as the predication cycle. In this way, the problem can be formulated as how to predicate the central fishing ground during the next week according to the information of aquatic products in this week (the position, the output, and size). Even so, the problem is quite difficult in that the position and size of the fishing ground are space data. Meanwhile, the information of the state of the sea involves about 600 pieces of space and un-space attributes, and so methods such as decision tree, regression, etc., are not very suitable. On the basis of the above consideration, we adopt CBR, a kind of Lazy Learning (Aha, 1997).

A rational, consistent case representation is essential in the process of case library building. A prominent question in a CBR system is how to combine situation, solution, and outcome to form a case representation. In our system, we employ the Object-Orientated Technologies to express the state of the sea and the fishing condition, and every instance of a class is captured by a record in database and created dynamically during system evolution.

Through the proper pretreatment, the initial data are turned into forms suitable for machine learning. The primitive records take the form of time, place, output, manner, etc. (records from some fishery company even have no output records), upon which we must compute the central fishing grounds. Meanwhile, for simplicity, we neglect fishing grounds' form and only take their sizes into consideration. We classify these primitive records into groups in terms of time and manner and can bring about some reduction in some clustering ways to find central fishing grounds, which can be revised in the following phase through human–computer interaction:

(1) combine the adjacent central fishing grounds around until there are no adjacent ones;
(2) eliminate the central fishing ground with output lower than a preset threshold;
(3) if the number of central fishing grounds is still big after the above processes, eliminate the fishing grounds with smaller size and modest output;
(4) combine the remaining fishing grounds to form the central fishing ground; the position of the central fishing ground is their geometric center, its size is the number of the component fishing grounds, and output is their accumulation.
(5) the result of the merge step (4) is submitted to the user in a visual manner, and the user is further adjusted according to the specific situation.
(6) the result is in the database.

We have developed the central fishing ground forecasting expert system for the domain experts to draw the central fishing ground as shown in Figure 6.5.

6.11.2 *Similarity Measurement*

A key point is CBR is how to retrieve the "best" similar cases. Case retrieval is based on the similarity comparison and totally determined by the definition of "similarity". It is hardly the case that we can find satisfactory cases with an improper definition of similarity. So, the similarity definition carries great weight in CBR systems. However, similarity is a notion that is always coarse, incomplete, and ever-changing. The optimum choice of cases usually follows the following rules: Compute the semantic, structure, target, and individual similarities using the corresponding algorithms to assess the overall similarities between cases, and then calculate the whole similarity according to the importance of these similarities in the question — it is similar to the total dynamic weighting.

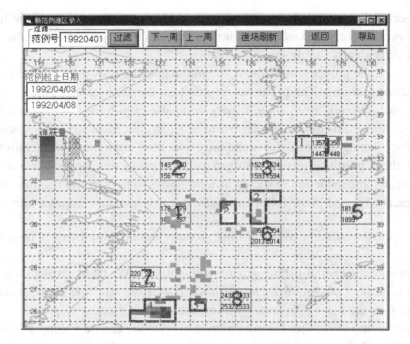

Fig. 6.5.   Central fishing grounds after clustering and human revision

In our system, we employ the following three methods to measure the similarities:

- Similarity in terms of position:

$$\text{sim } 1 = \frac{\sum (w_i \times \text{distance}(\text{pos(goal)} - \text{pos(source)}))}{\sum w_i}, \tag{6.8}$$

- Similarity in terms of temperature:

$$\text{sim } 2 = \frac{\sum (w_i * \text{difference}(\text{temp(goal)} - \text{temp(source)}))}{\sum w_i}, \tag{6.9}$$

- Similarity in terms of temperature gradient:

$$\text{sim } 3 = \frac{\sum (w_i * \text{difference}(\text{delta(goal)} - \text{delta(source)}))}{\sum w_i}, \tag{6.10}$$

where w_i is the weight. The closer the temperature test spot to the central fishing ground (d_i), greater is the w_i. Suppose $d_{\max}$ is the diameter of the marine area, $w_i = 1$ when $d_i = 0$, and $d_i = d_{\max}$, w_i is a preset value w_0 (can be modified by users), otherwise

$$w_i = 1 - \frac{d_i(1 - w_0)}{d_{max}}. \qquad (6.11)$$

6.11.3 *Indexing and Retrieval*

Case reuse is the process of choosing the best matching case from the stored ones and adapting its solutions to solve the new problem. The process can be divided into analogy mapping and analogy conversion. A precondition of the adaptation of base case to problem solving in the target case is a one-to-one mapping between the features of the target and base cases and the choice of relations and structures that can be used in the target case. So, in analogy mapping, two primary problems are the following: the identification and mapping of features and choice of mapping relations and structures.

Case indexing involves assigning indices to cases to facilitate their retrieval. The main indexing methods include near neighbor, induction, knowledge guide, or their combinations. The main difficulty in our system lies in the fact that the information of the state of the sea and the fishing condition is related to space and time. For clarity, we conduct the following simplification. Suppose C_{t1} is the state of the sea at time t_1, which is a precondition (condition attribute) of fishing grounds, and G_{t1} is the fishing ground at t_1, including output, size, and decision attributes. Case at $t_1 I_{t1} = (C_{t1}, G_{t1})$ is a vector with high dimension. $I_{t1-tn} = \{I_{t1}, I_{t2}, \ldots, I_{tn}\} = \{(C_{t1}, G_{t1}), (C_{t2}, G_{t2}), \ldots, (C_{tn}, G_{tn})\}$ is a case sequence, where t_{i+1} is the next week of t_i, and $\Delta G_t = G_{ti+1} - G_{ti}$ is the change of the fishing ground in a week.

Suppose $\Gamma_{s'1-s'k}$ and $\Gamma_{t'1-t'k}$ are subsets of I_{s1-sm}, I_{t1-tn} with k-elements and total order, and that $\text{sim}(\cdot)$ is the similarity measurement function. If $\forall I_{s'i} \in \Gamma_{s'1-s'k}, \forall I_{t'i} \in \Gamma_{t'1-t'k}, \text{sim}(I_{s'_i}, I_{t'_i}) \geq \delta_{(1 \leq i \leq k)}$, written as $\Gamma_{s'1-s'k} \approx \Gamma_{t'1-t'k}$, then I_{s1-sm} and I_{t1-tn} are $k - \delta$ totally similar, where δ is the predefined threshold value between 0 and 1. Obviously, the bigger k and δ are, the bigger the degree of the similarity between I_{s1-sm} and I_{t1-tn}.

Suppose $C'_{s'1-s'k}$ and $C'_{t'1-t'k}$ are k-element subsets of condition sequences $C_{s1-sm} = \{C_{s1}, \ldots, C_{sm}\}$ and $C_{t1-tn} = \{C_{t1}, \ldots, C_{tm}\}$. If $\forall C_{s'i} \in C'_{s'1-s'k}, \forall C_{t'i} \in C'_{t'1-t'k}, \text{sim}(C_{s'i}, C_{t'i}) \geq \delta_{(1 \leq i \leq k)}$, written as $C_{s'1-s'k} \approx C_{t'1-t'k}$, then I_{s1-sm} and I_{t1-tn} are $k - \delta$ conditional similar, where δ is the predefined threshold value between 0 and 1.

Suppose $I_{u-cur} = \{I_u, I_{u+1}, \ldots, I_{cur}\}$ is a fishing ground sequence of length $cur - u + 1$ from time u to time cur, and $I_{u-cur+1} = \{I_u, I_{u+1}, \ldots, I_{cur}, I_{cur+1}\} = \{I_{u-cur}, I_{cur+1}\}$ represents the evolvement of fishing grounds from time u to the time cur $+ 1$, where $I_{cur+1} = (C_{cur+1}, G_{cur+1})$, C_{cur+1} can be gathered accurately in the way that the meteorological phenomena is analyzed, and G_{cur+1} is the fishing ground in the next week that needs to be predicted. Suppose $\Gamma_{u'1-u'k}$ is a total order subset of $I_{u-cur+1}$ with elements I_{cur} and I_{cur+1}. Our task is to find a history sequence I_{v-w} with sub-sequence $\Gamma_{v'1-v'k}$ $k - \delta$ totally similar to $\Gamma_{u'-u'k}$. $\Gamma_{u'1-u'k} \approx \Gamma_{v'1-v'k}$ implies $C'_{u'1-u'k} \approx C'_{v'1-v'k}$, which implies in turn $G_{cur+1} = G_{u'k} \approx G_{v'k}$. Finally, we can fix the position of G_{cur+1} by $G_{v'k}$.

As demonstrated by experiments, the condition for total similarity is very strong. The notion of conditional similarity serves well. Suppose $C'_{u'1-u'k}$ is a total order subset of $C_{u-cur+1}$ with elements C_{cur} and C_{cur+1}. Our task is to find a history sequence C_{v-w} with sub-sequence $C'_{v'1-v'k}$ $k - \delta$ conditionally similar to $C'_{u'1-u'k}$. $C'_{u'1-u'k} \approx C'_{v'1-v'k}$ implies $G_{cur+1} = G_{u'k} \approx G_{v'k}$, then $G_{cur+1} = G_{cur} + \Delta G$ and $\Delta G = G_{v'k} - G_{v'k-1}$ are the changes in the fishing grounds this week from fishing grounds for the next week. This is the very reason we introduced several similarity measurements in the previous section.

Due to the fact that it is difficult to set the value of δ, we adopt k-nearest neighbor method to retrieve k nearest neighbors, based on which the central fishing ground of next week can be calculated with great robustness and no value of δ.

6.11.4 *Revision with Frame*

Frame, as a knowledge representation method, was suggested by Marvin Minsky for recognition, natural language dialog, and other complex actions in 1975 (Minsky, 1975). A frame is a data structure for representing a stereotyped entity, such as a situation, a concept, or an event. As for a new situation, we can get an instance of the entity by filling the values into the structure. The frame structure also offers a way for prediction of a particular entity under a concrete context where we can find the needed information. Slots are the places in frame structures where predication information is stored. A frame comprises a number of slots, and each slot has its own name and the values that go into it. The values in the slot describe the attributes of the entity the frame represents. Usually, the slots are complex structures that have facets describing their properties, and every facet describes the characteristic of the slot from one viewpoint. Each facet takes one or more values, which are described by one concept or a few concepts. Frame theory is an important knowledge representation technology and has gained extensive application prospects as it organizes knowledge in a human-like and concise manner. But the existing frame systems still lack a way of dealing with conflicts in prediction and uncertain knowledge.

According to the prediction and study on marine fishery resources, we defined a frame system KBIF with the power to express uncertain knowledge with different importance. The main characteristics of KBIF include the following: Weight — the influence degree of every slot on the frame, trust factor — the degree of every slot can be believed, and preference factor — the inclination degree in inheritance from parent frames.

Fish migration is influenced by many factors and is too complicated to be described using traditional mathematical methods and models. The prediction algorithm in CBR can only make a predication based on some factors accumulated through a large amount of historical data, while expert knowledge of the fishing grounds is inaccurate and incomplete. The key point in prediction accuracy is how to revise the prediction results about the central fishing grounds effectively. Knowledge representation in *KBIF* adopts three kinds of knowledge processing models: frame model, blackboard structure, and fuzzy reasoning, and accordingly, expert revision systems are divided into three parts: atom set, rule set, and conclusion set. The application of the three models confers *KBIF* with great expansibility and flexibility in rule definition.

Model One: Frame Model *KBIF*. The knowledge (mainly many kinds of restriction factors) in *KBIF* is coded in terms of rules and the domain experts can define the impact factors flexibly. These factors form a consistent system through inter-factor communications and reach the goal collaboratively.

The atom set is constructed as follows: First of all, collect the restricting factors in the formation of central fishing grounds and divide them as primitive elements of prediction rules. Each element is an atom of prediction rules, while all these elements form the atom set, i.e., the frame. The atom set utilizes the knowledge representation principle of *KBIF* to express all influence factors that can be expressed in the prediction algorithm, and every factor can be treated as a slot in the frame. The frame is named as "The rule set of revision system" and layered into the following three layers: The station data, flow rate of the Yangtze River, and flow divisions. The station data include wind speed, wind direction, precipitation, temperature, atmospheric pressure, time, water temperature, salinity, name of station, etc. The flow rate data comprises time and month average. The flow divisions data include surface temperature, surface temperature gradient, surface salinity, surface salt gradient, vertical water temperature gradient, vertical salt gradient, ground salinity, ground salt gradient, time, and water temperature of the ground. Atom sets can be extended along with the enhancement of domain experts' understanding and meet the expanding requirement on the prediction of the central fishing grounds.

Model Two: Blackboard structure. We have developed the subsystem of blackboard in a broad sense on the basis of *KBIF*, which plays an important role in the decision process. With this subsystem, users can divide the solution space into sub-structures, i.e., rule sets by homogeneity and heterogeneity cut arbitrarily.

We have defined the notion of virtual blackboard, which can be instanced to blackboard systems in accordance with the predication characteristics of fishery resources. It combines the knowledge sources, i.e., atom sets, rule generation set, and concrete application of fuzzy reasoning. The architecture of KBIF is a miniature blackboard, including a group of atom sets, a miniature blackboard, and a controller for rule production. The architecture offers an effective combination of a knowledge layer and an experience reasoning layer. Atom sets are coded in the system implicitly, corresponding to the frame model, and can be expanded if needed. The controller for rule production combines the atom sets according to the requirements of experts, then it fills the blackboard with these combinations and offers two kinds of functions (blocking and enumerating) to promote inference efficiency, and finally produces particular rules. This method offers the ability of rule production gradually, lightens the inference load of expertise reasoning, and avoids the omission of knowledge while keeping focus on the internal structure of knowledge. The visual interface that the system used to express such structure enhances the knowledge expression method and offers effective inference ability.

Model Three: Fuzzy reasoning. We use fuzzy methods to choose the rules to be used in the revision of prediction results, and thus more accurate results can be generated. In the rule set of the prediction and revision system, the positions, sizes, and outputs of central fishing ground (X axle, Y axle) are defined fuzzily, and new predication results can be reached by revising the results generated by CBR reasoning. After the whole predication process, we can revise the conclusion sets through a learning process on the sequence of conclusions ordered by some predefined credibility degrees. In this manner, we can constantly and gradually reach a believed solution.

6.11.5 *Experiments*

The architecture of the central fishing ground forecasting expert system is shown in Figure 6.6. The historical data are stored in the case library, after a series of pretreatments such as appropriate clustering and variation. In order to improve the predication precision, we employ multi-strategy retrieval and utilize different similarity computing technologies to find out the array of neighboring similar fishing grounds. Then, the prediction results will be revised in accordance with the rules already stored in the system. The joint employment of machine learning and expertise will further improve predication precision and system robustness.

While predicting the fishing grounds in winter, historical data in summer are not considered, and due to the fact that remote fishing grounds have little effects on the formation of central fishing grounds, we only choose those sea situations closer to central fishing grounds. In our experiments, we choose 150 out of 600 pieces of sea situations dynamically. In this way, calculation can be reduced greatly through filtration in terms of time and position while keeping prediction precision to a certain degree; the system response time is less than 7 seconds. A visual human–computer interaction module offers a friendly interface for input, output, inspection, and revision as shown in Figure 6.6.

We measure the predication results in terms of the following two factors: completeness, that is, the rate of predication fishing grounds over the actual ones: and precession, the difference between prediction fishing grounds and actual fishing grounds. Fishery experts think that the precision is up to 80% once the difference

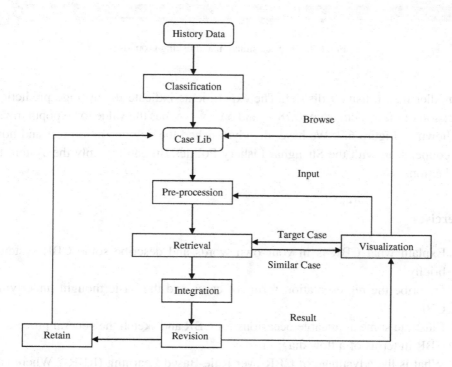

Fig. 6.6. Architecture of central fishing ground forecasting expert system

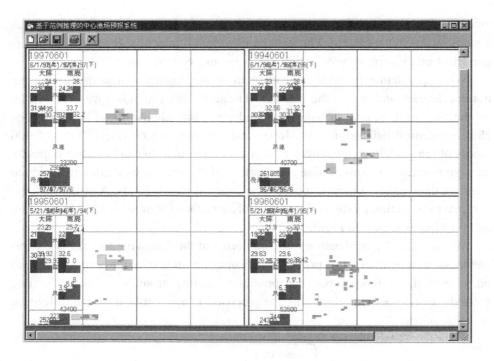

Fig. 6.7.   The sea situation and fishing grounds

is smaller than a fishing district. The experiments indicate the average prediction precision of the system is up to 78%, and our system has the value to be popularized as shown in Figure 6.7. We have already finished the demonstration test and now are cooperating with the Shanghai Fishery Politics Bureau to apply the system to production.

Exercises

6.1 Explain what CBR is in your own words and describe some CBR systems briefly.

6.2 Describe the representation forms of cases and the basic thought underlying CBR.

6.3 Illustrate some applicable occasions for CBR and sketch the general process of CBR in terms of a flow diagram.

6.4 What is the advantage of CBR over Rule-Based Learning (RBR)? Where can CBR (CBL) systems be applied?

6.5 List some kinds of similarities between the target cases and base ones, and try to compare the characteristics of some commonly used methods for similarity measurement.

6.6 Refer to relevant materials and introduce an application system based on CBR, and then discuss key challenges posed by CBR systems and how to overcome them.

6.7 Demonstrate the differences, by using examples, between CBR systems and expert systems.

Chapter 7

Inductive Learning

Inductive learning is one of the most widely studied methods in symbolic learning. Given a series of known positive examples and counterexamples about a concept, the task is to generalize a general concept description. Inductive learning can acquire new concepts, create new rules, and discover new theories. Its usual operations are generalization and specialization.

7.1 Introduction

Inductive learning is one of the most extensive approaches in symbol learning. Its task is to induct a general conceptual description from a series of known positive and negative examples given about a concept. Through inductive learning, new concepts can be obtained, new rules created, and new theories found. Generalization and specification are the general operations of inductive learning. Generalization is used to expand assumed semantic information so that it can include more positive examples and be applied in more situations. Specialization is an opposite operation of generalization. It is used to constrain the application range of conceptual description.

Inductive learning program is the procedure to describe the content mentioned above by a programming language. The language to write the inductive program is referred to as inductive programming language. The system which can execute inductive program and accomplish the specialized task of inductive learning is referred to as inductive learning system, which could be independent or embedded into another greater knowledge processing system. The input of general inductive program is the description of few observations in scientific experiments, while the output is the overall feature description of an object category or classification discriminative description of several object categories.

In contrast to deduction, the starting premise of induction is concrete fact rather than general truth while the reasoning objective is likelihood general assertion to explain fact in form and predict new truth. Induction attempts to lead to complete and correct description from a given phenomenon or part of its concrete observations. Induction has two aspects — generating likelihood assumption and its effectiveness (construction of truth value status). Only the former has preliminary significance in the research of inductive learning. The assumption effectiveness is secondary because the assumption generated by the hypothesis is discriminated by human experts and tested by known approaches of deductive reasoning and mathematical statistics.

Inductive learning can be classified into instance learning, observation, and discovery learning. The task of instance learning, also referred to as concept acquisition, is determined by general concept description, which should explain all given positive instances and exclude all given negative instances. These positive and negative instances are provided by the source of information. The source of information is very extensive. It can be a natural phenomenon or experimental results. Instance learning which learns from classified examples according to supervisor is a supervised learning algorithm.

Observation and discovery learning is also referred to as description generation. This kind of learning will generate and explain the disciplines and rules of all or most observations without the help of supervisor. It includes concept clustering, construction classification, discovery theorems, and expression theories. Observation and discovery learning which learn from observations without classification, or be discovered by functions itself, are unsupervised learning algorithms.

Since inductive reasoning leads to complete knowledge status from incomplete knowledge status, it is a kind of non-monotonous reasoning. However, inductive reasoning cannot verify whether the knowledge is right, while non-monotonic logic provides a theoretical foundation for us to handle non-monotonic generative knowledge.

The basic idea of the inductive principle is to formulate a scientific theory through assumption on the basis of a great deal of observations. All observations are singular propositions, while a theory is usually a universal proposition in domain. There is no logical inevitable implication relation between the singular proposition and universal proposition. They are usually default as facts cannot be observed. We use inductive assertion derived from inductive reasoning as knowledge from the database. Furthermore, they are used as default knowledge. When a new proposition contract with them has emerged, the original default knowledge derived from inductive reasoning would be thrown down so that the consistency of system knowledge can be kept.

A general definition of inductive learning from individual concept is as follows:

(1) Given an instance space constructed by all instances, each instance has several attributes.

(2) Given a description language, the descriptive capability of the language includes describing every instance (realized by describing its attributes) and describing some instance sets, which is referred to as concept.

(3) When learning executes, some instances are extracted from the instance space. The set constructed by these instances is referred to as positive instance set. Then, other instances are extracted from the instance space, which is referred to as negative instance set.

(4) If a concept A, which includes a positive instance set completely and whose intersection with negative instance set is empty set, can be found in limited steps, A is the individual concept for learning and learning is successful, otherwise it is a failure.

(5) If a definite algorithm exists so that learning is always successful for any given positive and negative instance set, the instance space is called acquisitive in the form of the language.

The representative approaches of inductive learning include version space, AQ11 algorithm, decision tree, etc., which will be discussed in this chapter.

7.2 Logic Foundation of Inductive Learning

7.2.1 *Inductive General Paradigm*

In order to depict conceptual inductive learning concretely, the general paradigm of inductive learning is given here (Michalski, 1983).

Given:

(1) premise statements (facts), F, its knowledge related to individual object in an object category, or partial features of an object;

(2) a tentative inductive assertion (which may be empty), its generalization item, or generalization description about objects;

(3) background knowledge that defines assumptions and constraints on observing statements and candidate inductive hypotheses, assertions generated by them, including any related general or domain-specific knowledge.

Find:

an inductive assertion (hypothesis), H, that is tautology or weak implication observing statements which should meet background knowledge.

A hypothesis H has a tautological implicit fact F, which means that F is the logic reasoning of H, i.e., $H \Rightarrow F$ holds. That is, if expression $H \Rightarrow F$ is always true in any explanation, it can be represented as follows: $H \vartriangleright F$, H is specialized to F or $F \ltimes H$. F *is* summed up or generalized to H.

Here, the procedure reasoning F from H is a tautological procedure. Since $H \Rightarrow F$ must hold according to the patterns mentioned above, if H is true, F must be true. On the contrary, the procedure reasoning H from fact F is a non-tautological procedure. That is, if fact F is false, H must be false.

Here, H has a weak implicit F, which means that fact F is not a definitive conclusion H, but a reasonable or partial conclusion H. With the concept of weak implication, this pattern has a possible and partial hypothesis which only needs to explain some of the facts. However, we still focus on the hypothesis of tautological implication facts.

With regard to any given fact set, innumerable hypotheses with regard to these facts could be generated. This needs background knowledge to provide constraints and optimal principles, so that these innumerable hypotheses could be decreased to one or several optimal hypotheses.

In order to formalize the logic foundation of conceptual inductive learning, basic symbols are given in Table 7.1, and the explanations to the symbol are appended.

7.2.2 *Conditions of Concept Acquisition*

In concept acquisition, the observed statements of facts F can be viewed as implications of the form:

$$F: \{e_{ik} ::> K_i\}, \quad i \in I, \tag{7.1}$$

where e_{ik} (training event of K_i) is symbol description of the number k instance of concept K_i. The conceptual predicate is K_i, where i is suffix set of K_i. $e_{ik} ::> K_i$ means that "all events in accordance with description e_{ik} can be asserted to be instances of concept K_i". The inductive hypotheses H seeked out by a learning program can be depicted by concept recognition rule set. Its form is as follows:

$$H: \{D_i ::> K_i\}, \quad i \in I, \tag{7.2}$$

where D_i is the description of concept K_i, i.e., expression D_i is the logic conclusion of events, which can be asserted as an instance of concept K_i.

Table 7.1. Basic symbols

Symbols	Significance
~	not
∧	conjunction (logic product)
∨	disjunction (logic add)
⇒	implication
⇔	logic equivalence
↔	item rewrite
⊕	exclusive or
F	fact set
H	hypothesis
▷	specialization
≺	generalization
⊨	reformalization
∃ v_i	existentially quantified variable v_i
∃ $I v_i$	value existentially quantified variable v_i
∀ v_i	universally quantified variable v_i
D_i	concept description
K_i	judge predicate of name of an concept
::>	implication conjunct concept description and concept name
e_i	an event (description of a situation)
E_i	predicate only if event is true for concept k_i
X_i	attribute
LEF	evaluation function
DOM(P)	domain of descriptor P

Using E_i to represent all description of training events in concept $K_i (i \in I)$, according to the definition of inductive assertion, it must that hold $H \triangleright F$. In order to let D_i become the description of concept K_i, using expressions (7.1) and (7.2) to replace H and F, respectively, the following condition must hold:

$$\forall i \in I \quad (E_i \Rightarrow D_i), \tag{7.3}$$

i.e., all training events of K_i must be in accordance with D_i. If every event only belongs to one concept, the following condition also holds:

$$\forall i, j \in I \quad (D_i \Rightarrow \sim E_i), \quad \text{if } i \neq j. \tag{7.4}$$

This means training events of every concept $K_i (j \neq i)$ are not in accordance with D_i.

Condition (7.3) is referred to as an integral condition. Condition (7.4) is referred to as a consistence condition. As accepted by the concept recognition rule, inductive assertion must meet these two conditions, so that the integrity and consistence can be assured. Integral condition and consistence condition provide a logical foundation for the conceptual algorithm of instance learning.

Description of one kind of objects is an expression satisfying integral condition, or a conjunction of these expressions. This kind of description judges the given category from all possible categories. Differences in the description of an object category is a expression satisfying the integral condition, or a disjunction of these expressions. Its objective is to label a given category into few other categories.

The main interest of knowledge acquisition lies in symbol description-oriented reasoning. This description should be easily understood and easily applied when generating an intelligence model which represents its information. Therefore, description generated by inductive reasoning should be similar to human knowledge representation.

In inductive learning classification, a guiding principle is choosing a language type for inductive learning which has some kind of a definitive form or a similar concept of common predicate logic, decision tree, generative rule, semantic network, framework, multi-value logic, modal logic, etc.

On the basis of predicate logic, representative capability can be improved through modifying and expanding, adding some extra forms and new concepts. Michalski *et al.* proposed annotated predicate calculus (APC), which is more appropriate for reasoning. The main differences between APC and common predicate calculus include the following:

(1) Every predicate, variable, and function is endowed with a label. The label is the set of background knowledge related to the learning problem of the descriptor, for example, a definition of the concept descriptor represents the relation between the label and other concepts, the effective range of descriptor, etc.

(2) Except for the predicate, APC also includes a compound predicate whose arguments can be compound items. A compound item is combined with several common items, such as $P(t_1 \lor t_2, A)$.

(3) The relation predicate among expressions are represented as a selective symbol relation, such as: $=, \neq, >, \geq, \leq, <$.

(4) Apart from universal quantified and existential quantification, there is also numeral quantification, which is used to represent the numerical information of an object satisfying an expression.

7.2.3 *Background Knowledge of Problems*

With regard to a given observation statement set, innumerable inductive assertions implicate that these statement could be constructed. Therefore, some additional information, i.e., background knowledge of problems, should be used to restrain the possible range of inductive assertion and decide on one or some optimal inductive assertions. For example, in the learning approach Star, background knowledge includes several parts:

(1) descriptor information used in observation statement is added in every descriptor label;
(2) form hypothesis about observation and inductive assertion;
(3) selection standard of attributes of list inductive assertion;
(4) various reasoning rules, heuristic rules, specific subprograms, and general and independent procedure, so that the learning system generates a logical conclusion and new descriptor of the given assertion and since the descriptor choice in the observation statement has an important influence on generating inductive assertion, the descriptor choice should be considered first.

The main content of learning system input is an observation statement set. The descriptor in these statements is an observable feature and has useful test data. Deciding on these descriptors is a main issue of inductive learning. Learning approaches can be depicted by an initial descriptor and a relation degree of the learning problem. The relations include the following:

(1) Related completely, that is, all descriptors in an observation statement set are directly related to the learning task. The learning task forms an inductive assertion relating these descriptors.
(2) Related partially, that is, there are many useless or redundant descriptors. Some of them are related. Now, the learning task must choose the most related descriptors and construct a rational inductive assertion based on these descriptors.
(3) Related indirectly, that is, the observation statement does not include descriptors directly related to problems. However, in the initial description, some descriptors can be used to generate related descriptors. The task of learning is to generate these related descriptors directly and get inductive assertion.

Descriptor labeling is background knowledge set related to descriptors and learning problems. It includes the following:

(1) type description of definition domain and descriptors;
(2) operator description related to descriptors;
(3) constraints and relation description among descriptors;
(4) significance and law of descriptors representing number in problems;
(5) features of descriptors applicable to objects;
(6) class including the given descriptor, i.e., parent node of descriptor;

(7) synonym that could replace the descriptor;

(8) definition of descriptors;

(9) typical example of given descriptors of objects.

The definition domain of a descriptor is a set of values that the descriptor can have. For example, human body temperature is between $34°C$ and $44°C$, then the value of descriptor "body temperature" can only be in this range. Descriptor type is decided by the relation of elements in the definition domain of the descriptor. According to the structure of the definition domain of the descriptor, it is of three basic types:

(1) **Nominal descriptor.** Definition domain of this descriptor is composed of an independent symbol or name. That is, values in the value set have no structural relation, such as fruit, people's name.

(2) **Linear descriptor.** Elements in a value set with this kind of descriptors are in accordance with a totally ordered set. For example, funds, temperature, weight, and product are all linear descriptors. Variables representing ordinal numbers, interval, ratio, and absolute calibration are specific instances of a linear descriptor. Functions which map a set to a totally ordered set are linear descriptors too.

(3) **Structural descriptor.** Its value set is a tree-forming graphical structure, reflecting generative levels among values. In such a structure, the parent node represents a more general concept than the child node. For example, in value set "place name", "China" is the parent of "Beijing", "Shanghai", "Jiangsu", "Guangdong", etc. The definition domain of a structural descriptor is defined by a group of reasoning rules explained by the background knowledge of problems. A structural descriptor can be further subdivided into ordered and unordered structural descriptor. Descriptor type is very important to determine the operation of an applied descriptor.

In the learning system Star, the basic form of assertion is c-expression, which is defined as a conjunction normal form:

$$\langle \text{quantifier form} \rangle \langle \text{conjunction of relation statement} \rangle, \qquad (7.5)$$

where $\langle$ quantifier form $\rangle$ represents none or many quantifiers and $\langle$ relation statement $\rangle$ is a specific form of predicate. Following is an example of c-expression:

$$\exists P_0, P_1([\text{shape}(P_0 \wedge P_1) = \text{box}][\text{weight}(P_0) > \text{weight}(P_1)]),$$

i.e., the shape of objects P_0 and P_1 are boxes, and object P_0 is more weighty than object P_1.

An important specific form of c-expression is a-expression, i.e., atomic expression, which does not include "inter disjunction". Inter conjunction and disjunction mean "and" and "or" of conjunction items, respectively; outer conjunction and disjunction mean "and" and "or" of conjunction predicate, i.e., "and" and "or" in common sense.

7.2.4 *Selective and Constructive Generalization Rules*

A generalization rule transforms a description into a more general description. A more general description tautologically implicates the initial description. Since generalization rule is non-tautological, if $F \vdash H$, then for all facts that make F to be false, they make H to be false ($\sim F \Rightarrow \sim H$).

In concept acquisition, if a rule $E ::> K$ is transformed into a more general rule $D ::> K$, it must hold that $E \Rightarrow D$. So we can get generalization rules using tautological implication in formal logic. For example, formal logic holds that $P \wedge Q \Rightarrow P$, then it can be transformed into a generalization rule:

$$P \wedge Q ::> K \ \vdash \ P ::> K. \tag{7.6}$$

If using labeling predicate calculus to represent these generalization rule, we should mainly consider transforming one or more statements into a single, more general generalization rule:

$$\{D_i ::> K_i\} \ i \in I \ \vdash \ D ::> K \tag{7.7}$$

Equals

$$D_1 \wedge D_2 \wedge \ldots \wedge D_n ::> K \ \vdash \ D ::> K. \tag{7.8}$$

The rule indicates that if an event meets the entire description D_i ($i \in$ I), it must meet a more general description D.

A basic characteristic of generalization transform is as follows. What it gets is only a hypothesis, and this must be tested using new data. Furthermore, the generalization rule does not assure that the descriptor obtained from it is rational or useful. Generalization is divided into two categories: constructive and selective. If in generating a concept description D, all descriptions used have appeared in the initial concept description D_i ($i \in$ I), then it is called selective generalization rule; otherwise, it is constructive generalization rule.

1. Selective generalization rules

Assume that CTX, CTX_1, and CTX_2 represent arbitrary expressions.

(1) Condition elimination rule:

$$CTX \wedge S ::> K \;\mid\!\!< \; CTX ::> K \qquad (7.9)$$

where S is a predicate or a logic expression.

(2) Add selective item rule:

$$CTX_1 ::> K \;\mid\!\!< \; CTX_1 \vee CTX_2 ::> K \qquad (7.10)$$

generalize concept description through adding the selective item rule, such as:

$$CTX \wedge [color = red] ::> K \;\mid\!\!< \; CTX \wedge [L = R_2] ::> K$$

(3) Enlarge quote range rule:

$$CTX \wedge [L = R_1] ::> K \;\mid\!\!< \; CTX \wedge [color: red \wedge blue] ::> K \qquad (7.11)$$

where $R_1 \subseteq R_2 \subseteq DOM(L)$, DOM(L) is a domain of L, L is an item, and R_i is a set of values L can have.

(4) Closed interval rule:

$$\left. \begin{array}{l} CTX \wedge [L = a] ::> K \\ CTX \wedge [L = b] ::> K \end{array} \right|\!\!< CTX \wedge [L = a \cdots b] ::> K \qquad (7.12)$$

where L is a linear descriptor, and a and b are specific values of L.

(5) Climbing generalization tree rule:

$$\left. \begin{array}{l} CTX \wedge [L = a] ::> K \\ CTX \wedge [L = b] ::> K \\ \quad\vdots \\ CTX \wedge [L = i] ::> K \end{array} \right|\!\!< CTX \wedge [L = S] ::> K \qquad (7.13)$$

where L is a structural descriptor in the generalization tree domain of L, and S represents the lowest parent node whose successors are $a, b, \ldots, i$.

(6) **Rule transforming constant into variable:**

$$\left.\begin{array}{c} F[a] \\ F[b] \\ \vdots \\ F[i] \end{array}\right| \Bigg\Vert \forall x\, F[x] \tag{7.14}$$

where $F[x]$ is a descriptor dependent on variable x, and $a, b, \ldots, i$ are constants. For descriptor $F[x]$, if some values of x $(a, b, \ldots, i)$ make $F[x]$ hold, then we can get the assumption: for all values of x, $F[x]$ holds.

(7) **Rule transforming conjunction into disjunction:**

$$F_1 \wedge F_2 ::> K \quad \Vdash F_1 \vee F_2 ::> K \tag{7.15}$$

where F_1 and F_2 are arbitrary descriptions.

(8) **Rule enlarging quantifier range:**

$$\forall x\, F[x] ::> K \quad \Vdash \exists x\, F[x] ::> K \tag{7.16}$$

$$\exists_{(i_1)} x\, F[x] ::> K \quad \Vdash \exists_{(i_2)} x\, F[x] ::> K \tag{7.17}$$

where I_1 and I_2 are the domain of quantifiers (set of integer), and $I_1 \subseteq I_2$.

(9) **Generalization decomposition rule:**

Used in concept acquisition:

$$\left.\begin{array}{c} P \wedge F_1 ::> K \\ \sim P \wedge F_2 ::> K \end{array}\right| \Bigg\Vert F_1 \vee F_2 ::> K \tag{7.18}$$

Used in description generalization

$$P \wedge F_1 \vee \sim p \wedge F_2 \Vdash F_1 \wedge F_2 \tag{7.19}$$

where P is the predicate.

(10) **Anti-enlarge rule:**

$$\left.\begin{array}{c} \mathrm{CTX}_1 \wedge [L = R_1] ::> K \\ \mathrm{CTX}_2 \wedge [L = R_2] ::> \sim K \end{array}\right| \Bigg\Vert [L \neq R_2] ::> K \tag{7.20}$$

where R_1 and R_2 are disjunction expressions.

Given an object description which belongs to concept K (positive instance) and an object description that does not belong to concept K (negative instance), the rule will generate a more general description which includes these two descriptions. This is the basic idea of learning difference description from instances.

2. Constructive generalization rule

Constructive generalization rule can generate some inductive assertions. The descriptors they used do not appear in the initial observation statement, that is, these rules transform the initial representing space.

(1) General constructive rule:

$$CTX \wedge F_1 ::> K \Big|_{F_1 \Rightarrow F_2} < CTX \wedge F_2 ::> K \qquad (7.21)$$

The rule states that if a concept description consists of a part F_1, and F_1 implicates another concept F_2, a more general description can be obtained by using F_2 to replace F_1.

(2) Computing variable rule:

Computing quantifier (CQ rule):

$$\exists_{V1, V2, ..., Vk} F[V_1, V_2, \ldots, V_k]$$

CQ rule will generate a new descriptor "#v-COND", representing the number of v_i meeting a certain condition COND. For example, "#v_i-length-2..4" represents the number of v_i whose length is between 2 and 4.

Computing number of predicate (CA rule): in descriptions, a descriptor is a relation which possess several variables $REL(v_1, v_2, \ldots, v_k)$, and the CA rule will compute the number of predicates which meet the condition COND in relation REL.

(3) Generating link attribute rule:

In concept description, if variables in a concept description formulate a link because of the difference of transfer relation, the rule can generate descriptors of some particular objects in the depicting link. This kind of object may be as follows:

- LST-object: "minimum object", or starting object of link,
- MST-object: ending object of link,
- MID-object: middle object of link,
- Nth-object: the Nth object of link.

(4) Rule detecting dependence relation of descriptors:

Assume that given an object set representing a concept, we use attribute description to depict features of the object. The description defines attribute values of the object and does not depict structural features of it. Assume that in all fact descriptions, the values of linear descriptor x are ascending ordered, while values of another linear descriptor y are ascending or descending ordered, then a 2D descriptor $M(x, y)$ is generated, which indicates that there is a monotonic relation between x and y. Descriptor has value ↑ when value y is ascending, otherwise descriptor has value ↓.

7.3 Inductive Bias

Bias plays an important role in concept learning. Bias means all factors affecting assume selection in concept learning except for a positive and negative example. These factors include the following: (a) language describing assumption; (b) assumption space considered by program; (c) assumption procedure according to what order; and (d) admit definitive criterion, that is, a research procedure with known assumption could be terminated, or proceed to select a better assumption. Employing the bias approach, learning partial difference assumption will result in different inductive leaps. Bias has two features (Utgoff, 1986):

(1) A strong bias is one that focuses concept learning on a relatively small number of hypotheses. On the contrary, a weak bias is one that allows the concept learner to consider a relatively large number of hypotheses.
(2) A correct bias is one that allows the concept learner to select the target concept. Conversely, an incorrect bias cannot select the target concept.

Figure 7.1 shows the role of bias in inductive learning. From the figure, we can know that given any training examples with a specific order, induction becomes an independent variable function. When bias is strong and correct, concept learning can select the available objective concept. When bias is weak and incorrect, concept learning is difficult because no guide can select the hypothesis. In order to transform a weaker bias, the following algorithm could be employed:

(1) Recommend new concept descriptions to be added to the concept description language through heuristics;
(2) Translate the recommendations into new concept descriptions formally represented by the concept description language;

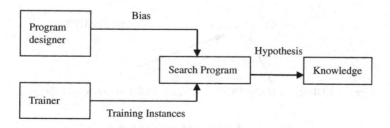

Fig. 7.1. Role of bias in inductive learning

(3) Assimilate newly formed concepts into the restricted space of hypotheses in a manner that maintains the organization of the hypothesis space.

In the algorithm mentioned above, step 1 determines a better bias. The machine executes transforming in steps 2 and 3, resulting in a new concept description language that is better than the former description language.

To realize inductive learning, it is necessary to study a good bias. As for the fundamental problem of bias transform, it includes tasks about assimilate generating knowledge and question acquisition, computing initial bias, approaches of goal freedom and goal sensitivity, etc. It needs to be studied further.

7.4 Version Space

Version space takes the whole rule space as the initial assumed rule set H. According to the information in training examples, it makes a generalization or specialization to a set, increasingly reducing the set H. Finally, H is converged into rules that only include quest. The term "version space" is used to refer to this set because it contains all plausible versions of the emerging concept.

In 1977, Mitchell pointed out that rules in rule space can build a partial order according to their general degree. Figure 7.2 shows a partial order in a rule space, where TRUE means that there is no condition, and this is the most general concept. Concept $\exists x$: CLUBS(x) means that at least a club is more specific than the former. Concept $\exists x, y$: CLUBS(x)∧HEARTS(y) means that at least a club and a heart exist and they are more specific than the former. Arrows in the figure point to a more general concept from a specific concept.

Figure 7.3 is the sketch map after ordering the general rule space. The highest point in the figure is the most general rule (concept). It is a point without description, i.e., a point without condition. All examples are in accordance with the concept. Points on the lowest line correspond to concepts of positive training examples. Each

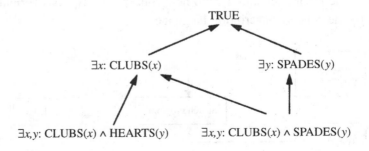

Fig. 7.2. A partial order in rule space

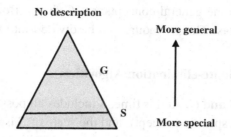

Fig. 7.3. Sketch map of general rule space ordering

point corresponds to a positive example. For example, every example shows the suit and rank of a card C, such as

$$\text{SUIT(C, clubs)} \wedge \text{RANK(C, 7)}.$$

This is a positive training example; at the same time, it is the most specific concept. Concept RANK(C,7) are points at the middle of rule space. It is more specific than no description, and more general than the positive training example.

When searching the rule space, we use a possible rational set of hypothesis rule H. H is the subset of rule space. It is a segment of rule space. The subset composed of the most general elements of H is referred to as set G; the subset composed of the most specific elements of H is referred to as set S. In rule space, H is a segment between the upper bound G and lower bound S. So, set H can be represented by G and S.

The initial set G of version space is the highest point (the most general concept); the initial set S is points of the lowest line (positive training examples); the initial set H is the whole rule space. In the search procedure, set G increasingly drops (specialization); set S increasingly rises (generalization); and set H increasingly reduces. Finally, H is converged into a request concept. Several algorithms are introduced in the following.

7.4.1 *Candidate-Elimination Algorithm*

Mitchell proposed an algorithm named candidate-elimination algorithm. It represents set H using bound sets G and S. Set H is called version space. All concept descriptions in H meet all positive examples provided, and do not meet any negative example provided.

At the beginning, H is the whole rule space. After accepting the positive training instances, the program is generalized. Through eliminating some specific concepts, set S arises. After accepting negative training instances, the program is specialized.

Through eliminating some general concepts, set G drops. Both of them eliminate some candidate concepts. The procedure can be divided into four steps (Mitchell, 1977).

Algorithm 7.1 (Candidate-elimination Algorithm).

1. **Initialize the sets S and G.** At this time, S includes all possible positive training instances (the most specific concept), and the scale of S is too great. The initial set S of the actual algorithm only includes the first positive training instance, and this kind of H is not the whole space.
2. **Accepting a new training instance.** If it is a positive instance, first eliminate the concept that does not cover the new positive instance from G, then modify S to the most specific result generalized from the new positive instances and original elements of S (that is, as less as possible modifying S, but S is required to cover the new positive instances). If it is negative instances, first eliminate the concept that covers the new the negative instance from S, then modify G to the most general result specialized from the new negative instances and original elements of G (that is, as less as possible modifying G, but G is required not to cover the new negative examples).
3. If $G = S$ and it is a single-element set, go to step 4, otherwise go to step 2.
4. Output the concept in H (i.e., G and S).

The following is an example. We use feature vectors to describe an object. Every object has two features: size and shape. The size of an object could be large (lg) or small (sm). The shape of an object could be circular (cir), square (squ), or triangular (tri). To let the program know the concept "circle", this can be represented as $(x,$ cir), where x represents any size.

Initial set H is the rule space. Sets G and S are as follows, respectively,

$$G = \{(x, y)\}$$

$$S = \{(\text{sm squ}), (\text{sm cir}), (\text{sm tri}), (\text{lg squ}), (\text{lg cir}), (\text{lg tri})\}.$$

The initial version space H is shown at Figure 7.4.

The first training example is a positive example (sm cir), which means that a small circle is a circle. After modifying algorithm S, we can get

$$G = \{(x\ y)\}$$

$$S = \{(\text{sm cir})\}.$$

Figure 7.5 shows the version space after the first training instance. Four concepts linked by arrows construct the version space. These concepts meet the first training

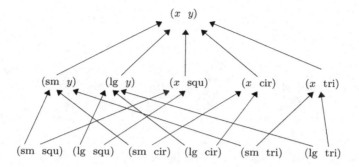

Fig. 7.4. Initial version space

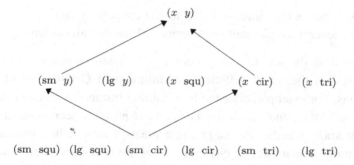

Fig. 7.5. Version space after the first training example

instance, and no other concepts do. In the actual algorithm, this is taken as the initial version space, not what is given in Figure 7.4.

The second training instance is the negative example (lg tri), which means that a large triangle is not a circle. This step specializes the set G, and it can get:

$$G = \{(x \text{ cir}), (sm \text{ } y)\}$$

$$S = \{(sm \text{ cir})\}.$$

Figure 7.6 shows the version space after the second training instance. At this time, H only includes three concepts, which meet the previous concept, but do not meet all concepts of this negative instance.

The third training instance is the positive instance (lg cir), which means that the large circle is a circle. This step first eliminates the concepts that do not meet the positive instance and then generalizes S and the positive instance. It gets:

$$G = \{(x \text{ cir})\}$$

$$S = \{(x \text{ cir})\}.$$

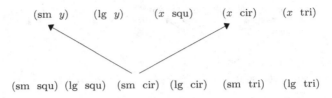

Fig. 7.6.　Version space after the second training example

The algorithm ends at this time, and outputs the concept (x cir).

There are several supplement explanations about this algorithm:

(1) Understanding the sets G and S. As for new instances that meet the required concepts, S is the set of sufficient conditions, and G is the set of necessary conditions. For example, after the first training instance, (sm cir) is a sufficient condition. That is, small circle must meet the required concept when the program does not know whether the large circle meets it or not. In addition, after the second training instance, (x cir) and (sm y) are necessary conditions. That is, the instance which meets the required concept is either a circle or is small. When the algorithm ends, $G = S$, i.e., it meets the necessary and sufficient condition.

(2) When learning the positive instances, S is generalized, and this often makes S enlarged. When learning the negative examples, G is specialized, and this often makes G enlarged. The scale of G and S is too large, which will make the algorithm difficult to apply. Algorithm is breath-first search for the rule space under the guide of training examples. As for a large rule space, the algorithm is too slow to accept.

7.4.2　*Two Improved Algorithms*

Basic learning algorithms of version space are very difficult to apply, so people proposed some improved algorithms. There are two improved algorithms among them that only employ positive instance learning. They are similar to the procedure mentioned above to modify S.

The first algorithm is collision match algorithm. It is used to learn the concept represented by "parameterized structural representation". In the procedure mentioned above to modify S, it always does as less generalization as possible so that it can cover a new positive example. If descriptive form is a predicate expression, the procedure is equal to find the largest public sub-expression. This only needs to eliminate the least conjunction condition. For example, set S is as follows:

$$S = \{BLOCK(x) \wedge BLOCK(y) \wedge SQUARE(y) \wedge RECTANGLE(x)$$
$$\wedge ONTOP(x, y)\},$$

which means block x is a rectangle, block y is a square, and x is on y. If the next positive training example I_1 is as follows:

$$I_1 = \{BLOCK(w) \wedge BLOCK(v) \wedge SQUARE(w) \wedge RECTANGLE(v)$$
$$\wedge ONTOP(w, v)\}$$

it means block w is a square, block v is a rectangle, and w is on v.

Through the procedure to modify S, the following public subset will be generated:

$$S' = \{S_1, S_2\},$$

where

$$S_1 = BLOCK(a) \wedge BLOCK(b) \wedge SQUARE(a) \wedge RECTANGLE(b)$$
$$S_2 = BLOCK(c) \wedge BLOCK(d) \wedge ONTOP(c, d).$$

S_1 equals the assumption that position ONTOP is not related to the required concept. S_2 equals the assumption that block shape is not related to the required concept. It should be noted that, when x corresponds to w and y corresponds to v, position relations between S and I_1 are matched while shape features are not matched. On the contrary, when x corresponds to v and y corresponds to w, shape features are matched while position relations between S and I_1 are not matched. This phenomenon is collision in match. In order to solve the collision, we use two elements in S' to consider these two sides, respectively.

The second approach is to maximize unified generalization. This algorithm is used to find the maximum unified generalization of predicate expression. It is similar to collision match algorithm, but the representative language it uses allows a many-to-one argument link in match.

Version space has two main shortages:
(1) **Lacks anti-noise ability.** All data-driven algorithms (include version space) find it hard to handle training instances with noise. Since concepts obtained from algorithms should meet the request of every training instance, a training instance would have make a big influence. Sometimes, wrong instances make

the program produce wrong concepts, and sometimes even no concepts. At this time, H becomes an empty set.

In order to solve the problem Mitchell proposed an approach to save multiple sets of G and S. For example, S_0 meets all positive instances, and S_1 meets all other positive instances except one, if S_2 etc. are similar. If G_0 exceeds S_0, H_0 is an empty set. This means that no concept meets all instances. So, the program finds G_1 and S_1, so that we can get H_1. If H_1 is empty too, it gets H_2.

(2) **Learns disjunction concept.** Version space cannot learn the disjunction concept. Some concepts are in disjunction form. For example, PARENT may be father or mother. This can be represented as PARENT(x) = FATHER(x) $\vee$ PARENT(x) = MOTHER(x). Since sets G and S are of conjunction form, the above-mentioned algorithm cannot find disjunction concepts.

The first solution uses representation language without a disjunction connective. It repeats many times to eliminate candidate elements so that it can find many conjunction descriptions covering all examples.

Algorithm 7.2 (Algorithm to Learn Disjunction Concept).

1. Set S is initialized to include one positive instance, and set G is initialized to include no description.
2. As for every negative instance, modify set G.
3. Select a description g in G and take g as a conjunction term of the solution set. g does not cover any negative instance, but it will cover part of the positive instances. Then eliminate all positive instances more specific than g from positive instance set (i.e., positive instances covered by g).
4. For residual positive instances and negative instances, repeat steps 1, 2, and 3 until all positive instances are covered. The disjunction of g obtained from each repeat is a required concept.

The disjunction does not cover any negative instance, and every g does not cover any negative instance either. The disjunction covers all positive instances, and every g covers positive instances eliminated by it. Note that, since there is no procedure to modify S, g does not cover all positive instances. However, g at least covers the positive instance at first step, so g should at least eliminate this positive instance.

The second solution is referred to as AQ algorithm (Michalski, 1975), which is similar to the former algorithm. But AQ algorithm uses heuristics to select a positive instance at the first step, requiring the positive instance to not be covered by several past g. Larson improved the AQ algorithm and applied it to spread predicate calculus representation.

7.5 AQ Algorithm for Inductive Learning

In 1969, Michalski proposed the AQ learning algorithm, which is an example-based learning algorithm. The AQ algorithm generates disjunction of a selected assumption, which covers all positive examples but does not cover any negative example. Its basic algorithm is as follows:

Algorithm 7.3 (Simple AQ Learning Algorithm).

1. Randomly select one positive example as a seed.
2. Generate consistent generalization expression of the example (referred to as star).
3. According to bias standard, select the optimal generalization expression from star. If needed, it specializes the assumption.
4. If this hypothesis covers all positive examples, then go to step 2.

Michalski proposed AQ11 in 1978 (Michalski and Larson, 1978). AQ11 algorithm searches rule space, repeatedly eliminates candidate elements, and gets general rules. AQ11 algorithm turns problems of learning discriminative rules into a series of problems of learning a single concept. In order to get rules of class C_i, it takes examples of class C_i as positive examples and all examples of other classes as negative examples. It can get descriptions that cover all positive examples but do not cover any negative example, which can be taken as rules of C_i. Discriminative rules found may overlap in the unobserved region of the example space.

In order to find a classification rule set which does not overlap, AQ11 takes examples of class C_i as positive examples, and negative examples include all examples of other classes $C_j (j \neq i)$ and all examples in the positive example region of various unhandled classes $C_k (1 \leq k \leq i)$. Then, class C_2 only covers parts that class C_1 does not cover. Parts that class C_3 covers are parts that neither class C_2 nor C_1 cover.

Discriminative rules obtained from AQ11 correspond to the most general description set meeting the training examples. That is, set G of various classes, such as G_1, G_2, etc. Sometimes the most specific description sets meet training examples, which need to be used. That is, set S of various classes, such as S_1, S_2, etc.

Michalski *et al.* employed the AQ11 program in learning the diagnosis rules for sick soy plants. In the program, 630 descriptions of plants with soy sickness have been provided. Each description has 35 feature vectors. At the same time, expert diagnosis conclusions have been pooled. The program of selecting examples selects 290 sample plants as training examples. The selective principle makes the distance between examples as large as possible. The other 340 plants are taken as a test set to check the acquired rules.

7.6 Constructing Decision Trees

A particularly efficient method for exploring the space of concept descriptions is to generate a decision tree. Hunt, Marin, and Stone have developed concept learning system (CLS) (Hunt *et al.*, 1966). CLS uses a lookahead strategy similar to minimax. At each stage, CLS explores the space of possible decision trees to a fixed depth, chooses an action to minimize cost in this limited space, then moves one level down in the tree. It intends to solve single-concept learning tasks and uses the learned concepts to classify new instances.

The main idea of the CLS algorithm is the following: First, start from an empty decision tree and improve the original decision tree by adding new a discriminative node until a decision tree could correctly classify the training examples.

Algorithm 7.4 (CLS Algorithm).

1. Let initial status of decision tree T only include a root (X, Q), where X is a set of all training examples, and Q is a set of all test attributes;
2. If all leaf nodes (X', Q'), of T have following status — when all training examples of the first vector X' belong to same class, or the second vector Q' is void — cease the execution of the learning algorithm, and the learning result is T;
3. Otherwise, select a leaf node (X', Q') without the status mentioned in step 2;
4. As for Q', we select the test attribute according to certain rules. Assume that X' was divided into m non-intersect subsets X'_i, $1 \leq i \leq m$, by different values of b. Sticking m branches from (X', Q'), each branch represents different values of b, then formulate m new leaf nodes $(X'_i, Q' - \{b\})$, $1 \leq i \leq m$;
5. Go to step 2.

It can be seen from the description of the CLS algorithm that the construct procedure is a procedure of hypothesis specialization, and so CLS algorithm can be seen as a learning algorithm with only one operator, which can be represented as: through adding a new discriminative condition (discriminative node), specialize current hypothesis. CLS algorithm recursively calls the operator, acting at every leaf node, and constructs a decision tree.

In step 2 of Algorithm 7.4, if there exists no contradiction within a training set, which means there does not exist two examples without the same attribute belonging to the same class, then if the second condition is met (i.e., Q' is empty), the first condition will be met too (i.e., all training examples of X' belong to same class). This means the cease condition should be chosen from one of them. However, as for the existing contradiction training set, the above-mentioned statement must not hold.

In step 4, the algorithm should meet $m > 1$ or the classification is pointless. However, because there are contradiction training examples, it is difficult to assure $m > 1$.

In step 4, the algorithm does not give the selective standard of test attributes, so CLS has been improved through many ways.

7.7 ID3 Learning Algorithm

Algorithm 7.4 did not give a method on how to select test attribute b, so Hunt had proposed several selective standards. In various decision tree learning algorithms, the most influential is the ID3 algorithm proposed by Quinlan in 1979. ID3 algorithm takes the decline velocity of information entropy as the selective standard of test attribute. Decline of information entropy is decline of information uncertainty.

7.7.1 *Introduction to Information Theory*

In 1948, Shannon proposed and developed information theory, studying information and mathematic measure, which measures the magnitude of information through eliminating the uncertain degree of various symbols in the information source. A series of concepts has been proposed:

(1) **Self-information.** Before receiving a_i, the uncertainty of the receiver sending a_i to an information source is defined as self-information $I(a_i)$, i.e., $I(a_i) = -\log p(a_i)$, where $p(a_i)$ represents the probability of a_i sent by the information source.

(2) **Information entropy.** Self-information reflects the uncertainty of symbols, while information entropy can be used to measure uncertainty of the whole information source X. It is defined as follows:

$$H(X) = p(a_1)I(a_1) + p(a_2)I(a_2) + \cdots + p(a_r)I(a_r)$$

$$= -\sum_{i=1}^{r} p(a_i) \log p(a_i), \tag{7.22}$$

where r represents all possible number of symbols of information source X. Information entropy is defined as the average self-information content provided by the information source when it sends a symbol. Here, log is logarithm taking 2 as base.

(3) **Condition entropy.** Condition entropy $H(X/Y)$ is used to measure the receiver receiving the random variable Y; random variable X still exists in uncertainty

when information source X and random variable Y are not mutually indepen-dent. Let X be correspondent to source symbol a_i, Y be correspondent to source symbol b_j, then $p(a_i/b_j)$ is the probability, the condition entropy as follows:

(4) **Average mutual information.** It is used to represent the amount of information about X provided by signal Y, represented as $I(X, Y)$:

$$H(X/Y) = - \sum_{i=1}^{r} \sum_{j=1}^{s} p(a_i/b_j) \log p(a_i/b_j), \tag{7.23}$$

$$I(X, Y) = H(X) - H(X/Y). \tag{7.24}$$

7.7.2 Attribute Selection

In Algorithm 7.4, we only have one empty decision tree when learning starts, not knowing how to classify examples according to attributes. In terms of training set, we should construct the decision tree to partition the whole example space based on attributes. Let the training set be X and it will be divided into n classes. Assume that the number of training examples belonging to the ith class is C_i, the total number of training examples in X is $|X|$. If the probability that an example belongs to the ith class is written as $P(C_i)$, then:

$$P(C_i) = \frac{C_i}{|X|}. \tag{7.25}$$

At this time, uncertainty of decision tree partition C is

$$H(X, C) = - \sum P(C_i) \log P(C_i). \tag{7.26}$$

In context, without confusion, $H(X, C)$ is simply written as $H(X)$.

Decision tree learning procedure is a procedure that the increasing decision tree diminishes the uncertainty of the partition. If we select attribute a to test, when we know $a = a_j$

$$H(X/a) = - \sum_i \sum_j p(Ci; a = a_j) \log p(Ci/a = a_j)$$

$$= - \sum_i \sum_j p(a = a_j) p(Ci/a = a_j) \log p(Ci/a = a_j)$$

$$= - \sum_j p(a = a_j) \sum_i p(Ci/a = a_j) \log p(Ci/a = a_j). \tag{7.27}$$

Assume that the number of examples belonging to the ith class is C_{ij}, written as $P(Ci, a = a_j) = \frac{C_{ij}}{|X|}$, i.e., $P(C_i, a = a_j)$ is the probability of belonging to the ith class when test attribute a is a_j. At this time, the uncertainty degree of decision tree classification is the condition entropy of the training set to attribute X:

$$H(X_j) = -\sum_i p(Ci/a = a_j) \log p(Ci/a = a_j). \tag{7.28}$$

After selecting test attribute a, for every leaf node X_j meets $a = a_j$, the information entropy about classification information is

$$H(X/a) = \sum_j p(a = a_j) H(X_j). \tag{7.29}$$

The amount of information provided by classification of attribute a is $I(X; a)$:

$$I(X, a) = H(X) - H(X/a). \tag{7.30}$$

The less the value of expression (7.29), the larger the value of expression (7.30) would be. This means the more information provided by test attribute a, the less uncertainty degree for classification after selecting a. Quinlan's ID3 algorithm selects the attribute which makes $I(X; a)$ maximum to be the test attribute, i.e., selects attribute a which makes expression (7.29) minimum.

7.7.3 ID3 Algorithm

Except for using information measure as standard, ID3 algorithm introduces increment learning techniques. In CLS algorithm, since the algorithm needs to know all training examples at the beginning, when the training example set is too large, examples cannot be immediately put into memory and have some problems. Quinlan introduces windows for increment learning to solve the problem. The following is the ID3 algorithm (Quinlan, 1983).

Algorithm 7.5 (ID3 Algorithm).

1. Select random subset X_1 with scale of W from the whole training example set X (W is window scale, and subset is referred to as window);
2. With the standard that makes the value of Expression (7.29) minimum, select each test attribute to form current decision tree;
3. Scan all training examples sequentially, and find the current exception of the current decision tree; if there is no exception, the algorithm ends.
4. Combine some examples of current window and some exceptions in step 3 to form a new window, go to step 2.

In order to construct new window in step 4, Quinlan tried two different strategies: one is to retain all examples of window and add appointed exceptions obtained from step 3. This strategy will make the window larger. The other strategy corresponds to retaining a training example for each node of the current decision tree while other examples are deleted from the window and replaced by exceptions. The experiments showed that both approaches work well, but if the concept is so complicated that windows with fixed scale W cannot be found, the second approach may be not converged.

7.7.4 *Application Example of ID3 Algorithm*

Table 7.2 shows that a data set may have noise. There are four attributes: Outlook, Temperature, Humidity, and Wind. It is divided into two classes, P and N, representing positive examples and negative examples, respectively. What we should do is construct a decision tree and classify the data.

Table 7.2. Daily weather classification

Attribute	Outlook	Temperature	Humidity	Wind	Class
1	Overcast	Hot	High	Not	N
2	Overcast	Hot	High	Very	N
3	Overcast	Hot	High	Medium	N
4	Sunny	Hot	High	Not	P
5	Sunny	Hot	High	Medium	P
6	Rain	Mild	High	Not	N
7	Rain	Mild	High	Medium	N
8	Rain	Hot	Normal	Not	P
9	Rain	Cool	Normal	Medium	N
10	Rain	Hot	Normal	Very	N
11	Sunny	Cool	Normal	Very	P
12	Sunny	Cool	Normal	Medium	P
13	Overcast	Mild	High	Not	N
14	Overcast	Mild	High	Medium	N
15	Overcast	Cool	Normal	Not	P
16	Overcast	Cool	Normal	Medium	P
17	Rain	Mild	Normal	Not	N
18	Rain	Mild	Normal	Medium	N
19	Overcast	Mild	Normal	Medium	P
20	Overcast	Mild	Normal	Very	P
21	Sunny	Mild	High	Very	P
22	Sunny	Mild	High	Medium	P
23	Sunny	Hot	Normal	Not	P
24	Rain	Mild	High	Very	N

Since the number of examples belonging to classes P and N is 12 at the beginning, the entropy value is:

$$H(X) = -\frac{12}{24} \log \frac{12}{24} - \frac{12}{24} \log \frac{12}{24} = 1.$$

If Outlook is selected as the test attribute, then according to formula (7.23), condition entropy is

$$H(X/\text{Outlook}) = \frac{9}{24} \left(-\frac{4}{9} \log \frac{4}{9} - \frac{5}{9} \log \frac{5}{9} \right) + \frac{8}{24} \left(-\frac{1}{8} \log \frac{1}{8} - \frac{7}{8} \log \frac{7}{8} \right)$$

$$+ \frac{7}{24} \left(-\frac{1}{7} \log \frac{1}{7} - \frac{6}{7} \log \frac{6}{7} \right) = 0.5528.$$

If Temperature is selected as test attribute, then

$$H(X/\text{Temp}) = \frac{8}{24} \left(-\frac{4}{8} \log \frac{4}{8} - \frac{4}{8} \log \frac{4}{8} \right) + \frac{11}{24} \left(-\frac{4}{11} \log \frac{4}{11} - \frac{7}{11} \log \frac{7}{11} \right)$$

$$+ \frac{5}{24} \left(-\frac{4}{5} \log \frac{4}{5} - \frac{1}{5} \log \frac{1}{5} \right) = 0.6739.$$

If Humidity is selected as test attribute, then

$$H(X/\text{Humid}) = \frac{12}{24} \left(-\frac{4}{12} \log \frac{4}{12} - \frac{8}{12} \log \frac{8}{12} \right)$$

$$+ \frac{12}{24} \left(-\frac{4}{12} \log \frac{4}{12} - \frac{8}{12} \log \frac{8}{12} \right) = 0.9183.$$

If Wind is selected as test attribute, then

$$H(X/\text{Windy}) = \frac{8}{24} \left(-\frac{4}{8} \log \frac{4}{8} - \frac{4}{8} \log \frac{4}{8} \right) + \frac{6}{24} \left(-\frac{3}{6} \log \frac{3}{6} - \frac{3}{6} \log \frac{3}{6} \right)$$

$$+ \frac{10}{24} \left(-\frac{5}{10} \log \frac{5}{10} - \frac{5}{10} \log \frac{5}{10} \right) = 1.$$

We can see that $H(X/\text{Outlook})$ is minimum, which means that information about Outlook is of great help for classification, providing the largest amount of information, i.e., $I(X, \text{Outlook})$ is maximum. Therefore, Outlook should be selected as the test attribute. We can see $H(X) = H(X/\text{Windy})$, i.e., $I(X, \text{Windy}) = 0$. Information about Wind cannot provide any information about classification. After selecting Outlook as the test attribute, the training example set is divided into three

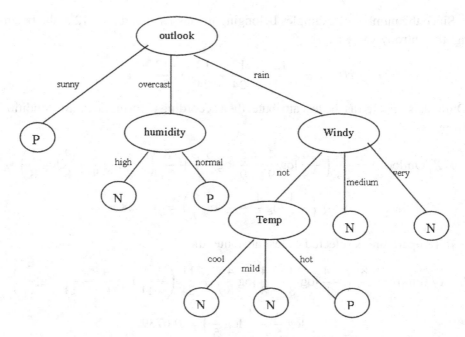

Fig. 7.7.   Decision tree generated by training Table 7.2

subsets, generating three leaf nodes. Using the above procedure to each leaf node in order, we can get a decision tree, as shown in Figure 7.7.

ID3 algorithms have extensive applications. The most famous is C4.5 (Quinlan, 1993). The new function of C4.5 is to transform a decision tree into an equivalent rule representation. In addition, C4.5 solves data learning problems of continuous value.

7.7.5 *Dispersing Continuous Attribute*

A decision tree is mainly used to learn the approach that takes discrete variables as attribute type. To learn continuous variable, it must be dispersed. However, in some algorithms (such as C4.5), it is easier to select the dispersed continuous attribute than to select the discrete attribute. In these algorithms, for a continuous attribute, first order different values of the stored training examples, then select each pair of neighboring central points as standard to the differential attribute values. Since these dispersed attributes are only represented by one example, the continuous attribute will be selected in priority.

Dougherty employs an information entropy-based procedure to disperse the continuous attribute. They disperse the continuous global variable before generating the decision tree, rather than disperse the local variable based on examples of a node like C4.5. Since local data are less, it is easily influenced by the noise of the data. Based on information entropy, this approach recursively divides continuous value into many discrete attributes. In addition, it employes MDL standard. They find this approach does not drop the classification accuracy when used in C4.5. On the contrary, it sometimes raises the accuracy and decreases the size of trees in C4.5.

Auer proposed an approach to disperse a continuous variable using the local method. His T2 algorithm divides continuous variables into many discrete variables but not a binary continuous variable. It is not doing recursive divide as above, but doing a complete search to find a group of intervals so that the error in the training example set is minimum. The default value of m is $C + 1$, where C is the number of partition classes. Therefore, the complexity of T2 is proportional to $C^6 f^2$, where f is the number of attributes.

In C4.5 Release 8 (R8), Quinlan proposed a local, MDL-based approach to penalize a continuous attribute if it has too more values.

Experimental data show that the C4.5 R8 approach has better performance in most situations, but the Dougherty approach of global discretization has better performance in a small data set. T2 works well when data are partitioned into less classes.

7.8 Bias Shift-Based Decision Tree Algorithm

The key to constructing a good decision tree is to select good attributes. In common, among a great deal of decision trees which can fit the given training examples, the smaller the size of the tree, the more the prediction capability of the tree. To construct these as small as possible, the key is to select proper attributes. Since the problem of constructing a minimum tree is an *NP* complete problem, most of the research can only employ heuristics to select good attributes. Attribute selection depends on impurity measures of various example subsets. Impurity measures include information gain, ratio of information gain, Gini index, distance measures, J-measures, G-statistics, χ^2 statistics, P^0 zero-probability assumption, evidence weights, minimal description length (MDL), orthogonal approach measures, correlation degree and Relief, etc. Different measures have different effects, so the difference between a single-variant decision tree and a multi-variant decision tree has emerged. The conclusions of deeply studying these measures are not agreeable. Not one algorithm has absolute predominance in solving problems of attribute selection, data noise, data increase, pre-pruning and post-pruning, pruning cease standard, etc. Empirical and intuitive feeling replaced strict and complete theory proof.

In fact, the above problems are bias problems in decision tree learning. Bias plays an important role in concept learning. Utgoff points out that inductive learning does not exist without bias. Inductive bias means all factors except primitive training instances and includes language describing hypothesis, program space considering hypothesis, order of hypothesis procedure, admitting definitive standard, etc. Bias has two features: one is that a strong bias focuses on concepts learning in relatively less number of hypotheses. On the contrary, a weak bias focus on concept learning in relatively more number of hypotheses; another feature is that correct bias permits concept learning selecting the target concept, while incorrect bias cannot select a target concept. When bias is strong and correct, the concept can select a useful target concept immediately; when bias is weak and incorrect, the task of concept learning is very difficult.

Bias can be divided into two categories: representation bias and procedure bias. Since the family of ID3 algorithms lack support of background knowledge, it is an inductive learning algorithm with the support of relatively weak bias. We strengthen the bias of a decision tree through shifting of representation bias and procedure bias.

7.8.1 *Formalization of Bias*

First of all, we define the basic concepts of bias formally.

Definition 7.1. S is a search space defined in $\langle A, C, F, T, L \rangle$, where attribute vector $A = \{a_1, \ldots, a_m\}$ has definite or infinite elements; classification vector $C = \{c_1, \ldots, c_k\}$ has definite elements. For given A and C, F is a set of all concepts; T is a set of training examples with n tuples; L represents a learning algorithm family.

Definition 7.2. A learning algorithm l defines a map from T to F, that is

$$t\{t \in T\} \xrightarrow{l(t,f)} f\{f \in F\}, \quad l \in L. \tag{7.31}$$

Definition 7.3. $D_{A \times C}$ is a probability distribution on $A \times C$; t is n tuples which is defined on $A \times C$ and suffices $D_{A \times C}$. Let D_c be a probability distribution on C, and identity of attribute set $IA(A_1, A_2)$ means the probability that puts a random attribute to the same class given concepts f and D_c. That is,

$$(T_0(A_1, f)) = l(T_0(A_2, f))), \quad l \in L \cap T_0 \subseteq T \cap A_1, \ A_2 \subseteq A \cap f \in F.$$

Definition 7.4. Let f_g be the target concept, then correctness of bias $\mathrm{Corr}B$ can be defined as

$$\mathrm{Corr}\,B = P_{D_A}(f_g(a) = f(a)), \quad f \in F \cap a \in A. \tag{7.32}$$

Definition 7.5. Let $|S|$ be the number of elements in S, then bias strength StrB can be defined as:

$$\text{Str}\,B = \frac{1}{|S|}. \tag{7.33}$$

Definition 7.6. Let $\text{State}_0(S) = \langle A_0, C, f, T, l \rangle$ and $\text{State}_1(S) = \langle A_1, C, f, T, l \rangle$ be two states of search space, then bias shift BSR is defined as:

$$\text{State}_0(S) \xrightarrow{\text{BSR}} \text{State}_1(S).$$

Definition 7.7. Let D_A be a probability distribution on A, and identity of learning algorithm $IL(l_1, l_2)$ means the probability that puts a random training example t to the same class given concepts f and D_A. That is,

$$IL(l_1, l_2) = P_{D_A}(l_1(t, f) = l_2(t, f)), \quad t \in T \cap l_1, \ l_2 \in L \cap f \in F. \tag{7.34}$$

Definition 7.8. Predict accuracy PA of a learning algorithm l is defined as

$$PA(l) = P_{D_{A \times C}}(f_{l(t)}(a) = c), \quad f \in F \cap t \in T \cap c \in C. \tag{7.35}$$

Definition 7.9. Let $\text{State}_0(S) = \langle A, C, f, T, l_0 \rangle$ and $\text{State}_1(S) = \langle A, C, f, T, l_1 \rangle$ be two states of search space, the procedure bias shift BSP is defined as

$$\text{State}_0(S) \xrightarrow{\text{BSP}} \text{State}_1(S).$$

Theorem 7.1. *Let l_1 and l_2 be learning algorithms, when $PA(l_1) \geq PA(l_2)$ holds, selecting l_1 has more correct bias.*

Proof. When $PA(l_1) \geq PA(l_2)$ holds, the classifier generated by l_1 can classify more examples correctly. That is,

$$P_{D_{A \times C}}(f_{l_1(t)}(a) = c) \geq P_{D_{A \times C}}(f_{l_2(t)}(a) = c). \tag{7.36}$$

After we project bias correctness to distribution $D_{A \times C}$, we can get:

$$\text{Corr}\,B = P_{D_{A \times C}}(f_g(a) = c).$$

Since target concept is embodied to a large extent by the classifier generated by learning algorithms, bias correctness can be adapted as:

$$\text{Corr}\,B = P_{D_{A \times C}}(f_{l(t)}(a) = c).$$

Substituting algorithms l_1 and l_2 in the above formula and combining with formula (7.36), we can get following:

$$\operatorname{Corr} B_1 = P_{D_{A \times C}}(f_{l_1(t)}(a) = c) \geq \operatorname{Corr} B_2 = P_{D_{A \times C}}(f_{l_2(t)}(a) = c).$$

Selecting l_1 has more correct bias. Theorem 7.1 is proved.   □

7.8.2 *Bias Shift Representation*

Decision tree learning algorithm is actually efficient, but because of lacking support of background knowledge, it cannot handle various generalizations. As for inductive algorithms based on predicate logic (e.g., AQ11, INDUCE), this function is the most preliminary and inseparable from learning procedure. One result of lacking background knowledge is that the procedure of constructing becomes complicated and is not easily understood by domain experts.

Many systems attempt to solve this problem, such as: algorithm PRISM of Cendrowska, INDUCT algorithm of Gaines, and other techniques introduced by Quinlan, Lavrac, etc., which make decision tree easier and more precise. However, they only focus on information included in historical data in an attempt to mine more useful resource.

We propose a pre-processing algorithm which can make use of learning algorithm based on representation transform and can handle various generalizations. This approach first pre-processes the primitive training instances, calls generalization algorithm CGAOI, makes primitive training instances achieve the appointed concept level, and then pre-processes the primitive training instances again.

In order to realize the proposed algorithm, first concept level is introduced.

Definition 7.10. A concept level is a mapping sequence from inferior concepts to superior concepts. These mapping sequences are organized in a tree to generate a concept-level tree.

Definition 7.11. A primitive training example set E^0 corresponds to a concept-level forest $F = \{F_1, \ldots, F_i, \ldots, F_\varpi\}$, where F_i is a set of concept-level trees corresponding to the ith attribute A_i, $1 \leq i \leq \varpi$. $F_i = \{T_1, \ldots, T_j, \ldots, T_\tau\}$, where T_j is the jth concept-level tree of attribute A_i, $1 \leq j \leq \tau$.

Definition 7.12. When there is no concept-level tree in attribute A_i, $F_i = \text{NULL}$.

Definition 7.13. A concept-level database D is used to save the history of concept-level trees.

In all attributes of the primitive training set, many attributes have their own fixed concept level. For example, if a commodity is made in Beijing, we can say it is made in China. Furthermore, we also can say it is made in Asia. This is a concept level of {Product Places: Beijing, China, Asia}.

Concept level is used to represent the requested background knowledge to control the procedure of generalization or specialization. Through organizing concepts of different levels into a tree classification, concept space can be represented as partial order from specialization to generalization. The most general concept is description with empty meaning, which can be represented as "ANY"; the most specific concept is leaf in a tree classification. Making use of concept level, we can represent found rules as simpler, easier, more special, and more logical.

7.8.3 *Algorithms*

1. Classification-guided attribute-oriented inductive algorithm

Classification-guided attribute-oriented inductive algorithm (CGAOI) can generalize the original relation into the appointed concept level. We thus propose the classification-guided attribute-oriented inductive algorithm CGAOI. This approach is a supervised approach. As a guide of classification learning task, it preprocesses primitive training instances and softly outputs generalization relation of the appointed level.

In the guide of classification feature of primitive training instances, the algorithm realizes the basic operations oriented by attribute induction, such as attribute eliminating, concept refining, attribute threshold controlling, and frequency propagating. At the same time, it realizes generalization consistency examination, data noise elimination, automatic concept-level generation, etc.

Algorithm 7.6 (Classification-Guided Attribute-Oriented Inductive Algorithm, CGAOI).

Input: Primitive training instance subset E^0, attribute set A^0, current attribute A; concept-level tree T, appointed concept-level tree L; appointed attribute controlling threshold Y; current concept-level, current attribute controlling threshold Y^0.

Output: appointed concept-level training example subset E, attribute set A, frequency C^T.

1. Call algorithm GCCC to generalize consistency check and noise elimination, return Ret1;
2. If generalization consistency check fails, then return failure;
3. Do concept improving operation under the control of Y and L;

4. Attribute elimination and frequency propagation;
5. Return success.

Theorem 7.2. *The representative bias shift will be stronger and more accurate through CGAOI processing.*

2. Pre-processing algorithm PPD

In the algorithm, we take the specific attribute value of a database as a bound of generalization and specification. When attribute controlling threshold is larger than the current attribute value (or level lower than current level), it calls generalization procedure; on the contrary, it calls specialization procedure to reduce the primitive training instances subset to the corresponding concept level.

Algorithm 7.7 (Preprocessing Algorithm PPD).

Input: Primitive training instance subset E^0; attribute set A^0; concept-level forest F; concept-level database D; appointed concept level L; appoint attribute controlling threshold Y; current concept level; current attribute controlling threshold Y^0;

Output: Appointed concept-level training example subset E; attribute set A;

1. Carry out operation on each attribute A_i in attribute set A^0;
2. Check whether concept-level tree F_i of A_i is empty;
3. if it is empty, then call algorithm AGCH to generate concept-level tree F_i of A_i
   automatically, return Ret1;
4. Ret1$= -1$, go to step 1;   // Ai have no concept-level tree
5. If $(Y = Y^0 \cap L = L^0)$, then go to step 1;
6. If $(Y < Y^0 \cup L > L^0)$, then call generalization algorithm CGAOI, return Ret2;
7.   Ret2 $= -1$, go to step 1;   // if fail, then abandon generalization
8.   Ret2 $= 0$, go to step 11;   // generalization success
9. If above conditions are not met, then go to step 1;
10. Call algorithm MEA to train example subset and maintain attribute set;
11. Call algorithm STCH to store concept-level tree of A_i into concept-level database D;
12. Go to step 1.

7.8.4 *Procedure Bias Shift*

Various decision tree learning algorithms have their own advantage, and the basic point of our proposed decision tree learning algorithm based on bias shift is to employ their advantages. At the same time, the learning algorithm has a complicated relation with its learning task and attributes of the training set, such as size, dimension, domain, etc., so we cannot use simple controlling branch sentence to realize the selection of seek optimum algorithm. Therefore, we introduce the concept of two-level decision tree learning algorithm based on bias transform (see Figure 7.8).

The algorithm is designed based on the idea of two-level and multiple strategies. Two-level learning places the focus on the first level being case-based reasoning used to select the most proper algorithm to solve a primitive training example set from various decision tree learning algorithms with different evaluation standards, adaptive domain, and size of training examples; and the second learning task being used to construct a classifier, that is, using selected decision tree algorithms, infer classification rules of decision tree representative form from cases without order and rule.

Case-based reasoning is a strategy that gets the source case in memory based on the prompt of the target case and guides target case solving from source cases.

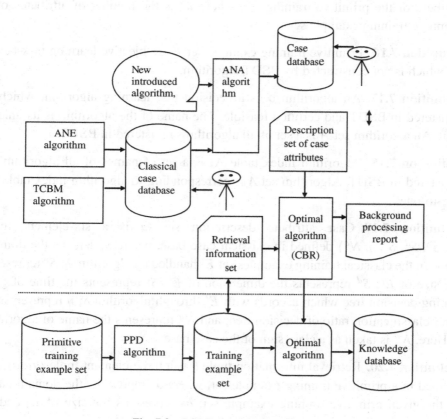

Fig. 7.8. BSDT algorithm structure

Here, target cases are generated from the classical case base of various decision tree algorithms. For a given primitive training instance subset, we first extract its retrieval information tuple θ to retrieval in case base. Similarity in retrieval procedure meets optimal index ζ in Definition 7.24.

Multi-strategy learning is not constrained in one learning algorithm. It also provides a mechanism to introduce new algorithms and classical examples. The mechanism provides a seamless link among the original register algorithm, the new classical case set, and the original register classical case set. The mechanism is realized by human–machine interaction and the classical case base-maintained algorithm.

Definition 7.14. Bias coefficient $C^b = [C_1^b, \ldots, C_{\varpi}^b]^T$ represents relativity between various attributes of primitive training set and learning task, where ϖ is the number of attributes of a primitive training example set.

Definition 7.15. Cost coefficient $C^c = [C_1^c, \ldots, C_{\varpi}^c]^T$ represents cost to get every attribute of the primitive training set, where ϖ is the number of attributes of a primitive training example set.

Definition 7.16. Primitive training example set E is objective learning task-based set which is not constructed by BSDT algorithm.

Definition 7.17. An algorithm α is a decision tree learning algorithm which is registered in BSDT and certified feasible. The name of the algorithm is its unique sign. An algorithm set A is a set of all algorithms registered in BSDT.

Definition 7.18. Algorithm index table AI is a set of names of all algorithms α registered in BSDT. Algorithm set A is corresponding to algorithm index table AI one-to-one.

Definition 7.19. Case attribute description set Θ is a six-element tuple $\langle \pi, S^e, S^d, S^t, \eta, N^a \rangle$ defined in classical case base, where π denotes the domain name of the classical training examples set E^t handled by algorithm δ; S^e represents the size of E^t; S^d represents the dimension of E^t; S^t represents the time of generating decision tree which accords with E^t through algorithm δ; η represents the error classification ratio of decision tree; and N^a represents the name of algorithm δ. Here, N^a is taken as a class sign of the case base.

Definition 7.20. Retrieval information tuple θ is a three-element tuple $\langle a_1, a_2, a_3 \rangle$ defined in a primitive training example set, where a_1 represents the domain name of the given primitive training example set; a_2 represents the size of E; and a_3 represents the dimension of E.

Definition 7.21. Case base CE is a set of cases generated by BSDT algorithm. Its six attributes are described by case attribute description set; category $N^a \in$ algorithm index table AP; example ce $\in$ CE is generated by algorithm ANA.

Definition 7.22. Domain name $\pi \in$ domain name set Π. In BSDT, $\Pi =$ {1-agriculture, 2-industry, 3-commence, 4-education, 5-electronics, 6-physics, 7-chemistry, 8-mathematics, 9-medicine, 10-others}.

Definition 7.23. Classical case base TEB = example index table EI$\cup$ classical case table TET. Example index table EI is a set of all domain names π registered in algorithm BSDT; Classical example table TET is a set of examples which are obtained from a domain and named by a domain name π.

Definition 7.24. An optimal index ζ is a case retrieval standard decided by both case attribute description set Θ and retrieval information tuple θ. It is determined by the following formula:

$$\zeta = (a_1 = \pi) \wedge (|a_2 - S^e| < \lambda_1) \wedge (|a_3 - S^d| < \lambda_2) \wedge (S^t \bullet \eta < \lambda_3),$$

where λ_1, λ_2, and λ_3 are tuple threshold, dimension threshold, and tree controlling threshold, respectively, and can be tuned in running time. In BSDT, the default values of λ_1, λ_2, and λ_3 are (where T_{in}, E_S, and E_η are tuple interval, error classification ratio, and expectation of generating time, respectively):

$$\lambda_1 = 0.1 \times T_{in}, \lambda_2 = 2, \lambda_3 = \frac{E_S \times E_\eta}{\sqrt{2}}.$$

Definition 7.25. An algorithm is an optimum algorithm Γ if and only if it meets optimal index ζ and makes λ_3 minimum.

Definition 7.26. The background handling report REP is a text file ErrRep.txt. When BSDT cannot find optimum algorithm Γ in appointed path, it will record error information and inform the manager to handle it.

Definition 7.27. In BSDT algorithm, the register procedure should do following tasks:

(1) Store the name of an algorithm N^a into the algorithm index table AI, and store the algorithm itself in a directory appointed by BSDT.
(2) Store the name of an example set N^{es} into the example index table EI, and store the classical case table TET in the classical case base.

7.8.5 *Bias Shift-Based Decision Tree Learning Algorithm*

BSDT algorithm first calls seek optimum algorithm SM to get optimum algorithm Γ. Then seek the algorithm in the system directory and current working directory. If no algorithm is found, it should be eliminated from the case base and algorithm index table, in order to avoid failure in the next search.

In fact, seek optimum algorithm SM is a procedure using case-based reasoning. As for a given primitive training set, we first extract its retrieval information tuple θ, then search the optimum algorithm that meets the optimal index ζ in the case base. When the case base is empty or SM algorithm fails, take GSD as a default selection of optimum algorithm.

Since inference in algorithm running should be decreased, BSDT journal can be taken as a means for the manager to intervene in the system.

Algorithm 7.8 (Bias Shift-Based Decision Tree Learning Algorithm BSDT).
    Input: primitive training example set;
    Output: target knowledge base;

1. Call pre-processing algorithm PPD;
2. Call seek optimum algorithm SM to get optimum algorithm Γ;
3. Search algorithm Γ in appointed path;
4. If algorithm exists,
5.   then Call Γ;
6. Generate decision tree and/or production rule set;
7. Store learning result into target knowledge base;
8. If algorithm does not exist,
9.   then let $\rho = 3$, call case base maintain algorithm CBM to delete Γ from case base and corresponding data structure;
10.   go to step 2;
11. Fill out the journal for BSDT.

7.8.6 *Typical Case Base Maintain Algorithm*

Algorithm TCBM realizes various operations of a typical case base, such as adding a new example set, example set version updating, deleting an example set, deleting example set and adding or deleting examples of example base, etc. Only when adding or deleting new examples or modifying existing example subset can the algorithm be activated. Because of employing hierarchical activating mode, after TCBM algorithm modifies the classical case base, it would automatically call each algorithm in the algorithm index table to execute again to construct the case base in accordance with the content of the classical case base. Case base and modification of related data structure are selected to influence the optimum algorithm directly.

Algorithm 7.9 (Typical Case Base Maintain Algorithm, TCBM).

Input: Primitive case base, case index table, case set S_0, domain name π, maintain operator ρ

Output: Modified case base, case index table

1. IF $\rho < 1$ and $\rho > 5$ THEN return;
2. IF $\rho = 1$, THEN   /* adding new case set */
Call ANE algorithm to add new case;
3. IF $\rho = 2$, THEN   /* typical case base version updating */
4. examine whether example index table and domain name π exists;
5. IF exists
6. delete corresponding table from case base;
7. delete related items in case index table;
8. call algorithm ANE to introduce new case set;
9.   IF $\rho = 3$, THEN   /* deleting case set */
10. Examine whether example index table and domain name π exists, if not, return;
11. Delete corresponding table from base;
12. Delete domain name π from example index table;
13. IF $\rho = 4$, THEN   /* adding examples to example base */
14. IF domain name π is not in the index table
call algorithm ANE to add new domain;
15. Check the appropriateness of record value and discard inappropriate record value; store training set S_0 into corresponding table in order;
16. IF $\rho = 5$, THEN   /* deleting examples of example base */
17. IF domain name π is not in index table, then return;
18. Delete cases in table;
19. Extract(S_0, π);   /* generating case for typical case base */
20. Store cases;

7.8.7 *Bias Feature Extracting Algorithm*

Features of candidate algorithms can help us to select the optimum bias automatically using the optimal algorithm. These features are organized according to the form of Definition 7.19. The procedure will be activated when the typical case base or algorithm index table varies.

Algorithm 7.10 (Bias Feature Extracting Algorithm).

Input: classical example base CEB, register algorithm RA, example set ES, example index table EI, algorithm index table AI, case base CB, operator OP

Output: modified CB

1. If op = 1   // CB is empty
2.   then {If EI = NULL || AI = NULL} return
3.   For i = 1 to maxRA
4.   For j = 1 to maxEI
5.   For k = 1 to Interval do
6.   {using algorithm AI(i) to generate a classifier in example set EI(j)
7.   and generate a data item according to definition 7.19
8.   store data item into CB; }
9. Else if op = 2   // adding a new algorithm
10.   then { For i = 1 to maxEI
11.   For j = 1 to Interval do
12.   {using algorithm RA to generate a classifier in example set EI(j)
13.   and generate a data term according to definition 7.19
14.   store data into CB;}
15. Else if op = 3   // adding a new example set
16.   then {For i = 1 to maxRA
17.   For j = 1 to Interval do
18.   {using algorithm AI(i) to generate a classifier in example set EI(j)
19.   and generate a data term according to definition 7.19
20.   store data into CB; }
21. Else if op = 4   // deleting an old register algorithm
22   . thenDelete related item of RA from CB
23. Else if op = 5   // deleting an old register example set
24.   then   Delete related item of ES from CB;
25. Else return failed;
26. Modify Interval according to the size of CEB

7.8.8 *Improved Decision Tree Generating Algorithm GSD*

We use cost coefficient C^c and bias coefficient C^b for constructing attribute selecting function ASF, and set their default value. The following gives the constructing method of attribute selecting function ASF.

Definition 7.28. $E^0 = \{e_1^0, \ldots, e_v^0\}$ is a set of primitive training examples, $A^0 = \{A_1^0, \ldots, A_v^0\}$ is an attribute set of E^0, where v is the maximum number of primitive training examples, ϖ is the maximum number of attribute of E^0; and $A_i = \{V_1, \ldots, V_v\}$ represents v different values of attribute i.

Definition 7.29. $E = \{e_1, \ldots, e_n\}$, $A^T = A \cup A^X = \{A_1, \ldots, A_m\} \cup A^X = \{A_1, \ldots, A_m, A_{m+1}\}$, which are a training example set and an attribute set through pre-processing under the introduction of background knowledge and algorithm *CGAOI*, where $1 \leq n \leq v, 2 \leq m \leq \varpi$.

Definition 7.30. $A^X = C^T = [C_1^T, \ldots, C_n^T] T$ is the propagate frequency obtained from the algorithm *CGAOI*.

Definition 7.31. $C = \{C_1, \ldots, C_k\}$ are k possible classes in the primitive training example set E. P_i represents the probability of class C_i in E.

Definition 7.32. In the process of generating a decision tree, each attribute-oriented test must make the value of attribute selecting function *ASF* maximum.

Definition 7.33. *ASF* function is defined as

$$ASF(A_i) = \frac{f(A_i) \bullet g(A_i)}{h(A_i)},$$

where $f(A_i)$ indicates the benefit of the attribute i; $g(A_i)$ indicates the bias of the attribute i; $h(A_i)$ indicates the cost of the attribute A_i, $1 \leq i \leq k$.

(1) The following formula gives the definition of $f(A_i)$, where U^I represents useful information; N^I represents useless information; T^I represents total information $= U^I + N^I$:

$$f(A_i) = \frac{U^I}{T^I} = 1 - \frac{N^I}{T^I}.$$

Let

$$\Delta I = H(T^I) - H(N^I),$$

$$-\Delta I = H(N^I) - H(T^I) = \log_2(N^I) - \log_2(T^I) = \log_2\left[\frac{N^I}{T^I}\right],$$

$$2^{-\Delta I} = \left[\frac{N^I}{T^I}\right] = 1 - \left[\frac{U^I}{T^I}\right] = 1 - f(),$$

$$f(A_i) = 1 - 2^{-\Delta I},$$

$$\Delta I = \text{Gain}(A_l, E) = I(E) - \text{Ent}(A_l, E),$$

$$I(E) = -\sum_{j=1}^{k} P_j \log_2 P_j, \; P_j = \frac{|E \cap C_j|}{|E|} \bullet CT_j,$$

$$\text{Ent}(A_l, E) = \sum_{i=1}^{v} \frac{|E_i|}{|E|} I(E_i),$$

$$f(A_i) = 1 - 2^{-\text{Gain}()}.$$

(2) $g(A_i)$ is defined as

$$g(A_i) = C_i^b.$$

(3) $h(A_i)$ is defined as

$$h(A_i) = C_i^c+,$$

from which we can get the expression

$$\text{ASF}(A_i) = \frac{(1 - 2^{-\text{Gain}()}) \bullet C^b}{C^c + 1}.$$

Our decision tree-generating algorithm GSD is a modified version of Quinlan's C4.5 algorithm. The modification is embodied in two aspects: input and attribute selecting. The input of GSD employs pre-process algorithm PPD to output the appointed concept-level training example subset. Furthermore, it uses the attribute-selecting function ASF to replace the attribute-selecting standard of C4.5.

Algorithm 7.11 (Decision tree generating algorithm GSD).
   Input: Training set
   Output: Decision tree, rule set

   1. Select standard CR from Gain, Gain Ratio and ASF;
   2. If all data items belong to one class, then decision tree is a leaf labeled with the class sign;
   3. Else, use optimum test attribute to divide data items into subset;
   4. Recursively call steps 2 and 3 to generate a decision tree for each subset;
   5. Generate decision tree and transform to rule set.

7.8.9 Experiment Results

BSDT algorithm uses the following data set (Table 7.3).

   Parts of the data set come from the UCI test database (ftp://ics.uci.edu/pub/machine-learning-database). The following measure is used to test the data set.

Table 7.3.   Experiment data set

Data set	#Training example number	#Attribute number	#Class number	#Example number of test set
Anneal	898	38	5	—
Breast-cancer	699	10	2	—
Credit	490	15	2	200
Genetics	3,190	60	3	—
Glass	214	9	6	—
Heart	1,395	16	2	—
Hypo	2,514	29	5	1,258
Letter	15,000	16	26	5,000
Sonar	208	60	2	—
Soybean	683	35	19	—
Voting	300	16	2	135
Diabetes	768	8	2	—

Use the random-selecting approach to divide a data set DS without given data set (such as: anneal, breast-cancer, etc.) into test set TS and learning set LS, and let $TS = DS \times 10\%$:

(1) Classifier C_0 is generated by using C4.5 algorithm and testifying 10 times in learning set LS, which has predict accuracy P_0 after testing in TS.
(2) Classifier C_1 is generated by using algorithm BSDT and testifying 10 times in learning set LS, which has predict accuracy P_1 after testing in TS.
(3) Classifier C_2 is generated by using algorithm BSDT with attribute selecting function ASF and testifying 10 times in learning set LS, which has predict accuracy P_2 after testing in TS.
(4) For each algorithm, we compute the average value of 15 experiments, so that we get a stable predict model.
(5) Compare results of P_0, P_1, and P_2, and the predict accuracies are listed in Table 7.4.

It can be seen from Table 7.4 that after being classified by decision tree classification predict model generated by algorithm BSDT, the precision of all data set is improved. The predict precision of ASF function defined by cost coefficient and bias coefficient is obviously improved. The experimental results show that ASF function and algorithm BSDT are effective.

We implement a method integrating various decision tree learning algorithms in algorithm BSDT. It is an effective approach to integrate various machine learning

Table 7.4.   Predict accuracy comparison

Data set	P_0	P_1	P_2
Anneal	96.9 ± 10.4	97.1 ± 9.7	97.8 ± 10.8
Breast-cancer	95.7 ± 2.1	96.2 ± 1.7	97.2 ± 2.5
Credit	84.8 ± 2.5	87.4 ± 1.8	89.5 ± 2.1
Genetics	98.7 ± 4.4	98.7 ± 4.4	98.7 ± 4.4
Glass	68.9 ± 9.2	75.2 ± 6.5	75.2 ± 6.5
Heart	77.8 ± 4.3	79.6 ± 3.9	79.8 ± 3.7
Hypo	93.2 ± 4.2	92.7 ± 3.9	92.7 ± 3.9
Letter	88.4 ± 9.8	93.7 ± 8.7	93.7 ± 8.7
Sonar	65.4 ± 7.1	74.7 ± 12.1	74.7 ± 12.1
Soybean	78.9 ± 5.9	84.8 ± 6.5	84.8 ± 6.5
Voting	95.8 ± 1.3	95.9 ± 1.6	95.9 ± 1.6
Diabetes	74.3 ± 3.0	76.1 ± 3.1	77.2 ± 2.3

algorithms, and it assures optimum selection of representation bias and procedure bias, and so it supports multiple strategy learning algorithm.

7.9 Computational Theories of Inductive Learning

Computational theories of learning mainly study the sample and computation complexity of learning algorithm. This section focuses on Gold learning theory and Valiant learning theory.

Computational learning theory is very important for building the science of machine learning; otherwise, it is difficult to recognize the scope of applicability of a learning algorithm or analyze the learnability in different approaches. Convergence, feasibility, and approximation are essential issues which require computational learning theory to give a satisfying learning framework containing reasonable restrictions. In computational learning theory, early efforts along these aspects are based primarily on Gold's framework (Gold, 1967). In the context of formulization linguistic learning, Gold introduces the concept of convergence, which handles the problem of learning from examples. Learning algorithm allows to propose many assumptions without knowing when they are correct, only determining the point where their computations are correct assumptions. Because of the high complexity of Gold algorithm, this style is not applied in practical learning.

Based on Gold's learning framework, Shapiro proposed a model reasoning algorithm to study the relation between formal language and its explanation, that is, relation between grammar and semantics of formal language. Model theory takes formula, sentence theory, and their explanation — model as mathematical objects to study. Shapiro model reasoning algorithm can get a theory output when only definite input facts need to be input (Shapiro, 1981).

In 1984, Valiant proposed a new learning framework (Valiant, 1984), which requires high approximation with objective concept and does not require accurate identification of object concept. Kearns, Li, Pitt, and Valiant gave some new results to the concept which can be represented as Boolean formula. Haussler applied the Valiant framework to analyze problems of version space and inductive bias and gave a computing formula of computational complexity.

7.9.1 *Gold's Learning Theory*

The research of Gold's linguistic learning theory introduces two basic concepts, i.e., limit identification and enumeration identification, which played important roles in early theory research of inductive reasoning (Gold, 1967).

Limit identification takes inductive reasoning as an infinitive procedure. Ultimate or limit act can be seen as its successful standard. Assume M is an inductive reasoning approach which attempts to describe unknown rule R correctly. Assuming M runs repeatedly, the example set of R becomes more and more large, forming an infinite sequence $g_1, g_2, \ldots$ speculated by M. If there exists a number m, that would make g_m the correct description of R,

$$g_m = g_{m+1} = g_{m+2} = \cdots,$$

Then the limit of the example sequence M can identify R correctly. As unknown rules are learned more and more, M can successfully modify the speculation about R. If M stops modifying its speculation after a definite number of times, and the final speculation is the correct description of R, then M correctly identifies R at the limit of the example sequence. Notice that M cannot confirm whether it can converges into a correct assumption because whether there exists a contradiction between new data and current speculation is unknown.

Enumeration identification is the first approach to speculate the abstraction of multinomial sequence, that is, it systematically searches the possible rule space, until it finds a speculation in accordance with all data so far. Suppose that concrete domain of rule is prescribed, there is an enumeration, i.e., $d_1, d_2, d_3, \ldots$, such that each rule in the enumeration has one or multiple description. Given an example set of a rule, through the table, enumeration identification will find the first description d_1, that is, if it is compatible with the given example, then speculation is d_1. This approach cannot confirm whether it can achieve correct limit identification.

If example representation and compatible relation meet the following two conditions, enumeration approach assures the limit identifying all rules of that domain:

(1) A correct assumption is always compatible with given examples.
(2) Any wrong assumption is not compatible with sets with examples large enough for all sets.

In order to compute the enumeration approach, enumeration $d_1, d_2, d_3, \ldots,$ must be computable; it must compute that a given description is compatible with a given example set.

Algorithm 7.12 (Enumeration Identification Algorithm).

Input:
- The set of a group of expressions $E = e_1, e_2, \ldots$
- Oracle TE to provide enough objective example set.
- Oracle LE of ordering information.

Output:

A series of hypotheses $H_1, H_2, \ldots,$ each hypothesis H_i is in E, and is consistent with the ith example.

Procedure:

1. Initialize: $i \leftarrow 1$;
2. examples $\leftarrow$ emptyset;
3. Loop:
4.   call TE(), add example to set examples;
5.   While LE($e_i, +x$) = no, for positive example set $+x$, or
6.   LE($e_i, -x$) = yes, for negative example set $-x$,
7. $i \leftarrow i + 1$;
8. Output e_i.

7.9.2 *Model Inference*

A model inference problem is an abstraction from scientific problems. In this abstraction, we try to find some unknown model M which can explain some results. Shapiro gave the following definition of the model inference problem. Suppose that a first-order language L and two subsets of it, an observational language L_o and a hypothesis language L_h, are given. In addition, an oracle for some unknown model M of L is given. The model inference problem is to find a finite L_o-complete axiomatization of M. In order to solve the model inference problem, Shapiro has developed a model inference algorithm in terms of Gold's theory (Shapiro, 1981).

L sentence is divided into two subsets: observable language L_o and hypothesis language L_h. Assuming that

$$\square \in L_o \subset L_h \subset L',$$

where $\square$ is empty sentence, then the model inference problem can be defined as follows: given one-order language L and two subsets: observable language L_o and hypothesis language L_h. Further, given a handle mechanism oracle to an unknown model M of L, the model inference problem finds a definite L_o of M — completed axiomatization.

The algorithm to solve model inference problem is referred to as model inference algorithm. Enumeration of model M is an infinite sequence F_1, F_2, F_3, ..., where F_i is the fact about M, each sentence α of L_o is taking place at fact $F_i = \langle \alpha, V >, i \rangle 0$. Model reasoning algorithm reads the enumeration of observable language L_o once. A fact which generates a definite set of sentences of hypothesis language L_h is referred to as speculation of algorithm. A kind of model inference algorithm is as follows:

Algorithm 7.13 (An Enumeration Model Inference Algorithm (Shapiro, 1981)).
1. Let h be a total recursive function
2. Set S_{false} to $\{\square\}$, S_{true} to $\{\}$, k to 0
3. Repeat
4.   read the next fact $F_n = \langle \alpha, V \rangle$
5.   add α to S_v
6.   while there is an $\alpha \in S_{\text{false}}$ such that $T_{kn}\alpha$
7.   or there is an $\alpha_i \in S_{\text{true}}$ such that $T_k \neg_{n(i)} \alpha_i$ do
8. $k = k + 1$
9.   output T_k
10. Forever

where, $\alpha_1, \alpha_2, \alpha_3, \ldots$ are a fixed effective enumeration of all sentences of L_o, $T_1, T_2, T_3, \ldots$ are a fixed effective enumeration of all finite sets of sentences of L_h; and M is a model for L. Symbol $T_n \alpha$ denotes that one can derive α in n derivation steps or less, $T \neg_{n(i)} \alpha$ denotes that T cannot derive α in n steps or less.

Algorithm 7.13 is not feasible because of its global nature. Whenever it finds that a set of sentences is not an axiomatization of the model, it simply discards it and searches through all finite sets of sentences until it finds the next plausible conjecture. In order to overcome this problem, Shapiro developed an incremental inference algorithm which is called the contradiction backtracking algorithm, since it can trace a contradiction between a conjecture and the facts back to its source, which is a false hypothesis (Shapiro, 1981).

7.9.3 *Valiant's Learning Theory*

Valiant claims that a learning machine must have the following properties (Valiant, 1984):

(1) The machine can learn the concept of all classes. Furthermore, these classes can be characterized.
(2) Concept class is proper and uncommon for general knowledge.
(3) The computational process of machine deduction program is required within a feasible number of steps.

Learning machine is composed of learning protocols and deduction procedure. Learning protocols prescribe the approach to get information from the outer. Deduction procedure is a mechanism, and a correct recognition algorithm of learning concept is deductive. From a general point of view, the approach to study learning is to prescribe a possible learning protocol. Using this learning protocol to study concept class, recognition program can be deducted in multinomial time. Concrete protocol provides two kinds of information. The first is access to typical data, which are positive examples of concepts. To be precise, assume that these positive examples essentially have an arbitrary probability distribution, it calls subprogram EXAM-PLES to generate positive examples whose relative probability distribution is definite. The second available information source is ORACLE. In the basic version, when submitting data, it will tell whether learning the data is a positive example of concept.

Assuming that X is an example space, a concept is a subset of X. If an example is in concept, it is a positive example, else it is a negative example. Concept representation is a concept description; concept class is a group of concept representation. The learning model has effective learnability of concept class. Valiant learning theory only requires that good approximation to objective concept has high probability. It permits concept description generated by the learner, and objective concept has a small bias, which is an argument of the learning algorithm. In addition, the probability of permitting learner fail is δ, which is also an input argument. Differences between two concepts employ probability distribution D in example space X to evaluate

$$\operatorname{diff}_D(c_1, c_2) = \sum_{x \in X, c_1(x) \neq c_2(x)} D(x). \tag{7.37}$$

According to the protocol, a concept class C is learnable if and only if there exists an algorithm which uses protocol to represent all objective concepts $c^* \in C$ and all distribution D

(1) Executive time is multinomial related to $\frac{1}{\varepsilon}, \frac{1}{\delta}$, number of c^*, and other arguments.

(2) Concept c in output C has probability $1 - \delta$

$$\text{diff}_D(c, c^*) < \varepsilon.$$

In Valiant's learning theory, there are two complexity measures. One is sample complexity, which is the number of random examples used to generate high probability and low error. Another computational complexity is performance complexity, which is defined as the computing time needed to generate the assumption with a given number of samples in the worst case.

Assuming that L is learning algorithm, C is a kind of object concept in example space X. For any $0 < \varepsilon, \delta < 1$, $S_\varepsilon^L(\varepsilon, \delta)$ represents the minimum number of samples m so that in any objective concept $c \in C$, any distribution in X, given m samples of c, L generates an assumption whose probability is at least $1 - \delta$ and error is at most ε. $S_\varepsilon^L(\varepsilon, \delta)$ is referred to as L sample complexity of target class c. In the following, we discuss sample complexity of two learning algorithms.

1. Classification algorithm of learning conjunction concept

The content of the algorithm is as follows:

(1) For a given sample, find the minimum main atom of each attribute. These atoms perform conjunction to form an assumption h.

(2) If h does not include negative examples, then it returns h, else gets the result and holds that sample is not in accordance with any pure conjunction concept. Haussler (1988a) analyzed this algorithm and concluded that its sample complexity $S_c^L(\varepsilon, \delta)$ is

$$C_0 \left(\log\left(\frac{1}{\delta}\right) + n \right) / \varepsilon \leq S_c^L(\varepsilon, \delta) \leq C_1 \left(\log\left(\frac{1}{\delta}\right) + n \log\left(\frac{1}{\varepsilon}\right) \right) / \varepsilon,$$

$$(7.38)$$

where C_0 and C_1 are positive constants.

2. Greedy algorithm of learning pure conjunction concept

Algorithm 7.14 (Greedy Algorithm of Learning Pure Conjunction Concept).

1. As for given samples, find the minimum main atom of each attribute.
2. At the beginning, pure conjunction assumption h is empty, when there is negative examples in samples, do
3. In all attributes, find the minimum main atom, which deletes most negative examples and add them to h. If no minimum main atom, then any negative example can be deleted. The loop ends.

4. Eliminate deleted negative examples from samples.
5. If there is no negative examples, then return h, else report samples are inconsistent with any pure conjunction concept.

Haussler discussed the problem of sample complexity of the algorithm in his paper (Haussler, 1988b) and gave the following result:

$$C_0 \left(\log \left(\frac{1}{\delta} \right) + s \log \left(\frac{n}{s} \right) \right) \Big/ \varepsilon$$

$$\leq S_c^L(\varepsilon, \delta) \leq C_1 \left(\log \left(\frac{1}{\delta} \right) + s \left(\log \left(\frac{sn1}{\varepsilon} \right) \right)^2 \right) \Big/ \varepsilon, \qquad (7.39)$$

where C_0 and C_1 are positive constants, and s is the maximum number of atoms in pure conjunction concept.

We can see from this that Valiant's learning theory only requires assumption generated by a learning algorithm that can approach the objective concept well with high probability and does not require the identification of a target concept precisely. This kind of learning theory is "approximately correct" identification, sometimes simply called Probably Approximately Correct (PAC) Theory. Valiant's learning theory has more practical significance than Gold's learning theory.

Exercises

7.1 What is inductive learning? What are its main characteristics?
7.2 Through examples, explain the application of selective and constructive generation rules.
7.3 What is the bias problem in decision tree learning? Describe in simple terms several bias learning algorithms.
7.4 What is hypothesis space? Describe the relation among hypotheses in hypothesis space.
7.5 What are the inductive reasoning patterns which AQ learning approach complies with? Why do we say the procedure of AQ learning is a procedure of searching the hypothesis space?
7.6 Combining with the figure of rule space ordering, describe the basic idea of version space.

7.7 Give the procedure that a candidate-deleting algorithm is used in the following data set:

Positive example:　(a) object (red, round, apple)
　　　　　　　　　　(b) object (green, round, mango)
Negative example:　(a) object (red, large, banana)
　　　　　　　　　　(b) object (green, round, guava)

7.8 Explain decision tree learning approach and its applicable situation.

7.9 In the procedure of constructing decision tree, what principle for selection of test attribute should be employed? How to realize it?

7.10 Explicate the basic idea and building steps of ID3 algorithm.

7.11 Given the following data, answer the questions.

Studied hard	Hours slept before	Breakfast	Got A
No	5	Eggs	No
No	9	Eggs	No
Yes	6	Eggs	No
No	6	Bagel	No
Yes	9	Bagel	Yes
Yes	8	Eggs	Yes
Yes	8	Cereal	Yes
Yes	6	Cereal	Yes

(1) How much is the initial entropy of GotA?
(2) Which is the attribute that the decision tree (ID3) will select as root node?
(3) Construct the decision tree.

7.12 In what aspects can C4.5 learning algorithm improve ID3 learning algorithm?

7.13 What is the sample complexity and computational complexity of the learning algorithm?

7.14 Why Valiant's learning theory has more practical significance than Gold's learning theory?

Chapter 8

Statistical Learning

Statistical learning refers to a set of tools for modeling and understanding complex data sets. With the explosion of "Big Data" problems, statistical learning has become a very hot field in many scientific areas as well as economy, finance, and other business disciplines. People with statistical learning skills are in high demand.

8.1 Introduction

The statistical method is to perform the external quantity of the object to infer its possible regularity. The scientific regularity is always hidden deeper. At first, some clues are always seen through statistical analysis from its quantitative performance, and then certain hypotheses or doctrines are proposed for further in-depth theoretical research. When theoretical research makes certain conclusions, it often needs to be verified in practice. That is to say, when observing some natural phenomena or specially arranged experimental data, whether it is consistent with the theory, to what extent, and which direction it may take, need to be treated by statistical analysis.

Statistics has been greatly developed in the last hundred years. We can roughly describe the process of statistical development using the following framework:

- 1900–1920 — data description;
- 1920–1940 — the dawn of statistical models;
- 1940–1960 — mathematical Statistics Era;
- 1960–1980 — challenges of stochastic model assumptions;
- 1980–1990 — relaxation Structure Model Hypothesis;
- 1990–1999 — modeling complex data structures.

Among them, from 1960 to 1980, there was a revolution in the field of statistics. It is sufficient to estimate the dependencies from the observed data, as long as the general properties of the set of functions to which the unknown dependencies belong are known. Leading this revolution are the four discoveries of the 1960s:

(1) the principle of regularization on the resolution of ill-posed problems found by Tikhonov, Ivanov, and Philips;
(2) non-parametric statistics found by Parzen, Rosenblatt, and Chentsov;
(3) the Law of large numbers in universal function spaces found by Vapnik and Chervonenkis, and its relationship to the learning process;
(4) the complexity of algorithm and its relationship with inductive reasoning discovered by Kolmogorov, Solomonoff, and Chaitin.

These four findings have also become an important basis for statistical learning research. The traditional statistics mainly studies the asymptotic theory, that is, the statistical properties when the sample tends to infinity. The statistical method mainly considers the hypothesis of the test and the data model fit. It relies on an explicit basic probability model.

Common statistical methods include regression analysis (multiple regression, autoregressive, etc.), discriminant analysis (Bayesian discriminant, Fisher discriminant, non-parametric discriminant, etc.), cluster analysis (system clustering, dynamic clustering, etc.), and exploration analysis (principal element analysis, correlation analysis, etc.). The support vector machine (SVM) is based on the principle of structural risk minimization of computational learning theory. The main idea is to find a hyperplane as a two-class segmentation in high-dimensional space for two types of classification problems to ensure the minimum classification error rate (Vapnik *et al.*, 1997). An important advantage of SVM is that it can handle linear indivisible situations.

Vapnik and his research group have studied machine learning based on finite samples since 1960s. A complete theory, statistical learning theory, was established in the 1990s (Vapnik, 1995). Moreover, a new universal learning algorithm, Support Vector Machine (SVM), has been proposed. SVM minimizes the probability of classification error based on the structural risk minimization inductive principle. The main idea of SVM is mapping the nonlinear data to a higher dimensional linear space where the data can be linearly classified by hyperplane (Vapnik *et al.*, 1997). One advantage of SVM is the capacity of disposing linearly non-separable cases.

8.2 Statistical Learning Problem

8.2.1 Empirical Risk

We consider the learning problem as a problem of finding a desired dependence between input and output (or supervisor's response) using a limited number of observations. Learning problems could generally be represented to find an uncertain dependency relationship between variables y and x, where the joint probability distribution function $F(x, y)$ is unknown. The selection of the desired function is based on a training set of n independent and identically distributed observations:

$$(x_1, y_1), (x_2, y_2), \ldots, (x_n, y_n). \tag{8.1}$$

Given a set of functions $\{f(x, w)\}$, it aims at choosing a best function to approximate the supervisor's response $f(x, w_0)$, which makes the risk function be minimal:

$$R(w) = \int L(y, f(x, w)) d F(x, y), \tag{8.2}$$

where $\{f(x, w)\}$ is the set of expected functions, w are functional general parameters. $L(y, f(x, w))$ measures the loss, or discrepancy between the response y of the supervisor to a given input x and the response $f(x, w)$ provided by the learning machine. Different types of learning problems have diverse formal loss function.

Empirical risk minimization inductive principle is used in the classical methods of a learning problem. Empirical risk is defined on the basis of the training set:

$$R_{\text{emp}}(w) = \frac{1}{l} \sum_{i=1}^{l} L(y_i, f(x_i, w)). \tag{8.3}$$

Machine learning designs a learning algorithm for minimizing $R_{\text{emp}}(w)$.

8.2.2 VC Dimension

Statistical learning theory is inductive learning theory on the basis of the small sample size. One significant concept is Vapnik–Chervonenkis Dimension (VC Dimension) in pattern recognition. The VC dimension of a set of indicator functions $f(x, w)$ is equal to the largest number h of vectors that can be separated into different classes in all the 2^h possible ways using this set of functions (i.e., the VC dimension is the maximum number of vectors that can be shattered by the set of functions). The VC dimension is equal to infinity if there exists a set of vectors that any number of samples can be shattered by the functions $f(x, w)$. The VC dimensions of a set of bounded real functions are defined by transformed indicated functions with threshold.

The VC dimension of the set of functions (rather than the number of parameters) is responsible for the generalization ability of the learning machine. Intuitively, learning machines with high VC dimensions have more complexity and power. At the moment, there is no universal theory to calculate the VC dimension of an arbitrary function set. In an n-dimensional real space Rn, the VC dimension of linear classification and linear real function is $n + 1$. However, the VC dimensions of $f(x, \alpha) = \sin(\alpha x)$ are infinite. In the statistical learning theory, it is still a problem to calculate the VC dimension using theoretical and experimental methods.

8.3 Consistency of Learning Processes

8.3.1 *Classical Definition of Learning Consistency*

In order to construct algorithms for learning from a limited number of observations, we need an asymptotic theory (consistency is an asymptotic concept). We describe the conceptual model for learning processes that are based on the empirical risk minimization inductive principle. The goal of this part is to describe the necessary and sufficient conditions for the consistency of learning processes that minimize the empirical risk.

Definition 8.1. The Empirical Risk Minimization Inductive Principle (Vapnik, 1995).

We say that the principle (method) of the empirical risk minimization (ERM) is consistent for the set of functions $L(y, w)$ and for the probability distribution function $F(y)$ if the following two sequences converge in probability to the same limit (see the schematic Figure 8.1):

$$R(w_l) \xrightarrow[l \to \infty]{P} \inf_{w \in \Lambda} R(w), \tag{8.4}$$

$$R_{\text{emp}}(w_l) \xrightarrow[l \to \infty]{P} \inf_{w \in \Lambda} R(w). \tag{8.5}$$

In other words, the ERM method is consistent if it provides a sequence of functions $L(y, w_l), l = 1, 2, \ldots$, for which both expected risk and empirical risk converge to the minimal possible value of risk. Equation (8.4) asserts that the values of achieved risks converge to the best possibility, while Equation (8.5) asserts that one can estimate the minimal possible value of the risk on the basis of the values of empirical risk.

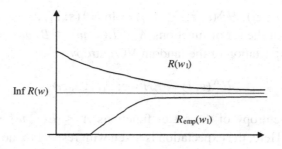

Fig. 8.1. Consistency of Learning Process

8.3.2 *Key Theorem of Learning Theory*

In 1989, Vapnik and Chefvonenkis proposed the key theorem of the learning theory as follows (Vapnik and Chefvonerkis, 1991):

Theorem 8.1. *Let $L(y, w)$, $w \in \Lambda$ be a set of functions that satisfy the following condition:*

$$A \leq \int L(y, w)dF(y) \leq B \quad (A \leq R(w) \leq B). \tag{8.6}$$

Then for the ERM principle to be consistent in the following sense

$$\lim_{l \to \infty} P\{\sup_{w \in \Lambda} R(w) - R_{\text{emp}}(w) > \varepsilon\} = 0, \quad \forall \varepsilon > 0, \tag{8.7}$$

it is necessary and sufficient that the empirical risk $R_{\text{emp}}(w)$ converges uniformly to the actual risk $R(w)$ over the set $L(y, w)$, $w \in \Lambda$. We call this type of uniform convergence uniform as one-sided convergence.

8.3.3 *VC Entropy*

Definition 8.2. Let $A \leq L(y, w) \leq B, \omega \in \Lambda$, be a set of bounded loss functions. Using this set of functions and the training set $z_1, \ldots, z_l$, one can construct the following set of lD vectors:

$$q(w) = (L(z_1, w), \ldots, L(z_l, w)), \quad w \in \Lambda. \tag{8.8}$$

This set of vectors belongs to the lD cube and has a finite minimal ε-net in the metric C (or in the metric L_p).

Let $N = N^\Lambda(\varepsilon; z_1, \ldots, z_l)$ be the number of elements of the minimal ε-net of this set of vectors $q(w)$, $w \in \Lambda$. Note that $N^\Lambda(\varepsilon; z_1, \ldots, z_l)$ is a random variable, since it is constructed using random vectors $z_1, \ldots, z_l$. The logarithm of the random value $N^\Lambda(\varepsilon; z_1, \ldots, z_l)$, $H^\Lambda(\varepsilon; z_1, \ldots, z_l) = \ln N^\Lambda(\varepsilon; z_1, \ldots, z_l)$ is called the random VC entropy of the set of functions $A \le L(y, w) \le B$, $w \in \Lambda$, on the sample $z_1, \ldots, z_l$. The expectation of the random VC entropy

$$H^\Lambda(\varepsilon; l) = EH^\Lambda(\varepsilon; z_1, \ldots, z_l)$$

is called the VC entropy of the set of functions $A \le L(y, w) \le B$, $w \in \Lambda$ on samples of size l. Here, the expectation is taken with respect to the product measure $F(z_1, \ldots, z_l)$.

Theorem 8.2. *For a uniform two-sided convergence, it is necessary and sufficient that the equality*

$$\lim_{l \to \infty} \frac{H^\Lambda(\varepsilon, l)}{l} = 0, \quad \forall \varepsilon > 0, \tag{8.9}$$

be valid. In other words, the ratio of the VC entropy to the number of observations should decrease to zero with increasing numbers of observations.

Corollary 8.1. *Under some conditions of measurability on the set of indicator functions $L(y, w)$, $w \in \Lambda$, the necessary and sufficient condition for uniform two-sided convergence is $\lim_{l \to \infty} \frac{H^\Lambda(l)}{l} = 0$, which is a particular case of equality (8.9).*

Theorem 8.3. *In order for the uniform one-sided convergence of empirical means to their expectations to hold for the set of totally bounded functions $L(y, w)$, $w \in \Lambda$, it is necessary and sufficient that for any positive δ, η, and ε, there exist a set of functions $L^*(y, w^*)$, $w^* \in \Lambda^*$ satisfying*

$$L(y, w) - L^*(y, w^*) \ge 0, \quad \forall y,$$
$$\int (L(y, w) - L^*(y, w^*))dF(y) \le \delta, \tag{8.10}$$

such that the following holds for the ε-entropy of the set $L^*(y, w^*)$, $w^* \in \Lambda^*$, on samples of size l:

$$\lim_{l \to \infty} \frac{H^{\Lambda^*}(\varepsilon, l)}{l} < \eta.$$

According to these key theorems, we study the learning theory. Moreover, we describe a sufficient condition for the consistency of the ERM principle by using different methods and functions. On the basis of these functions, three milestones of learning theory are constructed as follows:

(1) We use VC entropy to define the following equation describing a sufficient condition for the consistency of the ERM principle:

$$\lim_{l \to \infty} \frac{H^\wedge(l)}{l} = 0. \tag{8.11}$$

(2) We use the annealed VC entropy to define the following equation describing a sufficient condition for the consistency of the ERM principle:

$$\lim_{l \to \infty} \frac{H^\wedge_{\text{ann}}(l)}{l} = 0, \tag{8.12}$$

where the annealed VC entropy $H^\wedge_{\text{ann}}(l) = \ln E N^\wedge(z, \ldots, z_l)$.

(3) We use the growth function to define the following equation describing a sufficient condition for the consistency of the ERM principle:

$$\lim_{l \to \infty} \frac{G^\wedge(l)}{l} = 0, \tag{8.13}$$

where the growth function $G^\wedge(l) = \ln \sup_{z, \ldots, z_{l1}} N^\wedge(z, \ldots, z_l)$.

8.4 Structural Risk Minimization Inductive Principle

Statistical learning theory systematically analyzes the relationship a of inhomogeneous function set, empirical risk and actual risk, and the bounds on the generalization ability of learning machines (Vapnik, 1995). Here, we will only consider functions that correspond to the two-class pattern recognition case for the set of indicator functions (including the function minimizing empirical risk). Now, choose some η such that $0 \le \eta \le 1$. Then for losses taking empirical risk $R_{\text{emp}}(w)$ and actual risk $R(w)$ with probability $1 - \eta$, the following bound holds (Burges, 1998):

$$R(w) \le R_{\text{emp}}(w) + \sqrt{\frac{h(\ln(2l/h) + 1) - \ln(\eta/4)}{l}},$$

where h is a non-negative integer called the Vapnik Chervonenkis (VC) dimension and l is the total of samples.

It follows that statistical learning's actual risk $R(w)$ has two parts: one is empirical risk $R_{\text{emp}}(w)$ defined to be just the measured mean error rate on the training set (for a fixed, finite number of observations); another is VC confidence. The confidence interval reflects the maximal difference between the actual risk and empirical risk. Meanwhile, it reflects that risk brings structural complexity. There are some relations between the confidence interval, VC dimension h, and sample number l. The inequality (8.14) could simply be expressed as

$$R(w) \le R_{emp}(w) + \Phi(h/l). \tag{8.14}$$

According to the second term on the right-hand side of the inequality (8.14), $\Phi(h/l)$ increases while the VC dimension, h increases. Therefore, the confidence interval increases while learning a machine's complexity and the VC dimension increases. Moreover, the difference between actual risk and empirical risk increases when learning machines use a small sample of training instances.

Note that the bound for the generalization ability of learning machines is a conclusion in the worst case. Furthermore, the bound is not tight in many cases, especially when the VC dimension is higher. When $h/l > 0.37$, the bound is guaranteed to be not tight (Burges, 1998). When VC dimension is infinite, the bound does not exist.

To construct small sample size methods, we use both the bounds for the generalization ability of learning machines with sets of totally bounded non-negative functions, $0 \le L(z, w) \le B$, $w \in \Lambda$ (Λ is abstract parameters set). Each bound is valid with probability of at least $1 - \eta$:

$$R(w_l) \le R_{emp}(w) + \frac{B\varepsilon}{2}\left(1 + \sqrt{1 + \frac{4R_{emp}(w_l)}{B\varepsilon}}\right), \tag{8.15}$$

and the bound for the generalization ability of learning machines with sets of unbounded functions,

$$R(w_l) \le \frac{R_{emp}(w_l)}{\left(1 - a(p)\tau\sqrt{\varepsilon}\right)_+}, \tag{8.16}$$

where

$$a(p) = \sqrt[p]{\frac{1}{2}\left(\frac{p-1}{p-2}\right)^{p-1}} \qquad \varepsilon = 2\frac{\ln N - \ln \eta}{l}.$$

There are two methods to minimize the actual risk. One is to minimize the empirical risk. According to the upper formula, the upper bound of actual risk decreases while the empirical risk decreases. The other is to minimize the second term on the right-hand side of the inequality (8.15). We have to make the VC dimension a controlling variable. The latter method conforms to the small sample size.

Let the set S of functions $L(z, w)$ be provided with a structure consisting of nested subsets of functions $S_k = \{L(z, w), w \in \Lambda_k\}$, such that (see Figure 8.2)

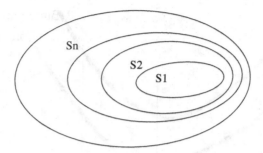

Fig. 8.2. A structure on the set of functions is determined by the nested subsets of functions

(Vapnik, 1995)

$$S_1 \subset S_2 \subset \cdots \subset S_n, \tag{8.17}$$

where the elements of the structure satisfy the following two properties:

(1) The VC dimension hk of each set S_k of functions is finite. Therefore,

$$h_1 \leq h_2 \leq, \ldots, \leq h_n, \ldots.$$

(2) Any element S_k of the structure contains either a set of totally bounded functions, $0 \leq L(z, w) \leq B_k$; $\alpha \in \Lambda_k$ or a set of functions satisfy the following inequality for some pair (p, τ_k):

$$\sup_{w \in \Lambda_k} \frac{\left(\int L^p(z, w) dF(z) \right)^{\frac{1}{p}}}{\int L(z, w) dF(z)} \leq \tau_k, \quad p > 2. \tag{8.18}$$

We call this structure an admissible structure.

For a given set of observations $z_1, \ldots, z_l$, the structural risk minimization (SRM) principle chooses the function $L(z, w_{kl})$ minimizing the empirical risk in the subset S_k for which the guaranteed risk (determined by the right-hand side of the inequality (8.15) or by the right-hand side of the inequality (8.16) depending on the circumstances) is minimal.

The SRM principle defines a trade-off between the quality of the approximation of the given data and the complexity of the approximating function. As the subset index n increases, the minima of the empirical risks decrease. However, the term responsible for the confidence interval increases. The SRM principle takes both factors into account by choosing the subset S_n for which minimizing the empirical risk yields the best bound on the actual risk as shown in Figure 8.3 (Vapnik, 1995).

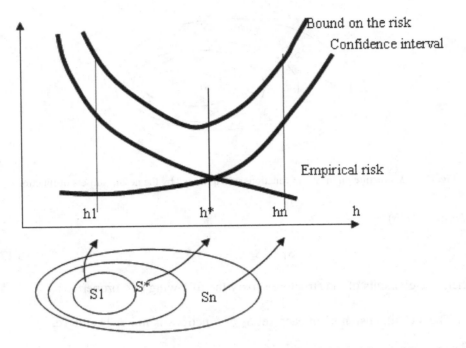

Fig. 8.3.   The bound on the structural risk is the sum of the empirical risk and the confidence interval

8.5 Support Vector Machine

Support vector machine (SVM) is a new type of universal learning machine proposed recently. SVM has extra advantages for pattern classification.

8.5.1 *Linearly Separable Case*

Suppose the training data $(x_1, y_1), \ldots, (x_l, y_l)$, $x \in R_n$, $y \in \{+1, -1\}$, where l is the sample size and n is the dimension of the input data. We can construct a hyperplane to absolutely separate two-class samples for the case where the training data are linearly separable. The hyperplane be described as

$$(w \bullet x) + b = 0, \tag{8.19}$$

where $\bullet$ denotes the vector dot products. To describe the separating hyperplane, let us use the following form:

$$w \bullet x_i + b \geq 0, \quad \text{if } y_i = +1,$$

$$w \bullet x_i + b < 0, \quad \text{if } y_i = -1,$$

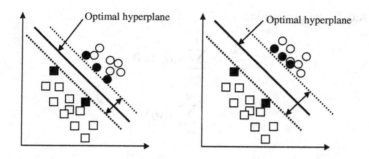

Fig. 8.4. The optimal separating hyperplane

where w denotes hyperplane's normal direction, $\frac{w}{||w||}$ denotes a unit normal vector, and $||w||$ denotes the Euclid modular function.

We say that this set of vectors is separated by the optimal hyperplane (or the maximal margin hyperplane) if the training data are separated without error and the distance between the closest vector to the hyperplane is maximal (see Figure 8.4).

For a linearly separable case, to find the optimal separating hyperplane we have to solve the following quadratic programming problem. Given the training samples, we find a pair consisting of a vector w and a constant (threshold) b such that they minimize the function

$$\min \Phi(w) = \frac{1}{2}||w||^2 \qquad (8.20)$$

under the constraints of inequality type

$$y_i(w \bullet x_i + b) - 1 \geq 0 \quad i = 1, 2, \ldots, l. \qquad (8.21)$$

Optimize function $\Phi(w)$ has quadratic form, and the constraint condition is linear. Thus, it is a typical quadratic programming problem that can be solved by the Lagrange multiplier method. Introduce Lagrange multipliers $\alpha_i \geq 0$, $i = 1, 2, \ldots, l$,

$$L(w, b, \alpha) = \frac{1}{2}||w||^2 - \sum_{i=1}^{l} \alpha_i \{y_i(x_i \bullet w + b) - 1\}, \qquad (8.22)$$

where the extremum of L is the saddle point of equality (8.22). To find the saddle point, one has to minimize this function over w and b and to maximize it over the non-negative Lagrange multipliers α. At the saddle point, the solutions w^*, b^*, and

α^* should satisfy the conditions

$$\frac{\partial L}{\partial b} = \sum_{i=1}^{l} y_i \alpha_i = 0, \tag{8.23}$$

$$\frac{\partial L}{\partial w} = w - \sum_{i=1}^{l} y_i \alpha_i x_i = 0, \tag{8.24}$$

where $\frac{\partial L}{\partial w} = \left(\frac{\partial L}{\partial w_1}, \frac{\partial L}{\partial w_2}, \ldots, \frac{\partial L}{\partial w_i} \right)$.

Therefore, through solving the quadratic programming problem, SVM attains the corresponding α^* and w^* satisfying the following equality:

$$w^* = \sum_{i=1}^{l} \alpha_i^* y_i x_i, \tag{8.25}$$

and the optimal hyperplane is shown in Figure 8.4.

For transforming the linearly separable case, the original problem becomes the following problem:

$$\max_{\alpha} W(\alpha) = \sum_{i=1}^{l} \alpha_i - \frac{1}{2} \sum_{i=1}^{l} \sum_{j=1}^{l} \alpha_i \alpha_j y_i y_j x_i \bullet x_j = \Gamma \bullet I - \frac{1}{2} \Gamma \bullet D\Gamma, \tag{8.26}$$

satisfying the following constraints

$$\sum_{i=1}^{l} y_i \alpha_i = 0 \quad \alpha_i \geq 0 \quad i = 1, 2, \ldots, l, \tag{8.27}$$

where, $\Gamma = (\alpha_1, \alpha_2, \ldots, \alpha_l), I = (1, 1, \ldots, 1), D$ is a $l \times l$ symmetric matrix, and each element is as follows:

$$D_{ij} = y_i y_j x_i \bullet x_j. \tag{8.28}$$

This fact follows from the classical Karush–Kuhn–Tucker (KKT) theorem, according to which the necessary and sufficient conditions for the optimal hyperplane are such that the separating hyperplane satisfies the conditions:

$$\alpha_i \{ y_i (w \bullet x_i + b) - 1 \} = 0 \quad i = 1, 2, \ldots, l. \tag{8.29}$$

According to equality (8.25), only those samples satisfying $\alpha_i > 0$ determine the classification result while those samples satisfying $\alpha_i = 0$ do not. We will call these samples satisfying $\alpha_i > 0$ as support vectors.

We train samples to attain vectors α^* and w^*. Selecting a support vector sample x_i, we attain b^* by the following equality:

$$b^* = y_i - w \bullet x_i. \tag{8.30}$$

For a test sample x, calculate the following equality:

$$d(x) = x \bullet w^* + b^* = \sum_{i=1}^{l} y_i \alpha_i^* (x \bullet x_i) + b^*. \tag{8.31}$$

According to the sign of $d(x)$, determine which class x belongs to.

8.5.2 *Linearly Non-separable Case*

In a linearly separable case, decision function is constructed on the basis of Euclid distance, i.e., $K(x_i, x_j) = x_i \bullet x_j = x_i^T x_j$. In a linearly non-separable case, SVM maps the input vectors x into a high-dimensional feature space H through some nonlinear mapping (see Figure 8.5). In this space, an optimal separating hyperplane is constructed. The nonlinear mapping $\Phi : R^d \to H$

$$x \to \Phi(x) = (\phi_1(x), \phi_2(x), \dots, \phi_{i(x)}, \dots)^T, \tag{8.32}$$

where $\phi_i(x)$ is a real function.

Feature vector $\Phi(x)$ substitutes the input vector x, and the equalities (8.28) and (8.31) are transformed as follows:

$$D_{ij} = y_i y_j \Phi(x_i) \bullet \Phi(x_j), \tag{8.33}$$

$$d(x) = \Phi(x) \bullet w^* + b^* = \sum_{i=1}^{l} \alpha_i y_i \Phi(x_i) \bullet \Phi(x) + b^*. \tag{8.34}$$

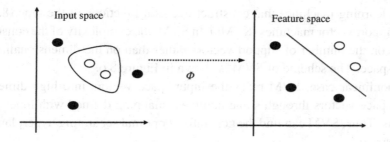

Fig. 8.5. The SVM maps the input space into a feature space

The optimize function equality (8.26) and decision function equality (8.31) only refer to inner product $x_i \bullet x_j$ of training samples. Therefore, we calculate the inner product in high-dimensional space using inner product functions in the input space. On the basis of relational theory, a kernel function $K(x_i \bullet x_j)$ is parallelism of inner product in a certain space if it satisfies Mercer's condition (Vapnik, 1995).

Using some appropriate inner product function $K(x_i \bullet x_j)$, SVM maps the input space vectors into feature space vectors through some nonlinear mapping. Moreover, the complexity of calculation does not increase. The object function equality (8.26) is transformed to the following equality:

$$\max_{\alpha} W(\alpha) = \sum_{i=1}^{l} \alpha_i - \frac{1}{2} \sum_{i=1}^{l} \sum_{j=1}^{l} \alpha_i \alpha_j y_i y_j K(x_i, x_j). \tag{8.35}$$

Thus, the corresponding classifying function becomes the following equality:

$$d(x) = \sum_{i=1}^{l} y_i \alpha_i^* K(x, x_i) + b^*. \tag{8.36}$$

This is called support vector machine (SVM) as shown in Figure 8.6 (Vapnik, 1995).

For a given $K(x, y)$, the corresponding function $\Phi(x)$ exists under certain condition. It is necessary and sufficient that the condition is satisfied as follows:

Given an arbitrary function $g(x)$, if $\int_a^b g(x)^2 dx$ is finite,

$$\int_a^b \int_a^b K(x, y)g(x)g(y)dxdy \geq 0. \tag{8.37}$$

Equation (8.37) is valid.

This decision condition is not feasible. It is well known that the polynomial function satisfies Mercer's condition. Therefore, $K(x, y)$ satisfies Mercer's condition if it approaches some polynomial function.

The learning machines that construct decision functions of the type (8.36) are called support vector machines (SVMs). In SVM, the complexity of the construction depends on the number of support vectors rather than on the dimensionality of the feature space. The scheme of SVM is shown in Figure 8.6.

In nonlinear case, SVM maps the input space vectors into high-dimensional feature space vectors through some nonlinear mapping defined with inner product functions. Thus, SVM can find the generalized optimal separating hyperplane in the feature space.

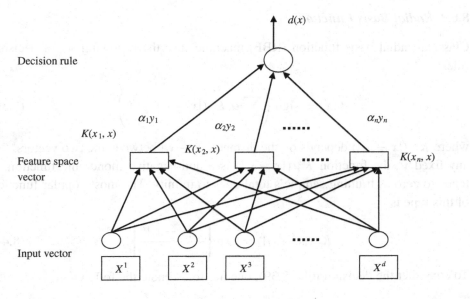

Fig. 8.6. Support vectors machine

8.6 Kernel Function

Using different functions for convolution of the inner product kernel function, one can construct learning machines with different types of nonlinear decision surfaces in the input space. At present, prevalent kernel functions are polynomial kernel function, radial basis function, multi-layer perceptron, and dynamic kernel function.

8.6.1 *Polynomial Kernel Function*

Polynomial kernel function is

$$K(x, x_i) = [(x, x_i) + 1]^d. \tag{8.38}$$

We construct a d-dimensional polynomial decision function of the form

$$f(x, \alpha) = \text{sign}\left(\sum_{\text{support vector}} y_i \alpha_i [x_i \bullet x) + 1]^d - b\right).$$

8.6.2 *Radial Basis Function*

Classical radial basis function (RBF) machines use the following set of decision rules:

$$f(x) = \text{sign}\left(\sum_{i=1}^{l} \alpha_i K_\gamma(|x - x_i|) - b\right), \tag{8.39}$$

where $K_\gamma(|x - x_i|)$ depends on the distance $|x - x_i|$ between the two vectors. For any fixed γ, the function $K_\gamma(|x - x_i|)$ is a non-negative monotonic function. It tends to zero as training sample's total goes to infinity. The most popular function of this type is

$$K_\gamma(|x - x_i|) = \exp\left\{-\frac{|x - x_i|^2}{\sigma^2}\right\}. \tag{8.40}$$

To construct the decision rule (8.39), one has to estimate the following:

(1) the value of the parameter γ,
(2) the number N of the centers x_i,
(3) the vectors x_i, describing the centers,
(4) the value of the parameters α_i.

In contrast to classical RBF methods, each center denotes a support vector in this method. Furthermore, all four types of parameters are chosen to minimize the bound on the probability of the test error.

8.6.3 *Multi-Layer Perceptron*

Multi-layer perceptron defines inner product kernel function using the sigmoid function. The number N of hidden units (the number of support vectors) is found automatically. The sigmoid kernel satisfies Mercer conditions as follows:

$$K(x_i, x_j) = \tanh(\gamma x_i^T x_j - \Theta). \tag{8.41}$$

Using this arithmetic, we avoid local minima problem that puzzles the neural network.

8.6.4 *Dynamic Kernel Function*

Amari and Wu proposed a method of modifying a kernel function to improve the performance of a support vector machine classifier (Amari *et al.*, 1999). This is based on the structure of the Riemannian geometry induced by the kernel function. U denotes feature mapping $U = \Phi(x)$, then

$$dU = \sum_i \frac{\partial}{\partial x_i} \Phi(x) dx_i,$$

$$\|dU\|^2 = \sum_{i,j} g_{ij}(x) dx_i dx_j,$$

where

$$g_{ij}(x) = \left(\frac{\partial}{\partial x_i} \Phi(x)\right) \bullet \left(\frac{\partial}{\partial x_j} \Phi(x)\right).$$

The $n \times n$ positive-definite matrix $(g_{ij}(x))$ is the Riemannian metric tensor induced in S. $ds^2 = \sum_{ij} g_{ij}(x) dx_i dx_j$ is the Riemannian distance. The volume form in a Riemannian space is defined as

$$dv = \sqrt{g(x)} dx_1, \dots, dx_n,$$

where $g(x) = \det(g_{ij}(x))$. Factor $g(x)$ represents how a local area is magnified in U under the mapping $\Phi(x)$. Therefore, we call it the magnification factor. Since $k(x, z) = (\Phi(x) \bullet \Phi(z))$, we can get

$$g_{ij}(x) = \frac{\partial}{\partial x_i \partial z_j} k(x, z)|_{z=x}.$$

In particular, for the Gaussian kernel function $k(x, z) = \exp\left\{\frac{|x-z|^2}{2\sigma^2}\right\}$, we have

$$g_{ij}(x) = \frac{1}{\sigma^2} \delta_{ij}.$$

In order to improve the performance of a SVM classifier, Amari and Wu proposed a method of modifying a kernel function. To increase the margin or reparability of classes, we need to enlarge the spatial resolution around the boundary surface in U. Let $c(x)$ be a positive real differentiable function and $k(x, z)$ denote a Gaussian kernel function, then

$$\tilde{k}(x, z) = c(x)k(x, z)c(z), \tag{8.42}$$

which also is a kernel function, and

$$\tilde{g}_{ij}(x) = c_i(x)c_j(x) + c^2(x)g_{ij},$$

where $c_i(x) = \frac{\partial}{\partial x_i} c(x)$. Amari and Wu defined $c(x)$ as

$$c(x) = \sum_{x_i \in SV} h_i e^{\frac{\|x - x_i\|^2}{2\tau^2}}, \tag{8.43}$$

where τ is a positive number, h_i denotes coefficient. Around the support vector x_i, we have

$$\sqrt{\tilde{g}(x)} \approx \frac{h_i}{\sigma^n} e^{\frac{nr^2}{2\gamma^2}} \sqrt{1 + \frac{\sigma^2}{\tau^4} \gamma^2},$$

where $\tau = \|x - x_i\|$ is the Euclid distance between x and x_i. In order to ensure $\sqrt{\tilde{g}(x)}$ is larger near the support vector x_i and is smaller in other region, we need

$$\tau \approx \frac{\sigma}{\sqrt{n}}. \tag{8.44}$$

In summary, the training process of the new method consists of the two steps:

(1) Train SVM with a primary kernel k (Gaussian kernel), then modifying the training result according to equalities (8.42), (8.43), and (8.44), we attain $\tilde{k}$.
(2) Train SVM with the modified kernel $\tilde{k}$.

When SVM uses the new training method, the performance of the classifier is improved remarkably, and the number of support vectors decreases such that it improves the velocity of pattern recognition.

Exercises

8.1 Compare Empirical Risk Minimization (ERM) Inductive Principle and Structural Risk Minimization (SRM) Inductive Principle.
8.2 What is the meaning of VC dimensions? Why does VC dimension reflect a function set's learning capacity?
8.3 What are the three milestones of the statistics learning theory? What problem was resolved in each milestone?
8.4 Describe support vector machine's primitive idea and mathematical model.
8.5 Why is statistical learning theory regarded as the foundation of support vector machine theory, and in which areas does it represent so?

8.6 Under linearly separable case, a hyperplane is defined as follows:

$$w^T x + b = 0,$$

where w denotes a weight vector, b denotes bias, and x denotes an input vector. If a set of input pattern $\{x_i\}_{i=1}^N$ satisfies the following conditions

$$\min_{i=1,2,\ldots,N} |w^T x_i + b| = 1$$

(w, b) is called the canonical pair of hyperplane. Prove that conditions of canonical pair-conduced distance between bounds of two classification is $2/\|w\|$.

8.7 Briefly narrate the primitive concept that support vector machine solves the nonlinearly separable problem.

8.8 Two-layer perceptron's inner product kernel is defined as

$$K(x, x_i) = \tan h(\beta_0 x^T x_i + \beta_1).$$

Under which values of β_0 and β_1, the kernel function does not satisfy Mercer's condition?

8.9 What are the advantages and limitations of a support vector machine and radial basis function (RBF) network while they, respectively, solve the following assignments?

(1) Pattern recognition
(2) Nonlinear regression

8.10 In contrast to other classification methods, what are support vector machine's significant advantages? Explain theoretically.

Chapter 9

Deep Learning

Deep learning is used to imitate the information processing mechanism of the human brain multi-layer neural network. It combines low-level features to form more abstract high-level representation attributes to explain the semantics of data, such as images, sounds, and texts.

9.1 Introduction

Deep learning as an exciting new technology has had rich history. Broadly speaking, there have been three waves of development of deep learning: deep learning known as cybernetics in the 1940s–1960s, deep learning known as connectionism in the 1980s–1990s, and the current resurgence under the name deep learning beginning in 2006 (Goodfellow *et al.*, 2016).

The first wave started with cybernetics in the 1940s–1960s, with the development of theories of biological learning. In 1943, McCulloch and Pitts published their paper in a neurons modeling group (McCulloch and Pitts, 1943). In their classic paper, McCulloch and Pitts combined the study of neurophysiology and the mathematical logic and described the logical analysis of a neural network. In their model, neurons were assumed to follow the yes–no model law. If the number of such simple neurons is enough and connection weights are appropriately set and synchronously operated, McCulloch and Pitts proved that in principle, any computable function could be calculated with such a network. In Hebb's book *"Behavior Histology"* (Hebb, 1949), he clearly explained the amendment to the physiological synaptic learning rules. In 1958, Rosenblatt proposed the first model called the perceptron (Rosenblatt, 1958) allowing the training of a single neuron. Rosenblatt's works on perceptron reveal a new method of pattern recognition and a new method of supervised learning (Rosenblatt, 1962).

The second wave started with the connectionist approach of the 1980–1995 period, with back-propagation to train a neural network with one or two hidden layers. In 1986, Rumelhart, Hinton, and Williams reported the development of the back-propagation algorithm. The same year, the famous book *Parallel Distributed Processing: Exploration of the Microstructure of Cognition,* edited by Rumelhart and McClelland was published (Rumelhart and McClelland, 1986). This book had a significant impact on the use of the back-propagation algorithm. It has become the most common multi-layer perceptron training algorithm. In fact, back-propagation learning was found independently at the same time in two other places. In the mid-1980s after the back-propagation algorithm was found, we found that as early as August 1974 in Harvard University, Werbos in his Ph.D. thesis had described it (Werbos, 1974). Werbos' doctoral thesis is the first documentation of an effective back-propagation model to describe the gradient calculation, and it can be applied to the general network model, including neural networks as its special case. The basic idea of back-propagation can be further traced back to the book by Bryson and Ho *Applied Optimal Control.*

The current and third wave, deep learning, started around 2006 (Hinton and Salakhutdinov, 2006). Hinton showed that a kind of neural network called a deep belief network could be efficiently trained using a strategy called greedy layer-wise pretraining. This wave of neural networks research popularized the use of the term deep learning to emphasize that researchers were now able to train deeper neural networks than had been possible before and to focus attention on the theoretical importance of depth. The third wave began with a focus on new unsupervised learning techniques and the ability of deep models to generalize well from small data sets.

In June 2012, the Google Brain project in *New York Times* attracted the attention of the public. This project is led by Andrew Ng and Jeff Dean at Stanford University. The parallel computation platform with 16,000 CPU cores is used to train the deep neural networks with 10 billion nodes. The mass data are directly loaded into the algorithm and let the data speak. The system will automatically learn from data.

In November 2012, Microsoft publicly demonstrated a fully automatic simultaneous interpretation system in Tianjin, China. The speaker made a speech in English, and the backend computer automatically accomplished speech recognition, machine translation from English to Chinese, and Chinese speech synthesis. The key technology that supported this backstage phenomenon was also deep learning.

On April 24, 2014, Baidu held the fourth technology Open Day in Beijing. During the Open Day, Baidu announced that they would officially launch a large data engine, including the core big data capability with the three major components Open Cloud, Data Factory, and Baidu Brain. Baidu provides big data storage, analysis, and mining techniques to the public through the large data engine. This is the first open big data engine in the world.

Deep learning is a new field in machine learning, and its core idea is to simulate the hierarchy abstraction structure of the human brain, analyze the large-scale data by unsupervised methods, and reveal the valuable information contained in big data. Deep learning was designed to research big data, which provides a deep thinking brain.

Suppose that there exists a system S with n layers $(S_1, \ldots, S_n)$. The system with input I and output O can be visually represented as $I \Rightarrow S_1 \Rightarrow S_2 \Rightarrow \cdots \Rightarrow S_n \Rightarrow O$. If the output O is equal to the input I, then the information of the input I is not lost after system transformation. To remain the same, this means that the input I after each layer S_i does not lose any information, that is, in any layer S_i, it is just another kind of representation of the original information.

The idea of deep learning is to stack multiple layers, and the output in the current layer serves as the input for the next layer. In this way, layer-wise representation of the input information can be realized.

In addition, the hypothesis presented above that the input is equal to the output is too strict. This limitation can be slightly loosened so that the difference between the input and the output is, as far as possible, little. This loosening principle can result in other deep learning methods. The above presentation is the basic idea of deep learning.

9.2 Human Brain Visual Mechanism

The human brain's visual mechanism is shown in Figure 9.1. For a long time, people have conducted research the human brain visual system.

In 1981, the Nobel Prize in medicine was awarded to David Hubel, Torsten Wiesel, and Roger Sperry. The main contribution of the first two people was in finding the information processing of the vision system: the visual cortex was graded like in Figure 9.2. The low-level V1 extracted the edge features. V2 extracted the shape or object parts, etc. The higher level regions extracted the entire object, the behavior of object, etc.

In 1958, David Hubel and Torsten Wiesel studied the correspondence between pupillary regions and cerebral cortical neurons at the John Hopkins University. They opened a 3-mm hole in a cat's hindbrain skull, inserted electrodes into the hole, and measured the activity of the neurons. Then, in front of the kitten's eyes, they showed objects of various shapes and brightness. Also, when each object was displayed, the position and angle at which the object was placed were also changed. They hoped

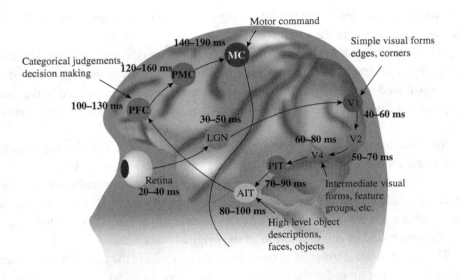

Fig. 9.1. Human brain visual system

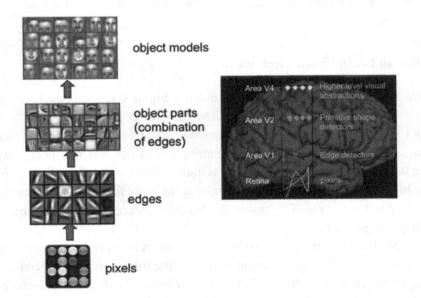

Fig. 9.2. Visual cortex grading handling

that through this method that the kittens would feel the stimulation of different types and different strengths. The reason for conducting this experiment was to prove a guess. There is a certain correspondence between different visual neurons located in the posterior cortex and the stimulation of the pupil. Once the pupil is subjected to a certain stimulus, a certain part of the neurons in the posterior cortex will be activated.

David Hubel and Torsten Wiesel discovered a neuron called the Orientation Selective Cell. When the pupil finds the edge of the object in front of the eye and the edge points in a certain direction, the neuron cell is active. This discovery has inspired people to think further about the nervous system. The neural–central-brain working process may be an iterative, continuous abstraction process. There are two keywords here, one is abstraction and the other is iteration: from the original signal, to low-level abstraction, and gradually to high-level abstraction. Human logical thinking often uses highly abstract concepts.

9.3 Autoencoder

Autoencoder is a single-hidden-layer neural network with the same number of nodes in the input layer and the output layer as shown in Figure 9.3. The aim of designing an Autoencoder is to reconstruct the input signal of the neural network as far as possible. This means that we need to solve the function $h_{W,b}(X) \approx x$, namely the output of the neural network is equal to the input as expected.

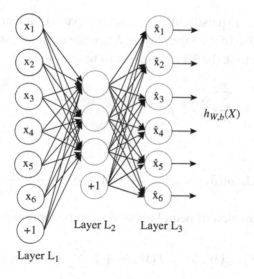

Fig. 9.3. Autoencoder

Suppose there exists a sample set $\{(x^{(1)}, y^{(1)}), \ldots, (x^{(m)}, y^{(m)})\}$ containing m samples. The batch gradient descent method can be used to solve the neural networks. In particular, for a single sample (x, y), the cost function is

$$J(W, b; x, y) = \frac{1}{2}||h_{w,b}(x) - y||^2. \tag{9.1}$$

Equation (9.1) is a variance cost function. Given a data set containing m samples, we can define the entire cost function as follows:

$$J(W, b) = \left[\frac{1}{m}\sum_{i=1}^{m} J(W, b; x^{(i)}, y^{(i)})\right] + \frac{\lambda}{2}\sum_{l=1}^{n_l-1}\sum_{i=1}^{s_l}\sum_{j=1}^{s_{l+1}}(W_{ji}^{(l)})^2$$

$$= \left[\frac{1}{m}\sum_{i=1}^{m}\left(\frac{1}{2}||h_{w,b}(x^{(i)}) - y^{(i)}||^2\right)\right] + \frac{\lambda}{2}\sum_{l=1}^{n_l-1}\sum_{i=1}^{s_l}\sum_{j=1}^{s_{l+1}}(W_{ji}^{(l)})^2. \tag{9.2}$$

The first item $J(W, b)$ in Equation (9.2) is a mean square error. The second item is a weight decay. Its aim is to reduce the scope of weight to prevent over-fitting.

$a_j^{(2)}(x)$ indicates the activation value of the input vector x on the hidden unit j. The average activation value of the hidden unit j is

$$\hat{\rho}_j = \frac{1}{m}\sum_{i=1}^{m}[a_j^{(2)}(x^{(i)})]. \tag{9.3}$$

In order to reach a sparsity, the least (most sparse) hidden units will be used to represent the feature of the input layer. When the average activation value of all hidden units is close to 0, the KL distance will be adopted:

$$\sum_{j=1}^{s_2} \rho \log\frac{\rho}{\hat{\rho}_j} + (1 - \rho)\log\frac{1 - \rho}{1 - \hat{\rho}_j}. \tag{9.4}$$

For ease in writing,

$$KL(\rho||\hat{\rho}_j) = \rho\log\frac{\rho}{\hat{\rho}_j} + (1 - \rho)\log\frac{1 - \rho}{1 - \hat{\rho}_j}. \tag{9.5}$$

So, the entire cost function of neural networks can be represented as

$$J_{\text{sparse}}(W, b) = J(W, b) + \beta\sum_{j=1}^{s_2} KL(\rho||\hat{\rho}_j). \tag{9.6}$$

The error computation formula $\delta_i^{(2)} = \left(\sum_{j=1}^{s_2} W_{ji}^{(2)} \delta_j^{(3)}\right) f'(z_i^{(2)})$, in back-propagation is modified as

$$\delta_i^{(2)} = \left(\left(\sum_{j=1}^{s_2} W_{ji}^{(2)} \delta_j^{(3)}\right) + \beta\left(-\frac{\rho}{\hat{\rho}_i} + \frac{1-\rho}{1-\hat{\rho}_i}\right)\right) f'(z_i^{(2)}). \qquad (9.7)$$

Therefore, the dimension of data can be reduced greatly. Only a few useful hidden units can represent the original data.

9.4 Restricted Boltzmann Machine

In 2002, Hinton, from the University of Toronto, proposed a machine learning algorithm called contrastive divergence (CD) (Hinton, 2002). CD can efficiently train some Markov random models with the simple architecture, including restricted Boltzmann machine (RBM) (Smolensky, 1986). This laid the foundation for the birth of Deep Learning later.

The RBM is a single-layer random neural network (generally the input layer is not included in the layer number of neural networks) as shown in Figure 9.4. RBM is essentially a probability graph model. The input layer is fully connected to the output layer, while there are no connections between the neurons in the same layer. Each neuron is either activated (the value is 1) or not (the value is 0). The activation probability satisfies the sigmoid function. The advantage of RBM is it gives a layer while the other one is independent. So it is convenient to randomly sample a layer when the other layer is fixed. Then this process is carried out alternately. Each update of the weights in theory needs all neurons to be sampled an infinite number of times, which is called contrastive divergence (CD). Because CD works too slowly, Hinton

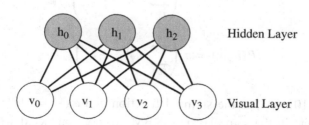

Fig. 9.4. Architecture of RBM

proposed an approximation method called CD-n algorithm in which the weights are updated once after sampling n times (Hinton, 2002).

If RBM has n visual units and m hidden units, the vectors $\mathbf{v}$ and $\mathbf{h}$ are, respectively, used to represent the states of the visual layer and the hidden layer. Here v_i indicates the state of the ith visual unit, and h_j indicates the state of the jth hidden unit. So given a set of states $\mathbf{v}$, $\mathbf{h}$, the system energy of RBM can be defined as

$$E(\mathbf{v}, \mathbf{h}) = -\sum_{i=1}^{n}\sum_{j=1}^{m} v_i W_{ij} h_j - \sum_{i=1}^{n} v_i b_i - \sum_{j=1}^{m} h_j c_j. \qquad (9.8)$$

In Equation (9.8), W_{ij}, b_i, and c_j are the parameters of RBM. They are real numbers, where W_{ij} indicates the connection intention between the visual unit i and the hidden layer j, b_i indicates the bias of the visual unit i, and c_j indicates the bias of the hidden unit j. The task of RBM is to solve the value of parameters to fit the given training data.

The states of RBM satisfy the form of the canonical distribution. That is to say, when the parameter is confirmed, the probability of the state v, h is

$$P(v, h) = \frac{1}{Z} \exp(-E(v, h))$$

$$Z = \sum_{v,h} \exp(-E(v, h)). \qquad (9.9)$$

Suppose RBM is at normal temperature $T = 1$, the temperature variable T is omitted. Based on the above definition, when the states for a layer of units are given, the conditional distribution of the states for another layer of units is

$$P(v_i|h) = \sigma\left(\sum_{j=1}^{m} W_{ij} h_j + b_i\right),$$

$$P(h_j|v) = \sigma\left(\sum_{i=1}^{n} v_i W_{ij} + c_j\right). \qquad (9.10)$$

In Equation (9.10), $\sigma(\cdot)$ is the sigmoid function and $\sigma(x) = 1/(1 + \exp(-x))$. Because the units in the same layer in RBM are not connected with each other, when the states for a layer of units are given, the conditional distribution of the state for another layer of units is independent, namely

$$P(v|h) = \prod_{i=1}^{n} P(v_i|h),$$

$$P(h|v) = \prod_{j=1}^{m} P(h_j|v). \tag{9.11}$$

This means that if we make a Markov chain Monte Carlo (MCMC) sampling on the distribution of RBM (Andrieu *et al.*, 2003), the block Gibbs sampling can be adopted. The block Gibbs sampling starts with an initial sate v, h, then $P(.|h)$ and $P(.|v)$ are alternatively used to compute the state transform of all visual units and hidden units. This shows the efficiency advantage of RBM in the sampling.

The unsupervised learning method can serve RBM through the maximum like-lihood principle (Hinton, 2010). Suppose there are training data $v^{(1)}, v^{(2)}, \ldots, v^{(d)}$, training RBM is equal to maximize the following objective function, where the biases b and c are omitted:

$$L(W) = \sum_{k=1}^{d} \log P(v^{(k)}; W) \equiv \sum_{k=1}^{d} \log \sum_{h} P(v^{(k)}, h; W). \tag{9.12}$$

In order to use the gradient ascent algorithm in the training process, we need to solve the partial derivatives of the objective function for all parameters. After the algebraic transformation, the final results are

$$\frac{\partial L(W)}{\partial W_{ij}} \propto \frac{1}{d} \sum_{k=1}^{d} v_i^{(k)} P(h_j|v^{(k)}) - \langle v_i h_j \rangle_{P(v,h;W)}. \tag{9.13}$$

Equation (9.13) can be split into two parts: positive phase and negative phase. The positive phase can be computed by Equation (9.10) based on the entire training data set. For the negative phase, $\langle f(x) \rangle_{P(x)}$ is defined as the average value of the function $f(x)$ on the distribution $P(\cdot)$. In RBM, this average value cannot be directly represented as a mathematical expression. That is the reason why training RBM is very difficult.

Obviously, the simplest method, MCMC, is used to solve the average value of the negative phase. In each MCMC sampling, the MCMC needs to make a large number of samples to ensure that they conform to the objective distribution. So we need to get a large number of samples to accurately approximate the average value.

These requirements greatly increase the computational complexity of the training RBM. Therefore, MCMC sampling is feasible in theory, but it is not a good choice in terms of efficiency.

Hinton proposed the contrastive divergence (CD) algorithm by considering the state of MCMC starts with the training data (Hinton, 2002). In CD algorithm, the computing process of the average value in the negative phase can be represented as follows. First, each training data are used for the respective initial states. After using Gibbs sampling, on a few state-timed transformations, the transformed state serves as the sample to evaluate the average value. Hinton found that with only a few times of state transformation, a good learning effect in practical application could be ensured.

The CD algorithm greatly improves the training process of RBM and makes a great contribution for the application of RBM and the rise of deep neural networks. The general maximum likelihood learning is similar to minimize the KL-Divergence between RBM distribution and training data distribution. In CD algorithm, this principle is inadmissible. Therefore, the essential of CD algorithm is not a maximum likelihood learning (Sutskever and Tielemant, 2010) as the model learned by CD algorithm has a bad model generation capability.

9.5 Deep Belief Networks

In 2006, Hinton proposed a deep belief network (DBN) in his paper (Hinton and Salakhutdinov, 2006), as shown in Figure 9.5. A deep neural network can be viewed as the stack of multiple RBMs. The training process can be carried out by the layer-wise training from the lower layer to the higher layer as the CD algorithm can be served to quickly train RBM. So, DBN can avoid the high complexity of directly training neural networks by splitting the entire network into multiple RBMs. Hinton suggested that the traditional global training algorithm can be used to fine-tune the whole network after the above training method. Then the model will converge to a local optimal point. This training algorithm is similar to the method initializing the model parameters to a better value by the layer-wise training method, and then further training the model through the traditional algorithm. Thus, the problem that the speed of the training model is slow can be solved. On the contrary, many experiments have proven that this method can produce very good parameter initialization values and improve the quality of the final parameters.

In 2008, Tieleman proposed a training algorithm called persistent contrastive divergence (PCD) (Tieleman, 2008), which improves the imperfection of the CD algorithm that is unable to read the maximization likelihood degree. The efficiency

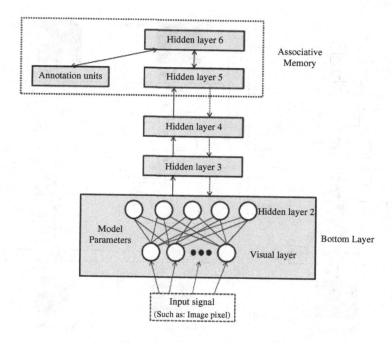

Fig. 9.5.   Deep belief networks

of PCD is the same as CD, and it does not destroy the training algorithm of the original objective function (maximum likelihood learning). In Tieleman's paper, a lot of experiments proved that RBM trained by PCD have stronger model generation capability compared with CD. In 2009, Tieleman further improved PCD and proposed a method employing additional parameters to increase the effect of training PCD (Tieleman and Hinton, 2009). He revealed the effect of Markov chain Monte Carlo sampling on training RBM. This laid the foundations for improving the subsequent learning algorithm about RBM. From 2009 to 2010, there existed a series of the tempered Markov chain Monte Carlo (tempered MCMC) RBM training algorithms based on Tieleman's research results.

The left figure in Figure 9.6 is a typical DBN with four layers. It compresses a high-dimensional image single into a representation with 30 dimensions corresponding to the top layer of size 30. We can also use the symmetry architecture of this network to map the 30 dimensions of the compressed signal to the original high-dimensional signal (the middle figure in Figure 9.6). If this network is employed to compress the signal, we can set that the output of the network equal to the input of the network. Then, BP algorithm is used to fine-tune the weights of the network (the right figure in Figure 9.6).

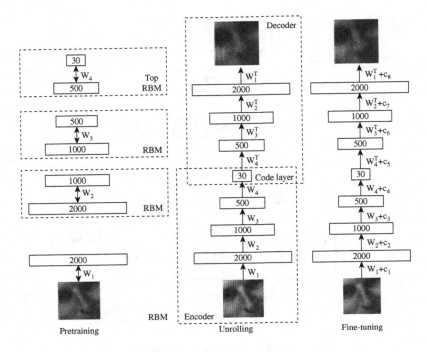

Fig. 9.6.   An example of DBN

9.6 Convolutional Neural Networks

Convolutional neural networks (CNN) is a multiple-stage of globally trainable artificial neural networks (LeCun *et al.*, 1989). CNN can learn the abstract, essential, and advanced features from the data with a little preprocessing or even with the original data. CNN has been widely applied in License Plate Detection, Face Detection, Handwriting Recognition, Target Tracking, and other fields.

CNN has better performance in 2D pattern recognition problems than multi-layer perceptron because the topology of the 2D model is added into the CNN structure, and CNN employs three important structure features: local accepted field, shared weights, sub-sampling ensuring the invariance of the target translation, shrinkage, and distortion of the input signal. CNN mainly consists of feature extraction and classifier. Feature extraction contains the multiple convolutional layers and sub-sampling layers. The classifier consists of one layer or two layers of fully connected neural networks. For the convolutional layer with the local accepted field and the sub-sampling layer with sub-sampling structure, they all have the character of sharing the weights. Figure 9.7 shows a CNN used to recognize the handwriting digits.

As can be seen in Figure 9.7, CNN has seven layers: one input layer, two convolutional layers, two sub-sampling layers, and two fully connected layers. Each input sample in the input layer has $32 \times 32 = 1,024$ pixels. C_1 is a convolutional layer with six feature maps, and each feature map contains $28 \times 28 = 784$ neurons. Each neuron in C_1 is connected to the corresponding local accepted field of size 5×5 in the input layer through the convolutional core of size 5×5 and the convolutional step of length 1. So, C_1 has $6 \times 784 \times (5 \times 5 + 1) = 122,304$ connections. Each feature map contains 5×5 weights and biases. Therefore, C_1 has $6 \times (5 \times 5 + 1) = 156$ trainable parameters.

S_1 is the sub-sampling layer containing six feature maps, and each feature map consists of $14 \times 14 = 196$ neurons. There is a one-to-one correspondence between the feature maps in S_1 and the feature maps in C_1. The window of sub-sampling S_1 is a matrix of size 2×2, and the step size of the sub-sampling defaults to 1. So, there are $6 \times 196 \times (2 \times 2 + 1) = 5,880$ connections in the S_2 layer. Each feature map in S_1 contains a weight and a bias. This means there are 12 trainable parameters.

C_2 is the convolutional layer containing 16 feature maps, and each feature map consists of $10 \times 10 = 100$ neurons. Each neuron in C_2 is connected to the local accepted field of size 5×5 in the k feature maps in S_1 through the k convolutional core of size 5×5, where $k = 6$ if the full connection way is adopted. So there are 41,600 connections in the C_2 layer. Each feature map in C_2 contains $6 \times 5 \times 5 = 150$ weights and biases, which means there are $16 \times (150 + 1) = 2,416$ trainable parameters.

S_2 is the sub-sampling layer containing 16 feature maps, and each feature map consists of 5×5 neurons. S_2 contains 400 neurons. There is a one-to-one correspondence between the feature maps in S_2 and the feature maps in C_2. The window of sub-sampling S_2 is a matrix of size 2×2. So there are $16 \times 25 \times (2 \times 2 + 1) = 2,000$

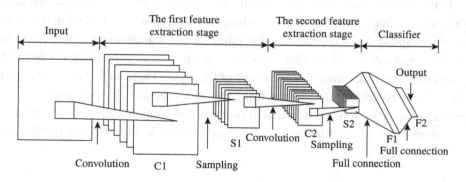

Fig. 9.7. CNN architecture of recognizing handwriting digits

connections in the S_2 layer. Each feature map in S_2 contains a weight and a bias. This means there are 32 trainable parameters in the S_2 layer.

F_1 is a full connection layer containing 120 neurons. Each neuron in F_1 is connected to the 400 neurons in S_2. So the number of connections or trainable parameters is $120 \times (400 + 1) = 48,120$. F_2 is a full connection layer and the output layer contains 10 neurons, 1,210 connections, and 1,210 trainable parameters.

In Figure 9.7, the number of the feature maps in the convolutional layer increases layer by layer. This can supplement the loss caused by sampling. On the contrary, the convolutional cores make the convolutional operation on the feature maps of the former layer produce the current convolutional feature maps. The produced different features expand the feature space and make the feature extraction more comprehensive.

The error back-propagation (BP) algorithm is mostly used to train CNN in a supervised way. In the gradient descent method, the error is back-propagated to constantly adjust the weights and biases. This allows the global sum of squared error on the training samples to reach a minimum value. BP algorithm consists of the four processes: network initialization, information flow feed-forward propagation, error back-propagation, and update of the weights and the biases. In error back-propagation, we need to compute the local variation value of the gradient on the weights and the biases.

In the initial process of training CNN, the neurons in each layer need to be initialized randomly. The initialization of the weights has a great influence on the convergence rate of the network. So the process of how to initialize the weights is very important. There exists a strong relationship between the initialization of the weights and the selection of the activation function. The weights should be assigned by the fastest changing parts of the activation function. The big weights or the small weights in the initialization process will lead to a small change on the weights.

In the feed-forward propagation of the information flow, the convolutional layer extracts the primary basic features of the input to make up several feature maps. Then the sub-sampling layer reduces the resolution of the feature maps. After convolution layer and sub-sampling alternatively complete feature extraction, the network obtains the high-order invariance features of the input. These high-order invariance features will be transmitted to the fully connected neural network and used for classification. After information transformation and computing in the hidden layer and output layer of the fully connected neural network, the network finishes the forward propagation process of the learning. The last results are output by the output layer.

The network starts the error back-propagation process when the actual output is not equal to the expected output. The errors are propagated from the output layer to the hidden layer, and then propagated from the hidden layer to the sub-sampling layer and convolutional layer in the feature extraction stage. The neurons in each layer start to compute the local changed value of the weights and biases when they get their output errors. At last, the network will enter the weights update process.

1. Feed-forward propagation of convolutional layer

Each neuron in the convolutional layer extracts the features in the local accepted field of the same location for all feature maps in the former layer. The neurons in the same feature map share the same weight matrix. The convolutional process can be viewed as the convolutional neurons seamlessly scan the former feature maps line by line through the weight matrix. The output, $O_{(x,y)}^{(l,k)}$, of the neuron located in line x column y in the kth feature map of the lth convolutional layer can be computed by Equation (9.14), where $\tanh(\cdot)$ is the activation function:

$$O_{(x,y)}^{(l,k)} = \tanh \left(\sum_{t=0}^{f-1} \sum_{r=0}^{kh} \sum_{c=0}^{kw} W_{(t,c)}^{(k,t)} O_{(x+r,y+c)}^{(l-1,t)} + \mathbf{Bias}^{(l,k)} \right). \tag{9.14}$$

From Equation (9.14), we need to traverse all neurons of the convolutional window in all feature maps of the former layer to compute the output of a neuron in the convolutional layer. The feed-forward propagation of the full connection layer is similar to the convolutional layer. This can be viewed as a convolutional operation on the convolutional weight matrix and the input with the same size.

2. Feed-forward propagation of sub-sampling

There are the same number of feature maps and a one-to-one correspondence relationship between the sub-sampling feature maps and the convolutional feature maps. Each neuron in the sub-sampling layer is connected to the sub-areas with the same size but is non-overlapping through the sub-sampling window. The output, $O_{(x,y)}^{(l,k)}$, of the neuron located in line x column y in the kth feature map of the lth sub-sampling layer can be computed by Equation (9.15):

$$O_{(x,y)}^{(l,k)} = \tanh\left(\mathbf{W}^{(k)} \sum_{r=0}^{sh} \sum_{c=0}^{sw} O_{(xsh+r,ysw+c)}^{(l-1,k)} + \mathbf{Bias}^{(l,k)}\right). \qquad (9.15)$$

3. Error back-propagation of sub-sampling layer

Error back-propagation starts from the output layer and enters the sub-sampling layer through the hidden layer. The error back-propagation of the output layer needs to first compute the partial derivative of the error about the neurons in the output layer. Suppose the output of the kth neuron is o_k for the training sample d. The expected output of the kth neuron is t_k for the sample d. The error of the output layer for the sample d can be represented as $E = 1/2 \sum_k (o_k - t_1)^2$. The partial derivative of the error E about the output o_k is $\partial E/\partial o_k = o_k - t_k$. Similarly, we can solve the partial derivatives of the error about all neurons in the output layer. Then we solve the partial derivatives of the error about the input in the output layer. Set $d(o_k)$ is the partial derivative of the error about the input of the kth neuron in the output layer. $d(o_k)$ can be computed by Equation (9.16), where $(1 + o_k)(1 - o_k)$ is the partial derivative of the activation function $\tanh(\cdot)$ about the input of the neuron. Then we start to compute the partial derivatives of the error about all neurons in the hidden layer. Suppose the neuron j in the hidden layer is connected to the output neuron through the weight w_{kj}. The partial derivative $d(o_j)$ of the error about the output of the neuron j can be computed by Equation (9.17). When we obtain the partial derivative of the error about the output of the hidden layer, the error is back-propagated to the hidden layer. Through a similar process, the error will be back-propagated to the sub-sampling layer. For convenience of expression, the partial derivatives of the error about the outputs of the neuron are called the output errors of the neuron. The partial derivatives of the error about the inputs of the neuron are called the input errors of the neuron:

$$d(o_k) = (o_k - t_k)(1 + o_k)(1 - o_k), \qquad (9.16)$$

$$d(o_j) = \sum d(o_k) W_{kj}. \qquad (9.17)$$

There are the same number of feature maps and a one-to-one correspondence relationship between the sub-sampling feature maps and the convolutional feature maps. So it is an intuitive process that the error is propagated from the sub-sampling layer to the convolutional layer. Equation (9.16) is used to compute the input errors of all neurons in the sub-sampling layer. Then the above input errors are propagated to the former layer of the sub-sampling layer. The sub-sampling layer is set to the *l*th layer, then the output error of the neuron located in line x column y in the kth feature map of the $(l-1)$th layer is computed by the following equation:

$$d(O_{(x,y)}^{(l-1,k)}) = d(O_{([x/sh],[y/sv])}^{(l,k)}) W^{(k)}. \tag{9.18}$$

All neurons in a feature map of the sub-sampling layer share a weight and a bias. So the local gradient variations of all weights and biases are related to all neurons in the sub-sampling layer. The weight variation $\Delta W^{(k)}$ and the bias variation $\Delta \mathbf{Bias}^{(l,k)}$ for the kth feature map in the lth sub-sampling layer can be computed by Equation (9.19) (9.20). In Equation (8.47), f_h and f_w, respectively, indicate the height and the width of the feature map in the lth sub-sampling layer:

$$\Delta \mathbf{W}^{(k)} = \sum_{x=0}^{fh} \sum_{y=0}^{fw} \sum_{r=0}^{sh} \sum_{c=0}^{sw} \mathbf{O}_{(x,y)}^{(l-1,k)} d(\mathbf{O}_{([x/sh],[y/sw])}^{(l,k)}), \tag{9.19}$$

$$\Delta \mathbf{Bias}^{(l,k)} = \sum_{x=0}^{fh} \sum_{y=0}^{fw} d(\mathbf{O}_{(x,y)}^{(l,k)}). \tag{9.20}$$

4. Error back-propagation of convolutional layer

There exist two error back-propagation ways in the convolutional layer: "push" and "pull". The "push" way (the left figure in Figure 9.8(a)) can be considered as that the neurons in the lth layer actively propagate the errors to the neurons in the $(l-1)$th layer. This is suitable for serial implementation. There is the "write conflict" problem in parallel implementation. The "pull" way (the right figure in Figure 9.8(b)) can be considered as that the neurons in the $(l-1)$th layer actively obtain the errors from the neurons in the lth layer. It is difficult to implement the "pull" way. Because of the border effect of the convolutional operation, we need to confirm which neurons

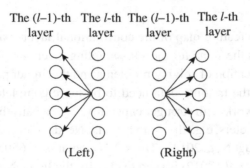

The $(l-1)$-th   The l-th   The $(l-1)$-th   The l-th
layer   layer   layer   layer

(Left)   (Right)

Fig. 9.8. Two ways of error back-propagation

in the feature map of the former layer are connected to the neurons in the current layer.

Here the "pull" way is used to describe the error back-propagation process of the convolutional layer. Equation (9.16) is employed to compute the input error of each neuron in the convolutional layer. Then the input error is propagated to the neurons in the former layer of the convolutional layer, like in the following equation:

$$d(\mathbf{O}^{(l-1,k)}_{(x,y)}) = \sum_{t=0}^{m-1} \sum_{(p,q)\in A} d(\mathbf{O}^{(l,t)}_{(p,q)})w, \qquad (9.21)$$

where A is the coordinate set of the neurons located in line x column y in the kth feature map of the lth layer and the neurons in the lth layer. W indicates the connected weight between the two neurons. The serial computational process by which the error in the convolutional layer is back-propagated to the former sub-sampling layer is described in the following:

> **for** each neuron i in the former layer of the convolutional layer
>> Confirm which neurons in the convolutional layer are connected to the neuron i
>> "Pull" the error from the relevant neurons in the convolutional layer using Equation (9.21)
> **end for**

The local gradient variation of the line r and the column y of the weight matrix describing the connection between the kth feature map in the convolutional layer and the tth feature map in the former layer can be computed by the following equation:

$$\Delta \mathbf{W}^{(k,t)}_{(r,c)} = \sum_{x=r}^{fh-kh+r} \sum_{y=c}^{fw-kw+c} d(\mathbf{O}^{(l,k)}_{(x,y)})\mathbf{O}^{(l-1,t)}_{(r+x,c+y)}. \qquad (9.22)$$

All neurons in a feature map of the convolutional layer share a bias. The computational method is the same for the sub-sampling layer.

With the complication of solving problems and the higher performance requirement for the CNN, the training data need to be more complete and larger. So we need to train the network with stronger capability. This means the network will have more trainable parameters, e.g., the famous ImageNet data set containing 14,197,122 labeled images (ImageNet, 2014). The CNN containing 650,000 neurons in the library (Krizhevsky *et al.*, 2012) is used to classify the ImageNet data set. There are 60,000,000 trainable neurons in the above CNN. A large number of training data and training parameters will significantly increase the computational time, especially the serial computation will cost a few months of computational time (Ciresan *et al.*, 2010). Therefore, the researchers began to research the parallel CNN. There exist at least five parallel ways, namely the parallelism of the samples, the parallelism between the former back layers, the parallelism between the feature maps in the same layer, the parallelism between the neurons in the feature map, and the parallelism of the neuron weights (Schmidhuber, 2014).

9.7 Recurrent Neural Networks

A recurrent neural network (RNN) is a class of artificial neural networks where connections between nodes form a directed graph along a sequence. This allows it to exhibit temporal dynamic behavior for a time sequence. Unlike feed-forward neural networks, RNNs can use their internal state (memory) to process sequences of inputs. This makes them applicable to tasks such as unsegmented, connected handwriting recognition or speech recognition. A typical RNN is shown in Figure 9.9.

RNNs contain input units, and the input set is labeled $\{x_0, x_1, \ldots, x_t, x_{t+1}, \ldots\}$, while the output set of the output units is marked as $\{y_0, y_1, \ldots, y_t, y_{t+1}, \ldots\}$. RNNs also contain hidden units, and we mark their output sets as $\{s_0, s_1, \ldots, s_t, s_{t+1}, \ldots\}$; these hidden units have done the most important work. You will find that in Figure 9.9 there is a one-way flow of information from the input unit to the hidden unit, while another one-way flow of information happens from the hidden unit to the output unit. In some cases, RNNs break the latter's limitations, and the boot information is returned to the hidden unit from the output unit. These are called "Back Projections", and the input to the hidden layer also includes the state of the last hidden layer, that is, within the hidden layer. Nodes can be self-connected or interconnected.

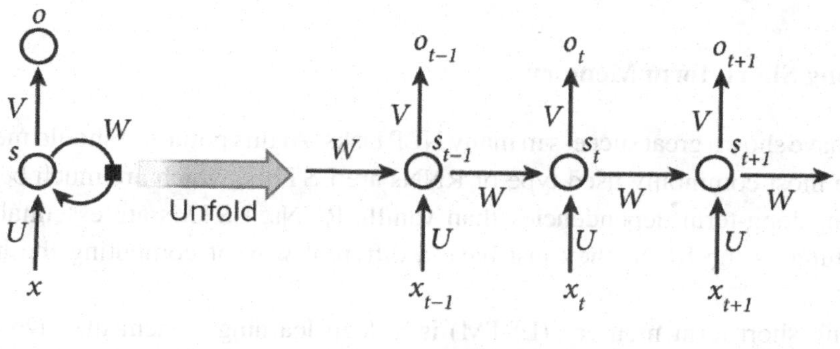

Fig. 9.9. A typical RNN structure

For example, for a statement containing five words, the expanded network is a five-layer neural network, with each layer representing a word. The calculation process for this network is as follows:

(1) x_t is the input at time step t. For example, x_1 could be a one-hot vector corresponding to the second word of a sentence.

(2) s_t is the hidden state at time step t. It is the "memory" of the network. s_t is calculated based on the previous hidden state and the input at the current step: $s_t = f(Ux_t + Ws_{t-1})$. The function f usually is a nonlinearity such as $\tan h$ (Hyperbolic tangent) or ReLU (rectified linear unit). s_{-1}, which is required to calculate the first hidden state, is typically initialized to all zeroes.

(3) o_t is the output at step t. For example, if we wanted to predict the next word in a sentence, it would be a vector of probabilities across our vocabulary, $o_t = \text{softmax}(Vs_t)$.

We can think of the hidden state s_t as the memory of the network. s_t captures information about what happened in all the previous time steps. The output at step o_t is calculated solely based on the memory at time t. As briefly mentioned above, it is a bit more complicated in practice because s_t typically cannot capture information from too many time steps back.

Unlike a traditional deep neural network, which uses different parameters at each layer, an RNN shares the same parameters $(U, V, W$ above) across all steps. This reflects the fact that we are performing the same task at each step, just with different inputs. This greatly reduces the total number of parameters we need to learn. Figure 9.9 has outputs at each time step, but depending on the task, this may not be necessary. For example, when predicting the sentiment of a sentence, we may only care about the final output, not the sentiment after each word. Similarly, we may not need inputs at each time step. The main feature of an RNN is its hidden state, which captures some information about a sequence.

9.8 Long Short-Term Memory

RNNs have shown great success in many NLP tasks. At this point, we should mention that the most commonly used type of RNNs are LSTMs, which are much better at capturing long-term dependencies than vanilla RNNs. LSTMs are essentially the same thing as the RNN; they just have a different way of computing the hidden state.

Long short-term memory (LSTM) is a deep learning system that avoids the vanishing gradient problem. LSTM is normally augmented by recurrent gates called "forget" gates (Gers *et al.*, 2017). LSTM prevents backpropagated errors from vanishing or exploding (Hochreiter and Schmidhuber, 1997). Instead, errors can flow backward through an unlimited number of virtual layers which unfold in space. That is, LSTM can learn tasks (Schmidhuber, 2015) that require memories of events that happened thousands or even millions of discrete time steps earlier. Problem-specific LSTM-like topologies can be evolved (Bayer *et al.*, 2009). LSTM works even given long delays between significant events and can handle signals that mix low- and high-frequency components.

LSTMs are explicitly designed to avoid the long-term dependency problem. Remembering information for long periods of time is practically their default behavior, not something they struggle to learn! All recurrent neural networks have the form of a chain of repeating modules of neural network. In standard RNNs, this repeating module will have a very simple structure, such as a single tanh layer. Figure 9.10 illustrates the repeating module in a standard RNN containing a single layer.

LSTMs also have this chain-like structure, but the repeating module has a different structure. Instead of having a single neural network layer, there are four, interacting in a very special way as shown in Figure 9.11. The key to LSTMs is the cell state, the horizontal line running through the top of the diagram. The cell state is kind of like a conveyor belt. It runs straight down the entire chain, with only some minor linear interactions. It is very easy for information to just flow along it unchanged. The LSTM does have the ability to remove or add information to the cell state, carefully regulated by structures called gates. Gates are a way to optionally let information through. They are composed out of a sigmoid neural net layer and a pointwise multiplication operation. The sigmoid layer outputs numbers between zero and one, describing how much of each component should be let through. A value of zero means "let nothing through", while a value of one means "let everything through!" An LSTM has three of these gates, to protect and control the cell state.

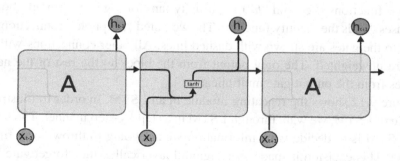

Fig. 9.10. Standard RNN containing a single layer

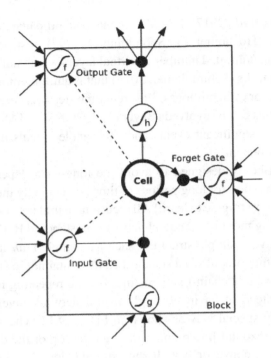

Fig. 9.11. LSTM block with one cell

Figure 9.11 shows the LSTM block with one cell. The three gates are nonlinear summation units that collect activations from inside and outside the block and control the activation of the cell via multiplications (small black circles). The input and output gates multiply the input and output of the call, while the forget gate multiplies the cell's previous state. No activation function is applied within the cell. The gate activation function 'f' is usually the logistic sigmoid, so that the gate activation functions are between 0 (gate closed) and 1 (gate open) The cell input and output activation functions ("g" and "h") are usually tanh or logistic sigmoid, though in some cases "h" is the identity function. The weighted "peephole" connections from the cell to the gates are shown with dashed lines. All other connections within the block are unweighted. The only output from the block to the rest of the network emanates from the output gate multiplication.

Figure 9.12 shows the repeating module in an LSTM. In order to illustrate the principle of LSTM, we walk through LSTM in a step-by-step manner. The first step in the LSTM is to decide what information we are going to throw away from the cell state. This decision is made by a sigmoid layer called the "forget gate layer". It looks at h_{t-1} and x_t, and outputs a number between 0 and 1 for each number in

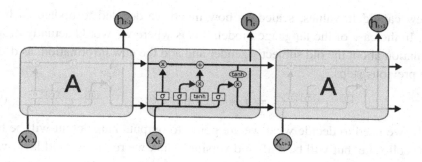

Fig. 9.12. The repeating module in an LSTM

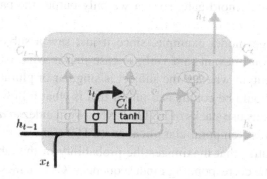

Fig. 9.13. Update a cell state

the cell state C_{t-1}. A "1" represents "completely keep this", while a "0" represents "completely get rid of this".

The next step is to decide what new information we are going to store in the cell state. This has two parts. First, a sigmoid layer called the "input gate layer" decides which values we will update. Next, a tanh layer creates a vector of new candidate values, $C_{\sim t}$, that could be added to the state. In the next step, we will combine these two to create an update to the state shown in Figure 9.13:

$$i_t = \sigma(W_i \cdot [h_{t-1}, x_t] + b_i), \tag{9.23}$$

$$\tilde{C}_t = \tanh(W_c \cdot [h_{t-1}, x_t] + b_C). \tag{9.24}$$

In the example of the language model, we would want to add the gender of the new subject to the cell state, to replace the old one we are forgetting. It is now time to update the old cell state, C_{t-1}, to the new cell state C_t. The previous steps already decided what to do, we just need to actually do it. We multiply the old state by f_t, forgetting the things we decided to forget earlier. Then we add $i_t * C_{\sim t}$. These are the new candidate values, scaled by how much we decided to update each state value. In the case of the language model, this is where we would actually drop the information about the old subject's gender and add the new information, as decided in the previous steps:

$$C_t = f_t * C_{t-1} + i_t * \tilde{C}_t. \tag{9.25}$$

Finally, we need to decide what we are going to output. This output will be based on our cell state, but will be a filtered version. First, we run a sigmoid layer which decides what parts of the cell state we are going to output. Then, we put the cell state through tan$h$ (to push the values to be between -1 and 1) and multiply it by the output of the sigmoid gate, so that we only output the parts we decided to (Figure 9.14).

For the language model example, since it just saw a subject, it might want to output information relevant to a verb, in case that is what is coming next. For example, it might output whether the subject is singular or plural, so that we know what form a verb should be conjugated into if that is what follows next.

Many applications use stacks of LSTM RNNs (Fernández *et al.*, 2007) and train them by connectionist temporal classification (CTC) (Graves *et al.*, 2006) to find an RNN weight matrix that maximizes the probability of the label sequences in a training set, given the corresponding input sequences. CTC achieves both alignment and recognition. LSTM can learn to recognize context-sensitive languages unlike previous models based on hidden Markov models (HMM) and similar concepts (Gers and Schmidhuber, 2001).

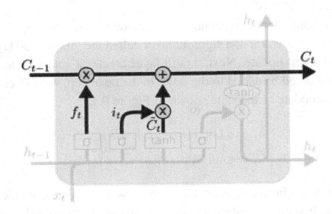

Fig. 9.14.   Generate the output

9.9 Neural Machine Translation

9.9.1 *Introduction*

The emergence of deep learning has dramatically changed machine translation. Since 2013, neural network-based machine translation has taken translation to a new level in terms of speed and accuracy. At the moment, owing to the fierce competition of technology giants and the study going on in academic circles, the level of machine translation is still evolving. In recent years, the biggest influence of deep learning on translation comes from neural machine translation (NMT), which greatly improves the accuracy of machine translation.

A decade ago, Google launched machine translation using phrase-based machine translation (PBMT). A few years ago, the Google Brain team began using a circular neural network (RNN) to directly learn the mapping between input sequences and output sequences. Phrase-based machine translation (PBMT) translates sentences into words and translates them separately, while neural machine translation (NMT) translates the input as a whole. The advantage of this is that the adjustments that need to be made during translation are much less.

When neural network machine translation technology first appeared, it achieved comparable results with PBMT on medium-sized public data sets. Since then, people engaged in machine translation studies have proposed a number of ways to improve NMT, including using attention to align input and output, split words into smaller units, or mimic external alignment models to deal with uncommon words. Despite this, the performance of NMT is still not enough for large-scale deployment of products.

It is not only Google that sees the great value of machine translation. Baidu, Huawei, Ali, and Tencent in China have started to research, and giants such as Facebook and Microsoft are not falling behind. This competitive situation will maximize the commercial deployment of machine translation and become more "available" to more people. Many novel techniques have been proposed to further improve NMT: using an attention mechanism to deal with rare words, a mechanism to model translation coverage, multi-task and semi-supervise training to incorporate more data, a character decoder, a character encoder, subword units also to deal with rare word outputs, different kinds of attention mechanisms, and sentence-level loss minimization. While the translation accuracy of these systems has been encouraging, let no take Google GNMT as an example to introduce the working principle of the neural translation machine (Wu *et al.*, 2016).

9.9.2 *Model Architecture*

GNMT follows the common sequence-to-sequence learning framework (Sutskever *et al.*, 2014) with attention (Bahdanau *et al.*, 2015). It has three components: an encoder network, a decoder network, and an attention network. The encoder transforms a source sentence into a list of vectors, one vector per input symbol. Given this list of vectors, the decoder produces one symbol at a time, until the special end-of-sentence symbol (EOS) is produced. The encoder and decoder are connected through an attention module which allows the decoder to focus on different regions of the source sentence during the course of decoding.

Let (X, Y) be a source and target sentence pair. Let $X = x_1, x_2, x_3, \ldots, x_M$ be the sequence of M symbols in the source sentence and let $Y = y_1, y_2, y_3, \ldots, y_N$ be the sequence of N symbols in the target sentence. The encoder is simply a function of the following form:

$$\mathbf{x_1}, \mathbf{x_2}, \ldots, \mathbf{x_M} = \text{EncoderRNN}(x_1, x_2, x_3, \ldots, x_M). \tag{9.26}$$

In Equation (9.26), $\mathbf{x_1}, \mathbf{x_2}, \ldots, \mathbf{x_M}$ is a list of fixed size vectors. The number of members in the list is the same as the number of symbols in the source sentence (M in this example). Using the chain rule, the conditional probability of the sequence $P(Y|X)$ can be decomposed as

$$P(Y|X) = P(Y|\mathbf{x1}, \mathbf{x2}, \mathbf{x3}, \ldots, \mathbf{xM})$$

$$= \prod_{i=1}^{N} P(y_i|y_0, y_1, y_2, \ldots, y_{i-1}; \mathbf{x_1}, \mathbf{x_2}, \mathbf{x_3}, \ldots, \mathbf{x_M}), \tag{9.27}$$

where y_0 is a special "beginning of sentence" symbol that is prepended to every target sentence.

During inference, we calculate the probability of the next symbol given the source sentence encoding and the decoded target sequence so far:

$$P(y_i|y_0, y_1, y_2, y_3, \ldots, y_{i-1}; \mathbf{x_1}, \mathbf{x_2}, \mathbf{x_3}, \ldots, \mathbf{x_M}). \tag{9.28}$$

The decoder is implemented as a combination of an RNN network and a softmax layer. The decoder RNN network produces a hidden state $\mathbf{y_i}$ for the next symbol to be predicted, which then goes through the softmax layer to generate a probability distribution over candidate output symbols. A deep stacked Long Short-Term Memory network is used for both the encoder RNN and the decoder RNN.

The attention module is similar to Bahdanau *et al.* (2015). More specifically, let y_{i-1} be the decoder-RNN output from the past decoding time step (or use the output from the bottom decoder layer). Attention context a_i for the current time step is computed according to the following formulas:

$$s_t = \text{attentionFunction}(y_{i-1}, \mathbf{x}_t) \quad \forall t, \quad 1 \le t \le M,$$

$$p_t = \exp(s_t) \Big/ \sum_{t=1}^{M} \exp(s_t) \quad \forall t, \quad 1 \le t \le M, \tag{9.29}$$

$$a_i = \sum_{t=1}^{M} p_t \cdot \mathbf{x}_t,$$

where AttentionFunction in GNMT implementation is a feed-forward network with one hidden layer.

In Figure 9.15, on the left is the encoder network, on the right is the decoder network, and in the middle is the attention module. The bottom encoder layer is bidirectional: the nodes with arrows pointing toward right direction gather information from left to right while the nodes with arrows pointing toward left direction gather information from right to left. The other layers of the encoder are unidirectional. Residual connections start from the third layer from the bottom in the encoder and decoder. The model is partitioned into multiple GPUs to speed up training. In fact, we have eight encoder LSTM layers (one bi-directional layer and seven uni-directional layers) and eight decoder layers. With this setting, one model replica is partitioned eight-ways and is placed on eight different GPUs typically belonging to one host machine. During training, the bottom bi-directional encoder layers compute in parallel first. Once both finish, the uni-directional encoder layers can

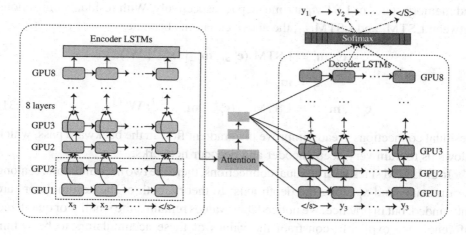

Fig. 9.15. The model architecture of GNMT

start computing, each on a separate GPU. To retain as much parallelism as possible during running the decoder layers, we use the bottom decoder layer output only for obtaining the recurrent attention context, which is sent directly to all the remaining decoder layers. The softmax layer is also partitioned and placed on multiple GPUs. Depending on the output vocabulary size, we either have them run on the same GPUs as the encoder and decoder networks or have them run on a separate set of dedicated GPUs.

9.9.3 *Quantized Inference*

Quantized inference using reduced precision arithmetic is one technique that can significantly reduce the cost of inference for these models, often providing efficiency improvements on the same computational devices. To reduce quantization errors, additional constraints are added to the model during training so that it is quantizable with minimal impact on the output of the model.

GNMT introduced residual connections among the LSTM layers in a stack. More concretely, let LSTM$_i$ and LSTM$_{i+1}$ be the ith and $(i + 1)$th LSTM layers in a stack, whose parameters are $\mathbf{W}^i$ and $\mathbf{W}^{i+1}$, respectively. At the tth time step, for the stacked LSTM without residual connections, we have

$$\mathbf{c}_t^i, \mathbf{m}_t^i = \text{LSTM}_i(\mathbf{c}_{t-1}^i, \mathbf{m}_{t-1}^i, \mathbf{x}_t^{i-1}; \mathbf{W}^i),$$

$$\mathbf{x}_t^i = \mathbf{m}_t^i,$$

$$\mathbf{c}_t^{i+1}, \mathbf{m}_t^{i+1} = \text{LSTM}_{i+1}(\mathbf{c}_{t-1}^{i+1}, \mathbf{m}_{t-1}^{i+1}, \mathbf{x}_t^i; \mathbf{W}^{i+1}), \tag{9.30}$$

where $\mathbf{x}_t^i$ is the input to LSTM$_i$ at time step t, and $\mathbf{m}_t^i$ and $\mathbf{c}_t^i$ are the hidden states and memory states of LSTM$_i$ at time step t, respectively. With residual connections between LSTM$_i$ and LSTM$_{i+1}$, the above equations become

$$\mathbf{c}_t^i, \mathbf{m}_t^i = \text{LSTM}_i(\mathbf{c}_{t-1}^i, \mathbf{m}_{t-1}^i, \mathbf{x}_t^{i-1}; \mathbf{W}^i),$$

$$\mathbf{x}_t^i = \mathbf{m}_t^i + x_t^{i-1},$$

$$\mathbf{c}_t^{i+1}, \mathbf{m}_t^{i+1} = \text{LSTM}_{i+1}(\mathbf{c}_{t-1}^{i+1}, \mathbf{m}_{t-1}^{i+1}, \mathbf{x}_t^i; \mathbf{W}^{i+1}), \tag{9.31}$$

Residual connections greatly improve the gradient flow in the backward pass, which allows us to train very deep encoder and decoder networks.

In an LSTM stack with residual connections, there are two accumulators: c_t^i along the time axis and $\mathbf{x}_t^i$ along the depth axis. In theory, both of the accumulators are unbounded, but in practice, we noticed their values remain quite small. For quantized inference, we explicitly constrain the values of these accumulators to be within $[-\delta, \delta]$ to guarantee a certain range that can be used for quantization later. The forward computation of an LSTM stack with residual connections is modified to the following:

$$\mathbf{c}_t'^i, \mathbf{m}_t^i = \text{LSTM}_i(\mathbf{c}_{t-1}^i, \mathbf{m}_{t-1}^i, \mathbf{x}_t^{i-1}; \mathbf{W}^i),$$

$$\mathbf{c}_t^i = \max(-\delta, \min(\delta, \mathbf{c}_t'^i)),$$

$$\mathbf{x}_t'^i = \mathbf{m}_t^i + \mathbf{x}_t^{i-1},$$

$$(9.32)$$

$$\mathbf{x}_t^i = \max(-\delta, \min(\delta, \mathbf{x}_t'^i)),$$

$$\mathbf{c}_t'^{i+1}\mathbf{m}_t^{i+1} = \text{LSTM}_{i+1}(\mathbf{c}_{t-1}^{i+1}, \mathbf{m}_{t-1}^{i+1}, \mathbf{x}_t^i; \mathbf{W}^{i+1}),$$

$$\mathbf{c}_t^{i+1} = \max(-\delta, \min(\delta, \mathbf{c}_t'^{i+1})).$$

Let us expand LSTM_i in Equation (9.32) to include the internal gating logic. For brevity, we drop all the superscripts i.

$$\mathbf{W} = [\mathbf{W}_1, \mathbf{W}_2, \mathbf{W}_3, \mathbf{W}_4, \mathbf{W}_5, \mathbf{W}_6, \mathbf{W}_7, \mathbf{W}_8],$$

$$\mathbf{i}_t = \text{sigmoid}(\mathbf{W}_1\mathbf{x}_t + \mathbf{W}_2\mathbf{m}_t),$$

$$\mathbf{i}_t' = \tanh(\mathbf{W}_3\mathbf{x}_t + \mathbf{W}_4\mathbf{m}_t),$$

$$\mathbf{f}_t = \text{sigmoid}(\mathbf{W}_5\mathbf{x}_t + \mathbf{W}_6\mathbf{m}_t), \qquad (9.33)$$

$$\mathbf{o}_t = \text{sigmoid}(\mathbf{W}_7\mathbf{x}_t + \mathbf{W}_8\mathbf{m}_t),$$

$$\mathbf{c}_t = \mathbf{c}_{t-1} \odot \mathbf{f}_t + \mathbf{i}_t' \odot \mathbf{i}_t,$$

$$\mathbf{m}_t = \mathbf{c}_t \odot \mathbf{o}_t.$$

When performing quantized inference, we replace all the floating point operations in Equations (9.32) and (9.33) with fixed-point integer operations with either 8-bit or 16-bit resolution. The weight matrix $\mathbf{W}$ above is represented using an 8-bit integer matrix $\mathbf{WQ}$ and a float vector s, as follows:

$$s_i = \max(\text{abs}(\mathbf{W}[i, :])),$$

$$\mathbf{WQ}[i, j] = \text{round}(\mathbf{W}[i, j]/s_i \times 127.0). \qquad (9.34)$$

All accumulator values ($\mathbf{c}_t^i$ and $\mathbf{x}_t^i$) are represented using 16-bit integers representing the range $[-\delta, \delta]$. All matrix multiplications (e.g., $\mathbf{W}_1\mathbf{x}_t$, $\mathbf{W}_2 m_t$, etc.) in Equation (9.33) are done using 8-bit integer multiplication accumulated into larger accumulators. All other operations, including all the activations (sigmoid, $\tanh$) and elementwise operations ($\odot, +$) are done using 16-bit integer operations.

We now turn our attention to the log-linear softmax layer. During training, given the decoder RNN network output $\mathbf{y}_t$, we compute the probability vector $\mathbf{p}_t$ over all candidate output symbols as follows:

$$\mathbf{v_t} = \mathbf{W_s} * \mathbf{y_t},$$
$$\mathbf{v'_t} = \max(-\gamma, \min(\gamma, \mathbf{v_t})), \tag{9.35}$$
$$\mathbf{p_t} = \text{softmax}(\mathbf{v'_t}).$$

In quantized inference, the weight matrix $\mathbf{W}_s$ is quantized into eight bits as in Equation (9.34), and matrix multiplication is done using eight-bit arithmetic. The calculations within the softmax function and the attention model are not quantized during inference.

The challenge of machine translation still exists. GNMT may still make mistakes that humans will never make, such as missing translations or misinterpreting proper nouns or rare words. The translation does not take into account the whole paragraph or even the full text. In short, there are still many areas for improvement in GNMT, but in any case, GNMT represents a major milestone.

Huawei Noah's Ark Lab proposed a new neural machine translation (NMT) model, introducing a loyalty index based on reconstruction. The results show that the model effectively improves the performance of machine translation.

The Ali translation team officially began to independently develop the NMT model since October 2016. In November 2016, the output of the NMT system was first applied for external evaluation in the Sino-British news communication scene and achieved good results. In 2017, Alibaba provided 300 billion translation services to customers worldwide, saving over $2.5 billion.

Exercises

9.1 What is deep learning? List the features of deep learning.

9.2 Compare the three deep learning methods: autoencoder, restricted Boltzmann machine, and deep belief networks.

9.3 Illustrate the architecture of convolutional neural networks.

9.4 Suppose a convolutional neural network is trained on the ImageNet data set (object recognition data set) and this trained model is then given a completely image as an input. What are the output probabilities for this input?

9.5 Error back-propagation starts from the output layer and enters the sub-sampling layer through the hidden layer in CNN. The error back-propagation of the output layer needs to first compute the partial derivative of the error about the neurons in the output layer. How to speed up this processing in CNN?

9.6 The bi-directional RNN is actually just two independent RNNs together. Construct a single-layer static bi-directional RNN network based on TensorFlow, using mnist handwriting as test case.

9.7 Try to build a simple time series prediction module in TensorFlow with LSTM RNN.

9.8 Try to build a neural machine translation (NMT) to translate Chinese to English using an attention model by bi-directional LSTM model.

Chapter 10

Reinforcement Learning

Reinforcement learning is the learning of mapping from situations to actions so as to maximize the scalar reward of a reinforcement signal. The learner does not need to be directly told which actions to take, as in most forms of machine learning, but instead discover which actions yield the most rewards by trying them and finding a balance between exploration and exploitation.

10.1 Introduction

People often learn by interacting with the outside environment. Reinforcement learning (RL) is a computational approach to the study of learning from interaction. RL is the learning of mapping from situations to actions so as to maximize the scalar reward of a reinforcement signal. The learner does not need to be directly told which actions to take, as in most forms of machine learning, but instead discover which actions yield the most reward by trying them. In the most interesting and challenging cases, an action may affect not only the immediate reward but also the next situation, and consequently all subsequent rewards. These two characteristics — trial-and-error and delayed reinforcement — are the two most important distinguishing characteristics of RL.

Reinforcement learning is not defined by characterizing learning methods, but by characterizing a learning problem. We consider any method that is well suited to solving that problem to be a reinforcement learning method. RL addresses the question of how an autonomous agent that senses and acts in its environment can learn to choose optimal actions to achieve its goals. RL is very different from supervised learning — the kind of learning studied in almost all current research in machine learning, statistical pattern recognition, and artificial neural networks. Supervised learning is learning under the tutelage of a knowledgeable supervisor, or "teacher",

351

which explicitly tells the learning agent how it should respond to training inputs. RL concerns a family of problems in which an agent evolves while analyzing consequences of its actions, with a simple scalar signal (the reinforcement) given out by the environment.

The study of RL develops into an unusually multidisciplinary field; it includes researches specializing in artificial intelligence, psychology, control engineering, statistical research, and so on. RL has particularly rich roots in the psychology of animal learning, from which it takes its name. A number of impressive applications of RL have also been developed. RL has attracted much attention in the past decade. Its incremental nature and adaptive capabilities make it suitable for use in various domains, such as automatic control, mobile robotics, and multi-agent system. Particularly with the breakthrough of the mathematical basis of reinforcement learning, the application of RL is on the rise, as one of the hotspots of the current research in the field of machine learning.

The history of reinforcement learning had two main threads, both long and rich, which were pursued independently before intertwining them into modern reinforcement learning. One thread concerned learning by trial-and-error and started in the psychology of animal learning. This thread runs through some of the earliest work in artificial intelligence and led to the revival of reinforcement learning in the early 1980s. The other thread concerned the problem of optimal control and its solution using value functions and dynamic programming. For the most part, this thread did not involve learning. Although the two threads were largely independent, exceptions revolve around a third, less-distinct thread concerning temporal-difference methods. All three threads came together in the late 1980s to produce the modern field of reinforcement learning.

In early artificial intelligence, before it was distinct from other branches of engineering, several researchers began to explore trial-and-error learning as an engineering principle. The earliest computational investigations of trial-and-error learning were perhaps by Minsky (1954) and Farley *et al.* (1954). In his Ph.D. dissertation, Minsky discussed computational models of reinforcement learning and described his construction of an analog machine, composed of components he called SNARCs (Stochastic Neural-Analog Reinforcement Calculators). Farley and Clark described another neural network learning machine designed to learn by trial-and-error. In the 1960s, one finds the terms "reinforcement" and "reinforcement learning" being widely used in the engineering literature for the first time. Particularly influential was Minsky's paper "Steps Toward Artificial Intelligence" (Minsky, 1961), which discussed several issues relevant to reinforcement learning, including what he called the credit assignment problem: how do you distribute credit for success among the many decisions that may have been involved in producing it? In 1969, Minsky got the Turin Award of ACM for the above contribution.

In 1994 and 1995, the interests of Farley and Clark shifted from trial-and-error learning to generalization and pattern recognition, that is, from reinforcement learning to supervised learning. This began a pattern of confusion about the relationship between these types of learning. Many researchers seemed to believe that they were studying reinforcement learning when they were actually studying supervised learning. For example, neural network pioneers such as Rosenblatt (1958) and (Widrow, *et al.*, 1960) were clearly motivated by reinforcement learning — they used the language of rewards and punishments — but the systems they studied were supervised learning systems suitable for pattern recognition and perceptual learning. Even today, researchers and textbooks often minimize or blur the distinction between these types of learning. Some modern neural network textbooks use the term trial-and-error to describe networks that learn from training examples because they use error information to update connection weights. This is an understandable confusion, but it substantially misses the essential optional character of trial-and-error learning.

The term "optimal control" came into use in the late 1950s to describe the problem of designing a controller to minimize the measure of a dynamical system's behavior over time. One of the approaches to this problem was developed in the mid-1950s by Richard Bellman and colleagues by extending a 19th century theory of Hamilton and Jacobi. This approach uses the concept of a dynamical system's state and a value function, or "optimal return function" to define a functional equation, now often called the Bellman equation. The class of methods for solving optimal control problems by solving this equation came to be known as dynamic programming (Bellman, 1957). Bellman also introduced the discrete stochastic version of the optimal control problem known as Markovian decision processes (MDPs), and Ron Howard devised the policy iteration method for MDPs in 1960. All of these are essential elements underlying the theory and algorithms of modern reinforcement learning.

Finally, the temporal-difference and optimal control threads were fully brought together in 1989 with Chris Watkins's development of Q-learning (Watkins and Dayan, 1989). This work extended and integrated prior work in all three threads of reinforcement learning research. By the time of Watkins's work, there had been tremendous growth in reinforcement learning research, primarily in the machine learning sub-field of artificial intelligence, and also in neural networks and artificial intelligence more broadly. In 1992, the remarkable success of Gerry Tesauro's backgammon playing program, TD-Gammon (Tesauro, 1992), brought additional attention to the field. Other important contributions made in the recent history of reinforcement learning are too numerous to mention in this brief account; we cite these at the end of the individual chapters in which they arise.

10.2 Reinforcement Learning Model

The reinforcement learning problem is meant to be a straightforward framing of the problem of learning from interaction to achieve a goal. The learner or decision-maker is called the agent. The thing it interacts with, comprising everything outside the agent, is called the environment. These interact continually, the agent selecting actions and the environment responding to those actions and presenting new situations to the agent. The model of RL is illustrated in Figure 10.1.

More specifically, the agent exists in an environment described by some set of possible state S. It can perform any set of possible action A. Each time it performs an action in some state, the agent receives a real-valued reward r_t that indicates the immediate value of this state–action transition. This produces a sequence of states s_i, actions ai, and immediate rewards r_i. The task of the agent is to learn a control policy $\pi : S \to A$ that maximizes the expected sum of these rewards, with future rewards discounted exponentially by their delay. The agent's goal, roughly speaking, is to maximize the total amount of reward it receives over the long run, as shown in Formula 10.1. In learning, the principle of RL is as follows: if the reward is positive, strengthen the action later, otherwise weaken the action:

$$\sum_{i=0}^{\infty} \gamma^i r_{t+i}, \quad 0 < \gamma \leq 1, \tag{10.1}$$

A task that satisfies the Markov property is called a Markov decision process, or MDP. If the state and action spaces are finite, then it is called a finite Markov decision process (finite MDP). Finite MDPs are particularly important to the theory of reinforcement learning.

Fig. 10.1. Reinforcement learning model

Markov decision process: An Markov decision process is defined by a four-tuples $\langle S, A, R, P \rangle$, where S is a set of possible state, A is a set of possible action, R is the reward function ($R : S \times A \to \mathcal{R}$), and P is the state transition function ($P{:}S \times A \to PD(S)$. $R(s, a, s')$ is the immediate reward after transition to state s' from state s by performing action a. $P(s, a, s')$ is the probability that action a in state s will lead to state s'. The task of the agent is to learn a policy, $\pi{:}S \to A$, for selecting its next action based on the current observed state st, that is, $\pi(st) = at$.

The nature of Markov property is as follows: given the state of the MDP at time t is known, transition probabilities to the state at time $t + 1$ are independent of all previous states or actions. If transition function P and reward function R are known, dynamic programming could be used to acquire the optimal policy. However, RL focuses on the solution of optimal policy when P and R are unknown.

To solve this problem, Figure 10.2 shows the relationship of the four basic components of RL: policy π, state transition function (value function) P, reward function R, and environment model. The bottom-up relations of the four elements are of a pyramid structure. At any given moment, the policy defines the main method of choice and action of the agent. This policy can be adopted by a group of production rules, or a simple table can be used to find it. As pointed out earlier, under specific circumstances, the policy may need an extensive search for a model or plan to process the results. It can also be random. The policy is the main component part of learning agents as it is sufficient to produce action at any time.

The policy is the decision-making function of the agent, specifying what action it takes in each of the situations that it might encounter. In psychology, this would correspond to the set of stimulus–response rules or associations. This is the core of a reinforcement agent, as suggested in Figure 10.2, because it alone is sufficient to define a full, behaving agent. The other components serve only to change and improve the policy. The policy itself is the ultimate determinant of behavior and performance. In general, it may be stochastic.

Fig. 10.2. Four components of RL

The reward function defines the goal of the RL agent. The agent's objective is to maximize the reward that it receives over the long run. The reward function thus defines what are good and bad events for the agent. Rewards are the immediate and defining features of the problem faced by the agent. As such, the reward function must necessarily be fixed. It may, however, be used as a basis for changing the policy. For example, if an action selected by the policy is followed by low reward, then the policy may be changed to select some other action in that situation in the future.

Whereas reward indicates what is good in an immediate sense, the transition function specifies what is good in the long run, that is, because it predicts reward. The difference between value and reward is critical to RL. For example, when playing chess, checkmating your opponent is associated with high reward, but winning his queen is associated with high value. The former defines the true goal of the task — winning the game — whereas the latter just predicts this true goal. Learning the value of states, or of state–action pairs, is the critical step in the RL methods.

The fourth and final major component of an RL agent is a model of its environment or external world. This is something that mimics the behavior of the environment in some sense. Not every RL agent uses a model of the environment. Methods that never learn or use a model are called model-free RL methods. Model-free methods are very simple and, perhaps surprisingly, are still generally able to find optimal behavior. Model-based methods just find it faster. The most interesting case is that in which the agent does not have a perfect model of the environment *a priori,* but must use learning methods to align it with reality.

The system environment is defined by the environment model. Because the model of P and R function are unknown, the system can only rely on the immediate reward received by each trial-and-error to choose policies. The objective is to find a policy that, roughly speaking, maximizes the total reward received. In the simplest formulation, the trade-off between immediate and delayed reward is handled by a discount rate $0 \leq \gamma < 1$. The value of following a policy π from a state s is defined as the expectation of the sum of the subsequent rewards, $r_1, r_2 \ldots$, each discounted geometrically by its delay as follows:

$$R_t = r_{t+1} + \gamma r_{t+2} + \gamma^2 r_{t+3} + \cdots = r_{t+1} + \gamma R_{t+1}, \tag{10.2}$$

$$V^\pi (s) = E_\pi \{ R_t \, | s_t = s \} = E_\pi \{ r_{t+1} + \gamma V (s_{t+1}) \, | s_t = s \}$$

$$= \sum_a \pi (s, a) \sum_{s'} P_{ss'}^a \left[R_{ss'}^a + \gamma V^\pi (s') \right]. \tag{10.3}$$

Values determine a partial ordering over policies, whereby $\pi_1 \geq \pi_2$ if and only if $V_{\pi 1}(s) \geq V_{\pi 2}(s)$, $\forall s$. Ideally, we seek an optimal policy π^*, one that is greater than or equal to all others. All such policies share the same optimal value function.

According to Bellman optimality equations, the value function $V^*(s)$ of optimal policy π^* at state s could be defined as follows:

$$V^*(s) = \max_{a \in A(s)} E\left\{r_{t+1} + \gamma V^*(s_{t+1}) \mid s_t = s, a_t = a\right\}$$

$$= \max_{a \in A(s)} \sum_{s'} P_{ss'}^a \left[R_{ss'}^a + \gamma V^*(s')\right]. \tag{10.4}$$

Dynamic programming methods involve iteratively updating an approximation to the optimal value function. If the state-transition function P and the expected rewards R are known, a typical example is value iteration, which starts with an arbitrary policy π_0, and then

$$\pi_k(s) = \arg\max_a \sum_{s'} P_{ss'}^a \left[R_{ss'}^a + \gamma V^{\pi_{k-1}}(s')\right], \tag{10.5}$$

$$V^{\pi_k}(s) \leftarrow \sum_a \pi_{k-1}(s, a) \sum_{s'} P_{ss'}^a \left[R_{ss'}^a + \gamma V^{\pi_{k-1}}(s')\right]. \tag{10.6}$$

In RL, without knowledge of the system's dynamics, we cannot compute the expected value by Equations (10.5) and (10.6). It is necessary to estimate the value by iteratively updating an approximation to the optimal value function, and Monte Carlo sampling is one of the basic methods. Keeping policy π, we can iteratively use Equation (10.7) to obtain approximate solutions:

$$V(s_t) \leftarrow V(s_t) + \alpha[R_t - V(s_t)]. \tag{10.7}$$

Combining the Monte Carlo method and dynamic programming method, Equation (10.8) gives the iterative equation of temporal-difference learning (TD):

$$V(s_t) \leftarrow V(s_t) + \alpha\left[r_{t+1} + \gamma V(s_{t+1}) - V(s_t)\right]. \tag{10.8}$$

10.3 Dynamic Programming

The term dynamic programming (DP) refers to a collection of algorithms that can be used to compute optimal policies given a perfect model of the environment as a Markov decision process (MDP). Classical DP algorithms are of limited utility in RL because of their assumption of a perfect model and their great computational expense, but they are still important theoretically. DP provides an essential foundation for the understanding of the methods presented in the rest of this book. In fact, all of these methods can be viewed as attempts to achieve the same effect as DP, with less computation and without assuming a perfect model of the environment.

First, we consider how to compute the state-value function V^π for an arbitrary policy π. This is called policy evaluation in the DP literature. We also refer to it as the prediction problem. For all s in S,

$$V^\pi(s) = \sum_a \pi(a|s) \times \sum_{s'} \pi(s \to s'|a) \times (R^a(s \to s') + \gamma(V^\pi(s'))), \quad (10.9)$$

where $\pi(a|s)$ is the probability of taking action a in state s under policy π, and the expectations are subscripted by π to indicate that they are conditional on π being followed. The existence and uniqueness of V^π are guaranteed as long as either $\gamma < 1$ or eventual termination is guaranteed from all states under the policy π. Figure 10.3 illustrates the first step of the computing process, and the three subsequent states of s_t are all known. As for policy π, the probability of the action a is $\pi(a|s)$. For each state, the environment may respond to one of the states, s', with a reward r. The Bellman equation is adopted to average the probability of these, without weight. It is noted that the value of the starting state must look forward to the discount value of the next state, γ, and the reward obtained with the path. In dynamic programming, if n and m are the number of states and actions, although the total number of the policy is nm, a dynamic planning method can be guaranteed in polynomial time to find the optimal strategy. In this sense, dynamic programming strategy is faster than any of the direct search index-classes and has polynomial time of action and states. However, if the state is based on the exponential growth of certain variables, of course, it will also appear dimensions of the disaster.

In dynamic programming iterative Equation (10.10) can be derived from Equation (10.4):

$$V_{t+1}(s) \leftarrow \text{MAX}_a \sum_{s'} P^a_{ss'}[\Re^a_{ss'} + \gamma V_t(s')], \quad (10.10)$$

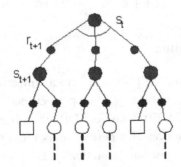

Fig. 10.3.   Dynamic programming method

$V_t(s) \rightarrow V^*(s)$ when $t \rightarrow \infty$. The award evaluation will be acquired until $|\Delta V|$ is less than a small positive number if repeated and iterated to each state.

The typical model of dynamic programming model has limited usage, as in many problems it is difficult to give the integral model of the environment. For example, simulation robot soccer poses such a problem that can be solved by real-time dynamic programming methods. In real-time dynamic programming, the environment model is not required to be given first, but it is necessary to have the environment model by testing in a real environment. The use of anti-nerve-state network can be used for generalization of states. The input unit of the network is the state of the environment s. The output of the network is the evaluation of the state $V(s)$.

DP methods update estimates of the values of states based on estimates of the values of successor states. That is, they update estimates on the basis of other estimates. We call this general idea bootstrapping. Many reinforcement learning methods perform bootstrapping, even those that do not require, as DP requires, a complete and accurate model of the environment. In Chapter 11, we explore reinforcement learning methods that do not require a model and do not bootstrap. In Chapter 12, we explore methods that do not require a model but do bootstrap. These key features and properties are separable, yet can be mixed in interesting combinations.

10.4 Monte Carlo Methods

Monte Carlo methods are a class of computational algorithms that rely on repeated random sampling to compute their results. Monte Carlo methods are often used when simulating physical and mathematical systems. Because of their reliance on repeated computation and random or pseudo-random numbers, Monte Carlo methods are most suited to calculation by a computer. Monte Carlo methods tend to be used when it is infeasible or impossible to compute an exact result with a deterministic algorithm. Unlike DP, the Monte Carlo methods do not assume complete knowledge of the environment. Monte Carlo methods require only experience — sample sequences of states, actions, and rewards from online or simulated interaction with an environment. Although a model is required, it need only generate sample transitions, not the complete probability distributions of all possible transitions that are required by dynamic programming (DP) methods. The term Monte Carlo method was coined in the 1940s by physicists working on nuclear weapon projects at the Los Alamos National Laboratory.

Monte Carlo methods are ways of solving the reinforcement learning problem based on averaging sample returns. There is no single Monte Carlo method; instead, the term describes a large and widely used class of approaches. However, these approaches tend to follow a particular pattern, that is,

(1) define a domain of possible inputs;
(2) generate inputs randomly from the domain and perform a deterministic computation on them;
(3) aggregate the results of the individual computations into the final result.

Here, we use it specifically for methods based on averaging complete returns (as opposed to methods that learn from partial returns, considered in chapter 11). Figure 10.4 gives the return reward by Monte Carlo sampling for one step during learning. Then through iterative learning, the actual obtained rewards are used to approximate the real value function.

Monte Carlo methods do not assume complete knowledge of the environment, but learn from online experience. Monte Carlo methods are ways of solving the reinforcement learning problem based on averaging sample returns. Given policy π, compute V^π for the subsequent state s_t under policy π, $R_t(s_t)$ is the long reward return, add $R_t(s_t)$ to the list Rs_i, $V(s_t) \leftarrow \text{average}(Rs_i)$.

The list could use incremental implementation,

$$V(s_t) \leftarrow V(s_t) + \frac{R_t(s_t) - V(s_t)}{N_{s_t} + 1},$$

(10.11)

$$N_{s_t} \leftarrow N_{s_t} + 1.$$

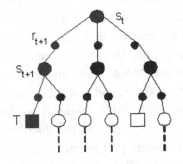

Fig. 10.4.   Monte Carlo Methods

Under Monte Carlo control, policy evaluation and improvement use the same random policy as

$$a^* \leftarrow \arg\max_a Q(s, a),$$

$$\pi(s, a) \leftarrow \begin{cases} 1 - e + \dfrac{e}{|A(s)|}, & a = a^*, \\[3mm] \dfrac{e}{|A(s)|}, & a \neq a^*. \end{cases} \tag{10.12}$$

In learning, if some actions are found to be good, then what action should the agent select in the next decision-making? One consideration is by making full use of the existing knowledge, select the current best action. But it has a drawback: maybe some better actions are not found; in contrast, if the agent always tests new actions, it will lead to no progress. The agent faces a trade-off in choosing whether to favor exploration of unknown actions (to gather new information), or exploitation of existing actions that it has already learned will yield high rewards (to maximize its cumulative reward). These are two main methods: e-greedy method and genetic simulated annealing. The selection probability of each action is related to its Q value:

$$p(a|s) = \frac{e^{Q(s,a)/T}}{\sum_{a'} e^{Q(s,a')/T}}. \tag{10.13}$$

10.5 Temporal-Difference Learning

Temporal-difference (TD) learning is a combination of Monte Carlo ideas and dynamic programming (DP) ideas. Like Monte Carlo methods, TD methods can learn directly from raw experience without a model of the environment's dynamics. TD resembles a Monte Carlo method because it learns by sampling the environment according to some policy. TD is related to dynamic programming techniques because it approximates its current estimate based on previously learned estimates (a process known as bootstrapping). TD learning algorithm is related to the temporal-difference model of animal learning.

As a prediction method, TD learning takes into account the fact that subsequent predictions are often correlated in some sense. In standard supervised predictive learning, one only learns from actually observed values: a prediction is made, and when the observation is available, the prediction is adjusted to better match the observation. TD(0) is the simplest case of temporal-difference learning and is described as follows.

Algorithm 10.1 (TD(0) Learning Algorithm).

    Initialize $V(s)$ arbitrarily, π to the policy to be evaluated

    Repeat (for each episode)

       Initialize s

       Repeat (for each step of episode)

       Choose a from s using policy π derived from V (e.g., ε-greedy)

       Take action a, observer r, s'

       $V(s) \leftarrow V(s) + \alpha \left[r + \gamma V(s') - V(s) \right]$

       $s \leftarrow s'$

    Until s is terminal

TD(0) learning algorithm contains two steps: determine the new action policy according to the current value function and evaluate the action policy by the immediate reward under the new action policy. The learning process is as follows:

$$v_0 \to \pi_1 \to v_1 \to \pi_2 \to \cdots \to v^* \to \pi^* \to v^*$$

until the value function and the policy reach the stable value. In TD learning, the computation of value function is shown in Figure 10.5.

    To illustrate the general idea of reinforcement learning and contrast it with other approaches, we consider the familiar child's game of tic-tac-toe. Two players take turns playing on a three-by-three board. One player plays $\diamond$s and the other $\bigcirc$s until one player wins by placing three marks in a row, horizontally, vertically, or diagonally.

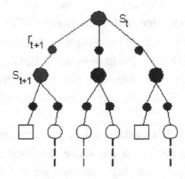

Fig. 10.5.   Temporal-difference Learning Method

If the board fills up with neither player getting three in a row, the game is a draw. Because a skilled player can play so as never to lose, let us assume that we are playing against an imperfect player, one whose play is sometimes incorrect and allows us to win. For the moment, in fact, let us consider draws and losses to be equally bad for us. How might we construct a player that will find the imperfections in its opponent's play and learn to maximize its chances of winning?

An evolutionary approach to this problem would directly search the space of possible policies for one with a high probability of winning against the opponent. Here, a policy is a rule that tells the player what move to make for every state of the game — every possible configuration of ◇s and ◯s on the three-by-three board. For each policy considered, an estimate of its winning probability would be obtained by playing some number of games against the opponent. This evaluation would then direct which policy or policies were considered next. A typical evolutionary method would hill-climb in policy space, successively generating and evaluating policies in an attempt to obtain incremental improvements. Or, perhaps, a genetic-style algorithm could be used that would maintain and evaluate a population of policies. Literally hundreds of different optimization methods could be applied. By directly searching the policy space, we mean that entire policies are proposed and compared on the basis of scalar evaluations.

Here is how the tic-tac-toe problem would be approached using reinforcement learning and approximate value functions. First we set up a table of numbers, one for each possible state of the game. Each number will be the latest estimate of the probability of our winning from that state. We treat this estimate as the state's value, and the whole table is the learned value function. State A has higher value than state B, or is considered "better" than state B, if the current estimate of the probability of our winning from A is higher than it is from B. Assuming we always play ◇s, then for all states with three ◇s in a row the probability of winning is 1, because we have already won. Similarly, for all states with three ◯s in a row, or that are "filled up", the correct probability is 0, as we cannot win from them. We set the initial values of all the other states to 0.5, representing a guess that we have a 50% chance of winning.

We play many games against the opponent. To select our moves, we examine the states that would result from each of our possible moves (one for each blank space on the board) and look up their current values in the table. Most of the time, we move greedily, selecting the move that leads to the state with the greatest value, that is, with the highest estimated probability of winning. Occasionally, however, we select randomly from among the other moves instead. These are called exploratory moves because they make us experience states that we might otherwise never see.

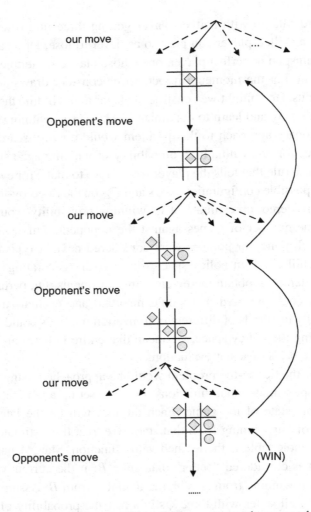

Fig. 10.6.   A sequence of tic-tac-toe moves. The solid lines represent the moves taken during a game; the dashed lines represent moves that we (our RL player) considered but did not make

A sequence of moves made and considered during a game can be diagrammed, as in Figure 10.6.

While we are playing, we change the values of the states in which we find ourselves during the game. We attempt to make more accurate estimates of the probabilities of winning. To do this, we "back up" the value of the state after each greedy move to the state before the move, as suggested by the arrows in Figure 10.6. More precisely, the current value of the earlier state is adjusted to be closer to the value of the later state. This can be done by moving the earlier state's value a fraction of the way toward the value of the later state. If we let s_n denote the state before the greedy move, and s_{n+1} the state after the move, then the update to the estimated value of s, denoted $V(s)$, can be written as

$$V(s_n) = S(s_n) + c(V(s_{n+1}) - V(s_n)), \tag{10.14}$$

where c is a small positive fraction called the step-size parameter, which influences the rate of learning. This update rule is an example of a temporal-difference learning method, so called because its changes are based on a difference, $V(s_{n+1}) - V(s_n)$, between estimates at two different times.

The method described above performs quite well on this task. For example, if the step-size parameter is reduced properly over time, this method converges, for any fixed opponent, to the true probabilities of winning from each state given optimal play by our player. Furthermore, the moves then taken (except on exploratory moves) are in fact the optimal moves against the opponent. In other words, the method converges to an optimal policy for playing the game. If the step-size parameter is not reduced all the way to zero over time, then this player also plays well against opponents who slowly change their way of playing.

This example illustrates the differences between evolutionary methods and methods that learn value functions. To evaluate a policy, an evolutionary method must hold it fixed and play many games against the opponent, or simulate many games using a model of the opponent. The frequency of wins gives an unbiased estimate of the probability of winning with that policy and can be used to direct the next policy selection. But each policy change is made only after many games, and only the final outcome of each game is used: what happens during the games is ignored. For example, if the player wins, then all of its behavior in the game is given credit, independently of how specific moves might have been critical to the win. Credit is even given to moves that never occurred! Value function methods, in contrast, allow individual states to be evaluated. In the end, both evolutionary and value function methods search the space of policies, but learning a value function takes advantage of information available during the course of play.

This simple example illustrates some of the key features of reinforcement learning methods. First, there is the emphasis on learning while interacting with an environment, in this case with an opponent player. Second, there is a clear goal, and correct behavior requires planning or foresight that takes into account delayed effects of one's choices. For example, the simple reinforcement learning player would learn to set up multi-move traps for a shortsighted opponent. It is a striking feature of the reinforcement learning solution that it can achieve the effects of planning and looking ahead without using a model of the opponent or conducting an explicit search over possible sequences of future states and actions.

While this example illustrates some of the key features of reinforcement learning, it is so simple that it might give the impression that reinforcement learning is more limited than it really is. Although tic-tac-toe is a two-person game, reinforcement learning also applies in the case in which there is no external adversary, that is, in the case of a "game against nature". Reinforcement learning also is not restricted to problems in which behavior breaks down into separate episodes, like the separate games of tic-tac-toe, with a reward only at the end of each episode. It is just as applicable when behavior continues indefinitely and when rewards of various magnitudes can be received at any time.

Finally, the tic-tac-toe player was able to look ahead and know the states that would result from each of its possible moves. To do this, it had to have a model of the game that allowed it to "think about" how its environment would change in response to moves that it might never make. Many problems are like this, but in others even a short-term model of the effects of actions are lacking. Reinforcement learning can be applied in either case. No model is required, but models can easily be used if they are available or can be learned.

10.6 Q-Learning

One of the most important breakthroughs in reinforcement learning was the development of an off-policy TD control algorithm known as Q-learning. Q-learning is a reinforcement learning technique that works by learning an action-value function that gives the expected utility of taking a given action in a given state and following a fixed policy thereafter. A strength of Q-learning is that it is able to compare the expected utility of the available actions without requiring a model of the environment.

The core of the algorithm is a simple value iteration update. For each state, s, from the state set S, and for each action, a, from the action set A, we can calculate an update to its expected discounted reward with the following expressions:

$$Q(s_t, a_t) \leftarrow (1 - c) \times Q(s_t, a_t) + c \times [r_{t+1} + \gamma \underset{a}{\text{MAX}} \, Q(s_{t+1}, a) - Q(s_t, a_t)],$$

$$(10.15)$$

where r_t is an observed real reward at time t, c are the learning rates such that $0 \leq c \leq 1$, and γ is the discount factor such that $0 \leq \gamma < 1$. Figure 10.7 illustrates the learning trace of V^* and Q^*.

Q-learning uses tables to store data. This quickly loses viability with increasing levels of complexity of the system it is monitoring/controlling. One answer to this problem is to use an (adapted) Artificial Neural Network as a function

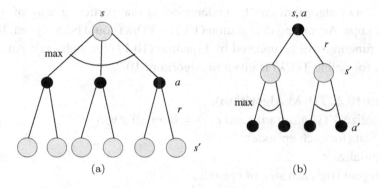

Fig. 10.7. (a) V^* and (b) Q^* Learning trace

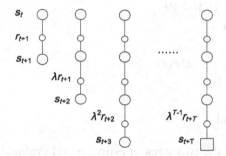

Fig. 10.8. λ-reward function

approximation, as demonstrated by Tesauro in his Backgammon-playing Temporal-Difference Learning research. An adaptation of the standard neural network is required because the required result (from which the error signal is generated) is itself generated at run-time.

Monte Carlo methods perform a backup for each state based on the entire sequence of observed rewards from that state until the end of the episode. The backup of Q-learning, on the contrary, is based on just the next reward, using the value of the state one step later as a proxy for the remaining rewards (Bootstrapping method). Thus, RL needs repeated learning to reach optimal policies. We construct a λ-reward function Rt' by rewriting Equation (10.8) as Equation (10.16). If the system reaches the end state at T step, the value function conforms to Equation (10.17). The theoretical meaning of λ-reward function is illustrated in Figure 10.8:

$$R'_t = r_{t+1} + \lambda r_{t+2} + \lambda^2 r_{t+3} + \cdots + \lambda^{T-1} r_{t+T}, \tag{10.16}$$

$$V(s_t) \leftarrow V(s_t) + \alpha \left[R'_t - V(s_t) \right]. \tag{10.17}$$

The TD(λ) algorithm can be understood as one particular way of averaging n-step backups. According to Equation (10.17), TD(λ) could be designed. In TD(λ), the value function will be updated by Equation (10.17) through $e(s)$. An complete algorithm for online TD(λ) is given in Algorithm 10.2.

Algorithm 10.2 (TD(λ) Algorithm).
> Initialize $V(s)$ arbitrarily and $e(s) = 0$ for all $s \in S$
> Repeat (for each episode)
>   Initialize s
>   Repeat (for each step of episode)
> $a \leftarrow$ action given by π for s(e.g., ε-greedy)
>   Take action a, observer r, s'
> $\delta \leftarrow r + \gamma V(s') - V(s)$
> $e(s) \leftarrow e(s) + 1$
>   for all s
> $V(s) \leftarrow V(s) + \alpha \delta e(s)$
> $e(s) \leftarrow \gamma \lambda e(s)$
> $s \leftarrow s'$
>   Until s is terminal

We could combine the two steps of estimate and evaluate of the value function to construct a value function of the state–action pair, Q function. In Q-learning, the learned action-value function Q, directly approximates Q^*, the optimal action-value function, independent of the policy being followed. The policy still has an effect in that it determines which state–action pairs are visited and updated. However, all that is required for correct convergence is that all pairs continue to be updated. This is the minimal requirement in the sense that any method guaranteed to find optimal behavior in the general case must require it. Under this assumption and a variant of the usual stochastic approximation conditions on the sequence of step-size parameters, Q_t has been shown to converge with probability 1 to Q^*. The Q-learning algorithm is shown in procedural form in Algorithm 10.3.

Algorithm 10.3 (Q-Learning Algorithm).
> Initialize $Q(s, a)$ arbitrarily
> Repeat (for each episode)
>   Initialize s
>   Repeat (for each step of episode)

Choose a from s using policy derived from Q (e.g., ε-greedy)

Take action a, observer r, s'

$$Q(s, a) \leftarrow Q(s, a) + \alpha[r + \gamma \max_{a'} Q(s', a') - Q(s, a)]$$

$$s \leftarrow s'$$

Until s is terminal

10.7 Function Approximation

RL is a broad class of optimal control methods based on estimating value functions from experience, simulation, or search. Most of the theoretical convergence results for RL algorithms assume a tabular representation of the value function, in which the value of each state is stored in a separate memory location. However, most practical applications have continuous state spaces, or very large discrete state spaces, for which such a representation is not feasible. Thus, generalization is crucial to scaling RL algorithms to real-world problems. The kind of generalization we require is often called function approximation because it takes examples from a desired function (e.g., a value function) and attempts to generalize from them to construct an approximation of the entire function. The mapping relations in RL include $S \rightarrow A, S \rightarrow R, S \times A \rightarrow R, S \times A \rightarrow S$, and so on. The nature of function approximation in RL is to estimate these mapping relations by parameterized functions.

Assuming the starting value of value function is V_0, then the sequence of value functions during learning are

$$V_0, \ \Gamma(V_0), \ \Gamma(\Gamma(V_0)), \Gamma(\Gamma(\Gamma(V_0))), \dots$$

where Γ represent Equation (10.8).

Most of the traditional RL algorithms adopt the lookup-table to save the value functions. Function approximation adopts parameterized functions to replace the lookup-table. The model of RL with function approximation is shown in Figure 10.9. In the model, value function V is the objective function, function V' is the estimated function, and $M : V \rightarrow V'$ is the estimated operator. Assuming the starting value of value function is V_0, then the sequence of value functions during learning are

$$V_0, \ M(V_0), \ \Gamma(M(V_0)), \ M(\Gamma(M(V_0))), \ \Gamma(M(\Gamma(M(V_0)))), \dots$$

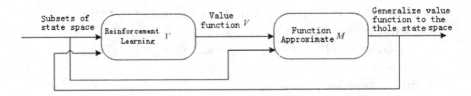

Fig. 10.9. RL model with function approximation

Like Q-learning, the equations of RL with function approximation are as follows:

$$Q(s, a) \leftarrow (1 - \alpha)V'(s, a) + \alpha(r(s, a, s') + \max_{a'} V'(s', a')), \quad (10.19)$$

$$V'(s, a) = M(Q(s, a)). \quad (10.20)$$

In RL learning with function approximation, two iterative processes work simultaneously. One is the iterative process of value function Γ. The other is the approximation process of value function M. The correctness and convergence of the approximation process M play a key role in RL. Function approximation is an instance of supervised learning, the primary topic studied in machine learning, artificial neural networks, pattern recognition, and statistical curve fitting, such as state aggregation, function interpolation, artificial neural networks, etc.

Aggregation is an intuitive and applicable technique to solve large-scale problems. In state aggregation, the state space of the Markov chain is partitioned, and the states belonging to the same partition subset are aggregated into one meta-state. The Markov chain is said to be lumpable if the transition process among meta-states is Markovian for every probability distribution of the initial state of the original Markov chain, and weakly lumpable if the transition process among meta-states is Markovian only for some initial probability distributions. It has been proved that the function approximation with state aggregation is convergent. However, it is possible that the convergent value is not the optimal value. To reach the optimal value, the step could be too long. Thus, it also suffers from the dimension tragedy for large MDP problems.

Function approximation with artificial neural networks has attracted much research of late. Though these new methods could accelerate the speed significantly, the convergence could not be ensured. Therefore, the new methods of function approximation, which have both convergence and high speed, are still one of the most important research topics in reinforcement learning.

10.8 Reinforcement Learning Applications

Reinforcement learning addresses the question on how an autonomous agent that senses and acts in its environment can learn to choose optimal actions to achieve its goals. In a Markov decision process (MDP), the agent can perceive a set S of distinct states of its environment and has a set A of actions that it can perform. At each discrete time step t, the agent senses the current state s_t, chooses a current action a_t, and performs it. The environment responds by giving the agent a reward $r_t = Q(s_t, a_t)$ and by producing the succeeding state $s_{t+1} = P(s_t, a_t)$. Here, the functions P and Q are part of the environment and are not necessarily known to the agent. In an MDP, the functions P and Q depend only on the current state and action, and not on earlier states or actions. Reinforcement learning is a useful way to solve MDP problems. Reinforcement learning reaches its goal by learning reward function $r_t = Q(s_t, a_t)$ and state transition function $P(s_t, a_t)$. Q-learning acquires the optimal policy by learning $r_t = Q(s_t, a_t)$.

RoboCup is an international robotics competition founded in 1993. The aim is to develop autonomous robots with the intention of promoting research and education in the field of artificial intelligence. The name RoboCup is a contraction of the competition's full name, "Robot Soccer World Cup". The following is the application of Q-learning algorithm to simulate robot soccer with three members (2 to 1). The training is aimed at trying to get to the main strategy of awareness in the attack when running. As can be seen in Figure 10.10, striker A controls the ball in the shoot region. But A has no angle to shoot; teammate B is also in the shoot region, and B has a good shot angle. Thus, A passes the ball to B, and B completes the shot. Then the cooperation is very successful. Through Q-learning approach in the training, the action A of passing ball to B is the best action in this state after training a large number of examples.

Figure 10.11 illustrates the description of states. The attack region is divided into 20*8 small regions. Each small region is a square with a length of 2 m. A 2D array $A_{i,j}$ ($0 \le i \le 19, 0 \le j \le 7$) can be used to describe the region. The attack state can be described by the location of three agents. Figure 10.11 shows the generalization of the state. The state in the same region can be considered as the similar state. Though the description of the state is not precise, it is a description of the strategic level that the agent can be running in the same strategic region actively. So, (S_A, S_B, S_G) describes a particular state, where SA is the regional code of the offensive team member A, S_B is the regional code of the offensive team member B, and S_G is the regional code of the offensive team member G. The regional code

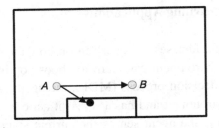

Fig. 10.10.   Robot soccer world cup training, 2–1

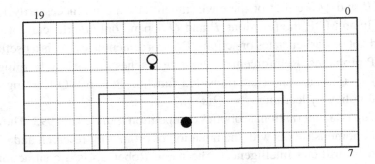

Fig. 10.11.   Position partition

is calculated as follows: $S = i*8 + j$. And the states are preserved by triples of the three regional codes.

The optional actions have {Shoot, Pass, Dribble}, described as follows:

Shoot: The strategy is obtained by learning through a strategy based on the probability of a shot.

Dribble: The strategy is always to reduce the threat and pass the ball to regions with a high probability to shoot the goal. In order to achieve this strategic objective, the offensive region can be divided into a number of strategic areas. In each strategic area, shot evaluation is recorded with the shooting success rate.

Pass: The strategy is very simple — just pass the ball between any two agents, and we do not choose the target agent. If the pass fails, then the state of adoption of this strategy is unsuccessful; through this training, an impossible path of passing the ball cannot be adopted.

All states in training include four absorption states. Assume that the offensive is in the left half, according to specifications of the standard soccer server, and the four states are play on, goal left, goal kick right, and free kick right. If taking the action and the state reaching the four absorption states, the agent will be given the ultimate reward r. For other actions, the agent will be given procedure rewards as immediate

Table 10.1. *Q* value

	Initial value	5,000	10,000	20,000
Shoot	1	0.7342	0.6248	0.5311
Pass	1	0.9743	0.9851	0.993
Dribble	1	0.9012	0.8104	0.7242

rewards. For example, the maximum reward value of goal left is 1, which means shooting the ball to the goal region.

The agent will obtain the ultimate reward by taking several actions through the corresponding states. At this time, the state–action pair will get the reward value. The core of Q-learning algorithm is that every state–action pair has its Q-value. The Q-values will be updated when getting the ultimate rewards. As the RoboCup simulation platform adds a smaller random noise in the design of the state transition, the model is non-deterministic MDP. The Q-value is updated by the following equation:

$$Q(s, a) = (1 - \alpha)Q(s, a) + \alpha(r + \gamma \max Q(s_{t+1}, a_{t+1})), \quad (10.21)$$

where $\alpha = 0.1$, $\gamma = 0.95$.

In actual training, the initial Q is 1. After about 20,000 trainings (to reach a state of absorption), the majority of items in Q value have changed and separated. Table 10.1 is the updated scene of Q-values with different training numbers.

Reinforcement learning has received much attention in the past decade. Its incremental nature and adaptive capabilities make it suitable for use in various domains, such as automatic control, mobile robotics, and multi-agent systems. A critical problem in conventional reinforcement learning is the slow convergence of the learning process. However, in most learning systems there usually exists prior knowledge in the form of human expertise or previously learned experience. Therefore, how to integrate other machine learning techniques, such as neural networks and symbol learning technology, to help accelerate the learning speed is an important direction of RL. At present, the main technical difficulty is as follows: how to prove and guarantee the convergence of learning algorithm from theoretical aspects. The development of effective models for complex MDP will also be an important direction in future research.

Exercises

10.1 Give a brief description of the main branches of reinforcement learning and its research history.

10.2 Explain the similarities and differences between reinforcement learning models and other machine learning methods.

10.3 Explain the decision process of MDP and its essence.

10.4 Give the basic ideas of Monte Carlo methods and discuss its applications in reinforcement learning.

10.5 Give the basic ideas of temporal-difference (TD) learning and illustrate its process taking into consideration the game of tic-tac-toe.

10.6 Consider the deterministic grid world shown below with the absorbing goal-state G. Here, the immediate rewards are in the figure for the labeled transitions and 0 for all unlabeled transitions. Give the V^* value for every state in this grid world. Give the $Q(s, a)$ value for every transition. Finally, show an optimal policy using $\gamma = 0.8$.

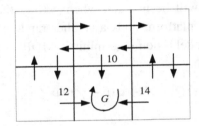

Chapter 11

Unsupervised Learning

Unsupervised learning does not require prior calibration of data. When the classification structure of data is unknown, objects are clustered into classes according to certain attributes of objects, so as to minimize similarity between classes and maximize similarity within classes. Using unsupervised learning, we expect to find intrinsic structural information hidden in the data set.

11.1 Introduction

Unsupervised learning is also called cluster analysis. The general clustering algorithm first selects several pattern points as the center of the cluster. Each center represents a category, and each pattern is attributed to the category represented by each cluster center according to a similarity measure (such as the minimum distance method) to form an initial classification. Then, the clustering criterion determines whether the initial classification is reasonable, and if it is unreasonable, the classification is modified, and the iterative operation is repeated until it is reasonable. Unlike supervised learning, unsupervised methods classify while learning, find the same category by learning, and then distinguish the class from other classes.

Unsupervised learning stems from many research areas and is driven by many application needs. For example, in complex network analysis, people want to find communities with inherently close associations; in image analysis, people want to segment images into regions with similar properties; in text processing, people want to find text subsets with the same theme. In lossy coding techniques, people want to find the code with the least loss of information; in customer behavior analysis, people want to find a customer group with similar consumption patterns in order to develop targeted customer management methods and improve marketing efficiency. These conditions can be classified as cluster analysis under appropriate conditions.

The usual way of clustering is to divide the set containing objects into disjointed parts, called cluster blocks. Given a data set $X = \{x_1, x_2, \ldots, x_n\}$, divide it into k subset classes, where $C_1, C_2, \ldots, C_K$, $C_i \subseteq X$, and $\bigcup_{i=1}^{K} C_i = X$, $\forall i \neq j$, $C_i \cap C_j = \emptyset$, $C_i \neq \emptyset$. The result of clustering can be expressed as a $n \times k$ rank matrix $U = (u_{ik})_{n \times K}$ where

$$u_{ik} = \begin{cases} 1, & i \text{ belongs to the cluster block } k, \\ 0, & i \text{ does not belong to the cluster block } k, \end{cases} \quad (11.1)$$

$$\sum_{k=1}^{K} u_{ik} = 1, \ i = 1, 2, 3, \ldots, n; \ k = 1, 2, 3, \ldots, K, \quad (11.2)$$

$$u_{ik} \in \{0, 1\} \ i = 1, 2, \ldots, n; \ k = 1, 2, \ldots, K. \quad (11.3)$$

The basic steps for typical data clustering are as follows:

(1) representation and preprocessing of the data set, including data cleaning, feature selection, or feature extraction;
(2) assess similarity or dissimilarity between given data and its definition method;
(3) according to the similarity, the data are divided, that is, clustered;
(4) evaluation of the clustering results.

At present, many clustering algorithms have been proposed including partitioning method, hierarchical method, density-based method, grid-based method, model-based method, fuzzy clustering, ant colony clustering method, high-dimensional data clustering method, constrained aggregation classes, self-organizing feature maps, etc. This chapter will introduce the first seven clustering methods.

11.2 Similarity Measure

The similarity between objects is the core of clustering. Object clustering uses distance or similarity coefficient to measure similarity, called Q-type clustering; attribute clustering often measures similarity according to similarity coefficient, called R-type clustering. The calculation of distances is described in Chapter 6. This section discusses similarity measures for similarity coefficients and attributes.

11.2.1 Similarity Coefficient

The similarity coefficient reflects the degree of similarity between objects, reflecting the degree of similarity between samples relative to certain attributes. There are many ways to determine the similarity coefficient. Here are some common methods that can be selected based on actual problems.

Set $O = \{x_1, x_2, \ldots, x_n\}$ to the entirety of the object to be classified, and $(x_{i1}, x_{i2}, \ldots, x_{im})$ to represent the feature data of each object. Let, $x_i, x_j \in O$, r_{ij} be the similarity coefficient between x_i and x_j, satisfying the following conditions:

(1) $r_{ij} = 1 \Leftrightarrow x_i = x_j$,

(2) $\forall x_i, x_j, r_{ij} \in [0, 1]$,

(3) $\forall x_i, x_j, r_{ij} = r_{ji}$.

The following methods are commonly used to determine the measure of similarity coefficients:

(1) **Quantitative product method:**

$$r_{ij} = \begin{cases} 1, & i = j, \\ \dfrac{1}{M} \displaystyle\sum_{k=1}^{m} x_{ik} x_{jk}, & i \neq j, \end{cases} \tag{11.4}$$

where M is a positive number and satisfies $M \geq \max_{i \neq j} (\sum_{k=1}^{m} x_{ik} x_{jk})$.

(2) **Angle cosine method:**

$$r_{ij} = \frac{\left| \sum_{k=1}^{m} x_{ik} x_{jk} \right|}{\sqrt{\left(\sum_{k=1}^{m} x_{ik}^2 \right) \left(\sum_{k=1}^{m} x_{jk}^2 \right)}}. \tag{11.5}$$

The cosine between the two vectors is used as the similarity coefficient, and the range is $[-1, 1]$. When the two vectors are orthogonal, the value is 0, indicating that they are completely dissimilar.

(3) **Correlation coefficient method:**

$$r_{ij} = \frac{\sum_{k=1}^{m} (x_{ik} - \bar{x}_i)(x_{jk} - \bar{x}_j)}{\sqrt{\sum_{k=1}^{m} (x_{ik} - \bar{x}_i)^2} \sqrt{\sum_{k=1}^{m} (x_{jk} - \bar{x}_j)^2}}, \tag{11.6}$$

where

$$\bar{x}_i = \frac{1}{m} \sum_{k=1}^{m} x_{ik}, \quad \bar{x}_j = \frac{1}{m} \sum_{k=1}^{m} x_{jk}$$

calculate the correlation between two vectors, in the range of $[-1, 1]$, where 0 means irrelevant, 1 means positive correlation, and -1 means negative correlation.

(4) **Maximum and minimum method:**

$$r_{ij} = \frac{\sum_{k=1}^{m} (x_{ik} \wedge x_{jk})}{\sum_{k=1}^{m} (x_{ik} \vee x_{jk})} \tag{11.7}$$

(5) **Arithmetic mean minimum method:**

$$r_{ij} = \frac{2 \sum_{k=1}^{m} (x_{ik} \wedge x_{jk})}{\sum_{k=1}^{m} (x_{ik} + x_{jk})} \tag{11.8}$$

(6) **Geometric mean minimum method:**

$$r_{ij} = \frac{\sum_{k=1}^{m} (x_{ik} \wedge x_{jk})}{\sum_{k=1}^{m} \sqrt{x_{ik} x_{jk}}} \tag{11.9}$$

(7) **Absolute value index:**

$$r_{ij} = e^{-\sum_{k=1}^{m} |x_{ik} - x_{jk}|} \tag{11.10}$$

(8) **Exponential similarity coefficient method:**

$$r_{ij} = \frac{1}{m} \sum_{k=1}^{m} e^{-(x_{ik} - x_{jk})^2 / s_k^2} \tag{11.11}$$

(9) **Absolute value reciprocal method:**

$$r_{ij} = \begin{cases} 1, & i = j, \\ \dfrac{M}{\sum_{k=1}^{m} |x_{ik} - x_{jk}|}, & i \neq j, \end{cases} \tag{11.12}$$

where, M is properly selected, so that r_{ij} is in $[0, 1]$ and separated.

(10) **Absolute value subtraction:**

$$r_{ij} = 1 - c \sum_{k=1}^{m} |x_{ik} - x_{jk}|, \tag{11.13}$$

where c is appropriately selected so that r_{ij} is separated in $[0, 1]$.

(11) **Non-parametric method:**

Let

$$x'_{ik} = x_{ik} - \bar{x}_i, \quad x'_{jk} = x_{jk} - \bar{x}_j,$$

$$n_{ij}^+ = \{x'_{i1} x'_{j1}, x'_{i2} x'_{j2}, \ldots, x'_{im} x'_{jm}\}, \text{ positive number,}$$

$$n_{ij}^- = \{x'_{i1} x'_{j1}, x'_{i2} x'_{j2}, \ldots, x'_{im} x'_{jm}\}, \text{ negative number,}$$

$$r_{ij} = \frac{1}{2} \left(1 + \frac{n_{ij}^+ - n_{ij}^-}{n_{ij}^+ + n_{ij}^-} \right). \tag{11.14}$$

(12) **Closeness method:**

If the characteristics of x_i, x_j are normalized,

$$\text{let} \quad x_{ik}, x_{jk} \in [0, 1] \quad (k = 1, 2, \ldots, m),$$

the degree of similarity is taken as the closeness

$$r_{ij} = 1 - c(d(x_i, x_j))^\alpha, \tag{11.15}$$

where c, α are the properly selected parameter values, $d(x_i, x_j)$ is the varied distances that are possible, and the Minkowski distance can be considered as

$$d(x_i, x_j) = \left(\sum_{k=1}^{m} |x_{ik} - x_{jk}|^p \right)^{1/p}. \tag{11.16}$$

When $p = 1$, it is the Hamming distance, if $p = 2$, it is the Euclidean distance.

(13) **Expert scoring:**

Experts are asked to directly rate the similarity between x_i and x_j and take the average as r_{ij}. Generally, percentage is used, and then divided by 100 to obtain a decimal in the interval $[0, 1]$ as the similarity coefficient of the objects.

11.2.2 *Similarity Measure of Attributes*

In the clustering process, clustering can also be performed based on the similarity between the attributes. Let the similarity coefficient between the attributes A_i and A_j be r_{ij}. The main calculation methods are as follows:

(1) **Correlation coefficient method:**

$$r_{ij} = \frac{\sum_{k=1}^{m} (x_{ik} - \bar{x}_i)(x_{jk} - \bar{x}_j)}{\sqrt{\sum_{k=1}^{m} (x_{ik} - \bar{x}_i)^2} \sqrt{\sum_{k=1}^{m} (x_{jk} - \bar{x}_j)^2}}, \tag{11.17}$$

where

$$\bar{x}_i = \frac{1}{m} \sum_{k=1}^{m} x_{ik}, \quad \bar{x}_j = \frac{1}{m} \sum_{k=1}^{m} x_{jk}.$$

(2) **Angle cosine method:**

$$r_{ij} = \frac{\left| \sum_{k=1}^{m} x_{ik} x_{jk} \right|}{\sqrt{\left(\sum_{k=1}^{m} x_{ik}^2 \right) \left(\sum_{k=1}^{m} x_{jk}^2 \right)}}. \tag{11.18}$$

(3) Correlation coefficient of binary attribute:

$$r_{ij} = \frac{1}{n}\chi^2 \tag{11.19}$$

(4) Correlation coefficient of multi-valued attributes:

If the attribute A_i has m different values and A_j has t different values, multiple correlation coefficients can be defined as

(1)

$$r_{ik}(1) = \left(\frac{\chi^2}{\chi^2 + n}\right)^{\frac{1}{2}}, \tag{11.20}$$

(2)

$$r_{ik}(2) = \left(\frac{\chi^2}{n \bullet \max(t-1, m-1)}\right)^{\frac{1}{2}}, \tag{11.21}$$

(3)

$$r_{ik}(3) = \left(\frac{\chi^2}{n \bullet \min(t-1, m-1)}\right)^{\frac{1}{2}}, \tag{11.22}$$

where, n is the sum of the number of objects in the $m \times t$ list of attributes A_i and A_j:

$$\chi^2 = n \sum_{i=1}^{m} \sum_{k=1}^{t} \frac{\left(n_{ik} - \frac{n_i n_k}{n}\right)^2}{n_i n_k}. \tag{11.23}$$

Since the result of clustering depends on the method of similarity measure, the method of measure must be carefully selected according to the specific characteristics of the actual problem.

11.3 Partitioning Clustering

A partitioning method (PAM) is a method of constructing k partitions for a database with n objects or tuples. Each is divided into a class (or cluster) and $k \leq n$. Each class contains at least one object, each of which must belong to and can only belong to one class (except for fuzzy partitioning calculations). The resulting clustering will optimize an objective partitioning criterion such that objects in one cluster are "similar" and objects in different clusters are "dissimilar".

11.3.1 *K-means Algorithm*

The formal definition of knowledge representation system is $S = (U, A)$, where U is the finite set universe of discussion and A denotes the attribute set which is non-empty and finite.

The most common methods of partitioning are the K-means algorithm and the k-center point algorithm. The K-means algorithm is an iterative clustering algorithm. During the iterative process, the objects in the class are continuously moved until the ideal class set is obtained. Each class is represented by the average of the objects in the class. The cluster obtained by the K-means algorithm has a high degree of similarity among objects in the cluster, and the degree of dissimilarity between objects in different clusters is also high. The process is as follows:

Algorithm 11.1 (K-means algorithm).

1. Randomly select k objects from n data objects as the initial cluster center.
2. Calculate the average of each cluster and use the average to represent the corresponding cluster.
3. Calculate the distance between each object and these central objects, and re-divide the corresponding objects based on the minimum distance.
4. Go to step 2 and recalculate the average of each (self-changing) cluster. This process is repeated until a criterion function no longer changes significantly or the clustered object does not change.

In general, the criterion function of the K-means algorithm uses a squared error criterion, defined as

$$E = \sum_{i=1}^{k} \sum_{p \in C_i} |p - m_i|^2, \qquad (11.24)$$

where, E is the sum of the mean-squared deviations of all objects in the data set and the corresponding cluster centers, p is the given data object, and m_i is the mean of the cluster C_i.

The K-means algorithm is relatively scalable and efficient for large databases. The time complexity of the algorithm is $O(tkn)$, where t is the number of iterations. In general, it ends with a local optimal solution. However, the K-means algorithm must be used when the average value is meaningful. It is not applicable to the categorical variables. The number of clusters to be generated is given in advance. It is sensitive to noise and abnormal data and cannot be used to deal with non-convex shape data.

11.3.2 *K-medoids Algorithm*

The K-medoids algorithm, also known as partitioning around medoids (PAM), is represented by an object that is close to the center point. First, a representative object is randomly selected for each cluster, and the remaining objects are allocated to the nearest cluster according to the distance from the representative object, and then the representative object is repeatedly replaced with the non-representative object to improve the quality of the cluster. The K-medoids algorithm is as follows:

Algorithm 11.2 (K-medoids Algorithm).

1. Initialize: randomly select k of the n data points as the medoids.
2. Associate each data point to the closest medoid ("closest" here is defined using any valid distance metric, most commonly Euclidean distance, Manhattan distance, or Minkowski distance).
3. For each medoid m

    3.1 For each non-medoid data point o

        3.1.1 Swap m and o and compute the total cost of the configuration.

4. Select the configuration with the lowest cost.
5. Repeat steps 2 ~ 4 until there is no change in the medoid.

When there is noise and abnormal point data, the K-medoids algorithm is better than the K-means algorithm, but the K-medoids algorithm has higher computational cost, and the time complexity of the algorithm is $O(tk(n-k)^2)$, which is not good. It is difficult to expand to a large database.

11.3.3 *Large Database Partitioning Method*

In order to solve the clustering problem of large databases, Ng *et al.* proposed the clustering large application based upon randomized search (CLARANS) algorithm (Ng and Han, 1994).

The CLARANS algorithm combines sampling techniques with PAM, randomly sampling one sample at each step of the search, and the number of samples (numlocal) is entered as a parameter by the user. The clustering process can be described as a search for a graph where each node is a potential solution, that is, a collection of k center points. The clustering result obtained after replacing a center point is called the neighbor of the current clustering result. The number of randomly tried neighbors (maxneighbor) is limited by a user-defined parameter. If a better neighbor is found, that is, it has a smaller square-one error value, CLARANS moves to that neighbor node and processing resumes; otherwise, the current cluster reaches a local optimum. If a local optimum is found, CLARANS starts looking for a new local optimum from the randomly selected nodes. The CLARANS algorithm is as follows:

Algorithm 11.3 (CLARANS Algorithm).

1. Enter the parameters numlocal and maxneighbor. Initialize i is 1, and let mincost be a relatively large number.
2. Randomly select k targets from n targets to form a set $\{O_1, O_2, \ldots, O_k\}$, and make them as *current*.
3. Let $j = 1$.
4. Randomly select one target O_S from the remaining $n - k$ target sets in step 2, and replace one $O_l(l \in \{1, 2, \ldots, k\})$ of the set $\{O_1, O_2, \ldots, O_k\}$ with O_S, get a new set $\{\{O_m\}_{m=1,2,\ldots,k,\ m \neq l} \cup O_S\}$. The set is represented by S, and then the cost differential(*) of the 2 sets is calculated.
5. If S has a smaller cost differential, then let S as *current*, then go to step 3.
6. Increase j by 1. If $j \leq$ maxneighbor, go to step 4.
7. When $j >$ maxneighbor, compare cost(**) in current with *mincost*. If the former is less than *mincost*, let *mincost* equal to the cost of current and let bestnode be current.
8. Increase i by 1. If $i >$ *numlocal*, output bestnode and stop. Otherwise, go to step 2.

Cost is an evaluation function used to evaluate the quality of the cluster. The smaller the value, the better the clustering effect. The *mincost* records the minimum value of the objective function in the search process. Output the *best* is the final solution.

The random search of CLARANS improves the efficiency of the algorithm, and the computational complexity of the algorithm is about $O(n^2)$. However, it is also possible to reduce the quality of clustering, and its clustering quality depends on the sampling method used. In addition, the CLARANS algorithm still has the same shortcomings as other partitioning algorithms. For example, data are required to be loaded into memory, and only a local optimal solution is obtained, and the result is affected by the initial value. Erosheva *et al.* proposed the Focused CLARANS algorithm (Erosheva *et al.*, 2004), using R^*-tree for sampling, and limiting the search for solutions on related clusters and related objects, improving the efficiency of the CLARANS algorithm. Since R^*-tree organizes data according to spatial position, the data stored in the same data page are also adjacent to each other in space, and a certain number of objects are extracted from each data page of R^*-tree, and the abstraction can better reflect the distribution of data.

11.4 Hierarchical Clustering Method

A hierarchical cluster method is clustering by organizing data into groups and forming a corresponding tree. The results of hierarchical clustering can be represented by a pedigree or a binary tree. Each node in the tree is a cluster. The lower cluster is the nesting of the upper cluster, and each layer constitutes a group.

Hierarchical clustering methods can be divided into two types: top-down splitting algorithm and bottom-up condensing algorithm. The bottom-up condensed clustering strategy is to first treat each object as a cluster and then merge the adjacent clusters into one large cluster until all objects are in one cluster, or a certain termination condition is satisfied. Most hierarchical clustering methods fall into this category, and they differ only in the definition of similarity between clusters. The top-down split clustering strategy is the opposite of the condensed hierarchical clustering, which first puts all objects into one cluster and then gradually subdivides it into smaller and smaller clusters until each object becomes a cluster, or a certain end condition has been reached: for example, the number of clusters that are desired is reached, or the distance between the two closest clusters exceeds a certain threshold.

In the condensed hierarchical clustering method and the split hierarchical clustering method, the user is required to specify the expected number of clusters as the termination condition of the clustering process. Hierarchical clustering methods, although simple, often encounter difficulties in merging or splitting point selection. Such a decision is critical because once a group of objects is merged or split, the next processing will take place on the newly generated cluster. The processing that has been done cannot be undone, and the objects cannot be exchanged between clusters. If the decision to merge or split is not well chosen at a certain step, it may result in low-quality clustering results. Moreover, this clustering method does not have good scalability because the decision to merge or split requires checking and estimating a large number of objects or clusters.

In order to improve the hierarchical clustering effect, hierarchical clustering is combined with other clustering techniques to form a multi-stage clustering method, mainly including balanced iterative reducing and clustering using hierarchies (BIRCH) algorithm, clustering using representatives (CURE) algorithm, robua clustering using links (ROCK) algorithms, and so on.

11.4.1 *BIRCH Algorithm*

By introducing clustering features and clustering feature tree concepts, Zhang *et al.* (1996) proposed the BIRCH algorithm. A clustering feature is a binary group containing clusters that give a summary of the information about the object's sub-clusters. If there are N d-dimensional points or objects in a sub-cluster, the sub-cluster is defined as CF $= (N, LS, SS)$, where N is the number of points in the subclass, and LS is the linear sum of N points, SS is the sum of the squares of the points. Stored in the clustering feature tree is information about clustering, which is a key metric for computing clustering and efficient use of storage. Each leaf node contains one or more sub-clusters, each of which contains one or more objects. A clustering feature tree has two parameters: a branching factor B and a threshold T. The branching factor B defines the maximum number of descendants of each non-leaf node, the maximum diameter, and the threshold parameter T gives the sub-cluster stored in the leaf nodes of the tree. The BIRCH algorithm mainly includes two stages of scanning database and clustering.

Algorithm 11.4. BIRCH algorithm procedure. The implementation of the entire algorithm is divided into four phases

1. Scan all data, create an initialized CF tree, divide dense data into clusters, and treat sparse data as isolated points.
2. This phase is optional. The global or semi-global clustering algorithm of phase 3 has the requirements of the input range to achieve the speed and quality requirements. Therefore, based on phase 1, a smaller CF tree is established.
3. Clustering the leaf nodes of the clustering feature tree by using a clustering algorithm.
4. (Optional and offline) Cluster refining.

The BIRCH algorithm has scalability. The time complexity of the algorithm is $O(n)$ (when the clustering feature tree is not reconstructed). A basic cluster is generated by the first scan of the data set, and the secondary scan further improves the cluster quality and processes outliers. The BIRCH algorithm has a faster processing speed, but it does not work well for non-spherical clusters.

11.4.2 CURE Algorithm

Guha *et al.* proposed that the clustering using representatives (CURE) algorithm uses representative points for clustering, which solves the problem that most clustering algorithms prefer spherical and similar sizes, and it is also easy to handle abnormal points with this (Guha *et al.*, 1998). The CURE algorithm selects a fixed number of representative points in the data space to represent the cluster, and then "shrinks" or moves it toward the center of the cluster according to a specific score or contraction factor. If the representative points of the two clusters are closest, the two clusters are merged.

Since each cluster has more than one representative point, the CURE algorithm can adapt to the non-spherical geometry, and the contraction or agglomeration of the cluster can control the influence of the abnormal point, so the CURE algorithm treats the abnormal point more robustly. For large databases, the CURE algorithm has good scalability and does not degrade the quality of the cluster. The main processing steps of the CURE algorithm are as follows:

Algorithm 11.5 (CURE Algorithm).

CURE (no. of points, k)

Input: A set of points S

Output: k clusters

1. For every cluster u (each input point), in u.mean and u.rep store the mean of the points in the cluster and a set of c representative points of the cluster (initially $c = 1$ since each cluster has one data point). Also u.closest stores the cluster closest to u.
2. All the input points are inserted into a $k - d$ tree T.
3. Treat each input point as separate cluster, compute u.closest for each u and then insert each cluster into the heap Q (clusters are arranged in increasing order of distances between u and u.closest).
4. While size(Q) > k.
5. Remove the top element of Q (say u) and merge it with its closest cluster u.closest (say v) and compute the new representative points for the merged cluster w.
6. Remove u and v from T and Q.
7. For all the clusters x in Q, update x.closest and relocate x.
8. Insert w into Q.
9. Repeat.

The time complexity of the CURE algorithm is $O(n)$, and the biggest problem is that the classification attribute cannot be processed.

11.4.3 *ROCK Algorithm*

In 1999, Guha *et al.* (2000) proposed a clustering algorithm ROCK for classification of attribute data. Its outstanding contribution is to use the global information of the common neighbor (link) number as a measure to evaluate the correlation between data points, rather than the traditional local measure function based on the distance between two points.

Algorithm 11.6 (ROCK Algorithm).
  Procedure cluster(S, k)
  1. begin
  2. link: $=$ compute_links(S)
  3. for each $s \in S$ do
  4. $q[s]$: $=$ build_local_heap(link, s)
  5. Q: $=$ build_global_heap(S, q)
  6. while size(Q) $> k$ do {
  7. u: $=$ extract_max(Q)
  8. v: $=$ max(q[u])
  9.   delete(Q, v)
  10. w: $=$ merge(u, v)
  11.   for each $x \in q[u] \cup q[v]$ {
  12.   link[x, w]:$=$link[x, u] $+$ link[x, v]
  13.   delete($q[x],u$); delete($q[x],v$)
  14.   insert($q[x],w,g(x, w)$);insert($q[w],x,g(x, w)$)
  15.   update($Q,x,q[x]$)
  16.   }
  17.   insert($Q,w,q[w]$)
  18.   deallocate($q[u]$); deallocate($q[v]$)
  19. }
  20. end

Note that there are two types of queues in the algorithm, the global queue Q and the normal queue $q[i]$. The compute_links(S) in the algorithm is the number of pre-computation calculation common points. The specific process is as follows:

Procedure compute_links(S)
  1.   begin
  2.   Compute inlist[i] for every point I in S
  3.   Set link[I, j] to be zero for all i, j
  4.   for i: $= 1$ to n do {
  5. N: $=$ inlist[i];
  6.   for j: $= 1$ to $|N| - 1$ *do*
  7.   for l: $= j + 1$ to $|N|$ *do*
  8.   link[$N[j]$, N[l]]: $=$ link[$N[j]$, $N[l]$] $+ 1$
  9.   }
  10.   end

In previous algorithms, the distance or similarity between two objects was only related to the two objects themselves, but not to other objects. The ROCK algorithm extends this local operation into a global operation. When calculating the distance or similarity between two objects, not only the two objects themselves but also the influence of neighbors are considered, and the anti-noise ability of the algorithm is enhanced. In order to be able to process large-scale data, ROCK also uses a random sampling method.

11.5 Density-Based Clustering

Centered on a point in space, the number of points in a unit volume is called the density of that point. Density-based clustering uses adjacent points of similar density as a cluster according to the difference in spatial density. Density clustering continues clustering as long as the density of adjacent regions (the number of objects or data points) exceeds a certain threshold. That is, for each data point in a given class, there must be at least a certain number of points in a given region. In this way, the density clustering method can be used to filter the "noise" abnormal point data and find clusters of arbitrary shape.

In the density clustering algorithm, there is the Density-based Spatial Clustering of Application with Noise (DBSCAN) algorithm based on a high-density connection region, Ordering Points To Identify the Clustering Structure (OPTICS) algorithm based on object sorting, and Density based Clustering (DENCLUE) algorithm for function clustering.

In 1996, Ester *et al.* proposed a density-clustering algorithm DBSCAN, which clusters by growing enough high-density areas to find clusters of arbitrary shapes from spatial databases containing noise (Ester *et al.*, 1996). The DBSCAN method defines a cluster as a set of "density-connected" points. Some of the concepts involved in the basic idea of DBSCAN are as follows:

(1) **The ε-neighborhood of an object:** This is the area within the radius of the given object.
(2) **Core point:** A ε-neighbor of an object contains at least a minimum number of (MinPts) objects, which is called a core point.
(3) **Direct density reachable:** Given a set of object sets D, if p is in the ε-neighborhood of q and q is a core point, then the object p is said to be directly reachable from the object q.
(4) **Density up to:** If there is an object chain $p_1, p_2, \ldots, p_m$, where $p_1 = p$, and $p_m = q$, for $p_1 \in D, (1 \leq i \leq n)$, p_{i+1} is from p_1 with the direct density of ε and MinPts is reachable, then the object p is reachable from the object q with respect to the density of ε and MinPts.

(5) **Density connection:** If there is an object o in the object set D such that the objects p and q are reachable from o about ε and MinPts, the objects p and q are connected with respect to the density of ε and MinPts.

(6) **Boundary point:** It is the non-core point, which is directly accessible from a certain core point.

(7) **Noise:** It is a point that does not belong to any cluster at the end of clustering.

The DBSCAN algorithm first needs the user to give the radius of the cluster object an ε-neighborhood and the minimum number of objects MinPts in the ε-neighborhood, and then the algorithm checks the number of objects in an object ε-neighbor. If the number of objects is greater than MinPts, this object is the core object, and a new cluster with the object as its core is built. Then, repeatedly looking for objects from these core objects in the ε-neighborhood, this search process may merge some clusters until no new objects can be added to any cluster. A density-based cluster is the largest collection of density-connected objects based on density reachability. Objects not included in any cluster are considered "noise".

The source code for the DBSCAN algorithm in Weka is placed in the weka.clusterers package with the file name DBScan.java. The two procedures, buildClusterer and expandCluster, are the core modules. buildClusterer is the interface module for all clustering methods, and expandCluster is used to extend the high-density connection region of the sample object collection. There is also a module called epsilonRangeQuery, which is located in the Database class and is used to query the collection of sample objects of the specified object in the ε-neighborhood.

In the buildClusterer module, the expandCluster module is called for each un-clustered sample point to find the largest set of sample objects connected by the density starting from this object. The main code processed in this method is as follows. When the expandCluster module returns true, it indicates that a cluster has been formed and a cluster label is taken.

Algorithm 11.7 (DBSCAN Algorithm in WeKa).

```
Weka.DBSCAN
1.  while (iterator.hasNext()) {
2.      DataObject dataObject = (DataObject) iterator.next();
3.      if (dataObject.getClusterLabel() == DataObject.UNCLASSIFIED){
4.          if (expandCluster(dataObject)) {
5.              clusterID++;
6.              numberOfGeneratedClusters++;
7.          }
8.      }
9.  }
```

The code in the module buildClusterer is relatively simple, mainly to provide a processing entry. Let us look at the module expandCluster, which takes a sample object as a parameter. In this module, mainly do a few things: determine whether the sample object is a core object; if it is a core object, then determine each object in the ε-neighbor of the sample object and check if they are core objects; if it is a core object, merge it into the current cluster.

Procedure List seedList = database.epsilonRangeQuery(getEpsilon(), dataObject);
// Judgment if dataObject is a core object
1.   if (seedList.size() < getMinPoints()) { // Set it to a noise point if it
is not a core object
2.   dataObject.setClusterLabel(DataObject.NOISE); // After setting it
as a noise point return false to prevent the increase of
cluster number
3.   return false;
4.   }
5.   // If the sample object dataObject is a core object, then process each object
in its neighborhood
6.   for (int i = 0; i < seedList.size(); i + +) {
7.   DataObject seedListDataObject = (DataObject) seedList.get(i);
8.   // Set the cluster ID of each sample object in the dataObject neighborhood
and classify it as a cluster
9.   seedListDataObject.setClusterLabel(clusterID);
10.   // If the sample object in the neighborhood is the same object as the
current dataObject, delete it. If you don't do this, it will cause an
infinite loop.
11.   if (seedListDataObject.equals(dataObject)){
12.   seedList.remove(i);
13. i- -;
14.   }
15.   }
16.   // Processing each sample object in the ε-neighbor of the dataObject
17.   for (int j = 0; j < seedList.size(); j++) {
18.   //Take a sample object seedListDataObject from the neighborhood
19.   DataObject seedListDataObject = (DataObject) seedList.get(j);
20.   // Find the ε-neighbor of the seedListDataObject and get all the
sample objects in it
21.   List seedListDataObject_Neighborhood =
database.epsilonRangeQuery(getEpsilon(), seedListDataObject);

22. // Judgment if seedListDataObject is a core object

23. if (seedListDataObject_Neighborhood.size() >= getMinPoints())

24. for (int $i = 0$; i < seedListDataObject_Neighborhood.size(); $i++$){

25. DataObject $p =$
  (DataObject)seedListDataObject_Neighborhood.get(i);

26. // If the seedListDataObject sample object is a core object then the sample object is in the neighborhood all un-clustered objects are added to the seedList

27. // And setting the cluster label of the un-clustered object or the noise object as the current cluster label

28. if (p.getClusterLabel() == DataObject.UNCLASSIFIED ||
  p.getClusterLabel() == DataObject.NOISE) {

29. if (p.getClusterLabel() == DataObject.UNCLASSIFIED)

30. // Adding a sample object to the seedList list here is a breadth-first method. This method is used to gradually expand the current cluster.

31. // This is a very important statement. If you don't have this sentence, you can't form an extended search trend, find a full density connection area.

32. seedList.add(p);

33. }

34. p.setClusterLabel(clusterID);

35. }

36. }

37. }

38. // Remove the currently processed sample points for the same purpose as before, in order to avoid infinite loops

39. seedList.remove(j);

40. j--;

41. }

42. // After finding a complete density connection area, return true completion processing

43. return true.

The remarkable feature of DBSCAN is that it has a fast clustering speed and is not sensitive to noise. It can discover clusters of arbitrary shapes in space. If spatial indexing is used, the computational complexity of DBSCAN is $O(n \log n)$; otherwise, the computational complexity is $O(n^2)$. The algorithm is sensitive to user-defined parameters. When clustering is identified with fixed parameters, the natural structure of the cluster may be destroyed. The algorithm is based on density connectivity and density reachability. The former is symmetric non-transitive, the latter is asymmetric, and the maximal and connectivity contradictions may divide a connected cluster into two clusters.

11.6 Grid-Based Clustering

The grid clustering method quantizes the object space into a finite number of cells to form a grid structure, and all clustering operations are performed on the grid structure (quantized space). The main advantage of this method is that the processing speed is fast, and its processing time is independent of the number of data objects, only related to the number of cells in each dimension in the quantization space.

In the grid-clustering method, there is the Statistical Information Grid-based Method (STING) algorithm that uses the statistical information stored in the grid-unit to cluster, the WaveCluster method that clusters using the wavelet transform method and high-dimensional data space query, and Clustering and density-based CLIQUE (Clustering In Quest) clustering method.

The STING algorithm is a grid-based multi-resolution clustering technique that divides a spatial region into rectangular elements. For different levels of resolution, there are usually multiple levels of rectangular cells that form a hierarchy: each cell at a higher level is divided into multiple lower level cells. Statistics about each grid cell attribute (used to answer the query) are pre-computed and stored. The steps of the STING algorithm are as follows:

Algorithm 11.8 (STING Algorithm (Wang *et al.*, 1997)).
1. Determine a layer to begin with.
2. For each cell of this layer, we calculate the confidence interval (or estimated range) of probability that this cell is relevant to the query.
3. From the interval calculated above, we label the cell as *relevant* or *not relevant*.
4. If this layer is the bottom layer, go to step 6; otherwise, go to step 5.
5. We go down the hierarchy structure by one level. Go to step 2 for those cells that form the *relevant* cells of the higher-level layer.
6. If the specification of the query is met, go to step 8; otherwise, go to step 7.
7. Retrieve those data that fall into the *relevant* cells and do further processing. Return the result that meets the requirement of the query. Go to step 9.
8. Find the regions of *relevant* cells. Return those regions that meet the requirement of the query. Go to step 9.
9. Stop.

When STING scans the database, the spatial area is divided into rectangular units to establish a hierarchical structure. Each unit has 4 subunits, which store statistical information of each unit, such as the number of objects, center, variance, maximum value, minimum value, and data distribution type. The information of the upper unit is calculated by the subunit.

In 1996, Schikuta proposed a grid-based hierarchical clustering algorithm Balanced and Nested Grid (BANG) which clusters according to the location stored in the grid file (Schikuta, 1996). The BANG algorithm is basically as follows:

Algorithm 11.9 (Grid-based hierarchical clustering algorithm, BANG).

1. Insertion of patterns into the Grid Structure
2. Calculation of density indices
3. Sorting of the blocks with respect to density indices
4. Identification of cluster centers
5. Traversal of neighbor blocks

Later, Schikuta and Erhart (1997) developed the BANG-clustering algorithm based on the BANG structure.

Sheikholeslami *et al.* (1998) introduced the principle of wavelet transform into clustering research and proposed the WaveCluster method. The method first summarizes the number by imposing a multidimensional grid structure on the data space. According to each grid element, a set of information mapped to the points in the unit is summarized, and then a wavelet transform is used to transform the original feature space. The summary information is used in the wavelet transform, and then found in the transformed space: Cluster area. The algorithm of WaveCluster is as follows:

Algorithm 11.10 (WaveCluster Algorithm).

Input: Multidimensional data objects' feature vectors

Output: clustered objects

1. Quantize feature space, then assign objects to the units.
2. Apply wavelet transform on the feature space.
3. Find the connected components (clusters) in the sub-bands of transformed feature space, at different levels.
4. Assign label to the units.
5. Make the lookup table.
6. Map the objects to the clusters.

Due to the characteristics of wavelet transform, the algorithm has many advantages: it can effectively process large data sets, find clusters of arbitrary shape, successfully process isolated abnormal points, is insensitive to the order of input, and does not require specifying the number of result clusters or Input parameters, and neighborhood radius. The experimental analysis found that WaveCluster is superior to CLARANS and DBSCAN in efficiency and clustering quality, while WaveCluster can process up to 20-D data, and the speed is very fast, and the complexity is $O(n)$.

11.7 Model-Based Clustering

The model-based clustering method assumes a model for each cluster, looking for the best fit of the data to a given model. It attempts to optimize the adaptability between the given data and certain mathematical models. Model-based methods often assume that the data are generated based on the potential probability distribution. The algorithm mainly has two kinds of statistics and neural network.

In 1987, Fisher proposed the COBWEB algorithm (Fisher, 1987). COBWEB is a popular simple incremental concept clustering algorithm. Its input object is described by a pair of classification attributes. COBWEB creates hierarchical clusters in the form of a classification tree. The classification tree is different from the decision tree. Each node in the classification tree corresponds to a concept that contains a probabilistic description of the concept, summarizing the objects that are classified under that node. The probability description includes the probability of the concept and the conditional probability of the form $P(A_i = V_{ij}|C_k)$, where $A_i = V_{ij}$ is the attribute–value pair and C_k is the concept class (the count is accumulated and stored in each node of the calculated probability). This is different from the decision tree, which determines that the tree marks branches rather than nodes and uses logical descriptors instead of probability descriptors. A sibling at a certain level of the classification tree forms a division. To classify an object with a classification tree, a partial matching function is used to move down the tree along the path of the "best" matching node.

COBWEB uses classification utility as a heuristic evaluation metric to aid in the construction of the tree. The classification utility is defined as follows:

$$\frac{\sum_{k-1}^{n} P(C_k)\left[\sum_i \sum_j P(A_i = V_{ij}|C_k)^2 - \sum_i \sum_j P(A_i = V_{ij})^2\right]}{n}, \quad (11.25)$$

where, n is the number of nodes, concepts, or categories that form a partition $\{C_1, C_2, \ldots, C_n\}$ at a certain level of the tree. The probability $P(A_i = V_{ij}|C_k)$ represents intra-class similarity. The larger the value, the larger the proportion of class members sharing the attribute–value pair, and it is more predictable that the attribute–value pair is a class member. The probability $P(C_k|A_i = V_{ij})$ represents the dissimilarity between classes. The larger the value, the fewer pairs of attribute–values that objects in the control class share with the attribute, and the more predictable that the attribute–value pair is a class member.

COBWEB also has its limitations. First, it is based on the assumption that the probability distributions on each attribute are independent of each other. Since attributes are often related, this assumption is not always true. Furthermore, the probability distribution representation of clustering makes updating and storing clusters rather expensive. Because time and space complexity depends not only on the number of attributes but also on the number of values for each attribute, this is especially true when the attribute has a large number of values. Moreover, classification trees are not highly balanced for skewed input data, which can lead to dramatic changes in time and space complexity.

AutoClass is a data-clustering algorithm based on Bayesian theory (Cheeseman *et al.*, 1996). By processing the data, the probability value of each data belongs to each category, and the data are clustered. AutoClass can accurately and automatically cluster complex data. You can set the number of categories in advance to let AutoClass find it automatically. After the search is finished, you can get the probability that each piece of data belongs to each category. The AutoClass program was developed in 1995 by Cheeseman and Stutz and is available on the website (http://ti.arc.nasa.gov/ic/projects/bayes-group/autoclass/autoclassc).

Compared to other algorithms, AutoClass has the following advantages:

(1) Clustered data do not require pre-specified categories of data, but each data member is defined.
(2) It can process continuous or discrete data. In AutoClass, each set of data is represented by a vector, each of which represents a different attribute, which can be continuous or discrete.
(3) AutoClass requires data to be stored in two parts: Data File and Header File. This allows users to freely mix Data File and Header File to save time on input data.
(4) The missing value data can be processed. AutoClass can still cluster this set of data when there are gaps in certain attribute values in a set of data.

At the same time, AutoClass also has the following disadvantages:

(1) The premise of the AutoClass probability model is that the attributes are independent of each other, and this assumption is not true in many fields.

(2) AutoClass is not a fully automated clustering algorithm that requires subjectively determining the appropriate population range of data, but this problem is a major problem of clustering.

(3) When using AutoClass to process data, it is necessary to repeat the assumptions and tests and combine professional knowledge and procedures to get good results, which takes a lot of time.

(4) There is no *a priori* criterion to predict whether a set of data can be clustered, and thus there is a certain degree of stagnation. There is no post-test method to assess whether the results of the classification are trustworthy.

Due to these advantages and disadvantages of AutoClass, it is necessary to apply professional knowledge in clustering to first make a reasonable judgment on the data, overcome the shortcomings of AutoClass itself, and exert its advantages, so that scientific and reasonable clustering results can be obtained.

11.8 Semi-Supervised Clustering

Among all methods for unsupervised learning, clustering is possibly the most widely used technique. One of the research areas that has been receiving increasing attention in the last decade is the use of additional information regarding the problem, incorporated to the problem by using constraints that the elements must satisfy. This area is called "constrained clustering" (Basu *et al.*, 2008) and has been applied to a wide range of fields.

There are two different approaches reported in the literature for constrained clustering, and both are based on the concept of "Must-Link" and "Cannot-Link" restrictions. The first set of constraints indicates that two elements must always belong to the same cluster, whereas the second one does not permit the presence of two elements in the same cluster. In 2001, Wagstaff *et al.* (2001) proposed the constrained k-means clustering algorithm COP-KMEANS. The algorithm takes in a data set (D), a set of must-link constraints $(Con=)$, and a set of cannot-link constraints $(Con\neq)$. It returns a partition of the instances in D that satisfies all specified constraints.

Bravo *et al.* developed a constrained clustering with filtering (CCF) algorithm as follows (Bravo and Weber, 2011):

Algorithm 11.11 (Constrained Clustering with Filtering (CCF) Algorithm).
    Procedure CCF(Dataset X, R_1, R_2, b_1, b_2)
    1. $C = (C_1, C_2) \leftarrow$ Random(size(2))
    2.   Flag $\leftarrow 1^N$ {If element is used or outlier}

3.   while Movement in C > ε do
4.   Assign elements to closest cluster
5. $M_1 \leftarrow X(\text{cluster} = 1)$
6. $M_2 \leftarrow X(\text{cluster} = 2)$
7.   Calculate ext_1 and ext_2 from vectors $M_2 \cdot b_2$ and $M_1 \cdot b_2$
8.   Violations $\leftarrow 0$, Eliminated $\leftarrow 0$
9.   while Eliminated $< 0.01N$ or Violations $> \varepsilon$ do
10.   for $i = 1$ to N do
11.   if Flag$(i) = 0$ then
12.   Skip i
13.   end if
14.   if Cluster$(x_i) = 1$ then
15. $R \leftarrow R_1 \cdot x_i$
16.   else
17. $R \leftarrow R_2 \cdot x_i$
18.   end if
19.   if Element i violates conditions then
20.   Change cluster of element
21.   Violations $\leftarrow$ Violations $+1$
22.   end if
23.   end for
24.   if Violations $> \varepsilon$ then
25.   Flag$(I(\text{ext}_2)) \leftarrow 0$, Flag$(I(\text{ext}_1)) \leftarrow 0$
26.   Eliminated $\leftarrow$ Eliminated $+2$
27.   end if
28.   Recalculate$(M_1, M_2, \text{ext}_1, \text{ext}_2)$
29.   end while
30.   Recalculate(C)
31.   end while

CCF algorithm takes into account the constraints that must be satisfied and takes advantage of the fact that the linear restrictions are bound to possess a maximum or minimum value in the data set, that is, that given a fixed distribution of elements in the cluster, only the values ext_1 and ext_2 have to be checked against the elements of the cluster. The procedure starts with random centroids, and in each iteration the elements in the cluster are compared to the extreme value of the other cluster, i.e., if the element is in cluster 1, then it is checked whether restriction $R_1 \cdot x_i^1 (\geq \vee \leq)\text{ext}_1$ is satisfied with the largest or smallest element present in cluster 2, according to what is necessary. In case at the end of the movements the conditions are not fulfilled by all cases, then the extreme values in both clusters are removed from the analysis and the process is repeated. The algorithm continues until both the violations are below a threshold and the values of the centroids do not move more than a given tolerance.

The elements in each cluster have to satisfy the restrictions against most of the elements in the other cluster, and this is accomplished by eliminating a small number of extreme cases in each iteration and ensuring that all others satisfy the constraints. At each step, the minimum variance cluster is approximated, and it is this one solution that is perturbed by moving the elements according to the constraints. The convergence of the algorithm is ensured, since at worst case (infeasible problem) only two elements will remain and the method will stop with one element per cluster.

11.9 Evaluation of Clustering Methods

The clustering results reflect the distribution characteristics of the data, and the clustering method is used to analyze the unknown data, and a meaningful pattern can be found. Since clustering is unsupervised learning, clustering seems to be difficult to assess without the given class labeling. Classification or association learning has an objective criterion for success, that is, whether the prediction of test data is accurate or incorrect, but clustering is not. Moreover, the objective functions of the clustering process are different, and there are a large number of different cluster types. To measure the performance of data clustering algorithms, there are usually the following indicators

(1) **Scalability.** If an algorithm is applied to both small data sets and clustering on large databases without biased results, the algorithm is highly scalable.

(2) **The ability to handle different types of attributes.** Some algorithms can only be used to cluster numerical data, but in some applications cluster non-numeric data are required.

(3) **Discover clusters of arbitrary shapes.** Many distance-based algorithms can only find spherical clusters with similar dimensions and densities. It is important for the algorithm to find clusters of arbitrary shape, such as spirals.

(4) **The minimum parameters and domain knowledge to determine the parameter values.** Many clustering algorithms require the user to enter certain parameters, such as the number of clusters that are desired to be generated. The clustering results are very sensitive to the input parameters, and the input parameters add a burden to the user, so it should be avoided as much as possible.

(5) **The ability to process noise data.** Most databases contain isolated points, vacancies, unknown data, or erroneous data, and algorithms should minimize the impact of these data.

(6) **It is not sensitive to the order of input records.** The algorithm can be independent of the input order of the collection.

(7) **High dimensionality.** The algorithm can handle high-dimensional data while coping with low-dimensional data. For example, very sparse, highly skewed data in high-dimensional space.

(8) **Constraint-based clustering.** Real-world applications may require clustering under various constraints.

(9) **Interpretability and usability.** The user desires that the clustering results are interpretable, understandable, and usable.

The purpose of clustering is to give an optimal partition of the data. The so-called "optimal" is to divide similar data into the same cluster as much as possible, and the same data are not divided into different clusters as much as possible. For this purpose, homogeneity and heterogeneity are defined.

The homogeneity of a cluster is defined as the average similarity between members belonging to the cluster. Suppose the similarity between two objects x_i, x_j is $\text{sim}(x_i, x_j) \in [0, 1]$, the homogeneity of cluster C_p is calculated as follows:

(1)
$$\text{Hom}_1(C_p) = \min_{i,j=1}^{|C_p|} \text{sim}(x_i, x_j) \tag{11.26}$$

(2)
$$\text{Hom}_2(C_p) = \frac{1}{|C_p|^2} \sum_{i=1}^{|C_p|} \sum_{j=1}^{|C_p|} \text{sim}(x_i, x_j) \tag{11.27}$$

Similarly, the formulas for calculating the heterogeneity of two clusters $C_p, C_q (p \neq q)$ are as follows:

(1)
$$\text{Het}_1(C_p, C_q) = \max_{i,j=1}^{|C_p|,|C_q|} \text{sim}(x_i, x_j) \tag{11.28}$$

(2)
$$\text{Het}_2(C_p, C_q) = \frac{1}{|C_p||C_q|} \sum_{i=1}^{|C_p|} \sum_{j=1}^{|C_p|} \text{sim}(x_i, x_j) \tag{11.29}$$

The quality of the cluster can be evaluated by the compactness within the cluster and the separation between the clusters. Compactness reflects the degree of similarity between members belonging to the same cluster, expressed as

$$\text{Compactness}(C) = \sum_{i=1}^{k} \frac{\text{Hom}(C_i)}{k}. \tag{11.30}$$

The degree of separation of clusters reflects the degree of similarity between members belonging to different clusters, expressed as

$$\text{Seperation}(C) = 1 - \sum_{i=1}^{k} \sum_{j=1}^{k} \frac{\text{Het}(C_i, C_j)}{k^2}. \tag{11.31}$$

Using the compactness within the cluster and the degree of separation between the clusters to evaluate the quality of the cluster overcomes the limitations of the objective function, so that the evaluation of the clustering results is not affected by the number of clusters.

Exercises

11.1 What is unsupervised learning? What is the difference between it and supervised learning?

11.2 Object clustering uses distance or similarity coefficient to measure similarity. List the main methods to compute the similarity coefficient.

11.3 Briefly describe clustering methods, partitioning clustering, density-based methods, grid-based methods, and model-based methods. Give an example for each method.

11.4 Use the Euclidean distance as the distance function and use the k-means algorithm to cluster the following 8 points:

$$A_1(2, 10), \ A_2(2, 5), \ A_3(8, 4),$$
$$B_1(5, 8), \ B_2(7, 5), \ B_3(6, 4),$$
$$C_1(1, 2), \ C_2(4, 9).$$

11.5 The model-based clustering method assumes a model for each cluster, looking for the best fit of the data to a given model. Illustrate the principle by example.

11.6 Explain the characteristics of semi-supervised clustering methods.

Chapter 12

Association Rules

Association rule learning is a rule-based machine learning method for discovering interesting relations between variables in large databases. It is intended to identify strong rules discovered in databases using some measures of interestingness, extracted if-then rules from a set of data.

12.1 Introduction

The purpose of the association rule mining is to find out a hidden associated relation between different sets of data fields in a database. It is one of the most widely used and more studied data mining methods. The association rule model is an important model among knowledge models in data mining. The concept of the association rule was proposed by Agrawal *et al.* (1993). It is a kind of simple but very practical rule about data relations. The model of association rule belongs to the description pattern and the algorithm, which discovers the association rule belonging to non-supervised learning.

At the present, the trends of the research on association rules are as follows:

(1) *Discover association rules from the concept with single layer to multiple layers*: That is, the mining rule should effect on different layers of the database. For example, in the analysis of sell database of a supermarket, if only the original fields of table, such as "bread", "milk" were mined, it will be difficult to discover interesting rules. When some abstract concept about original fields, such as "food", is considered for mining, some new and abstract rules will be probably found. So, mining on different abstract layers in the database to discover rules and metarules is a new research direction.

(2) *Improve the efficiency of mining algorithm*: Usually, large quantities of data were processed in association rule mining and database may be scanned many times. So, it is important to improve the efficiency of the mining algorithm. There exist three methods: one is to reduce the number of times of a database is scanned, which it would improve the efficiency greatly. Another is sampling technology, which selects the data sets for data mining. This method is efficient in the applications which pay attention to efficiency. The other method is parallel data mining. Because large-scale data in the database are often located in different nodes in network, parallel data mining can improve the efficiency apparently. This method is often used in Web mining on Internet.

(3) Besides, key research topics also contain how to control the total scale of association rules, how to select and deal with the acquired rules, and how to discover fuzzy association rules and the mining algorithm with high efficiency. From the point of view of the mining object, a valuable problem to consider is how to extend rule mining from relation database to text and Web data in the future.

Association rules mine mainly from the transaction database, such as sales data in supermarkets, also called basket data. A transaction typically includes a unique transaction identity number and a list of the items making up the transaction. In transaction databases, we will investigate transactions with many items. Suppose product A appears in transaction 1, product B appears in transaction 2, we want to know how products A and B appear in a transaction. In the knowledge discovery of database, association rule is a knowledge pattern which describes how some products appear in a transaction. Association rule learners are used to discover elements that co-occur frequently within a data set consisting of multiple independent selections of elements (such as purchasing transactions), and to discover rules, such as implication or correlation, which relate to co-occurring elements. Questions such as "if a customer purchases product A, how likely is he to purchase product B?" and "What products will a customer buy if he buys products C and D?" are answered by association-finding algorithms. This application of association rule learners is also known as market basket analysis. As with most data mining techniques, the task is to reduce a potentially huge amount of information to a small, understandable set of statistically supported statements.

Let $R = \{I_1, I_2, \ldots, I_m\}$ be a itemset, and W be a set of transactions. Each transaction T, which is in W, is an itemset, $T \subseteq R$. Suppose A is an itemset, T is a transaction and $A \subseteq T$, we call transaction T supports set A. A_n association rule is an implication of the form $A \Rightarrow B$, where A, B are two itemsets, $A \subset R$, $B \subset R$, and $A \cap B = \emptyset$. Usually, the following four parameters are applied to describe the attributes of rules:

(1) **Confidence:** Suppose $c\%$ transactions which support itemset A in W also support itemset B at the same time, then $c\%$ is the confidence of association rule $A \Rightarrow B$. That is, confidence stands for the probability that an itemset A occurs in the transaction T and an itemset B also occurs in transaction T. The rule $A \Rightarrow B$ has confidence c in the transaction set W, where c is the percentage of transactions in W containing A that also contains B. This is taken to be the conditional probability, $P(B|A)$. That is,

$$\text{confidence}(A \Rightarrow B) = P(B|A). \tag{12.1}$$

For example, suppose 70% of consumers who bought bread also bought butter, then the confidence is 70%.

(2) **Support:** Suppose $s\%$ transactions in W support both the itemsets A and B, $s\%$ is called the support of rule $A \Rightarrow B$. The rule $A \Rightarrow B$ holds in the transaction set W with support s, where s is the percentage of transactions in W that contain $A \cup B$, that is, the union of set A and B. This is taken to be the probability, $P(A \cup B)$ which indicates a transaction contains the union of set A and set B. For example, suppose there are 1,000 customers in a supermarket some day and among them 100 customers purchased both bread and butter, then the support of $A \Rightarrow B$ is 10%(100/1,000).

(3) **Expected Confidence:** Suppose $e\%$ transactions in W support the itemset B, then e% is called the expected confidence of rule $A \Rightarrow B$. Expected confidence reflects the probability of the itemset B occurring in all transactions when there are no other restrictions. For example, suppose there are 1,000 customers in a supermarket and 200 customers purchased butter, then the expected confidence of $A \Rightarrow B$ is 20%.

(4) **Lift:** Lift is the ratio of confidence to the expected confidence. Lift reflects the influence with the occurrence of itemsets A to the occurrence of itemset B. Because the expected confidence is the probability of the occurrence of set B in all transactions, the confidence is the probability of the occurrence of set B in the transactions in which set A is presented. Then the ratio of confidence to the expected confidence reflects the change of probability of the occurrence of set B when the precondition "the occurrence of set A" is added. The lift between the occurrence of A and B can be measured by computing

$$\text{lift}(A, B) = \frac{P(A \cup B)}{P(A)P(B)}. \tag{12.2}$$

In the above example, the lift is $70\%/20\% = 3.5$.

Table 12.1.   Formula of the four parameters

Name	Description	Formula
Confidence	The probability of the occurrence of itemset B when itemset A occurs	$P(B|A)$
Support	The probability of the occurrence of both itemset A and itemset B	$P(A \cup B)$
Expected confidence	The probability of the occurrence of itemset B	$P(B)$
Lift	The ratio of confidence to the expected confidence	$P(B|A)/P(B)$

Let $P(A)$ be the probability of the occurrence of itemset A, $P(B|A)$ be the probability of the occurrence of itemset B when itemset A occurs, then the above four parameters can be expressed as shown in Table 12.1.

Confidence is a precise measure for an association rule. Support is a measure for the importance of an association rule. Support stands for the importance of a rule and the more the support is, the more important the rule is. There are rules which are with high confidence but low support, which means that the rule is neither important nor practical.

Expected confidence describes the support of itemset B where there is no influence from itemset A. Lift describes the influence of itemset A on itemset B. A great lift shows a great influence of itemset A on itemset B. Generally, the lift is often greater than 1 when the rule is practical for applications. Only when the confidence is greater than the expected confidence, the presence of A has promoted the effect on the presence of B and it shows itemsets A and B are related on some grade. If the lift is less than 1, it shows that the rule has no meaning.

Note that among the four parameters, confidence and support are used frequently.

12.2 The Apriori Algorithm

The association rule mining is to discover the rules with the minimum support (minsup) and the minimum confidence (minconf) defined by users from transaction databases. The problem of association rule mining can be decomposed into the following two sub-problems:

(1) **Find all large itemsets (or frequent itemsets) in a transaction database:** The large itemset is defined as the itemset X with support(X) no less than the minsup defined by user.

(2) **Generate association rules from large itemsets:** For every large itemset A, if $B \subset A$, $B \neq \emptyset$, and confidence($B \Rightarrow (A - B)$) $\geq$ minconf, then construct the rule $B \Rightarrow (A - B)$.

The second sub-problem is easier than the first one. Most research works focus on the first sub-problem. So, we introduce the algorithm which is concerned with the first sub-problem.

The famous Apriori algorithm concentrates on mining frequent itemsets for Boolean association rules (Agrawal *et al.*, 1993, 1994). The name of the algorithm is based on the fact that the algorithm uses prior knowledge of frequent itemset properties. Apriori employs breadth-first search, where k-itemsets are used to explore $(k + 1)$-itemsets. First, the set of frequent 1-itemsets is found by scanning the database to accumulate the count for each item, and collecting those items that satisfy minimum support. The resulting set is denoted as L_1. Next, L_1 is used to find L_2, the set of frequent two-itemsets, which is used to find L_3, and so on, until no more frequent k-itemsets can be found. We give the classical Apriori algorithm as follows:

Algorithm 12.1 (Apriori Algorithm (Agrawal, 1994)).
    Input: DB, a database of transactions;
        minsup, the minimum support count threshold.
    Output: L, frequent itemsets in DB
    Method:
    1. L_1 = find_frequent_1-itemsets(DB);
    2. for $(k = 2; L_{k-1} \neq \emptyset; k++)\{$
    3. C_k = apriori_gen(L_{k-1});
    4.   for each transaction $T \in$ DB{ //scan DB for counts
    5. C_T = subset(C_k ,T); //get the subsets of T that are candidates
    6.   for each candidate $c \in C_T$
    7. c.count++
    8.   }
    9. L_k = $\{c \in C_k | c$.count$\geq$minsup$\}$
    10. }
    11. return $L = \bigcup_k L_k$

Procedure apriori_gen(L_{k-1}: frequent($k - 1$)-itemsets)
    1. for each itemset $l_1 \in L_{k-1}$
    2.   for each itemset $l_2 \in L_{k-1}$
    3.   if($l_1[1] = l_2[1]$) $\bigwedge (l_1[2] = l_2[2])$ $\bigwedge \cdots \bigwedge (l_1[k - 2] = l_2[k - 2]) \bigwedge (l_1[k - 1] = l_2[k - 1])$ then{
    4. $c = l_1 \bowtie l_2$; //join step: generate candidates

5.   if has_infrenquent_subset(c, L_{k-1}) then
6.   delete c; //prune step: remove unfruitful candidate
7.   else add c to C_k;
8.   }
9.   return C_k.

Procedure has_infrequent_subset(c: candidate$k$−itemset;
                    L_{k-1}: frequent($k - 1$)-itemsets; //use prior knowledge
1.   for each ($k - 1$)-subset s of c
2.   if $s \notin L_{k+1}$ then
3.   return TRUE;
4.   return FALSE.

Apriori algorithm scans DB several times and calculates k-itemsets in k times. If the number of elements in the top itemset is k at most, then the algorithm will scan DB k times, or $k + 1$ time. Hash approach was used to improve Apriori algorithm. It minuses the verified record T to support the calculation of C_k by means of reducing the number of candidate itemsets, reducing the length of record and reducing the total number of records. There is the concept of negative boundary in the sampling algorithm. It utilizes the downward closeness of frequent itemsets. Suppose there is a downward close power set of an itemset SI, if all subsets of the itemset s are subsumed by S and the set is not subsumed by S itself, then the set will be an element of the negative boundary. All elements with these attributes form negative boundary, which is marked as Bd(S). For example, if $I = \{A, B, C, D, E\}$, $S = \{\{A\}, \{B\}, \{C\}, \{E\}, \{A, B\}, \{A, C\}, \{A, E\}, \{C, E\}, \{A, C, E\}\}$, then Bd($S$) $= \{\{B, C\}, \{B, E\}, \{D\}\}$. S is the superset of itemsets with high frequency if none of the sets in Bd(S) is with high frequency.

For database DB in Figure 12.1, we can get the candidate itemsets C_1 when we count the number of every item by scanning the whole sets of transaction in the first scanning of database. If the minimum support is 2, then the single dimension of itemsets L_1 is produced. Because there is the minimum support of any subset of large itemsets, Apriori calculates the L_2 using $L_1 * L_1$. The operation $*$ is defined as

$$L_1 * L_2 = \{X \cup Y | X, Y \in L_{k,} |X \cap Y| = k - 1\}.$$

Then the candidate itemset C_2 is produced and L_2 is produced from the minimum support. From L_2 to C_3, the two itemsets which have the same head item $\{BC\}$ and $\{BE\}$ will be confirmed. Then the rear itemsets $\{BC\}$ and $\{BE\}$, which are defined as $\{CE\}$, are tested if they are satisfied with the minimum support. Because they are satisfied with the minimum support, all the two-dimension subsets of $\{BCE\}$

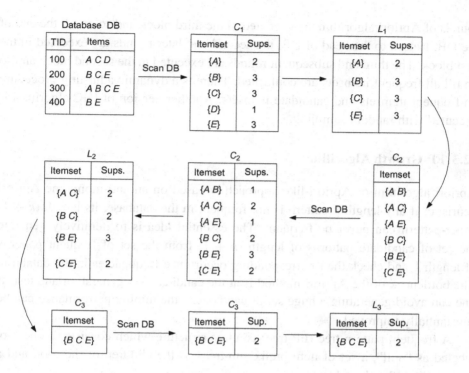

Fig. 12.1. Generation of candidate sets of items and sets of items

are large itemsets, so {*BCE*} is a candidate itemset. Because there are no any three-dimensional candidate itemsets from L_2, C_3 is confirmed and L_3 is gained. Then there are no higher dimension itemsets any more. So, the whole large itemsets are confirmed.

Except Apriori algorithm, sampling algorithm and DIC algorithm are classical association rule mining algorithm. The main idea of the sampling algorithm is to define a value lowsup which is less than minsup and to calculate the itemsets which Support(db(X)) >lowsup on sampling data with the help of algorithm of sampling. This itemset is marked as S. Suppose S is the super set of frequent itemsets. Negative boundary Bd(S) is calculated. Scanning DB and S and the support of Bd(S) are calculated. If no set in Bd(S) is a frequent itemset, then S is the super set of frequent itemsets. Otherwise, failure is reported and frequent itemsets in Bd(S) are added into S. The negative boundary of Bd(S) is calculated and DB is scanned and so on until no frequent itemsets can be added into S.

A DB is divided by M blocks in DIC algorithm. The first around of Apriori algorithm is executed in the first block. The first and the second rounds of Apriori algorithm are executed in the second block. The first, the second, and the third rounds of Apriori algorithm are executed in the third block and so on till the end of the DB. Return to the head of DB, the second and later rounds are executed in the first block. The third and subsequent rounds are executed in the second block and so on till all frequent itemsets are confirmed. There is a dynamic adjusting procedure on frequent itemsets and candidate itemsets. Another version of DIC algorithm is executed with random sampling.

12.3 FP-Growth Algorithm

Apriori algorithm or Apriori-like approach is based on an anti-monotone Apriori heuristic: if any length k pattern is not frequent in the database, its length $(k + 1)$ super-pattern can never be frequent. The essential idea is to iteratively generate the set of candidate patterns of length $(k + 1)$ from the set of frequent patterns of length k and check their corresponding occurrence frequencies in the database. The bottleneck of the Apriori method is at the candidate set generation and test. If one can avoid generating a huge set of candidates, the mining performance can be substantially improved.

A frequent pattern tree (FP-tree) is a tree structure which consists of one root labeled as "null", a set of item prefix sub-trees as the children of the root, and a frequent-item header table.

Each node in the item prefix sub-tree consists of three fields: item-name, count, and node-link, where item-name registers which item this node represents, count registered number of transactions represented by the portion of the path reaching this node, and node-link links to the next node in the FP-tree carrying the same item-name, or null if there is none. Each entry in the frequent-item header table consists of two fields, item-name and head of node-link, which points to the first node in the FP-tree carrying the item-name. FP-tree construction algorithm is as follows:

Algorithm 12.2 (FP-tree construction (Han *et al.*, 2000)).
    Input: DB, a database of transactions;
            minsup, the minimum support count threshold.
    Output: FP-tree, frequent pattern tree.
    Method:

1. Scan the transaction database DB once. Collect the set of frequent items F and their support s. Sort F in support descending order as L, the list of frequent items.

2. Create the root of an FP-tree, T, and label it as "null". For each transaction T in DB, do the following. Select and sort the frequent items in T according to

the order of L. Let the sorted frequent item list in T be $[p|P]$, where p is the first element and P is the remaining list. Call insert_tree($[p|P]$, T).

Procedure: insert_tree($[p|P]$, T)

1. if T has a child N and N.item-name = p.item-name, then increment N's is counted by 1;

2. else create a new node N, and let its count be 1, let its parent link be linked to T, and its node-link be linked to the nodes with the same item-name via the node-link structure;

3. if P is non-empty, call Insert_tree(P, N) recursively.

Table 12.2 lists a transaction database. We can use Algorithm 12.2 to construct an FP-Tree shown in Figure 12.2. First, a scan of DB derives a list of frequent items, $\{(f:4), (c:4), (a:3), (b:3), (m:3), (p:3)\}$, in which items are ordered in frequency descending order. This ordering is important since each path of a tree will follow this order. Second, one may create the root of a tree, labeled with "null". Scan the DB the second time. The scan of the first transaction leads to the construction of the first branch of the tree: $\{(f:1), (c:1), (a:1), (m:1), (p:1)\}$. For the second transaction, since its (ordered) frequent item list $\{f, c, a, b, m\}$ shares a common prefix $\{f, c, a\}$ with the existing path $\{f, c, a, m, p\}$, the count of each node along the prefix is incremented by 1, and one new node $\{b:1\}$ is created and linked as a child of $\{a:2\}$ and another new node $\{m:1\}$ is created and linked as the child of $\{b:1\}$. For the third transaction, since its frequent item list $\{f, b\}$ shares only the node $\{f\}$ with the f-prefix sub-tree, f's count is incremented by 1, and a new node $\{b:1\}$ is created and linked as a child of $\{f:3\}$. The scan of the fourth transaction leads to the construction of the second branch of the tree, $\{(c:1), (b:1), (p:1)\}$. For the last transaction, since its frequent item list $\{f, c, a, m, p\}$ is identical to the first one, the path is shared with the count of each node along the path incremented by 1. To facilitate tree traversal, an item header table is built in which each item points to its occurrence in the tree via a head of the node-link. Nodes with the

Table 12.2. Transaction database (Han *et al.*, 2000)

TID	Items bought	(Ordered) Frequent items
100	f, a, c, d, g, i, m, p	f, c, a, m, p
200	a, b, c, f, l, m, o	f, c, a, b, m
300	b, f, h, j, o	f, b
400	b, c, k, s, p	c, b, p
500	a, f, c, e, l, p, m, n	f, c, a, m, p

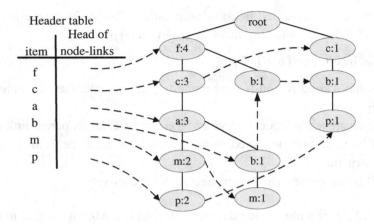

Fig. 12.2.   A FP-tree in Table 12.1

same item-name are linked in sequence via such node-links. After scanning all the transactions, the tree with the associated node-links is built and shown in Figure 12.2 (Han *et al.*, 2000).

FP-tree based association rules mining method transforms the problem of finding long frequent patterns to search for shorter ones recursively and then concatenating the suffix. It uses the least frequent items as suffix, offering good selectivity. FP-growth algorithm is summarized as follows:

Algorithm 12.3 (FP-growth Algorithm).
   Input: FP-tree, constructed based on Algorithm 12.2;
            minsup, the minimum support count threshold.
   Output: The complete set of frequent patterns.
   Method: FP-growth (FP-tree, α).
   1.   if FP-tree contains a single path P then
   2.   for each combination (denoted as β) of the nodes in the path P
   3.   generate pattern $\beta \cup \alpha$ with support_count = minimum support count
               of nodes in β;
   4.   else for each a_i in the header of FP-tree {
   5.   generate pattern $\beta = a_i \cup \bigcup \alpha$ with support_count = a_i.support_count;
   6.   construct β's conditional pattern base and then β's conditional FP-tree;
   7.   if FP-tree$_\beta \neq \emptyset$ then
   8.   call FP-growth (FP-tree$_\beta$, β);
   9.   }

The FP-growth method shows that it is efficient and scalable for mining frequent patterns. The method substantially reduces the search cost and is about an order of magnitude faster than the Apriori algorithm.

12.4 CFP-Tree Algorithm

In FP-growth algorithm, there are six fields in the FP-tree node, containing item-name, count, parent-link, child-link, sibling-link, and next-link (a pointer to the next node that has the same item-name). However, child-link and sibling-link are only used in the FP-tree constructing process, parent-link and next-link are only used in the mining process. So, we can reduce the number of fields by joining child-link with parent-link as cp-link which is first pointing to its child-node and after construction pointing to its parent node, and joining sibling-link with next-link as sn-link which is first pointing to its sibling-node and finally pointing to the next node (Qin *et al.*, 2004).

The compact FP-tree (CFP-tree) has similar structure as FP-tree, but there are several differences between them as follows:

(1) Each node in CFP-tree has four fields, item-no (which is the sequential number of an item in frequent 1-itemsets according to frequency descending order), count, cp-link and sn-link. Therefore, CFP-tree requires only 2/3 memory spaces of FP-tree.
(2) FP-tree is bidirectional, but CFP-tree is single directional. After the construction, CFP-tree only exists paths from leaves to the root.

The CFP-tree is constructed by Algorithm 12.4.

Algorithm 12.4 (CFP-tree Construction).
　Input: DB, a database of transactions;
　　　　minsup, the minimum support count threshold.
　Output: CFP-tree, compact frequent pattern tree.
　Method:

　　1. Scan the transaction database DB once. Collect the set of frequent items F and their supports. Sort F in support descending order as L, the list of frequent items.

　　2. Create the root of an FP-tree, T, and label it as "null". For each transaction in DB, do the following. Select the frequent items and replace them with their order in L, and sort them as Is. Let the sorted Is be $[p|P]$, where p is the first element and P is the remaining list. Call insert tree($[p|P]$, T).

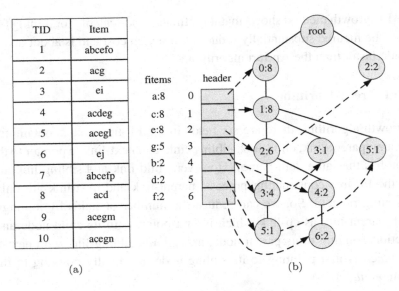

TID	Item
1	abcefo
2	acg
3	ei
4	acdeg
5	acegl
6	ej
7	abcefp
8	acd
9	acegm
10	acegn

(a)

(b)

Fig. 12.3.   CFP-tree (minsup = 20%)

Procedure: insert_tree([$p|P$], T).

1. If T has no child or cannot find a child in which its item-no= p, then create a new node N. N.item-no= p, N.count=1, N.cp-link= T; Insert N before the first node in which item-no is greater than p.

2. If T has a child N such that N.item-no= p, then increment N.count by 1.

3. If P is not empty, then call insert_tree(P, N) recursively.

After the construction of the CFP-tree, we should change the sn-link from sibling-link to next-link and reverse the cp-link. The processing procedure is as follows: Traverse the tree from the root. Add current node CN to the link of header [CN.item-no] as the last node. If CN has no child or all of its children and siblings have been processed, then let CN.cp-link = CN's parent, else process its children and its siblings recursively.

Figure 12.3(a) shows an example of a database and Figure 12.3(b) is the CFP-tree for that database.

Here, we give a CFP-tree mining algorithm based on constrained sub-tree and array-based technique (Grahne and Zhu, 2003). The following is the pseudocode of the CFP-tree mining algorithm.

Algorithm 12.5 (CFP-tree Mining Algorithm).

Input: A CFP-tree T

Output: The complete set of FI's corresponding to T

Method:

1. patlen=1;
2. for (k=flen-1; k>=0; k--) { // flen is the length of frequent itemset
3.   pat[0]=fitem[k];
4.   output {pat[0]} with support count[k];
5.   generate ST(k).EndArray[];
6.   mine(ST(k));
7. }

Procedure mine(ST($i_k, \ldots, i_2, i_1$)) {

1. generate ST($i_k, \ldots, i_2, i_1$).fitem[] and ST($i_k, \ldots, i_2, i_1$).count[], let the length be listlen;
2. if (listlen==0) then return;
3. if (listlen==1) then { pat[patlen] = ST($i_k, \ldots, i_2, i_1$).fitem[0]; output pat with support ST($i_k, \ldots, i_2, i_1$).count[0]; return}
4. if ST($i_k, \ldots, i_2, i_1$) has only single path then
    { output pat $\cup$ all the combination of ST($i_k, \ldots, i_2, i_1$).fitem[];
    return; }
5. patlen++;
6. for (k=listlen-1; k>=0; k--) {
7.   generate array;
8.   generate ST($i_k, \ldots, i_2, i_1, k$).EndArray[];
9.   if ST($i_k, \ldots, i_2, i_1, k$).EndArray[] is not NULL then
10.   mine(ST($i_k, \ldots, i_2, i_1, k$));
11.   }
12.   patlen--;
13. }

In the mine procedure, line 1 generates frequent itemset in the constrained sub-tree ST($i_k, \ldots, i_2, i_1$). Lines 2–3 process the condition while listlen is 0 or 1. Line 4 processes the condition while the constrained sub-tree has only a single path. Lines 6–11 generate a new array and constrained sub-tree, then mine the new sub-tree.

Because the CFP-tree could have millions of nodes, it takes plenty of time for allocating and deallocating the nodes. Just like Grahne and Zhu (2003), we also implement unified memory management for CFPmine algorithm. In the recursive mining process, the memory used in it is not frequently allocated and freed. It allocates a large chunk before the first recursion, and when a recursion ends, it does not really free the memory, and only changes the available size of the chunk. If the chunk is used up, it allocates more memory. It frees the memory only when all the recursions have been finished.

12.5 Mining General Fuzzy Association Rules

The main method of mining association rules about digital attributes to disperse continuous data transforms the mining association rules about digital attributes into the mining association rules about Boolean attributes. One method is to divide the universe of discourse about attributes into non-overlapping intervals, and then map the discreted data into these intervals. Non-overlapping interval may ignore elements which are near the boundaries of some intervals. This may lead to the ignorance of meaningful interval. The other method is to divide the universe of discourse about attributes into overlapping intervals, and then the elements near the boundary may be located in two intervals meanwhile. This may lead to over-emphasis on some intervals because of the contribution of elements nearby boundary. The main weak point of the above two methods is that the boundary is too rigid. A solution proposed by Jianjiang Lu is too vague about the boundary with fuzzy set which is defined on the domain of attributes (Lu, 2000) because the fuzzy set can supply a smooth transition between elements in set and elements not in set. With this transition, all elements nearby boundary will not be excluded and will not be overemphasized. The degree of membership of the elements of the fuzzy set in the domain of attributes is the language value. The language value is expressed as closed positive fuzzy number and zero fuzzy number with boundary. So, the problem of mining association rules about digital attributes is transformed into the problem of mining association rules about fuzzy association rules.

Definition 12.1. Suppose R is real number field, the closed interval $[a, b]$ is called the number of the closed interval, and $a, b \in R$, $a \leq b$.

Definition 12.2. Suppose $[a, b]$, $[c, d]$ are two closed intervals, and $0 \notin [c, d]$, then

$$[a, b] + [c, d] = [a + c, b + d]$$

$$[a, b] - [c, d] = [a - d, b - c]$$

$$[a, b] \times [c, d] = [ac \wedge ad \wedge bc \wedge bd, ac \vee ad \vee bc \vee bd]$$

$$[a, b] \div [c, d] = \left[\frac{a}{c} \wedge \frac{a}{d} \wedge \frac{b}{c} \wedge \frac{b}{d}, \frac{a}{c} \vee \frac{a}{d} \vee \frac{b}{c} \vee \frac{b}{d} \right], \quad 0 \notin [a, b]$$

Definition 12.3. Suppose A is a fuzzy set on R

(1) A is called closed convex fuzzy set on R if and only if $\forall \lambda \in (0, 1]$, $A\lambda$ is a closed convex set, that is to say, $A\lambda$ is a closed interval.

(2) *A* is called regular fuzzy set on *R* if and only if $\exists x_0 \in R$ then $A(x_0) = 1$, x_0 is called regular point of *A*.

(3) If $\forall \lambda \in (0, 1]$, and $A\lambda$ is a set with boundary, *A* is called fuzzy set with boundary.

(4) A regular convex fuzzy set on *R* is called a fuzzy number, a regular closed convex fuzzy set is called a closed fuzzy number and a regular closed convex fuzzy set with boundary is called a closed fuzzy number with boundary. $\tilde{\theta}$ is a zero fuzzy number and

$$\tilde{\theta} = \begin{cases} 1, & x = 0, \\ 0, & x \neq 0. \end{cases}$$

(5) Suppose *A* is a fuzzy number, if all numbers in supp $A = \{x \in R | A(x) > 0\}$ is positive real number, then *A* is called positive fuzzy number. All the positive fuzzy numbers with boundaries are marked as G, $\tilde{G} = G \cup \{\tilde{\theta}\}$.

Definition 12.4. "$\leq$" in $\tilde{G}$ is defined as $\forall A, B \in \tilde{G}$, $A \leq B$ if and only if for $\forall \lambda \in (0, 1]$, $a_1^\lambda \leq b_1^\lambda$ and $a_2^\lambda \leq b_2^\lambda$. $A_\lambda = [a_1^\lambda, a_2^\lambda]$, $B_\lambda = [b_1^\lambda, b_2^\lambda]$. "$\leq$" is partial order in $\tilde{G}$.

Definition 12.5. Suppose $A, B \in \tilde{G}$, then:

$$(A + B)(z) = \bigvee_{x+y=z} (A(x)) \wedge B(y)), \quad \forall z \in R,$$

$$(A - B)(z) = \bigvee_{x-y=z} (A(x)) \wedge B(y)), \quad \forall z \in R,$$

$$(A \times B)(z) = \bigvee_{x+y=z} (A(x)) \wedge B(y)), \quad \forall z \in R,$$

$$(A \div B)(z) = \bigvee_{x+y=z} (A(x)) \wedge B(y)), \quad \forall z \in R,$$

$$(kA)(z) = A\left(\frac{z}{k}\right), \quad k \neq 0, \quad \forall z \in R.$$

Theorem 12.1. *Suppose* $A, B \in \tilde{G}$, *for* $\forall \lambda \in (0, 1]$, *then* $(A \pm B)_\lambda = A_\lambda \pm B_\lambda$; $(A \times B)_\lambda = A_\lambda \times B_\lambda$; $A/B_\lambda = A_\lambda/B_\lambda$, $B \neq \bar{\theta}$, $(kA)_\lambda = kA_\lambda$, $k \neq 0$.

Note 1: From Theorem 12.1 and Definition 12.2, it is clear that suppose $A, B \in \tilde{G}$ then $A + B \in \tilde{G}$, $A \times B \in \tilde{G}$, $A/B \in \tilde{G}(B \neq \bar{\theta})$, $kA \in \tilde{G}(k > 0)$.

We will discuss the calculation about fuzzy association rules in a general sense. If there is a database $T = \{t_1, t_2, \ldots, t_n\}$, t_i denotes the *i*th tuple $I = (i_1, i_2, \ldots, i_n)$ which is the set of attributes, $t_j[i_k]$ denotes the value of the attribute ik on the *j*th tuple. Suppose $X = \{x_1, x_2, \ldots, x_p\}$, $Y = \{y_1, y_2, \ldots, y_q\}$ are the subsets of *I*, and $X \cap Y = \emptyset$, $D = \{f_{x1}, f_{x2}, \ldots, f_{xp}\}$, $E = \{f_{y1}, f_{y2}, \ldots, f_{yq}\}$, $f_{xi}(i = 1, 2, \ldots, p)$

is the fuzzy set in the domain of attribute xi and $f_{yj}(j = 1, 2, \ldots, q)$ is the fuzzy set in the domain of attribute y_j. The degree of membership of elements of these fuzzy sets is language value. The language value is expressed as closed positive fuzzy number with boundary or zero fuzzy number. Suppose ε' is a valve value, α' is the minimum rate of support. β' is the minimum confidence, α', β', ε' are closed positive fuzzy numbers with boundaries. The form of fuzzy association rules in general sense is "if X is D then Y is E".

Suppose $f_{xj}(t_i[x_j]) = x'_y$, $i = 1, 2, \ldots, n$; $j = 1, 2, \ldots, p$; $f_{yj}(t_i[y_j]) = y'_{ij}$, $i = 1, 2, \ldots, n$; $j = 1, 2, \ldots, q$; both x'_{ij} and y'_{ij} are closed positive fuzzy numbers with boundaries or zero fuzzy numbers. Suppose

$$\bar{x}'_{ij} = \max\{x \in R | x'_{ij}(x) = 1\}, \quad i = 1, 2, \ldots, n; \quad j = 1, 2, \ldots, p;$$

$$\bar{y}'_{ij} = \max\{x \in R | y'_{ij}(x) = 1\}, \quad i = 1, 2, \ldots, n; \quad j = 1, 2, \ldots, q;$$

$$\bar{\alpha}' = \max\{x \in R | \alpha'(x) = 1\}, \quad \bar{\beta}' = \max\{x \in R | \beta'(x) = 1\};$$

$$\bar{\varepsilon}' = \max\{x \in R | \varepsilon'(x) = 1\}, \quad M = \max\{\bar{x}'_{ij}, \bar{y}'_{ij}, \bar{\alpha}', \bar{\beta}', \bar{\varepsilon}'\};$$

$$x_{ij} = \frac{x'_{ij}}{M}, \quad i = 1, 2, \ldots, n; \quad j = 1, 2, \ldots, p,$$

$$y_{ij} = \frac{y'_{ij}}{M}, \quad i = 1, 2, \ldots, n; \quad j = 1, 2, \ldots, q,$$

$$\alpha = \frac{\alpha'}{M}, \beta = \frac{\beta'}{M}, \gamma = \frac{\gamma'}{M}.$$

x_{ij}, y_{ij}, α, β, ε are closed positive fuzzy numbers with boundaries or zero fuzzy numbers, their regular points are in the interval of $[0, 1]$.

Definition 12.6. The general support rate S about the general fuzzy association rules in general sense "if X is D then Y is E" is defined as

$$S = \frac{\sum_{i=1}^{n} \left[\prod_{j=1}^{p} \bar{a}(x_{ij}) \times \prod_{j=1}^{q} \bar{a}(y_{ij}) \right]}{n}, \quad \bar{a}(x) = \begin{cases} x, & x \geq \varepsilon', \\ \tilde{\theta}, & \text{others}. \end{cases} \quad (12.3)$$

Definition 12.7. The general confidence C about the general fuzzy association rules "if X is D then Y is E" is defined as

$$C = \frac{S}{\frac{1}{n} \sum_{i=1}^{n} \left[\prod_{j=1}^{p} \bar{a}(x_{ij}) \right]}, \quad \bar{a}(x_{ij}) = \begin{cases} x_{ij}, & x_{ij} \geq \varepsilon', \\ \tilde{\theta}, & \text{others}. \end{cases} \quad (12.4)$$

When $\frac{1}{n} \sum_{i=1}^{n} [\prod_{j=1}^{p} \bar{a}(x_{ij})] = \tilde{\theta}$, then $S = \tilde{\theta}$, and the rule will not be adopted. Suppose $\frac{1}{n} \sum_{i=1}^{n} [\prod_{j=1}^{p} \bar{a}(x_{ij})] \neq \tilde{\theta}$, it is easy to find that S in Definition 12.6 and C in Definition 12.7 belong to $\tilde{G}$. Meanwhile, all regular points of x_{ij} are in [0, 1]. So, the regular points of $\frac{1}{n} \sum_{i=1}^{n} [\prod_{j=1}^{p} \bar{a}(x_{ij})]$ are in [0, 1] also. That is, the maximum regular point of C will not be less than the maximum regular point of S, so C will not be less than S. Because S, C, α, β are in $\tilde{G}$, S can be compared with α, C, and β. When $S \geq \alpha$ and $S \geq \beta$, the rule "if X is D then Y is E" will be suitable.

12.6 Distributed Mining Algorithm for Association Rules

The typical application of association rules mining is market-basket analysis, where the items represent products, and the records represent point-of-sales data at large grocery stores or department stores. Other application domains for association rules mining include customer segmentation, catalog design, store layout, and telecommunication alarm prediction. Because data are increasing in terms of both the dimensions and size, association rules mining algorithm should handle massive data stores. Sequential algorithms cannot provide scalability, in terms of the data dimension, size, or runtime performance, for such large databases. Therefore, we must rely on high-performance parallel and distributed computing.

Two dominant approaches for using multiple processors have emerged: distributed memory and shared memory. A shared-memory architecture has many desirable properties. Each processor has direct and equal access to entire system's memory. Parallel programs are easy to implement on such a system. In a distributed-memory architecture, each processor has its own local memory, which only that processor can access directly. For a processor to access data in the local memory of another processor, message passing must send a copy of the desired data elements from one processor to the other. Although a shared-memory architecture offers programming simplicity, a common bus's finite bandwidth can limit scalability. A distributed memory, message-passing architecture cures the scalability problem by eliminating the bus, but at the expense of programming simplicity. A very popular paradigm combines the best of the distributed- and shared-memory approaches. Included in this paradigm are hardware or software distributed shared-memory systems. These systems distribute the physical memory among the nodes but provide a shared global address space on each processor.

Figure 12.4 shows where each parallel association rule mining method falls in the design space (Zaki, 1999). Distributed memory methods form the dominant platform, and a mix of data- and task-parallel approaches have been explored. However, all schemes use static load balancing or very limited dynamic load balancing. The

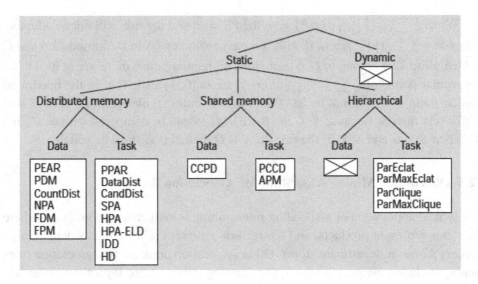

Fig. 12.4.   Parallel and distributed association rules mining algorithms

main design issues in distributed memory methods are minimizing communication and evenly distributing data for good load balancing.

David Cheung and his colleagues proposed the fast distributed mining (FDM) algorithm for association rules (Cheung *et al.*, 1996). The main difference between parallel and distributed data mining is the interconnection network latency and bandwidth. David Cheung and his colleagues discovered that there exist valuable properties between local and global large data sets. One should maximally take advantages of such properties to reduce the number of messages to be passed and confine the substantial amount of processing to local sites. Fast distributed mining has three editions: FDM-LP, FDM-LUP, FDM-LPP. They all have similar structure, but different pruning algorithms. FDM-LP only discusses local pruning; FDM-LUP discusses local pruning and upperbound pruning; FDM-LPP discusses local pruning and step-by-step pruning.

12.6.1 *Generation of Candidate Sets*

It is important to observe some interesting properties related to large itemsets in distributed environments since such properties may substantially reduce the number of messages to be passed across the network at mining association rules. There is an important relationship between large data sets and distributed database: every global large data sets must be local large data sets in some site. If a data set X in site

S_i is global large data set and local large data set, then X in site S_i is called gl-large at site S_i. All gl-large data sets in one site will form a basis for the site to generate its own candidate sets.

There are two features about local large data sets and gl-large data sets: First, if an itemset X at site S_i is locally large, all its subsets at site S_i are also locally large. Second, if an itemset X at site S_i is gl-large, all its subsets at site S_i are also gl-large. Obviously, there is a similar relation in centralized environment. Hereinafter, we show important results, adopting the technology of effectively creating candidate sets in distributed environment.

Let GL_i denote the set of gl-large itemsets at site S_i, and $GL_i(k)$ denote the set of gl-large k-itemsets at site S_i. If $X \in L_{(k)}$, then there exists a site S_i, such that all its size-$(k-1)$ subsets are gl-large at site S_i, i.e., they belong to $GL_i(k-1)$. In a straightforward adaptation of Apriori, the set of candidate sets at the kth iteration, denoted by $CA_{(k)}$, which stands for size-k candidate sets from Apriori, would be generated by applying the Apriori_gen function on $L(k-1)$. That is,

$$CA_{(k)} = \text{Apriori\_gen}(L_{(k-1)}).$$

At each site S_i, let $CGi(k)$ be the set of candidates sets generated by applying Apriori_gen on $GL_{i(k-1)}$, i.e.,

$$CG_{i(k)} = \text{Apriori\_gen}(GL_{i(k-1)}),$$

where CG stands for candidate sets generated from gl-large itemsets. Therefore, $CG_{i(k)}$ is generated from $GL_{i(k-1)}$. Since $GL_{i(k-1)} \subseteq L_{(k-1)}$, $CG_{i(k)}$ is a subset of $CA_{(k)}$. In the following, let $CG_{(k)}$ denote the sets $\cup_{i=1}^{n} CG_{i(k)}$

For every $k > 1$, the set of all large k-itemsets $L_{(k)}$ is a subset of $CG(k) = \cup_{i=1}^{n} CG_{i(k)}$, where $CG_{i(k)} = \text{Apriori\_gen}(GL_{i(k-1)})$. Therefore,

$$L_{(k)} \subseteq CG_{(k)} = \cup_{i=1}^{n} CG_{i(k)} = \cup_{i=1}^{n} \text{Apriori\_gen}(GL_{(k-1)}). \tag{12.5}$$

It indicates that $CG_{(k)}$ is a subset of $CA_{(k)}$, and may be much smaller than $CA_{(k)}$, and then it can be a candidate set for the size-k large itemsets. The differences between $CG_{(k)}$ and $CA_{(k)}$ depend on the distributing degree of the itemsets. The set of candidate sets $CG_{i(k)}$ can be generated locally at each site S_i at the kth iteration. After the exchange of support counts, the gl-large itemsets $GL_{i(k)}$ in $CG_{i(k)}$ can be found at the end of that iteration. Based on $GL_{i(k)}$, the candidate sets at S_i for the $(k+1)$st iteration can then be generated. By using this approach, the number of candidate sets generated can be substantially reduced to about 10–25% of that generated in Count Distribution.

12.6.2 *Local Pruning of Candidate Sets*

When the set of candidate set $C'G_{(k)}$ is generated, to find the globally large itemsets, the support counts of the candidate sets must be exchanged among all the sites. Notice that some candidate sets in $CG_{(k)}$ can be pruned by a local pruning technique before count exchange starts. The general idea is that at each site S_i, if a candidate set $X \in CG_{i(k)}$ is not locally large at site S_i, there is no need for S_i to find out its global support count to determine whether it is globally large. This is because in this case, either X is small or it will be locally large at some other site, and hence only the site(s) at which X is locally large need to be responsible to find the global support count of X. Therefore, in order to compute all the large k-itemsets, at each site S_i, the candidate sets can be confined to only the sets $X \in CG_{i(k)}$ which are locally large at site S_i. For clarity, the notations used in this section are listed in Table 12.3.

The local pruning procedure of candidate sets it as follows:

(1) **Candidate set generation:** Generate the candidate sets $CG_{i(k)}$ according to global large itemsets found at $(k-1)$st iteration at site S_i using formula $CG_{i(k)} =$ Apriori_gen$(GL_{(k-1)})$.

(2) **Local pruning:** For each $X \in CG_{i(k)}$, scan each local database DB_i to compute local support total count $X.sup_i$. If X at site S_i is not local large, it will be deleted from candidate data sets $LL_{i(k)}$. This pruning only deletes X from candidate data sets of site S_i, X may be present at candidate data sets of other sites.

(3) **Support count exchange:** Broadcast the candidate sets in $LL_{i(k)}$ toward other sites to collect support counts. Compute global support count and obtain all global large k-data sets in site S_i.

(4) **Broadcast the results of mining:** Broadcast all global large k-itemsets computed toward other sites.

In the above processes for finding globally large candidate itemsets, step 2 "local pruning" and step 3 "support count exchange", each site S_i should have two

Table 12.3.   Notation list

D	Number of transaction in DB
S	Minimum support minsup
$L_{(k)}$	Globally large k-itemsets
$CA_{(k)}$	Candidate sets generated from $L_{(k)}$
$X.sup$	Global support total count of X
D_i	Number of transactions in DB_i
$GL_{i(k)}$	Gl-large k-itemsets at site S_i
$CG_{i(k)}$	Candidate sets generated from $GL_{i(k-1)}$
$LL_{i(k)}$	Local large k-itemsets in $CG_{i(k)}$
$X.sup_i$	Local support total count at site S_i

support count sets. For local pruning, S_i should find out the local support counts of its local candidate sets $CG_{i(k)}$. For support count exchange, S_i should find out different local support counts with global support count sets in other sites. A simple approach would be to scan two times, first to find out local support count based on local candidate $CG_{i(k)}$; second is to respond to quests of support count from other sites. However, this would substantially degrade the performance.

In fact, it is unnecessary to scan the database two times. At site S_i, before kth iteration $CG_{i(k)}$ was obtained, some other relative sets also could be obtained. For example, $CG_{j(k)}$ ($j = 1, \ldots, n, j \neq i$). All $GL_{i(k-1)}$ ($i = 1, \ldots, n$) were broadcast toward each site, and candidate $GL_{i(k-1)}$ ($i = 1, \ldots, n$) could be computed from the corresponding $GL_{i(k-1)}$, after $(k-1)$-st iteration. That is, because all global large data sets created by previous iteration were broadcast toward all sites, at the beginning of iteration, each site could compute candidate itemsets in other sites. Therefore, local support count of all candidate itemsets could be obtained in a scan and be stored in a structure similar to Apriori algorithm Hash-tree. Two different support count sets can be searched in this structure in exchange of local pruning and support count.

12.6.3 *Global Pruning of Candidate Sets*

The local pruning at site S_i only makes use of the local support counts in DB_i to prune the candidate sets. In fact, local support counts in other sites are also pruned, adopting global pruning technology to realize prune. The main technology is to obtain all local and global support counts of candidate itemsets X after each iteration. After confirming one candidate data set to be global and large, local and global support count can be broadcast toward all sites. Using this information, candidate itemsets can be pruned in the process of iteration.

After finishing each iteration, if one candidate itemset is globally large, the system automatically broadcasts local support count of each candidate elements toward other sites. Suppose X is a size-k candidate itemset. Therefore, the local support counts of all the size-$(k - 1)$ subsets of X are available at every site. For a partition database DB_i ($1 \leq i \leq n$), maxsup$_i(X)$ stands for minimum local support count of all size-$(k - 1)$ subsets for X, that is, maxsup$_i(X) = \min\{Y.\text{sup}_i | Y \subset X \text{ 且 } |Y| = k - 1\}$. According to the relation of superset and subset, maxsup$_i(X)$ is upper bound of local support count $X.\text{sup}_i$. Therefore, maxsup(X) stands for the sum of these upper boundary functions in a distributed database, namely, the upper boundary of $X.\text{sup}$. $X.\text{sup} \leq \text{maxsup}(X) = \sum_{i=1}^{n} \text{maxsup}_i(X)$. Note that maxsup$(X)$ can be computed in each site, at the beginning of one iteration. Because maxsup(X) is the upper boundary of its global support count, it can be pruned globally. That is, if maxsup$(X) < s \times D$, X is impossible to be one candidate data set. This technology goes by the name of global pruning.

Global pruning can be combined with local pruning to form different pruning strategies. Two particular variations of this strategy will be adopted when we introduce several versions of FDM. The first method is called upper-bound pruning and the second one is called polling-site pruning. A possible upper bound of the global support count of a candidate set X is the sum

$$X.\text{sup}_i + \sum_{j=1,\, j \neq i}^{n} \text{maxsup}_j(X), \tag{12.6}$$

where $X.\text{sup}_i$ is found already in the local pruning. Therefore, this upper bound can be computed to prune the candidate set X at site S_i.

12.6.4 *Count Polling*

In general, few candidate itemsets are locally large at all the sites. Therefore, the FDM algorithm will usually require much less than $O(n^2)$ messages for computing each candidate itemset. To ensure that FDM requires only $O(n)$ messages for every candidate itemset in all the cases, a count polling technique is introduced.

This technology uses an assignment function to the candidate itemset X, which acts on X's Hash function that maps X to a polling site (suppose that this function can be quoted in any sites). There is no relation to X's polling site and the sites of X being locally large. The polling site of each candidate itemset X is used to compute if X is globally large. To realize the purpose, the corresponding X's polling site should broadcast X's polling request toward all the other sites, collect local support counts, and compute global support counts. Because there is only one polling site for each candidate item X, the number of X's total exchange information can be reduced to $O(n)$.

At the kth iteration, after the pruning phase (both local and global pruning) has been completed, FDM uses the following procedure at each site S_i to do the count polling.

(1) **Send candidate sets to polling sites:** At site S_i, find out candidate elements belonging to set $LL_{i(k)}$ and polling site S_j for each polling site S_j, which will be stored in $LL_{i,j(k)}$ (that is, store candidate elements according to group of their polling site). Each local support count of candidate itemsets is also stored in corresponding $LL_{i,j(k)}$. Send each $LL_{i,j(k)}$ to the corresponding polling site S_j.

(2) **Poll and collect support count:** If S_i is a polling site, S_i will receive all $LL_{i,j(k)}$ from other sites. S_i first find out original address list, whose X is sent, for each

candidate itemset X, then broadcast polling request to other sites, which is not in the original site list, to collect support count.

(3) **Compute global large itemsets:** S_i accepts support count from other sites and computes global support count for each candidate elements, then finds out globally large itemsets. Eventually, S_i broadcasts gl-large itemsets with their global support count to other sites.

12.6.5 *Distributed Mining Algorithm of Association Rules*

Here, we first introduce distributed mining algorithm FDM-LP which is an FDM with local pruning, including candidate set reduction and local pruning.

Algorithm 12.6 (FDM-LP Algorithm (Cheung *et al.*, 1996)).

Input: $DB_i (i = 1, \ldots, n)$, the database partition at each site S_i
Output: L, all global large data sets
Method:

1.   if $k = 1$ then
2. $T_{i(1)} = \text{get\_local\_count}(DB_i, \emptyset, 1)$
3.   else {
4. $CG_{(k)} = \cup_{i=1}^{n} CG_{i(k)}$
             $= \cup_{i=1}^{n} \text{Apriori\_gen}(GL_{i(k-1)})$;
5. $T_{i(k)} = \text{get\_local\_count}(DB_i, CG_{(k)}, i)$;}
6.   for_all $X \in T_{i(k)}$ do
7.   If $X.sup_i \geq s \times D_i$ then
8.   for $j = 1$ to n do
9.   if polling_site$(X) = S_j$ then
                        insert $\langle X, X.sup_i \rangle$ into $LL_{i,j(k)}$;
10.   for $j = 1, \ldots, n$ do send $LL_{i,j(k)}$ to site S_j;
11.   for $j = 1, \ldots, n$ do {
12.   receive $LL_{j,i(k)}$;
13.   for_all $X \in LL_{j,i(k)}$ do {
14.   if $X \notin LP_{i(k)}$ then
                            insert X into $LP_{i(k)}$;
15.   update $X.large\_sites$; } }
16.   for_all $X \in LP_{i(k)}$ do
17.   send_polling_request(X);
18.   reply_polling_request$(T_{i(k)})$;
19.   for_all $X \in LP_{i(k)}$ do {
20.   receive $X.sup_j$ from the sites S_j,

where $S_j \notin X.large\_sites$;

21. $X.sup = \sum_{i=1}^{n} X.sup_i$;

22.   *if* $X.sup \geqq s \times D_i$ *then*
                 insert X into $G_{i(k)}$; }
23.   broadcast $G_{i(k)}$;
24.   receive $G_{j(k)}$ from all other sites S_j, $(j \neq i)$;

25. $L_{(k)} = \cup_{i=1}^{n} G_{i(k)}$.

26.   divide $L_{(k)}$ into $GL_{i(k)}$, $(i = 1, \ldots, n)$;
27.   return $L_{(k)}$.

In FDM-LP algorithm, first, every S_i is initially a "home site" of the candidate sets, then as polling site to respond the request from other sites. Finally, S_i is transformed into a remote site to support local support count to other polling sites. We explain the above procedure according to different roles and activities of steps in the FDM-LP algorithm as follows:

(1) **Home site:** generate candidate itemsets and submit to polling sites (lines 1–10);
(2) **Polling site:** receive candidate itemsets and send poll requests (lines 11–17);
(3) **Remote site:** return support count to polling site (line 18);
(4) **Polling site:** receive support count and find out large itemsets (lines 19–23);
(5) **Home site:** receive large itemsets (lines 24–27).

In the following discussions, by using two different global pruning technologies, we show two more refined editions of FDM-LP algorithm.

Algorithm 12.7 (FDM-LUP Algorithm). FDM algorithm of local and upper bound pruning
   Method:
   The program fragment of FDM-LUP is obtained from FDM-LP by inserting the following condition (line 7.1) after line 7 of Algorithm 12.6.

(7.1)   *if* $g\_upper\_bound(X) \geq s \times D_i$ *then*

update FDM-LUP algorithm is that append upper bound pruning (line 7.1). Function g_upper_bound computes the upper bound for each candidate itemset. In other words, g-upper-bound returns an upper bound of X as the sum

$$X.sup_i + \sum_{j=1, j \neq i}^{n} maxsup_j(X)$$

$X.\text{sup}_i$ was computed in the process of local pruning, and $\text{maxsup}_j(X)$ ($j = 1, \ldots, n, j \neq i$) can be computed by local support count after $(k-1)$st iteration. If upper bound is a smaller number than global minsup, it is used to prune X. Compared with FDM-LP algorithm, FDMLUP should usually have a smaller number of candidate sets for count exchange.

Algorithm 12.8. FDM-LPP, FDM algorithm of local and poll address pruning

Method: The program fragment of FDM-LPP is obtained from Algorithm 12.6 by replacing its line 17 with the following two lines.

(16.1)   if $p\_upper\_bound(X) \geq s \times D_i$ then

(17) $end\_polling\_request(X)$;

FDM-LPP algorithm appends a new step, which is polling site pruning. In this step, polling site S_i accepts requests from other sites to perform polling. Each request includes local large itemset X and its local support count $X.\text{sup}_j$. S_j is site from which itemset X delivers to S_i. Note that $X.\text{large\_sites}$ is the set of all the originating sites from which the requests for polling X are being sent to the polling site (line 15). For every site $S_j \in X.\text{large\_sites}$, the local support count $X.\text{sup}_j$ has been delivered to S_i. For a site $S_q \notin X.\text{large\_sites}$, because X in S_q is not locally large, $X.\text{sup}_q$ is smaller than $s \times D_q$. $X.\text{sup}_q$ is bounded by the value $\min(\text{maxsup}_q(X), s \times D_{q-1})$. Therefore, an upper bound of $X.\text{sup}_q$ can be computed by following formula:

$$\sum_{j \in X.\text{large\_Sites}} X.\text{sup}_j + \sum_{q=1, q \neq X.\text{large\_sites}}^{n} \min(\text{maxsup}_a(X), s * D_q - 1). \quad (12.7)$$

In the FDM-LPP algorithm, S_i uses function p_upper_bound and the above formula to compute upper bound for $X.\text{sup}$. This upper bound will be pruned when it is smaller than the global support count.

Similar to the above discussion, FDM-LUP and FDM-LPP can obtain candidate itemset less than FDM-LP. However, they request more storage and communication messages for local support counts. Their efficiency mainly depends on the data distribution.

12.7 Parallel Mining of Association Rules

Data mining researchers expect parallelism to relieve mining methods from the sequential bottleneck, providing scalability to massive data sets and improving response time. The main challenges include synchronization and communication

Table 12.4.   Parallel algorithm for association rules

Algorithms	Characteristics
Count Distribution(CD)	**Apriori-base**
PEAR	**Candidate prefix tree**
PDM	Hash table for 2-itemsets, parallel candidate **generation**
NPA	Only master does sum reduction
FDM	Local and global pruning, count polling
FPM	Local and global pruning, skewness handling
CCPD	Shared memory
Data Distribution	Exchange full database per iteration
SPA	Same as Data Distribution
IDD	Ring-based broadcast, item-based candidate partitioning
PCCD	Shared memory (logical database exchange)
Hybrid Distribution	Combines Count and Data Distribution
Candidate Distribution	Selectively replicated database, asynchronous
HPA	No database replication, exchange itemsets
HPA–ELD	Replicate frequent itemsets
ParEclat	Eclat-based, asynchronous, hierarchical
ParMaxEclat	MaxEclat-based, asynchronous, hierarchical
ParClique	Clique-based, asynchronous, hierarchical
ParMaxClique	MaxClique-based, asynchronous, hierarchical
APM	DIC-based, shared memory, asynchronous
PPAR	Partition-based, horizontal database

minimization, workload balancing, finding good data layout and data decomposition, and disk I/O minimization. The parallel design space spans three main components: hardware platform, type of parallelism, and load-balancing strategy.

Table 12.4 shows the essential differences among the different methods and groups together with related algorithms (Zaki, 1999). As you can see, there are only a handful of distinct paradigms. The other algorithms propose optimizations over these basic cases. For example, PEAR, PDM, NPA, FDM, FPM, and CCPD are all similar to Count Distribution. Likewise, SPA, IDD, and PCCD are similar to Data Distribution, whereas HPA and HPAELD are similar to Candidate Distribution. Hybrid Distribution combines Count and Data Distribution techniques. ParEclat, ParMaxEclat, ParClique, and ParMaxClique are all based on their sequential counterparts. Finally, APM is based on the sequential DIC method, and PPAR is based on Partition.

12.7.1 *Count Distribution Algorithm*

Count Distribution (CD) is a parallel version of Apriori. It is one of the earliest proposed and representative parallel algorithms for mining of association rules (Agrawal *et al.*, 1996). Here, we describe briefly its steps. The database D is partitioned into $D_1, D_2, \ldots, D_n$ and distributed across n processors. The program fragment of CD at processor p_i, $1 \leq i \leq n$, for the kth iteration is outlined. For convenience, we use $X.\text{sup}_{(i)}$ to represent the local support count of an itemset X in partition D_i. In step 1, every processor computes the same candidate set C_k by applying the aprior_gen function on L_{k-1}, which is the set of large itemsets found at the $(k-1)$th iteration. In step 2, local support counts (support in D_i) of candidates in C_k are found. In steps 3 and 4, local support counts are exchanged with all other processors to get global support counts (support in D) and globally large itemsets (large with respect to D) L_k are computed independently by each processor. CD repeats steps 1–4 until no more candidate is found.

Algorithm 12.9 (Count Distribution Algorithm).
1. $C_k = \text{apriori\_gen}(L_{k-1})$;
2. scan partition D_i to find the local support count $X.sup(i)$ for all $X \in C_k$;
3. exchange $\{ X.sup(i) | X \in C_k \}$ with all other processors to get global support
   counts $X.sup(i)$
        for all $X \in C_k$;
4. $L_k = \{X \in C_k | X.sup(i) \geq minsup \times |D|\}$.

12.7.2 *Fast Parallel Mining Algorithm*

David Cheung and Yongqiao Xiao recently proposed a parallel version of FDM, called Fast Parallel Mining (Chenug and Xiao, 1999). The problem with FDM's polling mechanism is that it requires two rounds of messages in each iteration: one for computing the global supports and one for broadcasting the frequent itemsets. This two-round scheme can degrade performance in a parallel setting. FPM generates fewer candidates and retains the local and global pruning steps. But instead of count polling and subsequent broadcast of frequent itemsets, it simply broadcasts local supports to all processors. The more interesting aspect of this work is a metric Cheung and Xiao define for data skewness (the distribution of itemsets among the various partitions). For an itemset X, let $pX(i)$ denote the probability that X occurs in partition i. The entropy of X is given as

$$H(X) = -\sum_{i}^{n} pX(i) \log(pX(i)). \qquad (12.8)$$

The entropy ensures the distribution of the local support counts of X among all partitions. FPM is an enhancement of CD. The simple support count exchange scheme in CD is retained in FPM. The main difference is the incorporation of both the distributed and global prunings in FPM to reduce the candidate set size. In FPM, the first iteration is the same as CD. Each processor scans its partition to find out the local support counts of all size-1 itemsets and uses one round of count exchange to compute the global support counts. At the end of the first iteration, in addition to L_1, each processor also finds out the gl-large itemsets $GL_1(i)$, for $1 \le i \le n$. For the kth iteration of FPM, $k > 1$, the program fragment executed at processor i, $1 \le i \le n$, is described as Algorithm 12.10.

Algorithm 12.10 (FPM Algorithm).

   1. compute candidate sets $CG_k = \cup_{i=1}^{n} \texttt{apriori\_gen}(GL_{k-1(i)})$; (distributed pruning)

   2. prune candidates in CG_k by global pruning

   3. scan partition D_i to find the local support count $X.\text{sup}(i)$ for all remaining candidates $X \in CG_k$

   4. exchange $\{X.\text{sup}(i)|X \in CG_k\}$ with all other processors to get global support counts $X.\text{sup}(i)$ for all $X \in CG_k$

   5. $GL_{k(i)} = \{X \in CG_k|X._{\text{sup}} \ge minsup \times |D|, X._{\text{sup}(i)} \ge minsup \times |D_i|\}$ compute for all i , $1 \le i \le n$

   6. return $L_k = \cup_{i=1}^{n} GL_{k(i)}$

12.7.3 *DIC-Based Algorithm*

The DIC algorithm proposed by Sergey Brin and others is a generalization of Apriori (Brin *et al.*, 1997). The database is divided into p equal-sized partitions so that each partition fits in memory. For partition 1, DIC gathers the supports of single items. Items found to be locally frequent (only in this partition) generate candidate 2-itemsets. Then DIC reads partition 2 and obtains supports for all current candidates. That is, the single items and the candidate 2-itemsets. This process repeats for the remaining partitions. DIC starts counting candidate k-itemsets while processing partition k in the first database scan. After the last partition p has been processed, the processing wraps around to partition 1 again. A candidate's global support is known once the processing wraps around the database and reaches the partition where it was first generated.

   DIC is effective in reducing the number of database scans if most partitions are homogeneous. If data are not homogeneous, DIC might generate many false positives (itemsets that are locally frequent but not globally frequent) and scan the database more than Apriori does. DIC proposes a random partitioning technique to reduce the data–partition skew.

Cheung and colleagues have proposed the Asynchronous Parallel Mining algorithm, which is based on DIC (Cheung *et al.*, 1998). APM uses FDM's global-pruning technique to decrease the size of candidate 2-itemsets. This pruning is most effective when there is high data skew among the partitions.

However, DIC requires that the partitions be homogeneous.

APM addresses this problem by treating the first iteration separately. APM logically divides the database into many small, equal-sized virtual partitions. The number of virtual partitions l is independent of the number of processors p, but usually $l \geq p$. Let m be the number of items. APM gathers the local counts of the m items in each partition. This forms an $l \times m$ data set, with one item support vector in an m-dimensional space. APM groups these l vectors into k clusters, maximizing intercluster distance and minimizing intracluster distance. Thus, the k clusters or partitions are as skewed as possible, and they are used to generate a small set of candidate 2-itemsets. APM now prepares to apply DIC in parallel. The idea is to divide the database into p homogeneous partitions. Each processor independently applies DIC to its local partition.

However, there is a shared prefix tree among all processors, which is built asynchronously. APM stops when all processors have processed all candidates, whether generated by themselves or others, and when no new candidates are generated. To apply DIC on its partitions, each processor must divide its local partition into r sub-partitions. Furthermore, DIC requires that both the p interprocessor partitions and the r intraprocessor partitions be as homogeneous as possible. APM ensures that the p partitions are homogeneous by assigning the virtual partitions from each of the k clusters of the first pass in a round-robin manner among the p processors. Thus, each processor gets an equal mix of virtual partitions from separate clusters, resulting in homogeneous processor partitions. To get intraprocessor partition homogeneity, APM performs a secondary k clustering. That is, they group the r partitions into k clusters, and again assign elements from each of the k clusters to the r partitions in a round-robin manner.

In the APM Algorithm, preprocessing contains the following: all processors scan their partitions to compute local supports of size-1 itemsets in their intervals; compute L_1 and generate $C_2 = $ Apriori_gen(L_1); perform a k-clustering on the intervals and a virtual partition pruning on C_2; initialize the shared trie with the remaining size-2 candidates; perform inter-partition interval configuration and intra-partition interval configuration to prepare a homogeneous distribution. The preprocessing is to serve two purposes: (1) reduce the number of size-2 candidates by a virtual partition pruning and initialize the trie with the remaining size-2 candidates; (2) perform inter-partition and intra-partition interval configurations to increase the homogeneity of the itemset distribution.

Algorithm 12.11 (APM Algorithm (Cheung *et al.*, 1998)).

// Parallel execution: every processor i runs the following fragment on its partition D_i

1. while (some processor has not finished the counting of all the itemsets on the trie on its partition)

2.   {while (processor i has not finished the counting of all the itemsets on the trie on D_i)

3.   {scan one more interval on D_i and count the supports of the item-sets on the trie;

4.   found out the locally large itemsets among the itemsets on the trie for the interval scanned;

5.   generate new candidates from these locally large itemsets;

6.   perform pruning on these candidates and insert the survivors into the trie;

7.   remove globally small itemsets on the trie;

8.   }

9.   }

Every processor in APM performs dynamic generation and counting. The new candidates generated by each process go through a pruning similar to the partition pruning before the survivors are inserted into the trie. Before a processor starts a new round of counting on the next interval, it traverses the trie to remove itemsets which are found to be globally small. This will keep the size of the trie minimum. If all the processors have counted all the itemsets on the trie, then APM terminates.

12.7.4 *Data Skewness and Workload Balance*

In a database partition, two data distribution characteristics, data skewness and workload balance, have orthogonal effects on prunings and hence on the performance of FPM. Intuitively, the data skewness of a partitioned database is high if the supports of most large itemsets are clustered in a few partitions. It is low if the supports of most large itemsets are distributed evenly across the processors.

David Cheung and Yongqiao Xiao have developed a skewness metric based on the well-established notion of entropy. Given a random variable X, its entropy is a measurement on how even or uneven its probability distribution is over its values. If a database is partitioned over n processors, the value $px(i) = \frac{X.\sup(i)}{X.\sup}$ can be regarded as the probability of occurrence of an itemset X in partition D_i, $1 \le i \le n$. The entropy $H(X) = - \sum_{i=1}^{n} (px(i) \times \log(px(i)))$ is a measurement of the distribution of the local supports of X over the partitions For example, if X is skewed completely into a single partition D_k, $(1 \le k \le n)$, i.e., it only occurs in D_k, then $p_x(k) = 1$ and $p_x(i) = 0, \forall i \ne k$. The value of $H(X) = 0$ is minimal in this case. On the contrary, if X is evenly distributed among all the partitions, then $px(i) = 1/n, 1 \le i \le n$, and the value of $H(X) = \log(n)$ is the maximal in this case. Therefore, the following metric can be used to measure the skewness of a data partition.

Definition 12.8. Given a database partition D_i $(1 \le i \le n)$, the skewness $S(X)$ of an itemset is defined by

$$S(X) = \frac{H_{\max} - H(X)}{H_{\max}}, \tag{12.9}$$

where $H(X) = - \sum_{i=1}^{n}(px(i) \times \log(px(i)))$ and $H_{\max} = \log(n)$.

The skewness $S(X)$ has the following properties:

(1) $S(X) = 0$, when all $p_x(i), 1 \le i \le n$, are equal. So, the skewness is at its lowest value when X is distributed evenly in all partitions.
(2) $S(X) = 1$, if $\exists k \in [1, n]$ such that $p_x(k) = 1$, and $p_x(i) = 0$ for $\forall i \ne k$, $1 \le i \le n$. So, the skewness is at its highest value when X occurs only in one partition.
(3) $0 < S(X) < 1$ in all the other cases.

Workload balance is a measurement of the distribution of the support clusterings of the large itemsets over the partitions at the processors. We define $W_i = \sum_{x \in L_s} w(X) \times px(i)$ to be the itemset workload in a partition D_i, where L_s is the set of all the large itemsets. Intuitively, the workload W_i in partition D_i is the ratio of the total supports of the large itemsets in D_i over all the partitions. Note that $\sum_{i=1}^{n} W_i = 1$.

Definition 12.9. For a database partition D_i $(1 \le i \le n)$, of a database D, the workload balance factor $TB(D)$ of the partition is given by

$$TB(D) = \frac{- \sum_{i=1}^{n} W_i \log(W_i)}{\log(n)}. \tag{12.10}$$

The metric $TB(D)$ has the following properties:

(1) $TB(D) = 1$ when the workload across all processors are the same.
(2) $TB(D) = 0$ when the workload is concentrated on one processor.
(3) $0 < TB(D) < 1$ in all the other cases.

The data skewness metric and workload balance factor are not independent. Theoretically, each one of them could have values ranging from 0 and 1. However, some combinations of their values are not admissible.

Association rule mining has become a mature field of research with diverse branches of specialization. The fundamentals of association mining are now well established with some important exceptions. Current research appears to focus on the specialization of fundamental association mining algorithms, many areas of which are still emerging. These include fields, such as measures of interest, the inclusion of domain knowledge and semantics, quantitative mining, disassociation mining, privacy mining, incremental mining, iterative, and interactive or guided mining, and higher order mining.

Exercises

12.1 Illustrate what is meant by support, confidence, minsup, minconf, and large itemset.

12.2 The following table shows four transactions with the minsup being 60%. Find out one frequent itemset.

TID	Date	Items_bought
1	01/05/2005	I_1, I_2, I_4, I_6
2	02/05/2005	I_1, I_2, I_3, I_4, I_5
3	03/05/2005	I_1, I_2, I_3, I_5
4	04/05/2005	I_1, I_2, I_4

12.3 Describe classical Apriori algorithm.

12.4 Do association rule mining based on the distributed system.

12.5 What are positive and negative relations? Give an example.

12.6 Summarize how to effectively mine the following rule, "A free commodity possibly triggers 200 total shopping in identical transaction" (agrees the price of each kind of commodity not negative)?

12.7 The following table includes nine transactions. Suppose the minsup is 20%, give all the frequent itemsets.

TID	Items
1	I_1, I_2, I_5
2	I_2, I_4
3	I_2, I_3, I_6
4	I_1, I_2, I_4
5	I_1, I_3
6	I_2, I_3
7	I_1, I_3
8	I_1, I_2, I_3, I_5
9	I_1, I_2, I_3

12.8 Develop an incremental algorithm for association rule mining.

Chapter 13

Evolutionary Computation

Evolutionary computation can provide highly optimized solutions in a wide range of problem settings, making them popular in computer science. Many variants and extensions exist, suited to more specific families of problems and data structures.

13.1 Introduction

Evolutionary computation is a computing system which applies natural evolution and adaptive thought (Yao and Xu, 2006). Darwin's evolutionism is a robust mechanism for searching and optimization, which has great impacts on the development of computer science, in particular artificial intelligence. The majority of organisms evolve by natural selection and sexual reproduction. Natural selection determines which individuals in a population can survive and reproduce, while sexual reproduction is the guarantee of gene mixture and recombination in the next generation. The principle of natural selection is "to select the superior and eliminate the inferior, survival of the fittest".

In the early 1960s, the above features of natural evolution had drawn Holland's great interest. In those years, he and his students were studying about how to establish a machine learning system. He found that machine learning can be realized not only by an individual's adaptation but also by plurivoltine evolutions of a population. Inspired by Darwin's evolution thought, Holland realized that in order to obtain an excellent learning algorithm, a reproduction of a population with multiple candidate strategies, instead of only one strategy, should be built and improved. As this idea originated from genetic evolution, Holland called this research field genetic algorithm. Genetic algorithm was not well known until his currently famous monograph *Adaptation in Natural and Artificial Systems* (Holland, 1975) was published in 1975. This monograph systematically introduces the basic theory of genetic algorithm and forms a foundation for genetic algorithm. In the same year, De Jong finished his doctoral dissertation "An Analysis of the Behavior of a Class of Genetic Adaptive Systems". In this doctoral dissertation, De Jong applied Holland's schema theory to his experiments and drew some important conclusions and presented some effective methods, which have come to have prodigious influence on the application and development of genetic algorithm.

The idea of genetic algorithm originates from the biological evolution process. It is essentially a class of stochastic search algorithms based on the information present in genetic mechanism and the principle of natural selection, including the principle of adaptation and struggling for existence in the evolution process. In genetic algorithm, a state space is expressed as a set of character strings. It is by applying a probability search process that genetic algorithm searches in state space and generates new individuals. A comparison of genetic algorithm and natural evolution is presented in Table 13.1.

The adaptation process is pivotal to artificial genetic systems. It generates a new structure by a population's structures and genetic operations, such as crossover and mutation, not by a simple structure. In a population, every structure has its own fitness value, which is used to determine which structures can generate new structures.

The simplest learning system based on genetic algorithm is shown in Figure 13.1. The system consists of two subsystems. One is a genetic algorithm-based learning subsystem, which leads to proper change of structures. The other is an executive subsystem, which results in improvement of a system's behaviors.

Table 13.1.   Comparison of genetic algorithm and natural evolution

Natural evolution	Genetic algorithm
Chromosome	Character string
Gene	Character feature
Allele	Feather value
Locus	Location in a string
Genotype	Structure
Phenotype	Parameter set, decoding structure

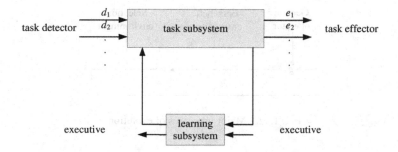

Fig. 13.1. Execution-oriented learning system

In 1988, Mayr had proposed neo-Darwinism, whose major viewpoints are as follows (Mayr, 1988):

(1) An individual is a basic goal of selection.
(2) Stochastic process plays a great role in evolution, while most genetic variations are accidental phenomena.
(3) Most genotypic variations, especially mutations, are the products of recombination.
(4) Gradual evolution is possibly related to uncontinuous phenotype.
(5) Not all the changes of phenotype are the inevitable result of natural selection.
(6) Evolution varies with diversified forms, including changing genes.
(7) Natural selection is based on the probability model and not on the deterministic model.

At present, evolutionary computation mainly includes genetic algorithm, evolutionary strategy, and evolutionary programming, which are introduced in the following.

13.2 Formal Model of Evolution System Theory

Evolution plays its roles in population. Waddington showed the importance of the relationship between genotype and phenotype (Waddinton, 1974). Population rejects the heterogeneous environment and the "epigenetic environment" is a multidimensional space. The interaction of genotype with environment determines the phenotype, which then acts through heterogeneously selecting the environment. Note that this multidimensional space is different from "epigenetic environment". At this

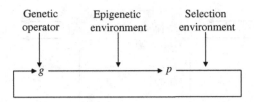

Fig. 13.2.   Major processes of evolution

time, adaptability is the product of the phenotype space and the selected environment space. It usually is a 1D function, denoting the contribution of many offspring to the next generation.

Based on the above idea, Muhlenbein and Kindermann presented a model which was called formal model of evolution system theory (Muhlenbein and Kindermann, 1989). Figure 13.2 shows the relationship of this model. Genotype space (GS) and phenotype space (PS) are defined by genotype and phenotype, respectively:

$$GS = \{g = (a_1, \ldots, a_n), \ a_i \in A_i\}, \tag{13.1}$$

$$PS = \{p = (p_1, \ldots, p_m), \ p_i \in IR\}, \tag{13.2}$$

where g denotes genotype and p denotes phenotype. The possible value of gene g_i is called allele. In Mendel's genetics, it is assumed that there are finite alleles in each gene.

Given an epigenetic environment set:

$$EP = \{EP_1, \ldots, EP_k\}$$

and transformation function:

$$f : GS \times EP \to PS,$$

$$p = f(g, EP). \tag{13.3}$$

In fact, the transformation function presents a model which shows that the change of phenotype is due to the interaction of the gene with the environment, and this change is higher order nonlinear. The final phenotype has all the characteristics, while the initial one just has a simple one-to-one correspondence. Quality function q expresses the quality of the phenotype in a given selection environment ES_i, and it is defined as follows:

$$q(p, ES_i, t) \to IR^+. \tag{13.4}$$

This quality function is in fact a fitness function, which is used for Darwinian selection. So far, there are three general models:

(1) Mendel's genetics;
(2) genecology;
(3) evolutionary gamete.

In Mendel's genetics, genotype is modeled in detail, but phenotype and environment are almost left in the basket. In genecology, the case is just the opposite. The theory of the evolutionary gamete is a model induced from sociobiology.

Let's first discuss the selection model in Mendel's genetics. For simplicity, assume that there are n alleles $a_1, \ldots, a_n$ in a gene. Double-genotype is expressed as a 2-tuple (a_i, a_j), and $p_{i,j}$ is defined as the frequency of genotype (a_i, a_j) in a population. Suppose that genotype is equal to phenotype. Quality function is used to assign a value to each phenotype:

$$q(a_i, a_j) = q_{i,j},$$

where $q_{i,j}$ can be explained as the difference between birth rate and death rate.

Suppose that $p'_{i,j}$ is the frequency of the next generation's phenotype. Then, Darwin's selection adjusts the distribution of phenotype according to selection equations:

$$p'_{i,j} = p'_{i,j} \frac{q_{i,j}}{\overline{Q}}, \tag{13.5}$$

$$\overline{Q} = \sum_{i,j} q_{i,j} p_{i,j}, \tag{13.6}$$

where $\overline{Q}$ is the average fitness of population. Assume that p_i is the frequency of alleles of population. If

$$p_{i,j} = p_i p_j,$$

then a selection equation in GS is obtained as follows:

$$p'_i = p_i Q_i / \overline{Q}, \tag{13.7}$$

$$Q_i = \sum_j q_{i,j} p_j. \tag{13.8}$$

The above discrete selection equation can be approximated with the following continuous equation:

$$\frac{dp_i}{dt} = p_i (Q_i - \overline{Q}) / \overline{Q}. \tag{13.9}$$

If $q_{i,j} = q_{j,i}$, then

$$\frac{dp_i}{dt} = p_i(Q_i - \overline{Q}).$$ (13.10)

It is easy to verify that

$$\frac{d\overline{Q}}{dt} = 2(E(Q^2) - \overline{Q}^2) = 2\text{Var}(Q) \geq 0.$$ (13.11)

This result is called Fisher's fundamental theorem, which shows that average fitness is proportional to the difference of fitness. In fact, only some of all possible genotypes are realized. This is the task of genetic operations: to search genotype space with a small number of individuals. These genetic operations are the main origin of the genetic variation of a population, and the most important genetic operations are mutation and recombination.

In genecology, it is usually assumed that dominance is inherited by interactions between gene loci. At each gene locus, two alleles are separated, and the dominant value increases by one, while the other decreases by one.

An individual's phenotypic value is expressed as

$$P_{i,j} = \mu + G_i + E_{i,j} + (GE)_{i,j},$$

where μ is the average of dominant value, G_i denotes the ith phenotype, $E_{i,j}$ is the ith gene in the jth individual, and GE denotes the interaction of the genotype and the environment.

The complex relationship prevents the population from directly accessing some of the "best phenotypes". This relationship constrains the selection. The important constraint has no genetic variation, interaction of genes, and nonlinear transformation from genotype to phenotype.

In the theory of evolutionary gametes, each individual can suit N strategies. Suppose that p_i is the frequency of strategy i in the next generations, $E_{i,j}$ is the profit of strategy i resisting strategy j. The quality of strategy i is

$$Q_i = \sum_j p_i E(i, j).$$

The average fitness of the population is

$$\overline{Q} = \sum_i p_i Q_i.$$

Suppose the number of asexually reproducing individuals is proportional to their fitness. This can be expressed by the familiar selection equation

$$p_i' = p_i \frac{Q_i}{Q}. \tag{13.12}$$

Evolution gamete theory requires dynamical attractors, which are called evolutionarily stable strategy (ESS). For $p_i, p_j \neq 0$, ESS is characterized by $Q_i = Q_j$.

13.3 Darwin's Evolutionary Algorithm

According to quantitative genetics, Darwin's evolutionary algorithm uses simple mutation/selection kinetics. Darwin's algorithm can be formalized as follows:

$$(\mu/\rho, \lambda)(\mu/\rho + \lambda), \tag{13.13}$$

where μ is the number of the parents and λ is the number of offspring. Integer ρ is called "hybrid" number. If two parents' genes are mixed, then $\rho = 2$. Individuals are allowed to generate offspring only if μ is the best. The comma denotes that parents have no choice while plus sign denotes that the parents have a choice.

An important part of Darwin's algorithm is that the range of mutation is not fixed but inherited. It adapts itself to the environment by way of evolutionary process. Darwin's algorithm is described as follows:

Algorithm 13.1 (Darwin's Evolutionary Algorithm).
1. Construct an initial population;
2. Generate offspring by mutation:
$$s_1' = s g_1$$
$$x_1' = x + s_1' Z_1$$
$$\vdots$$
$$s_\lambda' = s g_\lambda$$
$$x_\lambda' = x + s_\lambda' Z_\lambda$$
3. Selection:
$$Q(x) = \max_{1 \leq i \leq \lambda} \{Q(x')\}$$
4. Goto step 1.

In Darwin's evolutionary algorithm, random vector Z_i usually has distributed components, and $g_i s$ comes from distributed normative logs. Therefore, the algorithm generates λ offspring near the parents. By inheriting and the adaptive neighbor's property, the model can be extended to one with $2n$ genes, while the whole individual mutation is limited in n-dimensional space.

13.4 Classifier System

Holland and his colleagues had proposed a cognitive model of the classifier system, where rules are not expressed as a rule set, but the internal entity is manipulated by genetic algorithm. Figure 13.3 presents a general structure for the classifier system. As can be seen from Figure 13.3, a classifier system consists of three parts: executive subsystem, credit assignment subsystem, and discovery subsystem.

Executive subsystem is at the lowest level in the general structure and reacts directly with the environment. It is the same as the expert system, which consists of production rules. However, they are based on message passing. These kind of rules are called classifier.

For classifier system-based learning, the environment needs to be capable of providing feedback and affirming whether the wanted state arrives or not. The system will validate the effectiveness of these rules. These activities are usually called credit assignments, such as barrel chain algorithm.

The last level is the discovery subsystem, which generates new rules and substitutes some rules of little usefulness. The system generates rules by cumulative experiences and performs genetic selection, recombination, and substituting rules according to fitness.

The Classifier system is a system which is executed concurrently and is based on the message passing and rules. In a simple way, a message is expressed with a given character set and fixed length. All the rules are expressed in the form of

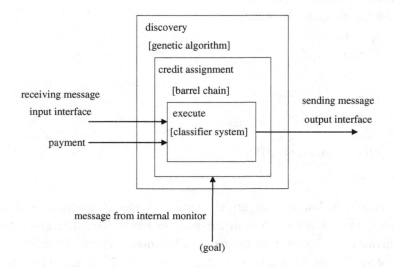

Fig. 13.3.   General structure of classifier system

"condition/action". Each condition defines all the required information, and then each action defines the related message to be sent when the condition is satisfied. For simplicity, suppose a message is expressed with a binary character string whose length is l and character set is $\{1, 0, \#\}$, where # means that it can match both 1 and 0. For example, the character string $11 \ldots 1\#$ defines a subset consisting of two messages, i.e., $\{11 \ldots 11, 11 \ldots 10\}$. The more general expression is as follows:

$$< s_1, s_2, \ldots, s_j, \ldots, s_l >, \quad s_j \in \{1, 0, \#\}.$$

This is a subset defined by only one character. Suppose

$$< m_1, m_2, \ldots, m_j, \ldots, m_l >, \quad m_j \in \{1, 0\},$$

is a l-bit message, which belongs to the following subset:

(1) If $s_j = 1$ or $s_j = 0$, then $m_j = s_j$.
(2) If $s_j = \#$, then m_j can be either 1 or 0.

All messages meeting the above requirement constitute a subset, which is a hyperplane in message space. A classifier system consists of a set of classifiers $\{C_1, C_2, \ldots, C_N\}$, a message table, an input interface, and an output interface. Figure 13.4 presents the basic structure of a classifier system. Each part's function is as follows:

(1) The current environment state is transformed into a standard message through an input interface.

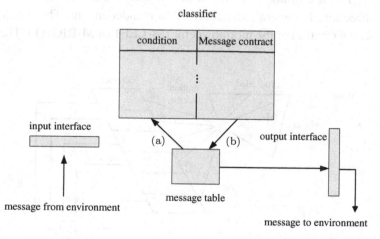

Fig. 13.4. Basic structure of classifier system (a) all messages for condition test and (b) the selected messages from classifier

(2) Classifier defines the process of dealing with the message according to the given rules.

(3) Message table contains all current messages.

(4) Messages are transformed into effector's action, thus amending the environment state.

Algorithm 13.2 (Classifier's Basic Algorithm).
1. Put all messages from input interface into message table;
2. Compare all messages in message table with all conditions in classifiers and record all matching;
3. For all matching satisfying classifier's condition, put the message that is defined by its action into message table;
4. Let all messages in message table be replaced with newly generated messages;
5. Standardize messages in message table so that they satisfy output interface, forming current system's output;
6. Go to step 1.

In order to show the interaction of classifiers and the influence of rule-based learning, we introduce a simple visual classifier system in this section, presented in Figure 13.5. Every object in the receptive field generates a message in the input interface. Detectors and their values are defined according to practical needs. There are three kinds of effectors in the system that determine the actions in the environment. One is to control the visual vector, which denotes the position of an object in the receptive field. The visual vector can increasingly rotate by a time-step (V-LEFT or V-RIGHT, 15° at a time). The system also has a motion vector, which denotes its motion direction. In general, visual direction is independent. The second vector then controls the rotation of the motion vector (M-LEFT or M-RIGHT). The second

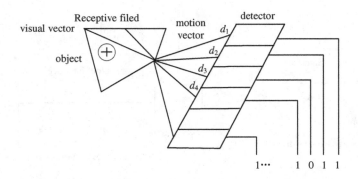

Fig. 13.5.   A simple visual classifier system

effector can also align the motion vector and visual vector, or oppose them (ALIGN or OPPOSE). The third effector is used to set up movement rate (FAST, CRUISE, SLOW, STOP) in a given direction. Classifiers are used to deal with the information that is generated by the detector and provide the effector with command sequences so as to get to a given target. Detector defines the right six bits in the message from the input interface (Figure 13.5). Property detector defines the following values

$$d_1 = \begin{cases} 1, & \text{if object is moved} \\ 0, & \text{other} \end{cases}$$

$$(d_2, d_3) = \begin{cases} (0, 0), & \text{if object is at the center of receptive field} \\ (1, 0), & \text{if object is on the left of the center} \\ (0, 1), & \text{if object is on the right of the center} \end{cases}$$

$$d_4 = \begin{cases} 1, & \text{if system is near to objects} \\ 0, & \text{other} \end{cases}$$

$$d_5 = \begin{cases} 1, & \text{object is large} \\ 0, & \text{other} \end{cases}$$

$$d_6 = \begin{cases} 1, & \text{object is flat and long} \\ 0, & \text{other} \end{cases}$$

Consider an irritation-reaction classifier which has the following rules:

IF a prey (small, moving, non-striped object) is centered and non-adjacent
THEN quickly move toward the object (ALIGN), (FAST).

In order to realize this rule, detection value is used as condition, which is expressed in the form of #'s. The 2-tuple (0, 0) denotes the message generated in input interface. According to the above definition, the classifier has the following condition:

$$00\#\#\#\#\#\#\#\#000001,$$

where the leftmost two bits are label, # is irrelevant to bits, and the rightmost six bits are the values of prescriptive detectors. If the condition is satisfied, the following message is sent out by the classifier:

$$0100000000000000,$$

where the prefix 01 shows that this message does not come from the input inter-face. This message can be used to set the condition of effector of output interface.

The whole rule is as follows:

00##########000001/0100000000000000,   ALIGN,   FAST.

In a warning system, the following rule can be used to determine whether the system is in a warning state

IF   there is a moving object in the visual field,
THEN   set up a warning timer and send out a warning message.
IF   the warning timer is not zero,
THEN   send out a warning message.
IF   there is no moving object in the visual field and the timer is not zero,
THEN   cancel the warning timer.

There are two effectors used to build a classifier by using the above rules. The effectors include SET ALERT, DECREMENT ALERT, as well as a detector

$$d_9 = \begin{cases} 1, & \text{if the timer is not zero} \\ 0, & \text{other} \end{cases}$$

The classifier can realize the following three kinds of rules, which have the following forms:

00##############1/0100000000000011,   SET ALERT,

00#####1########/0100000000000011,

00#####1#######0/DECREMENT ALERT.

A classifier system can be expressed as a network. The most direct method is to use each node in a network to denote the related classification. Figure 13.6 gives such a network chart. If a moving object appears in the visual field, then ALERT node is labeled. If the nodes ALERT, SMALL, and NOT STRIPED are labeled, then TARGET node is labeled. In order to make this network become a classifier, every node is associated with an identification tag. In Figure 13.6, the five prefix bits are used as tags.

From Figure 13.6, if a MOVING node is labeled by detector d_1, then the directed arc from MOVING to ALERT can be built by the following classifier:

00##############1/01001###########,

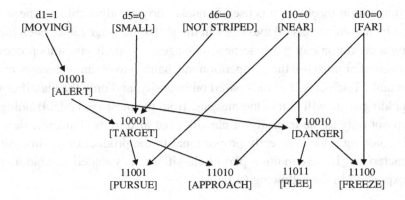

Fig. 13.6.   A network chart

The directed arc from SMALL, NOT STRIPED, and ALERT to TARGET can then be built by a single classifier:

$$00\#\#\#\#\#\#\#\#00\#\#\#\#, \quad 01001\#\#\#\#\#\#\#\#\#\# \; /$$

$$10001\#\#\#\#\#\#\#\#\#\#.$$

The other part in the network can be similarly accomplished.

13.5 Bucket Brigade Algorithm

A classifier system is a highly time-parallel learning system based on rules. It can continuously build and improve its environmental model, which is built by using obtained experience. The basic units of the classifier system consist of message and classifier (rules). However, the combination of the two units and default classifier can generate very complex knowledge structure.

Two kinds of learning mechanisms are used in the classifier system:

(1) **Bucket brigade algorithm.** According to the contribution to the system, every rule is assigned a credit value.
(2) **Algorithm for discovering rules.** This kind of algorithm may include genetic algorithm, which can discover new rules, so as to improve the system's knowledge database.

Based on the whole availability of the classifier system, the bucket brigade algorithm endows the classifier with a credit value. By modifying the executing cycle, competition mechanism is used in bucket brigade algorithm. In the working cycle, each classifier scans all messages in the global message table. Each message satisfying a condition can generate new messages. By modifying this process, the satisfied classifier must use the competition mechanism to obtain messages from the message table. Each classifier bids based on intensity, and only the classifier with a higher bidding scale will obtain the message from the message table. Bidding scale is related not only to the intensity of classifier but also to its characteristics. More precisely, bidding scale is directly proportional to the product of the intensity and the characteristic. If the condition part of classifier C is satisfied, the bidding scale can be expressed in the following form

$$\text{Bid}(C, t) = cR(C)S(C, t), \tag{13.14}$$

where $R(C)$ denotes characteristic, equaling the ratio of the number of bits which are not equal to # with the number of all bits in the condition part; $S(C, t)$ denotes the intensity of C at moment t; c is a constant smaller than 1, such as 1/8 or 1/16.

Victorious bidders put message in the message table, and at the same time their intensities reduce the bidding scale. Take classifier C for example

$$S(C, t + 1) = S(C, t) - B(C, t), \tag{13.15}$$

while classifier $\{C'\}$ for matching message sent by victorious bidders increase their intensities, their values are equal to bidding scale

$$S(\underline{C'}, t + 1) = S(C', t) + aB(C, t), \tag{13.16}$$

where $a = 1/(\text{the cardinality of } \{C'\})$.

Figure 13.7 presents the two purposes of a bid: supporting service and shift of bid by message flow. In addition, bid is used to modify the provider's intensity.

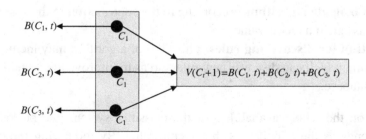

Fig. 13.7.   Intensity of classifier is modified by bid

If the system can learn effectively and work steadily, and related results are acceptable, then the decentralization of rule intensity can be reduced. If the decentralization cannot be controlled, the system may adopt the rules with high intensity, leading to loss of useful rules with low intensity. For changes of bidding competition and that of mechanism of message generation, some of them require "parasitic" rules to be controlled, while some require the finite message table to be utilized effectively.

13.6 Genetic Algorithm

Holland had abstractly analyzed the adaptive process of the natural system and designed an artificial system having adaptive features of the natural system. In this kind of artificial system, an adaptive process is described as a search process in changing structural space. He pointed out that (1) many complex structures can be coded in the simple form of bit strings; and (2) these bit strings can be gradually improved by some simple transforms, so that they transform in a good direction. Based on the above ideas, he proposed the genetic algorithm to simulate the evolution process of structures.

In genetic algorithm, the structure is first coded in the form of a character string, and each character string is called an individual. Then a set of character strings, which is called a population, is iteratively operated on. Each iteration is called a generation, which contains the process of the keeping the superior structure in population and that of information transform among structural and stochastic character strings. Similar to natural evolution, genetic algorithm gets a good chromosome by operating genes in the chromosome, so as to solve a related problem. Similar to nature, genetic algorithm knows nothing about the problem to be solved. It just needs to evaluate each chromosome and selects the chromosome according to the evaluation value, so that the chromosome with higher value has more chances to propagate. In genetic algorithm, a bit string serves as a chromosome, while the single bit serves as a gene. A population is randomly generated, and each individual in the population is a bit string. Each individual is endowed with a numerical value, which is called fitness. An individual with low fitness is deleted while one with high fitness is then selected for further operations. The common genetic operators mainly include reproduction, crossover, mutation, and inversion.

Compared with the traditional optimization algorithm, genetic algorithm has the following features:

(1) Genetic algorithm does not directly operate parametric variables, but utilizes related codes of parametric variables.

(2) Genetic algorithm's searching starts with one point which is from the population but not from the problem space.
(3) Genetic algorithm utilizes a fitness value, not differential coefficient or other information.
(4) Genetic algorithm utilizes probabilistic transition rules, not deterministic rules.

Genetic algorithm can solve the hard problem through a coding technique and breed mechanism to simulate the complex phenomenon. In particular, it is not constrained by the restriction hypothesis of search space and does not require the searching space to be continuous and derivative; it can get the global optimal solution with high probability from discrete, multiple-extremum, and noising high-dimensional problems. In addition, genetic algorithm's inherent parallelism makes it very suitable for massively parallel computing. At present, it is widely applied in various domains, such as optimization, machine learning, and parallel processing.

13.6.1 *Major Steps of Genetic Algorithm*

In order to use genetic algorithm to solve problems, the preparation is divided into the following four steps

(1) confirm the expression scheme;
(2) confirm the method to measure the fitness value;
(3) confirm the parameters and variables controlling the algorithm;
(4) confirm the method to get results and a criterion of how to terminate the algorithm.

In addition to genetic algorithm, the expression scheme is used to express every possible point in search space as a string with fixed length. Confirming the expression scheme requires the selection of a character string's length l and alphabet's size k. Binary bit string is usually used to express chromosomes in genetic algorithm. The measurement of fitness associates a fixed length string with a fitness value. The main parameters that are used to control genetic algorithm include the size N of the population, the maximum generation number M, and other parameters including selection probability p_r, crossover probability p_c, mutation probability p_c, etc. The criterion for algorithm termination is determined by concrete problems. After these preparation steps are finished, we can utilize genetic algorithm.

Algorithm 13.3 (Basic Genetic Algorithm).

1. Randomly generate a population which consists of fixed length strings;
2. Iteratively perform the following steps on the population until the selected criterion is satisfied:

    (a) Calculate the fitness value for every individual in the population;

    (b) Use the following three operators (first two operators at least) to generate new population:

    - Reproduction: reproduce the existing individual string to a new population.
    - Crossover: generate new strings by randomly choosing and recombining two existing individual strings.
    - Mutation: randomly select a gene in a string and variate this gene.

3. The individual string with the highest fitness value is used as the operation result of genetic algorithm, which is regarded as the solution to the problem (or approximate solution).

Figure 13.8 presents the flow chart of basic genetic algorithm, where variable GEN is currently the evolution generation number.

13.6.2 *Representation Schema*

For the genetic algorithm, let us consider an alphabet $V_+ = \{0, 1, *\}$ and use it to express schema. The so-called schema is a structure which is used to describe a subset of strings. All strings in this subset take the same values at some positions. The symbol "*" denotes an uncertain letter; that is, the symbol "*" matches both "0" and "1" at a given position. For example, consider a schema $H =^* 11^*0^{**}$ with length 7. Let string $A = 0111000$, then A is a representation of H; H can match A at the second, third, and fifth positions.

There are 3^l schemas with length l. In general, if the alphabet contains k letters, there are totally $(k + 1)^l$ schemas with length l. The order of a schema is defined as the number of symbols which is not equal to "*" in the schema, denoted by $o(H)$. For a binary string, its order is equal to the number of 1 and 0. For example, the order of schema 011^*1^{**} is equal to 4, denoted by $o(011^*1^{**}) = 4$; $o(0^{******}) = 1$.

The number of the symbol which is not equal to "*" in the schema is denoted by $o(H)$. For a binary string, its order is equal to the number of 1 and 0. For example, the order of schema 011^*1^{**} is equal to 4, denoted by $o(011^*1^{**}) = 4$; $o(0^{******}) = 1$.

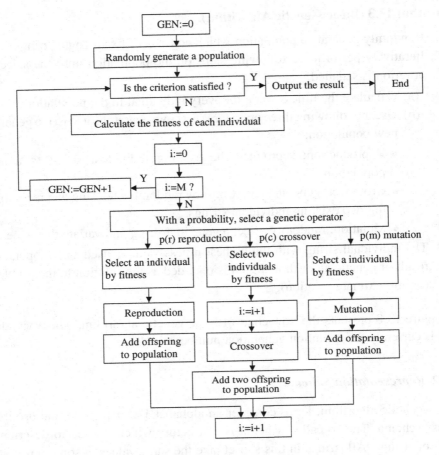

Fig. 13.8.   Flow chart of basic genetic algorithm

The length of a schema is defined as the distance between the first determining position and the last determining position in the schema, denoted by delta(H). For example, let $H = 011*1**$, then delta(H) = 4. This is because the first determining position in this schema is 1, while the last determining position is 5, then the distance between them is $5 - 1 = 4$.

Suppose at the moment t, schema H has M representations, which are contained in population $B(t)$, denoted by $M = M(H, t)$. At the reproduction stage, every string is reproduced according to its fitness value. String B_i's reproduction probability is

$$p_i = \frac{f_i}{\sum_{j=1}^{n} f_j}. \qquad (13.17)$$

After population $B(t)$ is replaced with a population consisting of n strings which are not superposed, we hope that there are $M(H, t + 1)$ representations of schema H in population $B(t + 1)$ at moment t. This can be calculated by the following equation:

$$M(H, t + 1) = M(H, t) \cdot n \cdot \frac{f(H)}{\sum_{j=1}^{n} f_j}, \tag{13.18}$$

where $f(H)$ denotes average fitness value of strings of schema H at moment t. Because the average fitness value of the whole population can be written as

$$\overline{f} = \sum_{j=1}^{n} \frac{f_j}{n}, \tag{13.19}$$

the reproduction growth equation of the schema can be expressed by

$$M(H, t + 1) = M(H, t) \frac{f(H)}{\overline{f}}. \tag{13.20}$$

This shows that the size of a particular schema is directly proportional to the ratio of the average fitness of the schema to that of the population. In other words, the schema whose average fitness value is higher than that of population can generate more representation strings in next generation, while the representation strings of a schema with lower average fitness will reduce in the next generation. Suppose the schema H's average fitness value is greater than that of the population by value $c\overline{f}$, where c is constant, then growth equation of a schema is

$$M(H, t + 1) = M(H, t) \frac{\overline{f} + c\overline{f}}{\overline{f}} = (1 + c) \cdot M(H, t). \tag{13.21}$$

Further, we can conclude that

$$m(H, t) = m(H, 0) \cdot (1 + c)^t. \tag{13.22}$$

Expression (13.22) shows that the representation strings of a schema whose average fitness is higher than that of population will grow exponentially with the generation; on the contrary, for the schema whose average fitness is lower than that of population, its representation strings will reduce at an exponentially decaying rate.

13.6.3 *Crossover Operation*

Crossover operation is a process of information exchange among structural random strings. Suppose that population $B(t)$ is a set of schemas, where historical information is expressed in the form of instances, which are saved in $B(t)$. Crossover operation is to generate new instances of the existing schemas. At the same time, new schemas are also generated. A simple crossover operation can be divided into three steps:

(1) Select two strings from population $B(t)$: $a = s_1 s_2 \ldots s_l$, $a' = s_1' s_2' \ldots s_l'$.
(2) Randomly select an integer $x \in \{1, 2, \ldots l - 1\}$.
(3) Exchange the elements on the left of the position x in a and a', and then generate two pieces of new strings: $s_1 \ldots s_x s_{x+1}' \ldots s_l'$ and $s_1' \ldots s_x' s_{x+1} \ldots s_l$.

If each string is endowed with intensity $S(C_j, T)$, then the genetic algorithm is described as follows:

Algorithm 13.4 (Genetic Algorithm with Intensity).

1. At the moment t, randomly generate population $B(t)$ with the number of M. Calculate the average fitness of this population, denoted by $v(t)$, and then endow each string in $B(t)$ with the standardizing value $S(C_j, t)/v(t)$.
2. Endow each string in $B(t)$ with a probability value, which is directly proportional to the standardizing value. Then, select n pairs of strings from $B(t)$ based on probability, where $n \ll M$, and reproduce them.
3. For every pair of replicated strings, cross one string with the other, forming $2n$ new strings.
4. Use newly generated $2n$ strings in step (3) to replace $2n$ strings with the smallest intensities in $B(t)$.
5. Let $t = t + 1$, go to step (1).

To show how the above genetic algorithm works, we give a simple example in Figure 13.9. In this example, there are eight strings which constitute a population.

$$
\begin{array}{ll}
C_1 & 111011101 \ldots \beta_1 \\
C_2 & 110011110 \ldots \beta_0 \\
C_3 & 000111110 \ldots \beta_2 \\
C_4 & 011010011 \ldots \beta_0 \\
C_5 & 100011101 \ldots \beta_2 \\
C_6 & 011001100 \ldots \beta_2 \\
C_7 & 100100101 \ldots \beta_0 \\
C_8 & 100010010 \ldots \beta_1
\end{array}
$$

where the value on the right of arrowhead is intensity of corresponding string C_i in $B(t)$. The strings C_2, C_3, C_6 are all the instances of schema ******1*0*···*, denoted by H_1; the strings C_3, C_5, C_8 are the instances of schema *00*1**···*, denoted by H_2. Calculate each schema's average intensity:

$$v(H_1) = \frac{0+2+2}{3} = 1.33,$$

$$v(H_2) = \frac{2+2+1}{3} = 1.67.$$

Then, we endow each string C_i with the standardizing value $S(C)/v(H)$ and then with a probability value according to the standardizing value. Select 3 pairs of strings for a crossover based on probability distribution. When crossing, select a position at random and then exchange the elements on the left of the position. This simple operation may lead to subtle influence. Figure 13.9 shows the whole influences on schema, where C_2, C_3, C_6 are the instances of schema ******1*#.

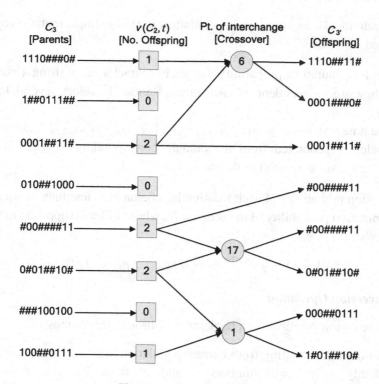

Fig. 13.9. Genetic operators

The average intensity of this schema is as follows:

$$v(*****1*\#) = \frac{0+2+2}{3} = 1.33.$$

C_3, C_5, C_8 is the instances of schema *00*#*****. Its average intensity is as follows:

$$v(*00*\#*****) = \frac{2+2+1}{3} = 1.67.$$

In genetic algorithm, if only the simple crossover operator is applied, then after a generation, the average proportion of each schema H from $B(t)$ in the population changes as follows:

$$P(H, t+1) \geq \left(1 - p_c \frac{\delta(H)}{l-1}(1 - P(H, t))\right) \frac{f(H, t)}{\overline{f}(t)} P(H, t), \qquad (13.23)$$

where p_c denotes crossover probability. It can be concluded that as long as $f(H, t) \geq \left[1 + \frac{\delta(H)}{l-1}\right] \overline{f}(t)$, the number of instances of schema H will increase.

13.6.4 *Mutation Operation*

For each individual $a = s_1 s_2 \ldots s_l$ in population $B(t)$, the simple mutation operation is described as follows:

(1) There is a mutation probability for each character in a string (individual), and they are independent of each other. Randomly select several locations: $x_1, x_2, \ldots, x_l$.

(2) Create a new string $a' = s_1 \ldots s_{x1-1} s'_{x1} s_{x1+1} \ldots s_{x2-1} s'_{x2} s_{x2+1} \ldots s_l$, where s'_{x1} is randomly generated from the domain corresponding to location x_1, and $s'_{x2}, \ldots, s'_{xk}$ are generated in the same way.

If the mutation probability of each location in schema H is less than or equal to p_m, then the mutation probability of the schema H, whose order is supposed to be o(H), is as follows:

$$1 - (1 - p_m)^{o(H)} \approx o(H) p_m, \quad (p_m \ll 1/l). \qquad (13.24)$$

13.6.5 *Inversion Operation*

A simple inversion operation can be described through three steps:

(1) Randomly select a string from current population: $a = s_1 s_2 \ldots s_l$.

(2) Randomly select two numbers i' and j' from $\{0, 1, \ldots, l+1\}$, and let $i = \min\{i', j'\}$, $j = \max\{i', j'\}$.

(3) Inverse the elements between locations i and j, and then a new string is obtained:
$s_1 s_2 \ldots s_i s_{j-1} s_{j-2} \ldots s_{i+1} s_j \ldots s_l$.

Inversion operation can change the location of a character in a string (individual). Any kind of arrangement of characters in a string can be obtained by using related inversion operations in turn. The main influence of inversion operation on schema H is to randomly change the length of schema H and the relationship among effective characters in schema H.

Besides reproduction, crossover, mutation, and inversion operations, there are other genetic operations, such as intrachromosomal duplication, elimination, translocation, and segregation.

13.7 Parallel Genetic Algorithm

Discrete Mandl's model-based genetic algorithm consists of the following six parts:

(1) chromosome representation for a given problem solving;
(2) original species for problem solving;
(3) quality function serving as environment;
(4) selection process for generating offspring;
(5) genetic operators, such as mutation and recombination;
(6) parameters for controlling the algorithm itself.

In the natural world, selection operation in an individual's environment is accomplished locally. Natural selection equation which is abstracted from the environment may lead to the risk of repetition. Parallel genetic algorithm has been successfully applied to solve many combinatorial problems. Each species is simulated on a processor. A parallel genetic algorithm can be described as follows:

(1) Given N individuals with different initial phenotypes;
(2) Calculate the local maximum value of each individual;
(3) Selection: select near-neighbor individuals for mating;
(4) Create an offspring by recombination and mutation;
(5) Goto step 2.

There are two differences between parallel genetic algorithm and classical genetic algorithm. One is that individual mating is locally finished; the other is that the individual utilizes the hill climbing method.

Therefore, the parallel genetic algorithm utilizes genotype learning and phenotype learning. Further, each individual survives in a certain environment, and crossover and selection are accomplished in such environment, such as the 2D grid. The individual's neighbor does not connect to the grid of genotype and phenotype space. Parallel genetic algorithm originates mainly from classical genetic algorithm. In genetic algorithm, the individual is regarded as the result of selecting "the best behavior". On the contrary, parallel genetic algorithm is based on the internal driver. Parallel genetic algorithm has more differences over general genetic algorithm. Its evolution is based on the driver of internal self-organization.

13.8　Classifier System Boole

In 1987, Wilson developed a classifier system for solving the boolean problem: Boole (Wilson, 1987). A boolean function is a mapping from strings with length L to $\{0, 1\}$. A learning function means the ability to correctly map any input(a string) till 0 or 1 is obtained.

Every Boole classifier consists of a class name and an action. For an input string with L-bit, the length of its class name is L; action is simply a bit of 0 or 1, which denotes one of the possible two values of boolean function. If class name matches the current input string, the system will make a decision. Classifier population $[P]$ is initialized with 0,1 or # based on a certain random rules. Action is initialized in a similar way. For example, the classifier with length of $L = 6$ is:

$$1\,0\,\#\,0\,\#\,1 \,/\, 1.$$

In Boole, $[P]$ contains 400 classifiers, which are initialized based on uniform distribution. The initial intensity is 100.

During the executing cycle, when a string is input, the system will output 0 or 1. Its executing cycle can be divided into two steps:

(1) Match input strings and form matching set $[M]$.
(2) Probability distribution is used in the intensity of $[M]$ classifier. A classifier is selected from $[M]$; that is, a particular classifier's selection probability is equal to the ratio of its intensity to the sum of all intensities of classifiers in $[M]$. The action of the selected classifier is used as the system's decision.

After the executing cycle, enhanced components adjust the intensity of the classifier according to the profit obtained from the environment. Wilson used the following algorithm to do this:

Algorithm 13.5 An algorithm for adjusting the intensity of the classifier (Wilson, 1987).

1. Create a set of classifiers which have the same selected actions, called action set [A]. And the set of all classifiers which are not in [M] is denoted by MOT[A].
2. For each classifier in [A], its intensity is reduced by a fraction e.
3. If the system decides correctly, the profit R is assigned to intensity of [A].
4. If the system decides incorrectly, the profit $R'(0 \leq R' \leq R)$ is assigned to the intensity of [A], and [A]'s intensity is reduced by a fraction p, where one of R' and p is equal to 0.
5. NOT[A]'s intensity is reduced by a fraction t.

If the system makes a correct decision in step 3, the intensity of [A] can be calculated by the following formula:

$$S'_A = S_A - eS_A + R, \tag{13.25}$$

where S_A is the sum of intensity of [A] before profit is obtained, and S'_A is the sum of profit. Suppose that R of [A] is the same for all time, it can be proved that S_A is gradually closed to R/e. It is suggested that S_A is a function of the estimated value of classical profit under a relatively stable profit condition. Step 4 defines three kinds of different profit mechanisms: profit-punishment, $p \neq 0$; just considering profit, p and R' are all equal to 0; profit–profit, $R' \neq 0$. The first situation reflects the environment, showing that the result of the system is incorrect. The second situation responds to the environment, and there is no difference before a correct action is generated. The third situation then reflects a general case, where there is an action getting the maximal profit and the others get the same profit. In step 2, e is regarded as the cost of each classifier in [A] in order to obtain the profit. The total profit of [A] is assigned by distribution function D, and the simplest method is to share R with each classifier.

The discovery component is based on Holland's genetic algorithm, using reproduction, crossover, and elimination. Boole's genetic algorithm is presented as follows:

Algorithm 13.6 (Boole's Genetic Algorithm).

1. Select a classifier C_1 from [P] according to probability and intensity.
2. Similar to step 1, select classifier C_2 according to probability χ, and then cross C_2 with C_1; then select one result as offspring, and the other one is discarded.

3. If step 2 is not finished, reproduce C_1 so as to generate offspring.
4. Apply mutation operation to generated offspring, that is, change allele of each individual with probability μ.
5. If each parent's intensity is reduced by one-third through mutation operation, then let offspring's initial intensity by equal to the sum of the reduced intensity of parents, else that of C_1 is reduced by one half and initial intensity of offspring is equal to the reduced scale.
6. Add offspring to $[P]$.
7. Delete the classifier with the minimal intensity from $[P]$.

In each executing circle, the algorithm is called with probability ρ. This algorithm is basically the same as the normative genetic algorithm. The difference between this algorithm and the normative genetic algorithm lies in the fact that the former can generate only one offspring when it is called at a time, while the latter usually generates many offspring.

In addition, the discovery component also uses another mechanism — creation. Namely, if $[M]$ is empty in the executing circle, then a new classifier is created. The name of the created classifier is a replication of the currently input string. The probability of inserting # is equal to the proportion of # in $[P]$. In order to get a related location in $[P]$, we may apply the method in step 7 to delete a classifier. Then, $[M]$ is recalculated.

For example, let us consider learning the six-path multiplexer. For every integer $k > 0$, the length of the multiplexer of a binary character string is $L = k + 2k$. For every input string, there are k address bits a_i and data bits d_i. The related string is expressed in the following form:

$$a_0 a_1 \ldots a_{k-1} d_0 d_1 \ldots d_{2k-1}.$$

The function value is given by data bits (0 or 1). For example, the following are the six-path multiplexer's input string and correct output value, where $L = 6, k = 2$:

$$0\,0\,0\,1\,0\,1 \quad 0$$
$$1\,1\,0\,0\,0\,1 \quad 1$$
$$1\,0\,1\,1\,0\,1 \quad 0$$

Because $k = 2$, the first two address bits in the first example are 00, showing that the output value of the data bits is 0. For the second example, its data bits are 11, so the bit 3 must be considered and the output value is 1. The disjunctive normal form of the function is expressed in the following form:

$$F_6 = a_0' a_1' d_0 + a_0' a_1 d_1 + a_0 a_1' d_2 + a_0 a_1 d_3.$$

The 6-path multiplexer is as follows:

$$0\ 0\ 0\ \#\ \#\ \#\ /\ 0$$
$$0\ 0\ 1\ \#\ \#\ \#\ /\ 1$$
$$0\ 1\ \#\ 0\ \#\ \#\ /\ 0$$
$$0\ 1\ \#\ 1\ \#\ \#\ /\ 1$$
$$1\ 0\ \#\ \#\ 0\ \#\ /\ 0$$
$$1\ 0\ \#\ \#\ 1\ \#\ /\ 1$$
$$1\ 1\ \#\ \#\ \#\ 0\ /\ 0$$
$$1\ 1\ \#\ \#\ \#\ 1\ /\ 1$$

This set is denoted by $[S_6]$. Boole can find multiple members of a particular classifier. On trial, profit-punishment policy is adopted, where $e = 0.1$, $R = 1,000$, $R' = 0$, $p = 0.8$, $G = 4.0$, $\mu = 0.001$, $\chi = 0.12$, $\rho = 1.0$, and $t = 0.1$. The results of 13,000 tests are presented in Table 13.2. The top 8 classifiers in Table 13.2 are the members of $[S_6]$.

13.9 Rule Discovery System

In rule discovery system, the first task is to evaluate the quality of the existing rules in the system, and then improve them. Grefenstette (1988a) had developed a rule discovery system RUDI. Figure 13.10 presents its control structure. The levels of problem solving consist of the simplified classifier system. At the learning level, genetic operators are used to operate on a population of knowledge structures, which are expressed as a set of rule tables. The whole behavior of the knowledge structure is used to control the reproduction of these structures.

In RUDI, credit-valuating method, profit-sharing plan (PSP), and bucket brigade algorithm (BBA) are used to provide each rule with mutually complementary effective information. According to the expected exterior reward, PSP-intensity provides rule effectiveness with even more accurate evaluation. During problem solving, it is used to solve conflicts. On the contrary, BBA-intensity evaluates the dynamic correlations between rules. This kind of measure can be used to assist clustering rules.

Grefenstette had proposed a method to modify intensity, called profit-sharing plan (PSP). In this method, the problem-solving plan is divided into a series of plots, which are differentiated based on the exterior reward received. If a plot wins in the bidding competition, the related rule is considered to be active in this plot. In the

Table 13.2. Learning results of a six-path multiplexer

Instance No.	Concept (Class name)							(Action)	Intensity
56	0	1	#	0	#	#	/	0	7655
52	0	1	#	1	#	#	/	1	7541
48	0	0	0	#	#	#	/	0	7056
46	1	0	#	#	0	#	/	0	7095
45	0	0	1	#	#	#	/	1	6665
41	1	1	#	#	#	0	/	0	5964
39	1	1	#	#	#	1	/	1	6323
35	1	0	#	#	1	#	/	1	5145
7	#	1	#	1	#	1	/	1	1044
4	1	1	#	#	#	#	/	1	522
3	#	0	#	#	1	#	/	1	293
3	1	1	#	#	0	#	/	0	210
2	#	0	1	#	#	#	/	1	330
2	0	1	1	#	#	#	/	1	212
2	1	0	0	#	0	#	/	0	150
2	0	0	#	#	#	#	/	1	219
2	1	#	#	#	1	#	/	0	326
2	1	0	#	0	#	#	/	0	238
1	#	1	#	0	#	#	/	0	129
1	1	0	#	#	#	#	/	0	168
1	1	1	#	#	#	#	/	0	97
1	1	0	#	#	0	0	/	0	100
1	0	0	#	#	1	#	/	1	81
1	1	#	#	#	#	0	/	0	212
1	1	0	#	#	0	1	/	1	56
1	0	1	#	#	#	#	/	1	116

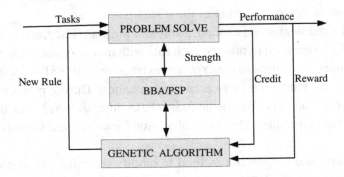

Fig. 13.10. Control structure of RUDI

plot t, PSP can modify the intensity $S_i(t)$ of each active rules

$$S_i(t+1) = S_i(t) - bS_i(t) + bp(t), \tag{13.26}$$

where $p(t)$ is the obtained exterior reward when the plot is finished; that is, when the exterior reward is obtained, each active rule collects the bids and offers a part of exterior reward. PSP's influence on a given rule R_i can be calculated by the following equation:

$$S_i(t) = (1-b)^t S_i(0) + b\sum_{i=1}^{t}(i-b)^{t-i}p(i-1), \tag{13.27}$$

where t is a plot in which rule R_i is active, namely, $S_i(t)$ is basically the average of exterior reward; $(1-b)$ is exponential attenuation factor. If b is small enough, $S(t)$ is equal to the average of $p(t)$. If exterior reward $p(t)$ is a constant p^*, S_i will converge to an equilibrium value S_i^*:

$$S_i^* = \lim_{t\to\infty}\left[(1-b)^t S_i(0) + b\sum_{i=1}^{t}(i-b)^{t-i}p^*\right] = p^* \tag{13.28}$$

Under the case of constant profit, it is in accord with equation (13.27), and the error $E_i(t) = p^* - S_i(t)$ is reduced by the following rate $E_i(t) = p^* - S_i(t)$:

$$\begin{aligned}
\Delta E_i &= E_i(t+1) - E_i(t) \\
&= S_i(t) - S_i(t+1) \\
&= -b(p^* - S_i(t)) \\
&= -bE_i(t). \tag{13.29}
\end{aligned}$$

The difference between current intensity and equilibrium intensity is reduced by a factor b every time the intensity is changed. For example, assume that $p^* = 500$, $b = 0.1$, and $S_i(t) = 100$, then $S_i(t+1) = 100 - 10 + 50 = 140$. Note that the error $p^* - S_i$ is reduced from 400 to 360; that is, this error is reduced by 10%.

We can find that under the case of constant reward, each rule's intensity can quickly converge to equilibrium intensity, and the reward can be evaluated when the plot is over. A possible restriction of PSP is that credit must be assigned in the interval corresponding to the plot differentiated by exterior reward. It is very important to select such a plot.

Suppose that rule R_i is ignited at step τ and rule R_j at step $\tau + 1$. Then BBA uses the following formula to modify the intensity S_i of rule R_i:

$$S_i(\tau+1) = S_i(\tau) - bS_i(\tau) + bS_j(\tau). \tag{13.30}$$

Except that plot index t is replaced with step index τ and exterior reward $p(t)$ is replaced with the intensity S_j of rule R_j, this formula is the same as (13.26). The first change means that the number of modifying rule's intensity in a given plot is larger than one. The second modification leads to the basic difference between PSP and BBA. Consider two pieces of rule R_i and R_j. Rule R_i is ignited after rule R_j. Assume that R_i and R_j are ignited in a plot no more than one time, then we have

$$S_i^* = \lim_{t \to \infty} \left[(1 - b)^t S_i(0) + b \sum_{i=1}^{t} (i - b)^{t-i} p^* \right] = p^*,$$

$$S_i(t) = (1 - b)^t S_i(0) + \sum_{i=1}^{t} b(1 - b)^{t-i} S_j(i - 1), \tag{13.31}$$

where the range of t is the whole plot and the two activities. In other words, the intensity of R_i follows that of R_j. If S_j can converge to a constant S_j^*, then S_i can also converge:

$$S_i^* = \lim_{t \to \infty} S_i(t) = \lim_{t \to \infty} \left[(1 - b)^t S_i(0) + \sum_{i=1}^{t} (1 - b)^{t-i} S_j(i - 1) \right] = S_j^*. \tag{13.32}$$

Similarly, formula (13.29) shows that S_j can converge to S_j^* (the internal payoff for R_i). This kind of analysis can be extended to any rule chain. For example, when $\langle R_1, R_2, \ldots, R_n \rangle$ are ignited in turn, only rule R_n can receive an exterior reward. In the balance condition, all rules in the chain have the same intensity. In the unbalance condition, all rules in the chain are described by (13.31), not by (13.32). In any case, if the expected reward received by the rule chain is consistent, then the intensity of the rules in the chain will converge to the general level.

To compare PSP with BBA, let's consider Figure 13.11. This figure presents 10 states, including initial states A and B, and terminal states H, I, and J. The exterior rewards generated in states H, I, and J are 1,000, 0, and 300, respectively.

In this example, the classifier system uses PSP or BBA to modify the intensity of the rule. All initial intensities are set to be 100, and bidding rate b is 0.1. In addition, interior rewards are distributed to 1,000 plots. This means that each classifier system consists of 3,000 steps. The obtained intensities of rules are presented in Table 13.3.

13.10 Evolutionary Strategy

Evolutionary strategy (ES) is a method to solve parameter optimization problems by simulating the natural evolution process. Early evolution treatment is based on a population consisting of many individuals and an operator: mutation. Evolutionary

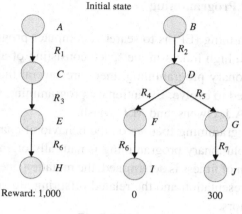

Fig. 13.11. Comparison of PSP and BBA

Table 13.3. Different methods to modify intensity

Rule	PSP's intensity	BBA's intensity
R_1	1,000	498
R_2	299	567
R_3	1,000	645
R_4	4	644
R_5	300	300
R_6	999	531
R_7	300	300

strategy operates mainly at the individual level. It can be simply described as follows:

(1) The defined problem is to find an n-dimensional real vector x, such that the maximum value of function $F(x): R^n \to R$ is obtained.
(2) The initial population of the parental vector is randomly selected from the feasible range of each dimension.
(3) The offspring vector is created by adding the parental vector with the Gaussian random variable with mean square deviation of zero.
(4) The next generation's parents are created by selecting vectors according to the minimum error principle.
(5) The process terminates if the standard deviation of vectors remains unchanged, or there is no effective calculation method.

13.11 Evolutionary Programming

Evolutionary programming (EP) is to search a computer program, which is coded as an individual, with high fitness in the space consisting of all possible computer programs. In evolutionary programming, there are several thousands of computer programs that are used to evolve. Evolutionary programming was first proposed in 1962 by L.J. Fogel, A.J. Owens, and M.J. Walsh.

Evolutionary programming focuses on the behavioral changes of species. The representation of evolutionary programming is naturally oriented to the task level. Once a representation of fitness is determined, the mutation operation can be defined based on such a representation and the related offspring are created based on concrete parental behaviors.

Evolutionary programming starts with an initial population consisting of randomly generated computer programs, which consist of the functions suitable for problem space. Thus, functions can be normal arithmetic function, normal programming operation, logic function, or particular function. Each individual (computer program) in the population is evaluated by a fitness value, which is related to a particular field.

Evolutionary programming is capable of reproducing new computer programs so as to solve problems. It consists of the following three steps:

(1) Generate an initial population, which randomly consists of the functions (programs) related to the problem.
(2) Repeat the following sub-steps until the selection criterion is satisfied:

   (i) Perform each program in the population and endow it with a fitness value according to its ability to solve the problem.
   (ii) Use related operations, such as mutation, to generate new computer programs, and then form a new population. Probabilistically select a computer program from the population based on a fitness value and then use a related operation to deal with this program. Replicate the existing computer program to a new population. Create new computer programs by randomly recombining two computer programs

(3) In the final population, the computer program with the highest fitness value is regarded as the result of evolutionary programming. This result is possibly the optimal or approximate solution to the problem.

Exercises

13.1 Describe the theoretical model of evolution systems.

13.2 Give Darwin's evolutionary algorithm.

13.3 Expatiate the definition of classical genetic algorithm and explain its basic elements.

13.4 Genetic algorithm attempts to keep genetic diversity as well as some important features (genetic schemas). Design a different genetic operator, so that genetic algorithm can reach both the targets.

13.5 What is simple mutation? Give its brief description.

13.6 What is simple inversion operation? Give its brief description.

13.7 For TSP problem, discuss the problem of its effective coding and design-related genetic operations and fitness functions.

13.8 Design a genetic algorithm for solving the TSP problem.

13.9 Explain how to express chromosomes and genes in a genetic algorithm.

13.10 For two parent individuals 1110###0# and 1##0111##, suppose that crossover location is 6. Use point crossing operator only to create their offspring.

13.11 Use a programming language to develop a program for parallel genetic algorithm.

Chapter 14

Multi-Agent Systems

Multi-agent systems mainly research how to solve the problem using physically or logically distributed systems. Agent computing is not only a hot topic of artificial intelligence but also an important breakpoint for next-generation software development. In this chapter, a brief survey of multi-agent systems' different attributes such as architecture, communication, coordination strategies, decision-making, and learning abilities have been presented.

14.1 Introduction

Solving large and complex problems usually needs many professional persons or social groups to work together. Since 1970s, distributed intelligence has become a hot research topic gradually with the development of computer networks, communication, and parallel program design technology. From 1990s, the rapid development of Internet has provided great conditions for novel information systems and decision support systems. They greatly increase the scale, scope, and degree of complexity. Distributed intelligence became the key point of these systems which have following characteristics:

(1) The data, knowledge, and control are distributed not only on logic but also on physical. It has no central control for the whole system.
(2) Each problem solver is connected by the computer network. The cost of communication is much less than the problem solution cost.
(3) Every component collaborates with each other to solve the problem which one component cannot solve alone.

The implementation of distributed artificial intelligence can remedy the shortage of the traditional expert system and greatly improve the performance of the knowledge system. The main advantages are as follows:

(1) **Improve problem-solving capacity.** Because of the distributed characteristics of the intelligent system, its problem-solving capacity increases substantially. First of all, once high reliability, communications path, processing nodes, as well as knowledge of redundancy and failure are known, the whole system just reduces the response time or solving accuracy and will not be completely paralyzed. Second, the system is easy to expand. To increase the processing units, the system's scale can be expanded, thus increasing the problem-solving ability. Third, module characteristics will enable the design of the whole system to be very flexible.

(2) **Improve the efficiency of problem solving.** Because the nodes of the distributed intelligent system need to be parallel to solve problems, we can develop parallelization to solve problems and increase the efficiency of problem solving.

(3) **Expand the scope of application.** Distribution of intelligent technology can break the restriction of the current knowledge engineering field only by using an expert. In distributed intelligent systems, different areas, and even different experts from the same field, can collaborate to solve a problem that particular experts cannot. At the same time, many non-experts can cooperate to solve the problem which may also meet or exceed the expert-level responses.

(4) **Reduce the complexity of the software.** A distributed intelligent system will break down a task into sub-tasks to solve a number of relatively independent sub-tasks. The result is a reduction in the complexity of problem solving.

Distributed intelligent research can be traced back to the late 1970s. Early distributed intelligent research focused on distributed problem solving (DPS). Their goal was to create a large size of cooperative groups to work together to solve a problem. In distributed problem-solving systems, data, knowledge, and control systems are distributed in the various nodes. There is no overall control and knowledge of the overall data and storage. Because no system in the node has enough data and knowledge to solve the whole problem, each node needs to exchange information, knowledge, and problem-solving state. They thus work through mutual cooperation for solving complex problems, i.e., through collaboration. In a pure DPS system, the problem is broken down into tasks. For solving these tasks, we need to design a specific task execution system for the problem. All the interactive strategies have been integrated as part of the overall system design. This is a top-down design of the system because the system is designed to meet the needs of the top requirements.

Hewitt and his colleagues developed an ACTOR model-based concurrent programming design system (Hewitt and DeJong, 1983). ACTOR model provides parallel computing theory in a distributed system, a group of experts, and the ability for ACTOR to acquire intelligence. Hewitt in 1991 proposed open information system semantics (Hewitt, 1991). He pointed out that competitiveness, commitment, cooperation, and negotiation should be the scientific bases of a distributed intelligent system. He attempted to provide a new basis for distributed artificial intelligence. In 1980, Davis and Smith proposed contract net (CNET) (Smith, 1980b). CNET use the bid–contract ways to implement task distribution in multi-nodes. The Contract Net system provides an important contribution to distributed tasks by mutual agreement and negotiation.

Distributed vehicle test monitoring (DVMT) system is also one of the earliest and most influential researches in the distributed artificial intelligence field. Lesser, Corkill, and Durfee from the University of Massachusetts were responsible for this project (Lesser and Erman, 1980). The system could track and monitor travelling vehicles in an urban area. Under this environment, they took on many kinds of research on distributed problem solving (Durfee *et al.*, 1987). DVMT used the distributed sensor network data as a background to research on the complex interaction between problem solving and blackboard to provide a method of abstracting and modeling a distributed system.

In 1987, Gasser developed a system named MACE, which is an experimental environment of distributed artificial intelligence system development (Gasser *et al.*, 1987). Every computing unit in MACE was named an agent. They have knowledge and reasoning ability. The agents communicate through message transmission. MACE is similar to object-oriented environment, but avoiding the complicated inherits issue in an object-oriented system. Every component in MACE can compute in parallel and provide the description language, the demons tracking mechanism. The research focused on the implementation of a distributed intelligent system and maintained clarity of the concepts.

Zhongzhi Shi and his colleagues at the Institute of Computing Technology, Chinese Academy of Sciences developed a distributed knowledge processing system DKPS. The system uses logic–object knowledge model and research on knowledge sharing and collaboration to solve problems (Shi, 1990b). Based on the ACTOR model, Ferber developed a reflection ACTOR Mering IV language in 1991 (Ferber, 1991). In this model, the actor is an active object that interacts through asynchronous transmission. Mering IV is a reflection language that can represent itself through structure and operation. A reflection of the system demonstrates that different sizes are seen, and the size of the agents can enable interaction in a uniform manner.

In the 1990s, multi-agent systems (MAS) became a hot research topic in distributed intelligence. A multi-agent system mainly researches on intelligent behavior coordination between multiple agents. For a common global goal or different goals, they share the knowledge of problem and solving approaches and collaborate for problem solving. Based on the concept of agent, people proposed a new definition of artificial intelligence: "Artificial intelligence is a branch of computer science. Its goal is to construct an intelligent agent with showing certain intelligent behaviors". Therefore, the research on intelligent agent is the core problem of artificial intelligence. Hayes–Roth from the computer science department of Stanford University said in the special report of the IJCAI'95: "intelligent computer is the first goal and ultimate goal of the artificial intelligence". Now, the research on intelligent agent attract attention not only from artificial intelligence researchers but also from scientists involved in data communications, human–computer interface design, robotics, and concurrent engineering.

14.2 The Essence of Agent

14.2.1 *The Concept of Agent*

In English, there are three main meanings for the term "agent": First, it refers to people being held accountable for their actions; second, agent is defined as an article used to produce a certain effect, i.e., physical, chemical, or biological significance of active things; third, the delegate is a person who receives a commission and carries out actions on behalf of other persons. In computer sciences and artificial intelligence, an agent can be viewed as an entity which perceives its environment through sensors and acts upon that environment through effectors. If the agent is a person, the sensors are eyes, ears, and other organs, while the hands, legs, mouth, and other parts of the body are the effectors. If it is a robot, cameras are sensors and all moving parts constitute the effector. Generally, an agent has a structure as shown in Figure 14.1 (Russell and Norvig, 1995). It has some or all of the following characteristics:

(1) **Autonomy.** This is a basic characteristic of an agent, that is, it can control its own behavior. The autonomy of the agent is reflected in the following: the acts of agent should be active and spontaneous; the agent should have its own goals or intentions. According to the requirements of the goal and environment, the agents should plan for their own short-term actions.

(2) **Interaction.** This is the awareness of and influence by the environment. This is applicable whether the agent survives in the real world (such as robots, Internet

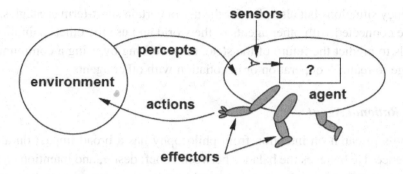

Fig. 14.1.   The agent structure

services on the agent, etc.) or the virtual world (such as the agents in virtual shopping malls, etc.). They are able to sense the environment and can change it through behaviors. An agent cannot be called an "Agent" if it cannot affect the environment.

(3) **Collaboration.** Usually the agent is not alone there, but survives along with a lot of agents in the agent world. Good and effective cooperation among agents can greatly enhance the multi-agent system performance.

(4) **Communication.** This is also a fundamental characteristic of an agent. Communication is a means of information exchange between the agents. Furthermore, the agents and people should be able to carry out "conversation" in a certain sense. To undertake tasks, an agents' collaboration and negotiation are required, which are based on communication.

(5) **Longevity (or coherence time).** Traditional procedures are activated when needed, or stopped when the operator ends. An agent is different. It should last at least "fairly long" enough to run. Although not an indispensable characteristic of agents, it is generally believed that it is one of the important ones.

In addition, some scholars also raised the idea that the agent should be adaptive and have a personality, among other characteristics. In practical applications, the agent needs to take actions under conditions of restrictions of time and resources. Therefore, the agents in the real world should have real-time characteristics besides the general nature.

At present, the research on multi-agent systems is very active. Multi-agent systems are trying to use agents to simulate human behaviors. Agents are used in the real world and by the community simulation, robots and intelligent machinery, and in other fields. In the real-world survival, the agents need to face a changing environment. In such an environment, agents not only must provide a timely response to emergency situations but also plan for the use of certain short-term strategies. Thus, they are connected with other agents in the world and use the other main modeling methods to predict the future of the state, thus working by using a communication language to realize cooperation or negotiation with other agents.

14.2.2 *Rational Agent*

Bratman's research on intention from philosophy has a broad impact on artificial intelligence. He believes the balance between belief, desire, and intention can solve the problem effectively. In the open world, rational agents cannot be driven by intention, desire, and their combination since there is a belief-based intention that exists between desire and planning. The reasons are as follows:

(1) Agent actions are restricted to limited resources. Once agents decide what to do, they build a limited format commitment.
(2) In multi-agent environments, agents need commitment to coordinate the actions of all agents. If there is no commitment, no actions are existent. The intention is the choice of commitment.

In an open and distributed environment, the actions of a rational agent are restricted by intention. The intention is represented as follows:

(1) If an agent wants to change its intention, it needs reasons to do so;
(2) An agent cannot insist on its unimportant intention without considering the changes in the environment.

The main purpose of rational balance is to make a rational act in conformity with the characteristics of the environment. The so-called characteristics of the environment not only refer to the objective conditions but also include environmental factors in social groups, such as social groups on the rational judgement of the law. Bratman presented the intention–action principle: If A takes action B since the current intention is reasonable, then Agent A changes its intention to an action. Action B is thus reasonable.

In a specific time, an agent is assessed as follows:

(1) Performance test provides performance measure of the degree of success.
(2) Agents can percept all things; we will call this sense of history as the perception sequence.
(3) Agents know the environment.
(4) Agents can perform actions.

An ideal agent can be defined: for each sequence after perception, the ideal rational agents, on the basis of the evidence provided by the perception sequence and their inherent knowledge, should undertake the desired actions to make the performance the largest.

14.2.3 *BDI Model*

BDI agent model can be described by the following elements:

(1) a group of beliefs about the world;
(2) a group of goals that agents want to achieve;
(3) a plan base to describe how to reach the goal and change the belief;
(4) an intention structure to describe currently how the agent achieves the goal and changes the beliefs.

14.3 Agent Architecture

14.3.1 *Agent's Basic Architecture*

An agent can be seen as a black box. It perceives the environment through the sensor and affects the environment with the actor. If we consider a human being an agent, we perceive the environment with eyes, ear, nose, etc., and affect the environment using hands, legs, etc. A robot agent usually holds some cameras for getting environmental information and the motor is their actor. A software agent uses codes as their sensors and actors (Figure 14.2).

Besides communication with environment, most agents need to deal with the received information to achieve their goals. Figure 14.3 shows the work process of an intelligent agent. After receiving information, the first step for agents is syncretizing the information to make it acceptable to the knowledge base of agents. Information syncretizing is very important because the results from different communication components are often heterogeneous and the representation is different. For example,

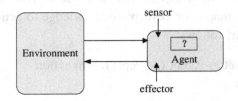

Fig. 14.2. Agent interaction with environment

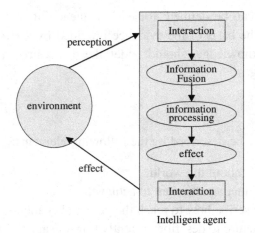

Fig. 14.3.   The work process of an intelligent agent

for the same thing, the information provided by human beings and received by agents may be different. So, information syncretizing must identify and differentiate this kind of variance correctly.

Once the agent has received external information, the information process becomes the key task of the agent since it reflects the real function of every agent. The purpose of information processing is explaining the useful data and forming the concrete plan. Because every agent has its own goal, the impact of inner goal must be considered as a part of whole impact. If agents know the impact, they need to adopt actions to realize the goal. To form a plan, agents may prescribe knowledge, including new conditions to reflect concrete actions. However, this is not obligatory since sometimes agents need not have plans when they take actions. If communicating with environmental objects, the action model will adopt the proper communication component. The control task is also part of the action component.

From the discussion above, agents can be defined as forming a map from perceptive knowledge to actions. Suppose O is the perceptive set, A is the possible actions which can be achieved by agents. The agent function $f: O^* \rightarrow A$ defines the actions of all agents. The task of artificial intelligence is to design agent programs which can realize the map from perceptive knowledge to actions. The skeleton of the agent program is as follows:

Algorithm 14.1. Skeleton-Agent (percept) return action
    Input static: memory
    Method:
    1. *memory* ← Update-Memory (*memory, percept*);

2. *action* ← Choose-Best-Action (*memory*);
3. *memory* ← Update-Memory (*memory, action*);
4. return *action*.

The agents will change their memory to reflect the new percept after every function call. An ideal rational agent hopes to achieve the best performance for every percept.

Not every agent's action is the reflection of new conditions. Agents can also create new plans. In this condition, the knowledge of the information provider is useful only at a specific time. This is the main difference between reactive agents and deliberative agents.

14.3.2 *Deliberative Agent*

A deliberative agent (or cognitive agent) is a distinct symbol model which possesses reasoning ability about the environment and can make intelligent actions. It follows the tradition of classical artificial intelligence. It is a knowledge-based system. Environmental model is implemented in advance to form the main knowledge base. There are two problems of this architecture:

Conversion problem: how to translate the real world to the correct symbol description?

Representation/reasoning problem: how to represent the real entity and process. How to let the agents in possession of the ability to make a decision according to reasoning of information do so in limited time.

The first problem results in research on computer vision and natural language processing. The second problem induces research on knowledge representation, autonomic reasoning, and planning. In the real world, these problems are a bit difficult since the representation is very complex. So, the deliberative agents have their limitations in the dynamic environment. Without necessary knowledge and resources, it is difficult to add new information and knowledge about the environment into the existent model.

A deliberative agent is a kind of active software. Different from concrete domain knowledge, it has knowledge representation, problem solution representation, and environment representation and communication protocol. According to the way of thinking, deliberative agents can be divided into abstract thinking agents and visual thinking agents. Abstract thinking agents have abstract concepts. They think through symbol information processing. However, visual thinking agents think using visual material. It adapts the connection theory of nerve mechanism.

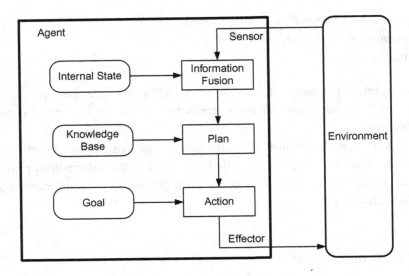

Fig. 14.4. The architecture of a deliberative agent

Figure 14.4 gives the architecture of a deliberative agent. The agent gets external information through the sensors. Then, it syncretizes the information according to the internal states and generates the description of the current state. Then, a plan is created with the support of the knowledge base. Finally, agents can form a series of actions, which are then performed by actors to affect the environment.

Algorithm 14.2 (Deliberate-Agent Algorithm).

Input: static: *environment*, //describing the current world environment

　　　　　　　 Kb,　　　　　 //knowledge base

　　　　　　　 plan　　　　 // Plan

　 Method:

1. *environment* ← Update-World-Model (*environment, percept*)
2. *state* ← Update-Mental-State (*environment, state*)
3. *plan* ← Decision-Making (*state, kb, action*)
4. *environment* ← Update-World-Model (*environment, action*)
5. return *action*

In the above program, the Update-World-Model function generates an abstract description of the current world environment from percept. The Update-Mental-State function revises the agent's inner mental state according to the percept environment. The knowledge base includes general knowledge and real knowledge. Agents apply the knowledge to make decisions with the Decision-Making function.

BDI model, which is a typical deliberative agent, can be described with the following elements:

- a group of beliefs about the world;
- current goals;
- a plan base which describes how to achieve the goal and revise the belief;
- an intention structure to describe how to achieve the current goals and revise the current beliefs.

According to BDI Architecture, Rao and Georgeff proposed a simple BDI interpreter (Rao and Georgeff, 1992).

Algorithm 14.3 (BDI-Interpreter).

```
1.   BDI-Interpreter () {
2.   initialize-state();
3.   do
4.       options := option-generator(event-queue, B, G, I);
5.       selected-options := deliberate(options, B, G, I);
6.       update-intentions(selected-options, I);
7.       execute(I);
8.       get-new-external-events();
9.       drop-successful-attitudes(B,G,I);
10.      drop-impossible-attitudes(B,G,I);
11.  until quit
```

14.3.3 *Reactive Agent*

The problems in traditional artificial intelligence are reflected in a deliberative agent without any change. The main criticism focuses on rock-bound architecture. The agents work in a dynamic environment. So, they need to make a decision according to the current conditions. However, their intention and plan were developed on the symbol model of a previous specific time. There is little change in that. Rule-based rock-bound extends the disadvantage since the conversion between planner, scheduler, and executor is the time cost. The implementation of the condition of the scheduler changes more or less. The symbol algorithms of deliberative agents are often ideal and decidable, which lead to much complication. In a dynamic environment, it is more important to meet the requirement than look for plan optimization. However, deliberative agents are good at mathematical proof of plans.

Different from the deliberative agents, reactive agents include no world model. They have no complex symbol reasoning (Wooldridge and Jennings, 1995).

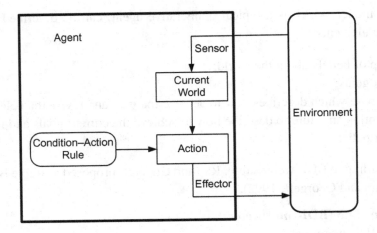

Fig. 14.5.   The architecture of reactive agent

Figure 14.5 gives the architecture of reactive agents. The condition–action rules connect the cognition and actions. The rectangle in the figure represents the current inner states of decision process. The ellipse shows the background knowledge which is used in the process.

Algorithm 14.4 (Reactive-agent Algorithm).

    Reactive-agent (percept) returns action

        static: state, describe the current world state

            rules, a group of condition–actions rule

1. state $\leftarrow$ Interpret-Input (percept)
2. rule $\leftarrow$ Rule-Match (state, rules)
3. action $\leftarrow$ Rule-Action [rule]
4. return action

In the program, the Interpret-Input function generates the abstract description of the current states from the percept. The Rule-Match function returns a rule which is matched with the description of current states.

The term reactive agents was coined by Professor Brooks in MIT who proposed behavior-based artificial intelligence (Brooks, 1991b). He thought that intelligent behaviors are the result of communication between agents and the environment. Brooks is not only a critic but also a practice expert. He implemented some robots without symbol reasoning. These robots were based on a subsumption architecture system. Subsumption architecture is a hierarchical behavior which can finish tasks. Every behavior tries to control the robot, which cause competition between them. The behaviors in the base layer represent the relative original behaviors which have high priority. As a result, the implementation of this kind of architecture is relatively simple (Figure 14.5). Brooks alleged that the agent with this kind of architecture can finish tasks by symbol-based artificial intelligence.

14.3.4 *Hybrid Agent*

We have discussed the architecture of a reactive agent and a deliberative agent. They reflect the characteristics of behavior-based artificial intelligence. However, both pure reactive agent and deliberative agent architecture are the best ways to build agent. People have begun to propose the hybrid agent which connects classic and non-classic artificial intelligence.

The obvious architecture is of an agent with two subsystems. One is deliberative agent which has the symbol-based world model and can generate the plan and decision. The other is the reactive agent which can react to the environment without reasoning. Generally speaking, the reactive agent has higher priority than the deliberative agent since this can make the reactive agent react quicker to important events happening in the environment.

Multi-agent processing environment (MAPE) is a parallel programming environment with a special language (Shi *et al.*, 1994). The agent architecture is of a hybrid style, as shown in Figure 14.6. Each agent contains modules for perception, action, reflection, model, planning, communication, decision-making, and so on.

In 1998, agent-oriented software development environment (AOSDE) was constructed at Intelligence Science Laboratory (Shi *et al.*, 1998). Figure 14.7 shows the agent model which consists of three layers, that is, virtual machine layer, logic layer, and resource layer.

Virtual machine layer is intended to be a general interface to the environment which provides the agent's communicative, sensoric, and actoric links to the outside world. The communicative part provides the functionality of sending message to and receiving message from other agents using software agent communication language (SACL) or other languages. An agent can sense its environment through the sensoric part. Actors will carry out the physical actions the agent may perform. This layer provides a set of primitives to the upper layer, and so hides the difference of real machines. Through this layer, the upper layers can run successfully without interfering with the network, operating system, or hardware configuration. Resource layer is a set of resources, such as knowledge base, database, model base, image base, and so on, that are used by a special agent.

Logic layer is a core component of the agent model. We defined agent as an entity that can execute some specific actions and communicate with its environment. Although agents may differ in many aspects from each other, they do have many

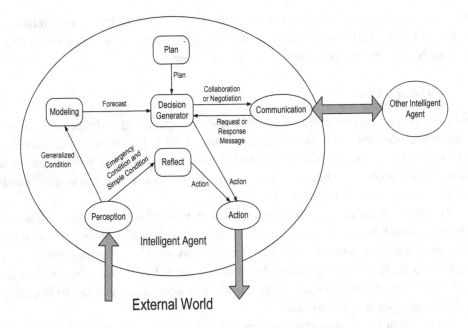

Fig. 14.6.   Hybrid architecture of MAPE agent

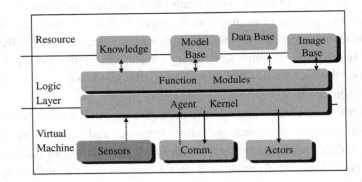

Fig. 14.7.   The agent model of AOSDE

features in common. For example, their communication method, execution engine, and representation of mental states can be the same. The differences are only in the decision-making strategies, actions they may perform, and representation of knowledge. By separating these parts, we can get a kernel of agents, which is the same for all agents. We make some slots on the kernel, so the decision-making methods and domain-related function modules can be inserted to the kernel very conveniently, as shown in Figure 14.8.

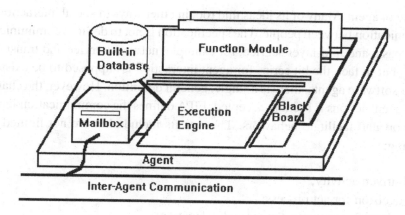

Fig. 14.8. Illustration of agent kernel

The agent kernel is like the mainframe of a computer, while the function modules are just like some functional cards inserted into the slots. The mailbox is a device used to perform inter-agent communication, and the blackboard is for communication within the agent, that is, between function modules or between the function module and the execution engine. The agent kernel also has a built-in database, where it records useful information of itself and other agents.

14.4 Agent Communication Language

Foundation for intelligent physical agents (FIPA) is an IEEE Computer Society standards organization that promotes agent-based technology and the interoperability of its standards with other technologies. FIPA, the standards organization for agents and multi-agent systems, was officially accepted by the IEEE as its eleventh standards committee on June 8, 2005.

FIPA was originally formed as a Swiss-based organization in 1996 to produce software standards specifications for heterogeneous and interacting agents and agent-based systems. Since its foundation, FIPA has played a crucial role in the development of agent standards and has promoted a number of initiatives and events that contributed to the development and uptake of agent technology. Furthermore, many of the ideas that originated and were developed in FIPA are now coming into sharp focus in the new generations of Web/Internet technology and related specifications.

FIPA defines a language and support tool. For example, the protocol is used for communication with each other. Software agent technology adopts a high view for this kind of agent. Many of its ideas find root in other ways of social interaction, e.g., communication between people. The specification is not to define a communication-related basic and mid-layer service, for example, network service and transmission service, but in fact, the bit series for agent interaction is supposed to be existent.

For software agents, there is a single, general definition. However, the characteristic of agent actions is broadly accepted. FIPA defines the communication language to support and facilitate behaviors. These traits include but are not limited to the following:

- goal-driven activity;
- self-decision for act process;
- interaction through negotiation and delegation;
- mental state model, for example intention belief desire plan and promise;
- the adaptation to environment and requirement.

14.4.1 *Agent Communication Introduction*

Abstract characteristics can be described by an agent's mental states.

(1) Belief that a group of facts which the agent think as true. If an agent accepts a false proposition, it indicates the agent thinks the proposition is false.
(2) Indetermination. It shows that the agent cannot determine whether the proposition is true or false. Worth the whistle, indetermination does not impede proposition to adopt some support proposition format, for example, probability. To be more accurate, indetermination provides a smallest promise mechanism for different representation methods.
(3) Intention indicates a choice, or a group of characteristics that the desire is true or the current state is not true. To accept this intention, the agent will form a series of actions. These actions will cause the generation of a specific society state.

For a proposition P, believe P, not believe P, the determination of P, and indetermination of P are inconsistent.

Besides, agents understand and can execute some actions. In a distributed system, an agent can realize its intention through affecting other agent's actions.

Affecting other agents' behaviors is realized by a kind of specific class named communication action behavior. Communication action is taken from one agent to other agents. To execute a communication action, the agent needs the mechanism to send code action message. So, communication action initiator and acceptor are the message's sender and receiver.

The message of the FIPA definition is gathered by core sets. It means a correspondence action, but this correspondence action tries the general balance definition, expresses ability and simplicity, and is related with the understanding of the agent developer. The correspondence action that the message type is defined is carried out. The one who combines appropriate realm knowledge, corresponding to the letters of the language, can ensure the meaning of the news contents.

With regard to the mental state and from the sender's view to the accepter's view, mental state generation of the expectation is expressed by a precondition. However, because the sender and receiver are independent, the expectation result cannot be guaranteed.

If two agents want to interact through communication, they need a common point for message transmission. The message transmission service attribute discussion is taken cave of by the FIPA committee 1-agent management.

The contribution of agent technology to the complex system action and interaction process manifests on high interaction. The ACL in FIPA is based on this view. For example, the communication action described by the book is used to inform facts, request complex action, and negotiate protocol. The mechanism mentioned cannot compete with the basic network protocol, for example TCP/IP, OSI seven protocols, and cannot compare with them. They are also not a substitute for CORBA, Java RMI, and Unix RPC. However, their functions are the same as some of the above examples. At least, the ACL message is transmitted by this mechanism.

After considering the goal of FIPA general open-agent system, the function of ACL is clear. Other mechanisms, for example CORBA, have the same goal. However, some constraints are added to the object interface during implementation. Historical experience tells us that the agent and the agent system can be implemented by a diversified interface mechanism; existent examples include using the TCP/IP socket, HTTP, SMTP, and GSM short message for agents. ACL tries to reduce to the smallest to respect the diversification. Especially, the smallest message transmission is defined as the text through the small bit stream. This is the method adopted by KQML. This broad method is used for high performance. This system's message is very high. FIPA defined a substitute transmission method, including other transmission expressions. They satisfy the high performance of the request.

At the same time, ACL is transmitted as a group request.

The message service can transmit a bit series to the message to the destination. Through the message service interface, the agent can find whether it can deal with the 8-bit stream.

Under normal circumstances, the message service is reliable (the message package can reach its destination), accurate (the form of receipt is the same as what was sent), and orderly (from agent A sent to an agent B, when the message arrives at B it will be sent in a different order). Unless specified, an agent will be considered to have the following three characteristics.

If the messaging services cannot guarantee one or all of the above characteristics, it will represent through the message transmission services interface that in some way it wants out.

The agents will be able to choose whether to pause and wait for the results of the news or continue to other unrelated tasks when waiting for the reply information. The effectiveness of action is in implementing the details, but whether or not to support such actions must be clear.

It will impart information of the parameters of action, for example, if there is no response time, not in the message that is there at this level, but if the messaging services are a part of the interface.

Message transmission services will find and report errors and return to agents, e.g., the form of an error message, not transmission, if it could not find agents. Based on the errors circumstances, it will return a value of message send interface, or through an error message related to return to.

A principal will have a name that makes messaging services move the news to reach the right destination. Messaging services can determine the correct transmission mechanism (TCP/IP, SMTP, HTTP, etc.), allowing the main location of the change.

14.4.2 *FIPA ACL Message*

FIPA has defined the types of information, especially information on the format and types of information meaning. Message type is a reference to grammar rules; these types give meaning for the entire message and information content.

For example, if i notices j "Bonn in Germany": the content of the message from i to j is "Bonn in Germany", and the action is to inform this act. "Bonn in Germany" has a certain significance, but also for the two symbols "Bonn" and "Germany" to have any reasonable explanation of the circumstances as being true, the significance of information includes the principal role of i and j. A decision on the nature of these roles i and j is a private matter, but as the result of this meaningful communication is imminent, the role of these will be that reasonable expectations are met.

Clearly, the news content in the areas of knowledge will be unrestricted. ACL does not mandate that the content of the message be there in any formal way. The agent itself must be able to correctly interpret any of the known content of the message. The ontology share issues will be discussed later. This was announced by the specification regulating the content independent of the meaning of the rules. A set of standard communication movements and their implications are outlined in detail.

It is worth noting that there is a balance between action capacity and norms. A large set of very detailed action types that convey subtle differences in meaning may be the same as a small set of more general action types, but this set of action types will have different representations and execution restrictions on the subject. This type of action group targets can be expressed as: (a) covering all large-scale communications; (b) not allowing the burden of agent design from becoming too heavy; and (c) allowing for the agent action to provide communications services using choice, reducing redundancy, and becoming fuzzy. In short, the objectives of ACL language definition are as follows: integrity, simplicity, and concision.

The basic viewpoints of ACL are that the message is expressed as a communication action. In order to ensure elegance and consistency in the dialogue, communications and actions should be handled similarly; a known communication action is one of the actions an agent can complete. The terminology messages in this paper have two different meanings: message can be a synonym for communications action or refer to the computing structure speech of the messaging service.

ACL communication language specification is based on a precise form of semantics. It gives a clear meaning to the communication action. In fact, this formal base also led to effective interactive communication. On this foundation, message parameters are defined by describing the form of information to be defined. Similarly, the norm agents used, such as information exchange protocol, are only a description of the operational semantics.

1. The agent requirement

Here, we introduce some predefined message types and protocols for agents. However, not all messages require implementation of all agents. The following is a list of minimum requirements for the FIPA ACL compatible agent:

(1) If agents receive message that they do not know or if they could not address the content of the message, they send "not-understood". The agents must receive and address "not-understood" messages from other agents.
(2) The agents can choose to implement the predefined type and source of any protocols or a subset. The implementation of the information provided by the action must be consistent with the definition of semantics.

(3) The agent that uses the communication act defined in the article must be in line with the definition.

(4) The agent can use another definition of communication act that this article did not define. It has the responsibility to ensure that the agent understands the meaning of the action. But the agent should not define new matching with standard actions.

(5) The agent will be able to correct the grammatical form of good message and generate a consistent form of transmission. Similarly, the agent must also be able to transfer the good form of grammar translated into a sequence of character-related messages.

2. Message Structure

Figure 14.9 shows the main elements of a message.

In transmission, messages are represented in the *s*-form. The first element of the message determines the communication act and the main meaning of the message. This is followed by message keyword parameters separated by a colon to guide, and there is no space between the colon and the keyword parameters. One parameter contains message content using some form of coding. Other parameters are used to help the messaging services correctly transmit the information (such as the sender, receiver), help the recipient explain the implications of information (such as language, ontology), or help the receiver reply more cooperatively (such as reply-with, reply-by).

The transmission form is the serial bit stream transferred by the messaging service. The receiver agent is responsible for bit stream decoder, decoding elements

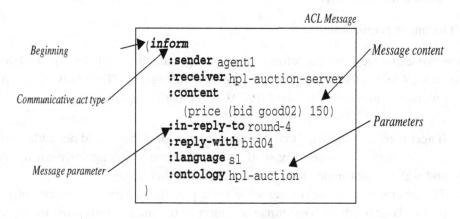

Fig. 14.9. Message structure

of messages and correctly handling it. The communication act of a message corresponds to a performative in KQML.

3. Message Parameter

As mentioned earlier, a message includes a group of one or more parameters. These parameters in the message can be in any chronological order. Only one of the parameters — receiver is indispensible — in the messaging service can correctly transmit message. Obviously, the message is useless if it does not have the recipient of the message. However, parameters for effective communication are different under different circumstances.

Predefined message parameter:

Message Parameter	Meaning
:sender	message sender
:receiver	message receiver
:content	message content
:reply-with	reply the original message
:in-reply-to	the message act reply
:envelope	message service content
:language	act content decode
:ontology	The meaning of symbols as expressions
:reply-by	the time and date of sending message
:protocol	use protocol
:originator	delegate agent requested information
:reply-to	the agent answer to which agent
:protocol "(" ⟨protocol name⟩ +")"	use protocol nested
:conversation-id	the communications action sequences
"(" ⟨id⟩ +")"	the table is sub protocol
:conversation-id	the communications action sequence

4. The message content

The message content represents what the communication act applies for. If the communication act believes the message is a sentence, the content is grammatical elements. Generally, content is encoded in one language. The language is defined in the language parameter. The requirements for language content are that it should have the following characteristics:

A content language must represent proposition, objects, and actions. While any language can have more characteristics, here we do not need other features.

Language content must represent the data structure of act: the proposition notice, requesting action, and so on.

Proposition: Represents whether the sentence is true or false.

Object: A confirming structure representative of discussion in the area (may be abstract or concrete). Object does not necessarily mean object-oriented languages such as C++ and Java programming in the professional programming structure.

Action: An agent explanation of the grounds will complete some of the agent structure.

The most common situation is the agent content of a joint consultation language. However, the agent must overcome the content difficulty of the first step to begin a dialogue. So there must be a common reference point in advance that both sides know. To register a directory service and the implementation of other key agent management functions, this specification includes the following language definitions:

(1) FIPA specifies that the management of the agent content of language is the s-expressions that are used for the concept of life cycle management of the agent proposition, objects, and actions. Expressions are defined in the first part of the specification.

(2) The agent needs to execute standard agent management capacity through agent management content language and message in ontology. Language and ontology are represented in the corresponding parameters of the FIPA–agent–management field.

5. The representation of message content

The contents of a message refer to field expression of communications action. It is encoded in the message with content parameters. FIPA specification does not require a standardized content language.

In order to provide simple language coding services, ACL grammar, including the s-expression forms, allows for selection of the arbitrary length and complexity of the s-expression structure. Therefore, universal s-expression syntax language could be modified for effective ACL language. However, the agents usually need to embed a code with a symbol of expression, and not for the news, which by itself is a simple form of s-expression. ACL syntax provides two mechanisms. They should avoid the need for an ACL interpreter to explain the expression of any language problem.

(1) Using double quotes to include expressions makes it a string of ACL. A backslash symbol distinguishes between double quotes in double quotes. The note contents of the expression in the backslash character also need to be distinguished. For example,

(inform :content "owner (agent1,\"Ian\")"
    :language Prolog
. . .)

(2) Before the appropriate expression in a long string of code, expressions are processed to ensure that its structure has nothing to do with the vocabulary symbols. For example,

(inform :content #22 "owner (agent1, "Ian")"
    :language Prolog
. . .)

Therefore, the ACL interpreter will generate a language that is embedded in the vocabulary of symbols — a string. Once the message is explained via expression through symbols, language coding schemes based on parameters can be explained.

Table 14.1 shows the Communicative act directory.

Table 14.1. Communicative act directory

Communicative act	Information passing	Requesting information	Negotiation	Action performing	Error handling
Accept-proposal			✓		
Agree				✓	
Cancel				✓	
Cfp			✓		
Confirm	✓				
Disconfirm	✓				
Failure					✓
Inform	✓				
Inform-if (macroact)	✓				
Inform-ref (macroact)	✓				
Not-understood					✓
Propagate				✓	
Propose			✓		
Proxy				✓	
Query-if		✓			
Query-ref		✓			
Refuse				✓	
Reject-proposal			✓		
Request				✓	
Request-when				✓	
Request-whenever				✓	
Subscribe		✓			

14.5 Coordination and Cooperation

14.5.1 *Introduction*

In computer sciences, one of the most challenging goals is to build a computer system that can cooperate with other systems (Kraus, 1997). The computer system is becoming more and more complex. To integrate the intelligent agents is more challenging. Cooperation between agents is the key point for cooperative work. Besides, multi-agent cooperation is an important concept for distinguishing a multi-agent system from other forms of distributed computing, object-oriented system, and expert system (Doran *et al.*, 1997). Coordination and cooperation are the core problems of multi-agent research since they is based on the intelligent agent. Coordinating the knowledge, desire, intention, plan, and action to implement cooperation is the main goal of a multi-agent system.

Coordination is the characteristic by which multiple agents interact to finish a group of activities. Coordination is adaptation to the environment. Coordination changes the intention of agents. The reason for multiple agents to coordinate is so that the agents have intention. Cooperation is a special example of multi-agent coordination. Multi-agent research is based on the human society. In human societies, communication is indispensable. Communication is between conflict and non-conflict. At the same time, in an open, dynamic, multi-agent environment, agents with different goals and resources must coordinate with each other. For example, there will be a deadlock when resource conflict without coordination occurs. On the contrary, if one agent cannot finish the goal independently, it needs cooperation of other agents.

In a multi-agent system, cooperation only improves the ability of a single agent but also the performance of a multi-agent system and increases the agent's ability to solve the problem, thus making the system more agile. Through cooperation, multi-agents can solve more real problems and extend application. Although a single agent only cares about its own requirement and goal, its design and implementation can be independent of other agents. However, in the multi-agent system, agents do not exist alone. The agents' actions must meet society rules although they are compliant agents. The relationship between the multi-agent systems makes interaction and cooperation have great conditionality on an agent's implementation and design.

In the current phase, the research on multi-agent cooperation has two branches. One is by borrowing the approach from the research on multi-entities' behaviors (Kraus, 1997). The other is from the view of intention, goal, and plan to research multi-agent cooperation, e.g., FA/C model (Lesser, 1991), the Joint Intention Framework (Levesque, 1990), and share plan (Grosz and Kraus, 1996). The latter method has bigger application scope. Each theory is only adapted to some specific coordination environments. Once the environment changes, for example, the number of agents, type, and interaction relationship disagree with theory, the cooperation based on this theory loses its superiority. The latter approach focuses on the planning and solution of problems and assumes the process of coordination as being different. Some agents find cooperative partners first and then generate plans. Some may generate a plan for the problem first and then take cooperative actions. Some may generate a partial global planning, PGP, to regulate their actions for cooperative goals (Lesser, 1991). The latter two cooperative methods seem relaxed and lack the necessary disposal mechanism. They require a shared cooperative plan between agents. The first approach has bigger uncertainty, and cooperative plans are influenced by the cooperative team.

In a multi-agent system, the agent is autonomic. The knowledge, desire, intention, and behavior of agents are different. To coordinate cooperative work is the necessary condition for problem solving and for maintaining efficiency. Many researches on organization theory, politics, sociology, social psychology, anthropology, jurisprudence, and economics are applied in multi-agent systems. Multi-agent coordination is the process by which multiple agents interact with each other for a consistent way of work. Coordination can avoid the deadlock and livelock of multi-agents. Deadlock means a multi-agent cannot take the next action; livelock is the state in which a multi-agent can do consecutive work but there is no result. There are many coordination methods such as the following:

- organizational structuring;
- contracting;
- multi-agent planning;
- negotiation.

From the point of social psychology, multi-agent cooperation is of the following types:

(1) **Cooperation:** put its own interest second;
(2) **Selfish:** put cooperation second;
(3) **Completely selfish:** does not consider any cooperation;
(4) **Complete cooperation:** does not consider its own interest;
(5) A hybrid of cooperation and selfish.

The interaction between agents has two kinds of relationship: negative and positive. A negative relationship causes conflict. The resolution of conflicts results in coordination. A positive relationship represents the plan of multi-agent overlapping or of some agent having an exclusive ability. Every agent can get help through cooperation.

Before the mid-1980s, research on coordination and cooperation in distributed intelligence mainly focused on helping each other to realize the goal without conflict. This kind of research is used in distributed problem solution. In the mid-1980s, Rosenschein undertook deep research for his doctoral thesis on multi-agent interaction when agents had goal conflicts. He applied game theory to build the static model for rational agent interaction (Genesereth, *et al.*, 1986). It then became the theoretical foundation for multi-agent coordination and cooperation. After that, many researchers used game theory to formalize the multi-agent cooperation. All of these researches were done to build a model to coordinate the actions or through cooperation to realize the goal in case of inconsistent goal condition. Some of the research considered time preference. Some of the research was open environment oriented.

The research done at MIT adopted meta-communication to coordinate multi-agent computing under the foundation of intensifying FA/C and PGP approaches. Macintosh applied the heuristic approach to introduce the cooperation to machine theorem proof. Sycara researched the negotiation-based labor and capital problem (Sycara *et al.*, 1996). The approach applied the heuristic and constraint satisfaction technology to solve the distributed search problems. It adopted the asynchrony trace to resume the inconsistent search policies. The disadvantage is this approach needs an arbitrage machine to solve conflicts. Conry researched multi-steps negotiation using multiple goals and resources. Hewitt proposed the distributed artificial intelligence approach which challenges Rosenschein's static interaction model. The real world is open and dynamic. Coordination and cooperation are also open and dynamic. Computing bionomics argues that the agents need not have a strong reasoning ability in the open and dynamic environment. They can gradually coordinate relationship with the environment through consecutive interaction to make the whole system have evolutionary ability. That is similar to an ecosystem. The BDI model emphasizes agent intention and the rational balance between desire and intention in the interaction process.

Shohan proposed that the artificial agent society needed a law to regulate the agents' actions. Every agent must follow the law and believe that other agents also abide the law. This law can regulate the agents' behaviors on one hand. On the other hand, it can ensure other agents' action style. This guarantees the realization of agents' behaviors. Decker proposed a dynamic coordination algorithm in a distributed sensor network (Decker, 1995). The agent can revise the sensor domain according to the unified standard which can automatically reach coordination. This dynamic reconstruction domain can realize the system load balance in the whole system. Its performance is better than the static sub-area algorithm. Especially, this approach can decrease the fluctuation in performance, which is more adapted to dynamic real condition.

In multi-agent planning, agents can regulate the pertinence of goals to realize autonomic behavior coordination. German Wei proposes an approach to form an action and the goal's correlation value for a specific problem through distributed learning. The other autonomic coordination approach is the Markov process proposed by Kosoresow. The Markov process is a quick probability coordination approach when the agent's goal and preference is consistent. If Markov process is applied as the agent's reasoning mechanism, it can analyze the astringency of multi-agent interaction and average the astringency time. When the agent's goal and preference are not consistent, it can check the inconsistence at a specific time point and solve the conflict by submitting it to a higher coordination protocol. In order to describe a group of agent actions, we need a common intention to connect the member's behavior. Jennings adopts a common duty concept to emphasize the function of intention as the action controller. It prescribes how the agents act in the cooperative problem solution. This common duty can provide functional instruction for architecture design, provide a standard for inspecting problem solution, and provide exceptional dispose. They realized this common duty in the GRATE system.

14.5.2 *Contract Net Protocol*

In 1980, Smith proposed the contract net protocol for distributed problem solution (Smith, 1980b). This protocol was widely applied in multi-agent coordination. The communication among agents has the same message format. The real contract net system provides a contract protocol based on the contract net protocol. It prescribes task assignment and the roles of agents. Figure 14.10 shows the architecture of a node in contract net protocol.

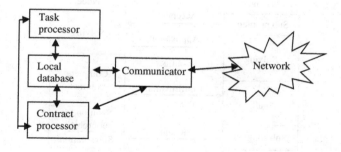

Fig. 14.10. Architecture of a node in contract net protocol

The local database includes the knowledge base related to the node which is used to negotiate information in the current state and the problem solution process. The other three components execute their tasks according to the local knowledge base. The communicator is in charge of communicating with other nodes. The node can only connect with the network through the communicator. Especially, the communicator should understand the messages that are sent and received.

The contract processor judges the tasks, sends the application, and finishes the contract. It can also analyze the reached information. Finally, the contract processor executes the coordination for the whole node. The task of the task processor is to deal with the tasks. It receives the tasks from the contract processor and applies the local database for solutions and returns the result to the contract processor.

Contract net protocol partitions the task into sub-tasks. It designates a node as the manager node. The manager node is familiar with the sub-tasks (Figure 14.11).

The Manager node provides the bids. Those are part of the unsolved sub-problems contract. The message format in the contract net protocol is as follows:

For example:

TO:	All nodes
FROM:	Manager
TYPE:	Task bid announcement
ContractID:	xx-yy-zz
Task Abstraction:	⟨description of the problem⟩
Eligibility Specification:	⟨list of the minimum requirements⟩
Bid Specification:	⟨description of the required application information⟩
Expiration time	⟨latest possible application time⟩

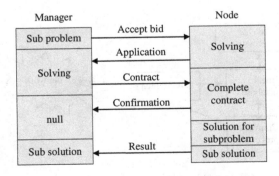

Fig. 14.11.　The negotiation process in contract net protocol

The bids are open for all agents. They solve the bids through the contract processor. They apply the local database to solve the current resources and agent knowledge. The contract processor decides which tasks are worth doing. If they want to perform a task, they need to inform the manager using the following message format:

TO:	Manager
FROM:	Node X
TYPE:	Application
ContractID:	xx-yy-zz
Node Abstraction:	(description of the node's capabilities)

The manager must select some nodes and give the contract to the most proper node in the whole application. It visits the concrete knowledge solution approach to select the best performance and assign the sub-problem to the node. According to the message, the assignment contract is as follows:

TO:	Node X
FROM:	Manager
TYPE:	Contract
ContractID:	xx-yy-xx
Task Specification:	(description of the subproblem)

The communicator sends the confirm message to the Manager to accept the contract. Once the problem is finished, the solved problem is sent to the Manager. The promising node is in charge of the solution of the problem. The contract net protocol is for task allocation. The node cannot accept other agents' current state information. If the node cannot finish the task because of resource or ability limitation, it can divide the task into some sub-tasks and allocate the sub-tasks to other nodes. In this condition, the node has a manager role and provides the bids. Every node can be a manager, bid applicant, or contract member.

The traditional contract net protocol is extended to inference the negotiation process. One of these extensions is publicizing the bid file. All the nodes can join the bid process. This requires communication and abundant resources. The manager must evaluate many bid files and use a lot of resources. The big load of the manager is caused by publicizing the bid files. First, the manager needs the ability to inform part of the nodes. You can image that if the manager has knowledge of every node, it can estimate the candidate nodes for dealing with the sub-problems. Second, the common bid request can be cancelled. If the unsolved problems can use the previous methods, the manager can contact the nodes that solved the previous problem. Once the resource can be used, the manager and the node write down the contract. Besides, the node can self-bid. In this condition, many open bids only investigate the new tasks. The bid request is only needed when the proper bids cannot be found.

The second side of contract net system extension is influencing real contract assignment. In the traditional protocol, the manager needs to wait to receive the node's information after the assignment. Before information arrives, the manager does not know whether the node has accepted the contract. The node cannot create a contract and build the constraint of contract after bid. Some suggestion for the extension is to build the contract constraint early. For example, when a node bids, it can provide the possible clause of accepting promise. The acceptance is not an easy acceptance or refusal. It can hold some reference and conditions. The biggest time limit for contract confirmation is extending it further. If there is no confirmation for the contract within a limited time, the manager will stop the contract. The contract process can send the information and avoid the manager to enable waiting for a long time. The managers can assign the contract again before the longest time interval.

14.5.3 *Partial Global Planning*

The most important trait of the partial global planning (PGP) approach is that the ability of each agent is determined in a multi-agent system (Durfee and Lesser, 1991), that is, collecting the current states to reach the goals. The agents can optimize their tasks with knowledge. PGP provides a flexible concept and coordinates the distributed problem solution component.

The basic condition to apply the PGP is there are several agents for the whole problem to work. An agent is a part of PGP and considers the other agents' action and relations to reach their own conclusion. This knowledge is seen as partial global planning. Figure 14.12 gives an example to explain the basic work principle. Two agents work for two sub-problems (A or B). Each agent sends information to their cooperative agent. Agent 1 informs agent 2 its current sub-problem A. At the same time, agent 2 informs its sub-problem B. Every agent can know the cooperative agent's condition according to the information. For example, agent 1 knows its sub-problem A2 is determined by agent 2's sub-problem B. It can thus inform agent 2. PGP's process can be divided into the following four steps:

(1) each agent creates partial planning;
(2) communication and exchange of rules happen between agents;
(3) create partial planning;
(4) revise and optimize the partial global planning.

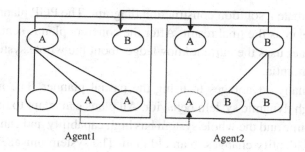

Fig. 14.12. Partial global planning

At the beginning of the coordination, each agent must create a partial planning process and solve the assigned tasks. Every partial planning has at least two different layers. The whole structure includes the important steps for solving the problem, which reflects the long-term planning for solving the problem. It includes detailed information about every sub-problem.

Once the partial plan is finished, agents exchange the knowledge among themselves. Each agent needs to have some specific organization knowledge. It can determine other agents' roles and which information is of interest. Meta-organization determines the layers of the agents. Once agents received the plan information from the other agents, they must organize the information in the PGP format. They also need to check if there is new information including the dependence to the inner plan. Then, they form logic components with the sub-plans. PGP consists of the following components:

(1) **Goal.** Goal includes the basic information, the reason for existence, long goal, and the comparable priority.
(2) **Plan activity diagram.** It includes other agents' tasks and their current states, detailed plan, expected result, and some experiments.
(3) **Solution construction diagram.** This diagram includes how the agents communicate and cooperate with each other. The size and time of the sent plan are very important.
(4) **State.** State includes reporting PGP's whole important information, e.g., other agents' plan and time mark.

The PGP core planner analyzes the information sent by the other agents and determines if they work for the same goal. The PGP planner integrates the knowledge by planning the activity diagram. It can forecast the behavior and result of the other agents. This plan activity diagram forms the foundation of future work. Plan activity compares the partial plan and new knowledge to create a revised partial plan. During this time, they create a solution construction diagram. The PGP planner generates a revised partial plan as the final result. After the concrete plan is sent to the specific agents, the planner uses the current knowledge about the whole system to optimize and enrich the minutia.

There are many advantages to using the partial planner. The most important advantage is high dynamic system behavior. All plans can adapt to the environment solution at any time and the whole system has high capability and can bring about an effect. PGP can identify changes in an old plan. The system must send the revision to the node as soon as possible since revision can influence their work. If any small revision needs to be sent to the node, the whole system will be on a high load. In this condition, PGP agrees on small inconsistences and only informs about the big revisions. The system developers must develop the fault tolerance system and designate a threshold to indicate that the revision is important. The second advantage is that it is effective and can avoid redundancy. If two or more agents have similar problems and register their PGP, then reassignment and construction take place. The work assignment is very effective.

The old PGP model had many constraints especially in the heterogeneous agents' different solutions to problems. How to deal with dynamic agents changing the solution policy again? How to finish concrete tasks within a limited time? How to negotiate between agents? There are some methods to extend the PGP model. For example, using general partial global planning provides new components to meet the needs (Decker, 1995).

Osawa proposed an approach to construct a cooperative plan in an open environment based on collaboration between the robots (Osawa, 1993). In the approach, a rational agent used the "multi world model" to construct an incomplete single-agent plan and then according to the effect-based model balance the cost. This process can be described as follows:

(1) requestor sends RFP to call-board;
(2) leisure agent applies RFP from call-board;
(3) call-board sends RFP to leisure agents;
(4) leisure agent generates the plan;
(5) leisure agent sends it to requestor;
(6) requestor investigates the possibility of cooperation;
(7) requestor sends cooperation rewards;
(8) applicants form cooperative plan.

Utility is computed using the following formula:

$$\text{utility}(a, g) = \text{worth}(a, g) - \text{cost}(\text{plan}(a, g))$$

The average utility is the principal of cooperation. Although Osawa solved the cooperative problems in an open environment, it is not a good way to add the utility to be divided for an average value since the utility is only the order relation of the agent to the goal. We cannot compare the utilities between different kinds of agents.

14.5.4 *Planning Based on Constraint Propagation*

In a multi-agent system, the coordination work of agents can be realized by situated action and planning. The method-based situated action emphasized the interaction between agents and environment and the effects of perception — action looping upon agent actions. The planning method decides the sequence of agent actions for execution, and the sequence will be decided in a searching manner. Compared with situated action, planning can make the agent actions more correct and more rational, and therefore, planning is applied generally in a deliberative agent.

Because of the lack of considering coordination and cooperation among agents in a multi-agent system, generally planning algorithms, like UCPOP, GraphPlan, and SNLP, cannot be applied directly. In a multi-agent environment, the actions among agents are concurrent and not controlled by a single agent. An agent can make a system coordinate more by communication and protocol to try to change the actions of other agents, and to complete the work which cannot be complicated itself by requesting the cooperation of other agents. Classical planning algorithms assure that an agent is the only one who can change the environment; therefore, the planning result cannot ensure that there is no conflict with the other agents, and the solution capability of the agent is limited. The distributed planning in dynamic environment hypothesizes that the paroxysm in an environment is not foreseeable and that planning and executing are handled alternately. This method cannot ensure reliability and completeness of planning.

A planning, especially partial-order planning, can be assured by constraints in the planning steps as follows: Using temporal constrains to designate the time sequence of executing steps; using code signation constraints to designate the executing steps. Planning solving is a process which adds and refines constraints gradually. The resolution of the conflict between coordination and cooperation among agents can be accomplished by designating temporal constraints and code signation constraints. The resource confliction of agent actions and the services which are offered by one agent for the other agents can be presented by a causal link and can be solved by adding temporal constraints to agent actions. At the same time, cooperative actions among agents, such as two agents cooperating to lift up a desk, must be described by a single action description. The correctness of agent planning is assured by truth criterion in a multi-agent system. We propose a multi-agent concurrent partial order planning algorithm (Shi *et al.*, 2002). Each agent is planning for the target to be accomplished in parallel. When an agent decides to add a new action, it accomplishes the coordination of a multi-agent system by constraint propagation with other agents.

To describe the planning action, there are too many constraints in the accomplishment of practical scheduler using STRIPS, and it is very difficult to use situated checking computations.

In 1989, Pednault proposed a kind of action-described language ADL (Pednault, 1989). We expand ADL to describe the planning actions in a Multi-agent System (Shi *et al.*, 2002). It is more powerful than STRIPS, but less powerful than first-order logic.

The semantic of ADL is based on the mathematical structure which describes the world statements. An action a is represented by a statement couple $\langle s, t \rangle$ in ADL, and action a produces a statement "t" when it is executed at statement s. The relations between a statement s and a statement description ϕ are represented by a symbol $\models$, denoted as $s \models \phi$.

The action template in ADL represents a set of possible actions which is described by four selectable clauses: Precond, prerequisite; Add and Delete, the set of formulas added or deleted in relation R on statement t; and Update, a set of relations which describe the functions how to transform from s to t.

Multi-agent planning means that one or more concurrent processes of an agent search their respective targets in their respective planning space simultaneously. In order to coordinate actions of different agents, we have to add a partial constraint between actions which may lead to conflict among themselves. The partial constraint distributes in different agents, so there could be a problem on judging consistency in the partial constraint.

Algorithm 14.5. Consistency Checking of distributed partial-order constraint.
calculate_transition_closure(α, A_i)

   Input: planning $\langle S, B, O, L \rangle$, constraint $A_i \prec A_j$,
   Output: transitive closure $T_<(A_i)$.

   1.   send information to all agents to set temporal constraint O in its planning
to read-only mode;

   2.   compute of local transitive closure $T_\leq^\alpha(A_i)$ of action A_i in agent α;

   3. $T_<(A_i) = T_\leq^\alpha(A_i)$;

   4.   let SET(agentn) be actions of the agent in $T_<(A_i)$.

   5.   start a new thread for every nonempty SET(agentn)

6. {
7. $T_<(A_i) = T_<(A_i) +$ request (calculate_transition_closure(agentn,
        SET(agentn));
8.   return.
9. }
10. after all subthreads return, return $T_<(A_i)$;
11. demand of all agents to disable the read-only mode of constraint.

In Algorithm 14.6, the cooperation between agents involves two phases: task assignment for every agent and sub-goal planning of agent. Task assignment means that the global goal of the multi-agent system is decomposed and is assigned to one or a group of agents in the system so as to accomplish the target. Here we emphasize the later problem, or say, in the beginning of planning every agent has its own goal, which may be assigned to the agent or be formed to meet its own interest. Furthermore, for a multi-agent system and agents in the system we assume:

(1) Any effect of all actions is a deterministic function of system status when the job and action is being preformed.
(2) Agent possesses all the knowledge of its own action, actions of other agents, and the initial states of the system.
(3) The change of system can only be caused by actions of agents.
(4) No matter whether an agent could make planning successfully, it will keep the promise of actions with other agents in the planning phase so as to enable other agents to accomplish their planning.

Communication between agents is in accord with the message transmission protocol in communication language ACL Specification. In particular, the communication should be without delay, and the message sent to the same target will arrive according to the sequence of the message sending.

The architecture of agents is given in Figure 14.13. Due to requirements of negotiation between agents and judging consistency in constraint, in every agent there are three independent threads, which are

Planning thread: responsible for executing Algorithm 14.6 for solving its own planning problems.

Constraints maintenance thread: calculating the local transitive closure of the action on its own actions set S and judging consistency in the distributed partial-order planning.

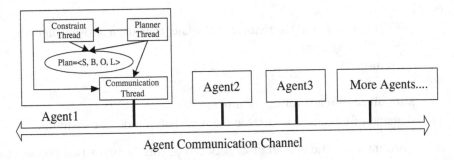

Fig. 14.13.   The architecture of planning agents

Communication and negotiation thread: responsible for sending action constraints and accomplishing cooperation and coordination of actions between agents.

Every agent could solve its own sub-goal planning according to Algorithm 14.6. In Algorithm 14.6, agents construct and maintain planning according to the UCPOP framework; when the need arises for requesting services from and cooperating with other agents to judge consistency in the distributed partial-order constraint, agents communicate with each other.

Algorithm 14.6 (Planning Algorithm).

planning $(\langle S, B, O, L \rangle, G, \Lambda)$

1. Termination conditions: if G is empty, return $\langle S, B, O, L \rangle$;
2. Targets resolution: get a target $\langle Q, A_c \rangle$ from G,
    (a) If Q is a conjunction of Q_i, add every $\langle Q_i, A_c \rangle$ into G, and go to step 2;
    (b) If Q is a disjunction of Q_i, randomly choose a Q_k, and add it into G, and go to step 2;
    (c) If Q is a character and $A_p \xrightarrow{\neg Q} A_c$ exists in L, return failure.
3. Select operator: randomly choose an action existing in S, or from Λ choose a new action A_p, which has effection e and an universal clause p, where $p \in T(\theta_\ell)$ and $MGU(Q, p) \neq \perp$ (Q and p have a general resolution); if there is not any action satisfying conditions in Λ and there is a agent β whose action $A_{\beta j}$ satisfies conditions, send a request to β; if there are joint-actions satisfying conditions, send requests to all executors of joint-actions; the agent which receives a request executes the step 4 and 5 in its planning P_b, if it succeeds, β returns Comm($A_{\beta j}$) and add joint-actions or Comm($A_{\beta j}$) into S, and go to 2; otherwise, β returns failure.
4. Enabling new action: Let $S' = S$, $G' = G$. If $A_p \notin S$, add A_p into A', and add $\langle preconds(A_p) \backslash MGU(Q, R, B), A_p \rangle$ into G', and add non-cd-constraints(A_p) into B'.

5. Protection of Causal Link: for every causal link $l = A_i \xrightarrow{P} A_j$ and every action A_t which may be a threat to l, choose one from following three solutions (if do not choose any solution, return failure)

   (a) Upgrade: for O judge consistency in the distributed partial-order constraint, if constraint is consistent, $O' = O' \cup \{A_j < A_t\}$

   (b) Degrade: for O judge consistency in the distributed partial-order constraint, if constraint is consistent, $O' = O' \cup \{A_t < A_j\}$

   (c) Facing: if 1 which A_t becomes a threat to is a conditional conclusion, let condition be S and conclusion be R, and add $\langle \neg S \backslash MGU(P, R), A_t \rangle$ into G'.

6. Recursive call: if B is inconsistent, return failure; otherwise, call $(\langle S', B', O', L' \rangle, G, \Lambda)$.

Algorithm 14.6 is sound but not complete. Soundness means that for a planning problem if an agent found a planning using a planning algorithm, the planning is the solution for the problem. Algorithm 14.6 is not complete because there is a temporal and equivalent constraint relationship when an agent and other agents search in the planning space, which means the planning space of agents has been limited. In particular, in order to not cause parallel planning be too complex and prolix, we do not provide a mechanism for when an agent cannot find a solution after backtracking process if it could ask other agents to adopt backtracking process or to relax constraints, which will expand its current solution space and thus the agent could continue searching.

14.5.5 *Ecological-Based Cooperation*

At the end of 1980s, a new subject — the ecology of computation — was presented. It is a subject that researches the behavior and resource application. It spurns the traditional closed, static algorithm for solving a problem. It thinks the world is an open, evolved, concurrent ecosystem which solves the problem by collaboration. Its development is related with the research of an open information system.

The distributed system is similar to a society and a biological organization. This kind of open system is different from the current computer system. It computes tasks asynchronously. Its nodes can generate the process in other machines. These nodes can make decisions according to incomplete and late knowledge. There is no central control node. It solves the problem by communication with and cooperation of many nodes. These characteristics consist of a concurrent combination. Its communication, policy, and competition are similar to the ecosystem. Hewitt (1991) proposed an open information system concept. He argued that incomplete knowledge, asynchronous computing, and inconsistent data are inevitable in an open computing system. Human society, and especially the problems in sciences, can be solved by cooperation.

Computing bionomics considers the computing system as an ecosystem. It introduces biological mechanisms, e.g., mutations in a computing system. This revision causes the change of the life gene, which diversifies to improve the ability to adapt to the environment. This mutation policy becomes a method to improve its own ability in the artificial intelligence system. Miller and Drexler discussed a series of evolution models, for example, the ecosystem and a commerce market and pointed the difference between the ecosystems. They thought that a direct computing market was the most ideal system model.

Because incomplete knowledge and late information are the inner characteristics of a computing ecosystem, the dynamic activities research under these constraints is important. Huberman and Hogg (1987) proposed and analyzed the process of dynamic games. They pointed that if there are many choices when the processes finish the tasks, the dynamic graduate process may undergo nonlinear fluctuation and chaos. This indicates that a stable policy for computing a biologic system is not existent. They also discussed possible common rules and the importance of cooperation and compared the biologic ecosystem with human organization. Similar to dynamic theory, Rosenschein and Geneserth proposed static policy theory to solve the conflicts in nodes with different goals.

Famous ecosystem models include biologic ecosystem model, species evolution model, economic model, and the sciences group's society model. A large ecosystem's intelligence surpasses that of any single intelligence.

1. Biologic ecosystem model

It is the most famous ecosystem which has typical evolution characteristics and hierarchical traits. This trait is reflected in the food chain. For a complex biologic ecosystem, all the species consist of a close network, i.e., food chain. This system's main roles are those of hunters and preys. The life is dependent on life. The large ecosystem consists of small ecosystems.

2. Species evolution model

Species evolution is dependent on genes. From plant heredity to model genetics, researchers have demonstrated the combination of gene's importance in species evolution. The gene pool consists of a group of genes from a species. The gene is the carrier of biological information. If the environment changes, the selection mechanism will change. This change inevitably causes a change in the gene pool.

The change of a specific species is called gene stream. A species is always experiencing isolation, gene flow, and change as a continuous cycle. At the beginning, a geographically isolated group develops alone and the gene quickly flows in the inner structure. Because of the opening, the system can communicate and compete to realize the survival of the fittest.

3. Economics model

The economic system is similar to a biologic ecosystem. In the commerce market and ideal market, evolution determines economic entities' decision. The choices mechanism is a market encouragement mechanism. The evolution is rapid. The relationship is between the enterprise and consumer, and the inter-enterprise relationship is dependent on both parties. A decision-maker can adopt the effective approaches in order to pursue long interest, and especially sustain losses in business in short time.

14.5.6 *Game Theory-Based Negotiation*

In a multi-agent system, negotiation has many meanings. One point of view is that negotiation is about allocation of resource and sub-problems. Another view thinks that negotiation is peer-to-peer direct negotiation. The goal of negotiation is to build cooperation among a group of agents. Agents have their own goals. The negotiation protocol provides the possible basic rules for the negotiation process and forms the foundation of communication. The policy of negotiation is decided upon by the concrete agents. Although the agent developers provide different extents to the ability of negotiation, it must guarantee the match between protocol and policy. That is to say, the policy can run in the protocol.

For a single agent, the goal of negotiation is to improve its own state and support other agents without getting affected. The agents must make a trade-off to maintain the ability of the whole system. From this view, negotiation communication can be divided into the following types:

(1) **Symmetry cooperation.** The result of negotiation is better that the past result and the inference by other agents is positive.
(2) **Symmetry trade-off.** Agents would like to achieve their goals. Negotiation means trade-off of participants, which will decrease the effects. However, negotiation cannot ignore the existence of other agents. They can only take the policy of trade-off and make the participants accept the result.
(3) **Asymmetry cooperation/trade-off.** The effect of cooperation on one agent is positive, but for the other agent a trade-off is required.

(4) **Conflict.** Because of the conflicts of goals of multi-agents, they cannot reach an acceptable result. The negotiation must stop before the result.

14.5.7 *Intention-Based Negotiation*

Grosz applied the belief, desire, and intention theory to agent negotiation (Grosz and Kraus, 1996). This method does not use the sub-plan, but uses the intention for negotiation to decrease communication. BDI theory thinks that the agents' actions were not the desire and plan but the result of a combination of belief and desire. The sub-plan to realize intention is generated by this intention. One intention is correspondence with some sub-plans. An agent's communication need not lead to exchange of the sub-plans and can only involve exchange of intentions. However, Grosz's approach assumes the agents are completely cooperative.

Zlotkin's work greatly improves the static negotiation theory between two agents. However, his approach is not applicable to an open multi-agent system. Current BDI team approaches lack tools for quantitative performance analysis under uncertainty. Distributed partially observable Markov decision problems (POMDPs) are well suited for such analysis, but the complexity of finding optimal policies in such models is highly intractable. Nair and Tambe have proposed a hybrid BDI–POMDP approach, where BDI team plans are exploited to improve POMDP tractability and POMDP analysis improves BDI team plan performance (Nair and Tambe, 2005).

14.5.8 *Team-Oriented Collaboration*

Coordination between large teams of highly heterogeneous entities will change the way complex goals are pursued in real-world environments. Scerri and his colleagues proposed a Machinetta approach which combines team-oriented programming and proxy architecture to overcome the limitations of effective coordination between very large teams of highly heterogeneous agents (Scerri *et al.*, 2004). The main advantages to Machinetta approach display one or a combination of the characteristics: large scale, dynamic environment, and integration of humans. By connecting the Machinetta proxies with the graphical development tool for constructing team plans, the Team Oriented Programming programmer gains a good idea of what is going on in the plan and how to make effective changes in it.

Token-based coordination is a process by which agents attempt to maximize the overall team reward by moving tokens around the team. If an agent were to know the exact state of the team, it could use an Markov decision process (MDP) to determine the expected utility-maximizing way to move tokens. Unfortunately, it is not feasible for an agent to know the complete state; however, it is illustrative to look at how tokens would be passed if it were feasible. Then, by dividing the monolithic joint activity into a set of actions that can be taken by individual agents, we can decentralize the token routing process where distributed agents, in parallel, make independent decisions of where to pass the tokens they currently hold. Thus, we effectively break a large coordination problem into many small ones.

Algorithm 14.7. Token pass local model which makes the decision process for agent α to pass incoming tokens (Xu *et al.*, 2005).

Method:
```
1.   while true do
2.       Tokens(α) ← getToken(sender);
3.       for all Δ ∈ Tokens(∈) do
4.           if Acceptable(Δ, α) then
5.               if Δ.type == Res then
6.                   Increase(Δ,threshold);
7.               end if
8.           else
9.               Append(self,Δ.path);
10.              for all Δᵢ ∈ Hα do
11.                  Update(Pα[Δ],Δᵢ);
12.              end if
13.              if (Δ.type == Res)||(Δ.type == Role) then
14.                  Decrease(Δ.threshold);
15.              end if
16.              acquaintance ← Choose(Pα[Δ])
17.              Send(acquaintance,Δ);
18.              AddtoHistory(Δ);
19.          end if
20.      end for
21.  end while
```

In the above model, $P\alpha$ is the decision matrix agent that α uses to decide where to move tokens. Initially, agents do not know where to send tokens, but as tokens are received, a model can be developed and better routing decisions made. That is, the model, $P\alpha$ is based on the accumulated information provided by the receipt of previous tokens. Algorithm 14.7 shows the reasoning of agent α when it receives incoming tokens from its acquaintances via the function getToken (sender) (line 2). For each incoming token Δ, function Acceptable (α, Δ) determines whether the token will be kept by α (line 4). When a resource is kept, its threshold is raised (line 6). If α decides to pass Δ, it will add itself to the path of Δ (Line 9) and Update $(P\alpha[\Delta], \Delta_i)$ will update how to send Δ according to each previously received token Δi in α's history (line 11). If Δ is a resource or role token, its threshold will be decreased (line 14). Then, α will choose the best acquaintance to pass the token to according to $P\alpha[\Delta]$ (line 16) and record Δ in its history, $H\alpha$ (line 18).

14.6 Mobile Agent

Along with the development of Internet applications, especially information retrieval, distributed computing, and electronic commerce, people hope to acquire the best service within the scope of the whole Internet, to build the network as a whole, and to make a software agent move freely in the whole network. The concept of mobile agent was conceived gradually at this time.

At the beginning of the 1990s, General Magic proposed the mobile agent concept for the first time in industry when it released its business system Telescript. A mobile agent was defined as a kind of agent that can independently move from one host to another in the heterogeneous network environment. A mobile agent is a special software agent that can communicate with other agents and resources. Besides the basic characteristics, autonomy, activity, and reasoning, it also has a mobility function. It can delegate the users to finish the task by moving from one host to another host. This mobility can reduce the network load, and thus increase the efficiency of communication. It can adapt to the dynamic environment and has good security and fault tolerance ability.

A mobile agent can be seen as a combination of agent technology and distributed computing technology. It is not similar to the traditional computing model. Different from remote procedure call (RPC), a mobile agent can move from one node to another. This mobility can be selected according to the requirement. A mobile agent is also different from the common process move because a common process cannot allow the process to select when and where to move. However, the mobile agent can decide where and when to move at any time. A mobile agent is also different from the Applet in Java Language. Applet can only move from server to client machine. A mobile agent can move both from the server and from the client.

Although the architecture of mobile agent is different, almost all mobile agent systems include a mobile agent (MA) and a mobile agent environment (MAE), which builds the correct and secure environment for mobile agents to run. It also provides basic services (including create, transmit, and execute), constraint mechanism, fault tolerance policy, security control, and communication mechanism. MA's mobility and problem-solving ability are decided by MAE's services. Generally speaking, MAE includes the following services:

(1) **Transaction service:** realizing creation, mobility, persistence, and environment allocation for mobile agents;
(2) **Event service:** including agent transfer and communication protocol, realizing events move in mobile agents;
(3) **Directory service:** providing locating and routing services;
(4) **Security service:** providing a secure run environment;
(5) **Application service:** providing service interface for special task.

In general, an MAE can only locate one machine. However, an MAE can run in multiple machines if the hosts are connected by a fast network. MAE uses agent transfer protocol to realize mobility and allocate the run-time environment and service interface. MA runs in MAE, and they communicate between themselves by agent communication language (ACL) and access the services provided by MAE.

Based on the architecture of mobile agent, MA can be divided into two types: user agent (UA) and server agent (SA). UA can move from an MAE to anther MAE. It runs in MAE and communicates with other MAs through ACL. It can access the services provided by an MAE. SA cannot move and its main function is to provide services for local and visiting MA. An MAE holds several SAs that provide different services. Because SA cannot move and can only be controlled by the local MAE administrator, it ensures that SA cannot be vicious. It cannot directly access the system resource. It can, only through the SA's interfaces, access the restrictive resources, thus preventing hostile agents from attacking the hosts. This is the common security policy in a mobile agent system.

Mobile agent is a novel concept that has no unified definition. However, almost all mobile agents have the following characteristics:

(1) **Unique identification:** Mobile agents must have a specific identification which can help them delegate the tasks of users.
(2) **Autonomic mobility:** Mobile agents can automatically move from one node to another. This is the basic characteristic of a mobile agent which distinguishes it from other kinds of agents.
(3) **Continuous run:** Mobile agents must have the ability to run consecutively at different addresses. Specifically, mobile agents can hang the state when they begin to move to another node and run again at the hang state when they reach the destination.

Currently, mobile agents have already come into practical applications from theoretical research. Researchers have built a series of mature development platforms and run environments. Theoretically speaking, mobile agents can be coded by any language (such as C/C++, Java, Perl, Tcl, Python, etc.) and can run on any machine. However, since mobile agents need to support different software and hardware environments, it is better to choose an expositive, platform-independent language to develop mobile agents. Java is an ideal development language for mobile agents currently since Java binary code after compilation can run on any system that has the Java virtual machine (JVM), having good cross-platform characteristic.

Although the mobile agent has been a hot topic in academic research for many years, the first really applicable mobile agent system was not created until 1996. Currently, the mobile system can be divided into three types: traditional expositive language based, Java language based, and CORBA platform based. We introduce several typical mobile agent systems which represent the direction and trend of mobile agents.

1. General Magic's Odysses

During early exploration, the Telescript that was developed by General Magic Company has been widely adopted in the last few years. Telescript is a kind of object-oriented expositive language. The mobile agents coded by Telescript have two formats in communication. First, one agent can call other agents' methods if they are in the same place. Second, mobile agents can build the connection to transfer the computable mobile objects if they are in different places. Telescript was a relatively successful mobile agent system since its emergence. It was secure and robust. The performance is also excellent. Telescript's three basic concepts (agent, place, and go) gave a clear description for mobile agents: agent go places.

With the development of Java language and cross-platform technology, Telescript lost its superiority and attraction. Under this condition, General Magic began to change its policy. They developed a Java-based system called Odyssey that could support Java RMI, Microsoft DCOM, and CORBA IIOP. Odyssey inherited many characteristics of Telescript and became a widely used mobile agent development platform.

2. IBM's Aglet

Aglet is one of the earliest mobile agent systems based on Java. Its name is the combination of agent and applet. It can be seen as an applet object which has agent characteristics. Aglet was produced as a thread on one machine. It can stop running work at any time and transfer the unfinished work to another machine. From concept, an aglet is a mobile object. It supports autonomic running and can be moved from one machine to another that has the aglet running environment.

Aglet built a simple but all-sided mobile agent programming framework. It provided a dynamic and effective communication mechanism for mobile agent communication. It also held a detailed and easy-to-use security mechanism. These features simplified mobile agent development.

3. Recursion's Voyager

Voyager can be seen as an improved object request broker. Compared with the other mobile agent systems, Voyager has a deeper relation with Java language. It can be used to develop mobile agent systems and create distributed systems. Voyager is a pure Java distributed computing platform which can quickly generate high-performance distributed application programs. It is a good mobile agent development platform which represents the current technology level.

14.7 Multi-Agent Environment MAGE

Multi-agent environment (MAGE) is an agent-oriented software development, integration and run environment developed by Intelligence Science Laboratory, Institute of Computing Technology, Chinese Academy of Sciences (Shi *et al.*, 2003). It provides users a software deployment and system integration mode which includes requirement analysis, system design, and agent generation. It also provides a multi-software reuse mode, which is beneficial for agent software. It can also wrap other legacy systems to quickly integrate as a new software.

14.7.1 *The Architecture of MAGE*

The MAGE System framework includes requirement analysis and modeling toolkit AUMP, visual agent studio, and multi-agent run-time environment MAGE. The structure of MAGE is shown in Figure 14.14. AUMP supports agent-oriented analysis and design. VAStudio can realize the model to programs, including different agent behaviors. Finally, agents can run in the agent-supporting environment.

14.7.2 *Agent Unified Modeling Language*

Agent unified modeling language (AUML) is an agent-oriented modeling language. Its main function is help the software designers and programmers to model the software and describe the software development process from the beginning to the end. AUML unifies the agent-oriented and object-oriented methods.

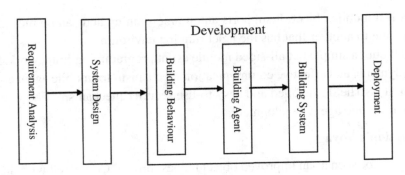

Fig. 14.14.   MAGE architecture

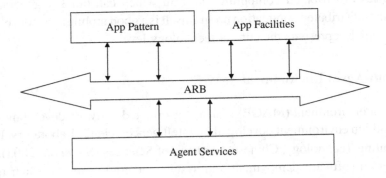

Fig. 14.15.   CARBA architecture

AUMP is a multi-window application software which runs on the Windows platform. It provides a Graphic User Interface for users to edit and revise the models.

14.7.3 *Visual Agent Development Tool*

On the agent-oriented distributed platform, we combine the common object request broker agent and Internet to build the common agent request broker architecture (CARBA) (Cao and Shi, 1998). As can be seen in Figure 14.15, CARBA consists of an agent request broker (ARB), agent application facilities (AppFacilities), an agent domain pattern (appPattern), and agent services.

CARBA is a distributed management mechanism which uses the ARB as its core component. It defines the way distributed agents send requests and receive responses. AppFacilities provide the agent components from horizontal and vertical directions. AppPattern builds the templates according to the domain requirement, e.g., agent life circle, agent library, name, etc. CARBA can realize the following objectives:

(1) decompose the system according to the function in a heterogeneous and distributed environment;
(2) integrate the components according to requirement.

Based the above method, we developed a visual development toolkit named Visual Agent Studio (VAStudio). The objective for designing this toolkit was to provide a user-friendly GUI to support agent-oriented development. It is not just a programming editor but a design and coding environment. It can use GUI to generate the agents step-by-step. It also provides a series basic tool, e.g., components management tool, behavior library, agent library, etc. (Figure 14.16).

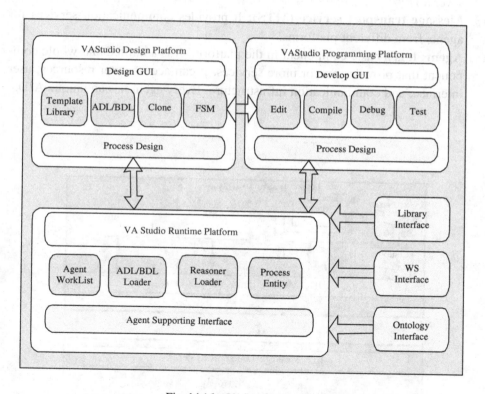

Fig. 14.16.   VAStudio structure

14.7.4 *MAGE Running Platform*

MAGE platform follows the rule of FIPA. It is a realization of FIPA standard. It provides agent generation, localization, registration, communication services, and mobility and exit services (Figure 14.17).

(1) **Agent management system (AMS):** It is an indispensable component in the MAGE platform. AMS controls agent access and use in the platform. One platform has only one AMS which records the agent directory, including agent name and address. AMS also provides white-page services for other agents. Every agent must register on AMS to get an effective Agent ID.

(2) **Directory facilitator (DF):** It also indispensable in the platform. DF provides yellow-page services for other agents. Agents can register their services on DF and can search services provided by other agents. One platform can have several DFs.

(3) **Message transport service (MTS):** It provides communication services for agents from different platforms.

(4) **Agent:** It is a basic component in the platform. It is a unified and whole component that provides one or more services. It can access outer resources, user interface, and communication infrastructure. Every agent has an unique AID.

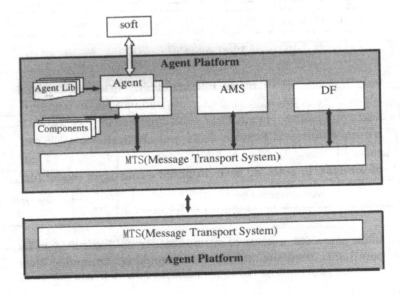

Fig. 14.17. MAGE running platform

(5) **Agent platform (AP):** It provides a physical infrastructure for agents that includes machine, operation system, agent support software, agent management components (DF, AMS, MTS), and agents.

(6) **Software:** It includes all non-agent software. Agents can access them, e.g., adding new service, acquiring new service protocol and new security protocol/algorithm, new negotiation protocol, and accessing supporting toolkits.

(7) **Agent library (Agent Lib).**

14.8 Agent Grid Intelligence Platform

Web Services provide a means of interoperability that was essential to achieve large-scale computation with a focus on middleware to support large-scale information processing. In a Grid, the middleware is used to hide the heterogeneous nature and provide users and applications with a homogeneous and seamless environment by providing a set of standardized interfaces to a variety of services. In 2002, we proposed a four-layer model for agent-based grid computing to combine agent computing with grid computing through the middleware concept, shown in Figure 14.18 (Shi *et al.*, 2002).

(1) **Common resources:** Consist of various resources distributed in the Internet, such as mainframe, workstation, personal computer, computer cluster, storage equipment, databases or data sets, or others, which run on Unix and other operating systems.

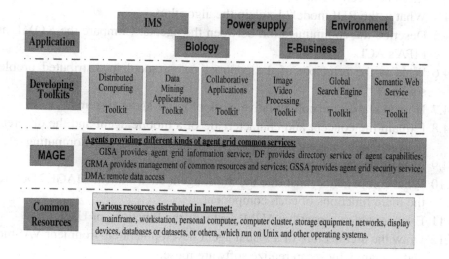

Fig. 14.18. Model of AGEGC

(2) **MAGE environment:** It is the kernel of Grid computing which is responsible for resource location and allocation, authentication, unified information access, communication, task assignment, agent developing tools, and others.

(3) **Developing toolkit:** Provide developing toolkits, containing distributed computing, data mining applications, collaborative applications, image and video processing, global search engine, semantic Web services, and negotiation support, to let users effectively use middleware resources.

(4) **Application service:** Organize certain agents automatically for specific-purpose applications, such as power supply, oil supply, e-business, distance education, e-government, etc.

In terms of the model of AGEGC, we have developed Agent Grid Intelligence Platform (AGrIP), which is a powerful developing environment for complex and large distributed intelligent systems. AGrIP has been applied to develop many group intelligent decision support systems, such as agent grid-based city emergency interactive response system (GEIS), residential power demand simulator based on MAS (RSMAS), and so on.

Exercises

14.1 Describe briefly the solution process of distributed problem solving.

14.2 Explain briefly the concept of agent and its basic structures.

14.3 What is a deliberative agent? What is a reactive agent? Compare the differences between them.

14.4 What is the BDI model? Explain the algorithm.

14.5 Describe the communication between the agents. Compare the KQML and FIPA's ACL.

14.6 What is the principle of the contract net protocol in distributed problem solving?

14.7 How to realize the collaborative work of multi-agent systems?

14.8 Explain the concept and characteristic of a mobile agent and the difference between mobile agent technology and traditional network computing.

14.9 Investigate several typical mobile agent systems.

14.10 What components constitute the multi-agent environment MAGE? Describe the main functions of each component.

14.11 Explain which aspect for AUML extends the functions of UML?

14.12 Draw the architecture of a visual agent development environment VAStudio and explain why it can realize software reuse.

Chapter 15

Internet Intelligence

The Internet is a major innovation in the history of human civilization and has revolutionized the development of information technology and artificial intelligence. Numerous information resources are connected through the Internet to form a global information system and become an interactive platform for artificial intelligence.

15.1 Introduction

In 1962, Licklider of the US Defense Advanced Research Projects Agency and others proposed the idea of interconnecting computers through the Internet (Licklider and Clark, 1962). In December 1969, ARPANET connected four major computers in the southwestern United States, including the University of California, Los Angeles, the Stanford Institute of Research, the University of California, Santa Barbara, and the University of Utah. By June 1970, the Massachusetts Institute of Technology, Harvard University, BBN, and the San Damonica Systems Development Corporation of California joined. In 1972, ARPANET was shown to the public, and email appeared. ARPANET was transferred to the TCP/IP agreement in 1983. NSFNET, founded by the National Science Foundation in 1995, is connected to 50,000 networks worldwide, and the Internet has taken shape.

The development history of the Internet over the past 50 years can be divided into four stages, namely, computer interconnection, Web page interconnection, user real-time interaction, and semantic interconnection.

(1) **Computer interconnection stage:** The first host connected to ARPANET in the 1960s marked the birth of the Internet and the beginning of the development phase of network interconnection. At this stage, with the advent of IBM 360, the first personal computer, the Unix operating system, and the advanced programming language, computers gradually became popular, forming a relatively

unified computer operating system, with convenient computer, software programming languages and tools. People try to connect computers distributed in different places through communication links and protocols, creating the Internet, forming a universal standard TCP/IP protocol for network interconnection and transmission protocols, and a universal and unified standard for network address allocation and domain name resolution. Based on the Internet, people can develop various applications on it. For example, the phase of emergence of remote login, file transfer, e-mail, and other simple applications has effective and far-reaching Internet uses.

(2) **Web page interconnection stage:** In March 1989, while at the European Quantum Physics Laboratory, Tim Berners-Lee, developed a master–slave distributed hypermedia system. As long as people use simple methods, they can get rich information quickly and conveniently through the Web. In the process of accessing information resources with Web browsers, users do not need to care about technical details, so the Web was welcomed as soon as it was launched on the Internet. In 1993, Web technology made a breakthrough, which solved the problems of text display, data connection, and image transmission in remote information service, making the Web a very popular way of information dissemination on the Internet. Web pages all over the world are connected by the text transfer protocol, which has become a prominent feature of the development of the Internet at this stage. Through this stage of development, common resource location method, document format, and transmission standard, such as uniform resource locator (URL), hypertext markup language (HTML), and hypertext transfer protocol (HTTP), have been formed. WWW services became the most sought-after service with the most traffic on the Internet, and various Web applications have been developed.

(3) **User interaction stage:** With the development of computers and the Internet, the capacity of computing devices and storage devices connected to the Internet has been greatly improved. By the late 1990s, the World Wide Web was no longer simply a content-based platform, but was moving toward providing greater and richer user interaction capabilities, such as blogs, QQ, wikis, social bookmarking, and so on. This stage is different from the second stage of Web page interconnection. This stage takes the comprehensive interconnection of all kinds of resources, especially the interconnection of application programs as the main feature. Any application system will more or less rely on the Internet and all kinds of resources on the Internet. The application system is gradually transferred to the Internet and the World Wide Web for development and transportation.

(4) **Semantic interconnection stage:** Semantic interconnection is to solve interoperability problems among different applications, enterprises, and communities. This interoperability is guaranteed by semantics, and the interoperability environment is a heterogeneous, dynamic, open, and globalized Web. Each application has its own data, such as a calendar with itineraries and a Web with bank accounts and photos. Integrating software is required to understand the data on a Web page, which retrieves and displays photo pages, discovers the date, time, and description of the photos taken; understands transactions in online bank statements; understands various views of an online calendar; and knows which parts of the Web page indicate which dates and time. Data must be semantically able to interoperate between different applications and communities. Through semantic interconnection, the computer can read the content of the web page and support the user's interoperability on the basis of understanding.

With the large-scale application of the Internet, various Internet-based computing modes have emerged. In recent years, cloud computing has attracted wide attention. Cloud computing is a paradigm of distributed computing which emphasizes the establishment of information technology infrastructure such as large-scale data centers on the Internet and provides infrastructure capabilities for various users through a service-oriented business model. In the user's view, cloud computing provides a large-scale resource pool. Resource pool manages resources including computing, storage, platforms, and services, and resources in the resource pool can be abstracted and virtualized and are dynamically scalable. Cloud computing has the following characteristics:

(1) **Service-oriented business model.** At different levels, the cloud computing system can be viewed as "software as a service" (SaaS), "platform as a service" (PaaS), "infrastructure as a service". (IaaS), and so on. In the SaaS mode, the application software is uniformly deployed on the server side, and the user uses the application software through the network, and the server side can provide a service according to a fine-grained service quality guarantee agreement between the server and the user. The server side uniformly allocates and optimizes the computing, storage, and bandwidth resources required by the application software of multiple tenants and can perform performance expansion according to the actual load.

(2) **Resource virtualization.** In order to pursue economies of scale, cloud computing systems use virtualization, which breaks down the division of data centers, servers, storage, networks, and other resources in physical devices; abstracts

physical resources; and schedules and dynamically optimizes virtual resources as a unit.

(3) **Centralized sharing of resources.** The resources in the cloud computing system are shared among multiple tenants, and the cost and energy consumption are reduced through centralized management of resources. Cloud computing is the product of typical scale economies.

(4) **Dynamic scalability.** A key feature of cloud computing systems is that it can support users to dynamically adjust the amount of resources used, without the need for users to pre-install, deploy, and run the resources required for peak user requests.

15.2 Semantic Web

According to the World Wide Web Consortium (W3C), the semantic Web provides a common framework that allows data to be shared and reused across applications, enterprise, and community boundaries. The Semantic Web is therefore regarded as an integrator across different contents, information applications, and systems.

In 1999, Web founder Berners-Lee first proposed the concept of "Semantic Web". In February 2001, W3C officially established "Semantic Web Activity" to guide and promote the research and development of the Semantic Web, and the status of the Semantic Web was officially established. In May 2001, Berners-Lee and others published an article in the *Scientific American* magazine proposing the vision of the Semantic Web (Berners-Lee *et al.*, 2001).

The Semantic Web must provide sufficient and appropriate semantic description mechanisms (Davies, 2006). From the perspective of the entire application concept, the Semantic Web needs to realize the sharing of information at the knowledge level and the interoperability at the semantic level. This requires a semantic "common understanding" between different systems (Berners-Lee *et al.*) "The Semantic Web is not another Web, it is an extension of the existing Web, where information is given a well-defined meaning, so that computers can work better with people" (Berners-Lee *et al.*, 2001). Ontology naturally becomes the theoretical basis for guiding the development of semantic Web. In 2001, Berners-Lee gave the original Semantic Web architecture (Figure 15.1). In 2006, Berners-Lee gave a new semantic Web hierarchical model (Berners-Lee *et al.*, 2006), which is shown in Figure 15.2.

There are seven layers, namely UNICODE and URI, XML and namespace, RDF schema, OWL and rules, unified logic, proof, and trust in the hierarchical model of semantic Web. The functions of each layer are briefly introduced in the following.

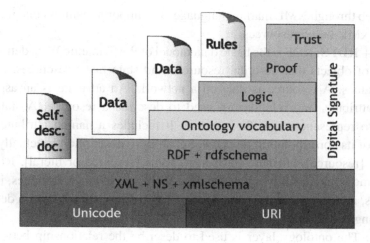

Fig. 15.1. Basic architecture of semantic Web

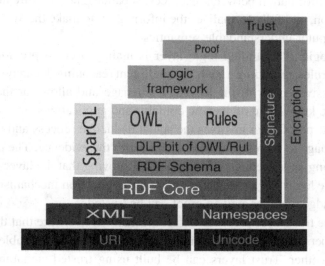

Fig. 15.2. Hierarchical model of semantic Web

(1) **UNICODE and URI:** UNICODE and URI form the basis of the Semantic Web. The encoding of UNICODE processing resources ensures that the international common character set is used to realize the unified encoding of information on the Web. A URI is a superset of Uniform Resource Locator, URLs, that supports the identification of objects and resources on the Semantic Web.

(2) **XML and namespace:** This layer includes a namespace and XML Schema, which separates the structure, content, and data representation of resources on

the Web through XML markup language and supports seamless integration with other XML-based resources.

(3) **RDF + RDFS:** RDF is the basic data model of the Semantic Web, defining three types of objects that describe resources and state facts: resources, attributes, and values. A resource is data on a network. An attribute is an aspect, feature, attribute, and relationship used to describe a resource. A statement is used to represent a specific resource. It includes a named attribute and the value of its corresponding resource. So, an RDF description is actually a triple: object [resource], attribute [property], value [resource or literal]. RDFS provides modeling primitives that organize Web objects into hierarchies, including classes, attributes, subclass and sub-attribute relationships, domain definitions, and range constraints.

(4) **OWL:** The ontology layer is used to describe the relationship between various resources, expressed in OWL. The ontology reveals the complex and rich semantic information between resources, separates the structure and content of information, and fully formalizes the information to make the Web information have computer-understandable semantics.

(5) **Unified logic:** The unified logic layer is mainly used to provide axiom and inference rules, providing a basis for intelligent reasoning. It can further enhance the expressive power of the ontology language and allow for the creation of descriptive knowledge of specific domains and applications.

(6) **Proof:** The proof layer involves the actual deductive process and the use of the Web language to represent evidence and verify the evidence. The proof focuses on providing an authentication mechanism, proving that the layer performs the rules of the logical layer, and combining the application mechanism of the trust layer to judge whether a given proof can be trusted.

(7) **Trust:** The trust layer provides a trust mechanism to ensure that the user agent provides personalized services on the Web and secure and reliable interactions with each other. Trust layers can be built using trusted signatures and other certification authorities by using digital signatures and other knowledge. When the operation of the agent is secure, and the user trusts the operation of the agent, and the services it provides, the semantic Web can fully exert its value.

Semantic Web provides a convenient information exchange and resource-sharing platform for people all over the world to better connect people. Due to the wide range of applications and the rapid development of Web technology, the evolution roadmap of Web technology is shown in Figure 15.3 (Spivack, 2008). The abscissa of the graph represents the semantics of social connection, that is, the degree of connection between people; the ordinate represents the semantics of

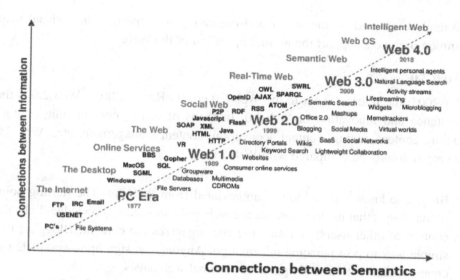

Fig. 15.3.   The evolution of Web technology

information connection, that is, the degree of connection between information; and the dotted lines with arrows represent the evolution of Web technology, including PC era, Web 1.0, Web 2.0, Web 3.0, and Web 4.0.

1. Web 1.0

The Web links highly distributed documents on the Internet to form a spider-like structure. Documentation is one of the core concepts of the Web. Its extension is very extensive, in addition to containing text information, it also contains audio, video, pictures, files, and other network resources.

The way the Web organizes documents is called hypertext, and the link between connected documents is called hyperlink. Hypertext is a kind of text. Unlike traditional text, it is the way text is organized. Traditional text takes a linear approach to text organization, while hypertext is organized in a nonlinear manner. Hypertext organizes the relevant content in the text through links, which is close to the human mindset, allowing users to quickly view relevant content in the text.

The basic architecture of the Web can be divided into three parts: client, server, and related network protocols. The server takes on a lot of tedious work, including processing and management of data, execution of applications, and generation of dynamic Web pages. The client mainly sends a request to the server through the browser, and after processing the request, the server returns the processing result and related information to the browser. The browser is responsible for parsing the information returned by the server and presenting it to the user in a visual way. Common protocols support the normal operation of the Web.

2. Web 2.0

After 2003, the Internet went to the Web 2.0 era (O'Reilly, 2005). Web 2.0 is the inheritance and innovation of Web 1.0. In terms of usage, content unit, content creation, content editing, content acquisition, content management, etc., Web 2.0 has greatly improved compared with Web 1.0.

(1) Blog, also known as weblog, is abbreviated from Web log. The starting point of the blog is that the user weaves the web, publishes new knowledge, links the content of other users, and the blog site organizes the content. Blogging is a simple way to post personal information. Anyone can sign up to complete the creation, distribution, and update of personal web pages.

The blog's model takes full advantage of the interaction and updation of the network to allow users to get the most valuable information and resources as quickly as possible. Users can express their infinite expressiveness, instantly record and publish personal life stories, and flash inspiration. Users can also meet friends, meet and gather friends, and conduct in-depth communication. Blogs are divided into basic blogs, group blogs, family blogs, collaborative blogs, public community blogs, and commercial, corporate, and advertising blogs.

(2) Wiki is a multi-person collaborative writing tool. Wiki sites can be maintained by multiple people, and everyone can post their own opinions or expand and explore common themes. A wiki is a hypertext system that supports collaborative writing for the community and a set of supporting tools to support this writing. Wiki text can be browsed, created, changed, and run much less expensively than HTML text. The wiki system supports collaborative writing for the community and provides the necessary assistance for collaborative writing. Wiki writers naturally form a community, and the Wiki system provides a simple communication tool for the community. Wikis are easy to use and open to help you share knowledge within the community.

The word Wiki comes from the Hawaiian word "wee kee wee kee" which originally meant "fast hurry", and it specifically refers to Wikipedia. The most famous example of Wiki is Wikipedia, created by Jimmy Wales and Larry Sanger on January 15, 2001. As of early 2009, Wikipedia had articles in more than 250 languages used in the world. Chinese Wikipedia was formally established on October 24, 2002. Baidu Encyclopedia (http://baike.baidu.com) began in April 2006.

Web 2.0 has attracted widespread attention, and the way software developers and end users use the Web has changed. For Web 1.0 applications, the interaction between users and the Web was limited to publishing and acquiring content. For Web 2.0 applications, the interaction between users and the Web has extended from publishing and acquiring content to participating in the creation, contribution, and rich interaction with Web content. In Web 2.0, users will play bigger and bigger roles. They provide content, establish relationships between different contents, and create new value by using various network tools and services.

3. Web 3.0

Web 3.0 is a smart filter and diversified demand satisfaction platform based on user needs. The most essential feature of Web 3.0 is the precision of semantics. In essence, Web 3.0 is a Semantic Web system that implements more intelligent communication between people and people and between people and machines. It is an integration of a series of applications.

Web 3.0 transforms the Internet itself into a generic database with cross-browser, hyperbrowser content delivery, and request mechanisms, using artificial intelligence to reason and using 3D technology to build websites and even virtual worlds. Web 3.0 will bring a richer and more relevant experience to users. The software foundation for Web 3.0 will be a set of application programming interfaces (APIs) that allow developers to develop applications that take advantage of a certain set of resources.

4. Web 4.0

Web 4.0 will be the intelligent Web. It efficiently acquires the required knowledge through cross-media, distributed search on the cloud infrastructure. Web 4.0 era has a close relationship with IPv6. IPv6 solves the address problem and provides the foundation for industrial Internet and Industry 4.0, cloud computing and big data, and fifth-generation mobile communications. Further, IPv6 needs to be secure, trustworthy, and manageable.

15.3 Ontology

After a long period of study, the ontology has matured. In various literatures, although the usage of concepts and terms related to ontology is not completely consistent, the use of facts has emerged. We first list several representative definitions of ontology, and then briefly describe related concepts. Several representative definitions of ontology are as follows:

(1) Ontology is a philosophical term meaning "the theory of existence", especially the branch of philosophy. It studies the natural existence and the composition of

reality. It tries to answer questions like "what is existence", "what is the nature of existence", and so on. From this point of view, formal ontology refers to an area that determines the possible states of objective things as a whole and determines the individualized needs that each objective thing must satisfy. Formal ontology can be defined as a system of all forms and patterns of existence.

(2) Ontology is a clear expression of conceptualization. In 1993, Gruber of Stanford University's Knowledge Systems Laboratory (KSL) gave the first formal definition of an entity widely accepted in the field of information science (Gruber, 1993). Gruber argues that conceptualization is an abstract, simplified observation of the world expressed for a specific purpose. Every knowledge base, information system based on knowledge base, and subject based on knowledge sharing contains a conceptual world, which is explicit or implicit. Ontology is an explicit explanation for a conceptualization. Objects in ontology and their relationships are described by a lexicon of knowledge expression language. Therefore, an ontology can be defined by defining a set of terminologies for knowledge expression, which can be understood to describe entities, objects, relationships, and processes in the domain world, and through formal axioms to limit and standardize the interpretation and use of these terms. Therefore, strictly speaking, ontology is a declarative description of a logical theory. According to Gruber's interpretation, the explicit expression of conceptualization means that an ontology is a description of concepts and relationships that may exist for an agent or group of agents. This definition is consistent with the description of ontology in concept definition, but it is more universal. In this sense, ontology is very important for knowledge sharing and reuse. Borst made a slight modification to Gruber's ontology definition, arguing that ontology can be defined as a form of specification that is shared conceptually.

(3) Ontology is a set of concepts or terms used to describe or express knowledge in a domain. It can be used to organize a higher level of knowledge abstraction in a knowledge base and can also be used to describe knowledge in a specific domain. Think of ontology as a knowledge entity rather than a way of describing knowledge. The term ontology is sometimes used to refer to a knowledge entity that describes a domain. For example, Cyc often refers to its representation of knowledge in a domain as an ontology. That is, the representation vocabulary provides a set of terms used to describe facts in the domain, and the knowledge entities that use these terms are a collection of facts in the field. However, this difference between them is not obvious. An ontology is defined as a knowledge that describes a domain, usually a general domain of knowledge, using the representative vocabulary mentioned above. At this time, ontology is not just

vocabulary but the entire upper knowledge base (including the vocabulary used to describe this knowledge base). A typical application of this definition is the Cyc project, which defines its knowledge base as an ontology for use by other knowledge base systems. Cyc is a massive, multi-relational knowledge base and inference engine.

(4) Ontology belongs to the content theory in the field of artificial intelligence. It studies object classification, object attributes, and relationships between objects in specific domain knowledge. It provides terminologies for the description of domain knowledge.

It can be seen that different researchers, from different angles, will have different understandings of the definition of ontology. However, basically, ontology should contain the following meanings:

(1) Ontology describes the existence of objective things, which represents the essence of things.
(2) Ontology is independent of the description of ontology. Any description of ontology, including people's conceptual understanding of things, and human language descriptions of things, are projections of ontology on certain media.
(3) Ontology is independent of the individual's understanding of ontology. Ontology does not change because of personal differences. It reflects a consistent "knowledge" that can be recognized by the group.
(4) Ontology itself does not have errors with objective things because it is the essence of objective things. But the description of ontology, that is, any ontology written in formal or natural language, as a projection of ontology, may be inaccurate with ontology itself.
(5) The described ontology represents a public perception of people's knowledge in a particular field. This public concept can be shared and reused, thus eliminating the inconsistencies of different people's understanding of the same thing.
(6) The description of ontology should be formal, clear, and unambiguous.

According to the different levels of the ontology, it is divided into top-level ontology, domain ontology, task ontology, and application ontology, as shown in Figure 15.4. Among them, the concepts of top-level ontology research, such as space, time, events, behavior, etc., are independent of specific fields and can be shared and reused in different fields. Domain ontology at the second level studies the vocabulary and terminology in specific areas (such as books, medicine, etc.) to model the domain. Task ontology at the same level mainly studies the solvable problem-solving method, which defines common tasks and reasoning activities.

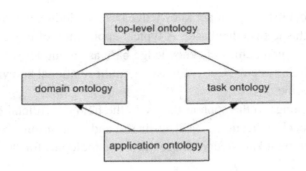

Fig. 15.4.   Hierarchical model of ontology

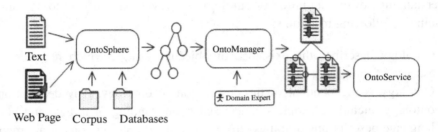

Fig. 15.5.   Ontology-based knowledge management framework

Both domain ontology and task ontology can refer to the vocabulary defined in top-level ontology to describe their own vocabulary. Application ontology at the third level describes the specific application, which can simultaneously refer to concepts in specific domain ontology and task ontology.

Ontology knowledge management generally requires the following basic functions: (a) support for multiple representation languages and storage forms of ontology, with ontology navigation function; (b) support basic operations of ontology such as ontology learning, ontology mapping, ontology merging, etc.; (c) provide ontology version management functions and support for the extensibility and consistency of the ontology. Figure 15.5 shows an ontology knowledge management framework consisting of three basic modules:

(1) The ontology of domain ontology learning environment — OntoSphere — the main functions of which include Web corpus acquisition, document analysis, ontology concept and relationship acquisition, expert interaction environment, and finally establishment of high-quality domain ontology that meets application requirements.
(2) The ontology management environment — OntoManager — which provides management and modification editing of the existing ontology.

(3) Subject-based knowledge service — OntoService — which provides semantic-oriented multi-agent knowledge services.

15.4 Knowledge Graph

With the development of the Internet, the content of network data has exploded. Due to the large-scale, heterogeneous, and diversified structure of Internet content, it poses a challenge for people to effectively obtain information and knowledge. Knowledge graph, with its powerful semantic processing ability and open organization ability, laid the foundation for the knowledge organization and intelligent application in the Internet era.

The research and application of large-scale knowledge graph libraries has attracted enough attention in academia and industry. The knowledge graph is intended to describe the entities that exist in the real world and the relationships between entities. The knowledge graph was officially proposed by Google on May 17, 2012. The original intention was to improve the search engine's ability to improve the user's search quality and search experience. With the development and application of artificial intelligence technology, knowledge graph has gradually become one of the key technologies and has been widely used in the fields of intelligent search, intelligent question and answer, personalized recommendation, content distribution, and so on.

In essence, the knowledge graph is used to describe the various entities or concepts and their relationships that exist in the real world, which constitute a huge semantic network diagram, with nodes representing entities or concepts, and edges composed of attributes or relationships. The current knowledge graph has been used to refer to a variety of large-scale knowledge bases.

Acemap knowledge graph (AceKG), supported by Acemap, is now open to everyone for research and non-commercial use (Wang *et al.*, 2018). They hope this knowledge graph will benefit the research and development for academic data mining. AceKG describes 114.30 million academic entities based on a consistent ontology, including 61,704,089 papers, 52,498,428 authors, 50,233 research fields, 19,843 academic institutes, 22,744 journals, 1,278 conferences, and three special affiliations. In total, AceKG consists of 3.13 billion pieces of relationship information. An example of AceKG is provided in Figure 15.6.

The type of knowledge contained in the knowledge graph includes the following:

(1) **Entity:** Refers to something that is distinguishable and independent, such as a certain author, a certain paper, a certain field, and so on. Everything in the world consists of specific things, which refers to entities, as shown in Figure 15.6.

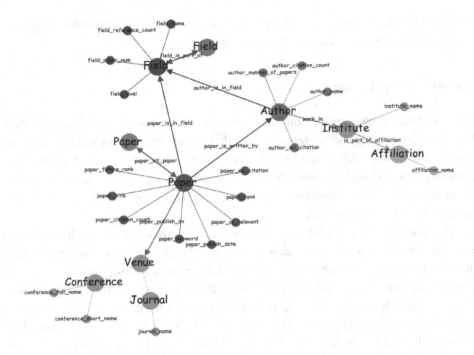

Fig. 15.6.   Knowledge graph example

The entity is the most basic element in the knowledge map, and there are different relationships between different entities.

(2) **Semantic class (concept):** A collection of entities with the same characteristics, such as fields, books, computers, etc. Concepts mainly refer to collections, categories, and object types, types of things, such as characters, geography, and so on.

(3) **Content:** Usually used as the name, description, interpretation, etc., of entities and semantic classes, which can be expressed by text, images, audio and video, and so on.

(4) **Attribute (value):** A property value that points to it from an entity. Different attribute types correspond to edges of different types of attributes. Attribute value mainly refers to the value of the specified attribute of the object. The "venue", "conference", and "journal" shown in Figure 15.6 are several different attributes. The attribute value mainly refers to the value of the specified attribute of the object.

(5) **Relationship:** Formalized as a function that maps k points to a Boolean value. On the knowledge map, the relationship is a function that maps k graph nodes (entities, semantic classes, and attribute values) to Boolean values.

Based on the above definition, the knowledge base uses a triple set. The basic forms of triples mainly include (entity 1 – relationship – entity 2) and (entity – attribute – attribute value). Each entity (extension of the concept) can be identified by a globally unique ID, each attribute–value pair (AVP) can be used to characterize the intrinsic properties of the entity, and the relationship can be used to connect two entities. Describe the connection between them. The three tuple is a general expression of knowledge graph.

Compared with other existing open academic KGs or data sets, AceKG has the following advantages: (a) AceKG offers a heterogeneous academic information network, i.e., with multiple entity categories and relationship types, which supports researchers or engineers to conduct various academic data mining experiments. (b) AceKG is sufficiently large (the size of this data set is nearly 100G) to cover most instances in academic ontology, which makes the experiments based on AceKG more convincing and of practical value. (c) AceKG is fully organized in structured RDF triples, which is machine-readable and easy to process.

In Acemap knowledge graph, the data set is hosted using Apache Jena framework (Wang *et al.*, 2018). Apache Jena framework stores the data in TDB database and provides access to linked data via a SPARQL search engine. In addition, it provides Fuseki HTTP service for any Web client and completes Java API to query the linked data. The data provision architecture is shown in Figure 15.7.

15.5 Cloud Computing

Cloud Computing is an emerging business computing mode. It distributes computing tasks across resource pools of large numbers of computers, enabling applications to acquire computing power, storage space, and various software services as needed. It is shared pools of configurable computer system resources and higher level services that can be rapidly provisioned with minimal management effort, often over the Internet. Since the launch of Amazon EC2 in 2006, the availability of high-capacity networks, low-cost computers, and storage devices as well as the widespread adoption of hardware virtualization, service-oriented architecture, and autonomic and utility computing has led to growth in cloud computing.

The National Institute of Standards and Technology's definition of cloud computing identifies five essential characteristics (Mell and Grance, 2011):

(1) **On-demand self-service:** A consumer can unilaterally provision computing capabilities, such as server time and network storage, as needed automatically without requiring human interaction with each service provider.

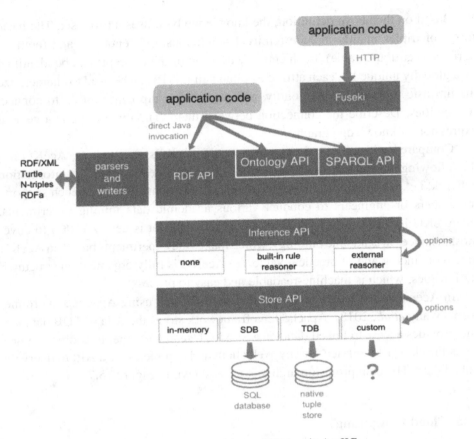

Fig. 15.7.   Data provision architecture in AceKG

(2) **Broad network access:** Capabilities are available over the network and accessed through standard mechanisms that promote use by heterogeneous thin or thick client platforms (e.g., mobile phones, tablets, laptops, and workstations).

(3) **Resource pooling:** The provider's computing resources are pooled to serve multiple consumers using a multi-tenant model, with different physical and virtual resources dynamically assigned and reassigned according to consumer demand.

(4) **Rapid elasticity:** Capabilities can be elastically provisioned and released, in some cases automatically, to scale rapidly outward and inward commensurate with demand. To the consumer, the capabilities available for provisioning often appear unlimited and can be appropriated in any quantity at any time.

(5) **Measured service:** Cloud systems automatically control and optimize resource use by leveraging a metering capability at some level of abstraction appropriate to the type of service (e.g., storage, processing, bandwidth, and active user

accounts). Resource usage can be monitored, controlled, and reported, providing transparency for both the provider and the consumer of the utilized service.

Cloud computing providers offer their "services" according to different models, of which the three standard models are Infrastructure as a Service (IaaS), Platform as a Service (PaaS), and Software as a Service (SaaS) as follows (Mell and Grance, 2011):

1. Infrastructure as a service

IaaS refers to online services that provide high-level APIs used to dereference various low-level details of underlying network infrastructure like physical computing resources, location, data partitioning, scaling, security, backup, etc. A hypervisor, such as Xen, Oracle VirtualBox, Oracle VM, KVM, VMware ESX/ESXi, or Hyper-V, LXD, runs the virtual machines as guests. Pools of hypervisors within the cloud operational system can support large numbers of virtual machines and have the ability to scale services up and down according to customers' varying requirements. Linux containers run in isolated partitions of a single Linux kernel running directly on the physical hardware. Linux cgroups and namespaces are the underlying Linux kernel technologies used to isolate, secure, and manage the containers. Container-isation offers higher performance than virtualization because there is no hypervisor overhead. Also, container capacity autoscales dynamically with computing load, which eliminates the problem of over-provisioning and enables usage-based billing. IaaS clouds often offer additional resources such as a virtual-machine disk-image library, raw block storage, file or object storage, firewalls, load balancers, IP addresses, virtual local area networks (VLANs), and software bundles.

IaaS cloud providers supply these resources on-demand from their large pools of equipment installed in data centers. The consumer is able to deploy and run an arbitrary software, which can include operating systems and applications. The consumer does not manage or control the underlying cloud infrastructure but has control over operating systems, storage, and deployed applications, and possibly limited control of select networking components. For wide-area connectivity, customers can use either the Internet or carrier clouds. To deploy their applications, cloud users install operating system images and their application software on the cloud infrastructure. In this model, the cloud user patches and maintains the operating systems and the application software. Cloud providers typically bill IaaS services on a utility computing basis: cost reflects the amount of resources allocated and consumed.

2. Platform as a service

The capability provided to the consumer is to deploy onto the cloud infrastructure consumer-created or -acquired applications created using programming languages, libraries, services, and tools supported by the provider. The consumer does not manage or control the underlying cloud infrastructure including network, servers, operating systems, or storage, but has control over the deployed applications and possibly configuration settings for the application hosting the environment.

In the PaaS models, cloud providers deliver a computing platform, typically including operating system, programming language execution environment, database, and Web server. Application developers can develop and run their software solutions on a cloud platform without the cost and complexity of buying and managing the underlying hardware and software layers. Some integration and data management providers have also embraced specialized applications of PaaS as delivery models for data solutions. A recent specialized PaaS is the blockchain as a service (BaaS) that some vendors such as IBM Bluemix and Oracle Cloud Platform have already included in their PaaS offering.

3. Software as a service

SaaS's capability provided to the consumers the ability to use the provider's applications running on a cloud infrastructure. The applications are accessible from various client devices through either a thin client interface, such as a Web browser (e.g., Web-based email), or a program interface. The consumer does not manage or control the underlying cloud infrastructure including network, servers, operating systems, storage, or even individual application capabilities, with the possible exception of limited user-specific application configuration settings.

SaaS is sometimes referred to as "on-demand software" and is usually priced on a pay-per-use basis or using a subscription fee. In the SaaS model, cloud providers install and operate application software in the cloud and cloud users access the software from cloud clients. Cloud users do not manage the cloud infrastructure and platform where the application runs. This eliminates the need to install and run the application on the cloud user's own computers, which simplifies maintenance and support.

15.6 Edge Computing

Edge computing is a distributed computing paradigm in which computation is largely or completely performed on distributed device nodes known as edge devices as opposed to primarily taking place in a centralized cloud environment. Edge computing is related to the concepts of wireless sensor networks, intelligent and context-aware networks, and smart objects in the context of human–computer interaction.

Internet of things (IoT) was first introduced to the community in 1999 for supply chain management, and then the concept of "making a computer sense information

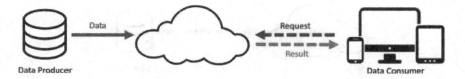

Fig. 15.8.   Cloud computing paradigm

without the aid of human intervention" was widely adapted to other fields, such as healthcare, home, environment, and transport. Now with IoT, we will arrive in the Internet of everything (IoE), where there will be a large quality of data generated by things that are immersed in our daily life, and a lot of applications will also be deployed at the edge to consume these data.

Figure 15.8 shows the conventional cloud computing structure. Data producers generate raw data and transfer it to cloud, and data consumers send request for consuming data to the cloud, as noted by the solid line. The dotted line in the left direction indicates the request for consuming data being sent from data consumers to cloud, and the result from the cloud is represented by the dotted line in the right direction. However, this structure is not sufficient for IoT. In the cloud computing paradigm, the end devices at the edge usually play roles as data consumer. However, people are also producing data nowadays from their mobile devices. The change from data consumer to data producer/consumer requires more function placement at the edge.

Edge computing refers to the enabling technologies allowing computation to be performed at the edge of the network, on downstream data on behalf of cloud services and upstream data on behalf of IoT services. Here, we define "edge" as any computing and network resources along the path between data sources and cloud data centers. Figure 15.9 illustrates the two-way computing streams in edge computing (Shi *et al.*, 2016). In the edge computing paradigm, the things are not only data consumers but also data producers. At the edge, the things can not only request service and content from the cloud but also perform the computing tasks from the cloud. Edge can perform computing offloading, data storage, caching, and processing, as well as distribute request and delivery services from cloud to user. With those jobs in the network, the edge itself needs to be well designed to meet the requirement efficiently in services such as reliability, security, and privacy protection.

In the cloud computing paradigm, most of the computations happen in the cloud, which means data and requests are processed in the centralized cloud. However, such a computing paradigm may suffer longer latency. In edge computing, the edge has certain computation resources, and this provides a chance to offload part of the workload from the cloud.

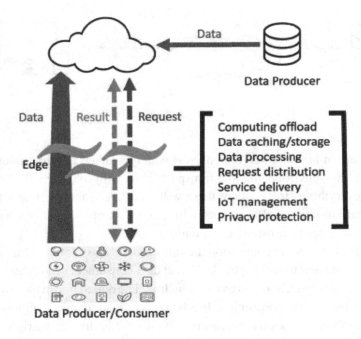

Fig. 15.9.   Edge computing paradigm

In edge computing, data are still owned by each stakeholder and rarely shared due to privacy concerns and formidable cost of data transportation, which significantly limits Internet of things (IoT) applications that need data input from multiple stakeholders. Weisong Shi and Quan Zhang *et al.* proposed a firework model for collaborative edge computing, shown in Figure 15.10 (Zhang *et al.*, 2016). Healthcare requires data sharing and collaboration among enterprises in multiple domains. A collaborative edge can fuse geographically distributed data by creating virtual shared data views. The virtual shared data are exposed to end users via a predefined service interface. An application will leverage this public interface to compose complex services for end users. These public services are provided by participants of the collaborative edge, and the computation only occurs in the participant's data facility such that the data privacy and integrity can be ensured. We use connected healthcare as a case study. A flu outbreak is the beginning of our case study. The patients flow to hospitals, and the electronic medical record of the patients will be updated. The hospital summarizes and shares the information for this flu outbreak, such as the average cost, the symptoms, data on the population, etc. A patient will theoretically follow the prescription to get the pills from a pharmacy. One possibility is that a patient did not follow the therapy. Then the hospital has to take the responsibility

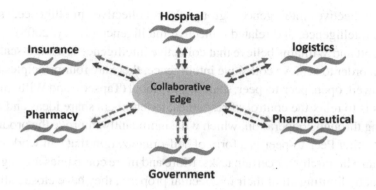

Fig. 15.10. Collaborative edge

for rehospitalization since it cannot get the proof that the patient did not take the pills. Now, via collaborative edge, the pharmacy can provide the purchasing record of a patient to the hospital, which significantly facilitates healthcare accountability.

15.7 Collective Intelligence

Collective intelligence is a kind of shared or group intelligence. It emerges from the cooperation and competition of many individuals, and there is no centralized control mechanism. According to Wikipedia, collective intelligence is defined as "shared or group intelligence that emerges from the collaboration, collective efforts, and competition of many individuals and appears in consensus decision making" (http://en.wikipedia.org/wiki/Collective_intelligence). Collective intelligence can be seen in bacteria, animals, humans, and computer networks and appears in many forms of consensus decision-making patterns.

The scale of collective intelligence varies from individual collective intelligence, interpersonal collective intelligence, group collective intelligence, activity collective intelligence, organizational collective intelligence, network collective intelligence, neighboring collective intelligence, community collective intelligence, urban collective intelligence, provincial collective intelligence, national collective intelligence, regional collective intelligence, etc. The collective intelligence of international organizations and the collective intelligence of all mankind are all the wisdom reflected by groups within a specific scope.

Forms of collective intelligence can be varied, including conversational collective intelligence, structural collective intelligence, evolutionary collective intelligence based on learning, communication-based information collective intelligence, thinking collective intelligence, group flow collective intelligence, statistical collective intelligence, and related collective intelligence (Tovey, 2008).

Tapscott and Williams believe that collective intelligence is a large-scale collaboration. In order to achieve collective intelligence, there are four principles that need to be followed: open, peer-to-peer, shared, and global (Tapscott and Williams, 2008). Openness is to relax the control of resources, to let others share ideas and apply for franchising through cooperation, which will significantly improve the products after rigorous testing Peer-to-peer is a form of self-organization that can work more efficiently than a hierarchy for certain tasks. More and more companies are beginning to realize that by limiting all of their intellectual property, they have closed all possible opportunities. Sharing something allows them to expand their market and launch products faster. Advances in communication technology have spurred global companies. Globally integrated companies have no geographical restrictions, but have global connections that enable them to acquire new markets, ideas, and technologies.

Collective intelligence systems are generally complex large systems, even complex giant systems. In the 1990s, Qian Xuesen proposed the concept of "open complex giant system (OCGS)" (Xuesen *et al.*, 1990) and proposed "a comprehensive integration method from qualitative to quantitative" as a complex giant system for dealing with openness. The methodology focused on the combination of human intelligence and computer high performance, based on noetic science and artificial intelligence, using information technology and network technology to build a "hall for metasynthetic engineering". The system deals with complex problems associated with open complex giant systems in an operational platform (Dai, 2006). With the widespread use of the Internet, this integrated hall for metasynthetic engineering is a collective intelligence system based on the Internet.

15.8 Crowd Intelligence

The Internet-based cyber-physical world has profoundly changed the information environment for the development of artificial intelligence, bringing a new wave of artificial intelligence research and promoting it into the new era of AI 2.0. As one of the most prominent characteristics of research in the AI 2.0 era, crowd intelligence has attracted much attention from both industry and research communities.

The last section explains collective intelligence as manifested by intelligent group activities and behaviors. Apparently, any kind of human group activity can fall into the scope of collective intelligence, as long as the interactions among the group members demonstrate intelligent features, such as generation of new knowledge, consensus decisions, and the emergence of smart behavior patterns. For crowd intelligence Li Wei *et al.* defined it as "beyond the limitation of individual intelligence, crowd intelligence emerges from the collective intelligent efforts of massive numbers of autonomous individuals, who are motivated to carry out the challenging computational tasks under a certain Internet-based organizational structure" (Wei *et al.*, 2017). This definition shows that crowd intelligence is an essentially Internet-based collective intelligence that has the following characteristics:

(1) Internet-based crowd intelligence emerges from massive numbers of individuals in online organizations and communities on online platforms. This definition emphasizes the importance of the Internet in the emergence of crowd intelligence.
(2) A crowd intelligence system interweaves crowd and machine capabilities seamlessly to address challenging computational problems. From the aspect of computing, the rise of crowd intelligence allows novel possibilities of seamlessly integrating machine and human intelligence on a large scale, which can be regarded as mixed-initiative intelligent systems. In such a system, AI machines and crowds can complement the capability of each other to function as enhanced AI systems.

Figure 15.11 illustrates crowd intelligence and related areas. Since Howe first proposed the concept of crowdsourcing in 2006 (Howe, 2009), this has been assigned

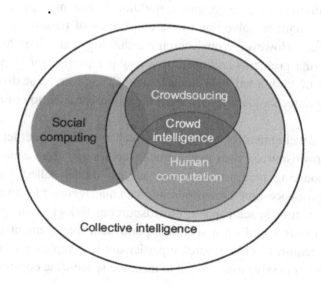

Fig. 15.11. Crowd intelligence and related areas

to non-specific solutions through an open Web platform. The distributed problem-solving model completed by the provider community is becoming increasingly popular, thanks especially to mobile Internet technology and the sharing economy model. Crowdsourcing is outsourcing a job traditionally performed by an employee to an undefined, generally large group of people via open call. Crowdsourcing technology can bring human experience into solving problems by gathering group intelligence, opening up a new perspective for breaking through the traditional data management challenges.

In the past 10 years, crowdsourcing technology has been closely related to people's daily lives. For example, early crowdsourcing platforms usually refer to "question and answer system" platforms such as Wikipedia, Yahoo! answers, Baidu Knows etc., but development has become a necessity for modern people to acquire knowledge. In recent years, due to the single type of tasks supported by the early crowdsourcing platform, it has been unable to meet the needs of current data types and task-complexing Web applications, thus prompting the birth of the new generation of "online crowdsourcing platform", namely, large online job recruitment and task subcontracting management platforms, such as Amazon mechanical turks (AMT), CrowdFlower, oDesk, etc. This type of crowdsourcing platform not only brought a new technological revolution but also created a huge market economy value. Therefore, crowdsourcing technology has brought enormous potential to the technological revolution in the Internet age. Crowdsourcing mode is the trend of the times. With the advent of the era of big data, although various data-driven applications continue to emerge, many traditional data management challenges will be more difficult to solve due to the constraints of traditional data management technologies. However, crowdsourcing technology can integrate human experience into solving problems and open up a new perspective for breaking through the challenges of traditional data management. Therefore, crowdsourcing-based data management technology has attracted the extensive attention of academia and industry.

The rapid development of technologies such as mobile Internet and IOT has transformed crowdsourced data management technology from a model based on online crowdsourcing platform to a new service model called "spatiotemporal crowdsourcing". Space-time crowdsourcing data management technology refers to the allocation of time-space-capable crowdsourcing tasks to non-specific crowdsourced participants based on a spatiotemporal data management platform. The core operation requires a crowdsourcing participant to complete the crowdsourcing task in an active or passive manner and to meet the space-time constraints specified by the task.

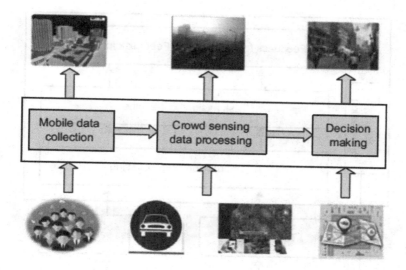

Fig. 15.12.   Mobile crowdsourcing major tasks

Mobile crowdsourcing is an extension of human computation from the virtual digital world to the physical world. Participatory sensing proposed by Burke *et al.* intends to organize mobile devices to form interactive and participatory sensor networks, which enable public and professional users to gather, analyze, and share local knowledge. (Burke *et al.*, 2006) Mobile crowdsensing greatly extends the capability of group perception and awareness in many areas, such as healthcare, urban planning and construction, as well as environmental protection. Figure 15.12 illustrates the major tasks and applications in both participatory sensing and mobile crowdsourcing.

A general problem-solving workflow of mobile crowdsourcing is shown in Figure 15.13 (Tong *et al.*, 2017). The participants in mobile crowdsourcing include "requesters of tasks" and "workers", who are connected through mobile crowdsourcing "platforms".

According to different task assignment strategies, the existing problem-solving approaches in mobile crowdsourcing can be described as the following two main models: matching-based model and planning-based model.

(1) **Matching-based model:** This model uses the bipartite graph matching model as the task assignment strategy where each task and worker corresponds to a vertex in the bipartite graph, and the relationship between the task and the worker is regarded as the edge in the bipartite graph. The matching-based model has a wide range of applications, such as the taxi-calling service and last-mile delivery.

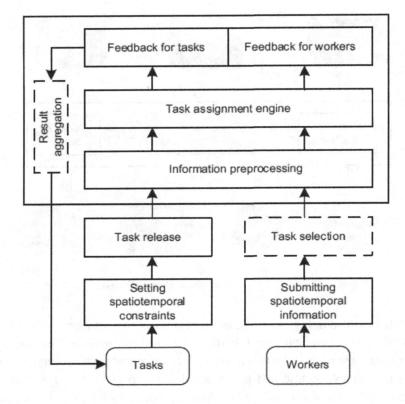

Fig. 15.13.   Workflow in mobile crowdsourcing

(2) **Planning-based model:** This aims to provide the optimal planning for each worker, according to the given spatiotemporal information and constraints of the tasks. In particular, the planning-based model can be widely used for on-wheel meal-ordering service, real-time ridesharing, etc.

Crowd intelligence may involve a wide range of crowd tasks, such as collective data annotation, collaborative knowledge sharing, and crowdsourcing-based software development, which demand different levels of expertise and dedication. To achieve the goals of these crowd tasks, one can adopt interaction patterns including collaboration, coordination, and competition to connect individuals and provide mediation mechanisms for them to work in a socialized environment.

A key scientific problem is how to grasp the pattern of crowd intelligence in different scenarios, reveal its internal mechanism, and guide the incentive mechanism and operation method to realize predictable crowd intelligent emergence. The quality of the submissions therefore has a great impact on the effectiveness of the system, which, however, often varies among different workers. How to assess, control, and guarantee the quality of the work and how to use the work even of low quality are important issues. To address these problems, new mechanisms and methods are needed for quality control to assure the quality of the whole crowd intelligent system.

For future research, there are some challenges that need to be solved in crowd intelligence, such as dynamic crowd organization, dynamic pricing, quality control on latency, etc.

Exercises

15.1 Give an example of the format of RDF. What is the meaning of RDF Schema?

15.2 What types of OWL are there? Explain its relationship with XML and RDF.

15.3 What are the basic guidelines for designing ontology? Give the basic steps of building an ontology and its main points.

15.4 Try to build a system for getting ontology from a Web page and from a relational database separately.

15.5 Take Cyc and e-Science as examples to illustrate the ways to build a large-scale knowledge system.

15.6 Give a Web technology evolution process and compare the main features of various Web types.

15.7 What is the knowledge graph? How to develop a large-scale knowledge graph system?

15.8 How to develop a collective intelligence system from methodology and technical approaches?

15.9 Mobile crowdsourcing is an extension of human computation from the virtual digital world to the physical world. Try to build a mobile crowdsourcing to gather, analyze, and share local knowledge.

Bibliography

Aamodt, A. and Plaza, E. (1994) Case-based reasoning: Foundational issues, methodological variations, and system approaches. *Artificial Intelligence Communications*, 7(1): 39–52.

Agrawal, R., Imieliski, T., and Swami, A. (1993) Mining association rules between sets of items in large database. In: *Proceedings of ACM SIGMOD International Conference on Management of Data (SIGMOD'93)*, May, pp. 207–216.

Agrawal, R. and Srikant. R. (1994) Fast algorithms for mining association rules. In: *Proceeding of the 20th International Conference on Very Large Data Bases (VLDB'94)*. Santiago, Chile, pp. 487–499.

Agrawal, R. and Shafer, J.C. (1996) Parallel mining of association rules: Design, implementation and experience. Special issue in data mining. *IEEE Trans on Knowledge and Data Engineering*, 8(6): 962–969.

Aha, D.A. (1990) Study of Instance-Based Algorithms for Supervised Learning Tasks: Mathematical, Empirical, and Psychological Evaluations. Ph.D. Thesis. Irvine: University of California.

Aha, D. (1997) *Lazy Learning*. The Netherlands: Kluver Academic Pub.

Aha, D., Kibler, G., and Albert, M.K. (1991) Instance-based learning algorithms. *Machine Learning*, 6(1): 37–66.

Amari, S. (1985) *Differential Geometrical Methods in Statistics*. Springer Lecture Notes in Statistic, Berlin: Springer, p. 28, Berlin: Springer.

Amari, S. and Wu, S. (1999) Improving support vector machine classifier by modifying kernel functions. *Neural Networks*, 12: 783–789

Amsterdam, J. (1988a) Extending the valiant learning model. In: *Proceedings of ICML* San Mateo, CA, p. 88.

Amsterdam, J. (1988b) Some philosophical problems with formal learning theory, In: *Proceedings of AAAI-88*, Saint Paul, Minnesota.

Andrieu, C., De Freitas, N., Doucet, A., *et al.* (2003) An Introduction to MCMC for Machine Learning. *Machine Learning*, 50(1): 5–43.

Baader, F., Calvanese, D., McGuinness, D., Nardi, D., and Patel-Schneider, P. (eds.), (2003) *The Description Logic Handbook: Theory, Implementation and Applications*. Cambridge: Cambridge University Press.

Bahdanau, D., Cho, K., and Bengio, Y. (2015) Neural machine translation by jointly learning to align and translate. In: *International Conference on Learning Representations*, San Diago, USA.

Basu, S., Banerjee, A., and Mooney, R.J. (2002) Semi-supervised clustering by seeding. In: *Proceedings of the 19th International Conference on Machine Learning (ICML)*, pp. 27–34.

Basu, S., Davidson, I., and Wagstaff, K. (2008) *Constrained Clustering: Advances in Algorithms, Theory, and Applications.* Chapman & Hall/CRC, Taylor & Francis Group.

Baum, L.E. and Petrie, T. (1966) Statistical inference for probabilistic functions of finite state Markov chains. *The Annals of Mathematical Statistics*, 37(6): 1554–1563.

Bayer, J., Wierstra, D., and Togelius, J., *et al.* (2009) Evolving memory cell structures for sequence learning. *Artificial Neural Networks — ICANN 2009. Lecture Notes in Computer Science.* Berlin, Heidelberg, Springer, 5769: 755–764.

Bellman, R. (1957) *Dynamic Programming.* Princeton University Press, New Jersey.

Berners-Lee, T., Hendler, J., and Lassila, O. (2001) The semantic web. *Scientific American*, 281(5): 29–37.

Berners-Lee, T., Hall, W., Hendler, J.A., O'Hara, K., Shadbolt, N., and Weitzner, D.J. (2006) A framework for web science. *Foundations and Trends in Web Science*, 1(1): 1–130.

Biberman, Y. (1994) A context similarity measure. *Machine Learning:* ECML-94, Berlin Heidelberg: Springer-Verlag.

Bies, R.R., Muldoon, M.F., Pollock, B.G., Manuck, S., Smith, G., and Sale, M.E. (2006) A genetic algorithm-based, hybrid machine learning approach to model selection. *Journal of Pharmacokinetics and Pharmacodynamics,* (Netherlands: Springer), pp. 196–221.

Blumer, A., Ehrenfeucht, A., Haussler, D., and Warmuth, A. (1986) Classifying learnable geometric concepts with the Vapnik–Chervonenkis dimension, In: *Proceedings of 18th Annual ACM Symposium on Theory of Computation*, Berkeley, CA.

Booker, L.B., Goldberg, D.E., and Holland, J.H. (1989) Classifier systems and genetic algorithms. *Artificial Intelligence*, 40(1): 235–282.

Bravo, C. and Weber, R. (2011) Semi-supervised constrained clustering with cluster outlier filtering. *Lecture Notes in Computer Science* vol. 7042, Berlin: Springer, pp. 347–354.

Brin, S., Motwani, R., Ullman, J.D., and Tsur, S. (1997) Dynamic itemset counting and implication rules for market basket data. *ACM SIGMOD Record*, 26(2): 255.

Brooks, R.A. (1991a) Intelligence without representation. *Artificial Intelligence*, 47: 139–159.

Brooks, R.A. (1991b) Intelligence without reasoning. In: *Proceedings of IJCAI'91*, Sydney.

Buntine, W. (1989) A critique of the valiant model. In: *Proceedings of IJCAI-89*, Detroit, Michigan, USA.

Buntine, W. (1991) Classifiers: A theoretical and empirical study. In: *Proceedings of IJCAI-91*, pp. 638–644.

Buntine, W. (1994) Operations for learning with graphical models. *Journal of Artificial Intelligence Research*, 2: 159–225.

Burges, J.C.J. (1998) A tutorial on support vector machines for pattern recognition. *Data Mining and Knowledge Discovery*, 2(2): 167.

Burke, J.A., Estrin, D., Hansen, M., *et al.* (2006) Participatory sensing. Workshop on World-Sensor-Web: Mobile Device Centric Sensor Networks and Applications, pp. 117–134.

Burke, R. and Kass, A. (1996) Retrieving Stories for Case-Based Teaching. *Case-Based Reasoning (Experiences, lessons, & Future Directions).* Menlo Park, CA/Cambridge, MA, AAAI/MIT Press, pp. 93–110.

Cao, Hu, and Zhongzhi Shi. (1998) CARBA: Common agent request broker architecture. *PRICAI'98*, Singapore. Cheung D.W., Han, J., Ng, V., Fu, A. and Fu, Y. (1996) A Fast Distributed Algorithm for Mining Association Rules. *Fourth International Conference on Parallel and Distributed Information Systems,* December, pp. 31–42.

Carbonell, J.G. (1986) Analogy in problem solving. In: Michalski, R.S., Carbonell, J.G. and Mitchell, T.M. (eds.), *Machine Learning II: An Artificial Intelligence Approach.* Los Alton, CA: Morgan Kaufmann.

Carbonell, J.G. (1989) Introduction: Paradigms for machine learning. *Artificial Intelligence*, 40(1): 1–9.

Cheeseman, P., and Stutz, J. (1996) Bayesian classification (Autoclass): Theory and results. In *Advances in knowledge discovery and data mining*, edited by U.M., Fayyad, etc. Menlo Park, CA/Cambridge, MA, AAAI/MIT Press, ISBN 0-262-56097-6.

Cheung, D.W., Ng, V.T., Fu, A. W., and Fu, Y. (1996) Efficient mining of association rules in distributed databases. *IEEE Transactions On Knowledge And Data Engineering,* 8: 911–922.

Cheung, D., Hu, K., and Xia, S. (1998) Asynchronous parallel algorithm for mining association rules on shared-memory multi-processors. In: *proceeding of the 10th ACM Symposium. Parallel Algorithms and Architectures*, New York, ACM Press, pp. 279–288.

Cheung, D.W. and Xiao, Y. (1999) *Effect of Data Distribution in Parallel Mining of Association, Data Mining and Knowledge Discovery*. Dordrecht: Kluwer Academic Publishers, 3: 291–314.

Chickering, D. and Heckerman, D. (1996) Efficient approximations for the marginal likelihood of incomplete data given a Bayesian network. Technical Report MSR-TR-96-08, Microsoft Research, Redmond, WA.

Ciresan, D.C., Meier, U., Gambardella, L.M., *et al.* (2010) Deep big simple neural nets excel on handwritten digit recognition. *Neural Computation — NECO*, abs/1003.0, (12), pp. 3207–3220.

Clark, P., and Niblett, T. (1989) The CN2 induction algorithm. *Machine Learning*, 3(4): 261.

Cooper, G.F. and Herskovits, E. (1992) A Bayesian method for the induction of probabilistic networks from data. *Machine Learning*, 1992(9): 309–347.

Cooper, M.C. (1989) An optimal k-consistency algorithm. *Artificial Intelligence*, 41: 89–95.

Dai, R. (2006) *Social Intelligence Science*. Shanghai: Shanghai Jiaotong University Press.

Davies, J. (2006) *Semantic Web Technology: Trends and Research*. New Jersey: John Wiley and Sons Ltd.

de Kleer, J. (1984) How circuits work. *Artificial Intelligence*, 24: 205–280.

de Kleer, J. (1986) An assumption-based TMS. *Artificial Intelligence*, 28: 127–162.

de Kleer, J. (1989) A comparison of ATMS and CSP techniques. In: *Proceedings of IJCAI-89*, Menlo Park, pp. 290–296.

de Kleer, J. (1993) A view on qualitative physics. *Artificial Intelligence*, 59: 105–114.

de Kleer, J. and Brown, J. (1984) A qualitative physics based on confluences. *Artificial Intelligence*, 24: 205–280.

Decker, K. (1995) Environment Centered Analysis and Design of Coordination Mechanisms. PhD Thesis, University of Massachusetts.

Deerwester, S., Dumais, S.T., Furnas, G.W., Landauer, T.K., and Harshman, R. (1990) Indexing by latent semantic analysis, *Journal of the American Society for Information Science*, 41(6): 391–407.

DeJong, G. and Mooney, R. (1986) Explanation-based learning: An alternative view, *Machine Learning*, 1(2): 145.

DeJong, K.A. (2006) *Evolutionary Computation: A Unified Approach*. Cambridge MA: MIT Press.

Dietterich, T. (2017) Steps toward robust artificial intelligence. *AI Magazine*, 38(3): 3–24.

Dietterich, T.G., Trimponias, G., and Chen, Z. (2018) Discovering and removing exogenous state variables and rewards for reinforcement learning. In: *Proceedings of the 35th International Conference on Machine Learning (ICML 2018), and Proceedings of Machine Learning Research*, 80: 1261–1269.

Doran, J.E., Franklin, S., Jennings, N.R., and Norman, T.J. (1997) On cooperation in multi-agent systems. http://eprints.ecs.soton.ac.uk/2193/1/FOMAS-PANEL-KER.pdf

Doyle, J. (1979) A truth maintenance system. *Artificial Intelligence*, 12(3): 231–272.

Durfee, E.H., Lesser, V.R., and Corkill, D.D. (1987) Cooperation through communication in a distributed problem solving network. *Distributed Artificial Intelligence*, Marshfield: Pitman Publishing.

Durfee, E.H. and Lesser, V.R. (1991) Partial Global Planning: A coordination framework for distributed hypothesis formation. IEEE *Transactions on Systems, Man, and Cybernetics*, Special Issue on Distributed Sensor Networks, SMC-21(5): 1167–1183.

Ellman, T. (1989) Explanation-based learning: Programs and perspectives, *ACM Computing Surveys*, 21(2): 163–221.

Erosheva, E., Fienberg, S., and Lafferty, J. (2004) Mixed-membership models of scientific publications [C]. *Proceedings of the National Academy of Sciences of the United States of America*, 101: 5220–5227.

Ester, M., Kriegel, H., Sander, J., and Xu, X. (1996) A density-based algorithm for discovering clusters in large spatial databases with noise. In: *Proceedings of the 2nd ACM International Conference on Knowledge Discovery and Data Mining (KDD)*, pp. 226–231.

Farley, B., Clark, W. (1954) Simulation of self-organizing systems by digital computer. *Transactions of the IRE Professional Group on Information Theory*, 4(4): 76–84.

Ferber, J. (1991) Actors and agents as reflective concurrent objects: A merging IV perspective. *SMC-21*, p. 991.

Fernández, S., Graves, A., and Schmidhuber, J. (2007) Sequence labelling in structured domains with hierarchical recurrent neural networks. In: *Proceedings of the 20th International Joint Conferences on Artificial Intelligence*, IJCAI, pp. 774–779.

Fisher, D.H. (1987). Knowledge acquisition via incremental conceptual clustering. *Machine Learning*, 2: 139–172.

Fisher, D.H. (1989) Noise-tolerant conceptual clustering. In: *Proceedings of IJCAI-89*, Detroit, Michigan, USA.

Freeman-Benson, B. and Borning, A. (1992) Integrating constraints with an object-oriented language. In: *Proceedings of the 1992 European Conference on Object-Oriented Programming*, pp. 268–286.

Freund, Y. and Schapire, R.E. (1995) A decision-theoretic generalization of on-line learning and an application to boosting. In: *Proceeding Of the Second European Conference on Computational Learning*.

Gasser, L., Bragaza, C., and Herman, N. (1987) MACE: A flexible testbed for distributed AI research, *Distributed Artificial Intelligence*. Marshfield: Pitman Publishing.

Genesereth, M. R., Ginsberg, M. L. and Rosenschein, J. S. (1986) Cooperation Without Communication. The National Conference on Artificial Intelligence, Philadelphia, Pennsylvania, August 1986, pp. 51–57.

Gers, F.A. and Schmidhuber, E. (2001) LSTM recurrent networks learn simple context-free and context-sensitive languages. *IEEE Transactions on Neural Networks*, 12(6): 1333–1340.

Gers, F. A., Schraudolph, Nicol N., Schmidhuber, J. (2003) Learning precise timing with LSTM recurrent networks. *The Journal of Machine Learning Research*, 3: 115–143.

Gold, E.M. (1967) Language identification in the limit. Information and Control, 10: 447–474.

Goldberg, D.E. (1989) *Genetic Algorithms in Search, Optimization, and Machine Learning*. Boston, MA: Addison-Wesley Publishing Com., Inc.

Goodfellow, I., Bengio, Y., and Courville, A. (2016) *Deep Learning*. Cambridge, MA: The MIT Press.

Grahne, G. and Zhu, J. (2003) Efficiently using prefix-trees in mining frequent itemsets. In: *First Workshop on Frequent Itemset Mining Implementation (FIMI'03)*, Melbourne, FL.

Graves, A., Fernández, S., and Gomez, F. (2006) Connectionist temporal classification: Labelling unsegmented sequence data with recurrent neural networks. In: *Proceedings of the International Conference on Machine Learning, ICML 2006*, pp. 369–376.

Grefenstette, J.J. (1988a) Credit assignment in rule discovery systems based on genetic algorithms. *Machine Learning*, 3(2): 225–246.

Grefenstette, J.J. (1988b) Credit assignment in genetic learning systems. In: *Proceedings of AAAI-88*, Saint Paul, Minnesota.

Grefenstette, J.J. (1989) Incremental learning of control strategies with genetic algorithms. In: *Proceedings of IWML-89*, Cornell University, Ithaca, New York.

Grosz, B. and Kraus, S. (1996) Collaborative plans for complex group actions. *Artificial Intelligence*, 86(2): 269–357.

Gruber, T.R. (1993) A translation approach to portable ontology specifications. *Knowledge Acquisition*, 5(2): 199–220.

Gruber, T.R. (1993) A translation approach to portable ontology specifications. *Knowledge Acquisition*, 5(2): 199–220.

Gu, J. (1992) Efficient local search for very large-scale satisfiability problems. *Sigart Bulletin*, 3(1): 8–12.

Guha, R.V. and Lenat, D.B. (1990) Cyc: A midterm report. *AI Magazine*, 32–59.

Guha, S., Rastogi, R., and Shim, K. (1998) CURE: An efficient clustering algorithm for large databases, *ACM SIGMOD*, pp. 73–84.

Guha, S., Rastogi, R., and Shim, K. (2000) ROCK: A robust clustering for categorical attributes. *Information Systems*, 25(5): 345–366.

Han J., Pei, J. and Yin, M. (2000) Frequent patterns without candidate generation. In: *Proceedings of the 2000 ACM-SIGMOD International Conference on Management of Data* (SIGMOD'00), pp. 1–12.

Han, J., Jian P., Yiwen Y., and Runying M. (2004) Mining frequent patterns without candidate generation. *Data Mining and Knowledge Discovery* 8: 53–87.

Han, J. and Kamber, M. (2006) *Data Mining: Concepts and Techniques* (2nd edition). San Francisco: Morgan Kaufmann.

Haussler, D. (1987) Learning conjunctive concepts in structural domains. In: *Proceedings of AAAI-87*, Seattle, Washington.

Haussler, D. (1988a) New theoretical directions in machine learning. Machine Leaning, 2(4): 281.

Haussler, D. (1988b) Quantifying inductive bias: AI learning algorithms and Valiant's learning framework. *Artificial Intelligence*, 36, 177–221.

Haussler, D. (1989) Generalizing the PAC model: Sample size bounds from metric dimension-based uniform convergence results. In: *Proceedings of the Second Annual Workshop on Computational Learning Theory*, Santa Cruz, CA.

Hebb, D.O. (1949) *The Organization of Behavior*. Hoboken, New Jersey: Wiley.

Heckerman, D. (1997) Bayesian networks for data mining. *Data Mining and Knowledge Discovery*, 1: 79–119.

Hewitt, C. and DeJong, P. (1983) Analyzing the roles of descriptions and actions in open systems. In: *AAAI*.

Hewitt, C. (1991) Open systems semantics for distributed artificial intelligence. *Artificial Intelligence*, 47: 79–106.

Hinton, G.E. (1989) Connectionist learning procedures. *Artificial Intelligence*, 40(1): 185–234.

Hinton, G.E. (2002) Training Products of Experts by Minimizing Contrastive Divergence. *Neural Computation*, 14: 1771–1800.

Hinton, G.E. and Salakhutdinov, R. (2006) Reducing the dimensionality of data with neural networks. *Science*, 313(5786): 504–507.

Hinton, G.E. (2010) A practical guide to training restricted Boltzmann machines. *UTML TR 2010–003*, University of Toronto.

Hochreiter, S. (1991) Untersuchungen zu dynamischen neuronalen Netzen. Diploma Thesis. Institut f. Informatik, Technische Univ. Munich.

Hochreiter, S. and Schmidhuber, J. (1997) Long short-term memory. *Neural Computation*, 9(8): 1735–1780.

Holland, J.H. (1971) Proceeding and processors for schemata. In: Jacks E.L. (ed.), *Associative Information Processing*, American Elsevier.

Holland, J.H. (1975) *Adaptation in Natural and Artificial Systems.* University of Michigan Press, Regents.

Holland, J.H. (1985) Properties of the bucket brigade algorithm. In: *Proceedings of an International Conference on Genetic Algorithms and Their Applications,* Pittsburg, PA.

Holland, J.H. (1986) Escaping brittleness: The possibilities of general-purpose learning algorithms applied to parallel rule-based systems. Michalski, R.S., Carbonell, J.G., and Mitchell, T.M. (eds.), *Machine Learning: An Artificial Intelligence Approach,* Morgan Kaufmann.

Holland, J.H., Holyoak, K.J., Nisbett, R.E., and Thagard, P.R. (1986) *Induction: Processes of Inference, Learning, and Discovery,* The MIT Press.

Howe J. *Crowdsourcing: Why the Power of the Crowd is Driving the Future of Business.* Newyork, NY: Crown Publishing Group.

Hu, X. (1995) Knowledge Discovery in Database: An Attribute-oriented Rough Set Approach. Doctoral Dissertation, University of Regina, Canada.

Huberman, B.A. and Hogg, T. (1987) Phase transitions in artificial intelligence systems. Artificial Intelligence, 33(2): 155–171.

Hunt, E.B., Marin, J., and Stone, P.T. (1966) *Experiments in Induction.* Salt Lake City: Academic Press.

ImageNet (2014) http://www.image-net.org/, Stanford Vision Lab, Stanford University.

Inmon, W.H. (1992) *Building the Data Warehouse.* QED Technical Publishing Group.

Jalali, V. and Leake, D. (2015) CBR meets big data: A case study of large-scale adaptation rule generation. Case-based reasoning research and development. In: *Proceedings of the Twenty-Third International Conference on Case-Based Reasoning, ICCBR-15,* Berlin: Springer-Verlag.

Jennings, N.R. (1993) Commitments and Conventions: The foundation of coordination in multi-agent system. *The Knowledge Engineering Review,* 8(3): 233–250

Jennings, N.R. (2000) On agent-based software engineering. *Artificial Intelligence Journal,* 117(2): 277–296.

Jennings, N.R., Cohn, A.G., Fox, M., Long, D., Luck, M., Michaelides, D. T., Munroe, S., and Weal, M.J. (2006) Interaction, planning and motivation. *Cognitive Systems: Information Processing Meets Brain Science* (Morris, R., Taressenko, L., and Kenward, M. (eds.)) Amsterdam: Elsevier, pp. 163–188.

Jiao, W. and Zhongzhi, S. (2000). Methodology for agent-oriented software analysis and design and its software-supporting environment. In: *The 16th IFIP World Computer Congress* (ICS2000) *International Conference on Software: Theory and Practice,* Beijing, China.

Keane, M.T. (1988) *Analogical Problem-Solving,* Ellis Horwood, Series in Cognitive Science. Prentice Hall, p. 385.

Kirsh, D. (1991) Foundations of AI: The big issues. *Artificial Intelligence,* 47: 3–30.

Koehn, P., Och, F.J., and Marcu, D. (2003) Statistical phrase-based translation. In: *Proceedings of the 2003 Conference of the North American Chapter of the Association for Computational Linguistics,* pp. 48–54.

Koller, D. and Friedman, N. (2009) *Probabilistic Graphical Models: Principles and Techniques.* Cambridge, MA, MIT Press.

Kolodner, J.L. (1993) *Case-Based Reasoning.* San Francisco: Morgan Kaufmann.

Kraus, S. (1997) Negotiation and cooperation in multi-agent environments. *Artificial Intelligence,* 94(1–2): 79–97.

Krizhevsky, A., Sutskever, I., and Hinton, G.E. (2012) ImageNet classification with deep convolutional neural networks [C]. In: *Annual Conference on Neural Information Processing Systems,* Lake Tahoe, pp. 1106–1114.

Lafferty, J., McCallum, A., and Pereira, F. (2001) Conditional random fields: Probabilistic models for segmenting and labelling sequence data. In: *Proceedings of the Eighteenth International Conference on Machine Learning (ICML),* pp. 282–289.

Laird, J.E., Rosenbloom, P.S., and Newell, A. (1986) Chunking in SOAR: The anatomy of a general learning mechanism, *Machine Learning*, 1(1): 11.

Laird, J.E. and Newell, A. (1983) A universal weak method: Summary of results. In: *Proceedings of IJCAI-83*, Karlsruhe, West Germany.

Laird, J.E. and Rosebbloom, P.S. (1984) Toward chunking as a general learning mechanism. In: *Proceedings of AAAI-84*, Austin, Texas.

Langley, P.W. and Zytkow, J.M. (1989) Data-driven approaches to empirical discovery. *Artificial Intelligence*, 40(1): 283–312.

Langton, C.G. (ed.), (1989) *Artificial Life*. Redwood City, CA: Addison-Wesley.

Langton, C.G., Taylor, C., Farmer, J.D., and Rasmussen, S. (eds.) (1992) *Artificial Life II*. Redwood City, CA: Addison-Wesley.

Langton, C.G. (Ed.), (2000) *Artificial Life: An Overview*. Cambridge: MIT Press.

LeCun, Y., Boser, B., Denker, J. S., *et al.* (1989) Handwritten digit recognition with a back-propagation network[C]. *Advances in Neural Information Processing Systems*. Denver: Morgan Kaufmann, pp. 396–404.

LeCun, Y., Bottou, L., Bengio, Y., *et al.* (1998) Gradient-based learning applied to document recognition. *Proceedings of the IEEE*, 86(11): 2278–2324.

Lesser, V.R. (1991) A retrospective view of fa/c distributed problem solving. *IEEE Transactions on Systems, Man, and Cybernetics*, 21(6): 1347–1362.

Lenat, D.B. (1995) CYC: A Large-scale investment in knowledge infrastructure. *Communications of the ACM*, 38(11): 32–38.

Lenat, D.B. (2005) Applied ontology issues. *Applied Ontology*, 1(1): 9–12.

Lenat, D.B., Guha, R.V., Pittman, K., Pratt, D., and Shepherd, M. (1990) CYC: Toward programs with common sense. *CACM*, 33(8).

Lesser, V.R. and Erman, L.D. (1980) Distributed interpretation: A model and experiment. *IEEE Transaction on Computer*, C-29: 1144–1163.

Levesque, H.J. (1990) All I know: A study in autoepistemic logic. *Artificial Intelligence*, 42: 263–309.

Li, W., Wen-jun W., Huai-min W., *et al.* (2017) Crowd intelligence in AI 2.0 era. *Frontiers of Information Technology & Electronic Engineering*, 18(1):15–43.

Liao, L., Zhongzhi, S., and Shijun, W. (1994) Influence-based backjumping combined with most-constrained-first and domain filtering. In: *DKSME-94*, pp. 657–662.

Licklider, J.C.R. and Clark W. (1962) On-line man computer communication. In: *Proceedings of the Spring Joint Computer Conference*, pp. 113–128.

Lin, F. and Reiter, R. (1994) How to progress a database (and why) I: logic foundations. In: *4th International Conference on Principles of Knowledge Representation and Reasoning*, Bonn, Germany.

Lu, J., Liu, H. (2000) Mining Generalized Fuzzy Association Rules in Database Chinese. *Journal of Engineering Mathematic*, 17(1): 117–120.

Mackworth, A.K. (1977) Consistency in networks of relations. *Artificial Intelligence*, 8(1): 99–118.

Mayr, E. (1988) *One Long Argument: Charles Darwin and the Genesis of Modern Evolutionary Thought*, Cambridge, MA, Harvard University Press.

McCarthy, J. (1980) Circumscription — a form of non-monotonic reasoning. *Artificial Intelligence*, 13(1–2): 27–39.

McCarthy, J. (1986) Applications of circumscription to formalizing commonsense knowledge. *Artificial Intelligence*, 28: 89–116.

McCarthy, J. (2005) The future of AI-A manifesto. *AI Magazine*, 26(4): 39.

McCulloch, W.S. and Pitts, W. (1943) A logic calculus of the ideas immanent in nervous activity. *Bulletin of Mathematical biophysics*, 5: 115–133.

McClelland, J.L. and Rumelhart, D.E. (1987) *Explorations in Parallel Distributed Processing: A Handbook of Models, Programs, and Exercises*. Cambridge, MA, The MIT Press.

McDermott, D. and Doyle J. (1980) Non-monotonic logic I. *Artificial intelligence*, 13(1–2): 41–72.

McDermott, D. (1982) Non-monotonic logic II: Non-monotonic modal theories. *JACM*, 29(1): 33–57.

Mell, P. and Grance, T. (2011) The NIST definition of Cloud Computing. (Technical report), National Institute of Standards and Technology: U.S. Department of Commerce. doi:10.6028/NIST.SP.800-145. Special publication 800-145.

Meng, Zuqiang, and Zhongzhi Shi (2009) A fast approach to attribute reduction in incomplete decision systems with tolerance relation-based rough sets. *Information Sciences*, 179: 2774–2793.

Michalski, R.S. (1973) Discovering classification rules using variable-valued logic system VL1. In: *Proceedings of IJCAI-73*, Stanford, California.

Michalski, R.S. (1975) Variable-valued logic and its applications to pattern recognition and machine learning. Rine, D.C. (ed.), *Computer Science and Multiple-valued Logic Theory and Applications*. The Netherlands: North-Holland.

Michalski, R.S. (1980) Knowledge acquisition through conceptual clustering: A theoretical framework and an algorithm for partitioning data into conjunctive concepts. *Policy Analysis and Information Systems*, 4(3): 219–244.

Michalski, R.S. (1983) A theory and methodology of inductive learning. Michalski, R.S. *et al.* (eds.), *Machine Learning*. Berlin Heidelberg: Springer-Verlag.

Michalski, R.S. (1986) Understanding the nature of learning. Michalski, R.S., Carbonell, J.G., and Mitchell, T.M. (eds.), *Machine Learning: An Artificial Intelligence Approach*, Morgan Kaufmann.

Michalski, R.S. and Larson, J.B. (1978) Selection of most representative training examples and incremental generation of VLI hypotheses: The underlying methodology and the description of programs ESEL and AQ11. Technical Report UIUCDCS-R–78–867. Department of Computer Science, University of Illinois,Champaign-Urbana, Illinois.

Michalski, R.S. and Stepp, R.E. (1981) An application of AI techniques to structuring objects into an optimal conceptual hierarchy. In: *Proceedings of IJCAI-81*, Vancouver, B.C.

Michalski, R.S., Stepp, R., and Diday, E. (1981) A recent advance in data analysis: Clustering objects into classes characterized by conjunctive concepts. Kanal, L. and A. Rosenfeld (eds.), *Pattern Recognition*, North-Holland.

Michalski, R.S., Carbonell, J.G., and Mitchell, T.M. (eds.), *Machine Learning: An Artificial Intelligence Approach*, New York, Tioga.

Michalski, R.S. and Stepp, R. (1983) Learning from observation: Conceptual clustering. Michalski, R.S., Carbonell, J.G., and Mitchell, T.M. (eds.), *Machine Learning: An Artificial Intelligence Approach*, New York, Tioga.

Michalski, R.S., Carbonell, J.G., and Mitchell, T.M. (1983) *Machine Learning: An Artificial Intelligence Approach*. New York, Tioga.

Michalski, R.S. (1984) Inductive learning as rule-guided generalization of symbolic descriptions: A theory and implementation. Bierman, A.W., Guiho, G., and Kodratoff, Y. (eds.), *Automatic Program Techniques*, Princeton, NJ: Macmillan.

Michalski, R.S., Carbonell, J.G., and Mitchell, T.M. (1986a) *Machine Learning: An Artificial Intelligence Approach*. Morgan Kaufmann.

Michalski, R.S., Amarel, S., Lenat, D.B., Michie, D., and Winston, P.H. (1986b) Machine learning: Challenges of the eighties. Michalski, R.S., Carbonell, J.G., and Mitchell, T.M. (eds.), *Machine Learning: An Artificial Intelligence Approach*, Morgan Kaufmann.

Minsky, M.L. (1954) *Theory of Neural-Analog Reinforcement Systems and Its Application to the Brain-Model Problem*. Princeton, NJ: Princeton University.

Minsky, M. (1961) Steps toward artificial intelligence. *Proceedings of the IRE*, 49(1): 8–30.

Minsky, M. (1975) A framework for representing knowledge. Winston, P.H. (ed.), *Psychology of Computer Vision*, New York, McGraw-Hill.

Minsky, M. (1985) *The Society of Mind*. New York, Simon and Schuster Inc.

Minsky, M. (1989) *Semantic Information Processing*. Cambridge, MA: MIT Press, Hall.

Minsky, M. (2006) *The Emotion Machine: Commonsense Thinking, Artificial Intelligence, and the Future of the Human Mind*. New York, Simon & Schuster.

Minsky, M. and Papert, S. (1969, 1988) *Perceptrons*. Cambridge, MA: MIT Press.

Mitchell, T.M. (1977) Version spaces: A candidate elimination approach to rule learning. In: *Proceedings of IJCAI-87*, Cambridge, MA.

Mitchell, T.M. (1980) The need for biases in learning generalizations. Technical Report CBM-TR-117, Rutgers University.

Mitchell, T.M. (1982) Generalization as Search. *Artificial Intelligence*, 18(2): 203–226.

Mitchell, T.M. (1983) Learning and problem solving. In: *Proceedings of IJCAI-83*, Karlsruhe, West. Germany.

Mitchell, T.M. (1984) Toward combining empirical and analytic methods for learning heuristics. Elithorn, A. and Banerji, R. (eds.), *Human and Artificial Intelligence*, The Netherlands: North-Holland.

Mitchell, T.M. (1997) *Machine Learning*. McGraw Hill.

Mitchell, T., Cohen, W., Hruschka, E., *et al.* (2015) Never-ending learning. *Proceedings of the AAAI Conference on Artificial Intelligence (AAAI)*.

Mitchell, T.M., Utgoff, P.E., Nudel, B., and Banerji, R. (1981) Learning problem — solving heuristics through practice. *Proceedings of IJCAI-81*, Vancouver, B.C.

Mitchell, T.M., Utgoff, P.E., and Banerji, R.B. (1983) Learning by experimentation: Acquiring and refining problem solving heuristics. Michalski, R.S., Carbonell, J.G., and Mitchell, T.M. (eds.), *Machine Learning: An Artificial Intelligence Approach*, New York, Tioga.

Mitchell T., Hutchinson, R., Just, M., Niculescu, R.S., Pereira, F., and Wang, X. (2003) Classifying instantaneous cognitive states from fMRI data. *American Medical Informatics Association Symposium*.

Mitchell, T.M., Mahadevan, S., and Steinberg, L.I. (1985) LEAP: A learning apprentice for VLSI design. In: *Proceedings of IJCAI-85*, Los Angeles, California.

Mitchell, T.M., Keller, R.M., and Kedar-Cabelli, S.T. (1986) Explanation-based generalization: A unifying view. *Machine Learning*, 1(1): 47.

Moore, R.C. (1985) Semantical considerations on nonmonotonic logic. *Artificial Intelligence*, 25(1): 75–94.

Moore, R.C. (1993) Autoepistemic logic revisited. *Artificial Intelligence*, 59(1–2): 27–30.

Muhlenbein, H. and Kindermann, J. (1989) The dynamics of evolution and learning — towards genetic neural networks. Pfeifer, R., Schreter, Z., Fogelman-Soulie, F., and Steels, L. (eds.), *Connectionism in Perspective*, The Netherlands: North-Holland.

Nair, R. and Tambe, M. (2005) Hybrid BDI-POMDP framework for multiagent teaming. *Journal of Artificial Intelligence Research*, 23: 367–420.

Newman, M.E.J. and Barkema, G.T. (1999) *Monte Carlo Methods in Statistical Physics*. New York, USA: Oxford University Press.

Ng, R. and Han, J. (1994) Efficient and effective clustering method for spatial data mining. In: *Proceeding of the 20th International Conference on VLDB*, Santiago de Chile, pp. 144–155.

Neal, R.M. (1993) Probabilistic inference using Markov chain Monte Carlo methods. Technical Reort, CRG-TR-93-1, Department of Computer Science, University of Toronto.

Newell, A. (1990) *Unified Theories of Cognition*. Cambridge, MA.: Harvard University Press.

Newell, A. (1992) Unified theories of cognition and the role of Soar. *Soar: A Cognitive Architecture in Perspective*, Michon, J. A. and Anureyk. A. (ed.), Dordrecht: Kluwer Academic Publishers.

Newell, A. and Simon, H.A. (1972) *Human Problem Solving*. Upper Saddle River, New Jersey, Prentice-Hall.

Newell, A. and Simon, H.A. (1976) Computer science as empirical inquiry: Symbols and Search. *Communications of the Association for Computing Machinery*, 19(3): 113–126.

Nigam, K., McCallum, A., Thrun, S., and Mitchell, T. (1998) Learning to classify text from labeled and unlabeled documents. In: *Proceedings of the Fifteenth National*

Nilsson, N.J. (1980) *Principles of Artificial Intelligence*. New York, Tioga.

Nilsson, N.J. (2005) Human-level artificial intelligence? Be serious! *The AI Magazine*, 26(4): 68–75.

Nilsson, N.J. (2007) The physical symbol system hypothesis: Status and prospects. Lungarella, M. *et al.* (eds.), *50 Years of AI, Festschrift*, Vol. 4850, LNAI Springer, pp. 9–17.

Nilsson, N.J., (2009) *The Quest for Artificial Intelligence: A History of Ideas and Achievements*. Cambridge University Press. In: *Conference on Artificial Intelligence (AAAI-98)*, pp. 792–799.

Osawa, E.I. (1993) A Schema for agent collaboration in open multiagent environments. In: *IJCAI-93*, pp. 352–359.

O'Reilly, T. (2005) What is Web 2.0. design patterns and business models for the next generation of software. http://oreilly.com/web2/archive/what-is-web-20.html.

Purdom, P.W. Jr. and Brown, C.A. (1983) An analysis of backtracking with search rearrangement. *SIAM Journal of Computing* 12(4): 717–733.

Qian, Xuesheng (1986) *On Noetic Science*. Shanghai: Shanghai People Press (in Chinese).

Qian, Xuesen, Jingyuan Yu, and Ruiwei Dai (1990) A new field of science: An open complex giant system and its methodology. *Nature magazine*, 13(1): 3–10 (in Chinese).

Qin, Liangxi, Ping Luo, and Zhongzhi Shi (2004) Efficiently mining frequent itemsets with compact FP-tree. *Intelligent Information Processing*, 397–406.

Quinlan, J.R. (1979) Discovering rules from large collections of examples: A case study. Michie, D. (ed.), *Expert Systems in the Micro Electronic Age*, Edinburgh, UK, Edinburgh University Press.

Quinlan, J.R. (1983) Learning efficient classification procedures and their application to chess endgames. Michalski, R.S., Carbonell, J.G., and Mitchell, T.M. (eds.), *Machine Learning: An Artificial Intelligence Approach*, New York, Tioga.

Quinlan, J.R. (1986a) Induction of decision trees. *Machine Learning*, 1(1): 81.

Quinlan, J.R. (1986b) The effect of noise on concept learning. Michalski, R.S., Carbonell, J.G., and Mitchell, T.M. (eds.), *Machine Learning: An Artificial Intelligence Approach*, San Francisco: Morgan Kaufmann.

Quinlan, J.R. (1987) Generating production rules from decision trees. In: *Proceedings of IJCAI-87*, Milan, Italy.

Quinlan, J.R. (1988) An empirical comparison of genetic and decision-tree classifiers. In: *Proceedings of ICML-88*, San Mateo, CA.

Quinlan, J.R. (1993) *C4.5: Programs for Machine Learning*. San Francisco: Morgan Kaufmann Publishers Inc.

Rabiner, L.R. (1989) A tutorial on hidden Markov models and selected applications in speech recognition. *Proceedings of the IEEE*, 77(2): 257–286.

Rao, A.S. and Georgeff, M.P. (1992) An abstract architecture for rational agents. In: *Proceedings of the 3rd International Conference on Principles of Knowledge Representation and Reasoning*, San Francisco: Morgan Kaufmann.

Reiter, R. (1978) On closed world data bases. Gallaire, H. and Minker, J. (eds.), *Logic and Data Bases*, New York, Plenum Press.

Reiter, R. (1980) A logic for default reasoning. *Artificial Intelligence*, 13(1–2): 81–132.

Richter, A.M. and Weiss, S. (1991) Similarity, uncertainty and case-based reasoning in PATDEX. *Automated reasoning, essays in honour of Woody Bledsoe*. Amsterdam, Kluwer pp. 249–265.

Rosenblatt, F. (1958) The Perceptron: A probabilistic model for information storage and organization in the brain. *Phychological Review*, 65, 386–408.

Rosenblatt, F. (1962) *Principles of Neurodynamics*. Washington D.C, Spartan Books.

Rosenbloom, P.S. (1983) The chunking of goal hierarchies: A model of practice and stimulus-response compatibility, Department of Psychology, Carnegie-Mellon University.

Rosenbloom, P.S., Laird, J.E., and Newell, A. (1987) Knowledge Level Learning in SOAR. In: *Proceedings of AAAI-87*.

Rumelhart, D.E. and McClelland, J.L. (eds.), (1986) *Parallel Distributed Processing: Explorations in the Microstructure of Cognition*, Vol. I, Cambridge, MA: MIT Press.

Russell, S.J. and Norvig. P. (1995, 2003) *Artificial Intelligence: A Modern Approach*. Upper Saddle River, New Jersey: Prentice Hall.

Scerri, P., Pynadath, D., Schurr, N., Farinelli, A., Gandhe, S., and Tambe, M. (2004) Team Oriented Programming and Proxy Agents. The Next Generation. *PROMAS 2003*: pp. 131–148.

Schank, R.C. (1972) Conceptual dependency: A theory of natural language understanding. *Cognitive Psychology*, 3(4): 552–631.

Schank, R.C. (1982) *Dynamic Memory*. Cambridge, MA: Cambridge University Press.

Schank, R.C. (1992) Story-Based Memory. Morelli, R. *et al.* (eds.), *Minds, brains, and computers*, Ablex, pp. 134–151.

Schank, R.C. and David B.L. (1989) Creativity and learning in a case-based explainer. *Artificial Intelligence*, 40(1): 353–385.

Schikuta, E. (1996) Grid-clustering: An efficient clustering method for very large data sets, *Technical Report No. TR-96201*, Institute of Applied Computer Science and Information Systems, University of Vienna, Austria.

Schikuta, E. and Erhart, M. (1997) The BANG-clustering system: Grid-based data analysis. In: International symposium on Intelligent Data Analysis, pp. 513–524.

Schmidhuber, J. (2014) Deep learning in neural networks: An overview. http://www.idsia.ch/~juergen/deep-learning-overview.html.

Schmidhuber, J. (2015) Deep learning in neural networks: An overview. *Neural Networks*, 61: 85–117.

Shafer, G.R. and Shenoy, P.P. (1990) Probability propagation. *Annals of Mathematics and Artificial Intelligence*, 2(1–4): 327–351. doi: 10.1007/BF01531015

Shapiro, E.Y. (1981) Inductive inference of theories from facts. *Research Report 192*, Department of Computer Science, Yale University, New Haven, CT.

Shapiro, E.Y. (1983) *Algorithmic Program Debugging*. Cambridge, MA, MIT Press.

Shanahan, M. (1997) *Solving the Frame Problem*. Cambridge, MA, The MIT Press.

Sheikholeslami, G., Surojit, C., and Zhang, A. (1998) WaveCluster: A multi-resolution clustering approach for very large spatial databases. *VLDB1998*, New York City, pp. 428–439.

Shi, W., Cao, J., Zhang, Q., Li, Y., and Xu, L. (2016) Edge computing: Vision and challenges. *IEEE Internet of Things Journal*, 3(5): 637–646.

Shi, Z., Zhongzhi S., Xi L., and Zhiping, S. (2008) *A Computational Model for Feature Binding. Science in China Series C Life Sciences*, 51(5): 470–478.

Shi, Z. (1984) Design and Implementation of FORMS. In: *Proceedings of International Conference on Computer and Applications*, Beijing.

Shi, Z. (1987) Intelligent scheduling architecture in KSS. In: *The Second International Conference on Computers and Applications*, Beijing.

Shi, Z. (1988a) On knowledge base system architecture. In: *Proceedings of Knowledge-Based Systems and Models of Logical Reasoning*, Cairo.

Shi, Z. (1988b) *Knowledge Engineering*. Beijing: Tsinghua University Press (In Chinese).

Shi, Z. (1990a) Hierarchical model of mind. Invited speaker. In: *Chinese Joint Conference on Artificial Intelligence Shi*, Zhongzhi. (2006a). *Intelligence Science*. Tsinghua University Press (in Chinese).

Shi, Z. (1990b) Logic — object based knowledge model. *Chinese Journal of Computer*, 10.

Shi, Z. (1990c) Neural Computer. In: *Proceedings of National Conference on Neural Network*.

Shi, Z. (1992a) Hierarchical model of human mind. Invited talk, In: *PRICAI-92*, Seoul.

Shi, Z. (1992b) *Principles of Machine Learning*. International Academic Publishers.

Shi, Z. (ed.), (1992c) *Automated Reasoning. IFIP Transactions A-19*, North-Holland.

Shi, Z. (1993) *Neural Computing*. Beijing: Electronic Industry Press (in Chinese).

Shi, Z. (1994) Artificial thought and intelligent systems, *AI Summer School'94*, 1994.

Shi, Z. (2000) *Intelligent Agent and Application*. Science Press (in Chinese).

Shi, Z. (2001a) *Knowledge Discovery*. Tsinghua University Press (In Chinese).

Shi, Z. (2001b) *Advanced Computer Network*. Electronic Industry Press (in Chinese).

Shi, Z. (2006a) *Intelligence Science*. Beijing: Tsinghua University Press (in Chinese).

Shi, Z. (1998, 2006b) *Advanced Artificial Intelligence*. Science Press (in Chinese).

Shi, Z. (2006c) Agent grid intelligence platform for collaborative working environment. Keynote Speaker, *SELMAS2006 (ICSE 2006)*, Shanghai, May 22–23.

Shi, Z. (2007) *Artificial Intelligence*. Defence Industry Press (in Chinese).

Shi, Z. (2008) *Cognitive Science*. University of Science and Technology of China Press (in Chinese).

Shi, Z. (2009a) *Neural Networks*. High Education Press (in Chinese).

Shi, Z. (2009b) On intelligence science. *International Journal on Advanced Intelligence*, 1(1): 39–57.

Shi, Z. (2012) *Intelligence Science*. Singapore: World Scientific Publishers.

Shi, Z. (2017) *Mind Computation*. Singapore: World Scientific Publishers.

Shi, Z., Hu, C., Yunfeng, L., Wenjie, W., and Tao, J. (1998a) A building tool for multiagent systems: AOSDE. In: *IT & Knows, IFIP WCC'98*.

Shi, Z., Yuan Chen, and Lejian Liao. (1996a) Constraint reasoning system COPS. *The Progress of Artificial Intelligence 1996*, pp. 69–73.

Shi, Z., Mingkai Dong, Haijun Zhang, and Qiujian Sheng (2002a) Agent-based grid computing. Keynote Speech, In: *International Symposium on Distributed Computing and Applications to Business, Engineering and Science*, Wuxi, December, pp. 16–20.

Shi, Z., Mingkai Dong, Yuncheng Jiang, and Haijun Zhang (2005). A Logic foundation for the semantic web. *Science in China, Series F Information Sciences*, 48(2): 161–178.

Shi, Z., He Huang, Jiewen Luo, Fen Lin, and Haijun Zhang (2006) Agent-based grid computing. *Applied Mathematical Modeling*, 30: 629–640.

Shi, Z., Youping Huang, Qing He, Lida Xu, Shaohui Liu, Liangxi Qin, Ziyan Jia, and Jiayou Li. (2007) MSMiner-A developing platform for OLAP. *Decision Support Systems*, 42(4): 2016–2028.

Shi, Z., Qijia Tian, Wenjie Wang, and Tao Wang (1996b) Epistemic reasoning about knowledge and belief based on dependence relation. *Advanced Software Research*, 3(2).

Shi, Z., Qijia Tian, and Yunfeng LI (1999) RAO Logic for Multiagent Framework. *Journal of Computer Science and Technology*, 14(4): 393–400.

Shi, Z. and Jun Wang, Applying case-based reasoning to engine oil design. *AI in Engineering*, 11: 167–172.

Shi, Z., Tao Wang, Chunhuan Mo, and Hui Tang (1994) MAPE: Multi-Agent Processing Environment. *PRICAI-94*, Beijing.

Shi, Z. and Zhihua Yu. (1990) *Cognitive Science and Computer*. Beijing: Scientific Popularization Press.

Shi, Z., Haijun Zhang, and Mingkai Dong (2003) MAGE: Multi-Agent Environment. In: *ICCNMC-03*, IEEE CS Press, pp. 181–188.

Shi, Z., Jian Zhang, and Jimin Liu (1998b) Neural field theory — A framework of neural information processing. *Neural Network and Brain Proceedings*, 421–424.

Shi, Z., Zhikun Zhao, and Hu Cao (2002b) A Planning Algorithm Based on Constraints Propagation. In: *International Conference on Intelligent Information Technology (ICIIT2002)*, September 22–25, Beijing, China, pp. 410–416.

Shi, Z. and Zheng Zheng (2007) Tolerance granular space model. Miao Teqian (eds.), *Granular Computing: Past, Present and Future*. Beijing: Science Press, pp. 42–82 (*in Chinese*).

Simon, H.A. (1983) Why should machines learning? Michalski, R.S., Carbonell, J.G., and Mitchell, T.M. (eds.), *Machine Learning: An Artificial Intelligence Approach*, New York, Tioga.

Simon, H.A. (1986) *Human Cognition: Information Processing Theory of Thinking*. Beijing: Science Press.

Smith, R. (1980a) A learning system based on genetic algorithms. PhD Thesis, Department of Computer Science, University of Pittsburgh.

Smith, R.G. (1980b) The contract-net protocol: High-level communication and control in a distributed problem solver. *IEEE Transaction on Computers*, C-29(12): 1104–1113.

Smolensky, P. (1986). Information processing in dynamical systems: Foundations of harmony theory. Rumelhart, D.E. and McClelland, J.L. (eds.), *Parallel Distributed Processing*, Vol. 1, MIT Press, Cambridge, pp. 194–281.

Spivack, N. (2008) http://www.slideshare.net/novaspivack/web-evolution-nova-spivack-twine.

Sutskever, I. and Tielemant, T. (2010) On the convergence properties of contrastive divergence. *Journal of Machine Learning Research — Proceedings Track*, 9: 789–795.

Sutskever, I., Vinyals, O., and Le, Q.V. (2014) Sequence to sequence learning with neural networks. In: *Advances in Neural Information Processing Systems*, 3104–3112.

Sutton, R.S. (1996) Generalization in reinforcement learning: Successful examples using sparse coarse coding. Touretzky, D., Mozer, M. and Hasselmo, M. (eds.), *Advances in Neural Information Processing Systems*, New York: MIT Press, pp. 1038–1044.

Sycara, K., Decker, K., Pannu, A., Williamson, M., and Zeng, D. (1996) Distributed artificial agents. http://www.cs.cmu.edu/~softagents/.

Tapscott, D. and Williams, A.D. (2008) *Wikinomics: How Mass Collaboration Changes Everything*. USA: Penguin Group.

Tesauro, G.J. (1992) Practical issues in temporal difference learning. *Machine Learning*, 8: 257–277.

Tian, Qijia, Zhongzhi Shi, Wenjie Wang, and Tao Wang (1995) An approach to autoepistemic logic, *ICYCS-95*, Beijing.

Tian, Qijia, and Zhongzhi Shi (1996) A model-theoretical approach to action and progression, *SMC-96*, Beijing, 1996.

Tian, Qijia, and Zhongzhi Shi (1997) Model-theoretical foundation of action and progression. *Science in China Series E-Technological Sciences*. 40(4): 430–438.

Tieleman, T. (2008). Training restricted Boltzmann machines using approximations to the likelihood gradient. In: *Proceedings of the 25th international conference on Machine learning*, pp. 1064–1071.

Tieleman, T. and Hinton, G. (2009) Using fast weights to improve persistent contrastive divergence. In: *Proceedings of the 26th Annual International Conference on Machine Learning*. New York, NY, USA.

Tong, Yongxin, Ye Yuan, Yurong Cheng, *et al.* (2017) A survey of spatiotemporal crowdsourced data management techniques. *Journal of Software*, 28(1): 35–58 (in Chinese).

Tovey, M. (2008) *Collective Intelligence*. Oakton, Virginia: Earth Intelligence Network.

Utgoff, P.E. (1984) Shift of Bias for Inductive Concept Learning. PhD Thesis, Department of Computer Science, Rutgers University.

Utgoff, P.E. (1986) *Machine Learning of Inductive Bias*. Dordrecht: Kluwer Academic Publishers.

Utgoff, P.E. (1988a) Perceptron trees: A case study in hybrid concept representations. In: *Proceedings of AAAI-88*, Saint Paul, Minnesota.

Utgoff, P.E. (1988b) ID5: An incremental ID3. In: *Proceedings of ICML-88*, San Mateo, CA.

Utgoff, P.E. and Mitchell, T.M. (1982) Acquisition of appropriate bias for inductive concept learning. In: *Proceedings of AAAI-82*, Pittsburgh, PA.

Vaithyanathan, S. and Dom, B. (1998) Model-based hierarchical clustering. PRICAI Workshop on Text and Web Mining.

Valiant, L.G. (1984) A theory of the learnable. *Communications of the ACM*, 27(11): 1134–1142.

Valiant, L.G. (1985) Learning disjunction of conjunction. In: *Proceedings of IJCAI-85*, Los Angeles, California.

Vapnik, V.N. (1995) *The Nature of Statistical Learning Theory*. New York: Springer-Verlag.

Vapnik, V.N. (1998) *Statistical Learning Theory*. Hoboken, NJ, Wiley-Interscience Publication, John Wiley & Sons, Inc.

Vapnik, V.N. and Chervonenkis, A. Ja. (1991) A necessary and sufficient conditions for consistency in the empirical risk minimization method. *Pattern Recognition and Image Analysis*, 1(3): 284–305.

Vapnik, V., Golowich, S., and Smola, A. (1997) Support vector method for function approximation, regression estimation, and signal processing. *Advances in Neural Information Processing Systems*, pp. 281–287.

Waddington, C.H. (1974) A catastrophic theory of evolution. *Annals of the New York Academy of Science*, 231: 32–42.

Wagstaff, K., Cardie, C., Rogers, S., and Schroedl, S. (2001) Constrained k-means clustering with background knowledge. In: *Proceedings of the Eighteenth International Conference on Machine Learning*, Morgan Kaufmann, pp. 577–584.

Wallach H. Efficient (2002) Training of Conditional Random Fields. M.Sc. Thesis, Division of Informatics, University of Edinburgh.

Waltz, D. (1975) Understanding line drawings of scenes with shadows. In The Psychology of Computer Vision, P.H. Winston (ed.), 19–91, McGraw Hill.

Wang, Ruijie, Yuchen Yan, Jialu Wang, *et al.* (2018) AceKG: A Large-scale Knowledge Graph for Academic Data Mining. In: *Proceedings of the 2018 {ACM} on Conference on Information and Knowledge Management*.

Wang, W., Yang, J., and Muntz, R.R. (1997) STING: A Statistical Information Grid Approach to Spatial Data Mining. In: *VLDB1997*, Athens, Greece, pp. 186–195.

Watkins, C. and Dayan, P. (1989) Q-learning. *Machine Learning*, 8: 279–292.

Werbos, P.J. (1974) Beyond Regression: New Tools for Prediction and Analysis in the Behavioral Sciences. Ph.D. Thesis, Harvard University, Cambridge, MA.

Widrow, B., Hoff, M.E. (1960) Adaptive Switching Circuits. IRE WESCON Convention Record, pp. 96–104.

Wilson, S.W. (1987) Classifier systems and the animat problem. *Machine Learning*, 2(3), 199.

Wooldridge, M. (2002) *An Introduction to MultiAgent Systems*. Hoboken, NJ: John Wiley & Sons Ltd.

Wooldridge, M. and Jennings, N.R. (1995) Intelligent agents: Theory and practice. *Knowledge Engineering*, 10(2): 115–152.

Wu, Yonghui, Schuster, M., Zhifeng Chen, *et al.* (2016) Google's neural machine translation system: Bridging the gap. arXiv:1609.08144v2.

Xu, Y., Scerri, P., Yu, B., Okamoto, S., Lewis, M., and Sycara, K. (2005) An integrated token-based algorithm for scalable coordination. In: *Proceedings of the Fourth International Joint Conference on Autonomous Agents and Multiagent Systems (AAMAS)*, Utrecht, NL, pp. 407–414.

Xu, Y., Scerri, P., Lewis, M., and Sycara, K. (2008) Token-based approach for scalable team. *Cooperative Networks: Control and Optimization*, Lypiatts, UK, Edward Elgar Publishing.

Yao, X., and Yong, X. (2006) Recent advances in evolutionary computation. *Journal of Computer Science and Technology*, 21(1): 1–18.

Yao, Y. (2001) Information granulation and rough set approximation. *International Journal of Intelligent Systems*, 16: 87–104.

Ye, S. (2001) Massive Data Reduction and Classification. PhD. Dissertation, Institute of Computing Technology, Chinese Academy of Sciences, Beijing, China.

Ye, S. and Zhongzhi, S. (1995) A necessary condition about the optimum partition on a finite set of samples and its application to clustering analysis. *Journal of Computer Science and Technology*, 10(6): 545–556.

Zadeh, L.A. (1997) Towards a theory of fuzzy information granulation and its centrality in human reasoning and fuzzy log ic. *Fuzzy Sets and Systems*, 19: 111–127.

Zadeh, L.A. (2005) Toward a generalized theory of uncertainty (GTU) — An outline. *Information Sciences*, 172: 1–40.

Zaki, M.J. (1999) Parallel and distributed association mining: A survey. *IEEE Concurrency*, 7(4): 14–25.

Zaki, M.J. (2000) Scalable algorithms for association mining. *IEEE Transforms on Knowledge and Data Engineering*, 12(3): 372–390.

Zaki, M.J. (2005) Efficiently mining frequent trees in a forest: Algorithms and applications. *IEEE Transforms on Knowledge Data Engineering*, 17(8): 1021–1035.

Zhang, B. and Ling, Z. (1992) *Theory and Applications of Problem Solving*, Elsevier Science Publishers B. V., the Netherlands, North-Holland.

Zhang, Q., Zhang, X., Zhang, Q., *et al.* (2016) Firework: Big data sharing and processing in collaborative edge environment. Fourth IEEE Workshop on Hot Topics in Web Systems and Technologies.

Zhang, T., Ramakrishnan, R. and Livny, M. (1996) BIRCH: An efficient data clustering method for very large databases. *Proceedings of the ACM SIGMOD International Conference on Management of Data*, ACM Press, pp. 103–114.

Zheng, Z., Hong, H., and Zhongzhi, S. (2005) Tolerance relation based information granular space, Heidelberg, Springer, *Lecture Notes in Computer Science*, 3641: pp. 682–691.

Zhou, H. (1993) Design of Internal Combustion Engine Oil Product Based on Case-based Learning. Ph.D. Dissertation, China University of Petroleum: Beijing.

Zhou, Z. (2016) *Machine Learning*. Beijing: Tsinghua University Press (in Chinese).

Author Index

Subject Index

A

absolute value index, 378
absolute value reciprocal method, 378
absolute value subtraction, 378
action description, 88, 92
action theory, 71
ACTOR, 471
AdaBoost Algorithm, 160
agent, 472
agent architecture, 475
agent communication language (*see also* ACL), 483, 485, 490
agent grid intelligence platform (*see also* AGrIP), 517–518
agent kernel, 483
agent structure, 473
Ali translation, 348
analogical mapping, 212
analogical learning, 210
analogical transformation, 213
analysis model, 212
angle cosine method, 377, 379
annotated predicate calculus, 252
APM algorithm, 430
approximate inference, 198, 205
Apriori algorithm, 404–405, 408
AQ learning algorithm, 267
AQ11 algorithm, 267
arc-consistent, 106
arithmetic mean minimum method, 378
ARPANET, 519
association rule, 401
assumption-based truth maintenance system, 108
ATMS, 69
AttentionFunction, 345

attribute selection, 270
AutoClass, 140
autoencoder, 323
autoepistemic logic, 43, 57–58, 62
autoepistemic theories, 58

B

back-propagation algorithm, 320
background knowledge, 252
backjumping, 112–114
backtracking, 102
backtracking algorithm, 103
BANG algorithm, 393
basic genetic algorithm, 452
Bayesian assumption, 137
Bayesian classification, 138
Bayesian formula, 144
Bayesian latent semantic, 176
Bayesian method, 136
Bayesian network, 135–136, 139, 163, 168, 171, 201–202
Bayesian probability, 140
Bayesian problem solving, 154
Bayesian theorem, 154, 156
Bayesian theory, 135–136
BDI-interpreter, 479
belief propagation, 197
bias feature extracting, 286
bias shift-based decision tree, 275
bias shift-based decision tree learning (*see also* BSDT) algorithm, 284
Big Data, 299
BIRCH algorithm, 384–385
Blocks World, 77
Boole's genetic algorithm, 459
Boolean combination, 98